THE ESSAYS,
ARTICLES AND REVIEWS OF
EVELYN WAUGH

Books by Evelyn Waugh:

PRB: An Essay on the Pre-Raphaelite Brotherhood (1926, 1982)
Rossetti: His Life and Works (1928)
Decline and Fall (1928)
Vile Bodies (1930)
Labels (1930)
Remote People (1931)
Black Mischief (1932)
Ninety-Two Days (1934)
Mr Loveday's Little Outing and Other Sad Stories (1936)
Waugh in Abyssinia (1936)
Scoop (1938)
Robbery Under Law (1939)
Put Out More Flags (1942)
Work Suspended (1942)
Brideshead Revisited (1945)
When the Going was Good (1946)
Scott-King's Modern Europe (1947)
Wine in Peace and War (1947)
The Loved One (1948)
Helena (1950)
The Holy Places (1952)
Men at Arms (1952)
Love Among the Ruins (1953)
Tactical Exercise (1954)
Officers and Gentlemen (1955)
The Ordeal of Gilbert Pinfold (1957)
Msgr. Ronald Knox (1959)
A Tourist in Africa (1960)
Unconditional Surrender (1961)
A Little Learning (1964)
Charles Ryder's Schooldays and Other Stories (1982)

THE ESSAYS,
ARTICLES AND REVIEWS OF
EVELYN WAUGH

EDITED BY
DONAT GALLAGHER

. ——— .

. Little, Brown and Company .

Boston　　　　　Toronto

. ——— .

To Mary, Felicity and Verity

. CONTENTS .

. ACKNOWLEDGEMENTS .

Such a large part of preparing the physical manuscript and standardizing the text of this book was done by Mary Gallagher, my wife, that I am indebted to her not so much for help as for collaboration. I must also thank her for limitless personal support over an extended period of difficulty. I am very grateful to the Evelyn Waugh Estate, particularly to Auberon Waugh, for encouragement and assistance, and to Michael Sissons of A. D. Peters and Co. for wise and friendly guidance. Father Philip Caraman, SJ generously transferred to me material he had collected over many years. He also gave me the benefit of experience gained as the friend and editor who published so many of Waugh's best pieces in the *Month.* Margaret Fitzherbert (née Waugh) and Harriet Waugh very kindly spoke to me about their father's interests. Of the many libraries which have helped in the collection of Waugh's fugitive pieces I can mention only the British Newspaper Library at Colindale and the Humanities Research Center of the University of Texas, Austin, which generously made available unique materials. Their staffs, like the reference staff of the James Cook University Library, in particular Helen Mays, and the librarian of the Catholic Central Library, London, were also extremely helpful. William Deedes, editor of the *Daily Telegraph,* and the archivists of the *Daily Telegraph, The Times,* the *Observer* and the *Daily Express* gave invaluable information.

I must record my great debt to Michael Davie and to Mark Amory, both for personal help and for their richly informative editing respectively of Waugh's diaries and letters, and to Professor Robert Murray Davis of the University of Oklahoma, Professor Charles E. Linck of East Texas State University and Dr Paul A. Doyle of Nassau Community College, for their pioneering work on Waugh's bibliography. It is also my pleasure to thank for information and trouble taken Sir Harold Acton, Basil Handford of Lancing College, Lady Lothian, Jean Marshall of J. M. Dent and Sons, Sir Fitzroy Maclean, Captain D. A. Oakley, RM, editor of the *Globe and Laurel,* Professor Hugh Trevor-Roper (now Lord Dacre) and Milton Shulman of the *Daily Express.* Geoffrey Strachan and Cathryn Game of Methuen London have been the kindest of publishers. Finally I must thank James Cook University of North Queensland for timely leave and financial assistance, Professor Anthony Hassall of the Department of English for most generous co-operation in overcoming difficulties, and the efficient and devoted departmental secretaries, Gloria Sargent and Julie-Anne Horwood, for typing the manuscript.

Donat Gallagher

. NOTE ON REFERENCES, BIBLIOGRAPHY AND SOURCES .

The contents of this volume are arranged chronologically, with some minor variation at the beginnings and ends of sections. The list of occasional writings not printed in this volume is also arranged chronologically. References to Waugh's journalism in introductions and notes are therefore made by dates enclosed in parentheses within the text, e.g. 'Fan-fare' (8 April 1946). Publication details will be found at the foot of each title page and in the list of occasional writings not printed in this volume.

References to Waugh's published diaries are to Michael Davie's *The Diaries of Evelyn Waugh*, first published by Weidenfeld and Nicolson in 1976. References to his published letters are to Mark Amory's *The Letters of Evelyn Waugh*, first published by Weidenfeld and Nicolson in 1980. As both collections now exist in a variety of editions, all chronologically ordered, reference is again made by date.

Unpublished letters, diaries and manuscripts quoted here are, with few exceptions, lodged at the Humanities Research Center, Austin, Texas. Letters cited as to or from 'Peters' were either written to or received from Mr A. D. Peters personally, or (rarely) one of his colleagues, in the firm of literary agents, A. D. Peters and Company, of London. Waugh dealt exclusively with A. D. Peters for the whole of his working life, and the correspondence between him and 'Peters' is the principal source of information about the motives for his journalism and the conditions under which it was written.

A list of Waugh's books is given opposite the title page of this book because journalism, novels, travel books and biographies so often throw light on each other.

. PREFACE .

Evelyn Waugh divided the contemporary literary world into 'those who can write but cannot think, those who can think but cannot write, and those who can neither think nor write but employ themselves at international congresses lecturing on the predicament of the writer in modern society'. Modesty constrained him from adding a fourth category, to which he certainly believed he belonged, of those who could both write and think. The appearance of this 'complete' collection of Evelyn Waugh's essays and articles is an invitation to reconsider his journalism in these lucid terms. Memories of famous jokes, insults and vividly eccentric posturings still persist and still determine his reputation. Of course they should be remembered, because the public 'front' they constituted, Mr Pinfold's 'character of burlesque', was in itself a fascinating creation and the pungent ingredient in the most idiosyncratic journalism. But claims to lasting attention must in the end rest on more solid ground. In Waugh's case they rest on exceptional talent as a writer, and vigour and independence as a thinker.

By being able to 'write' Waugh meant being able to write readably; and by readably he meant lucidly, elegantly and with individuality. Lively narrative – as found, for example, in popular newspaper stories – could survive 'verbal commonness'. The flavour of 'first-hand experience', even in an unliterary book, was always 'intoxicating'. But normally prose was expected to be exact, *pleasurable* in vocabulary and image and cadence, and marked by a unique 'tone of voice'. In these broad terms Waugh was himself outstandingly readable; he could write.

The more particular qualities of his prose are not so easy to define. Philip Toynbee once complained of its being 'a very elegant construction but also archaic, mandarin and even pompous'. The term 'construction' was exactly right. For Waugh did not aspire to naturalness, in the sense in which naturalness was prized from the turn of the century until the 1960s, and he always sought to complete a structure. In life he tended to act out theatrically, often to the point of farce, any role he happened to fill: as regimental soldier to become conspicuous for pedantic correctness of dress, as commando to become conspicuous for informality. Every piece of writing then was a construction, though a construction bearing the marks of irrepressible impulse, imagination and mischief. Every piece was, to some extent, a performance. For those reasons, perhaps, Waugh wrote a larger range of sharply contrasted, excellent styles than any other English author of this century: from maliciously pointed 'Waughspishness' to polemic of Macaulay-like vigour and amplitude; from rapid-fire assertion to luxuriant 'fine writing'. Versatility was Waugh's most obvious distinction. On the other hand a unique tang, a signature, marks all of his prose, in whatever style, and lends it permanent interest. This arises from the close alliance of the impulse to stylistic virtuosity with an unquenchable tendency to jokes and to malice, and with the tough habits of mind of an active, penetrating thinker.

By being able to 'think' Waugh meant being able to think consistently. His standard of the 'readable' was arguably so high as to exclude many able, widely enjoyed writers. But his standard of rationality was moderate. He expected no one to share his views, or even to be fair or unprejudiced. He merely expected writers' opinions to be consistent with their own principles or prejudices, and their statements to be consistent with one another. He was mostly disappointed, often by admired friends, always by the respected leaders of contemporary thought. The editor of a *New Statesman* anthology once described 'Newstatesmanship' as 'hard-headed and soft-hearted'. Waugh thought it the opposite: all soft-headed self-contradiction. This can be gathered from the analysis (27 July 1946) of Cyril Connolly's *Horizon* 'blue-print' for post-war society, since for present purposes Connolly's and *Horizon*'s liberal and socialist ethos can be equated with 'Newstatesmanship'. The 'significant feature' of the plan for Waugh was not that it was unworkable, but that it was irrational in a typical way. It was so full of 'internal contradictions' that it 'epitomized the confusion' of Connolly (pointedly described as 'the leader of the English intellectuals') and of all his contemporaries. In the following pages several studies generally regarded as profound, e.g. Romilly Fedden's *Suicide* (15 April 1938) and Harold Laski's *Faith, Reason and Civilization* (22 April 1944), are debunked for undefined premises and unwarranted conclusions.

Waugh displayed the virtues and vices of most sharply critical minds, allied to a superb talent for unexpectedness. He was an intellectual, in the sense that in his make-up intellect predominated. Though brilliantly capable of conveying visual impressions and of being funny and elegant, he seldom attempted an impression or humour or elegance without at the same time having something to *say*. Compare his *Daily Mail* article on the once topical subject of sunbathing (5 July 1930) with comparable pieces by E. V. Knox and 'Beachcomber', and instead of pure whimsy one finds an amusing sketch of the pleasures and pains of the sun followed by an attack on the self-righteousness of sun-bathers and of the protestors who gathered to stare them out of nakedness. But the true note of Waugh's thinking was putting familiar subjects in a surprising new light. Sometimes the surprise was melodramatic, as in 'I see boredom . . . everywhere' (28 December 1959):

> I am not the least nervous about the much-advertised threats of the nuclear scientists: First, because I can see nothing objectionable in the total destruction of the earth, provided it is done, as seems most likely, inadvertently . . .

But this was an exaggeration of a more interesting facility for making subjects, on which there already existed a full range of well-known opinions, come alive by sudden penetration and the discovery of a fresh viewpoint. An example concerning war and pacifism comes from a review of Guy Chapman's *Vain Glory* (29 July 1937):

> It is part of Mr Chapman's thesis that no one gains anything in war. This of course is true, absolutely. War is an absolute loss, but it admits of degrees; it is very bad to fight but it is worse to lose. That was the realistic attitude of the British soldier which brought him to victory.

On the other hand, though sharp in argument, Waugh was not given to developing arguments in the abstract. He refused to write 'pure essayism' or 'middles'; he scorned Belloc's 'banging about of ideas and a few facts'. His preferred subjects were books, people and places known at first-hand. And many of his best pieces, like the review of Ralph Dutton's *The Victorian Home* (28 November 1954), reveal a hobbyist–scholar's love of accurate detail.

The worst pieces, on the other hand, reveal the limitations common to very clear, logical minds, i.e. inability to see beyond a clear, logical point of view once it has been conceived, and inability to enter imaginatively into an opposing viewpoint. 'Logical' arguments may be profoundly unsatisfactory to those at whom they are directed, particularly when the subject matter of argument is inherently mysterious, as in some religious controversy; or when fundamental information is significantly incomplete or confused, as in so much political discussion. Waugh's contributions to religious controversy sometimes appear to rely on deductions from formulae which are themselves the real, if submerged, subject of dispute. The excellent essay on Graham Greene's *The Heart of the Matter*, in so far as it is an examination of Mr Greene's theology from the viewpoint of a 'logical rule-of-thumb' Catholic, perhaps best exemplifies the narrowness induced by overconfidence in logic and precise definition (16 July 1948).

Sharp intelligences tend to controversy and to opposition. Waugh was inclined to both, as well by habit of mind as by temperament and conviction. His important targets were not, however, the established reputations so beloved of most satirists but fashions, mass enthusiasms and the Spirit of the Age – anything popular and uncritically accepted. So contrasuggestible was he that he seems at times to have enjoyed fighting on the unpopular side simply because it was unpopular. But he was also convinced that opposition to everything destructive of civilized life was a duty. Active 'intolerance' became a principle by which he lived: 'There are still things which are worth fighting *against*' (2 April 1932) was the battle cry of a lifetime's campaign against declining qualitative standards, and against social and aesthetic and literary movements threatening traditional life and culture. Opposition in its various phases is, from one point of view, the key to Waugh's career.

As a boy living in a still predominantly bourgeois and traditional society, Evelyn was 'bolshie' and so radically 'ultra-modern' as to worry both father and form master. At Oxford he became dissolute and defiant and earned himself the incongruous reputations of extreme Hobbism at the Union and of avant-gardism as a member of Sir Harold Acton's hyper-aesthetic set. (As Sir Harold seems also to have awakened enthusiasm for Victorianism and Roman Catholicism, his influence was mixed.) On becoming a professional writer in 1928, in the very age of debunking and jazz and up-to-dateness, the Oxford pattern continued. Total up-to-dateness in style, and scorn of the suburbs, enabled Waugh to pass as ultra-modern, but he turned his conservative satiric talents primarily against the fashionable crazes of Youth, cocktails, Cocteau, telephones, talkies, functional ('good taste') furniture and architecture; and against socialism, sex and Merrie England arts-and-crafts. When the 1930s became the Political Decade, and the literary world turned *en masse* to the left, Waugh became politically right-wing. Mass indignation against Fascism in Abyssinia and Spain, mass enthusiasm for Peace and for socialism and for anti-Fascism, Waugh met with the conservative's cool distrust of 'fad and panic'. Since writers, publishers, artists and the universities tend to be particularly excitable and vocal at times of crisis, Waugh explained an intelligentsia's responsibilities in terms which defined his understanding of his own duty, which was 'to correct popular sentiments and give a call to order in times of hysteria':

> It is the natural inclination of any trade to provide the public with what it wants rather than what it needs; in the sphere of economics this produces a recurrent disastrous succession of slumps and booms. In matters of the mind exactly the same process is at work. It should be the proper function of an intelligentsia to correct popular sentiments and give the call to order in times of hysteria. Instead the editors and publishers, whose job it is to exploit the intelligence of others, see it as their interest to indulge and inflame popular emotion, so that the mind moves in feverish vacillation from one extreme to another instead of in calm and classical progress. People now use the phrase 'without contemporary significance' to express just those works which are of most immediate importance, works which eschew barbaric extremes and attempt to right the balance of civilization. (29 July 1937)

After 1945 Waugh went further still. The outcome of the Second World War had seemed to some Roman Catholic conservatives unspeakably tragic, entailing as it did widespread savage persecution of the Catholic Church in eastern Europe, the forced repatriation of large populations to countries where they would face certain death, and starvation and wickedness in half the world. Waugh was also disturbed by what seemed to him a reversal of real power within English society. He was now proud to call himself a reactionary, because he was in revolt, not against isolated follies or evils or political causes, but against the modern world and the Spirit of the Age. It was the artist's duty to refuse 'to go flopping along with the times'. Reaction, however, did not condemn the artist to being perpetually of yesterday. On the contrary the artist–reactionary was a 'creature of the *Zeitgeist*' and 'in the advance guard' (16 July 1948).

Waugh was five years old in 1908, the date of the first Post-Impressionist Exhibition, and of the first Welfare State measure, in England. The products of modern science and modern industry, the telephone and the motor-car, were just beginning to affect general social life. 1908 is therefore a convenient year from which to date the beginnings of modern and liberal England. In 1966 when Waugh died the precepts of Modernism and liberalism had become received opinion, the unconscious assumptions about art and society of socialists and Conservatives alike; and the surface of life had been transformed by motor-cars and aeroplanes, wireless and television, domestic appliances and the fearful weapons of modern war. A liberalizing movement had transformed the face of the Roman Catholic Church. Scarcely a whisper was heard in 1966 of a Post-Modern movement, or of popular disenchantment with industrialism, or of a conservative revival. Modernity felt as permanent as had Victorianism in 1866. Only Waugh foretold the tide's going out.

Waugh's life therefore spanned the Modern Period. But as the world had grown more accepting of Modernism and liberalism, he had grown increasingly antagonistic. And the world, which had once smiled on an ultra-modern young man's outrages, was now bitterly hostile towards his 'ultra-conservative' scourgings. Everyone in public life gradually acquires a *persona*, a public picture more or less defined and visible, which may bear little relation to the sort of person he or she is. In his last decades Waugh acquired a bold and garish *persona* which, though now less widely mistaken for an accurate portrait, still persists in some quarters. At its worst it was of a once lively writer grown narrow and dull, of a middle-class snob fatuously in love with Birth and brutally rude to 'inferiors'; of a would-be squire, a Roman Catholic bigot, an anti-Semite; of an insanely reactionary ultra-conservative. Yet Waugh could not be dismissed. 'His values,' wrote Philip Toynbee, 'are vulgar and absurd'; but he added that Waugh had haunted his dreams and imagination, 'a powerful and impressive figure whom I have tried but failed to please.' Malcolm Muggeridge has described similar feelings.

Why Waugh provoked such reactions will emerge more clearly in the introduction to Part 6. Suffice to say here that black depression and manic gaiety each led to occasional outrages, that exquisitely phrased attacks were sometimes unconscionably cruel, and so on; but that any fabled atrocity of Waugh's should be examined in the light of Cyril Connolly's warning that 'If the public want such an image [of a 'miserable ogre'] nothing can stop them creating it.' The Pinfold 'front' and a 'Garbo'-like remoteness helped Waugh become a national figure. But on a deeper level he compelled respect by the sheer courage and the style with which he opposed the most fundamental developments of his time. It is absurd to accuse him of naive Blimpishness. Certainly he had the Swiftian habit of carrying logic and commonsense to conclusions which went far beyond those of the merely sensible, and of pronouncing with reckless bitterness and provocativeness. But his essential contribution was to remain rationally – not nostalgically – in touch with what was permanently valuable in the past; with tastes and ideas that were neglected, perhaps ridiculed as 'ultra-conservative', in his own day, but which would, with the inevitable revolution of fashion, once again be honoured. In an age obsessed with mass movements and the Common Man, he insisted on his own individuality. He lived as he enjoyed to live, flaunting outmoded fashions in dress, wine and manners. In defiance of Modern functionalism, and because variety and ornament appealed to him, he 'Victorianized' his houses. Thus he dramatized his attachment to the energy, inventiveness and freedom of the 'immediate past', which had fostered individualism. Since the 1960s colourful diversity of clothes, a new enthusiasm for 'doing your own thing' and 'creating your own space', though foreign to Waugh in language and style and owing nothing to his influence, are evidence of recent abandonment of early twentieth-century attitudes against which he rebelled. Waugh was sceptical of the claims made for motor transport by avant-gardists like Aldous Huxley, who hymned it as a liberating miracle; the contemporary avant-garde is almost unreasonably hostile to the motor-car. Though essentially Modern in his art, Waugh rejected the extremes of Modernist experiment in literature, painting and architecture, and championed the Victorian narrative school of painters when it was universally despised. Picasso and Matisse have not yet been relegated to gallery basements as he predicted, and perhaps never will be; but Victorian painting is now widely exhibited and admired. It is not possible to itemize all of the matters about which Waugh differed from his contemporaries: he once said that he disapproved of *everything* invented since mid-Victorian times except electric light, which allowed him to read Victorian novels in bed. Nor is it possible to convey the depth of the disagreement, for he was profoundly critical of the twentieth century's most fundamental assumptions: that change implies progress, that widespread political activism is beneficial, that a stratified society is necessarily unjust, and that an institutional Church is incapable of providing serious religious experience.

But it is futile to attempt to boil Waugh's journalism down to a series of propositions, to a quintessence of Waughism. His thinking, like Shaw's, is digestible only in the form – or rather in the many diverse forms – in which it appeared over a writing life of forty years. Diversity is the hallmark of his *oeuvre*, comprising as it does the highly literate criticisms of an artist, bookman and aesthete, the 'forcefulness' of a spokesman for Youth, elegant Mayfair chat about all that was 'new and gay', traveller's tales from Abyssinia to the Arctic, the polemic of a hard-headed conservative correspondent, and the piety and bellicosity of a traditionalist Roman Catholic. Moods and motives, like subjects, range between extremes – from disinterested zeal to desperate need for money, from almost gloating pleasure in a fine book to bitter anger at an insult – as Waugh responded to the changes in personal and professional life, and to the national and ecclesiastical events, which determined his development.

This volume is divided into six parts chronologically arranged, corresponding to phases in Waugh's development: 'bookish teenager' and raffish student; 'ultra-modern' young novelist; adventurous traveller; right-wing propagandist; successful Catholic novelist in retreat from the modern world and the century of the common man; and self-appointed scourge of the classless society and progressive Catholicism. Many pieces, particularly literary essays and reviews, could of course appear indifferently in any phase. The main use of the division is to highlight material unique to each period and thus to emphasize the diversity of Waugh's career and output. Very few generalizations apply to his career. For example it is broadly true – both Waugh and A. D. Peters said it in different ways – that Waugh wrote journalism only when he badly needed money or was stirred by strong conviction. But in the immediate pre-war period, when he was very short of money, he could not get work; and in the immediate post-war period, when his income from *Brideshead Revisited* was so high as to make earnings from journalism a taxation embarrassment, offers of work involving travel, tax-free expenses and the opportunity to write about Roman Catholicism led to his most prolific period. Subjects chosen and approaches adopted are equally difficult to describe outside the circumstances obtaining during shortish periods of time.

Each part opens with an introduction offering, where appropriate, financial, personal, religious, political and aesthetic information. Its purpose is to make intelligible the amount of journalism Waugh sought and published, the quality he aimed at, the subjects he preferred and the attitudes he assumed. Where Waugh might have been expected to write about a subject (e.g. the Spanish Civil War) but did not, his reasons for not doing so are explained.

The collection is 'complete' in the sense that it is as comprehensive as the realities of publishing allow, and in that it seeks to include within one set of covers everything that any serious reader of Waugh might hope to find. The selection, in intention at least, is impersonal. Everything has been included that could reasonably be thought 'important', either on account of its quality or of its theme; so too has every piece known to have been commented on, favourably or unfavourably, by anyone; and everything that seems likely to be of assistance to students of Waugh. In other words I have tried to bring together everything notably funny, elegant, beautiful, profound or self-revealing, and anything that seems to define Waugh's own aims. A very few pieces without much intrinsic merit have been included in order to illustrate a kind of writing Waugh attempted, or an aspect of his thinking that would otherwise be unrepresented.

The selection has been made from essays, articles, prefaces and introductions, reviews, news reports and public letters. Pre-prints and reprints of travel books and biographies were not used. Two anomalous pieces, a 'Statement' Waugh contributed to an Official Note delivered by the Italian Government to the League of Nations, and the 'Warning' printed on the dust cover of the first edition of *Brideshead Revisited,* are included on account of their exceptional interest. Anything that could be dignified by the name of 'essay' has of course been included. Between articles, prefaces and reviews, no preference was exercised on grounds of form alone. Much of Waugh's best writing went into reviews, and many of his reviews are self-expressive. They are therefore well represented.

Every omission was made with regret, because Waugh rarely wrote without revealing *something* of his tastes, or standards of importance, or experiences. He never adopted a confiding tone, but everything he wrote carries the impress of individuality and speaks tellingly about its author. The obvious categories of exclusion were topical pieces lacking substance and point, cursory reviews of forgotten books, badly flawed pieces, repetitions (e.g. a preface to a book and an article on the author of the book covering the same ground) and news reports and letters to editors lacking significance outside their original context. It is fortunate that a number of important letters to editors have been reprinted by Mark Amory in his edition of Waugh's correspondence. A list of the journalism not included in this volume is placed at the back of the book for the convenience of those who wish to read more widely.

When more than one text is available, the one used here is that last revised by Waugh. He was an inveterate reviser. As A. D. Peters explained when urging Hamish Hamilton to send him a proof of an article being reprinted, Waugh was 'apt to rewrite, subtract and add extensively'. His changes were always improvements. For example 'Titus with a Grain of Salt' in the *Spectator* (2 September 1955) is manifestly inferior in finish and charm to the revised and expanded version from *Spectrum: A Spectator Miscellany* (1956) which is printed here. Had Waugh published a volume of essays as he planned to do, he would certainly have 'polished', and probably amplified, anything included. In this reprinting spelling and punctuation have been standardized in accordance with the house rules of the present publisher. Waugh only once complained to an editor about a matter of form, and that was to insist on 'Jones's' instead of 'Jones' '. Otherwise his work was printed according to the widely varying conventions of the magazines and newspapers which published it. Obvious misprints, spelling mistakes and grammatical blunders have been silently corrected. When there was evidence (e.g. from Waugh's corrections or from other printings) to support change, a few other alterations have been made and noted. Waugh used commas in a slightly eccentric way and was not an infallible grammarian. Whatever he deliberately wrote is of course left unaltered.

Waugh would never have consented to the reprinting of slight or inferior journalism during his lifetime, when he would have seemed to be endorsing its quality and sentiments. He was rightly ashamed of some newspaper work of the 1930s, and affected cynicism about much of what he wrote 'for money'. But no apology is needed for resurrecting 'beastly little articles' he wished forgotten, for in 'A Young Novelist's Heaven' (18 March 1930) the heavenly libraries contain 'all the books that the authors burned when they came back from the last publisher'. A piece so slight as 'Beau Brummells on £60 a Year' (13 February 1929) is therefore included here because, in revealing an unusual interest in clothes and a canny side to a nature often thought purely reckless, it satisfies legitimate curiosity about its author. It has also been mocked from time to time and is therefore interesting to scholars.

On the other hand, Waugh certainly intended to collect a number of his more substantial pieces of journalism, or 'essays', as he called them. Though a severe critic of his own work, he was satisfied with much of it and proud of some. When selling material for volume publication he occasionally warned A. D. Peters (unnecessarily) that rights were to be kept 'for my future book of collected essays'. In later years he proposed several specific selections.

This 'complete' collection will be valued because it embodies so much of the mind of an allusive novelist, whose fictions everywhere imply, and rarely state, his idiosyncratic tastes and opinions. It will also be valued for what it is in itself, a body of writing that is irresistibly readable. Waugh's highest distinction, pointed out many years ago by Alan Pryce-Jones, remains the simple fact that an unusually large number of people, whether friendly or hostile, cannot imagine seeing his name at the foot of a page and not wanting to read what lies above it. Perhaps they are drawn by a unique unpredictability of mind and personality, perhaps by writing so accomplished that it 'comes to one, not merely as printed words, but as a lively experience, with the full force of another human being personally encountered.'

I

. FIRST STEPS .
LANCING, OXFORD, BOHEMIA

NOVEMBER 1917 – OCTOBER 1928

'I feel that I must write prose or burst.'

Diary, 2 April 1921

. INTRODUCTION .

The first article of Waugh's to be printed, a defence of Cubism in *Drawing and Design*, appeared in 1917 when he was 14 years old. After the success of *Decline and Fall* had created a market for journalism, his first fully professional article was sold to the *Daily Express* by A. D. Peters in October 1928. The intervening years were spent at Lancing and Oxford, then in London and elsewhere, with Waugh drifting between polytechnic courses and schoolteaching jobs of ever-diminishing prestige. Socially Waugh moved away from the Georgian literary world of his boyhood home into a diverse circle of Oxford friends, to which he added the semi-bohemian London literary world of his brother.

It must be said at once that for most of this period writing of any sort was less important to Waugh than drawing, and that fiction was more important to him than non-fiction. And that as late as 1928 Waugh still thought of himself as 'an out-of-work schoolmaster': which means that he then hoped – as he continued to hope until 1945 – for a career other than painting or writing. He gave little sign of adopting literature as a profession. He wrote few essays or articles. But his early journalism cannot, on these accounts, be presumed negligible. Some pieces of course lack interest or are bad, others are youthfully over-written. Most are precociously assured. Of the better pieces several retain, at the very least, curiosity value; while one, the preface to Francis Crease's *Decorative Designs* (1927), would find a place in the smallest collection of Waugh's essays. The limited output of journalism comprises writing for and editing of school and university magazines, a brief stint on the *Daily Express* as a reporter, and some *belles-lettres*.

Editing and writing for magazines appealed to Waugh early. During 1916 at his private school, Heath Mount, he wrote, and his father had cyclostyled and stapled, five issues of *The Cynic*, a self-proclaimed rival to the official school magazine. This was cheeky in conception but tame in its cynicism. During his last term at Lancing (September–December 1921) Waugh edited the *Lancing College Magazine*, earning J. F. Roxburgh's praise: 'you have lifted the L.C.M. to an entirely different level' (see note to *The Poetic Procession*, November 1921). He now gave some scope to the 'bolshevism' that had been suppressed while he was seeking to become editor. His first editorial mocked the conventions rigidly limiting school friendships, and was followed by two pseudonymous letters (one of December 1921 printed) designed to stir up controversy. The response was gratifying. His second editorial (December 1921) fashionably espoused the cause of 'the youngest generation' against the 'old men who made the war'. It should be read in conjunction with the diaries, and both diaries and editorial should be read in conjunction with the articles on Youth published from 1928 to 1932.

In his first year at Oxford Waugh was Union reporter for the *Cherwell* from

January to April 1922, and business manager and Union reporter for the *Oxford Fortnightly Review* from October to December. The *Review* was a fierce Conservative organ replete with Bolshevik atrocities and Vatican plots against the Empire. A 'scoop' from the *Cherwell* and a report from the *Review* illustrating Waugh's analytical tendencies and attraction to the unpopular side are reprinted here. In the following year Harold Acton began the *Oxford Broom*: Waugh drew its cover and functioned as 'editor's support'; he wrote macabre stories for it, but no articles. On the other hand, the *Broom*'s manifesto, 'A Modern Credo' (February 1923, pp. 5–8) might be thought a source for the characteristics Waugh attributed to his generation in 'Too Young at Forty' (22 January 1929). From August 1923 drawings, stories and Union reports began to appear in the *Cherwell*, then recently acquired by a Philbrick-like eccentric (*A Little Learning*, p. 182), which tried to be brighter than the hearty *Isis*. It was in the *Isis* in the first six months of 1924 that most of Waugh's Oxford non-fiction appeared. From January to June he was sub-editor, film critic and Union reporter. He also contributed three feature articles. The film review printed here (23 January 1924) is one of seven to appear. The Union report (5 March 1924) is one of nine. To keep the Oxford journalism in perspective, it can be noted that during his Oxford years Waugh published approximately seventy caricatures, wood engravings, dust jacket designs, book plates, column heads and magazine covers, some of which continued to be used for many years. This was twice his output of stories, poems, articles and other miscellaneous pieces of writing.

From 12 April to 28 May 1927 Waugh worked on the *Daily Express* as a probationary reporter. As very little is known about this episode, and since the authorities (including Waugh) have described it variously, it may be useful to set out the ascertainable facts. In later life Waugh treated the experience as a joke: 'Then for three weeks I worked on a daily newspaper. "Worked" is too strong a term. I sat in the reporters' room and was occasionally sent out to cover unimportant stories. Nothing I wrote was ever printed' (2 December 1962). Earlier he had written more precisely to a *Life* executive, 'I was once a journalist for seven weeks' (*Letters*, 7 February 1946). Alec Waugh, who had an excellent memory, confirms one detail of his brother's account: 'They did not print a line he wrote' (*A Year to Remember*, London, 1975, p. 100). Waugh's diary entries regarding the job are significant for students of his journalism. 'I find the work most exhilarating' (9 May) indicates a temperamental attraction to observing life's oddities and to recording first-hand experience. 'Papers are full of lies' (23 May, the day Waugh was given notice) and 'Attended a fire in Soho where an Italian girl was supposed to have been brave but had actually done nothing at all' (1 July, referring to 27 May) indicate a scepticism fatal to a career in daily journalism.

The *belles-lettres* of the period reflect a predominant enthusiasm for art. It may be supposed that the young Waugh wrote a number of literary pieces, since he complains in the Dedicatory Letter to his 'nursery novel' that his surroundings were 'entirely literary' and filled with 'paper and print'. The Lancing diaries abound in acute criticism. But of the three reviews published at the time, only two are worth preserving: one is of J. F. Roxburgh's *The Poetic Procession* (November 1921), written in Waugh's last term at school when 'J.F.' was still an awe-inspiring 'mentor' (see *A Little Learning*, pp. 156–62). In 1927 the *Bookman* sent Waugh books for review and he sold review copies (*Diaries*, 27 August, 7 and 8 September 1927). Most *Bookman* reviews were anonymous, and it is impossible to trace Waugh's (possible) contributions. A signed review of R. Brimley Johnson's *English Letter Writers* appeared in the *Bookman* in March 1928, but it is not reprintable. All three essays of the period are about art and artists.

As this is the only period when Waugh's essays deal exclusively with art, a rough outline of his aesthetic, based on these and later essays and on unpublished notes, could be useful here. 'In Defence of Cubism' (November 1917) is a product of the only phase in Waugh's life when he was attracted by avant-gardism. He later described his modernism as 'aesthetic hypocrisy' (*A Little Learning*, pp. 116–23), but his performance was sufficiently convincing to cause his form master to warn in a term report against the 'ultra-modern'; and to lead Arthur Waugh to preface *Tradition and Change* (1919) with a Dedicatory Letter imploring Evelyn, whose 'studio' had become 'a temple of the most modern school of art', not to 'despise the old'. By the time Waugh came to write *Rossetti: His Life and Works* (1928) and 'Dante Gabriel Rossetti: A Centenary Criticism' (1 May 1928), he had rejected not only Cubism but modernist aesthetics. The brief theoretical chapters which frame the book, the few discreet sentences which conclude the article, scarcely hint at the thoughtfulness of the rejection, and as a matter of history were completely overlooked by all but two reviewers of the book. Only the annotations Waugh made (around 1926) in his copies of I. A. Richards's *Principles of Literary Criticism* (1925) and Hubert Waley's *The Revival of Aesthetics* (1926) explain his thinking at all fully. The more important marginalia with a fascinating exegesis can be found in pages 10–16 of Robert Murray Davis's *Evelyn Waugh, Writer* (1981). Briefly summarized in the order in which they crop up in Chapter 9 of *Rossetti*, Waugh's major points are (1) that there is no pure 'aesthetic emotion', and consequently no absolute distinction between 'beauty of picture and beauty of subject'; (2) that art is not necessarily, and only, 'a statement of formal relationships'; it may therefore be legitimately linked with 'representation' and other 'impure' elements. Waugh thus denied the intellectual bases of Post-Impressionist aesthetics, but he concluded by looking forward to a 'fusion' of modern and romantic theories that might result in a 'workable aesthetic'. One further point to emerge from the marginalia in Richards is the low value Waugh placed on the 'momentary consciousness' produced by the arts, and the high value he gave to the 'permanent modifications' they make to the mind. Waugh attacked Picasso in *The Times* (*Letters*, 18 December 1945) for merely 'sending' his devotees – working a 'mesmeric trick' on them – as against providing 'the sober and elevating happiness' gained from the masters. This was not, as it was assumed to be, mere teasing or philistinism of the 'excellent likeness' school, but an extension of a considered aesthetic. This applies with appropriately greater force to the major essay, 'The Death of Painting' (1956).

Rossetti and his circle remained a persistent theme in Waugh's journalism. Reviews about Rossetti (11 January 1935, 16 July 1945), Ruskin (17 July 1953, 17 September 1954) and Holman Hunt (14 October 1960) are reprinted in this volume. Reviews of books by Violet Hunt (8 October 1932), Vincent Brome (20 February 1959) and Gale Pederick (8 November 1964) have been omitted. Several other subjects figure prominently in Waugh's art criticism. Mid-Victorian furniture and decoration, as in 'The Philistine Age of English Decoration' (March 1938), in 'Victorian Taste' (3 March 1942) and in 'Those Happy Homes' (28 November 1954), enters in passing into many pieces of work. English narrative painting, generally despised by his contemporaries, was regarded by Waugh as a unique national school and a source of pride (9 July 1955). Architecture, broadly speaking, filled the place in Waugh's generation that nature had occupied in all generations since the Romantic Movement (26 February 1938). As for critical principles other than those already enunciated, or expressed in essays printed in this book, the foremost is 'that a work of art is not a matter of thinking beautiful thoughts or experiencing tender emotions (though these are its raw materials), but of intelligence, skill, taste, proportion, knowledge, discipline and industry' (Letters, 18 November 1960).

The preface to Francis Crease's Decorative Designs (1927) demands a particular comment because it displays, unmixed, the aestheticism and the attraction towards the secret and contemplative life which were permanently important to Waugh, though largely lost sight of in the dazzle created by the 'hard, bright' personae of maturity. The essay should be read in conjunction with the review of Edward Johnston's life (24 July 1959). The 'thrill and tremble of the heart' Waugh felt watching Johnston's 'swift, precise, vermilion strokes coming to life', the 'awe and exhilaration of the presence of genius', remained part of the Bright Young Novelist and of the 'hard-boiled' Man of the World. The portrait of Harold Acton (20 February 1924) is equally characteristic in its elegance, economy and felicity in praise.

. IN DEFENCE OF CUBISM[1] .

Art can, at the best of times, reproduce only an impression, and we have to employ such optical illusions as perspective by which to deceive the eye, and try

Drawing and Design, November 1917.
1 This is Waugh's first published essay, written when he was 14 years old. It was printed as an 'article' but not paid for, the editor claiming he had regarded it as a 'letter'. See A Little Learning, p. 121.

to give a flat surface the impression of depth. Thus that hackneyed argument, 'unlike life', is obviously quite fatuous. And yet, in twentieth-century Europe, a Europe prepared by the Impressionism of Turner and Manet, we find it cropping up again and again. 'That bears no possible resemblance to a figure' is a criticism which is repeated daily in every Cubist's studio – and yet it is recognized for what it is. Why?

Let us first consider the 'unlike life' argument. Should Art be like life? If we consult our greatest masters, Turner, Whistler, Manet, Constable, the answer is, No. If 'like life' means the irritating detail and impoverished sentiment of Frith, is it not best to shun such an ideal? And yet the anti-Cubist will ask, if not life, what should Art present? The answer is, surely the impression that objects give. Of course, we are not to suppose that the Cubist receives the impression of a maze of innumerable geometrical figures, but he must use some means of putting down his sensations. The black-and-white artist does not see life composed of black lines, but he translates his impressions into his own medium. Thus the resemblance to life does not in the least concern the merits of the picture.

The average person condemns Cubism unheard, frequently unseen. You hear the self-satisfied Philistine denouncing Cubism as pure affectation; you ask him what Cubist pictures he has seen; none, or perhaps one in a halfpenny paper reproduced by a smudged half-tone block printed on the cheapest paper by a rotary press – and quite probably a Futurist one. The would-be-funny cartoons entitled 'How to draw in Cubes', or 'Art (?) made easy', have given an already prejudiced public an entirely erroneous idea of the art.

Few people seem to realize that pictures in Cubes can be bad as well as good. They seldom, if ever, see a good Cubist picture. They see articles in magazines headed 'That Cubist', with reproductions of the most affected pictures, and judge the whole art by these. Such is the public for whom Art has to work!

In some few cases Cubism is a mode of expression which is dangerously rivalled by Impressionism. Most notable of these cases is the landscape, but this is only an exception. In most cases it is far superior to any medium in use. Its value as an advertising art has been shown. Will Scott has made it unequalled in the many-sided art of caricature. In fact, it is a Cubist poster (Will Scott's caricature of Sidney Drew) that has the honour of being the first artistic advertisement that is used outside the ordinary cinema. Roger Fry, and all the artists and craftsmen working co-operatively with him at the Omega workshops, has shown its value in house-decoration. Jean de Bochière has shown, by his portrait of himself, that Cubism is an unsurpassed medium for portraiture. Nevinson has demonstrated its use in almost every branch of painting and in some, notably one of a falling aeroplane, which is now on show at the Fine Arts Gallery, shows that it can attain effects where drawing of any other sort, either linear or academic painting, would fail.

And as to the coming years. I see before Cubism a glorious future. When it has passed through the fire of prejudice and contempt, it will emerge, purged of all the affectations which now beset it, as it really is. The public will accept it as it has accepted the Impressionists. The Academicians will fall and die unlamented, and Nevinson, Picasso and all the early Cubists who like 'The lone antagonists of destiny, who went down scornful before many spears' fought to the last against all the contempt and deliberate misunderstanding of a prejudiced public, will take their well-deserved places among the masters who · paved the way for their coming. But *'quod sit futurum cras fuge quaerere'*[1] – Let us not paint to produce fame in the future, but rather Art in the present.

. THE POETIC PROCESSION .

There will come a time when the most thrilling house match will be forgotten and the most intimate friendships lost and a very few things will be all that are essential and memorable of Lancing; of these, at least for all who have passed through the sixth form, one of the most vivid will be the personality of Mr J. F. Roxburgh,[2] and it is as a record of his personal taste that *The Poetic Procession* is of absorbing interest to all who have known him.

But those who look in it to find it couched in the language which has made him quoted wherever Lancing men meet, will find a different and a better thing. Now and then it bursts out like a happy, irresistible chuckle; the reference to Byron as 'that preposterous nobleman'; the comment on

> And half cut down a pasty, costly made
> Where quail and pigeon, lark and leveret lay
> Like fossil of the rock, with golden yolks
> Imbedded and ingellied.

'I have always liked that pie'; these have the 'J.F.' ring about them, and surely the note after 'Come live with me and be my love', 'I am sure she did go and live with him', is an echo of the inimitable 'Well, I daresay she did?'

But Mr Roxburgh is not speaking to the self-important immaturity of the sixth form; his audience are working men and he is telling them what poems he likes and why he likes them with the simplicity which comes of real erudition; and if one is surprised to find nearly four pages devoted to Tennyson and no

---

1 *Quid sit futurum cras, fuge quaerere et /quem Fors dierum cumque dabit, lucro appone.* 'Cease to inquire what the future has in store and take as a gift whatever today brings forth' (Horace, *Odes*, I, ix, 13).

Review of *The Poetic Procession*, by J. F. Roxburgh. *Lancing College Magazine*, November 1921.

2 J. F. Roxburgh was a master at Lancing and later Headmaster of Stowe. At Lancing he was one of Waugh's 'mentors' (see *A Little Learning*, pp. 156–62 and Waugh's review of *Roxburgh of Stowe*, by Noël Annan, *Observer*, 17 October 1965). In a letter of thanks for this review (which Waugh tipped into his copy of *The Poetic Procession*, now at Humanities Research Center, Texas), Roxburgh wrote: 'you have lifted the L.C.M. [*Lancing College Magazine*] to an entirely different level . . . if you use what the Gods have given you will do as much as any single person to shape the course of your generation.'

mention of Patmore or Yeats or the Pre-Raphaelites, it is because he is telling simple men the simplest poems he likes, very simply. In a half casual way, *The Poetic Procession* is full of subtle criticism. 'With Wordsworth it is always Sunday.' Of 'La Belle Dame sans Merci', 'I could not tell you what that poem means; I only know it means more to me every time I read it.' Of the 'Ode to the West Wind', 'I wonder if that could have been written if Coleridge had not written the "Ancient Mariner".'

The *Procession* ends – one might say that in a well-organized procession the most important people always bring up the end – with Rupert Brooke and Mr Masefield. One is glad that Mr Roxburgh did not go further and pour out his sarcasm on the Neo-Georgians; it has been a very fine procession and, as Mr Roxburgh says in the Preface, he has only allowed the most noble and most famous a place in it.

'The poet is a man who feels the same as you and I feel and sees the same sights, but who feels what he feels more intensely than we do, and sees when he sees more clearly, and because of this greater sensitiveness of his, he has ideas too that we have never had and can grasp truths that we have never reached. But – greatest gift of all – the poet can express what he feels and sees and thinks as common men cannot.'

Mr Roxburgh has said this of poetry; we might say it of his criticism.

. EDITORIAL .
THE COMMUNITY SPIRIT

'It is very beautiful,' said the foreigner, 'the life you must lead here. I, of course, have known nothing of this and only now, when you have shown me your school, can I realize what I have missed. It is the companionship – the community spirit of three hundred friends.'

We were standing on the steps of the lower quad looking out across the river. The school were trooping up the College Hill from leagues.[1] Three boys passed us.

'Look at those now,' he said, 'I feel I could be friends with everyone here.'

'I believe they are rather nice,' I said, 'but as a matter of fact I hardly know them. They're in another house, you see.'

A small, good-looking boy passed us, flushed with his game.

'And he – do you know him?'

'Yes – at least a little. He's a charming man. I used to like him rather a lot; but he's a good deal junior to me, you know, and it isn't encouraged by the authorities. They're quite right, of course, it wouldn't do, but it's rather bad luck when it is all right, isn't it?'

Lancing College Magazine, November 1921.
1 House Leagues was the Lancing inter-house football (or cricket) competition for average players. First Club was for the best players.

'It is,' said the foreigner, and then after a pause, 'And he – I can't think that he is so much junior to you?'

'Who, the man on the right? No, he used to be my best friend. I don't see much of him now – he's been made a house captain, you see. But I expect I shall be one next term and then it'll be all right.'

'But whom then have you chosen out of the three hundred to be your friends?'

'Well there's – oh I don't know really – I go about with Strang – he's a good fellow really, he only cares about motor-bikes and actresses, but he's about my place in the house and there's Dean, I don't like him much but he's good company, and several people like that.'

'I see,' said the foreigner.

. CORRESPONDENCE .

Dear Sir, – I feel that some reply is called for by your editorial in the last Magazine. Whether or no it is desirable to preface an official record with so controversial an article, I do not propose to discuss – that, of course, is for your own taste to decide. What I do wish to do is to take up your challenge and make some defence for the system of controlling friendship, either directly by authority or indirectly by public opinion, which is enforced at Lancing, as at all public schools.

Your first charge, Sir, is that boys are restricted in their choice of friends largely to their own house and to their own age. The first is inevitable in a school run upon the basis in which the house is the unit for all forms of athletics and society; the second is desirable, I think I need not remind anyone conversant with public school conditions.

The second charge, that on being made an house captain a boy usually drops most of his friends, may be defended upon two grounds. First, in the interests of discipline, it is essential that the officials shall form a caste apart; and, secondly, I do not think that anyone usually regrets the severance. Public-school friendship, I venture to think, is not so sacred an affair as people would suppose, and usually springs from the need of companionship. The term before anyone is made a house captain, he has the difficult task of impressing on those above him that he is both a sound character and also a formidable man to keep in the opposition. In the course of performing this task, he usually makes himself cordially detested by all his friends, and they are only too glad to

Lancing College Magazine, December 1921. The *nom-de-plume* comes from Macaulay's 'Epitaph on a Jacobite': 'For him I languished in a foreign clime/Grey-haired with sorrow in my manhood's prime,/Heard on Lavernia Scargill's whispering trees,/And pined by Arno for my lovelier Tees.'

take the occasion of his promotion as an opportunity of dropping him. I am
Faithfully yours,

LAVERNIA SCARGILL.

[We feel that we have given our own views on this question with sufficient
clearness, but would welcome further correspondence from the School and
Old Boys. – Ed.]

. THE YOUNGEST GENERATION[1] .

During the last few years, a new generation has grown up; between them and
the young men of 1912 lies the great gulf of the war. What will they stand for
and what are they going to do?

The men of Rupert Brooke's generation are broken. Narcissus-like, they
stood for an instant amazedly aware of their own beauty; the war, which old
men made, has left them tired and embittered. What will the young men of
1922 be?

They will be, above all things, clear-sighted, they will have no use for
phrases or shadows. In the nineteenth century the old men saw visions and the
young men dreamed dreams. The youngest generation are going to be very
hard and analytical and unsympathetic, but they are going to aim at things as
they are and they will not call their aim 'Truth'.

And because they are clear-sighted, they will not be revolutionaries and they
will not be poets and they will not be mystics; there will be much that they will
lose, but all that they have will be real.

And they will be reticent too, the youngest generation. The young men of
the nineties subsisted upon emotion and their poetry and their painting thrills
with it. They poured out their souls like water and their tears with pride;
middle-aged observers will find it hard to see the soul in the youngest generation.

But they will have – and this is their justification – a very full sense of
humour, which will keep them from 'the commission of all sins, or nearly all,
save those that are worth committing.' They will watch themselves with,
probably, a greater egotism than did the young men of the nineties, but it will
be with a cynical smile and often with a laugh.

It is a queer world which the old men have left them and they will have few
ideals and illusions to console them when they 'get to feeling old'. They will not
be a happy generation.

Editorial, *Lancing College Magazine*, December 1921.

1 A speech on Youth and Age given by Waugh and written into his diary 23–30 September 1920
explains most of the allusions in this editorial. See also diaries for 25 June 1920 and 22 November
1921, the latter for the influence of Rupert Brooke ('the beauty of living has gone out of the
youngest generation').

. FROM THE UNION .

At the second Public Business Meeting of the term, held on Thursday 2 February, the motion was:– 'That this House would welcome Prohibition.' During question time material proofs were forthcoming to the effect that the Junior Treasurer's practice fell short of his theory on this subject.

Mr W. Duncan (Pembroke) began his speech convincingly, but had only time to dissociate himself from Mr Pussyfoot Johnson and the Salvation Army when he was compelled to withdraw by indisposition, for which we were very sorry. His place was most promptly taken by

Mr H. F. Bagnall (St John's), who also disclaimed the sentimental views usually held by prohibitionists. It was not these people, but the men of experience such as doctors and schoolmasters, that were the real strength of the movement. He cautioned the Opposition against using as an argument the freedom of the individual. All law was a restraint of that. His speech was punctuated by the migrations of peoples, specially workers of the Church.

. THE UNION .

Anyone who went to the Union on 28 October hoping to hear a sane discussion of what party government really meant must have been disappointed. In fact, in reviewing the course of the debate one feels that disappointment must have been the result of any expectations; the evening was typical of the Union at its worst. The members seem to have quoted the couplet about the time when none was for the party and all for the state so often that they have become firmly convinced that all party strife and partisan allegiance must necessarily be treachery to the nation. One hoped in vain for a speaker who would show the case that resulted from the steady fruition of conflicting loyalties; everyone concentrated his energies – more or less successfully – upon abusing or defending the late coalition.

One of the most successful was Mr Gardiner; he made a very convincing speech, full of anecdotes and statistics, both of which he seems to regard as being, alike, no worse for exaggeration.

Mr Pares, who also spoke on the paper, was clever and scholarly – too clever, in fact, and too scholarly, for the Union. Mr Elwes, who spoke first, has a fragile and rather inconclusive fluency which delighted the House.

Maiden speeches were made by Mr Gordon, of Brasenose, and Mr Molson,

Cherwell, 7 February 1922. See *A Little Learning*, p. 182: 'My only scoop [as a reporter for the *Cherwell*] was . . . when Mr John Sutro stood up to speak . . . [after] he had been drinking heavily . . . . A special copy had to be printed for [Sutro's parents] with the passage deleted.'

Oxford Fortnightly Review, 4 November 1922.

of New College. Mr Gordon speaks with a quiet subtlety reminiscent of the School Debating Society, but shows promise of considerable success when he has adapted himself to the House. Mr Molson spoke at the very end, and was unable, through lack of time, to say all he wished. He said enough, however, to make the House expectant of future things from him.

The division showed an easy majority for the motion; it was interesting to observe that this decision against coalition was carried by a combination of Labour and Conservative opinion.

. MYSELF WHEN YOUNG .

Mr Waugh is a writer about whom it has been peculiarly difficult to form any just opinion. He is already the author of six books; the first of these, *The Loom of Youth*, was an enormous and immediate success and because this success was obviously due more to its interest as propaganda than its virtue as a work of art, the fact has largely been overlooked that it was a remarkably good novel. Mr Waugh's second novel, which appeared last year without any of the sensation of *The Loom*, encouraged one in the belief that he is a skilled and a thoroughly sincere artist; one could not, however, disregard the feeling that *The Lonely Unicorn* was too carefully built, too highly restrained; it was frankly hard to interest oneself in what interested Mr Waugh.

Myself When Young is a definite challenge to this doubt. Mr Waugh has set himself to write an intensely personal book which should be neither a novel or an essay, but simply a record of the sort of thing which he does and the sort of thing which interests him. He shows us how he works, what processes of thought go to build up his stories, what sort of persons he meets and likes writing about. He is, it would seem, making his position clear to the world. He seems to say, 'You cannot deny that I am an artist. There are the materials with which I propose to work. Whatever you think, there are the things which will always interest me. I hope you will like them. If you do not, I shall be the poorer man, but it is thus that I shall write.'

This seems, to us, at any rate, to be the attitude from which the book is written. Reviewers in quite reputable papers have, since the publication of the book, been unanimous in regarding it as the confession of a would-be middle-aged young man of the world. Perhaps the title was unfortunate. To us it seems that *Myself When Young* is essentially the work of a young man writing a preface to his future work. There is in the book very little assumption of age – though the sentimentalities of middle-aged men are undisguisedly one of the things which Mr Waugh finds interesting – it is on the contrary full of genuine hope for the future and a perfectly modest consciousness of strength.

Review of *Myself When Young*, by Alec Waugh. *Cherwell*, 10 November 1923. Unsigned, but included in E.W. scrapbook at the Humanities Research Center, Austin, Texas, USA.

The importance of the book, then, lies in the question 'Is it interesting?' and this is a question which every reader must decide for himself. To us it was intensely and quite surprisingly interesting. We did not know that there was so much romance in cricket and football. About a third of the book is devoted to such games, and it seems a great testimony to the writer's personality that one reader at least whose knowledge of them is limited to memories of 'junior house games' in the dim past should have been quite engrossed in his dissertations upon them.

There is also a great deal of literary criticism; Mr Waugh's opinions are those of the professional writer accustomed to the chatter of literary parties rather than of the aesthetician, but they are none the less valuable and far more entertaining for this; he regards writing essentially as a trade, but as a noble trade; he is shrewd and sincere in his judgments of fellow tradesmen.

But perhaps the most significant part of the book is the little collection of stories scattered about it. Here, it would seem, Mr Waugh is putting into practice his principles and one can say without hesitation that they are very good stories indeed. 'Last Love' is perhaps the finest. The story is peculiarly suited to him – the final romance of a successful man of the world and his realization of middle age. A simple and not very new plot, but told and interpreted in a way which gives it unbelievable subtlety and originality.

The whole book, as one would expect, is extremely well written and, in spite of its apparently haphazard nature, very closely knit together. The last three or four pages are one of the best achievements of pure style we have seen in any writer under 30. It is a book which might very easily have been a failure; Mr Waugh has made it a very definite success and has proved his claim to respect for his future books.

. SEEN IN THE DARK .
THE MERRY-GO-ROUND

The Merry-go-Round at the Super Cinema obviously sets out to be a 'big' film. It starts well in the grand manner with the awakening and toilet of an Austrian nobleman, and one settled down to expect a 'high life' drama of the Ingram-Ibanez sort. One was almost immediately engulfed, however, into a violent and sentimental circus life, with all the usual panoply of hunchbacks, flagellant ring-masters, gorillas and sorrowing clowns. It was rather a pity; one could with pleasure have seen more of the Viennese debauch, and, to be honest, the clown's dying wife was a little tiresome. There was only one unusual part of the story; one had, not unnaturally, supposed that the faithful hunchback would go to the war, be wounded, and emerge from the hospital whole and handsome. This did not happen; he won a lottery and solaced himself with his gorilla,

Review of *The Merry-go-Round. Isis*, 23 January 1924.

while the heroine married the wicked nobleman. For so much injustice one was grateful.

But, of course, the real charm of the cinema is in the momentary pictures and situations which appear. There were two of these in *The Merry-go-Round* which made any shortcomings immeasurably worth while. One was the gorilla standing in the window before it killed the circus-master, and the other, a little before it, was the scene in which the villain pursued the heroine round the half-lighted merry-go-round. The violent struggle in the strange, unmoving jungle of monstrous animals was almost Sitwellian.

It was a pity that the management did not show a comic film instead of *The Bolted Door*. It will be a sorry time when Oxford audiences become too stupid to appreciate Snub Pollard.

. WITTENBERG AND OXFORD .
'A little more than kin and less than kind.'

There is, I think, no reason for believing that Shakespeare went to Oxford; indeed, what little evidence there is for his having had any early life at all is almost entirely opposed to the idea. This perhaps is one of the most formidable arguments which might be brought forward by people who believe that other men wrote his plays for him; how else could he have written such a brilliant study of Oxford mentality? And yet it is a disquieting reflection that the finest Oxford studies have all been written by men who were not at the University. With every reason for their success, *Sinister Street, The City in the Foreground* and *Patchwork* all failed, while *Verdant Green* is completely successful. It may be that an Oxford education makes people too self-conscious or just too stupid – I do not know. Our immediate concern is with the success of the foreigner, not the failure of the native.

This week, for the first time in its history, the OUDS are producing the greatest undergraduate tragedy. It is strange that they should have existed so long without attempting it; it is quite incredible that from the Ruskin roofs of north Oxford and the more murky backways of Fleet Street protests have arisen against the impertinence of the attempt. Elsewhere in this paper will be found a detailed discussion of the merits of the production. Here it is only fitting that we should say this, that the OUDS are probably the only group of people who could hope to give an adequate interpretation of *Hamlet* for the simple reason that the whole significance of the play is that it is an under-graduate play; if they have realized this they will have succeeded, but it is a sec-ret well hidden under the shabby stage properties of 300 years. There are more phantoms about the pathetic prince than his murdered father; all about him, with well-schooled gestures, stand the shades of the great actors who have mouthed his lines and bowed to the cheers, waving their arms, shaking off the powder from their wigs and driving him on to destruction. It is no easy thing to escape from these grim beasts to the ordered simplicity necessary to understanding.

What is the story? An adultery, a poisoning, a ghost, a revenging son – the readiest stock-in-trade of the Elizabethan stage. Burbage must have had many like it growing loose-leaved among the foils and clothes' chests; it is not unlike the murder of Gonzago, a story extant and written in very choice Italian. It would require more than this to make a work of art a by-word among the less educated classes for 300 years.

Surely what gives *Hamlet* its whole charm and personality is that instead of the usual gang of Renaissance noblemen one sees slouching and swaggering about the prison palace of Elsinore a rather intelligent, well bred and wholly typical crowd of English undergraduates?

Mr Fagan[1] himself, I believe, remarked on this and suggested that the 'lick-spittle' courtiers, Rosencrantz and Guildenstern, would probably have edited the Wittenberg *Broom*.[2] Doubting, as in courtesy we must, the closeness of the analogy between these rather horrid young men and the contributors to our distinguished contemporary, we welcome this point of criticism. But surely the comparison might be carried further? From any window in Oxford it would not be hard to pick out twenty Osrics and 200 Horatios, and surely Polonius himself, napkin in hand, may be seen hobbling from dinner to the Senior Common Room.

But why not further still? Scholars and journalists are continually fretting themselves about the character of Hamlet; Mr Scaife has put his, Hamlet's, sanity forward to be discussed by the Union Society; even in the Senior Common Rooms, I am told, the thing is debated. And yet, and yet is it so densely obscure, so inextricably complex?

Hamlet is a prince by birth; he is surly at home and openly insolent to his father's friends; as a lover, half-hearted but romantic and not ungraceful; a tolerable sportsman, thoroughly self-assured when discussing the drama but a little at sea when discussing life; woefully worried about all the obvious sorts of difficulties like suicide and himself. If only these contentious scholars would look out of their windows; if only these journalists would take a train from Paddington to Oxford; surely their answer is here. Would they not see a hundred Hamlets pottering about the Broad Street and all mad north-north-west?

Tonight the Union intend debating 'Was Hamlet mad?' from eight until half-past eleven – I think I can see Hamlet doing exactly the same.

1 James Fagan, founder of the Oxford Playhouse.
2 A reference to the *Oxford Broom*. See following item.

. MR HAROLD ACTON (CHRIST CHURCH) .
EDITOR OF *THE OXFORD BROOM*; AUTHOR OF *AQUARIUM*

Mr Harold Acton was born in Florence in July 1904 and, after a decorous education at Wixenford and Eton, came up to Christ Church in October 1922. It was not long before he was recognized as one of the most remarkable figures in Oxford. It is quite extraordinary how Mr Acton always attracts attention by sheer distinction of manner while utterly eschewing the eccentricities by which lesser men seek to make themselves conspicuous. It is true that, like most of his countrymen, he wears what a recent Sunday paper was pleased to describe as 'sideboards', but, as he said himself, the victorious army at Waterloo wore them on the playing fields of Eton; he also has a very beautiful Benedictine-coloured waistcoat, but he seldom wears that in public. Ordinarily well-made clothes and a blackthorn stick, fairly short hair, and perhaps a copy of the *Isis* under his arm, are his chief 'properties'. His contempt for 'aesthetes' is unbounded, and not long ago, when accused of being one by a group of youths round the door of one of the smaller colleges, he waved his umbrella and scattered them with unexpected ferocity.

At Eton he collected Whistler pamphlets, helped to found the Art Society, and contributed to Mr Brian Howard's enterprising but rather formidable *Eton Candle*. In Oxford he found a more congenial atmosphere. He painted his room in Meadows bright yellow, and collected the most incredible Early Victorian decorations. He also purchased a megaphone through which he reads his own and the Sitwells' poetry in a way which, with all respect to the assiduity of the OUDS, is inimitable.

The *Oxford Broom* first appeared in the spring of last year, and, unlike most publications of this kind, shows no signs of dying. It is a paper which was badly needed. When Mr Acton came up to Oxford, he found the University, as far as literature was concerned, in a very sad way. There was a grim pipe-smoking intelligentsia who lived in Wellington Square, ran the 'Ordinary' and despised almost everything; there were a few ornamental and rather tiresome folk who were proud of having read Mallarmé; and there was the *Oxford Outlook* under the care of Mr Scaife, and Mr Murray and Mr Hollis. With the *Broom* high spirits entered into this foetid atmosphere. It was advertised with the impudence of a patent medicine – '*Are you a corpse mentally?*' – and fully justified its boast. It has proved a magnificent tonic for the sullen mind of the literary undergraduate.

Mr Acton's own book of poems, *Aquarium*, appeared in April 1923. It has already been reviewed in this paper, and further literary criticism would be out of place in this article. It is sufficient to say that whatever signs it bore of immaturity – and indeed many of the poems were written at Eton – it has very

Isis, 20 February 1924. Unsigned, but in a letter to the editor dated 11 January 1982 Sir Harold Acton confirmed that Waugh wrote it.

few signs of imitation – a quality curiously enough which was often attributed to it by the less discerning sections of the local and London press. *Aquarium* is a very fine expression of Mr Acton's personality, showing all the qualities of exuberance and charm which his friends associate with him.

One quality of Mr Acton's which he controls so well that few recognize its existence is an amazing erudition. Only after one has known him for quite a long time does one realize that there is no subject on which he has not got complete and highly specialized knowledge. It is a quality which, combined with exuberance, is of immeasurable value.

Oxford has every reason to be proud of Mr Acton, both for his poetry and for himself.

. LOST, LOST, O LOST .

Mr Evelyn Waugh regrets to announce that he has lost a walking-stick made of oak, preposterously short with a metal band round it. It is a thing of no possible value to anyone but himself; for him it is an incalculable loss. If it should fall into the hands of any honest or kindly man or woman, will he or she bring it to the *Isis* Office, and what so poor a man as Mr Waugh is can do, shall not be lacking.

. THE UNION .

The crowd at the Union on Thursday was prodigious. They began assembling at about tea-time, and were admitted at dinner-time; care had been taken to obstruct all the gangways with stewards; for sheer physical discomfort I have never known such a successful debate. It was successful for other reasons, too. All sorts of exceedingly important people came up for it; there was a general atmosphere about the room that we were all taking part in an historical event; one can easily forgive the President for his slightly nervous and self-important manner.

We began by standing up in silence at Mr Scaife's suggestion, in respect to those members of the Society who were 'no longer in the land of the living' – a curious phrase but a praiseworthy sentiment.

The question for debate was, 'That Civilization has advanced since this Society first met.'

Questions were severely dealt with, and Professor Gilbert Murray moved his motion. He admitted that there were many things which were not as good as they used to be – Windsor soup, and marmalade and things like that; famous beauties no longer moved his friends to tears and his brother never danced like

Isis, 5 March 1924.

From 'The Passing Hour'. *Isis*, 20 February 1924.

a frog. He saw hope, however, for our civilization in the fact that no one ever looked on anyone younger than himself as being really civilized.

Mr John Buchan, opposing, found it hard to pull this argument to pieces. He turned from it, and showed that this was a generation disillusioned of all the dreams of the founders of the Society; that young men had no prospect of adventure or discovery; that we were all moving between narrow walls; that we none of us spent our more emotional moments in reading Pickering 'on adult baptism'. This sounds a rather gloomy speech, but it was delivered with so much charm and wit that it left the House wholly undepressed and in a good mood to receive the metallic wit of Mr P. Guedalla.

It is hard to give an accurate impression of this ex-President's speech; every sentence of it had an unexpected form; every epithet was unusual; every argument twisted obliquely from its usual significance or spun inside out. It seemed to me to represent cosmopolitan Oxford oratory in its most exciting form.

He was followed by the Rev. Father R. A. Knox, who was almost wholly different from him in mentality, but clearly showed the same training. Father Knox showed how from the anthropological considerations of our present ideas about food and drink, the apportionment of work between men and women, burial customs and drama, we were rapidly approaching the civilization of the savage.

After Mr Buchan's speech an amendment had been proposed by Mr Gordon Bagnall, an ex-President from Mr Scaife's own college. Although it had not yet been opposed, the President proved himself a conscientious interpreter of the pleasure of the House by allowing Mr Wedderburn to move 'that the question be now put'. We rejected the amendment heavily.

Mr E. C. Bentley (Merton), ex-President, thought we were getting Americanized.

Dr H. A. James (St John's) knew that we had got profane.

Dr Rosslyn Bruce (Worcester) proposed an amendment which the President first declared to be in order and then on Mr Bagnall's insistence ruled out of order. Dr Bruce made a jolly speech, and held back all the crowds who were standing in the gangways intending to get away.

Dr A. J. Carlisle (University), ex-President, replied to Dr James with his usual generosity towards youth. It was a very charming speech.

Mr Gerald Gardiner was the first undergraduate to speak, and said all the right things and made an interesting little contribution to the debate.

Mr N. A. Beechman claimed to be the corpse at the epigrammarian's funeral.

Mr Bandaranaike thought that civilization was all right, because it only meant doing the same unpleasant things in a slightly more pleasant way.

There also spoke Mr J. S. Collis, Mr J. D. Woodruff, Mr L. C. Redmond Howard (Trinity College, Dublin), the Hon. H. Lygon (Magdalen) and Mr H. J. S. Wedderburn.

On a division there voted: ayes, 576; noes, 279.

The motion was carried by 297 votes. Then we went away to bed after really rather a good evening.

. OXFORD AND THE NEXT WAR .
A LETTER OF EXHORTATION FROM
AN UNDERGRADUATE TO A FRIEND ABROAD

Dear Bill,

It occurs to me that I have allowed almost the whole term to go by without writing to you. This was disgraceful. My only excuse can be your utter remoteness and the complete heart-breaking dreariness of everyone and everything in Oxford.

You did well to go down. I can think of nothing which has happened this term which could at all interest you. All your friends have behaved more or less abominably to each other, as they used in your time, and have fallen into various degrees of ill favour with the authorities. The Proctors have been peculiarly aggressive this term. You probably saw, or will have seen before you get this, that they banned our 1840 Exhibition without any sort of reason. They seem to be determined that we shall not enjoy ourselves. The other day I was walking home with a pickaxe which I borrowed to complete the costume of 'the Conservative Working Man' for a fancy-dress party, when I was stopped by a bowler-hatted servant and brought to the Proctors, who told me that it was not seemly to carry workmen's tools about. I wonder if it was just snobbery or ill nature, or whether he was afraid of being attacked.

The Union has been sadder than ever and has just been celebrating a centenary. I do think it is time that something was done to stop the thing. You cannot imagine what the debates have been like this term, with Scaife setting a tone of arrogant mediocrity and people like de Gruchy trying to clear things up. They have elected Gerald Gardiner President this term – do you remember him? A tall man with a jerky voice who is generally writing things in the OUDS.

The OUDS, by the way, have shown themselves in no way as contemptuous of the press as Scaife. I have never seen anything like the amount of comment and praise which Gyles's simple little performance of 'Hamlet' roused in the London papers. It was a thoroughly good amateur show; that is to say, everyone knew his part tolerably well, and the lights didn't go out or the curtains catch fire, or the wigs come off, or anything like that, but all the fuss in Fleet Street was utterly silly. It is a pity that all these editors and reporters treat Oxford so seriously. They even, some of them, swallowed poor Jim Fagan's lame little excuses about 'infinity' for his very commonplace 'geometry and curtains'.

Isis, 12 March 1924.

The Bicester have had to close down owing to foot-and-mouth disease, but that doesn't affect a poor man like myself. There has been quite enough to exasperate us all without that.

You know, Bill, what we want is another war. I become more and more convinced of that every day.

These tiresome historians always find causes for their wars in national expansion and trade rivalry and religion and such things. I don't know about these because, as you know, I am never up in time to read the newspapers, but I gather from those who do that things are pretty unsettled. What seems to me more important is that we have a great body of young men of all sorts of education just longing for another general disturbance. We all had the fortune to be brought up in easy familiarity with bombs and casualty lists and bad bread and all the things young men used to be warned about, and we know exactly how bearable and unbearable they are.

We also know that when there is a war the fighting people at least have moments of really intense enjoyment and really intense misery – both things which one wants at our age. As far as I can see, there is just no chance of any of us being able to earn a living, or at least a living decent enough to allow of any sort of excitement or depravity. Here we are with bills, over-fastidious tastes and a completely hopeless future. What can we do but long for a war or a revolution?

If on your travels you meet any traitors who want to levy war against the king, or kings who want to overthrow representative institutions, or fanatics who want to convert people by the sword to some ghastly religion, or jolly adventurers who want to kill all the Mormons or check the Yellow Peril, or restore the Hapsburgs or the Stuarts, or invade America in the cause of alcohol or China in the cause of opium, or France in the cause of Sabbatarianism, or the Vatican in the cause of compulsory vaccination, please tell them, him or her that we can raise a very jolly platoon of gentlemen-adventurers for them in Oxford if they, he or she will pay us handsomely and give us a good chance of a speedy death.

What a long letter, Bill!

Yours,
Evelyn.

. PREFACE TO THE DECORATIVE DESIGNS
OF FRANCIS CREASE .

Only one man could suitably have undertaken to write a preface for this collection of temperate and exalted designs; that is John Ruskin. I say this carefully, knowing very well that name and period have become so indissolubly wedded in modern criticism, that by a larger and less fastidious public than this book is intended to reach, such a statement would be regarded as pertly ironical. What I mean is not that there is the most remote connection between Mr Crease's art and the efflorescence of Venetian Gothic and aesthetic social-ism of the Ruskin period, but that the qualities for its just appreciation are exactly that fineness of perception and delicate equipoise of senses that Ruskin possessed in so high a degree and for which he found no adequate stimulus in the art of his own period. Ruskin would have risen exuberantly to these designs, and he alone could, without impertinence, descant upon their elo-quent excellencies. They belong to no period; they are the outcome of no particular school or training, but of an individual sensibility patiently con-cerned with the beauty of natural form and in intimate communion with other minds of the same temper, whether in their period they showed themselves in the profuse invention of luxurious textiles, or in the austere incision of gems. They are northern, rather than Mediterranean, more of Chartres than of Rome, but often, and particularly in the later designs, leaving a faintly discern-ible fragrance of the East as of a spiced wind borne to alien hills or of the Magi at some Flemish *Nativity*. They have little about them that is capricious, nothing that is mannered or superficial, nothing assertive, nothing crude, nothing debased.

It is just for these reasons that they are noticeably unsympathetic to the present period. Looking back upon the last few months in London, I think of three typical artistic events: M. Michel Sevier's Exhibition of Paintings, the Magnasco Society's Exhibition of Baroque Drawings, and the production of *Mercury* by the Russian ballet. These, with the Charvet ties and shell button-holes, Lord Lathom's interior decorations, the paper boys crying the news of Mrs Bonati's murder, and the gossip in the constricted foyer of the Prince's Theatre, make up 'the period'. They go together, the vital with the trivial; but Mr Crease's work is aloof from all this. It cannot become old-fashioned because it is not part of a fashion. It is intended for a small circle composed almost exclusively of his personal friends, and thus it is fitly produced in a narrowly limited edition, not aiming like most limited editions at creating an artificial rarity, but rare from its own nature, appealing to few, and steadfast in its appeal.

No doubt it seems presumptuous to insist so strongly upon the good qualities necessary for the appreciation of Mr Crease's work, and then to put

Preface to Francis Crease, *Thirty-Four Decorative Designs*. London, privately printed, 1927.

myself forward to express this appreciation. Let me explain how it is that I come to be writing this preface. I am Mr Crease's first and, so far, his only pupil; whatever I seem to be claiming for myself is derived directly from him.

It was, oddly enough, my house tutor at Lancing who first introduced me to him, when I was 16 years old. For some time I had observed him in Chapel on Sunday evenings, an incongruously elegant figure in the side aisle, who, drawn by the music, used to sit through most of the service in meditation, bear with the sermon, and then wrapping his cloak about him, would disappear mysteriously onto the downs.

I had some interest in heraldry at the time, and, being ecclesiastically minded, in illumination, and I won a prize of some sort for decorating a collect, an architect of eminence judging the award. I began to feel artistic, and, during harvest, wore a red poppy in my buttonhole, which was thought to be rather bad form. One afternoon I was changing after a boxing competition, in which I had been characteristically unsuccessful, when I received a summons to come to my house tutor's room, and to bring with me my prize prayer. I came sulkily. Mr Crease was at tea with him, enthroned among canes and lists. I presented my illumination and stood about uncomfortably until told to sit down. After a close inspection he politely commended the pretty colours, and then, with a touch of vehemence in his voice, deplored the 'unworthiness' of the script. It was not script at all, said Mr Crease, and then, with bewildering diffidence, he offered to teach me how it should be done; the illumination, he said, was beautiful, far superior to anything he could ever hope to do; it was shameful that the script should be unworthy of it; with great pains he had learned a little of the art; perhaps he could be of some use to me. It was an unusual way for a master's guest to address a gauche and recently pummelled schoolboy. I looked at my house tutor, and, to my surprise and lasting gratitude, he consented.

At the time Mr Crease was living at Lychpole, a secluded farm on the Sompting estate. Either there or to Sompting Abbotts I went every week for my lesson, and it is no exaggeration to say that from then until Mr Crease left Sussex, these meetings coloured and dominated everything that I did.

On the afternoon of my first visit to him, I was overtaken by a heavy storm on the top of Steep Down, and arrived very late, very wet and very shy. He lent me dry clothes, gave me tea in a handleless Crown Derby cup, and taught me with the utmost patience how to cut a quill pen. Everything about his rooms was tranquil and beautiful – the old furniture, the richly coloured china and embroidery on the chimney-piece, the silver candlesticks, the monochrome reproductions of the Sistine frescoes, and, epitomizing all that the place stood for, the *Winter-Cherry* design with the inscription –

> I love all beauteous things,
> I seek and adore them;
> God hath no better praise,
> And man in his hasty days
> Is honoured for them.

It was an intoxicating contrast to the rain outside and the discomfort and rancour of the school I had left. When he set me to write I found that the verses he had put out for me were some lines on Sherborne Abbey written by my brother.

I never became much good at script; I had not the time for practice or the patience – it is, after all, a mature accomplishment – but I learned far more. In writing, once the barest respect has been paid to the determining structure of the letter, the pen is free to flourish and elaborate as it will. In the control of these often minute variations of form, in the direction of serifs, the spacing and poising of shapes, the sense of historical propriety, there is scope for every talent required in the building of a cathedral. At the time my own predilection was for the most rigid fourteenth-century Gothic hand; Mr Crease's script was the freest possible adaption of the Celtic scripts of the ninth and tenth centuries. In learning to prefer his style, I gained for the first time some insight into the underlying motives of linear design. Ruskin started his pupils with a lichened twig or spray of ivy to teach them the alphabet; Mr Crease started me with the alphabet and led me to the lichened twig and the singularly lovely irises that grew in the garden at Sompting Abbotts.

I had lived for the most part in London among bricks and buses, and was very insensitive to natural beauty. I think that I was even disposed to regard a love of Nature as a sign of effeminacy and weakness of intellect. One afternoon Mr Crease set me to do a water-colour of the meadows below his window and the hill beyond, and then, leaning over my shoulder as I strained and niggled at the line of the larches, suddenly transfigured my drawing with great brushfuls of gold and crimson. He used to walk back with me sometimes as far as the turn in the Roman ditch round Steep Down where Lancing Ring suddenly comes into view, I eagerly questioning him about architecture or aesthetics or Limoges or Maiolica, he trying to turn me to the beauty of the evening and the downs.

Whatever he said was devoutly entered in my diary every evening.

'The tree which moves some to tears of joy,' he would quote, 'is in the eyes of others only a green thing which stands in the way . . . some scarce see Nature at all. But to the eyes of the man of imagination, Nature is Imagination itself.'

It is this transfusion of everything with the pure joy of Beauty, in which nothing is dissected or set aside, but everything is seen as part of one moment of worship, that is so characteristic of Mr Crease's work.

A letter of his written in March 1920 seems to me to express his attitude to Nature as I cannot hope to do in this preface, and to explain his designs.

My dear Evelyn Waugh [he wrote],
This evening whilst you were in Chapel was one of extraordinary splendour, and I wished you also might have been touched by it. For myself, the shadows of the prison house have fallen long ago, but now and again some shape of beauty lifts the shadow for a time. It is so much easier to feel one could write 'Resentment Poems' than 'Songs of Exuberance'; I hope it may never be so with you.
What I have in mind is the hope that you, like so many others of intelligence, may

not run after definitions of Art and Beauty and the like, feeling the definition and failing to feel the Beauty itself as it approaches on an evening like this evening. I can think of an Oxford friend at this moment who feels nature described in a sonnet and sitting in his arm-chair, but seems to fail in the open air. And again I remember a Don at Oxford learned in Greek Gems, telling me how all the other Dons would be interested in curious knowledge and facts about any gem, but its beauty always, or nearly always, escaped them. I often think of that fifteenth-century writer who said, 'I would rather feel compunction than know its definition.' Happily we are not thinking of compunction at this moment, but you see what I mean. No Flemish painter of the seventeenth century or English school of the nineteenth could hope to convey more than the suggestion of the visionary splendour of this evening – Wordsworth and Gray came nearest to such an atmosphere, so I believe.

One thing in my youth I had, and it was a verse or two of Gray repeated to me – I must be more thankful.

I wish you could have seen the flight of gulls in the fields on the left of the Ring, against the softer greys and greens, blue and rose colours; hundreds of them suddenly took their way home to the sea in one long stream following each other, and changing colour in the sunlight, and making sad music as a prelude to the coming symphony of colour. I always feel that those passing through Lancing have had all that I have never had – but it does seem sad that somehow or other it so often leads to the Hotel Metropole at Brighton as an Ideal, and not to the Truth which makes you free. Don't give this to Gordon to print! [my house tutor, who owned a small hand-press].

But I have no wish to write a history of my own aesthetic awakening or to detail a development that has been lamentably incomplete and impure; my only hope is to justify myself for this pressing forward first with my homage.

It is a particularly happy moment, it seems to me, for the collection of Mr Crease's work, for the decisive processes of stitching and pressing.

In a distinguished essay on the 'Art of Francis Crease' in the August number of the *Beacon*, 1922, Mr Osbert Burdett wrote:

For the return to nature that his instinct first led him to follow has been, as we already see, the first step on the road that runs beyond nature to the province of pure design, where the forms of the artist are filled entirely by imaginative life, though themselves organically derived from the motives he has left behind him.

This tendency, so acutely discerned five years ago, has become abundantly and gloriously evident in Mr Crease's latest designs. Compare for example No. 15 (folio 14) at the beginning of the book with Nos. 28 and 31 (folios 26 and 29) at the end, and you will see, fully achieved, the emancipation of the essential structure of design from its accidental resemblances – as fully as in the abstractions of the *Mercury* ballet. The procession climbs in decorous progress from the meadow-sweetness of the *Bats and Borage* (folio 4) to the superb luxuriance of the *Pride of the Peacock* (folio 9) and the *Wild-Carrot* (folio 10), to the almost mathematic *Cyclamen* (folio 22), and then, at another turn in the path, begins to emerge into austere and unpeopled heights, into a rarer atmosphere and more brilliant sunlight, while far below the groves of Lychpole have become a green place in the spreading horizon.

And surely another sheet is already stretched upon the drawing board?

. DANTE GABRIEL ROSSETTI:
A CENTENARY CRITICISM .

Centenaries have been crowding in upon us with rather embarrassing profusion during the last few years, each with its little crop of reprints and biographies, but, wearisome as no doubt they tend to become, they serve the very useful purpose of providing the occasion for reconsidering one by one and reassessing the great bulk of exalted reputations that was the legacy of the Victorian age. In no case is this more salutary than in that of Dante Gabriel Rossetti. His pictures hang in the public galleries, his poems are in the anthologies, his name is familiar to the least erudite, but there is, notwithstanding, a peculiar vagueness about his fame; he seems to stand in his period like some Dantesque figure in one of his own canvases, dominant but singularly ill-defined. His contemporaries are as much to blame for this as we are. During his lifetime a golden haze had already begun to accumulate about his melancholy and secluded genius, which Theodore Watts-Dunton's *Aylwyn* did little to dissipate. 'What a supreme man is Rossetti!' wrote Philip Bourke Marston, the blind poet. 'Why is he not some great exiled king that we might give our lives in trying to restore him to his kingdom?' 'You must not say anything about Rossetti,' said Whistler on his death-bed, 'Rossetti was a king.' When this species of admiration begins to fail its place is too often taken by ridicule or neglect. At the present time, a hundred years after Rossetti's birth, his fame seems in real danger of extinction. How far can we reconcile his contemporary eminence with modern critical standards, and how far, in surveying the course of his life, can we recapture a glimpse of that intangible vesture of romance which he wore so easily?

The circumstances of his childhood are significant. He was born on 12 May 1828, at No. 38, Charlotte Street, Fitzroy Square, the second of four highly gifted and receptive children born in successive years. His father, Professor Gabriele Rossetti, of King's College, had had an exciting youth in Italy. Born of illiterate peasant stock, he had risen to prominence under the Napoleonic regime, and had filled the posts of secretary to the Department of Instruction at Rome and curator of the bronzes at the Museo Borbonico at Naples. When 'Bomba' came back in 1815 he had become a liberal and an inflammatory poet. In 1820 he was among the organizers of a highly successful little revolution, and in 1821 was in hiding under sentence of death. Sir Graham More, an English admiral, rescued him and took him to Malta, from where he travelled to Bloomsbury. From then onwards his adventures were purely studious. He married Frances Polidori, a governess, half Italian by birth, and devoted himself to scholarship: a scholarship which had for its chief concern the detection of concealed messages in the works of the Italian poets.

This side of their father's life had little interest for the Rossetti children, and

Fortnightly Review, 1 May 1928.

the delight which later they all took in Dante was entirely of their own discovering and quite independent of any cyphers or anagrams his poems might contain. Nor were they interested in the political questions that were feverishly debated in their father's dining-room. It is impossible to suppose, however, that they were not deeply influenced by the atmosphere of the household. It was an atmosphere of exile, lamentation and intrigue. Almost every Italian who came to London, from the humblest organ-grinder to the liberal aristocrat of the Risorgimento, found himself at some time or another receiving the modest but ungrudged hospitality of the Rossettis; homeless and hunted people surrounded Rossetti from the first, and one can only surmise how much the character of the dark declivity of his later years may have been determined at his father's table in Bloomsbury.

From the first it was recognized that Rossetti was to be a poet or a painter, or both. Disturbing as it may have been in other ways, the Rossetti family was one in which artistic ability had every chance of development. They regarded art as a serious business of life, not as a fad or a hobby; and never even when their finances were most seriously embarrassed and Rossetti's output at its lowest did they ever question his ability or attempt to deflect him from following his vocation. In 1846 he entered the Academy Antique School of Drawing.

II

It is not possible in this essay to recount in detail the story of Rossetti's life and work, but it may be suggested very conveniently by considering five pictures painted at different stages in the development of his art and in widely different circumstances.

First, *Ecce Ancilla Domini*, or *The Annunciation* as it was renamed to clear it as far as possible from the taint of Popery. The original hangs in the National Gallery, and reproductions may be seen in night nurseries all over England. It represents the Virgin Mary and the Angel Gabriel; both are clothed in white, and there are pale flames round the angel's feet. Mary newly awakened shrinks back on her low bed in startled awe; the embroidered lily at which she has been working hangs by her feet; Christina Rossetti was the model from whom he worked. It is the second picture he ever painted, and after his name appear the initials P.R.B.

'Pre-Raphaelitism' is a phrase which has entered into the language with rather confused connotations. It may be taken loosely to mean the whole aesthetic-mediaeval movement from the publication of Ruskin's famous chapter, 'On the Nature of Gothic', to the foundation of the Grosvenor Gallery, including in its too ample embrace the Museums at Oxford and Swinburne's *Poems and Ballads*. In this movement Rossetti is gloriously eminent. But if we restrict Pre-Raphaelitism to mean the ideals of the Pre-Raphaelite Brotherhood, we find it to be totally foreign and intolerably oppressive to Rossetti's real inclination. Pre-Raphaelitism in this sense, as Holman Hunt understood it, was in essence a revolution against the baroque, or more positively a 'return to Nature'. Italian painting in the sixteenth century aimed at achieving an organized vitality of form in which each part of the composition was subordinate to the central scheme. The objects to be represented were more or less predetermined by the subject, but in painting the picture they were treated with negligence or emphasis according as they contributed to the structure of the whole. The tone values of light and shade were similarly regarded as qualities of the picture, decided by the intellect, not as the qualities of the scene perceived directly by the eye. After three centuries of unintelligent imitation these admirable principles had become debased into a code of rules whose inadequacy became the more painfully apparent as generation of mediocrities succeeded generation. In 1849 Landseer was the favourite of the public; Dyce of the connoisseur. Year by year the Academy was filled from ceiling to floor with characterless paintings, all of which observed the academic rules and sought to attract attention by prettiness or pathos of subject. Clearly it was time either to revert to the source or to try something new. The Pre-Raphaelites attempted to do the one and very nearly did the other. Photographic reproduction was in its infancy, and as Millais and Holman Hunt were too poor and too busy to travel they cannot be blamed for their ignorance of primitive Italian painting. They had never seen any of the works of Orcagna and Cimabue, nor, probably, had they even heard their names. The period before Raphael became in their minds a golden age in which artists had done what they themselves wished to do. Lured by the ancient fallacy of the noble savage, who lives by the light of Nature, they assumed that pre-Renaissance painting was less stylized than that of its successors, and taking the name of Pre-Raphaelites they set themselves the task of the conscientious transcription of Nature – a task, needless to say, that no real Pre-Raphaelite had ever attempted.

Rossetti, eager to paint before he could draw, attached himself to Holman Hunt as a pupil, and his first finished picture, *The Girlhood of the Virgin Mary*, constituted the whole of his training. *The Annunciation* was his second exhibition painting begun in accordance with Holman Hunt's precepts, and the last he ever finished. It deliberately eschews any rhythm. It was Holman Hunt's aim that his pictures should be 'like windows' opening from the walls of the gallery; the interest was to be diffused all over the canvas, each part of the composition being of equal importance as the reverent study of some natural object. The repose of *The Annunciation* is due to its instinctive balance. Rossetti has, unconsciously, echoed and repeated the lines of the frame, the horizontal and the perpendicular, dividing up his canvas into a diaper of agreeably disposed rectangles. It is the last time that the initials P.R.B. appear after Rossetti's name. It is also the last time Christina Rossetti sat to him for an important painting. His spirit was soon to break out in search of other types of beauty and other types of love. There is a tenderness and virginal simplicity in the conception that he was never to recapture; an austerity in its execution that he was never again to seek.

III

The fresco of *Launcelot and Guinever* in the library of the Union Society at Oxford has almost wholly vanished. One can just discern a vague discoloration of the plaster between the round windows; the other frescoes are as bad: that is all that is left of the band of brilliant colour which Coventry Patmore compared to the border of an illuminated missal.

Rossetti was now 30 years old; a boisterous, assertive young man at the forefront of 'the movement', with a reputation growing on all sides. The Pre-Raphaelite Brotherhood had for many years been a thing of the past. Millais was now accepted by the Academy, and was advancing steadily on the easy path that led to the presidency and to civil honours; Stephens had given up painting and taken to criticism; the pendulum of Collinson's religious vacillations had come to a standstill, leaving him in an artistic coma from which he rarely stirred; Deverell was dead; Holman Hunt and Woolner still pressed on imperturbably, but a personal quarrel separated them from Rossetti. In their places Rossetti had collected a circle of friends of whom he was the unquestioned leader, most of them considerably his juniors in age. 'Topsy' Morris and Edward Burne-Jones had gone up to Oxford with the intention of taking holy orders; here they had assembled a little coterie about them, mostly composed of theological students from Pembroke, whom Burne-Jones had known in Liverpool. At one time it was decided to devote 'Topsy's' considerable fortune to the endowment of a monastery from which they should wage 'a crusade of Holy War against the Spirit of the Age', but gradually they found that the architecture and the illuminated manuscripts usurped a more and more prominent place in their discussions, until the monastery became wholly secularized and devoted to the crusade against machine-made taste, which Ruskin was already prosecuting in his lecture tours all over the country. In this mood they met Rossetti, who, in his exuberance, his glowing incisiveness of speech, and his exquisite mediaeval water-colours, seemed the very embodiment of all they had been seeking. Morris and Burne-Jones settled near him in London at Red Lion Square. Morris had already begun on a career as an architect and as a poet, but Rossetti, at this stage, would not allow that anything was worth doing except painting. 'If any man has poetry in him, let him paint,' he said, 'for it has all been written already, and people are only just beginning to paint it.' Not only was Burne-Jones to become a painter, but Morris too. Two years followed of slangy good fellowship and gaiety. Rossetti was emancipating himself from the fastidious patronage of Ruskin, and building up a connection among the bourgeois picture buyers of the northern industrial towns. He was generally regarded as the founder of the Pre-Raphaelite Movement, a misconception of Ruskin's which he did nothing to contradict. Then in the Long Vacation of 1858 he was taken by Woodward, the arch-fiend of Oxford architecture, to see the new Union Society buildings. The debating hall, now the library, fired his imagination, and he offered to recruit a party of artists to decorate the provocative strip of bare wall between the gallery and the roof. He himself would do two, or possibly three, of the frescoes. The building committee agreed too readily, and in a few weeks Morris was at work, painting feverishly with small water-colour brushes upon the damp plaster. Rossetti, Val Prinsep, Spencer Stanhope, Hungerford Pollen, came down later, and for a time the work progressed pleasantly. The Union paid for their expenses, and when term began the artists found themselves in a delightful position. They dined at High Table and drank with Algernon Swinburne at Balliol, and lived very comfortably in the High; but the work never got finished. None of them knew anything of the very special technique required for mural decoration. While they were still at work damp began in places to absorb the colours, while in others the paint flaked off as soon as it was dry. Morris was cured of being a painter; the band of young artists disappeared, and a Mr Rivière was hired to finish the pictures off as best he could. Some sketches of Rossetti's composition have survived. The central figure is of a young girl of rich, almost exotic, beauty, whose abundant black hair and brooding eyes were to appear again and again in Rossetti's painting. She is Jane Burdon, who in 1860 became Mrs William Morris.

IV

Beata Beatrix and *Monna Vanna* hang within a few yards of each other in the Tate Gallery. Each is the half-length portrait of a singularly beautiful woman, the one of Elizabeth Siddal, the other of Fanny Cornforth. *Beata Beatrix* was painted after Elizabeth Siddal's death, the culmination of a long series of exquisitely tender studies. It was consciously designed as a memorial of Rossetti's tragic marriage. Walter Deverell originally discovered Miss Siddal working in a bonnet shop off Leicester Square, and until Rossetti finally engrossed her to himself she was the favourite model of the Pre-Raphaelite circle. Rossetti was probably engaged to her as early as 1851, but a peculiar secretiveness in the girl forbade any announcement even to their most intimate friends. He painted and drew from her continually, filling every drawer in his little rooms at Chatham Place with inspired studies. Ruskin remarked how it seemed to cure him of all his worst faults merely to look at her, but it was an incalculably distressing period, and one which overshadowed and embittered his entire life. Like the young lover in the *Heptameron*, he suddenly found himself confronted with mortality and corruption in the thing dearest to him, for from the time of their first acquaintance Elizabeth Siddal was a dying woman; her very beauty was symptomatic of underlying disease, and the time of their engagement was rendered wretched by her successive breakdowns. Ruskin did all he could to help. He sent her abroad, supplied her with money, and tended her like some precious work of art. In 1860, while she was still convalescent from a terrible and nearly fatal attack of illness, Rossetti married her. In 1862 she died in London from an overdose of laudanum, which the coroner's jury charitably attributed to 'misadventure'. *Beata Beatrix* is Rossetti's *amende*. It represents Elizabeth Siddal as Dante's Beatrice dehumanized and exalted in a death-like trance, while on the frame he has inscribed *'Quomodo sedet sola civitas'*.

Fanny Cornforth represents the 'Profane Love' of Rossetti's dichotomy. He found her eating nuts in the street in 1854, and from then until a few months before his death she remained his ideal type of physical beauty and physical love. She was by nature coarse and soulless, and no doubt rumours of his prolonged connection with her gave colour to the attacks levelled against him by Robert Buchanan in 1871. *Monna Vanna*, the most impassioned portrait of her, was painted in the prosperous and apparently happy years at Cheyne Row which succeeded the death of his wife. Rossetti was now earning an income of about £3,000 a year; he entertained largely, collected china, *bric-à-brac* and animals, and was to all outward appearance a thoroughly enviable man. With the help of an assistant he turned out a regular succession of replicas of his early work and new studies of female beauty, variously adorned, with an almost effortless profusion. *Monna Vanna*, in its opulence and facility, is typical of the series. He has forsaken the restraint of the Pre-Raphaelites, the fading romanticism of the aesthetes, the delicacy of his own early love, and is frankly enjoying commercial success and the physically good things of life.

V

Proserpine was painted at Kelmscott in 1874. Rossetti was now a very different man from the expansive hedonist of *Monna Vanna*. In 1870 he had published his collected poems, which had been received on all sides with a chatter of praise and admiration, most of the reviews being written by his personal friends. But there was one critic, Robert Buchanan, now almost forgotten, but well enough known in his time as poet, playwright and journalist, who for personal reasons had for some time been awaiting the opportunity for a direct attack upon the morals and taste of the Rossetti circle. The attack appeared pseudonymously in the *Contemporary Review* eighteen months after the publication of Rossetti's poems, and was printed as a pamphlet under his own name in the ensuing spring. This coarse and obviously ill-intentioned article, 'The Fleshly School', had an effect wholly out of proportion with its real significance or its author's intentions. Only Rossetti's intimate friends knew that the apparently robust and self-confident artist was actually on the verge of a serious breakdown. For some years he had been a victim to the grossest immoderation in the use of chloral, a newly discovered drug, which he had begun to use as a sleeping draught under the impression that it was comparatively innocuous. Buchanan's attack, coming upon him at a time when he was incapable of resistance, brought to the surface all the lurking morbidity of his temperament. He became temporarily insane, attempted suicide and never afterwards fully recovered his reason from the persecution mania which now beset him. In

1872 he took up his residence at Kelmscott, William Morris's home, a tragically incongruous figure in the sunny little Cotswold manor. *Proserpine* is his most important work in this period. It is a portrait of Jane Morris, standing in brooding melancholy in the subterranean light, torn from the clipt yews and water meadows to the netherworld of the ancients. All Rossetti's sense of exile and frustration have gone to the painting.

From the time that he left Kelmscott until the time of his death Rossetti lived a life of almost complete seclusion at Cheyne Row, rarely leaving his own garden except for an occasional midnight walk in Regent's Park. One might add one more picture to the list – *La Pia*, a distressing work of prematurely faltering hand and brain, ill-drawn and inhuman. It represents the wife of Italian romance imprisoned by her husband in a tower overlooking the poisonous Maremma marshes, slowly dying of their exhalations: a melancholy and symbolic conclusion to a life's work which began with the sweet girlhood of Mary the Virgin.

It is easy to see what it was in Rossetti's life and personality which captivated the imaginations of his contemporaries. His value to us is a different matter. All his art, poetry as well as painting, is essentially human and personal, two qualities which modern criticism does not regard with sympathy. While he was at work on *Proserpine*, Cézanne, unrecognized and unrequited, was painfully discovering new principles which were to make Rossetti's work seem singularly pretentious and immature to the next generation; but sooner or later his discoveries will have become commonplace. It is safe to say that anything which has ever given genuine pleasure to cultured people will do so again. Rossetti, in painting and poetry, gave melodious expression to the regrets and aspirations of baffled humanity, and cannot ever for very long suffer complete neglect, though it hardly seems conceivable that the full praises of his contemporaries will ever be re-echoed.

2

. ULTRA-MODERN? .

BRIGHT YOUNG NOVELIST – CONVERT TO ROME

OCTOBER 1928 – OCTOBER 1930

I think it would be so convenient if the
editors could be persuaded that I embodied
the Youth Movement so that they would refer
to me whenever they were collecting opinions.

Letter to A. D. Peters, c. 27 November 1928

It seems to me that a young man today aged say 20 or 21 must have an almost
insane buoyancy of temperament if he does not at times feel he is not wanted.
Unemployment in the great centres of organized industry is too obvious a
disaster to need comment; the physical suffering is so acute, the burden on the
rest of the community so oppressive that it is natural enough that this
phenomenon shall absorb most of the attention of the world. But the industrial
workers are not the only unemployed. . . In countless upper- and middle-class
homes all over Europe, healthy, morally responsible and in many cases expensively educated young men are facing the prospect of getting a job with
increasing despair . . . One will [therefore] expect, in that part of a society
which moulds the ideas, manners and art of its generation, psychological
symptoms of futility, inferiority and a revolt from culture and it is exactly these
things that are, in fact, coming to articulate expression today.

From an address 'To an Unknown Old Man', BBC, 28 November 1932

. INTRODUCTION .

On 20 October 1928 Waugh published his first newspaper article, a young novelist's view of censorship. It was a very modest piece in the *Daily Express*, about a third of a column, carrying a note introducing its author as 'a new writer whose work has been praised by Mr Bennett'. The reviews of *Decline and Fall* were still appearing, and Arnold Bennett, chief critic of the Beaverbrook press, had warmly commended the new novel a few days before in the *Evening Standard*. On 20 October 1930 the *Daily Express* printed 'Converted to Rome: Why It has Happened to Me' as a full-page spread, boldly headlined. Two leaders in the *Express* had already discussed the significance of Waugh's conversion. His long-heralded article was put at the head of a series, an eminent Protestant parliamentarian being brought in to make a reply, and a well-known Jesuit (oddly) to sum up the contending viewpoints. An entire page of the *Express* was given over to the ensuing letters. But by the time 'Converted to Rome' appeared, Waugh had left London for Addis Ababa, and had decisively broken out of the way of life and kind of writing that had led to this sort of prominence. The article had been boomed, not because of any religious significance it might have had, but because its author was notorious for his 'almost passionate adherence to the ultra-modern' (*Daily Express*, 30 September 1930, p. 8). In the gossip columns *Vile Bodies* was known simply as 'the ultra-modern novel'.

The two years following *Decline and Fall* had been crowded with incident and literary production: a Mediterranean cruise (February-June 1929); *Vile Bodies* (15 January 1930); a quiet divorce (17 January 1930); the much publicized conversion to Catholicism (29 September 1930); *Labels* (1 October 1930); and a hyper-active social life in the fastest, smartest young set whenever Waugh was in London. In only two years Waugh had established himself as a fully professional writer, earning a comfortable living by his pen alone. Newspaper journalism played a significant part in his success. Indeed mid-1930 was the most prolific period of journalism Waugh was to know. In four to five months he placed almost fifty pieces, and was 'elated' to find his 'regular income temporarily up to £2,500 per year' (*Diaries*, 20 May 1930). It was the only period when almost all of his articles appeared in newspapers rather than in magazines.

A word on the part often played by newspapers in a novelist's success during the 1920s and 1930s may be in order as conditions have markedly altered since then. In 1930 the quality press was still formidably austere; it lacked the features and literary pages (and the influence in literary matters) nowadays associated with the *Sunday Times* and *Sunday Telegraph*, *Guardian* and *Observer*. Nor did it pay well. Where sophisticated literature was concerned, the tabloid press did not come into calculation. But the 'popular' newspapers, among which Lord Beaverbrook's *Daily Express* and *Evening Standard* and Lord Northcliffe's *Daily Mail* stood out prominently, were immensely influential. Waugh's review of *Northcliffe: An Intimate Biography* (23 August 1930) gives useful insights into the workings of these wealthy enterprises. Three aspects of their operation were of benefit to novelists: 'gossip', or the obsession with getting 'names', including novelists' names, into the papers; 'talking points', or the continual stimulation of interest in debatable topics, like 'the Modern Girl', which required numberless feature articles; and their determination to attract eminent writers, largely by paying high fees. As for fees, where the quality *Manchester Guardian* paid four guineas for 'Consequences' (4 April 1929), the popular *Evening Standard* paid ten guineas for 'Too Young at Forty' (22 January 1929), an article of similar length and merit. Waugh sought to make as much use as he could of gossip columnists and interviewers, and of any opportunity for high-paying journalism.

To achieve success as a novelist, 'Literature' (22 February 1929) explains, 'the important thing is to make people talk'. Waugh's main means of self-promotion was doing interesting things (no doubt because he enjoyed them) and making sure newspapers reported them. Did he win a bet at a house party by climbing a tower, or give his tie to a woman who admired it in a restaurant ('Modern Raleigh'), or be late for a christening ('Waiting for Waugh', says Mrs Brian Guinness, 'is like waiting for a bride'), or pour African gold on to a nightclub table and distribute it to friends, then a newspaper made a story of it. Perhaps he was a little too assiduous with the kind of paragraph beginning, 'Visiting the Pollard Galleries with Lord Berners was . . .' Assiduity was certainly attributed to him. Lady Eleanor Smith, the gossip columnist of the *Sunday Dispatch*, titled a piece about Waugh 'Determined – to Impress'. Another columnist made the point, implying no discredit, that Waugh had achieved success 'by the intelligent application and advertisement of his own talent'.

The journalism of the period was undertaken, in part, for the same reason as gossip-column publicity: to make the author seem interesting to potential book-buyers. But it was by no means circumscribed by that motive. Even the most frankly commercial work had, as will emerge, elements beneath its ultra-modern surface which, if detected, could only have alienated fashionable opinion. Nor was the journalism homogeneous. *Decline and Fall* and *Vile Bodies* make convenient landmarks for a more particular description.

Decline and Fall caused uncontrollable laughter among Waugh's friends (as Christopher Sykes charmingly relates), but it sold fewer than 2,000 copies. It left Waugh genuinely poor. He had married in June, and had no income but what his pen could earn. He sought any work he could get, and was willing to satisfy any editor's whim: 'Yes I should be pleased to write Wyndham Lewis [D. B. Wyndham Lewis 'Beachcomber'] stuff or any other kind of 'stuff' that anyone will buy,' he wrote to A. D. Peters. 'Please fix up anything that will earn me anything – even cricket criticism or mothers welfare notes' (*Letters*, c.

12 November 1928). He made many proposals, too many to list fully, for stories and articles. The most prominent subjects to come up were men's fashions, interior decoration, religion, education, tourism, motor-racing. He had the great good sense to see the value of becoming recognized as a spokesman for Youth at a time when there was a 'boom in Youth' and young persons' opinions were constantly in demand. 'I think it would be so convenient if the editors could be persuaded that I embodied the Youth Movement so that they would refer to me whenever they were collecting opinions' (letter to Peters, c. 27 November 1928).

The journalism Waugh managed to secure after *Decline and Fall* was of three kinds. The first kind was rather bookish reviews for the *Observer,* such as that of Le Corbusier's *The City of Tomorrow.* Four signed *Observer* reviews appeared between 1928 and 1930; unsigned pieces, now untraceable, may have appeared as well. Among other literary work the critical appraisal of Ronald Firbank is outstanding as one of Waugh's finest and most self-defining essays. (Duckworth had just issued an edition-de-luxe of Firbank's novels, and contemporaries saw Firbank as Waugh's 'most direct literary ancestor': *Daily Express*, 13 February 1929, p. 19.) The humorous sketches from *Passing Show* (19 January to 23 February 1929) are part of a series of six. It is remarkable that, though these pieces are very happily satiric and playful, and appear effortless, Waugh found writing the series 'an awful strain'; he had 'the utmost difficulty' producing it (letters to Peters, 14 December and 31 October 1928). He wrote to Peters soon after, 'At the moment Wyndham Lewis is rather in abeyance. I prefer forcefulness' (c. 27 November 1928). Most of the newspaper pieces written from 1928 to 1930 were what the trade called 'challenging' and what Waugh called 'forceful'.

There is an exception, a fussy article of advice on how to dress cheaply but well, 'Beau Brummells on £60 a Year'. Understandably it has been used against Waugh from time to time: 'He practised journalism, telling young men how to be well dressed on £57.2.6d a year' suggests a pitiful limitation of range and depth. Waugh naturally did not wish to see such 'beastly little articles' (letter to Peters, 2 August 1950) disinterred and used to his discredit. But his most enthusiastic welcome to a proposal for work at this time was, as a matter of fact, for a series on men's clothes: 'Is this at all what they want? Naturally I am extremely anxious to keep this job. Would they like it more chatty?. . . May I mention shops by name?. . . ' Unfortunately the commissioning editor decamped, making the series a washout (letter to Peters, 29 March 1929), and leaving Waugh permanently suspicious of new or financially shaky magazines.

When *Vile Bodies* came out in 1930 it made Waugh a celebrity, partly because it popularized the doings and sayings of the ultra-glamorous Bright Young Things, but largely because it included recognizable portraits of prominent people. Editors now advertised Waugh's articles as by 'the brilliant young novelist whose *Vile Bodies* is one of the most discussed books of the season'. His work was sought by newspapers and magazines. Most wanted him for series such as 'What Do You Think of Heaven?' in which the 'young' novelist was balanced against an 'eminent' magistrate (18 March 1930); or for a debunking series 'Searchlight on a Classic', in which Flora Robson said that *The Merchant of Venice* was 'the worst of all plays', Arnold Bennett that he would 'not re-read *Westward Ho!* for £1,000', and Waugh (very feebly) that *Tess of the D'Urbervilles* was 'vulgar' (17 January 1930). 'Challenging' views on Youth, Marriage, Divorce and so on, were in demand. *Harper's Bazaar, John Bull, Fortnightly Review, Week-end Review* and the *Architectural Review* printed more substantial pieces, most of them pre-prints or preliminary versions of *Labels*.

But the major commissions of the period came from the *Daily Mail* and the *Graphic*. The *Mail* secured London's newest literary lion to do an exclusive weekly article, on a subject of his own choice, for three months, at thirty guineas each. At the same time the *Graphic*, a glossy magazine, gave him a weekly book page until the end of 1930, at ten guineas per week plus books. The prolific period did not last long. It came to an end when the *Daily Mail* refused to extend Waugh's contract; they felt, as Peters politely relayed their view to Waugh, 'that this weekly arrangement is not bringing out your best work' (1 August 1930). Then Waugh found himself 'spoiling for a fight with [Alan] Bott', editor of the *Graphic* (*Diaries*, 1–5 August 1930).

An unpublished fragment of autobiography explains that Waugh found London in the 1920s 'alight and alive with fun and variety'. He made many new friends among the most fashionable – and the rowdiest – young set, the Bright Young People. Furthermore, as *Vile Bodies* demonstrates, he was hyper-reactive to new fads and fashions; to aeroplane travel, films, revivalism, motor-racing, parties, cocktails, telephoning, gossip columns, penniless aristocracy, and the places where 'everyone' was going. The *Daily Mail* articles are also made out of up-to-the-minute Mayfair life – but in the sense that they deal with happenings in Waugh's life shortly before the article was written. A glance at the 19 May to 23 August diaries in conjunction with contemporaneous articles reveals, for example, that 'Such Appalling Manners' (14 June 1930) was written, as the diary of 11 June 1930 says, 'all against Baby Jungman who chucked my luncheon on Friday with particular insolence'. The frenetic pace of life recorded in the diaries for the summer of 1930 explains why these articles are not Waugh's 'best work'.

The *Graphic* book pages are good general reviewing, for Waugh was capable of treating most kinds of literature, even those in which he was not personally interested, entertainingly. He had the advantage of very strong connections with the book trade. On the other hand his *Graphic* reviews tend to be more critical – that is, more like critical studies – than those of his chattier predecessors and successors. Perhaps this created differences between himself and his editor; it certainly ensured that a proportion of his weekly reviews, by nature the most ephemeral of writings, would retain some interest.

A significant non-literary aspect of these reviews was Waugh's using them to feud with the journalistic belabourers of the Bright Young People. When

Charles Graves in *–And the Greeks* abused some Bright Young gatecrashers, Waugh defended them in a tone of hauteur: 'Is it conceivable that Mr Graves is suggesting in print that there are houses where it is natural for him to be received but not these ladies?' (7 June 1930). An acrimonious controversy developed. Similarly Ethel Mannin, a stern critic of the Younger Generation, 'made free' with the names of several of Waugh's 'friends', also Bright Young People, in *Confessions and Impressions*. Waugh ridiculed the book (12 July 1930) and Ethel Mannin's reply (9 August 1930). In these ways he identified himself with an anarchic group, few of whom had his compensating talent or seriousness, and exposed himself to the kind of criticism to which they were subject. The most notable attack came in a section of Percy Wyndham Lewis's *Doom of Youth* (1932) titled 'Winn and Waugh' (pp. 98–108), where 'youngergenerationconsciousness' was construed as 'revolutionary agitation'.

Entertaining a mass audience by discussing profound subjects, brightly, in a short space, always involves simplification and exaggeration, and often insincerity. To that extent any intelligent author writing for a newspaper on, say, divorce might send his article to his agent, as Waugh did, with a breezy cynicism: 'Here is some balls for. . .' Waugh's uneasiness went deeper. An historian tracing the immense shifts in popular sympathy during the 1920s and 1930s from Victorian to modern institutions would have to grant a powerful influence to newspaper features. A rough impression is that conservative opinion was ineffectually presented by retired headmasters (*pace* G. K. Chesterton), while liberal opinion was presented by Shaw, Wells, Bennett, Galsworthy, Priestley, Hardy, Huxley, Lawrence. . . and was serenely triumphant. A conservative would have felt it necessary to undermine the genre. Waugh's review of D. H. Lawrence's *Assorted Articles* (31 May 1930) attempts to do this by dismissing the topics discussed as 'trivial' and by attributing a 'tongue-in-cheek' attitude to all intelligent novelists caught up in the game:

> The average sophisticated novelist sits down to earn his . . . guineas from the penny daily in a mood of apology. He hopes that his friends will not see his article, and he puts in several sly allusions to make clear to any who do that his tongue is in his cheek. He tries to secure the rewards of popular acclamation while remaining aloof from popular sympathies.

The claims made here about other novelists are highly dubious, but the passage accurately defines Waugh's own aims. He was capable of writing popularly. The idiom and many of the attitudes of modernity – candour, anti-humbug, irreverence – came to him naturally. No one could mock Mrs Grundy and 'Jix' better than he. But in writing for 'popular acclaim', which he succeeded in gaining, he not only remained 'aloof from popular sympathies' but actively subverted them.

Perhaps the most permanently interesting journalism of this and the following period (apart from the essay on Firbank's technical discoveries, in which Waugh is clearly acknowledging a debt) are the articles on Youth. A long and (by 1928) tedious debate had raged for most of the 1920s between 'moderns' who believed that the 'paralysing hand of Age' was strangling the 'spirit and enterprise' of Youth, and the 'old-fashioned' who scorned the Young as merely irresponsible, insolent and soft. Waugh wrote the conventional rhetoric of youthful disrespect for Age without effort, and with still-entertaining gusto; but his articles are also significant personal statements. In defining the qualities of the neglected 'Youngest' generation, 'Too Young at Forty' states the more important of Waugh's own tendencies: rejection of Marx and Freud and Frazer, scorn for Georgian arts-and-crafts, a liking for disciplined religion, and a menacing lack of 'prudery': it was the age of 'debunking and of 'candour'; or, in the positive terms of the *Oxford Broom*, of 'violent sincerity'. 'The War and the Younger Generation' announces a theme that was to last Waugh a lifetime, revolt against declining 'qualitative standards'. A preference for the 'civilized' values begotten of Age is found in 'Why Glorify Youth?' (March 1932). And finally all of Waugh's attacks on Age, and his championing of the right to be Young, amount, if read alertly, to a profoundly conservative argument in favour of Age asserting its authority. Within the 'ultra-modern' young man in a modern and liberal era there was a conservative rebel on his way to Rome.

. TURNING OVER NEW LEAVES .

The summer is over; for two sunny months we have not had to bother ourselves about other people's books; those astute old satyrs, the publishers, have all been at their play awaiting the gestation of their spring adventures. For two happy months we have been engaged with our own books or old books or with no books at all. But now we are back in London; there are brown leaves in the squares and the smell of bonfires and, on our way to dinner, an unsuspected draughtiness about the windows of the motor-car. The autumn publishing season has begun; with the proud trepidation of parish workers decorating the church for the Harvest Festival, the publishers bring out their produce. And what a harvest! Each year this autumnal spate of literature becomes more formidable and so, no doubt, will continue to become until that salutary day when the expansion of broadcasting puts out of work all the amateurs and dilettanti and professional hacks and journalists, and literature again becomes the slightly discreditable pursuit of those who really have something to say. Meanwhile the granaries are bursting; there is barely room for choir or congregation, so encumbered is the church with various more or less ornamental forms of vegetation. We have much to be thankful for.

Reviews of *In the Beginning*, by Norman Douglas; *Life of HRH Duke of Flamborough*, by Laurence Housman; *Dialogues and Monologues*, by Humbert Wolfe; *Sceptical Essays*, by Bertrand Russell; *The Collected Poems of D. H. Lawrence*; *Youth Rides Out*, by Beatrice Kean Seymour. *Vogue* (London), 17 October 1928.

First there is the magnificently loaded vine of Mr Norman Douglas. I think that *In the Beginning* comes as near to being a faultless book as we shall find this side of mortality. In saying this I am, of course, making a distinction of degree, not of kind; it is not everyone, or even most intelligent people who like the kind of which this book is so lovely an example. That wistful company who are always hoping that Mr Douglas will write another *South Wind* are again disappointed, and I think that if they have an eye for the omens, they may take this disappointment as final. Satire is very much more boring to write than to read, and it now seems clear that Mr Douglas, having achieved, with superb facility, the only great satirical novel of his generation, has now resolutely turned his back upon the idiosyncrasies of his fellow men for the abiding delights of scholarship and imagination. *In the Beginning* is a story of the time when Gods and mortals lived on terms of intimacy, before moral ideas had tempered the simple pleasures of the flesh. It has no anthropological significance, and though for a few pages the story steers perilously near that horrid whirlpool, Allegory, a deft divagation takes it into the easy harbourage of a delightful debauch in the harem and of the philosophic satyrs, who alone know what they want, grumbling under the stars. It is a book to be deeply thankful for.

Then there is a redoubtable pumpkin grown by Mr Laurence Housman. He is still unaffectedly diverted by the antics of his fellow men; more than this, he has purpose in his satire. *The Life of HRH the Duke of Flamborough* is the story of a completely ordinary man, rather below the average of any class in intelligence, who by accident of birth finds himself in a position of eminence and popularity; he might quite easily have been king. The royal tradition was strong enough to support him triumphantly through a long life of incompetence, and in a tendentious and rather tiresome last chapter Mr Housman reflects how strong this tradition must be and how sad that it is not better employed. There is no need to worry about this nor about the undisguised similarities between the career of His Grace of Flamborough and that of a late royal duke. To an educated public it is only manner and not matter that can be shocking; Mr Housman's manner is delicate, humorous and tolerant. The first chapters are wholly delightful. 'Monkeys,' reflected the young Duke after a visit to the zoo, 'seem to have a language of their own, but not so advanced or easy to understand as parrots'; and again, 'My tutor tells me that I ought not lightly to invoke the name of my Maker except in Church.' As the Duke ages, the narrative necessarily gets heavier, and I was a little bored by his speech about whiskers; but his death is beautifully told, and the meetings of his morganatic wife and Queen Augusta, the illustrations, particularly the frontispiece, and the incident of the umbrella at the trooping of the colour are all quite charming.

I think that the metaphor of Harvest Thanksgiving may tend to be tiresome; otherwise two books of essays, *Dialogues and Monologues*, by Mr Humbert Wolfe, and *Sceptical Essays*, by Mr Bertrand Russell, might not inaptly be compared to pulpit decorations of chrysanthemums and 'red hot pokers'.

Neither book can be disregarded. Mr Wolfe has a sweetly persuasive manner and a real belief in the importance of the written word; in the dialogues he always sees to it, as he had every right to do, that he comes out best after courteously making his opponents' case more graceful, surely, than they could have done unaided. Mr Russell is of quite another temper; he has very little faith in the value or permanence of Art, and he thinks politeness often does more harm than good. He is in the direct descent from the aristocratic sceptics of the eighteenth century. Sure of himself as a thinking being, he maintains an admirable consistency in doubt of everything else. It is his triumph to carry commonsense inquiries to conclusions widely different from the customary assumptions of the sensible; he is able without a tremor to look into the common and unfathomable abysses of pessimism and turn aside with the judicial comment, 'Yes, I think it is probable that we shall all fall in.' The difficulty with most of Mr Russell's books is that they are so hard to understand. The present volume demands no more than ordinary attention and education.

The most important work of poetry of this year is clearly *The Collected Poems of D. H. Lawrence*. It is impossible, in the space before me, to say more than a very little of what one feels about Mr Lawrence. One curious contradiction I am conscious of after a careful reading of these two volumes of poems, and that is that Mr Lawrence's finest poetry is in his novels. There is nothing in either of these books which to my mind compares for poetic power with, for example, the scene in the Cathedral in *The Rainbow*. Verbally, in the meanest sense, Mr Lawrence is a most imperfect writer. Whenever his spiritual sense flags he is betrayed into a drabness and an uncouthness of phrase which Mr Wolfe, for example, would never permit. His great importance as a writer depends entirely upon the way in which images surge up subterraneously and, we might judge, in involuntary effusion. He writes upon volcanic crust; underneath, and liable at any moment to burst through, is the whole subconscious field so rarely accessible to civilized man. Sex, not as a polite pleasure of the senses, but as the procreative urge which takes possession and makes the lover a mere vehicle for its expression, lies behind everything he writes; procreation, the slow germination in the darkness of the womb and the warm earth, the tidal ebb and flow of life, the seasons of the earth, the antagonism of the sexes, asserting their right to individual independence against imperative fusion – these are Mr Lawrence's themes. Art can only be distilled gently and at second hand 'recollected in tranquillity', metamorphosed into 'significant form'; however the process may be explained, its importance is apparent in Mr Lawrence's work. In his long, shapeless narrations he can in some measure wear his demon down; his poems are ebullitions of vital stuff, flung up, inchoate, from unplumbed depths.

Finally, at this season, let us be duly grateful for the white and brown crisp-crusted, soft-centred daily bread of our women novelists. Where would the publishers be without them? *Youth Rides Out* is Mrs Seymour's seventh novel; it is, in fact, a direct offshoot of her sixth and develops with the same felicity and feminine insight the affairs of some of the minor, but no less lovable characters in *Three Wives*. It deals mostly with those mild domestic acerbities that women novelists understand so shrewdly, with physical comfort, social gradations and sexual differences. It is safe to predict that for everyone who reads Mr Douglas or Mr Lawrence there will be many, many library subscribers who will find recreation and delight in Mrs Seymour's seventh novel.

. YES, GIVE US A CENSOR[1] .

All professional writers, whatever their opinions, must be deeply interested in Mr James Douglas's article advocating the institution of an unofficial board of literary censors. The uncertainty of operation of the present laws is a nuisance to everyone except perhaps the public, who are not forced to read anything, and no doubt prefer to make their own choice of what is suitable for them. Writers and publishers would very greatly welcome a system by which they could get more guarantee that their work was not subject to sudden suppression.

The really difficult question about Mr Douglas's scheme is the constitution of his board. It must be one which writers will respect, and our bench of bishops or even the editors of Sunday newspapers might come in for ridicule which would entirely undo the efficacy of the scheme. If, on the other hand, it were composed of eminent writers, Mr Shaw, Mr Bennett, Mr Wells, for instance, it is extremely unlikely that the section of the public who go in for being shocked would be satisfied with the board's decisions. Again, a committee of 'men of the world', Lord Lonsdale, Lord Birkenhead, Mr Winston Churchill, would be likely to disagree and also would find their duties an intolerable imposition to their daily work. What is really needed is some committee representative of enlightened public opinion, and with that conclusion we come back to the beginning of the argument.

My suggestion is that a jury should be constituted in perpetual session, chosen by the same methods as a grand jury, who should be called on to decide on the one question, '*Can this book do harm?*' That is to say, is it inflammatory? Is it intelligible to children and the weak intellects who allow themselves to be led astray by their novel-reading? Is it offensive, either by reason of gross personal attacks on living or dead people, or by the use of those words which are called 'unprintable', and which custom has reserved for moments of uncontrollable vexation?

No doubt many books might escape condemnation on these grounds, which

Daily Express, 20 October 1928.
[1] Waugh wrote to Peters about this article c. 25 October 1928: ' they cut [it] about until it said the exact opposite of all I meant.'

might still shock some people in some places, but the public conscience would be at rest. They would know that the best was being done for them: they would still be under no obligation to read what they did not want to, and no one need feel that there was a slur upon either national purity or national freedom.

. TAKE YOUR HOME INTO YOUR OWN HANDS! .

I do not know who started the idea of 'good taste'. I strongly suspect that DORA[1] had a younger brother who went to art classes at an evening polytechnic, and that it all began with him.

Certainly no one worried much about it in the eighteenth century, when people who were rich enough put cupids all over their ceilings, and built fireplaces in a style happily based on a combination of Greek, Chinese and French Gothic. Nor, I think, did it much concern our grandparents who went on accumulating the grossest kinds of *bric-à-brac* in superb disregard of all that Mr Ruskin was saying in his clever books. But quite lately, with the advent of all the other worries which gave that hunted look to Mr Strube's 'Little Man',[2] came the plague of 'good taste'.

One has only to look around today at the bleak little parlours of the suburbs and the still bleaker great drawing-rooms of Belgrave Square to see the havoc it has caused. Some terrific voice from behind the bar seems to have said 'Time, gentlemen, please,' and forthwith everyone began carrying away her dearest possessions to the lumber-room or sending them down to a very chilly reception in the servants' hall.

In some mysterious way, for which I strongly suspect my fellow journalists in the Home Pages are largely responsible, everybody seems to have been bullied into an inferiority complex about their own homes.

In Victorian times people were terrified of being thought poor, and starved themselves in order to clothe a second footman. Nowadays we are all desperately poor and quite boastful about it, but I have yet to find anyone but myself who still says with absolute complacency, 'I don't know much about art, but I do know what I like.' I say that about three times a day and it always has the profoundly shocking effect that I hoped for.

Look around your own drawing-room. Where is the fire-screen with the family coat-of-arms worked in coloured wools by your Aunt Agatha? And why is that horrible earthenware pot, which someone else's Aunt Agatha made in a

---

Daily Express, 16 January 1929.

1 Defence of the Realm Act. An emergency Act often used during the 1920s by the Home Secretary, Sir Joynson Hicks ('Jix'), to ban books, plays, late shopping, etc. 'DORA' recalled Mrs Dora Grundy and stood for 'Jix's' bleak puritanism.

2 Strube was a newspaper cartoonist. One of his characters was a Pooter-like citizen, the Little Man.

suburb of Brighton, sitting so coldly on the mantelpiece? And do you really find it comfortable to read by that triangular lamp shade which throws all the light on the ceiling? And where is the stuffed parrot?

Have you made all these changes because you really like them or because someone has been at you about 'good taste'?

It may be that you really do like them, but it seems odd that Colonel Brown's wife who disagrees with you about politics and religion and how to bring up her daughters should see eye to eye with you on this point. And the vicar's drawing-room is exactly like yours, although you could never bear the vicar; and so is the doctor's wife's, who, they say, drinks far more than is good for her, and wears such extraordinary hats.

If by some odd coincidence you really do heartily agree with your neighbour's taste in house decoration, well and good; but if she likes to fill her window with arts-and-crafts pottery bowls of crocuses, and you like aspidistras better, just fill your house with aspidistras till it looks like a conservatory, and if you like Benares brass pots, put them in those, and if you like bamboo stands, put them on them. By all means hide the tiger's head which your Uncle George shot in India, if it keeps you awake at night, but if you like it, don't be bullied into putting it away by Mrs Brown who lives next door. March round with your umbrella and tell her that her hunting prints and Staffordshire pottery are 'middle class' or 'bad taste'.

And if you see sarcastic glances being cast on the family photograph album or the cup you won at the cycling gymkhana or at the tinted photograph of the Acropolis or the Landseer engravings, just you say very decisively, 'I don't know much about art, but I do know what I like'; then they will see that they are beaten, and Mrs Brown will say to the vicar's wife that it is so sad that you have no taste, and the vicar's wife will say to the doctor's wife that it really only shows what sort of people you are, but all three will envy you at heart and even perhaps, one by one, bring out from the attics a few of the things they really like.

. TOO YOUNG AT FORTY .
YOUTH CALLS TO THE PETER PANS
OF MIDDLE-AGE WHO BLOCK THE WAY

Every ten years or so an unaccountable wave of feeling seems to engulf the British Public and awaken them to the fact that there is a 'Younger Generation'. I do not know why this should be so, because, of course, people are born and grow up daily, and not in decades; it is, however, one of the many odd idiosyncrasies of the public mind that its recognition of the ordinary facts of growth should invariably take the form of sudden and indiscriminate booms in Youth. At the beginning of this century we had the Reforming Boom – Fabianism and feminism hand-in-hand; then there was the Merrie England

Evening Standard, 22 January 1929.

Boom – folk-dancing and beer-drinking eyeing each other askance; the last, or Conquering Hero Boom, at the end of the war, was stupendous and almost in proportion to the four years' slump in everything worthwhile which preceded it.

Ten years ago everyone was agog for Youth – young bishops, young headmasters, young professors, young poets, young advertising managers. It was all very nice, and, of course, they deserved it, but I hope that I shall not be thought ungrateful to the men who defended me when I was a helpless schoolboy in the OTC if I mention the fact that once again *there is a younger generation*.

Things have not been particularly easy for those of us who have grown up in the last ten years. In former years a young man or woman setting out on his career saw his progress marked out in a gentle gradation of seniority. It may have been slow, but it *was* progress. At the head of everything tottered 'the old man'; his second in command, a few years his junior, waited respectfully to take his place; another sharp winter and everyone would get a rise; a few more fogs, perhaps a railway accident or an epidemic, and another death would move the procession a step nearer its goal; success waited on succession.

But today things are very different. In business, in the professions, in art, in the public services the way is blocked by the phalanx of the Indestructible Forties. A fine, healthy lot, these ex-captains and majors work by day, dance by night, golf on Sundays, nothing is too much for them, and nothing is going to move them for another thirty years. How they laugh and slap their thighs and hoot the horns of their little two-seater cars. I don't suppose that I shall be heard at all when I diffidently whisper that *there is a younger generation*.

And yet I think I see signs that another boom in Youth is coming, though it is going to be quite different from all its predecessors. Always before it has been the younger generation asserting the fact that they have grown up; today the more modest claim of my generation is that we are young.

Our seniors cannot have it every way; they really must begin to grow up a little. They must cure themselves of the arrested development that seems to afflict them. In the Church we see tough old clergymen expounding the exploded heresies of the Dark Ages under the name of 'Modern' Churchmen. Cézanne died long before we were born and still his imitators proclaim their paintings as 'Modern' Art. In Society indefatigable maiden ladies of Chelsea and Mayfair, dyspeptic noblemen and bald old wits still caper in the public eye as 'the Bright Young People'. There are the Peter Pans of Bloomsbury, the skittish old critics who will not grow up, who must always be in the movement. Is there no one who will gently remind them of their silver hairs and explain to them, patiently and tactfully, that *there is a younger generation*?

A healthy system of classification has divided prominent people in three classes; from birth to the age of 40 they are spoken of as 'young and brilliant'; from 40 to 60 they are 'distinguished'; from 60 to death 'veteran'. Surely it is time that the pre-war *enfants terribles* became a little more circumspect in their demeanour, a little more thoughtful in their public utterances, a little more 'distinguished'?

'But,' I shall be asked, 'if these plump old soldiers whom we have so long looked upon as "modern" are not the younger generation, what is this younger generation like?' In reply I can mention five writers all known already to a considerable public who seem to me to sum up the aspirations and prejudices of my generation. These are, first, Mr Harold Acton, poet and novelist; Mr Robert Byron, the art critic; Mr Christopher Hollis, the Catholic apologist; Mr Peter Quennell, poet and literary critic; and Mr Adrian Stokes, philosopher. Each of these writers has already published more than one work and it is in them that the spirit of my generation can be read. They are all diverse in interests and method, but they have the unifying quality of Youth in them and in the other less articulate members of my generation [sic].

I see certain common tendencies which may be called the Spirit of the Age. One is a tendency to be bored with the problems of Sex and Socialism, which so vexed our seniors; another is the horror of the 'ye olde' picturesque, folk-dancing, art-and-crafty relaxations of our seniors; another is a disposition to regard very seriously mystical experience and the more disciplined forms of religion; another is a complete freedom from any kind of prudery, from either the Victorian facility of being shocked or the Edwardian will to shock; and, lastly, we all have the earnest wish that people will soon realize that *there is a younger generation*.

. CAREERS FOR OUR SONS: THE COMPLETE JOURNALIST .
SECRETS OF PRESS SUCCESS

Last week I told you how to become a reporter on one of our popular daily papers. For a month or so you will be able to identify yourself with that imponderable organization of occult influence and moral regeneration 'The Press'; you will be able to ring up total strangers with the magic '*Daily Excess* speaking' and be sure of a respectful hearing; your lightest word will reverberate to provincial breakfast tables, making and unmaking governments, creating fashions in table decorations and nursery furniture, banning novels, detecting murderers, probing the innermost secrets of national life. All round the reporters' room you will see the journalists at it, too. Lost in dreams of oriental power, you await your summons to take part in the work.

You may have to wait a long time. In one newspaper office an old man may be seen any day turning over the files, with an expectant eye, turning from time to time towards the news editor's door. He was engaged 'on space' during the war when journalists were scarce. He even wrote a quarter column interview with a station-master whose son had captured a spy. Since then the paper has changed hands and editors have come and gone but he is still hoping for another 'story'.

Passing Show, 26 January 1929.

A great deal depends on how you spend the first days in the office. There are a certain number of people who can be idle for long stretches of time without appearing bored. To these fortunate souls comes in its season every form of worldly prosperity. During the time when you are waiting for work you are confronted with the double problem of keeping cheerful and keeping sober. Only very experienced reporters may be drunk in the office.

Eventually you will be given a 'story'. You will see the news editor approaching. 'I say, Waugh,' he may say, 'a woman's body has just been found in one of the Sculpture Rooms at the Royal Academy. You might just go out and find the murderer,' or 'Here's a new novel by a man who once snubbed the editor. Just sit down and ban it, will you, there's a good chap,' or 'I'm sending you across to Port Said tonight by air. We want a series of articles on the night life of the native quarter.'

It is possible that he may say any of these things but it is more likely to be something like, 'Run down to the zoo will you, and write up a story about how the animals are preparing for Christmas?' (that is rather a favourite thing with editors), or 'There's a new reservoir being opened at Hendon. I don't suppose that there's a story in it, but you might as well be there in case anyone gets drowned,' or 'They say there is going to be a fashion in side-whiskers for men. Get some opinions about that – an actress, a bishop, a few lords.'

In cases like this the correct procedure is to jump to your feet, seize your hat and umbrella and dart out of the office with every appearance of haste to the nearest cinema. It is hardly ever any use to go and interview people. If they are at all nice to meet they will not want to meet you, and if they have refused an interview it is just possible that they will look in your paper next day. The thing to do is just to go and sit in a cinema for an hour or so and smoke a pipe and think of something they might have said. Even if the bishop in question does open your paper next day and learns that he is making every effort to stamp out side-whiskers in his diocese he is unlikely to do anything about it.

Society journalism is a separate craft, and one by which any young man or woman can earn quite a lot of money. Quite hard words are said about the 'selling of one's friends' by those who are never sold. The truth, of course, is that Society secretly adores its publicity. Once it becomes known that you are 'Mr Chit-Chat of the *Daily Excess*' your social popularity is assured and invitations from total strangers cover your chimney-piece.

That popular conception of an unbidden guest, lurking in hired evening clothes behind palms and curtains, scribbling upon his celluloid cuffs the scandals of the great, may once have had some foundation, but now things are very different. His chief difficulty is to avoid hurting the feelings of the smart old things who clamour for his attention. 'Poor Peter,' they say, 'he is not at all well off, and he's so brave trying to earn a living. It's only fair to help him when one can. I'll just ring him up and tell him what I'm going to wear at Lady C.'s tonight.' 'Exclusive' night-clubs beg him to join; restaurants offer him free meals; famous portrait painters volunteer astonishing details about their private lives. His telephone rings continually while eager voices 'rumour' their own engagements; everyone is so anxious to help him.

However, his career, too, is a brief one. In the jolly musical-chairs of Fleet Street there are frantic peeresses scrambling for his place. Names tend to repeat themselves in his column as his acquaintances grow more insistent; he will print a photograph of the Dowager Lady C. over the inscription 'Lady C., one of the Bright Young People who are to be seen any night at the Cocktail Club.' Something will go wrong and he will have to find another career.

. CAREERS FOR OUR SONS: LITERATURE .
THE WAY TO FAME

There is a great deal to be said for the Arts. For one thing they offer the only career in which commercial failure is not necessarily discreditable. Shabbiness of appearance and irregularity of life are not only forgiven to the artist but expected. Art offers scope for profound and prolonged laziness, and in the event of success gives rewards quite out of proportion to industry.

Of all the Arts the one most to be recommended to the young beginner is literature. Painting is messy; music is noisy; and the applied arts and crafts all require a certain amount of skill. But writing is clean, quiet, and can be done anywhere at any time by anyone. All you need is some ink, a piece of paper, a pen and some vague knowledge of spelling. Even the last is not essential if you employ a competent typist.

All you have to do is to write 'Chapter One' at the head of your paper and from then onwards for better or worse you are an author. Many people never get any further than that.

The best sort of book to start with is biography. If you want to make a success of it, choose as a subject someone very famous who has had plenty of books written about him quite recently. Many young writers make the mistake of choosing some forgotten Caroline clergyman or eighteenth-century traveller. They become deeply interested in their subject, spend dreary days in the British Museum Reading Room, and write a graceful, carefully documented work. But is it a success? No. The reason being that either the editor has never heard of your clergyman or traveller, and therefore does not take the trouble to have the book reviewed at all, or else it falls into the hands of someone who has himself been attracted by the same character, knows as much about him as you do and rather thought of writing the book himself. In which case he will jump on all the inevitable inaccuracies with terrific severity.

On the other hand, if you choose someone like Disraeli or Shakespeare or the elder Pitt, you can be quite certain of what is called a 'respectful hearing'. That means that all the famous critics who write weekly articles in learned journals see in your book a pleasant opportunity for once more printing their nicely turned opinions about Disraeli or Pitt, or whoever you have chosen. Every time a life of anyone really famous is published, they bring out the same old article they wrote when they were taking Schools at Oxford. It is two easy columns for them and if they are at all amiable at heart they will show their gratitude by prefacing their essays with some little allusion to your book. 'A new author, coming to his task with youthful exuberance but mature judgment,' they will write, 'has once again raised the perennially engrossing problem of the elder Pitt.'

You will not make very much money by this first book but you will collect a whole list of kindly comments which your publisher will be able to print on the back of the wrapper of your next. This should be a novel, preferably a mildly shocking one. Your biography has made you a 'man of letters' and established your integrity of purpose. Librarians who see that distinguished critics have spoken respectfully of your work will be slow to ban it.

The reviews matter very little in the case of a novel. The important thing is to make people talk about it. You can do this by forcing your way into the newspapers in some other way. Attempt to swim the Channel; get unjustly arrested in a public park; disappear. There are innumerable means of attracting public notice. Even a severe accident in a gale should be enough to secure you a commission for a series of articles on 'the Church' or some such topic.

From then onwards your fame is secure. Your advice will be enlisted over the telephone upon questions of public moment; photographers will offer you complimentary sittings; you will be inundated with letters from the wives of starving clergymen offering to do your typing for you if you will buy them a typewriter and a correspondence course. You will be asked to lecture in America and give expert advice in courts of law, and restaurants will bribe you to stage seductions there in your next book.

Finally, at the end of a happy and full life, you can look forward to a knighthood, a Civil List pension and a funeral in Westminster Abbey, if only you play your cards successfully at the beginning.

. CAREERS FOR OUR SONS: EDUCATION .
TRUTHS ABOUT TEACHING

The splendid thing about Education is that everyone wants it and, like influenza, you can give it away to anyone without losing any of it yourself.

As soon as we reach the age when we become intolerable in the home we are sent away to schools and kept there as long as our parents can afford. If they are really rich they can keep on 'educating' us all their lives, sending us from university to university all over the world. From their point of view the advantages of education are direct and wholly delightful. By one simple expedient they are relieved of the moral responsibilities and physical inconvenience of having us about the house. When we end up in prison they can say, 'Well, well, we did all we could. We gave him an excellent education.'

Once you have been educated you can never starve; you can always educate in your turn. Irregular, ill-paid and in most ways grossly unseemly as the employment of teaching may be it is always open to us, whatever our shortcomings. It is the great privilege from which no misfortune nor disgrace can ever exclude us, the proud right of the educated Englishman to educate others.

I once fell into conversation with a man in early middle age who seemed already to have suffered every mischance which man can incur in a civilized state. He had been expelled from his public school for theft and sent down from Cambridge for chronic alcoholism; he had been co-respondent in two divorce cases and served a term of hard labour for blackmail; he had been deprived of his commission during the war for offences too hideous to specify and had been saved from execution for desertion only by the Armistice. 'So you see,' he concluded, 'there was nothing left to do but become a schoolmaster.' He was at present teaching football and geometry at a fashionable private school. 'I don't keep my job long,' he admitted, 'but they always send me away with a good character. You see, they daren't admit that they ever engaged quite such a bad egg as me. Bad for the school's reputation.'

It must never be supposed that the life of the schoolmaster is an easy one. It is quite the reverse. The private schools of England are to the educated classes what the Union Workhouses are to the very poor. Relief is granted to all who come but it is provided in as unpalatable a form as possible. The early hours, the close association with men equally degraded and lost to hope as yourself, the derision and spite of indefatigable little boys, the gross effrontery of matrons and headmasters' wives, all these and many minor discomforts too numerous to mention are the price you must pay for bare subsistence.

Headmasters when they engage you will freely admit that 'there is no future in it'. No one knows how or where private schoolmasters die; perhaps when they become too old to resist further they are unobtrusively incinerated by their pupils.

However, some schools are less bad than others, and an old campaigner discovers ways to mitigate some of the more acute discomforts. It is the easiest thing in the world to get a job. You apply to an agency which introduces you to some headmasters. Dress quietly and cleanly for the interview, and choose the old boys' tie of some reputable public school. Do not allow the headmaster to cross-examine you about yourself. Take the initiative and start asking about his school. How big is the swimming bath? What percentage of boys learn music? How many matches did they win last season? What chances are there of getting a game of golf now and then? Is the vicar High Church?

Make it quite clear that *you* are interviewing *him*. After about ten minutes say, 'Well, I like the sound of your school, and I think I shall be happy there.

When does term begin?' He will say very diffidently, 'Oh, about salary?' Say, 'A hundred and fifty and laundry.' Then he will say, 'All right.'

When you arrive at the school, remember to be a man of the world with your colleagues. Compare the school unfavourably with others you have been at and hint that you are only doing this for a year or so until your uncle dies and leaves you a jolly little estate in the north. They will not believe you but they expect some such deception; it preserves the self-respect of the common room. Talk to them about some good 'binges' you have had in the 'hols' and hint at love affairs.

With the boys it is essential to adopt an attitude of uncompromising severity from the first. Any suggestion of humour or humanity will be observed to your discredit. Punish the first boy who sneezes or drops a book. A week or so of this establishes the right atmosphere of hostile submission. After that you will be able to let things run their own course. I was once taught by a mathematics master whose invariable formula on entering the room was 'Open your Algebras at page 116. Read the explanation of simple equations. Do as many as you can of each exercise. Look up the answers and give me your marks at the end of the hour.' He used then to open one of Mr Nat Gould's novels and we all spent the period in peace.

It is as well to draw some sort of diagram upon the blackboard in case of inspection. Most headmasters, however, learn that such visitations usually cause more harm than good to the reputation of the school.

. CAREERS FOR OUR SONS: CRIME .
HOW TO BE RICH AND DISHONEST

When all is said and done, there is no profession which offers such facile opportunities to young men and women of initiative and good sense as that of crime. Of course, nowadays, the modern fashion in legislation has made us all to some extent criminal. Mere law-breaking as such is of no value to anyone. No one gets nearer prosperity by buying his cigarettes late in the evening or by parking his car outside his neighbour's front door.

I do not propose to recommend a career of such minor offences nor of those superb orgies of degradation which carry our commercial peers into the dizzy heights of seven-figure income tax returns. I mean, rather, the steady routine of dishonesty and violence by which any capable young man can, with reasonable good fortune, support himself in some comfort and provide for a leisured old age.

In this career alone a youth of respectable upbringing and normal education starts in a superior position to his rivals. There is in all but one great nation

Passing Show, 23 February 1929.

today a slight slur attached to the calling still remaining from the theocratic days of the Dark Ages. Progressive America has succeeded in overcoming this prejudice and crime is openly practised by people of refined feelings and high social position. But in England, with a few honourable exceptions, the criminal class is recruited almost entirely from those of mean advantages. Bill Sikes outnumbers Raffles by a thousand to one. To start in crime with reputable middle-class antecedents; to be ready in case of apprehension with an easy 'Good evening, officer'; to have an episcopal cousin or two and a legal uncle to testify to your good character; all these things, though seemingly unimportant, count for a lot in the present organization of society.

Another great advantage which crime offers over other trades or professions is the holidays. It is not a whole time job. Some of our most successful burglars fill in their days as college tutors or bus conductors.

It is as well to start at once with something ambitious. Too many young men drift into crime with a series of ill-considered and barely profitable specula-tions; a ten shilling note from an unguarded till, sixpence from a blind beggar's cup, a yard or two of artificial silk from some bargain basement. Only after they have been detected and disgraced do they set about their career in earnest, and by that time their reputation, which is nine-tenths of their capital, has been squandered.

Murder is, of course, the king among crimes, but murder for profit is rarely successful, for by its nature it points to the murderer. By far the finest, all-round general utility crime is robbery with violence. All you have to do is to arm yourself with a hammer, cover the lower part of your face with a bandana handkerchief and conceal yourself behind a hedge in some unfrequented country lane. Wait until someone passes, make sure that he or she is decently dressed and of meagre physique. Then step out of your hiding and hit them on the head, take their money and return home in time to have a bath before dinner. Perhaps it is the very simplicity of the process that impels so many people to attempt more elaborate feats. It has, of course, the disadvantage of uncertain increment, but that one has to expect in all crimes except suicide.

An ingenious crime which can be committed about once a year is this. You enter an hotel and order a drink which you pay for with a five pound note. When the waiter brings you your change you say that surely you gave him a ten pound note. He says he is positive it was five pounds. 'Well,' you say, 'I know it was a ten pound note because I cashed a cheque for thirty pounds this morning. There are the other two. You see they have consecutive numbers. Look in the till and see whether there is not another ten pound note with a consecutive number.' The waiter goes there, finds that there is and returns with profuse apologies and five pounds change which you divide in whatever ratio seems equitable with your accomplice who, ten minutes before you entered, changed a ten pound note at the office.

Another crime which is committed with astonishing frequency is to go into Cartier's and say: 'I am Lord Beaverbrook. Please give me some diamonds,' and then to go away and sell them. This is called 'impersonation with intent to defraud'.

Housebreaking is more a craft than an art, and should not be attempted without expert assistance. It is a valuable tip whenever undertaking work of this kind to change into pyjamas and bedroom slippers; then if anyone interrupts you, you can pretend to be walking in your sleep.

Another similar precaution before attempting daylight burglaries is to have a friend dressed in the uniform of an asylum warder. If you are discovered, he has only to walk up and say, 'I'm sorry you were troubled, sir. The bloke is off his nut. Thinks he's Charles Peace,' and put you into a taxi and safety.

One last point: after each crime it is a good thing to bump off your accomplice. If you do not he will in all probability bump you off somehow later.

. BEAU BRUMMELLS ON £60 A YEAR .

Of course, there is really only one way of being perfectly dressed – that is, to be grossly rich. You may have exquisite discrimination and the elegance of a gigolo, but you can never rival the millionaire if he has even the faintest inclination towards smartness. He orders suits as you order collars, by the dozen. His valet wears them for the first three days so that they never look new, and confiscates them after three months so that they never look old. He basks in a perpetual high noon of bland magnificence.

It is useless to compete against him. If your object in choosing your clothes is to give an impression of wealth, you had far better adopt a pose of reckless dowdiness and spend your money in maintaining under a hat green and mildewed with age a cigar of fabulous proportions. If, however, you have no intention of deceit, but simply, for some reason, happen to like being well dressed, it is essential to have at least two tailors.

There are about a dozen first-rate tailors in London whose names you may always see quoted by the purveyors of 'mis-fit' clothing. Below them are about a hundred rather expensive eminently respectable unobtrusive shops in fashionable streets, where your uncles have bought their clothes since undergraduate days. Below them are several hundreds of quite cheap very busy little shops in the City and business quarters. The secret of being well dressed on a moderate income is to choose one of the first-rate and one of the third-rate tailors and maintain a happy balance between them.

There are some things, an evening tail-coat for instance, which only a first-rate tailor can make. On the other hand, the difference between a pair of white flannel trousers costing five guineas in Savile Row or George Street and one costing two guineas in the Strand is practically negligible. The same applies to almost all country clothes. It is not necessary or particularly desir-

Daily Express, 13 February 1929.

able that these, except of course riding breeches, should be obtrusively well cut.

The chief disadvantage of small tailors is that they usually have such a very depressing selection of patterns. It is a good plan to buy all your tweeds direct from the mills in Scotland and to have them made up. Another disadvantage of the small tailor is that he never knows what is fashionable. At least once every eighteen months you should spend fifteen guineas in getting a suit in Savile Row, which will serve as a model for him.

It is never wise to allow any one except a first-rate tailor to attempt a double-breasted waistcoat; in some mysterious way this apparently simple garment is invariably a failure except in expert hands. But you can safely leave all trousers which are not part of a suit, even evening trousers, which ought, in any case, to be of a rather heavier material than the coat, to your less expensive shop. The most magnificent-looking travelling coat I ever saw had been made up for four guineas from the owner's own stuff by the second-best tailor in a cathedral town.

It is usually an economy to buy your hosiery at an expensive shop. It is essential that evening shirts and waistcoats should be made to your measure; cheap ties betray their origin in a very short time.

There is only one completely satisfactory sort of handkerchief – the thick squares of red and white cotton in which workmen carry their dinners. Socks wear out just as quickly whatever their quality, and are the one part of a man's wardrobe which ought never to attract attention. Expensive shoes are a perfectly sound investment, particularly if you keep six or seven pairs and always put them on trees when they are not in use.

By taking trouble in this way a young man should be able to be more than ordinarily well dressed for less than £60 a year.

	£	s.	d.
One suit (Savile Row) cash price	13	13	6
One-third evening suit (one every three years;			
Savile Row) cash price	6	6	o
One suit (Strand)	7	7	o
Country clothes: flannels, part of tweeds, etc.			
made in Strand from own materials	10	o	o
One pair of shoes (best quality)	3	10	o
Hosiery, hats, etc	10	o	o
One-third town overcoat (Savile Row)	6	6	o
	£57	2	6

. RONALD FIRBANK .

It is no longer necessary to be even mildly defiant in one's appreciation of Ronald Firbank. There is, it is true, small probability of his ever achieving very wide recognition, and even among critics of culture and intelligence there will, no doubt, always be many to whom his work will remain essentially repugnant, but already in the short time which has elapsed since his death, his fame has become appreciably stabilized so that condemnation of him implies not merely a lack of interest in what may or may not have been the amiable eccentricities of a rich young man, but also the distaste for a wide and vigorous tendency in modern fiction.

Those who delight in literary genealogy will find his ancestry somewhat obscure. He owes something to *Under the Hill* and Baron Corvo, but the more attentively he is studied, the more superficial does the debt appear. His progeny is unmistakably apparent. In quite diverse ways Mr Osbert Sitwell, Mr Carl Van Vechten, Mr Harold Acton, Mr William Gerhardi and Mr Ernest Hemingway are developing the technical discoveries upon which Ronald Firbank so negligently stumbled.

These technical peculiarities are late in appearance in Firbank's work and are the result of an almost incommunicable sense of humour attempting to achieve means of expression. His early books are open to the charge, so indefatigably launched against them, of obscurity and silliness. When he had in *The Flower Beneath the Foot*, *Prancing Nigger* and *Cardinal Pirelli* fully developed his technical method the obscurity gives way to radiant lucidity and most of the silliness is discovered to be, when properly expressed, exquisitely significant. Some silliness, a certain ineradicable fatuity, seems to have been inherent in him. His introduction of his own name in *The Flower Beneath the Foot* and *Prancing Nigger* is intolerable *vieux jeu*; perhaps Firbank's sense of humour had reached a degree of sophistication when it could turn on itself and find the best fun of all in the doubly banal; if so it was a development where few will be able to follow him. His coy naughtiness about birches and pretty boys will bore most people with its repetition. He exhibits at times a certain intemperance in portraiture, indulging too gluttonously an appetite other novelists, even his most zealous admirers, struggle to repress. These defects, and perhaps some others, may be granted to his detractors, but when everything has been said which can intelligently be brought against him there remains a figure of essential artistic integrity and importance.

It is the peculiar temper of Firbank's humour which divides him from the nineties. His raw material, allowing for the inevitable changes of fashion, is almost identical with Oscar Wilde's – the lives of rich, slightly decadent people seen against a background of traditional culture, grand opera, the picture galleries and the Court; but Wilde was at heart radically sentimental. His wit is ornamental; Firbank's is structural. Wilde is rococo; Firbank is baroque. It is very rarely that Firbank 'makes a joke'. In *The Princess Zoubaroff* there is the much-quoted introduction:

NADINE: My husband.
BLANCHE [*genially*]: I think we've slept together once?
ADRIAN: I don't remember.
BLANCHE: At the opera. During *Bérénice*.

Even here the real wit is not in the pun, but in Adrian's 'I don't remember'; one of those suddenly illuminated fragments of the commonplace of which Firbank's novels are full and which, Mr Gerhardi has shown, are not inimitable. Any writer with a more or less dexterous literary sense can evolve 'jokes' without the least exercise of his sense of humour. In his later work the only verbal jokes are the proper names, Mrs Mouth, Lady Something, Mr Limpness, etc. The humour is no longer a mosaic of extricable little cubes of wit. It cannot be repeated from mouth to mouth prefaced by any 'Have-you-heard-this-one?'

> Floor of copper, floor of gold. . . . Beyond the custom-house door, ajar, the street at sunrise seemed aflame.
> 'Have you nothing, young man, to declare?'
> '. . . Butterflies!'
> 'Exempt of duty. Pass.'
> Floor of silver, floor of pearl. . .
> Trailing a muslin net, and laughing for happiness, Charlie Mouth marched into the town.
> Oh, Cuna-Cuna! Little city of Lies and Peril! How many careless young nigger boys have gone thus to seal their doom!

But by its nature Firbank's humour defies quotation. Perhaps it is a shade nearer to the abiding and inscrutable wit of the Chinese. It is there to be enjoyed by those who have a taste for it, but it is too individual and intangible to become a literary influence. The importance of Firbank which justifies the writing of a critical essay about him lies in his literary method. He is the first quite modern writer to solve for himself, quite unobtrusively and probably more or less unconsciously, the aesthetic problem of representation in fiction; to achieve, that is to say, a new, balanced interrelation of subject and form. Nineteenth-century novelists achieved a balance only by complete submission to the idea of the succession of events in an arbitrarily limited period of time. Just as in painting until the last generation the aesthetically significant activity of the artist had always to be occasioned by anecdote and representation, so the novelist was fettered by the chain of cause and effect. Almost all the important novels of this century have been experiments in making an art form out of this raw material of narration. It is a problem capable of many solutions, of which Firbank discovered one that was peculiarly appropriate and delicate.

His later novels are almost wholly devoid of any attributions of cause to effect; there is the barest minimum of direct description; his compositions are built up, intricately and with a balanced alternation of the wildest extravagance and the most austere economy, with conversational nuances. They may be compared to cinema films in which the relation of caption and photograph is directly reversed; occasionally a brief, visual image flashes out to illumine and explain the flickering succession of spoken words.

> One sunny May Day morning, full of unrest, Lady Parvula de Pantzoust left the Hotel for a turn on the promenade. It was a morning of pure delight. Great clouds, breaking into dream, swept slowly across the sky, rolling down from the uplands behind Hare Hatch House, above whose crumbling pleasances one single sable streak, in the guise of a coal black negress, prognosticated rain.
> 'Life would be perfect,' she mused. . . .

And the dialogue begins anew.

But nothing could be farther from Firbank's achievement than the 'novel of conversation'. In his dialogue there is no exchange of opinion. His art is purely selective. From the fashionable chatter of his period, vapid and interminable, he has plucked, like tiny brilliant feathers from the breast of a bird, the particles of his design.

> 'I would give all my soul to him, Rara . . . my chances of heaven!'
> 'Your chances, Olga – ,' Mademoiselle de Nazianzi murmured, avoiding some bird-droppings with her skirt.
> 'How I envy *the men*, Rara, in his platoon!'
> 'Take away his uniform, Olga, and what does he become?'
> 'Ah *what* –'

The talk goes on, delicate, chic, exquisitely humorous, and seemingly without point or plan. Then, quite gradually, the reader is aware that a casual reference on one page links up with some particular inflection of phrase on another until there emerges a plot; usually a plot so outrageous that he distrusts his own inferences. The case of the Ritz Hotel *v*. Lady Something in *The Flower Beneath the Foot* is typical of the Firbank method. The King at a dinner party employs the expression:

> 'I could not be more astonished if you told me there were fleas at the Ritz', a part of which assertion Lady Something, who was blandly listening, imperfectly chanced to hear.
> 'Who would credit it. . . ! It's almost *too* appalling. . . . Fleas have been found at the Ritz.'

Nothing more is said for forty pages, and then:

> 'Had I known, Lady Something, I was going to be ill, I would have gone to the Ritz!' the Hon. 'Eddy' gasped.
> 'And you'd have been bitten all over,' Lady Something replied.

Twenty pages pass and then an 'eloquent and moderately victorious young barrister' is mentioned as 'engaged in the approaching suit with the Ritz'. A few pages farther on it is casually observed that the Ritz is empty save for one guest.

In the same way in *Cardinal Pirelli* the scandal of the Cardinal's unorthodox baptism of the Duchess's pet dog is gradually built up. The actual baptism is described; then it is approached circumspectly from another angle, touched and left alone. There is a long scene in the Vatican, apparently without relation to the rest of the story; at the end the Cardinal's name is mentioned; another touch and then retreat. There is a social climber who wants *her* dog to be baptized. Suddenly the Cardinal is in disgrace.

In this way Firbank achieved a new art form primarily as a vehicle for bringing coherence to his own elusive humour. But in doing this he solved the problem which most vexes the novelist of the present time. Other solutions are offered of the same problem, but in them the author has been forced into a subjective attitude to his material; Firbank remained objective and emphasized the fact which his contemporaries were neglecting that the novel should be directed for entertainment. This is the debt which the present generation owes to him.

. CONSEQUENCES .

For some reason the row in which Mrs Chrystabel sat was neglected by the sidesmen. Behind her and in front the embroidered bags chinked from hand to hand. Mrs Chrystabel had her half crown ready, but the bag never came near her. It was not her fault and yet as she emerged into the morning sunshine and walked down the churchyard path into the village street she was aware of an inward voice reproaching her as when on one occasion she had left the omnibus without buying her ticket. She missed that agreeable Sunday morning sense of satisfaction. It was for this reason that when, on the way back to her house, she was accosted by Bill Scroggs she did not, as was her habit, pass him by with her customary 'You must apply to the proper source, my good man.' She felt a guilty kinship with the very disreputable figure as though her own soul confronted her fresh from the spoiling of the church.

'A very nice day, mum,' said Scroggs.

'Yes, indeed,' said Mrs Chrystabel, 'you would hardly know it was November.'

'Forgive me talking to you, mum,' said Scroggs, 'but you don't know anywhere where I could get a bite for me and my wife?'

'You should do your shopping on Saturday,' said Mrs Chrystabel severely; 'the shops are all shut today.'

'Just come all the way from Newcastle,' said Scroggs, irrelevantly. 'Looking for work,' he added.

'Well,' said Mrs Chrystabel. 'I think you would have done much better to have stayed there. There is very little casual work in the country during the winter. Still I am very sorry for you. Perhaps you will be able to get something for your wife with this?'

And she gave him the half crown.

'God bless you, lady,' said Scroggs, and Mrs Chrystabel went back to luncheon feeling that indeed she had been blessed and that there had been a special intervention of Providence to save for Scroggs the half crown she had intended for the assistant clergy fund.

Now Scroggs was not all that he said. In fact, though he did not know it, he was just the sort of character who gets into the appendices of works on sociology. He was a crying social problem. He had not come from Newcastle at all, and he had no wife, although the rates of many counties were supporting his offspring. The moment that Mrs Chrystabel's back was turned he made straight for the village public house, where he remained drinking until closing time. When at last he was induced to leave with threats of the village constable he had drunk so much that he walked unsteadily into the very middle of the road, where he was knocked down by a large motor-car that darted down the street at a reckless speed in discourteous defiance of the notice which Mrs Chrystabel had had placed at the end of the garden asking motorists, please, to drive slowly through the village.

'Damn,' said the driver, who was a millionaire. 'I suppose I ought to stop. Someone may have got my number.'

So he slowed down and turned round and came back and found Scroggs lying quite flat in the middle of the road surrounded by most of the village.

'I hope he is not dead,' said the millionaire, for there were three previous convictions out against him for dangerous driving.

They shook Scroggs and gave him some brandy and poured some cold water over him. Presently he sat up.

'Extraordinary thing,' he said. 'I thought something knocked into me.'

'That's all right, my man,' said the millionaire, 'you come with us.'

So the millionaire gave some money to the village policeman, who scratched out all that he had been writing in his notebook, and he took Scroggs to a doctor, who quite soon cured him because he had a fine, drink-hardened constitution. When Scroggs was cured the millionaire gave him a job in a large, well-ventilated factory where they made the ugliest possible things in the cheapest possible way.

Scroggs was soon a great favourite with all the other men in the factory. They made him secretary of the hockey team and president of the Ethical Society and treasurer of the biannual outing fund. He spent all the money on standing them drinks, and they liked him still more.

'We've made a man of Scroggs,' said the millionaire.

Soon Scroggs was made head of the trade union, and he had a strike and made the millionaire quite poor again. After that he became so famous that they sent him to Parliament. Scroggs was very popular in Parliament because he was always in the smoking-room giving other members whiskies and sodas to drink.

One day there was a great deal of difficulty in Parliament because the members could not decide whether to have a war or not. Some said it would be a good thing because then the people would have to buy a lot of steel and gunpowder, and the others said 'No,' it would not be at all a good thing, because if there was a war and bombs were dropped on all the castles and cathedrals the Americans would not come and visit them. Scroggs didn't worry either way because he hadn't got any steel factories or hotels, so he just stayed in the smoking-room drinking whisky with another Member of Parliament who didn't care either way because he had both. Presently they rang a bell in the smoking-room to say that they were going to decide whether there was to be a war or not. Most of the members of Scroggs's party were on the side of the hotels, so they said, 'Vote against the war, Scroggs.' He said 'Yes' but he did not really understand. In fact, he got talking to the steel manufacturers and walked with them into their lobby by mistake.

'Well,' said the Speaker, 'that decides it. There will be a war,' because Scroggs's vote made a majority of one in favour of the steel and gunpowder makers.

So there was a war, and a bomb was dropped on Mrs Chrystabel's house which blew her sky high and killed her.

This is rather a sad story, more interesting, as they say, to the student than the 'general reader'. The 'general reader' will be disappointed because, of course, she expects Scroggs to be made a lord and marry Mrs Chrystabel, but it is most interesting to the student because it shows the far-reaching result of cause and effect. If the sidesman had passed Mrs Chrystabel the bag that Sunday morning the poor old lady would never have been blown sky high, which only shows how careful sidesmen ought to be.

. THE WAR AND THE YOUNGER GENERATION .

One of the oddest results of the Great War is the vigour and accuracy which it has lent to the catch-phrases of the Ibsenite movement. Until ten years ago it was nonsense to talk in any general way about 'The Younger Generation'. Youth and age merged together in a gentle and unbroken gradation; even in single families the paradoxes of fecundity by which aunts were not infrequently born after their own nephews and nieces tended to weaken the arbitrary distinctions of the genealogical tree. But in the social subsidence that resulted from the war a double cleft appeared in the life of Europe, dividing it into three perfectly distinct classes between whom none but the most superficial sympathy can ever exist. There is (a) the wistful generation who grew up and formed their opinions before the war and who were too old for military service;

Spectator, 13 April 1929.

(*b*) the stunted and mutilated generation who fought; and (*c*) the younger generation.

Every accident of environment contributed to make of this latter generation the undiscriminating and ineffectual people we lament today. For their elders, the war was either a shocking negation of all they had represented, or a reckless, rather thrilling, plunge into abnormality. For the younger generation it was simply the atmosphere of their adolescence. Darkened streets, food rations, the impending dread of the War Office telegram, hysterical outbursts of hate and sentiment, untrustworthy sources of information and the consequent rumours and scares; these were the circumstances which war-time children observed as universal and presumed to be normal. The air-raids, for the vast majority of children, were rather amusing events, when servants appeared in improbable night clothes and everyone drank Bovril in the basement; the real and lasting injury was caused, not by danger, but by the pervading sense of inadequacy. Everything was a 'substitute' for something else, and there was barely enough even of that. The consequence is a generation of whom 950 in every thousand are totally lacking in any sense of qualitative value. It is absurd to blame them if, after being nurtured on margarine and 'honey sugar', they turn instinctively to the second-rate in art and life.

The only thing which could have saved these unfortunate children was the imposition by rigid discipline, as soon as it became possible, of the standards of civilization. This was still possible in 1918 when the young schoolmasters came back to their work. Unfortunately, a very great number, probably the more influential and intelligent among them, came with their own faith sadly shaken in those very standards which, avowedly, they had fought to preserve. They returned with a jolly tolerance of everything that seemed 'modern'. Every effort was made to encourage the children at the public schools to 'think for themselves'. When they should have been whipped and taught Greek paradigms, they were set arguing about birth control and nationalization. Their crude little opinions were treated with respect. Preachers in the school chapel week after week entrusted the future to their hands. It is hardly surprising that they were Bolshevik at 18 and bored at 20.

The muscles which encounter the most resistance in daily routine are those which become most highly developed and adapted. It is thus that the restraint of a traditional culture tempers and directs creative impulses. Freedom produces sterility. There was nothing left for the younger generation to rebel against, except the widest conceptions of mere decency. Accordingly it was against these that it turned. The result in many cases is the perverse and aimless dissipation chronicled daily by the gossip-writer of the press.

What young man today, for example, in choosing a career, ever considers for one moment whether, by its nature, any job is better worth doing than any other? There was once a prevailing opinion that 'the professions', which performed beneficial services to the community, were more becoming to a man of culture than 'trades' in which he simply sold things for more than he gave. Today that prejudice is suppressed and shop-keeping has become a polite hobby.

There seem signs, however, that a small group of young men and women are breaking away from their generation and striving to regain the sense of values that should have been instinctive to them. If this is so, there may yet be something done by this crazy and sterile generation. But it is too early at present to discern more than the vaguest hope.

. CITIES OF THE FUTURE .

The title which the publishers have chosen to fasten on to the translation of M. le Corbusier's well-known book *Urbanisme* is justifiable but slightly misleading. Speculation about the future is always stimulating; a series of modern pamphlets has won a well-deserved success by appealing to this deeply rooted instinct to play the amateur detective in contemporary history and to pick out from the conflicting influences of our own milieu the determining forces of the succeeding generations. But M. le Corbusier's book has won its wide reputation on the continent for quite different merits. He is not attempting any Utopian prophecy. The 'City of Tomorrow', which he discusses, exists for the Future only in the sense that it has not yet been built Today. He himself calls it the Contemporary City, and he presents it not as the probable result of present directions of development, but as a logical solution to a problem which already exists in an acute form all over the world.

There is practically no sense that is not violated every time we return from the country or the sea to Paris or London or New York. Towns that have grown up haphazard along footpaths and mule tracks have become the centre of vast, densely populated areas which look inward for their life. Congested systems of transport are sapping the economic vitality of the cities just as the noise or dirt and hurry are sapping the physical vitality of the workers. M. le Corbusier does not presuppose any golden age. He states the problem and with incisive, Gallic logic expounds his solution, postulating only the technical equipment of modern engineering. His four aims are: to de-congest the centres of cities, to increase the density of these centres, to modify the present conception of the street to allow rapid circulation of traffic, and to increase the area of green, open spaces to ensure the necessary degree of repose and recreation to the workers. His book contains a cogent and almost lyrical explanation of how this can be done. Garden suburbs separated from the city by protected areas of park land still feed the offices and works. These, with the tenement houses of the workers who live in the city, are conceived vertically, set at wide distances and constructed of steel, glass and concrete. Broad one-way arterial roads transect

Reviews of *The City of Tomorrow*, by Le Corbusier, trans. Frederick Etchells; *The New Interior Decoration*, by Dorothy Todd and Raymond Mortimer. *Observer*, 11 August 1929.

the city for the use of fast traffic; crossings exist only at distances of four hundred yards; lower roads provide for slow-moving traffic connecting at intervals with the speed ways. The general view of the city is of square towers of glass set at intervals between trees. Order and health make their own aesthetic.

There is, however, a doubt that arises out of the consideration of this sane and courageous plan. How much confidence can we have in the stability of an economic system that has so far directed itself almost unconcernedly towards chaos? and, with compensating optimism, how much fear need we have that the two determining factors of population and transport will inevitably advance in exactly their present ratio? M. le Corbusier's city is indefensible in war, and it presupposes the continued dependence of man upon horizontal methods of transport. If his city were in existence today it would clearly be the city perfectly suited to our present needs. If the next generation sees, as one may confidently suppose that it will see, a period of stationary or decreasing population and of aerial transport, M. le Corbusier's city will become as antiquated as Aigues-Mortes. Perhaps the chief value of *Urbanisme* is as a social document which shows what the great cities of the world might have made of this decade if they had not chosen to have a war instead.

Miss Todd and Mr Mortimer have a lot to say about M. le Corbusier in their book, but they approach his work from a purely aesthetic angle. Moreover, their outlook is notably obscured by *snobbisme*; they admire his work as being avant-garde rather than as a logical solution to a practical problem, but *The New Interior Decoration* makes a valuable companion to *The City of Tomorrow* on account of its admirable illustrations. The photography and diagrams in M. le Corbusier's book are poorly produced, often, one suspects, at second-hand. *The New Interior Decoration* contains a series of well-chosen and well-reproduced plates, which is quite the best of its kind that has appeared in England. The accompanying essay is of more doubtful quality. There are verbal repetitions that may be the result of imperfect collaboration. There is also a surfeit of sociological generalization and a good deal of gratuitous instruction about the history of art and taste with which anyone intelligent enough to buy the book might be assumed to be familiar. The authors, however, are to be congratulated on their championship of English decorators, whose peculiar genius for humour and the adaptation of traditional culture is too often overlooked by the more doctrinaire continental architects. One or two small questions present themselves. The authors assume that fresh air, light and cleanliness are important contributions to comfort. Surely they forget that there are still large numbers of people whose work is done in the open air and who derive particular satisfaction from shutting themselves up impenetrably during their leisure? Also, all the rooms illustrated are, naturally enough, photographed when they are completely new and completely tidy. How will M. le Corbusier's houses look in a hundred years' time when the patina of the concrete has weathered and the sharp angles have softened, and how do the interiors look when a family of normally disorderly habits has lived there for a few years? One cannot help feeling that iron furniture bent out of shape would be more offensive than worm-eaten wood, and discoloured concrete and rusted metal than mellowed brick and stone.

. A YOUNG NOVELIST'S HEAVEN .

I am not sure if I shall go to Heaven, but I think I shall. Anyway, I know almost exactly what it is like.

There is no harp-playing except for those that really like it, and they always have to hold their eisteddfod in a sound-proof chamber by themselves. In my particular bit of Heaven there will be no musical instruments of any kind, not even a gramophone, and no one will be allowed to sing folk songs, or dance or ring me up on the telephone, or make any noise except plain speech, and all conversation will be in English: that is most important.

Foreigners abound, particularly Chinese, but they all, when spoken to, answer wittily in perfectly modulated English. The Chinese are allowed to wear national costume, and there is a certain number of very lovely people without anything on at all, but otherwise clothes must be fashionable and becoming; there are none of those nasty peasant costumes, or kilts, or 'missionary' clothes. In the winter everyone wears very beautiful furs. I alone shall wear ermine.

The seasons are much the same as those on the Mediterranean northern coast, except that they are variable at will. Heaven is on the sea of course, and the sandy beach slopes down suddenly into the water, which is bright blue, but not too warm or too smooth. The grass is particularly noteworthy in the landscape, being very rich and green even in the hottest weather. There are no coniferous trees in Heaven, but plenty of well-grown oak, ash, beech and chestnut. There are magnificent formal gardens, with pools and grottoes and temples and admirable antique sculpture; the fields in summer are full of buttercups and Jersey cows. There are no mosquitoes.

I am not altogether clear about the animals. There are none of the rotund smooth-haired terriers I see on earth; I think, probably, only long-haired dogs and short-haired cats are permitted. There are plenty of very spirited horses, and I shall ride far better than I do at present.

The architecture is varied. There are no Tudor mansions or cottages with half-timbered fronts, but there are many examples of Italian seventeenth-century and English eighteenth-century domestic architecture; there are some very comic Gothic revival castles and a few genuine Gothic cathedrals.

Meals are elaborate and incessant; the wine magnificent and incredibly

Daily Chronicle, 18 March 1930.

intoxicating; no one ever feels the worse for anything in Heaven.

No one will write any more books once they reach Heaven, but there is an excellent library, containing all the books written up to date, including all the lost books and the ones that the authors burned when they came back from the last publisher.

There is a theatre which plays Russian ballet and American crook-drama on alternate nights. Everyone can see equally well from every seat, but, as a matter of fact, they will always keep the Royal Box for me. The actors and actresses go straight back to Hell after each performance, and there is no nonsense about their coming on to parties and making jokes.

One makes a lot of new friends in Heaven; all encumbering relationships such as marriage and parenthood are instantly broken at death. Love affairs are frequent, terminable at will and mutually satisfactory. Everyone gets rather better looking as time goes on.

No one in Heaven pays the smallest attention to the Earth. They have almost forgotten all about the beastly little place. They have one standing joke, and that is about Spiritualism.

Births are not infrequent; they are practically painless, but the mothers make rather a fuss about it and attract plenty of attention. Children go on being children just as long as the parents like. When they get old they are popped off to Hell, or, if they are very naughty, to Earth.

Up to date about a thousand light years of souls have been saved, but Heaven is indefinitely extensible, so that there is no sign of overcrowding.

I know at least three people for certain who will not get to Heaven.

. WHAT I THINK OF MY ELDERS .

It is a very sad thing that so many elderly people live under the delusion that they are objects of contempt to their juniors. This renders them either furtive or defiant, according to their temperament, and in either case they tend to bore us about it. It is sad because, as a matter of fact, elderly people are not more contemptible than anyone else. Young people are by no means unanimous in their admiration or affection for each other.

I, for one, would very much prefer the company of my seniors to that of any of my juniors and most of my contemporaries, if only they could get it out of their funny old heads that they must all the time be on their guard against veiled ridicule. I admire almost anything about old people. I admire their looks. By 'old' I mean poor people over 50, rich men over 60 and rich women over 70. It takes much longer for rich people to become nice looking. They are lovely up to the age of about 16; then they go through a bad period during

Daily Herald, 19 May 1930.

which they feel it incumbent on themselves to be 'attractive' and emerge like butterflies from their chrysalis in late old age.

Poor people, it seems to me, as far as looks are concerned, start hideous and get better looking steadily every year. The finished product, however, is more or less the same. I do not know anything more admirable in the animal kingdom than the faces of astute old sinners in club windows or tough old sailors and labourers in public houses.

I also admire the way that old people manage their lives. They don't worry themselves about large problems of philosophy or public policy. They have settled all that in their minds long ago. They concentrate themselves instead upon the details of their own comfort. Like the founders of the monastic orders they devote their thoughts to planning a harmonious daily routine. They know exactly what pleasures are worth their while. They know how they wish to apportion their income, what kind of tobacco they like, what kind of food and drink, what kind of friends. They do not run into debt. They do not – except in rare and wholly regrettable instances – fall in love.

I admire their lack of ambition. I admire their abstinence from all kinds of sport and competitive athletics. I admire the resolution with which they hold to their own opinions: their indifference to the traps and pitfalls of logical proof. I admire, though I cannot often share, their sense of humour: those curious, crude jokes, full of barbarous expressions and inscrutable allusions, which seem to gain lustre and pungency with each repetition. I admire their tenacity of life.

I admire their lack of scruple. It takes a great deal to rouse them, but when some feature of their personal comfort is really threatened, they will suddenly plunge into conflict with every artifice and act of violence which their long lives have taught them. I admire the capacity, enjoyed by almost all old people, of enslaving others. There are very few of them who have not at least one willing, devoted, entirely absorbed helper.

The sad thing is that, with all these and so many other radiant superiorities, old people should ever pretend to be young. It is dreary enough to pretend to be better. What can be more boring than to pretend to be something worse than one is? Why will silly old women try to 'keep up' with modern art and modern manners? Why will they wear themselves out in giving parties and attending meetings? Why will old men go on writing books? Why will they go back year after year to Parliament? Why will they make speeches and write to the papers and paint pictures and act in plays and serve on committees and muddle about at offices and factories? Why, with the whole beautiful life of old age at their feet, will they keep on doing the absurd things young men do because they do not know any better?

The reason, I am sure, lies in the reflection with which I began this article. They are afraid that young people will laugh at them if they admit to being fully grown-up. The trouble is that when they were young they were very disrespectful to their elders. They read books by Ibsen and Samuel Butler and Mr

Bernard Shaw, and the poor old things got wrong ideas. They thought that their parents were stupid and vulgar because they were old. The truth was that they were stupid and vulgar because they had been brought up in a stupid and vulgar age.

I have no doubt that our grandparents were still worse when they were young. Yes, our parents were given the wrong end of the stick by all those clever books they read, and now they are haunted with the fear of becoming like their own parents. Old age should be the time for leisure and enjoyment, while youth is the time for work. Old people only make themselves ridiculous by pretending to be young. There are far too many of them doing the work which ought to be left to the young. They are muddling politics and muddling their businesses and muddling the arts, simply because they won't settle down to enjoy themselves.

Every schoolboy going off to work at school ought to reverse the customary benediction, and, patting his grandfather on the head, should say, 'Old man, I wish I was your age. The best part of your life is before you. Make the best of it.'

. MY FAVOURITE FILM STAR .

I feel that nowadays, since the introduction of what are charitably known as 'Talking Pictures', writing about the cinema is like writing about the music-hall; it tends to become a mere lament of a disappearing art. Like the old men who are for ever eulogizing the beauty and talent of the 'stars' of their young days, I find myself thinking not of the films I hope to see in the future but of the films I saw in the past. But it is a very recent past, and the stars are still with us. Though nowadays all we see of them is an immobile reflection of what we once admired, and though our appreciation is dimmed by the intrusion of uncouth voices, which we strive to dissociate from the actors and actresses who have so often delighted us, we must still be grateful for the past.

I know that I am in the minority in this feeling, and I hope fervently that this disturbing new invention will soon be tamed so that we can once more look upon the cinema – silent or 'talky' – not as an imitation stage play but as genuine and self-sufficient art. It is in this light that I regard the cinema and try to choose a favourite among the many actresses who sweetened my adolescence.

The one essential requisite in a film star seems to me beauty of movement. Beauty of appearance means nothing in the films if it does not include this, and this is the one artistic expression which the cinema has fostered and developed. I have never been to Hollywood and I am unimpressed by my acquaintances who have been there and come back disillusioned. I know to my cost that

Daily Mail, 24 May 1930.

amusing writers are often boring to meet. I do not mind if film stars are disappointing in their homes. The essential point is that they should make a lovely and harmonious work out of their acting. And this they do – or did do as long as they were allowed to. The great difficulty which I find is to know them apart. They are all so attractive and so complete that although I read with avidity the details of their marriages and divorces, I can rarely be accurate in attaching the right names to the right actresses. One inevitably becomes the 'fan' of one or two stars who, through some distinguishing trick in one's psychology, make themselves peculiarly memorable.

The trouble about so many actresses, it seems to me, is that they concentrate above all things on 'sex appeal'. This makes their films highly enjoyable. I will wait in a queue of any length in order to see Miss Clara Bow or Miss Nancy Carroll or Miss Bebe Daniels. It is unmixed delight to watch them. Where I go wrong is that as soon as I have left the theatre I have only a warm and grateful feeling to them but no clear memory of their individual charms. Greta Garbo I can always recognize because I admire her hats. I am hopelessly in love with her all the time I am at the films, but the moment it is over there is the same feeling of uncertainty. After all, 'sex appeal' is only one feeling. It may be stirred up by a blonde or a brunette, by tall, short, plump, thin, smart or ragamuffin types, but when all is said and done *it is just the same appeal*. Only one of an infinite series of emotions is aroused. That is where, for a man at any rate, male actors are so much more interesting. One can give one's whole attention to an actor like Emil Jannings or Conrad Veidt. One's appreciation of his art is not dimmed by that warm, cosy feeling of sex attraction which ruins all one's other discrimination.

There are two leading film actresses who, for me, stand out unforgettably. These are Miss Elsa Lanchester (Mrs Charles Laughton) and Miss Anna May Wong. Miss Lanchester has worked in few films and for some reason they are rarely shown, but I have a feeling of personal pride about her because I produced her first film. It was taken on a half-size camera. It was called *The Scarlet Woman: An Ecclesiastical Melodrama.*[1] I produced it when I was an undergraduate at Oxford. The hero has now given up film-acting for the simpler duties of the House of Commons.[2] It was a film of incredible complexity of plot, acted for the most part on Hampstead Heath. Since then Miss Lanchester has 'starred' in a brilliant series of comedies produced by Ivor Montague, but I have still a feeling of parental pride about her.

I have also a feeling of pride about Miss Wong, only this is not personal but racial pride, because it was the much-despised British film industry which first

---

[1] Now at the Humanities Research Center, University of Texas, Austin. Waugh wrote the film and acted two parts. For plot and titles see Charles Linck, 'Waugh – Greenidge film', *Evelyn Waugh Newsletter*, Autumn 1969, pp. 1–7. For stills see *A Little Learning* (1964 edition), p. 214, and 'Film Clips: The Scarlet Woman', *Sight and Sound*, Summer 1967, pp. 154–5. Waugh acted in two other Oxford films, '666' (Labour Club) and 'Mummers' (Hypocrites Club).

[2] Viscount Elmley, who played the Lord Chamberlain.

recognized her transcendent talent. Everyone fell in love with her when she played a small part in *The Thief of Baghdad*. For some time we caught glimpses of her flitting through crook plays of Chinatown, but it was British taste and enterprise which made of her the star we all admire today. It is absurd to attempt any definition of her charm. She has in the highest degree that subtlety of movement and restraint of expression which the film particularly nurtures. She has, several times, been condemned to play in films of very slight merit of plot or direction, but always she has lifted them at once into a realm of genuine artistic merit through her individual and inimitable grace and poignancy.

But why should her talent be left where it is? I should like to see Miss Wong playing Shakespeare. We are used to seeing Englishmen acting Princes of Denmark. We now see the brilliant success that a Negro actor can make in the part of a Moor. Why not a Chinese Ophelia? It seems to me that Miss Wong has exactly those attributes which one most requires of Shakespearean heroines. I cannot see her as Lady Macbeth, but she seems to me perfectly suited for the role of Juliet or to any of the heroines of the comedies. We have learned from her 'talky' that she has an excellent speaking voice; her acting has exactly the balance and modesty and refinement which the average European star loses before she attains the first rank. It seems to me absurd that plays of artificial oriental setting should have to be manufactured for her because no one has the enterprise to put her into one of the traditional English parts.

. ASSORTED ARTICLES .

D. H. Lawrence's death, less than three months ago, left the English literary public in a divided mind. Five years earlier their verdict would have been unembarrassed. Everyone, even those who had least supported and understood him during his life, would have been eloquent in tribute to a novelist of exuberant promise.

Twenty-five years later, Mr Peter Quennell, or whoever has by that time established himself on the throne of weekly criticism, would have been able to survey a career in which such inglorious incidents, now fresh in our memory, as the exhibition of Lawrence's drawings, would have fallen into due obscurity. By that time, I have no doubt, English moral standards will be secure enough to allow us to judge *Lady Chatterley's Lover* as a literary work; today, though our reaction may be one of disgust or of agreeable surprise, it is inevitably confused. This, in fact, seems to have been Lawrence's intention.

Like a few other great artists, his conscious intentions were not primarily artistic. He had a great deal to say. He was at war with civilization – a civilization which, for him, was characterized by the drab streets of his up-

Review of *Assorted Articles*, by D. H. Lawrence. *Graphic*, 31 May 1930.

bringing. He was at war with the English tradition of sterile culture. Above all he was at war with what he took to be the English 'respectable' attitude to sex.

Glorification of sex becomes more and more predominant in his later work; it is responsible both for the finest passages in his writing and for the conflicts with the police which embittered his last years. But when he is not on the heights, in those flat periods of his writing when he is resting from an outburst or painfully working himself up for another, this propagandist inclination is a bore.

Assorted Articles is simply a book of Lawrence's propaganda divorced from Lawrence's art. As the name suggests, these essays were mostly written for the press. It is one of the first signs of recognition, nowadays, that a writer or painter or man of fashion is getting himself talked about that he should be invited to write for the papers, usually upon some rather trivial subject. Novelists for the most part accept these invitations half-heartedly for what they are worth in guineas and publicity. To Lawrence, however, they meant a pulpit; he had a 'message' to deliver, and the wider the public the better he was pleased.

Moreover, to him the subjects were far from trivial. He wanted to stir up the whole of social life, to revitalize personal relationships, to denounce everything that seemed to him drab and sham. The subjects of popular discussion – the modern girl, the economic independence of woman, sex education, popular religious sentiment, etc. – were all matters of absorbing importance.

The average sophisticated novelist sits down to earn his fifteen, twenty or twenty-five guineas from the penny daily in a mood of apology. He hopes that his friends will not see his article, and he puts in several sly allusions to make clear to any who do that his tongue is in his cheek. He tries to secure the rewards of popular acclamation while remaining aloof from popular sympathy. Lawrence plunged into the work of 'feature' journalism with all the gusto of a prophet.

'Men must work and women as well', 'Cocksure women and hensure men', 'Sex versus loveliness', are the titles of some of these essays. As his illness began to encroach more and more on his energy, and the fear grew to certainty that he would have to leave unaccomplished half of the work he had set himself, Lawrence became more impassioned and more lyrical. The Easter essay on 'The Risen Lord' is a magnificent piece of rhetoric ending with the almost drunken challenge, 'I hate it, Mammon, I hate you and am going to push you off the face of the earth, Mammon, you great mob-thing, fatal to man.'

This was written at the same time as Mr James Douglas was also writing an Easter essay, also for the popular press. It is interesting to compare the two, both emotional, both extravagant, but separated by such an impassable gulf of genuine spiritual distinction; one can then realize how sham and insignificant was the temporary triumph of Mr Douglas.

. PEOPLE WHO WANT TO SUE ME .

I suppose that a novelist's life is not more full of embarrassments than anybody else's. There is no art or profession, except possibly higher mathematics, which one can practise without exposing oneself to amateur criticism and interference.

A novelist's trade, however, is the only one in which his acquaintances insist on coming right into the workshop and playing with the tools.

One of the most mischievous forms which this interference takes is the attribution to him of living models for his characters. Nowadays the instinctive reply to the question 'Have you read So-and-so's new novel?' is 'No. Who is in it?'

I was introduced to a young woman the other day whose first words were, 'Oh, I'm so excited to meet you. Now you can tell me who all the characters in your book really are! Mary says that Mrs – is Lady So-and-so, but I'm sure it is really Mrs –. I *am* right, aren't I?'

Now, reluctant as any writer must be to discourage any motive that can lead people to buy his books, it should be pointed out how unfair this is to the author and to his friends. Obviously there must be a connection of some kind between a writer's work and his life. His knowledge of the world is limited by his own experience. It is practically impossible for those who live among poor people to write about the rich; a writer who has never been seriously in love cannot make his characters seem so; upbringing, education, experience of travel, of the war, etc., all circumscribe and determine the incidents of a book.

But here the connection ends. Nothing is more insulting to a novelist than to assume that he is incapable of anything except the mere transcription of what he observes.

It is the same with one's characters. When one is describing someone's appearance it is quite likely that one will subconsciously be led to describe someone one has seen – after all, there is a very limited number of physical characters which one can enumerate. The reader, thinking she recognizes the portrait, will then assume that the temperament and the adventures of the character are also taken from life.

In the same way it sometimes happens that one's fancy is taken by a remark or a trick of speech which one overhears; everyone immediately jumps to the conclusion that the character who uses it in the book must in all points be identical with the one who used it in real life. In this way one is liable to the loss of friends and to libel actions.

Another maddening misconception is that the author must be in sympathy with all the opinions uttered by his characters. A breach of the moral law or convention in one's books is treated by many elderly and semi-literate people as a breach committed by oneself.

Daily Mail, 31 May 1930.

There is a worse trouble than any of these, however. That is the people who insist on identifying themselves. 'You ought to meet So-and-so ,' I was told the other day. 'He is just the kind of character you ought to put into one of your books.' 'Dear young lady,' I answered. 'I don't put people into my books. *They take themselves out .*'

Not long ago I published a novel in which a few pages were devoted to the description of an hotel. In order to avoid trouble I made it the most fantastic hotel I could devise. I filled it with an impossible clientèle, I invented an impossible proprietress. I gave it a fictitious address, I described its management as so eccentric and incompetent that no hotel could be run on their lines for a week without coming into the police or the bankruptcy court. Here at least, I thought, I was safely in the realm of pure imagination.[1]

Imagine my surprise, therefore, when I received threatening letters from two irate old ladies in London, one in Newcastle and one in New York, all identifying themselves and their establishments with my invention!

I had the same experience with the heroine of the story. She was a young lady of crazy and rather dissolute habits. No one, I should have thought, would see herself in that character without shame. But nearly all the young women of my acquaintance, and many whom I have not had the delight of meeting, claim with apparent gratitude and pride that they were the originals of that sordid character.

If only the amateurs would get it into their heads that novel-writing is a highly skilled and laborious trade. One does not just sit behind a screen jotting down other people's conversation. One has for one's raw material every single thing one has ever seen or heard or felt, and one has to go over that vast, smouldering rubbish-heap of experience, half stifled by the fumes and dust, scraping and delving until one finds a few discarded valuables.

Then one has to assemble these tarnished and dented fragments, polish them, set them in order, and try to make a coherent and significant arrangement of them. It is not merely a matter of filling up a dust-bin haphazard and emptying it out again in another place.

. ALEC WAUGH .

I did not really begin to know Alec until after the war. He is five years my senior and five years is a very long time when it represents the gulf between nursery and public school. For the first fifteen or sixteen years of my life, he was a very

---

[1] Waugh's Preface to *Vile Bodies* (London, 1965) admits that the novel contains 'a pretty accurate description of Mrs Rosa Lewis and her Cavendish Hotel, just on the brink of their decline but still famous.'

Olympian being indeed, whose arrivals at our house in Hampstead were always the occasion of parties and theatre-going; his ties, socks, hair lotions and walking-sticks seemed to me the highest goal of elegance I might one day attain. Indeed it was more as a man of the world and athlete than as a writer that he figured in my youthful imagination. It was not that he did not write. My father used to read us Shakespeare and poetry, and Alec wrote sonnets and blank-verse dramas; he wrote a short story, of which I still retain a copy, called 'The Melbourne Derby'; he wrote a long Swinburnian ode to Queen Esther. But it was as an athlete that his triumphs were most spaciously celebrated at home; his second-fifteen colours, house colours, first-eleven colours, his captaincy of his house were all events observed with present-giving and general cheerfulness.

At Sherborne he was editor of the school magazine and winner of the Prize Poem; he got into the sixth form at the unusually early age of 16, but the war prevented him from competing for further academic honours. He joined up at 17 in the Inns of Court OTC; from there he transferred to the Royal Military College at Sandhurst and was gazetted as second lieutenant to the Dorset Regiment. It was while he was in training in England that he wrote *The Loom of Youth*, his first novel. It was an astonishing achievement. It is simply the story of a boy's life at school from the day he arrived until the day he left; there have been many such books since written by all sorts of boys and girls about all sorts of schools. Alec's seems to me to stand quite apart from all these. It is mainly autobiographical. He had no educational axe to grind. He did not want to 'show up' anything or point a moral or retaliate upon personal enemies, although all these motives were attributed to him in one quarter or another. His interest was simply in the development of his hero's character and in the dramatic coherence of the incidents of his life. It was a book which shocked a number of people because he omitted nothing from what seemed essential to his theme, even if it was in conflict with the accepted tradition of English public schools. He wrote at great speed, at odd moments early in the morning and late at night, snatched from the brief leisure of his military training. The manuscript was written in notebooks, on the back of maps, on odd scraps of YMCA note-paper. It was published in the summer of 1917, just when he was going out to France for the first time, and was an immediate success, attracting by its treatment the respect of responsible critics and, by its theme, enormous popular interest. Edition after edition was quickly exhausted. Alec came out of the army at the end of the war to find himself already famous before his twenty-first birthday. Since then he has written six novels, two books of short stories, a book of poems, two books of essays and two books – *The Prisoners of Mainz* and *Myself When Young* – which defy classification but are, I suppose, best described as autobiography.

I think that my favourite of his novels is still *The Loom of Youth*. He has advanced enormously since then in maturity of outlook and polish of style, but his first book has a peculiar fragrance of youth and enthusiasm about it. His later work, like that of all sincere artists, inevitably reflects the passage of time and the twelve years since the war have been difficult and deadening ones. *Card Castle*, which, oddly enough, was least successful commercially, comes next in my admiration, and after that *Three Score and Ten*. Of his non-fiction works I think that his last book, *The Coloured Countries* [published in the USA as *Hot Countries*] comes far and away ahead. If one had to attribute any ancestry to Alec's peculiarly individual style, one would first think of Mr George Moore, but of Mr Moore brought up to date, divorced from Paris of the nineties and Dublin of the early 1900s and plunged into the insecure world of post-war London; of George Moore disillusioned even of his last inviolable stronghold of belief in the Sanctity of Art. Nothing could be better suited to this style of writing than the compilation of a leisurely, discursive and acutely critical travel book, such as Alec has produced in *The Coloured Countries*. Moreover this book is very much more than the mere daily journal of the novelist on a holiday. It contains in the chapters about Haiti what I think we may predict will be the germ of Alec's future development. It seems to me that he is growing out of novel-writing; his narrative poems, his story-teller's instinct for significant detail, his ability to sort out tangled chains of motive, to assess probabilities, to render incidents dramatic and memorable, seem to me all to fit him for the role of historian. Steps are being taken to induce him to undertake a history of the West Indies, and I feel confident that if he decides to give up his time and powers to the task, we shall all be indebted to him for a really valuable work.

Perhaps I ought to add some personal sketch of him. It is difficult for a brother. I know him both so well and so little. We are on terms of cordial friendship but we meet each other most infrequently, I suppose, of all our friends. Neither of us knows the other's movements. One day I receive a postcard from him bearing a Cambodian or West African postmark, telling me succinctly of some astonishing encounter; the next day my telephone will ring and I shall hear, 'Mr Waugh's compliments to Mr Waugh and will he lunch with him at the Ritz on Friday?'

I look up the day in my engagement book. 'Mr Waugh's compliments to Mr Waugh; he is very sorry he is engaged on Friday. Will Mr Waugh lunch with him at Boulestin's on Monday?'

'Mr Waugh leaves for Berlin by air on Sunday morning.'

And the next I hear will be a postcard from New York or New Zealand. You may meet him anywhere at any time and in any sort of company. Alec is in no kind of set. He has more friends and acquaintances than anyone I know, but none of them know each other. At most houses when you are invited to dine, you have some idea whom you will meet. At Alec's flat you may meet a rajah or a best-selling novelist or an ultra-modern painter or a colonial governor or someone he met playing cricket in Burma or a man who lent him a tennis racquet in the club at Port Said. You may meet him standing in the crowd at a baseball match or at a café on the Promenade des Anglais or at a first night in

London or in a gambling den in Saigon. He will always be the same; short, sturdy, very smartly dressed, usually carrying some slightly incongruous burden, a parcel of provisions, a baize cricket bag, or a cinema-camera. He will greet you with the utmost amiability; establish connections with six of your friends and relations; stand you a cocktail and then – disappear. He is always 'just going'; his luggage is invariably packed. You will arrange to meet him at the station to see him off; but you will miss him. He will have taken an aeroplane or been offered a lift in a car or he will discover some new line of ship in which he has never travelled. You will meet him three years later at the other side of the globe and he will recognize you and continue the conversation imperturbably as though he was unaware of the interruption.

. HAPPY DAYS IN THE OTC .

The boys of a great public school have recently composed a protest against the 'torture' of service in their OTC. Protests against their protest are rising from shocked old public-school boys in all parts of the Empire. The question has been raised in the House of Commons. It has in fact become a subject of general controversy.

I was never a very distinguished member of the corps at my school. I served in it for five years, I went to camp twice, but I never rose higher than the rank of acting-lance-corporal. Most weeks found me detailed for 'defaulters' parade'. However, I can say without affectation that many of my happiest hours at school were spent in uniform. I was fortunate in belonging to a house which maintained a tradition of anti-militarism. We had a fairly high standard of athletics, and a very high one of intellect, but we took a peculiar pride in the inefficiency of our house platoon.

This time last year, on the slopes of Lycabettos, I watched a company of Greek infantry doing squad drill. One sergeant had great difficulty in stopping his men smoking; they kept dropping their rifles and exchanging jokes from four to four. I was poignantly reminded of the many jolly field days I spent on the Sussex Downs.

I must admit that it was only late in my career that I began to appreciate the humorous possibilities of the corps. At first it *was* very much like 'torture' for a small boy of 13 to plod about water-logged fields in an acutely unhygienic uniform, with big boots, tight puttees and a heavy service rifle. We used all to dread uniform parade day, and crowd into the matron's room to have our temperatures taken in the rarely realized hope of getting 'leave off'. If those earnest pacifists, nurtured in a gentler system of education, who complain that the OTCs inculcate militarist ideals in the governing class could have seen our house matron's room seething with malingerers on the morning of a uniform

Daily Mail, 7 June 1930. From early 1930 controversy raged over the Labour government's decision to withdraw the grant and official recognition from the Cadet Corps.

parade, or heard the grousing in the changing room while we were cleaning our buttons, their apprehensions would be quickly allayed.

As we grew up this feeling of resentment gave place to one of slightly malevolent ridicule. We began to look forward to parades as occasions for elaborate 'ragging'. They were admirably suited for this purpose: first, because we did genuinely detest the corps and all it stood for; secondly, because there was no adequate provision for punishing offenders; any indiscipline in school or at games or in the house could be soundly beaten out at once. All that the corps authorities were able to do was to give us extra drills, which, in turn, developed into 'rags'; their only alternative was to expel us from the corps, which most of us cordially desired. Thirdly, by its nature, military discipline is peculiarly vulnerable to ridicule, as it demands a rigidity many times stricter than any other part of education.

I was looking through some old diaries the other day which I kept while I was at school. I was surprised to find that at least half of them, and certainly the more vivid half, was devoted to the record of various concerted rags on the corps. They seem rather unfunny now. One day there was an examination for 'Certificate A'. Officials came from the War Office to judge it. We were handed over to a candidate from another house to drill. It was a very important day for his future career, as he was going into the army. He took us in platoon drill. We lost him his certificate.

We used all to come late on parade, marching in a body; we used to drop our rifles; once one of us pretended to faint, falling flat on his back in the middle of an inspection, giggling slightly until he was carried away. We used to do all we could to cultivate a ludicrous appearance, bending the wire of our caps and wearing them at odd angles, choosing tunics that did not fit, getting our bayonets on the wrong side of our belts; on one occasion we all came on parade with coloured laces in one boot. We wore enormous buttonholes on mufti parades. Once on a field day our section deliberately lost itself and spent a lovely summer afternoon smoking peacefully on the top of a haystack, to the embarrassment of the amateur strategists who had assigned us an important place in the attack. Once our platoon numbered off 'Ace, two, three . . . nine, ten, knave, queen, king, sergeant.'

'Glorious parade today,' I read in my diary. 'Fulford fell down . . .' Well, it all seems a little dreary nowadays, but so do the accounts of any 'rag'. I think we must have been a great bore to those kindly officers – many of them were clergymen in private life – who commanded us. But if we had not been a bore to them about that we should have been about something else. As it was, all our superfluous high spirits were worked off on parade and we were able to devote ourselves fairly seriously to the other parts of our education. If it had not been the corps it would have been the science laboratories or the divinity school which we should have ridiculed. Instead it became rather a point of honour to make it clear to our masters that our quarrel with them was only in a purely military capacity. After spending all the afternoon in exasperating our unfortunate company commander, we would spend the evening in doing him as good a prose as we could and in listening respectfully to his advice.

Of the three people who were most outrageous in their efforts to make the OTC ludicrous one got a very good scholarship at the university and the other two became in turn presidents of the Oxford Union.[1] It seemed as though the War Office, in rare concord with the Office of Education, had chosen to provide us with just the necessary butt for our humour, so that we could devote ourselves wholeheartedly to the more durable benefits of public-school education. It is only natural to waste a certain amount of time at that age. It seems an excellent arrangement that the waste should be made profitable by teaching the young that disrespect for militarism which has been a peculiarly English characteristic since the days of Cromwell.

. SUCH APPALLING MANNERS! .

A few days ago I read in this page an article by Mr Cecil Beaton in which he said that young people were no longer bad mannered. If this had been said by someone whom I did not know I should have been very envious. 'Here,' I should have said to myself, 'here at last there is someone I really want to meet, someone who has managed to collect about him a set of good-mannered friends.'

But I know Mr Beaton; we go to each other's parties and we seem to share a large number of the same friends. Where, I wonder, does he find these good manners he speaks of? Perhaps we are like the two children in the 'Eyes and No Eyes' series of nature books, as Mr Beaton, with hypersensitive powers of observation, goes through the same parties as I, noting little acts of courtesy which escape my grosser vision. But I doubt it. I think I know Mr Beaton's motive. There is no surer way of creating a fashion than by stating that it already exists. If we go on for long enough proclaiming the return of courtesy and etiquette they are sure to come. Meanwhile we still have to suffer.

I have been to very few luncheon or dinner parties during the last month where someone has not 'chucked' usually within an hour of the meal. Twice I have seen hostesses receive telephone messages while their party was assembled waiting, to say 'Miss So-and-so regrets that she will be unable to come today.' In most cases no letter of explanation followed. I met a girl the other evening who said to me, 'Are you lunching with – tomorrow? Do tell him that I'm sorry but I shan't be able to come after all. I have to go into the country.' But I think the feminine attitude was most happily summed up in the remark of an acquaintance of mine who was recently married. A friend asked her whether she had ever received a wedding present he had sent. Her answer was, 'Yes,

---

1 Waugh won the scholarship, Roger Fulford and (Sir) Hugh Molson became presidents of the Oxford Union. For accounts of their ragging see *Diaries* 1-11 October and 11-18 March 1921. *Daily Mail*, 14 June 1930. See *Diaries*, 11 June 1930 and p.38 above.

rather. Thank you so much. I suppose I ought to have written, but the trouble was that if we thanked for one we should have to thank for them all.'

The trouble comes entirely from young women, and, like most trouble from women, it is not due to any vice of selfishness or unkindness or arrogance, but simply to sheer incompetence. They just do not know how to organize their affairs. They accept all verbal invitations at once without troubling to verify the date. 'I accept all invitations on principle,' I heard one girl say. 'One never need go if one doesn't want to.' On principle. . . . It is the same with their letter-writing. A very few girls have a perverse idea that there is something actually derogatory in answering a letter; in some mysterious way they think that if they did so they would appear to be flattering their men friends or 'making themselves cheap', but for the most part, I am convinced, girls are full of every innocent intention. It is simply that they cannot brace themselves to the moral resolution and intellectual effort required to write a note. Many apparently sane girls cannot even do their own telephoning, but leave messages to be garbled by their servants.

It is odd that the trouble should come from women, because their social lives are important to them. Most young men attach very little value to the part of their day which they spend in this way, but they are able to organize it intelligently; girls, with nothing else to think about, muddle everything and make themselves unpopular. At least – and here I am getting to the point of this article – *they ought to make themselves unpopular*. Popularity is the one vital thing in their lives. As long as they think that they are preserving that one sacred thing they do not mind how unpleasant or ludicrous they make themselves. Mr Beaton has started an excellent campaign in telling them that they are being unfashionable if they are rude. It is time that they were also told that they are getting themselves disliked.

Elderly people have always been perfectly sensible about this. If young people were rude at their houses they were not asked again, and that was that. Some young people say, 'Well, who wants to go to their boring houses, anyway?' Others conform, but feel that they are making some peculiar allowance for the caprice of old age. 'What a funny stuffy old thing Lady –– is,' they think. 'She expects one to write a letter accepting an invitation, and to stick to it even if something more amusing turns up, and to come at the actual time she says. Still, one must remember she belongs to another generation. . . .'

The thing I should like to see is the declaration of a sex war against these young women by the men of their own generation. They should be taught that courtesy is not a foible of senility and that bachelors are just as capable of striking names off their lists of acquaintances as dowagers. What is more, the men are bound to win in any contest of this kind. Girls can get along perfectly well without going to formal, grown-up parties, but they cannot dispense with the society of their own generation. Most men can get along perfectly well without parties of any kind. They have innumerable other interests and occupations.

On the rare occasions when I give a party I am always filled with despondency and look aghast down the table wondering why in the world I have brought this thing on myself. Girls are only half alive until they find themselves in a crowd. Moreover, men's sociable inclinations are completely satisfied in their own society. No woman can have the remotest conception of the ease and amiability of a bachelor party. Women, proverbially, are boring to each other. It is time that young men formed among themselves the sort of league that exists occultly among the dowagers; a crusade to ignore all girls who are too scatter-brained to remember the simple precepts of social intercourse which they were taught in the school-room.

. A NEGLECTED MASTERPIECE .

A few days ago I came upon an illuminating paragraph in a Sunday newspaper. It was in the column where a lady of fashion dispenses advice to those who consult her about their private concerns. A correspondent wrote, '. . . I am not outstandingly brilliant at anything. I can't leave home as my mother is delicate, but I want to do something to earn not less than £3 a week. I've tried chicken farming and it doesn't pay.' The answer was, 'You might get a job as a reader to a publisher . . . that or book reviewing.'

That explains everything about our literary critics; they are young ladies, not outstandingly brilliant at anything, who have failed to make a success with poultry. It explains, too, the tepid and negligent reception accorded to Mr Henry Green's *Living*.

This novel has been out for nearly a year but I make no apology for writing about it. It is a work of genius. I am as sure about this as I am about any question of taste. And no one outside a very narrow circle has read it.

There are several reasons for its neglect. One is the author's name. From motives inscrutable to his friends, the author of *Living* chooses to publish his work under a pseudonym of peculiar drabness. Moreover, the book lacks many of the qualities that attract attention – it is neither abnormally long nor abnormally short, it is not about the war, it is not about unnatural vice or religious doubt, it is not translated from any foreign language, it does not 'contain easily recognizable portraits of people prominent in Society'. Above all it cannot be 'skipped'. It has to be read with great care and humility – if possible three or four times.

It deals with an iron foundry in Birmingham and it may be as well to explain here that 'Mr Green' knows this subject intimately. After a normal education at Eton and Magdalen, Oxford, he went for two years to work in a factory, living in a workman's dwelling and following a workman's daily routine. There are two sets of characters; there are the Duprets who own the factory and their friends in London. Young Mr Dupret is, in an indefinable way, the hero of the

Review of *Living*, by Henry Green. *Graphic*, 14 June 1930.

story, which begins with his visit to the Birmingham works.

In the course of the book old Mr Dupret dies and his son succeeds him as head of the business. Young Mr Dupret falls in love with a girl in London society but fails to make any impression on her; she in her turns falls in love with a genial bounder called Tyler and fails to make any lasting impression on him. All this part of the book is conceived with exquisite irony. Old Mr Dupret's illness and the attempts to stir him from his lethargy, the house party with Tom Tyler being 'the life and soul' of it, are satirical passages only equalled in modern literature by Miss Compton-Burnett's *Brothers and Sisters* (another book that is not half as well known as it should be). In the second half of *Living* the rich characters fade away, having done their part, and the field is left to the factory workers in Birmingham.

These are treated in a manner which, as far as I know, is unique. 'Mr Green' has no political or sociological axe to grind; he is not distracted by any Tolstoyan illusions about the dignity of manual labour. He sees the working class with a humorous sympathy; we are accustomed to seeing them treated by bourgeois writers either as brutes or noble savages. For Mr Green they are like a pack of unruly schoolboys, full of intense enmities and jealousies and odd superstitions (particularly a fear of the bourgeois professions of medicine and law). He shows them as tortured by continuous social embarrassments in their intercourse with each other, and by all kinds of ill-digested moral precepts.

At first the book is so much about the *whole* factory that it is impossible to distinguish the characters from their background.

Soon, however, if one reads carefully, five or six clearly articulated characters begin to assert their importance; those who live in the household of old Mr Craigan, 'the best moulder in Birmingham'. Joe Gates lives in the same house and Lily Gates, his daughter. Craigan wants her to marry a melancholy young man who works under him in the factory; he has saved money, owns the house, and is a powerful man. She wants to marry a still more melancholy young man called Jones.

Her abortive elopement with Jones, which forms the crisis of the narrative, is a superb piece of writing. Next door live the Eames family, who symbolize fecundity and nature as opposed to the mechanized lives of the other characters.

Technically, *Living* is without exception the most interesting book I have read. Those who are troubled with school-ma'am minds will be continually shocked by the diction and construction. In a great number of instances, Mr Green omits the definite article where we expect to find it; he does worse violence to our feelings by such sentences as 'this was only but nervousness because her he was taking in was so pretty,' and 'he still had some of his Friday's money which he had not been able to drink away all of it.'

These are the very opposite of slovenly writing. The effects which Mr Green wishes to make and the information he wishes to give are so accurately and subtly conceived that it becomes necessary to take language one step further than its grammatical limits allow. The more I read it the more I appreciate the structural necessity of all the features which at first disconcerted me.

There are no unrelated bits such as one finds in most books. A danger in novel-writing is to make one's immediate effect and then discard the means one employed. Modern novelists taught by Mr James Joyce are at last realizing the importance of re-echoing and remodifying the same themes. Note, for instance, the repeated metaphor of 'pigeons' in *Living*. (Dickens vaguely saw the importance of this, but he used it purely rhetorically – for instance, in the recurring image of Steerforth lying with his head on his arm as he had done at school.)

Let me add one other comparison, for one can in some way circumscribe and localize a book by stating its bearing in relation to other works. I see in *Living* very much the same technical apparatus at work as in many of Mr T. S. Eliot's poems – particularly in the narrative passages of *The Waste Land* and the two *Fragments of an Agon*. Space does not allow me to say more; let me conclude by urging everyone who has the energy to tackle a book which is modern in the real sense of the word, and which is not predigested for weak literary stomachs, to read and *study Living*.

. WAS OXFORD WORTH WHILE? .

Last weekend I went down to Oxford for an undergraduate party. It is near the end of term, and half the guests were just out of the schools in the middle of their final examinations. They replied to polite inquiries about their progress: 'Oh, I don't know. With any luck in my *viva* I may scrape a second' – which is the stock answer of everyone who hopes for a first. I said that six years ago. I got a third.

I have reached the age when most of my friends in the University are dons. They go on, term after term – hospitable, malicious, unchanged. It was an unusual experience to see so many undergraduates, most of them in the last days of their last year, in the absurd white bow ties that are supposed to convey an academic appearance. It set me wondering whether Oxford had been worth while.

When parents and schoolmasters ask themselves and each other that question they often mean only one thing: Is the money spent on university education a sound capital investment? From three to four years of a young man's life, at an age when he might be earning a certain amount of money, are occupied instead in spending it. The amount, of course, varies a great deal from one man to another, but I suppose that it costs on the average about £1,000 to take a degree. Is there a corresponding increase in the graduate's earning capacity? Would the money have been better employed at some technical training college?

Daily Mail, 21 June 1930.

From this point of view, as far as I can judge from my own experience and that of my friends, Oxford is certainly not worth while. When I went down the only job I could get was that of teaching elementary classics to turbulent little boys at the salary of £160 a year. Of my contemporaries only one is earning 'real money'; he is a film star at Hollywood; incidentally he was sent down for failing to pass his preliminary schools. Another friend, on the other hand, took high honours in Mods and Greats and has also devoted himself to cinema work. He gets a part in the crowd at Elstree about once a month. Another scholar who took a double first and was president of the Junior Common Room has become a curate. Another friend who had an exemplary career in all branches of university life was for a month last year actually starving until he was dis-covered; another, who had a brilliant reputation among his fellow-undergraduates, lives in a dingy bed-sitting room and does occasional reviews for journals of precarious financial stability. As far as direct monetary returns are considered, our parents would have done far better to have packed us off to Monte Carlo to try our luck at the tables.

But, of course, that is a narrow and silly way to regard education. A much more pertinent question is: Do Oxford and Cambridge maintain a tradition of genuine culture?

To judge by the blank faces and blanker conversation of the young men in a London ballroom one would suspect that they did not. To judge by the decoration of my tutor's rooms, one would say with certainty that they did not. Oxford is not up to date in the latest theories of aesthetics and psychology from Berlin and Paris. Many of the colleges are far from hygienic. A great number of the undergraduates express the heartiest contempt for everything to do with Art or intellect.

But there is another side. Oxford is architecturally a city of peculiar grace and magnificence, and it is impossible for anyone, however deep his apparent preoccupation with hunting or golf or bridge, to live there for three or four years without being influenced by it.

All the misunderstanding of the value of university life seems to me to come from two extreme heresies. On the one hand are those who expect a university to be a kind of insurance company into which so much money is paid and from which so much, eventually, is extracted. They expect a BA degree to be a badge which will gain them instant preference over poorer competitors, and in nine cases out of ten they are disappointed.

On the other hand, there are those who expect Oxford to be like an Oxford novel. A place of easy living, subtle conversation and illuminating friendships. They expect it to be a kind of microcosm of eighteenth-century Whig society, combined with an infinitely sophisticated modernism. They, too, are disappointed.

The truth is that Oxford is simply a very beautiful city in which it is convenient to segregate a certain number of the young of the nation while they are growing up. It is absurd to pretend that a boy of 18, however sound he has been as a school prefect, is a fully grown man. Those who choose or are obliged to begin regular, remunerative, responsible work at the moment they leave school, particularly if they have had a fairly carefully tended adolescence, often show signs of a kind of arrested development. It is just because Oxford keeps them back from their careers that it is of most value.

It gives them another four years in which to grow up gradually. It puts them out of the way of their fellow-citizens while they are making fools of themselves. They can learn to get drunk or not to get drunk; they can edit their own papers and air their opinions; they can learn how to give parties; they can find out, before they are too busy, what really amuses and excites them; and they can do all this in a town by themselves.

After that they can begin on the dreary and futile jobs that wait for most of them, with a great deal more chance of keeping their sense of humour and self-respect.

. ONE WAY TO IMMORTALITY .

I went to luncheon not long ago with some people who make it their hobby to collect prominent people as their guests. I was asked, at the last moment, to fill a gap in the table, and as I looked round the room and encountered face after face made famous to me by caricaturists and press photographers, I was overawed to discover that I was the only nonentity present. I was made conscious of this by my introductions: for the others their name alone was necessary: I had to be explained. 'This is Mr Waugh. He writes for the *Daily Mail*.' I stood in the corner very shy and oppressed.

There was one 'celebrity', however, whom I could not identify. His sombre clothes and unobtrusive manner made it clear that he was very distinguished. His eyes, too, had that vigilant, hunted look, which 'celebrities' acquire after a week or two in London. He sat opposite me at luncheon, and the woman next to him was clearly having the same difficulty as I. In those blissful moments when my two neighbours were talking away from me and I found myself isolated from the conversation, I was amused to watch her efforts to 'place' him. She tried him on politics, literature, art, archaeology, diplomacy, law, science. Each time he eyed her furtively and expressed complete ignorance of the subject. At last, exhausted but undefeated, she said, 'But surely you do *something*?' 'Why, yes,' he replied: 'I keep a diary.'

There happened to be a slight hush at the moment he said this, and the statement was heard by half the table and hastily repeated. The effect was instantaneous. He looked round, scared by the interest he had created, and made things worse by adding: 'Not an important diary, you know. I just write down all the places I go to and the people I meet and what they look like and what they say.' *What they look like and what they say*. . . A sudden self-consciousness descended on the party. Everyone began searching his memory. What had he been saying? Was it anything indiscreet or, still worse, anything silly? The women began brooding about their hats. We all felt ourselves face to face with posterity. Eventually, perhaps, under modern unreticent conditions, quite soon, during our lifetimes, this dangerous little man would publish his vile journal. We could imagine it. Four or five volumes. I could imagine how each of us, with trembling fingers, would turn to the index. Were we mentioned? And whether we were there or not, it would be equally humiliating. Those of the party whose attainments or ambitions led them to expect lasting fame began, I could see, to imagine their future biographers dipping into this man's diary for racy, contemporary reporting. A cold wind seemed to have breathed over all of us. The party was a failure.

I wonder how many people, apart from schoolgirls, are in the habit of keeping a diary. From time to time I purchase a thick notebook and record a few pages of my daily round, but I have a deep-rooted feeling that it is a mischievous and degrading habit to write anything which will not bring in an immediate pecuniary reward, so that the journal invariably languishes and dies in a week or two. But for people who are less mercenary and more ambitious than I am it seems a very simple way of securing importance and immortality.

Mr J. C. Squire once wrote a delightful story about a man who earned a CB by pretending to keep a diary. He went out to political receptions and was continually flattered by cabinet ministers, who wished to hand down to history their own version of the purity of their motives. At his death the row of bound volumes which had attracted so much curiosity was found to be empty.

But it is not necessary to be in touch with famous people in order to write a valuable diary. I still think that the funniest book in the world is Grossmith's *Diary of a Nobody*. If only people would really keep journals like that. Nobody wants to read other people's reflections on life and religion and politics, but the routine of their day, properly recorded, is always interesting, and will become more so as conditions change with the years.

All over the country there are people who secretly nurse literary ambitions. Half the young women I know are engaged in writing novels; the other half write articles for magazines, few of which are ever published. Amateurs will embark on dramas in blank verse, epics, sex novels, historical romances, treatises on philosophy and heaven knows what. Why won't they keep diaries instead? There is no one in the country whose life, properly recorded, would not make a thrilling book. The routine of life in an office or factory, with its various squabbles and jokes and occasional tragedy; the life of an English village with the conversation of the rectory and the manor and the pub, the intrigues of the Women's Institute and the Mothers' Union; the life of a commercial traveller with the continual change of company and scene; a hospital nurse with the succession of patients all encountered in a relationship which makes for immediate intimacy; a governess watching children develop; a farmer whose whole livelihood depends on observance of nature.

. THIS SUN-BATHING BUSINESS .

I have been reading with the deepest amusement the accounts of the scene at the Welsh Harp last weekend when a mixed but united party attempted to sun themselves on a stretch of private ground by the shores of the lake. If we ever tend to feel a little superior to the squabbles of our earnest fellow-subjects in India or Malta, let us remember with humility the outburst last weekend. This man boils salt water; that man takes off his shirt; all men are brothers.

Not that I have the smallest enthusiasm for sun-bathing myself. I hate the whole business. Now and then I am forced to do it.

The first effect of this extensive unclothing is a mild interest in one another's colour – sometimes envious, usually sympathetic. This, however, very quickly passes and is succeeded by a sensation of gentle intoxication and content. That, too, is of short duration. Complete stupefaction sets in succeeded, at a long interval, by irritation, inflammation, and other symptoms of sunburn. Then you rub on oil, and bits of sand and waste-paper adhere to you. At the end of the process you go indoors feeling completely tired out, as if you had been doing a decent afternoon's work, half awake and morose. If you are lucky you are now discoloured evenly all over, if you have fair hair you look ludicrous, if you are dark you are a tolerable imitation of a Spanish donkey-boy. But if you are unlucky, like me, you turn a mottled crimson, with white flakes in places as though you were afflicted with some noisome skin disease.

All this is supposed to be good for you. Doctors say so. Nowadays people believe anything they are told by 'scientists', just as they used to believe anything they were told by clergymen.

Of one thing, however, I am suspicious. I am doubtful whether all the addle-headed young women who encumber the country were really born as stupid as they seem. Their brown limbs give away their secret, like the scars of the cocaine taker. They have just lain out too long in the sun and their wits have got hard boiled. They have their annual orgy of stultification on the Riviera, and whenever they can get it in England – mercifully rarely – they fall back on their craving for their drug, sunlight. It is astonishing how alert and intelligent many of these poor dolts become by Christmas. However, that is their own look out.

If I had a daughter I should take good care to shut her up indoors. Hamlet gave just this advice to Polonius. The astonishing thing about the Welsh Harp incident was that large crowds of people assembled to disturb the sun-bathing of a number of total strangers. Moreover, they were not impelled by an officious solicitude for their poor baking brains, but by indignation that they should sit there on the grass imperfectly clothed.

Now, I can quite understand that many people may be depressed by the spectacle of naked humanity. Personally I cannot see that an ugly body is any more offensive than an ugly dress. This, however, is not the point. The people who made a fuss at the Welsh Harp simply detest the spectacle of bodies of any kind, beautiful or ugly. But do they cherish their over-delicate sensibility and avoid places where they are liable to shock? (After all, England is still full of places where one can be pretty certain that everyone will be fully clothed.) No. These astonishing people assemble in a large crowd at the one place where they know they will see the very thing which displeases them. There are some types of mind which it is hopeless to try to understand.

But there is another equally odd conclusion which emerges from the situation; that is, the devastating self-righteousness of all parties. The sun-bathers are not merely content to enjoy themselves in a fashionable but slightly idiotic manner. They must pretend that they are full of exalted moral purpose, martyrs in the cause of hygiene and true decency.

That is one of the queer characteristics of our countrymen. They will always quote the highest motives for whatever they do. If an Italian, say, overcharges one's bill or gives one the wrong change and is detected, he grins and admits failure. An Englishman will always attempt to prove himself right, will go on grumbling until one is out of earshot and will think one 'no gentleman' for pointing out his dishonesty.

So it is with the disturbers of the peace at the Welsh Harp. If only the sun-bathers will be frank and say: 'We like to lie and cook in the sun, because (a) someone told us it was fashionable; (b) it is rather fun seeing what our friends look like without their clothes; (c) it is comfortable to let our brains dry up completely so that we haven't got to bother about thinking.' If only the other side would say: 'It was a hot day and we felt pugnacious and thought it would be fun to push those cranks into a pond.'

But no. There must be all the usual clap-trap about 'Freedom', 'Health', 'Purity' and even, most fantastic cry of all, 'Save the children!' What a funny lot we are!

. CONFESSIONS AND IMPRESSIONS .

Mrs Mannin[1] seems to have caused a considerable stir with her book, *Confessions and Impressions*; wherever I have been during the last ten days I have met people who told me that they were looking for her head on a charger.

Review of *Confessions and Impressions*, by Ethel Mannin. *Graphic*, 12 July 1930.
1 Correctly, Miss Mannin.

For this reason, I began reading it with the expectation of being entertained and shocked. I was flatly disappointed. It is dull, cranky and pretentious.

> My candle burns at both ends
> It will not last the night;
> But ah, my friends, and oh, my friends
> It gives a lovely light.

Mrs Mannin has placed this ghastly quotation on her title page, and has thus happily summarized the tone of her writing. The book consists of two parts: the first an autobiography, and the second a series of character studies of the more or less prominent men and women whom Mrs Mannin has come across.

The first part sets out with a brave show of frankness and fearlessness, but it is actually more full of concealment, innuendo and genteel reserve than the most pompous memorial biography. The chapter entitled 'Tragedy', in which the author deals with some bereavement in her recent past, is an extreme example of her aptitude for talking about indiscretions from behind an impenetrable palisade of broken sentences and incomplete allusions.

However, there is some interest in this first half as there must be in the record of practically any human life, but, 'ah, my friends, and oh, my friends', the second half!

As a modern poet once remarked, 'Anyone in this world can meet anybody else – once.' Mrs Mannin has scraped acquaintance with quite a number of celebrated people.

As she herself makes very clear in the first part of this book, through circumstances over which she had no control, she had very little schooling; and her early surroundings were not such as would enable her to help out the inadequacy of her mental equipment with an intuition of good taste.

She is out to track big game, but she lacks all the requisite qualifications, and she goes romping along like a Girl Guide, whooping and whistling, and plunging suddenly out of bushes upon her alarmed quarry, and whether she finds a rabbit or an elephant or a tiger or a rattlesnake it is all one to her.

Sometimes we catch the whisk of tail as a real lion slips off into the under-growth – Mr Bertrand Russell, Mr Osbert Sitwell, Mr Paul Robeson. More often Mrs Mannin makes a great pounce and emerges with some lesser capture – Mr Gilbert Frankau or A. S. Neill, MA. But the huntress stuffs the head and sticks in a pair of glazed, artificial eyes and hangs up the specimen for our contemplation with unembarrassed enthusiasm.

In this book Mrs Mannin makes very free with the names of several of my friends, who, I know, have only the slightest acquaintance with her, but I do not blame her for this.

In conversation everyone gossips ignorantly and maliciously about people he barely knows. What is more, if he can do it amusingly, he earns quite a lot by it, in hospitality and reputation for wit. I don't see that there is very much difference between this and selling one's chatter outright at ten and sixpence a volume.

My complaint about Mrs Mannin is that she has done her work so clumsily and tritely and has tried to butter it over with so much second-hand and second-rate uplift.

She simply shows a drab and boring mind and however gay the incidents of her life, however intense and various her experience, however exalted the people she contrived to claim acquaintance with, she is bound to make drab and boring books until she takes less seriously the compliments she seems to be offered, becomes a little more critical of those she encounters and a great deal more critical of herself; learns a little about the real meaning of tradition, and, in fact, works herself up to a standard of culture and courtesy which less impetuous girls attain in the schoolroom.

POSTSCRIPT

One of the few abiding delights of literary criticism is the occasional letter of protest one receives from outraged authors. The editor of the *Graphic* has just forwarded me one from Miss Mannin, the authoress of *Confessions and Impressions*, which I reviewed a week or two ago.

She complains, justly, that I misquoted her quotation about 'Oh, my friends, and ah, my friends'. It should read, 'Oh, my foes, and ah, my friends'. I am sorry about this, but it is ludicrously bad in either version. She also has some personal gibes about me which I wish I had space to quote in full. Among other things she remarks that on the occasion she met me ('anyone can meet anyone else – *once*') I looked as though any minute I would burst into tears and demand to be taken home. Well, as a matter of fact, that is almost exactly how I did feel.

. FOR ADULT AUDIENCES .

The other morning I read in my morning paper, in the page where 'Onlooker' looks at life, that a peer, anxious to take his children to a cinema, had been forced to leave London in disappointment; he had been unable to find any programme suitable for them. Why, 'Onlooker' asked, does someone not start a children's cinema?

But, where, oh where, can one find a cinema to which one can decently take grown-ups?

There are, it is true, numerous films classified 'for adult audiences'. One can see these all over the country, and, if one goes to an afternoon performance, the dialogue will, as often as not, be completely submerged in the yells and catcalls of over-excited children.

Graphic, 9 August 1930.

Daily Mail, 25 July 1930.

But, in spite of their popularity, these films are not at all what one might expect. If one consulted an educated Martian about what films were exclusively suitable for grown-up people he would no doubt give some such answer as this:

'It is natural for the very young to be interested in violence, whether comic or dramatic; they will enjoy films showing any kind of chase or combat. They have not a fully developed sense of probability, consequently they applaud exaggerated feats of heroism; they like to see a single soldier hold back an army, they admire athleticism, and delight in seeing people jump from galloping horses on to moving trains; they are easily deceived by fake photography; they have no first-hand experience of love, and readily believe in permanent fidelity and felicity and other romantic fictions. They are easily amused and dazzled by great display in the production.

'Grown-ups, on the other hand, have more serious and penetrating interests. They want the characters and the details of a plot to be convincing; they do not want cheap sentiment, mother love, mock heroics; they will detect absurdities in historical facts; they do not want facetious comments in their "interest films"; they do not want to see film versions of their favourite books perverting the plots, sticking on happy endings, cutting out important scenes which might hurt undeveloped sensibilities, introducing "love interest" where it is inessential.

'Above all grown-ups will be bored by vulgarity and excess in the production. They will prefer to see one or two first-rate dancers to an army of chorus girls; they will appreciate subtlety in artistic effect. They will welcome experiment; they will not be taken in by mere eccentricity.'

These are the qualities one might reasonably expect in a film suitable for adult audiences. Instead, this label means only one thing – sex. It means the same silly, second-hand stuff about love, only in this case the situation is complicated by the marriage of one or both of the lovers. Either this, or it means that the characters besides being thieves, drunkards, blackmailers, murderers, and adepts at all the other crimes towards which children are assumed to be sympathetic, are also observed as indulging in irregular love affairs.

Every year there are produced in London four or five plays, at least, to which one can go quite wholeheartedly for enjoyment. There is hardly a single film for which one does not have to make allowances. One has to make a deliberate effort to put oneself into the state of mind to accept and enjoy the second-rate. Half one's pleasure has to come from laughing at, not with, the film, in detecting gross Americanisms and solecisms, in affecting an exaggerated concern for the welfare of impossible characters.

The truth is that the film industry will try to do too much. It will insist, as no other art or industry has ever tried to insist, upon everything being suitable for everybody.

The result is that it produces a commodity mildly unsuitable to almost everyone. It will not produce children's films or grown-ups' films. It aims instead at the adolescent. The pimply youth and the giggling girl who embody all the lamentable characteristics of both ages – childhood without its freshness and purity and credulity, age without wisdom or maturity or culture.

It is no wonder that they fail. It is as though a writer set out to compile a book which was to be both a fairy story and first reader, a textbook on psychology, a work of scholarship, a novel, an adventure story, tragedy, drama and comedy, an encyclopaedia, a cookery book and a daily newspaper in one. But because the commercial organization of the films is so far in advance of their artistic integrity they have secured a virtual monopoly of the market.

What the film magnates do not realize is that the mean is no greater than the extremes. The average of any series of numbers is one number. The policy of aiming at the adolescent and putting in a few stray sops for children and adults is not necessarily a wise one from the point of bookings. The adolescent is clearly a considerable factor in cinema audiences. The film producers make films suitable for him and for him only. They then look into their cinemas and say, 'The majority of our audience are adolescents. Therefore we must produce films suitable only for them.'

It is the old fallacy, which any sales manager can expose, of confusing an actual with a potential public. All over the country there are hundreds of thousands of mature, sensible men and women who will not go to cinemas because the performances bore and irritate them.

It is not a matter of a few highbrows, but of a vast, responsible public waiting for anyone with the initiative to start a cinema for grown-ups.

. ANGEL PAVEMENT .

In defiance of the superstition that no book can be published between the end of July and the middle of September, Messrs Heinemann are issuing next Monday a new novel by Mr J. B. Priestley. It is another large book printed in agreeably large type on 613 large pages. It seems to me greatly to the publishers' credit that they can produce a volume of this size and quality at the price of half a guinea. Clearly they are relying upon a big sale for it, and I can see no reason why they should be disappointed.

I do not think that anyone can grudge Mr Priestley the success which he achieved with *The Good Companions*. It was due to no craze or unpredictable wave of fashion, to personalities, scandal, self-advertisement or any of the less worthy means by which books can achieve prominence, but simply to its own outstanding qualities of technical precision and felicity, and the humour and humanity of its mood. It was a book of high literary excellence whose appeal was to a far wider public than that which concerns itself solely with literary qualities. Above all it was a friendly and cheerful book; the characters excited

Review of *Angel Pavement*, by J. B. Priestley. *Graphic*, 16 August 1930.

affection and sympathy in readers of the most diverse kinds; it was a comfortable and warm-hearted book.

That is the only fear I have for *Angel Pavement*; it will not disappoint any of *The Good Companions* readers who appreciated what was really best in that book, but I think it may disappoint that section of the public who saw only the good humour and the warm-heartedness and nothing more.

In that borderland of illiteracy where great sales are achieved, *Angel Pavement* may seem slightly subdued and chilling after its exuberant predecessor. The conclusion of the story is very far from being the 'happy ending' of conventionalized fiction; indeed, the elements of consolation are so lightly stressed as to be barely perceptible. More than this, there are few characters in it for whom we can feel any very deep affection or esteem.

As I have said, these objections will not damp the enthusiasm of Mr Priestley's more responsible admirers, but they may prevent *Angel Pavement* from enjoying quite that vast popularity which *The Good Companions* so justly enjoyed.

Angel Pavement is a side street in the City, populated by slightly decayed merchants, selling carnival novelties, incandescent gas fittings, tailors' trimmings, 'Kwik-work' razor blades and so on. Among these offices is that of Twigg and Dersingham, wholesale dealers in veneers for the cheap furniture trade. Each of the people employed in this small business is a clearly defined character; taken together in their various relationships, they form a microcosm of contemporary English middle- and lower-middle-class life.

There is Mr Dersingham, the head of the business, 'a year or two under forty, tallish, fairly well built, but beginning to sag a little . . . one of those young men who are haunted by a lost Oxford or Cambridge career. These are not scholars or brilliant athletes who have been denied their chance of distinction, but simply the fellows who have been robbed of an opportunity of acquiring more striped ties, college blazers and tobacco jars decorated with college coats of arms, in short, the fervent freshmen who never have the freshmen nonsense knocked out of them . . . a tremendous "old boy". . . Perhaps the shortest definition of Dersingham – and he himself would have asked for no other – was that he was an old Worrelian.'

Then, there is Miss Matfield, his secretary, the daughter of a doctor who had once played scrum half with 'The Alsatians'. This gives her a distinction in Mr Dersingham's eyes which somewhat embarrasses their business relations. Miss Matfield lives in a frightful girls' hostel in Hampstead, where the inmates call one another by their surnames and exchange furtive, romantic confidences.

There is Mr Goath, the arch-type of defeatist, antiquated, incompetent, who travels for the firm, booking fewer and fewer orders with a kind of relish for failure. There is Mr Smeeth, the subtlest of the characters, who looks, but is not, a grey drudge; his wife has odious friends and his son inherits this taste in a more dangerous form which brings him later into touch with the police. There is Turgis, a wretched, sexually obsessed clerk. There are the charwoman and the office boy, who both conform to type with perhaps too simple facility.

There are other characters: Mr Benenden, the tobacconist round the corner where Mr Dersingham buys his 'Sahib' cigarettes; there are the girls at Miss Matfield's hostel and the guests at Mrs Dersingham's dinner party. But the actual office staff are the important figures in the story. There must be hundreds of little groups of this kind all over London, symptomatic of a putrefying industrial and social organization.

Mr Dersingham's business is going very badly; it will be necessary to reduce the already meagre staff. Into this hopeless group there suddenly bursts a Mr Golspie. He is the only personally admirable character in the book; in fact, I think it is clear that Mr Priestley has deliberately keyed down the other characters in order to enhance the glamour of this formidable man. He is a swaggering, domineering adventurer, of gross and violent appetites. His origin and destination are alike equally obscure.

We first meet him slightly tipsy, with a trunk full of smuggled cigars, landing in London from a Baltic steamer. Besides the cigars he brings with him some samples of veneer made by a new and economical process. Chance brings him to Angel Pavement where he offers Mr Dersingham the agency for these veneers. His intention is to settle in London for some time with his daughter and devote himself to building up his fortunes with the co-operation of Twigg and Dersingham. In a few months, however, he is off again, leaving the business hopelessly ruined. He has found England intolerable and English people impossible to work with.

Angel Pavement is the story of his relations with Mr Dersingham's firm and the effects of the impact of his personality on those of the characters already mentioned. Their failure to cope with him, brilliantly told, is nothing more or less than a crushing indictment of English middle-class inadequacy.

There is a dinner party at the Dersinghams, described with agonizing penetration, at which Mr Golspie and his daughter are made to feel 'outsiders'. It is doubtful how much loyalty Mr Golspie was ever capable of feeling for his colleague, but from that evening he absolves himself from all obligation. Mr Dersingham, feeling that public-school honour does not apply to people outside the 'old Worrelian' pale, attempts to 'double-cross' him with pitiful results.

Miss Golspie is a flirt; her treatment of Turgis very nearly ends in tragedy. Miss Matfield falls in love with Mr Golspie. For some time she resists him; then she decides to surrender herself: she waits at the railway station in a state of high excitement to spend the week with him on the south coast. Mr Golspie, like his daughter, does not keep the appointment.

The firm of Twigg and Dersingham, complaining bitterly of lack of 'fair play', lapses into the inevitable bankruptcy from which Mr Golspie had seemed, for a moment, disposed to rescue them. Everyone loses his job.

These are the incidents of this long story. Outlined in this way they sound depressing enough, but the writing is so shot through and through with humour and ripe satire that it is never for a moment dull or sordid. Even in the final disaster there are suggestions that in the wreck of their finances, the characters manage to attain a kind of compensation in the enrichment of their personal relationships. In this way the Smeeths, the most pathetic of all the groups throughout the book, come off best. George, the troublesome son, sides loyally with his father and the vile Mr Mitty is routed. Poor Miss Matfield, who has done most to preserve her dignity, comes off the worst. It is a very just conclusion.

The writing, we need hardly say, is admirable; the first two pages of the prologue seem to me to be really fine prose; the conversations and the management of the various gradations of the idiom are incredibly accomplished. Mr Priestley is often compared to Dickens and there are times, as in the following sentence, when he seems to allow himself to be deliberately derivative: '. . . he picked up his hat (and in such a manner as to suggest that he could do some wonderful things even with that, if he wished to), brought his hat in front of the second button of his overcoat, gave three brisk nods, then wheeled about and made an exit like a torpedo from its tube.'

But in the last chapters, and particularly the last chapter of all, 'They go home', Mr Priestley shows a true sense of modernity which, for all who regard reading a book as an artistic adventure rather than a fireside recreation, reveals *Angel Pavement* as a finer and more interesting work than *The Good Companions*.

. TELL THE TRUTH ABOUT MARRIAGE .

There is nothing essentially 'modern' in making a mess of one's marriage, although, to hear people talk, you might suppose that there were. Unhappy marriages are as old as monogamy. The thing that is modern about them is the admission of failure and the cheerful readiness to start again.

A hundred years ago people were continually getting tired of their wives or husbands, just as they got tired of their neighbours and the district in which they lived and the colour of their own hair, but they just regarded these things as inevitable and put up with them. There were plenty of other things to amuse them. Nowadays, in spite of the enormous multiplication of ostensible amusements, people seem to grow more and more interested in the one amusement that civilization and mechanization have been quite unable to change: the simple old amusement of sex.

Responsible people – doctors, psychologists, novelists – write in the papers and say, 'You cannot lead a happy life unless your sex life is happy.' That seems to me just about as sensible as saying, 'You cannot lead a happy life unless your golf life is happy.' It is not only nonsense, it is mischievous nonsense. It means that the moment a wife begins to detect imperfections in her husband she thinks her whole life is ruined. It also means that the great number of young men and women who realize by looking in the looking-glass that they are of homely appearance and that there is only a small chance of their ever inspiring an ardent romantic passion in anyone regard themselves as condemned to perpetual unhappiness.

Do let us get away from this sentimental attitude. Sex instinct in most cases is a perfectly mild and controllable appetite which would never cause most of us any serious trouble at all if it was not being continually agitated by every sort of hint and suppression. Even in the case of peculiarly fiery natures, the sex interest only predominates for about half the active life. The modern attitude is to pretend that it is improbable for two people to remain married and faithful for the whole of their lives, and that the moment a couple's physical interest in each other begins to slacken, it is their duty to look for other mates. The Church is accused of being out of date because it has maintained its laws in disregard of this superstition.

The law of monogamy and indissoluble marriage has, of course, been one of the factors which has determined the development of western civilization. There is practically no branch of our art or history or of our daily lives that is not in some way influenced by it. It depended originally upon both a material and spiritual sanction. The material one was purely economic. It was assumed that every member of the community had divisible, tangible possessions of some kind which would be inherited by his children. It was assumed that marriage produced children; it was assumed that women required protection and financial support from men. The marriage laws of the West, with some variations from State to State, were framed to safeguard the situation created by these assumed conditions. It is fashionable to speak of these assumptions as false and consequently of the law as being obsolete. But are they? It is true that the trend of modern development is in a contrary direction, but it is still far too early to speak of any of the three assumptions I have quoted as being completely superseded. The present tendency is for workers to live in rented tenements and work with machines whose value, perhaps, exceeds their whole life earnings. But workers of this kind are only one section of the community, and the greater part of our agriculture and retail trade is still organized on a basis of property transferable from father to son. In all such cases a doubtful and divided parentage would be fatal. So, too, with birth control. This is a science still in an experimental stage. People speak as though it were something which mankind had completely mastered, something of which the knowledge was only withheld from prejudice or malice. So, too, with the economic independence of women. This is far from having become completely developed. We see these tendencies, but we have no knowledge of what hidden tendencies may also be present to frustrate them.

Law can only legalize existing conditions. If, however, the conditions hinted at, at present, do really come into being, then it seems to me the material basis for our marriage laws *has* completely altered, and it is the State's job to sanction this change.

On the other hand, the spiritual sanction, which is guarded by the Church, is completely unshaken because it rests, not on exterior transitory conditions, but deep in man's nature. It rests on the two great truths: first that man's sex life is only a part of his general activity. He owes an obligation to the rest of the community and he cannot fulfil that if he spends his whole time thinking about fresh love-affairs and his own sex-appeal. Secondly, one's sex-nature is most fully satisfied not in variety but in intensity of experience. By developing and broadening his relationship with one mate he can achieve a relationship which, when it ceases to be sexual, does so by becoming something more important.

There are a number of people who maintain that the only interesting part of a love-affair is the preliminary courtship and the first surrender. That shows a very silly disposition, and, to guard against it, Church law demands absolute fidelity to one mate. This law has in every age seemed unnecessarily rigid to some people. A great deal of the Church's influence has been wielded by condemning silly things as sins and threatening hell-fire. These threats have ceased to be terrifying to that part of the population – the less highly educated – to whom they were chiefly addressed.

There is only one way in which people can now be impressed with the unimportance of sex in its narrow sense and the importance of marriage in its widest sense; that is by allowing the greatest possible freedom to young people in finding out the truth. By the present system of education the one thing that is hidden is the actual facts about sex; as a natural result they regard this as the most important thing of all. When they find that after some time of marriage sexual relations are not so absorbingly interesting as they had been led to suppose, they think it is because they have made a mistake in their choice of a mate. Then they get into the divorce courts.

There seems to me only one modern and sensible way to deal with what is called the 'marriage problem'. Teach children the biology and hygiene of sex; teach them it is not infinitely important or infinitely satisfying. Teach them fully about birth control and encourage them to find out for themselves exactly how much sex is likely to mean in their own lives: they will not then marry out of curiosity or inexperience. Arrange a system of legal marriage, registered by the State, dissoluble, like any other legal contract, by mutual consent. Then leave it to the Church to show the sacramental importance of marriage to her own members. It is because the law of the Church rests upon a real human need that she need not fear for its survival.

. NORTHCLIFFE: AN INTIMATE BIOGRAPHY .

'If one could find in you some ultimate purpose, even some wholesome and honest hate, you would present a less pitiful spectacle to the world. You would at least be a reality. But you are nothing. In all this great and moving dream of humanity you represent no idea, no passion, no policy, no disinterested enthusiasm.'

These words, written in December 1914, in an open letter from Mr A. G. Gardiner, then editor of the *Daily News*, to Lord Northcliffe, express, in terms that became famous, one widely held estimate of the career of that dazzling figure.

In the many volumes of memoirs and contemporary history that have appeared in the last ten years, it has become more and more the habit of apologists, whether for themselves or their friends, to use Lord Northcliffe's already somewhat encumbered reputation as a dumping ground for all their unseemly litter. Did a politician give way to hysterical and ill-considered judgments? – Northcliffe had forced the words into his mouth. Was some military or governmental department inadequate to its work? – Northcliffe was to blame.

Gradually the great newspaper-omen has been made to assume grim proportions in the public mind – a figure of vast and malign influence. Mr Hamilton Fyfe's 'intimate biography' comes most opportunely to restore to us an important man in his true nature and dimensions.

This is a penetrating and lively study, written with a keen professional appreciation of the implications of Northcliffe's work and with wide knowledge of his private and public life.

In one particular way Mr Fyfe seems to overshoot the mark in his aim for vividness: that is his continual use of the historic present. At the best this is a literary device of somewhat dubious efficacy, and in many cases in this book it leads the reader into positive doubt of the actual meaning of the passage.

'So-and-so thinks . . .' one reads, and cannot in the face of it tell whether this is a contemporary incident or the present opinion of a living being, while in other cases one is left in doubt whether statements refer to isolated events or to continuous, habitual actions. This is all the more regrettable, as the book needs no such conscious effort to render it exciting.

It is of Northcliffe as the pioneer of modern journalism that Mr Fyfe deals. The popular daily paper, as we know it today, with its 'splash' headlines, gossip, 'human' articles, competitions, insurance, is the creation of Northcliffe.

He found newspapers that were quite unreadable except for very serious and very leisured people; they contained closely printed three-column leaders

Review of *Northcliffe: An Intimate Biography*, by Hamilton Fyfe, from 'Books You Read'. *Graphic*, 23 August 1930.

upon subjects of national importance; verbatim reports of speeches, long despatches from foreign correspondents whose chief aim was to take on as much as they could of the solemnity and verbosity of an already somewhat antiquated diplomatic service.

Anonymity was rigorously preserved; when an editor of *The Times* died, no obituary notice appeared in his own journal. A sub-editor was once instrumental in stopping a runaway elephant; not only did he neglect to report this to his news editor, but when a report was sent in from another quarter he consigned it to the waste-paper basket as 'too sensational'.

Lord Northcliffe introduced into Fleet Street the policy that 'if a dog bites a man, that's nothing; if a man bites a dog, that's news.' He specialized in the *flair* for 'news', which, as every reporter knows, is a thing quite distinct from mere accurate fact, but he also improved the machinery for obtaining accurate facts, until the *Daily Mail* frequently had information of important events before the government or the individuals most immediately concerned.

But more than this, Northcliffe specialized in the 'talking point'. In every paper of his, every day, he provided a subject for conversation. It is in this aim of his that he was most easily misunderstood and it is this point of his work which Mr Fyfe illuminates with particular interest. The *Daily Mail* would attempt to introduce a new kind of hat for men; for a week or so it would be full of the hat; then the subject disappeared from the pages and the hat disappeared from the shop windows and from the heads of the few people who had bought it.

People would say that the *Daily Mail* had failed, but in point of fact it had succeeded in exactly what it set out to do. It had no interest in what hat its readers wore. All it wished to do was to cause them a few days' interest; and that was exactly what it had done.

These 'talking points' changed from day to day; that was the essential thing about them and whether the 'talking point' of the moment was some trivial point of personal interest or some great national question, it was all one to the proprietor. It was not, however, always all one to the politicians, who resented their capricious elevations into prominence and sudden lapses into obscurity.

Details of Northcliffe's career are of enormous interest to anyone interested in the psychology of success; he was essentially the creation rather than the creator of the conditions of his time. He found the vast, literate but uncultured public which popular education had evolved, and he found that they had nothing to read.

George Newnes had made the same discovery and he gave them *Tit-bits*; Alfred Harmsworth gave them the *Daily Mail*. He was so sympathetic to the spirit of his age that he seemed to anticipate its developments. He began the *Daily Mirror* before the discovery that half-tone photographic blocks could be printed on rotary machines; the paper was a failure and was only saved from disaster by this very discovery.

Throughout much of his life, his paper was reviled by the educated classes as 'that rag' and 'the yellow press'. It attained recognition in the end by sheer wealth, until we now see leaders of fashion and writers of the highest literary reputation willingly contributing to its columns and those of its rivals.

Northcliffe introduced the policy of exorbitant payment to journalists, and all the passages in Mr Fyfe's book dealing with his relations with his employees are of the greatest value. He liked to encourage an atmosphere of uncertainty in his staff; there were continual drastic changes, sudden, generous rewards; sudden, ungenerous reprisals; all offices were known to be open to direct competition. In this he was perhaps deliberately Napoleonic, and in the eccentricities that preceded his death this characteristic was notably exaggerated. Mr Fyfe recounts the amusing story of the sudden mock-elevation of Mr Glover from the post of hall porter to that of advertising manager.

Mr Fyfe deals with great skill with that part of his life for which Lord Northcliffe was most bitterly attacked – his conduct during the last war. Here the journalist's 'talking point' had become a matter of life and death to thousands, and it is impossible to discern in his attitude then, or in the first confused months of the peace, that he had a very clear conception of the direction in which he ought to wield his influence. In the matter, however, of his attack upon Kitchener, Mr Fyfe shows his action as not only justifiable but laudable; he did not initiate that policy but allowed himself to accept all the obloquy for it, which rightly belonged to the politicians.

His quarrel with Mr H. G. Wells over the inconsistency of his policy in the newspapers, and his policy as head of the department of propaganda, delightfully illustrate the limitations of his character. He had that sort of arrested development that one sees in so many supremely successful men; a schoolboy spirit of 'bet-you-can't-do-this'.

He never attained to the civilized man's scale of values – the judgment of whether any particular thing was, in point of fact, worth doing. In his own career one can discern no set purpose. He wanted his papers to have a large circulation – no more; his interest was purely competitive. He was not a particularly avaricious man; nor at all self-indulgent; his large fortune, as such, meant little to him. He did not desire power or social success; he was not using his papers for anything except to ensure themselves. The self-exaltation which afflicted the last phase of his life must surely have been the result of having no unfulfilled ambition – because he never had any clearly defined ambition to fulfil.

. VILE BODIES .

The recent re-emergence into popularity of the drawing-room album was, no doubt, originally a part of the general return to Victorian fashion in decoration. These volumes of delicate engravings, verse and mild romance, relegated to

Review of *Sins of New York*, by Edward Van Every. *Week-end Review*, 10 October 1930.

house-keepers' rooms and nursery cupboard, attracted attention for their qualities as 'period' pieces, and were restored to modern drawing-rooms in company and on equal terms with wax fruit, glass domes, and *papier mâché*. It was not long, however, before they had asserted claims to individual existence, not as pretty articles of furniture, but as the mechanism of a valuable social function. Nothing was easier, when morose or too garrulous callers arrived, than to put albums into their laps and direct conversation along smooth lines, leaning on their shoulders, sharing the jokes and comparing preferences. A natural consequence was the appearance of modern Conversation Books. Last year there were Mr Beaton's *Book of Beauty*, Mr Peter Arno's *Parade*, and numerous exquisitely funny productions of the Nudist movement in northern Europe. There has lately been an admirable addition to this table library published under the title *Sins of New York*. I saw this book in action a few days ago; it worked perfectly. A car-load of rather simple country people were brought over one glum Sunday afternoon to inspect a neighbouring house party who were held to be eccentric. They were set down on a sofa and given the *Sins of New York*. It had all the qualities needed; it was up-to-date, odd and slightly shocking; the expected atmosphere was created with the minimum of exertion.

Sins of New York is essentially a book to be read in company. Alone, in a critical mood, one may find it rather flat. It is a selection of illustrations and extracts made by Mr Van Every, an American sporting journalist, from the pages of the *Police Gazette*. This periodical, the immediate ancestor of the 'tabloid' press of *Late Night Final* and the *Front Page*, flourished mainly in the barbers' shops of New York from the forties to the late eighties of the last century. It had much in common – in its later period even its colour – with the old *Pink Un*. It was partly devoted to sporting news, partly to crime and partly to pornography, lightly veiled in a cloak of outraged puritanism. Its files make a magnificent hunting ground for the editor. Mr Van Every could hardly have failed to produce from them a highly diverting book. More credit, in fact, is due to him for his choice of the raw material than for the use he has made of it; his editorial comments are often facetious, his taste blunt and obvious. Mr Sitwell, in *Victoriana*, was able to make an exquisite and fantastic book out of the sombre columns of *The Times* and the *Athenaeum*. One cannot help wishing that it was he who had edited *Sins of New York*. But these are the reflections of a solitary reader. It is churlish to complain. Taken as it stands as a jolly contribution to the rough and tumble of social intercourse, *Sins of New York* deserves a place anywhere.

For those who like horrors there are several murders of the grossest nature; there is the record of a sporting dog fight; the biography of Madame Restell, the abortionist, to whom little boys in the street used to shout, 'Yah! Your house is built on babies' skulls!' and of whom the *Gazette* wrote:

> How many who enter her halls of death may be supposed to expire under her execrable butchery? . . . Does funeral train ever leave her door? . . . No! An obscure

hole in the earth; a consignment to the savage skill of the dissecting knife, or a splash in the cold wave, with the scream of the night blast for a requiem, is the only death shrine bestowed upon her victims. Witness this, ye shores of Hudson! Witness this, Hoboken beach!

The letterpress is nearly all in this style, and it reads aloud very well, but, for myself, the chief delight of the *Sins of New York* is in the illustrations. These are all wood engravings of an alluring or sensational nature. Lurid pictures of low life, representing the dangers of opium, alcohol and harlots; pictures of women fighting or getting drunk (both these subjects occur with a frequency that must imply a pathological appeal); portraits of American criminals and beauties. Perhaps my favourite is an illustration of one of the 'whimsical freaks and fancies indulged in by the giddy girls of Gotham'; it represents a 'society belle' in oriental costume, reclining on a divan and surrounded by oriental *objets d'art* of frightful ugliness; kneeling and kissing her bare foot is an elderly American gentleman in frock coat and pince-nez; his top hat and cane lie on the tiger-skin rug. It is described as 'Queer homage exacted by imperious belle'.

What a delightful paper the *Police Gazette* must have been when it was still topical and had not been obscured for us by all the boring trappings of 'quaintness'. How meagre our own Sunday press appears beside it; and how lifeless our photographs compared with the gusto of these bawdy draughtsmen.

. THE NAME OF ACTION .

A second novel is always a difficult business. Mr Greene had a considerable success, both in sales and esteem, with his first book, *The Man Within*, a historical novel. In his new book, *The Name of Reason*,[1] he has taken a theme in modern, indeed, in future European politics, but by placing the action in an imaginary Rhenish state he has been able to preserve that slight, romantic remoteness which gives historical fiction its charm. He has a real sense of the importance of plot and the structure of narrative.

I can foresee his early elevation to the position of a respectable, romantic, best-seller. At present, however, I find many features of his style a little repugnant. It is all metaphor and simile, which often fails in its reason for existing by obscuring rather than illuminating the description. He has a sturdy sense of drama, however, and the ability to 'put across' sex appeal. These two qualities should be enough to ensure prosperity. But I wish he would write more freely and directly.

His plot this time is the expedition of a wealthy, quixotic Englishman to a city state in the Palatinate to help free it from a fairly benevolent dictatorship.

Review of *The Name of Action*, by Graham Greene, from 'Books You Read'. *Graphic*, 25 October 1930.
1 Correctly, *The Name of Action*. This is Waugh's first review of a novel by Graham Greene.

The revolutionaries prove rather disappointing; the dictator's wife is irresistible; political events tumble and mingle with the events of the hero's romance in the most agreeable way possible. Mr Greene, it is pleasant to note, never lets himself get deflected from his theme by casual descriptive interests.

I think he ought to repeat and augment his success with this book.

. SATIRE AND FICTION .

I have been reading an intensely interesting and amusing book. That is *Satire and Fiction*, Mr Wyndham Lewis's new pamphlet, dealing with the critics of his opulently conceived novel, *Apes of God*, which caused a stir in the spring of this year, when it was published in bulky format at three guineas.

It is very hard to define Mr Lewis's position in modern literature. It seems to me to be somewhat similar to that of Samuel Butler in his own day. Nowadays, Samuel Butler has ceased to have any formative influence – except on intellectual public schoolboys who can read such observations as 'Man is like thistledown blown upon the wind,' and take them seriously. But we think the worse of his contemporaries who were unaware of his importance because, in spite of all his preoccupation with posterity, it was purely as a critic of contemporary scientific-philosophical systems that he was valuable.

So with Mr Lewis. I do not think that he will enjoy many posthumous honours, but it is ridiculous to live at the same time as he and pretend that he is not an important writer. For one thing, he has the finest controversial style of any living writer. He is able to write genuine prose satire without sacrificing modernity of diction – a very rare feat. He also is unique in taking modern literature very seriously. Second-rate highbrow work stirs him to real fury.

Satire and Fiction is in three parts. The first is the history of a review of *Apes of God* written by the poet, Mr Roy Campbell, and rejected, on the grounds that it was too favourable, by the editor of a literary magazine. Mr Lewis reprints all the correspondence involved, and it makes very amusing reading.

The middle section is an intolerable bore. It consists of press cuttings and personal letters in praise or condemnation of the novel. It seems to me to show great personal weakness that Mr Lewis thought these tributes worth reprinting.

The third and most important section is a series of notes in Mr Lewis's inimitable manner upon the nature of Satire and Fiction. The whole of this part is immensely interesting, particularly the observations about the 'Outside and Inside' method of fiction. No novelist and very few intelligent novel readers can afford to neglect this essay.

Review of *Satire and Fiction*, by Percy Wyndham Lewis, from 'The Books You Read'. *Graphic*, 25 October 1930.

. CONVERTED TO ROME .
WHY IT HAS HAPPENED TO ME

Three popular errors reappear with depressing regularity in any discussion about a convert to the Roman Catholic Church. It may be useful to mention these before going on to a more positive explanation of my position. They are:

1. *The Jesuits have got hold of him.* I have heard this often the last few years and have come to realize that there are a great number of English people who regard this pious and erudite body as a kind of spiritual pressgang, out for head-money; millionaires and great noblemen are the real quarry, but if, in the course of the hunt, they can bag a novelist or two, so much the better. This is very far from the truth. Instruction is, of course, necessary for anyone who wants to join the Roman Catholic Church, and Jesuits, like other priests, are ready to give help to those who need it. There is no coaxing or tricking people into acquiescence. They state or explain their doctrine, and the proselyte decides for himself whether it is true.

2. *He is captivated by the ritual.* This is certainly arranged to a great extent as an aid to devotion, but it would be a very superficial person who would accept a whole theological and moral system on these grounds alone. Indeed it seems to me that in this country, where all the finest ecclesiastical buildings are in the hands of the Anglican Church, and where the liturgy is written in prose of unexampled beauty, the purely aesthetic appeal is, on the whole, rather against the Roman Church.

3. *He wants to have his mind made up for him.* The suggestion here is that the convert cannot face the responsibility of thinking problems out for himself, but finds it convenient to swallow whole a complete explanation of the universe. The answer to this is that if he has a lazy mind it is easy enough to stagnate without supernatural assistance, and if he has an active mind, the Roman system can and does form a basis for the most vigorous intellectual and artistic activity.

I think one has to look deeper before one will find the reason why in England today the Roman Church is recruiting so many men and women who are not notably gullible, dull-witted or eccentric.

It seems to me that in the present phase of European history the essential issue is no longer between Catholicism, on one side, and Protestantism, on the other, but between Christianity and Chaos. It is much the same situation as existed in the early Middle Ages. In the sixteenth and seventeenth centuries conflicting social and political forces rendered irreconcilable the division between two great groups of Christian thought. In the eighteenth and nineteenth centuries the choice before any educated European was between Christianity, in whatever form it was presented to him in the circumstances of his upbringing, and, on the other side, a polite and highly attractive scepticism. So great, indeed, was the inherited subconscious power of Christianity that it was nearly two centuries before the real nature of this loss of faith became apparent.

Today we can see it on all sides as the active negation of all that western culture has stood for. Civilization – and by this I do not mean talking cinemas and tinned food, nor even surgery and hygienic houses, but the whole moral and artistic organization of Europe – has not in itself the power of survival. It came into being through Christianity, and without it has no significance or power to command allegiance. The loss of faith in Christianity and the consequential lack of confidence in moral and social standards have become embodied in the ideal of a materialistic, mechanized state, already existent in Russia and rapidly spreading south and west. It is no longer possible, as it was in the time of Gibbon, to accept the benefits of civilization and at the same time deny the supernatural basis upon which it rests. As the issues become clearer, the polite sceptic and with him that purely fictitious figure, the happy hedonist, will disappear.

That is the first discovery, that Christianity is essential to civilization and that it is in greater need of combative strength than it has been for centuries.

The second discovery is that Christianity exists in its most complete and vital form in the Roman Catholic Church. I do not mean any impertinence to the many devout Anglicans and Protestants who are leading lives of great devotion and benevolence; I do find, however, that other religious bodies, however fine the example of certain individual members, show unmistakable signs that they are not fitted for the conflict in which Christianity is engaged. For instance, it seems to me a necessary sign of completeness and vitality in a religious body that its teaching shall be coherent and consistent. If its own mind is not made up, it can hardly hope to withstand disorder from outside. In the Anglican Church today matters of supreme importance in faith and morals are still discussed indecisively, while the holders of high offices are able to make public assertions which do violence to the deepest feelings of many of their people.

Another essential sign one looks for is competent organization and discipline. Obedience to superiors and the habit of submitting personal idiosyncrasies to the demands of office seem to be sure signs of a real priesthood. Any kind of 'crankiness' or individual self-assertion in the ministers of a religious body shakes one's confidence in them.

Most important of all, it seems to me that any religious body which is not by nature universal cannot claim to represent complete Christianity. I mean this as a difference in kind, not in extent. The Church in the first century, when its membership was numerically negligible, was by nature as universal as in the time of the Crusaders; but many religious sects seem to pride themselves upon exclusion, regarding themselves as a peculiar people set aside for salvation. Others claim regional loyalty. Those who regard conversion to Roman Catholicism as an unpatriotic defection – a surrender to Italian domination – seem to miss the whole idea of universality.

These are a few of the signs by which in its public affairs one would recognize the Church one is seeking. There also remain the devotional needs of the individual members, for, however imposing the organization of the Church, it would be worthless if it did not rest upon the faith of its members. No one visiting a Roman Catholic country can fail to be struck by the fact that the people do use their churches. It is not a matter of going to a service on Sunday; all classes at all hours of the day can be seen dropping in on their way to and from their work.

Roman Catholic people are notable for this ability to pray without any feeling of affectation, and the explanation of it seems to me that prayer is not associated in their minds with any assertion of moral superiority. You never see in Roman Catholics going to Mass, as one sees on the faces of many people going to Chapel, that look of being rather better than their neighbours. The Protestant attitude seems often to be, 'I am good; therefore I go to church,' while the Catholic's is, 'I am very far from good; therefore I go to church.'[1]

---

1 The *Daily Express* followed Waugh's article with three features: E. Rosslyn Mitchell (a Protestant MP), 'Rosslyn Mitchell Replies to Evelyn Waugh', 21 October; Father Woodlock, SJ, 'Is Britain Turning to Rome?', 22 October; and 'Today Readers Join in the Great Controversy', 25 October 1930.

3

. ROUGH LIFE .
ABYSSINIA TO THE ARCTIC

OCTOBER 1930 - JANUARY 1935

Those who grew up in the Wilsonian epoch lived in a world which, among other less attractive peculiarities, was uniquely accessible. For our fathers a trip to Antioch or Fez was something of an adventure; for us, with the exception of the Soviet Asiatic dependencies and the remote corridors of the Vatican, there was no closed territory. Money, leisure and energy – and no great superabundance even of these – were the sole requisites for universal travel. There are signs that this happy state of affairs is in the decline and that, soon, a generation who have watered their whisky in the rivers of Matto Grosso and Sinkiang will find it hazardous to visit St Moritz.

From a review of *Under the Pole Star*,
by A. R. Glen and N. A. C. Croft. *Tablet*, 15 January 1938

. INTRODUCTION .

When Waugh left London in October 1930 to report Haile Selassie's coronation in Addis Ababa, he was making the first of a series of increasingly
adventurous journeys, and opening up major new areas of subject matter. It
might be supposed that the enterprising travels of these years gave rise to
memorable descriptive and narrative articles. Disappointingly, they did not.
The first journey to Addis Ababa extended to remote Abyssinia and continued
through the Aden Protectorate, then with increasing difficulty through central
Africa and down to the Cape; it resulted in *Remote People* (1931) and *Black
Mischief* (1932), but apart from coverage of the coronation and two political
essays, it led to nothing in magazines. From December 1932 until February
1933 was spent in rough, solitary and sometimes dangerous travel in the remote
hinterland of British Guiana and Brazil; the literary results were Waugh's most
popular short story, 'The Man Who Liked Dickens' (1933), *Ninety-Two Days*
(1934), *A Handful of Dust* (1934) and some articles in the *Daily Mail* and *Passing
Show* which caused recriminations at the time and are too poor to reprint. A trip
to the Arctic in July–August 1934, narrowly retrieved from disaster, was the
last hazardous journey undertaken purely as 'travel'; it alone of Waugh's
adventures has been well described outside a travel book. 'The First Time I
Went to the North' (1935) was contributed to a friend's volume of 'first-time'
experiences.

'Travel – and Escape from Your Friends' (16 January 1933) explains why
Waugh became a 'travelmaniac'. He knew that travel was 'bad business' for
anyone who could write Mayfair novels, because 'people would much sooner
read about Mayfair than the jungle'. On the other hand he was 'inquisitive
about places' and interested in 'human nature in unfamiliar surroundings'; he
needed 'physical risk' and a 'holiday from his own life'. In the 1930s a
fashionable young man's going off on improbable journeys required no more
explanation than that. But Waugh must have sensed also that a milieu such as
London society, which was at once excessively distracting and unvaried, would
inhibit the growth and expansion of his talent. It was commonly said in the
1930s that 'Every young novelist is imitating Evelyn Waugh – except Evelyn
Waugh.' The striking new developments in the three novels after 1930 owe
most to travel: not simply because travel provided new locales, but because it
filled deep personal and imaginative needs, and stimulated a very active mind
to elaborate quite profound themes. Had Waugh merely travelled 'to gather
material', he would easily have exploited his experiences in facile articles. As it
was he had the greatest difficulty in making literary use of his travels outside a
connected narrative, in which there was opportunity for the full play of mind
and personality on simple events. There was therefore justice in Waugh's reply
to a complaint about a series on Guiana done for *Passing Show*, that

he was incapable of what was required: 'You can't tell me a thing I don't know about the low quality of my journalism . . . poor *Passing Show* were hoping to buy something that simply wasn't in the shop' (letter to Peters, 18 October 1933).

Journalism now became intermittent, largely on account of travel, but also because of a reasonably comfortable income. 'Evelyn Waugh has done no work for a long time,' Peters wrote on 13 May 1935. 'I will let you know just as soon as he gets under way which will be just as soon as he needs money.' No regular work was sought or offered. As Waugh became better established, he turned from newspapers to fashion magazines, and from articles to short stories. 'The Patriotic Honeymoon' (1932) was the first of a succession of twice-a-year stories later collected in volumes. Editors naturally preferred stories when they could get them. Nevertheless, after competently reporting the coronation and political situation in Abyssinia, Waugh wrote several elegant – including two significant – pieces for fashion magazines, some very poor newspaper features, and a series of interesting travel reviews.

An impression has been created that Waugh's decision to go to Addis Ababa in 1930 was unusually whimsical, but this is false. The *Daily Mail* had refused to renew his contract beyond August, and by the beginning of that month Waugh found himself 'spoiling for a fight' with the editor of the *Graphic* (*Diaries*, 1-5 August 1930). The intriguing preparations for the coronation – purchase of the ex-Kaiser's ceremonial coach, an order for a cake weighing $1\frac{1}{2}$ cwt, and so on – had been in the newspapers for months, as had sensational accounts of Haile Selassie's bloody rise to power. The *Daily Mail* and the *Daily Sketch* were each using a fast aeroplane and a famous pilot to race the news and the pictures of the coronation back to London. It is not surprising that Waugh found Addis Ababa tempting.

He covered the event as an accredited special correspondent for *The Times* (twelve despatches appeared under the by-line 'From Our Special Correspondent' between 27 October and 13 November) and as a special correspondent for the *Daily Express* (five despatches appeared under the by-line '"Daily Express" Special Correspondent' between 29 October and 6 November). The *Graphic*, to which Waugh had been contracted until the end of the year for a book page, and which had released him on conditions negotiated by A. D. Peters, printed three mailed articles from Abyssinia.

The coronation took place on a Sunday. Since Waugh's cable missed the following Monday morning editions, and since the *Express* sent a rebuke for this delay (*Diaries*, 4 November 1930) Waugh has sometimes been depicted as a joke reporter. This is unfair. The telegraph office in Addis Ababa was closed on Sunday, and *all* genuine coronation cables, e.g. in the *Daily Mail* and *Daily Telegraph*, appeared on Tuesday under the notice 'Delayed in Transmission'. 'Ethiopia Today' (22 December 1930), an essay on the historical significance of Abyssinia's coming under centralized 'modern' government for the first time, and on the undesirability of Abyssinia's being imagined a 'civilized' state by the world at large, reflects British Colonial Office thinking. Britain had opposed Abyssinia's admission to the League of Nations, with the status and immunities membership implied, when Italy promoted it. Perhaps Waugh benefited from conversations with his uncle, Sir Stewart Symes, Resident at Aden, and with various lesser official friends (*Diaries*, 6 November 1930: 'Talked Abyssinian politics most evening'). Another political article, not reprinted here, was written at Sir Stewart Symes's request to publicize British policy in the Aden Protectorate (17 March 1931).

Harper's Bazaar first printed Waugh in December 1929, when it carried a part of *Vile Bodies*. It was the beginning of a profitable and, on the whole, happy association. *Harper's Bazaar* was then advertised as 'the most luxurious fashion magazine in the world'. It was dedicated to all that was 'new and gay', and while publishing many well-known authors, it required them to preserve an appropriate lightness. The editor was Joyce Reynolds, a woman with whom Waugh had a generally amiable relationship. A passage from a letter to Peters happily summarizes his friendly feelings towards Miss Reynolds, and the differences between them arising from his writing:

> I am sorry Miss Reynolds finds my story ['Mr Loveday's Little Outing'] lacking in Yuletide cheer [it was for a Christmas number]. If it was anyone else I'd tell her to go to hell, but she's an old customer and has proved herself a girl of honour on more than one occasion so the best thing will be to offer her the story about the dog ['On Guard'] . . . It is a poor story but she may think it preferable. (1 November 1934.)

Had Waugh been content merely to exercise his powers of pleasing, no one would have excelled him in society journalism. Elegance, wit, spice, up-to-dateness and a hint of the outrageous were exactly what editors and a smart public expected of a modern society novelist. But Waugh could never content himself for long with such undemanding 'stuff'. He was incorrigible in always trying to say something. Consequently what he considered his best work, for example 'A Call to the Orders' (26 February 1938), *Harper's Bazaar* rejected. Miss Reynolds said it did not 'fit in' with her 'contemporary ideals', and Waugh said she had 'turned Bolshie' (letters from Waugh to Peters, 30 November 1937 and 25 January 1938).

Editors of other fashion magazines were neither as generous nor as tolerant as *Harper's Bazaar*. Elizabeth Penrose, editor of *Vogue*, who had been forced to pay twenty guineas for an article by Waugh where she would normally have given twelve (*Harper's* usually paid thirty guineas), replied to a suggestion from Peters that she use more of Waugh's articles: 'I would find it extremely difficult to use much of his work at the price I have to pay. I find I can get very good writers and very creditable articles for a good deal less money . . .' (16 May 1938). Waugh was as unenthusiastic about *Vogue* as a market as *Vogue* was about him as a contributor. He did occasionally publish in *Vogue* very happily. But as what he once said about it sums up his attitude towards journalism and money, it is worth quoting: 'Either one writes to be read by intelligent people . . . or for money. Vogue falls between stools' (letter to Peters, 14 June 1956). In most circumstances Waugh would write entertainingly for a high fee. He would write seriously for no fee (e.g. for the *Tablet*) or for a small fee (e.g. for the *Spectator*). But the market in between did not much interest him.

Returning to the work of the period under review, in the early 1930s *Harper's Bazaar* and *Women's Journal* carried six Waugh articles. Of the four printed here, one attacks cocktail parties and one promotes Venice rather than the much more popular Riviera. In each case Waugh knows all about the current fashion – but is opposed to it. Those on the nineties (November 1930) and Youth (March 1932) are of permanent interest because they define Waugh's attitudes towards period and modernity; and particularize his constantly invoked standard of judgment, the 'civilized'.

The five newspaper features of the period, and the series in *Passing Show* on travel in Guiana, were very poor. Indeed in 1934 the editor of the *Sunday Referee* dramatically expressed his opinion of an uninspired article on the Duke of Kent's wedding by initially paying Waugh three guineas instead of the agreed thirty (letter to Peters, 10 January 1935). Correspondence between Peters and various editors in 1932 and 1933 frequently refers to work not used or needing rewriting, or 'not up to Mr Waugh's usual standard'. Peters was led to apologize: 'Evelyn's work has not been up to much lately . . .' (21 September 1933); and 'Evelyn has not been doing his best lately . . . he agrees it is time he pulled up his socks' (19 October 1933). On the other hand, 'Was He Right to Free the Slaves?' (13 July 1933), which points out some of the advantages of slavery (from a slave's point of view) on Wilberforce's centenary, might seem to succeed by sheer audacity. Perhaps it is a normal peril of audacity that literal-minded critics sometimes cite the article as evidence of Waugh's having recommended slavery.

In 1929 the *Spectator* invited Waugh to open its new series of articles by 'young people under 30' (13 April). His next association with the magazine came on 9 April 1932 when he reviewed two travel books under the heading 'The Traveller'. These were the first of thirty travel reviews to appear from time to time between 1932 and 1939. Travel was thus the occasion of Waugh's first 'regular' connection with what was to become his favourite medium for addressing a literate audience. Frequent general reviewing did not begin until 1938. It lapsed during the war but resumed in July 1953 and continued until 1962. The *Spectator* published Waugh's major attack on 'Change' in the Roman Catholic Church, the last of several articles he placed there.

Aficionados of travel literature will find in the travel reviews the outline of a 'theory' of travel literature, its kinds and possibilities; for Waugh typically created an intellectual framework within which to discuss any subject. The reviews are also self-expressive. It comes as a surprise to those who do not know Waugh well to find him claiming membership of 'that small circle . . . who prefer all but the very worst travel books to all but the very best novels' (9 April 1932). The preference springs from his finding 'the flavour of first-hand experience . . . unmistakable and intoxicating'; so intoxicating as to overwhelm faults of style or attitude. After 1935 Waugh became very much more interested in politics and in religion than he had been, and something of a propagandist for causes he believed in. Even so he commendably refrained, as a general rule, from opining, in print, about subjects where he lacked 'first-hand experience'.

. DUSKY EMPEROR GREETS THE DUKE OF GLOUCESTER .
RECEPTION AT A STATION THRONE
RED UMBRELLA
Daily Express Special Correspondent

Addis Ababa
Tuesday, 28 October

The Emperor of Abyssinia, Ras Tafari, welcomed the Duke of Gloucester to his empire today. A special throne room had been built at the station at Addis Ababa. Here the Duke was formally presented to the Emperor and the Crown Prince, while an Abyssinian band played 'God Save the King'.

A band of Marines from the cruiser *Effingham* was on the platform. It did not compete with the native musicians today, but will play on all official occasions for the Emperor in place of the jazz band which was originally ordered from Cairo.

The Duke left the station first with the Crown Prince in an aluminium motor-car, and four cars followed. In the last, a scarlet car, sat the Emperor under a scarlet umbrella. The procession was escorted by a squadron of Lancers, the caps of the native officers being trimmed with lions' manes.

The extensive preparations for the coronation are still incomplete, in spite of intense activity, and some confusion prevails throughout the city. Efforts are being mainly directed towards the removal of any street scenes which might offend the visitors. Begging has been prohibited, lepers have been expelled, and caravans forbidden to enter. A high stockade has been erected to conceal the humbler dwellings. There are numerous new buildings with corrugated iron roofs, and triumphal arches. Lighting is being installed in the principal thoroughfares, which are all unfinished. Several macadamized streets are under construction in places where there were hitherto only rough tracks, and a steamroller and hundreds of navvies at work somewhat impede the vast crowds assembling from all parts of the empire. Local officials and nobles are each bringing an escort, mostly armed with rifles, proportionate to their rank. Welta Ras Hailu, the richest feudal chief, has 25,000 retainers.

Haile Selassie – Tafari's new title – personally supervises and directs all details, driving with a cavalry escort in his scarlet car, under his scarlet silk umbrella, on repeated tours of inspection. The new building for the accommodation of the delegates is practically finished. The authorities have also commandeered the Imperial Hotel. Other hotels are completely full. Large quantities of food have also been commandeered.

The currency has considerably appreciated recently, and the prices are consequently enormous. Conditions, indeed, are practically impossible for unofficial tourists.

Special trains are running from Djibouti (Somaliland) in thirty-six hours instead of the usual sixty. The American, German, Japanese, French, Dutch, Egyptian and Polish delegations are here; the remainder are expected in the course of the next few days. Each delegation is received at the station with great formality, the guard of honour wearing khaki uniforms and puttees, with bare feet and fixed bayonets. It has been specially trained by Belgian officers. There is also a brass band which plays recognizable versions of the respective national anthems.

. EMPEROR OF ETHIOPIA .
THE CORONATION CEREMONY
(From our Special Correspondent)

Addis Ababa, Nov. 2

The coronation of the Emperor of Ethiopia this morning, although a spectacle of extreme splendour, proved something of an ordeal to some of those concerned. Distinguished visitors, accustomed to a milder habit of life, found themselves obliged to rise at 5.30 a.m. and dress in full uniform. Long before dawn the streets were thronged by a vast concourse of people arriving on foot or on mules from the outlying districts. Many of the chiefs were paying their first visit to Addis Ababa, as they showed by their consternation at the sight of motor-cars.

The Emperor and Empress had spent a night of vigil in the Cathedral of St George. Like all Abyssinian churches, this is an octagonal structure with an inner sanctuary, where the Emperor and the archbishops remained. The service was of extreme liturgical interest, and was conducted throughout the night until 7.50 this morning amid continuous chanting, beating of drums and the brandishing of brass rattles. The priests danced, swaying their bodies and clapping their hands.

The coronation took place in a temporary church to the east of the Cathedral. The foreign missions and the high Abyssinian dignitaries began to arrive at 7 o'clock. Half the church was taken up with a carpeted dais, in the centre of which were two thrones, with silk canopies, facing a covered altar

The Times, 4 November 1930.

bearing the regalia. The priests sat behind. On either side of the dais facing inwards were rows of chairs, on the left for the Ethiopian notables and on the right for the foreign missions, among which was that headed by the Duke of Gloucester, representing King George.

Behind the thrones were seats for European and American visitors, the wives of diplomatists, and lower Ethiopian officials. The costumes and ornaments worn by the Ethiopians were of the utmost magnificence – brilliant under-skirts, coronets, jewelled swords, huge head-dresses of gold braid, jewels and lions' manes. The unofficial Europeans were dressed, some in morning and some in evening clothes. An interesting note was struck by an American woman who wore a tweed suit and a toque decorated with a small star-spangled banner. Few Ethiopian women were present. They wore heavy cloaks and large veiled hats.

CROWNING THE EMPEROR

The Emperor entered at 7.45 and was conducted by the Rases to the throne. He wore a white and silver cloak, and was followed at intervals by bishops and deacons of the Abyssinian Church. The Abuna entered singing, accompanied by cymbals and triangles, and followed by about eighty ecclesiastics. The service proceeded until 8.45, when the Emperor was invested with the crimson robes of state. At intervals during the next hour he received the orb, spears, spurs, sword and other emblems of majesty, and finally he was crowned with a magnificent golden crown of Abyssinian workmanship, studded with emeralds and rubies. There was an outburst of acclamation, which was taken up by the populace outside, a salute was fired from the forts, and the band of HMS *Effingham* played the Ethiopian national anthem.

After the solemn investiture and crowning of the Heir-Apparent, the Empress, Rases and ministers paid their homage. The coronation ceremony was followed by a further ceremony in the Cathedral, and at its close the Emperor proceeded to a stand, where he read a royal proclamation, in which he assured his people that he would work for the prosperity and happiness of the country.

At 12.30 the Emperor and Empress drove to their palace, followed by the missions, the members of which are attending a banquet in the palace tonight.

. CHAMPAGNE FOR BREAKFAST .
A JOURNEY TO ABYSSINIA

The arrivals and departures of Abyssinian mails are incalculable, but one thing seems certain: that by the time this article reaches England, everyone will have

Graphic, 20 December 1930.

forgotten all about Addis Ababa and the coronation of the Emperor of Ethiopia.

For the first week of November, this remote and murky empire was a centre of world-wide interest; there were members of two European royal families and gross regiments of cinema photographers and journalists. For a week Addis Ababa attained the prominence of Crumbles or Croydon or Les Baux. Earnest students opened their atlases and located the place. But that will all be forgotten and the English papers will not mention Abyssinia again until some startling political event – and Ethiopian history is full of such occurrences – brings it once more into the 'news'.

For us, however, who were there during the coronation, the last few days will remain one of the most memorable times in our experience. Except government officials and journalists, there were very few visitors in the town. I don't think that there were more than a dozen tourists in the city. For this reason, and also because the details of the various ceremonies have already been conveyed to Europe in many extravagantly phrased cables, it seems to me worth while setting down a few personal impressions of the coronation week as a whole.

First, the town of Addis. It is a large settlement of quite recent growth straggling out on a five miles diameter over a rough, upland plateau broken by two precipitous watercourses. Half the habitation consists of little thatched huts, often window-less and chimney-less, built of mud and sticks. These lie together in little clusters, exact counterparts of the country village, set between and behind the more pretentious bungalows and villas. The palace stands on a slight eminence – a ramshackle assembly of pavilions and barns without architectural plan. There are several churches, all built on the same circular or octagonal plan, with two concentric ambulatories round a closed sanctuary; there is a large native bazaar, the stalls of which consist of simple, unshaded heaps of stones and earth, and a few shops and cafés, mostly kept by a mongrel race of interbred Levantines, Indians and Arabs. There are numerous houses under construction, some abandoned at their initial stages, others progressing just perceptibly.

The crowds in the streets are practically all armed with obsolete rifles; they chat and bow and kiss one another. Occasionally a woman of high rank passes on a mule under a dome-shaped straw sunshade. She is voluminously draped and her face completely bandaged up in white shawls, leaving only dark apertures for her eyes. Women of lower rank are rarely seen except in the bazaars. They are kept too busy to share in the leisured promenading and gossip of their husbands.

Immense efforts had been made by the Emperor to tidy up the city for the arrival of his guests. High stockades of eucalyptus wood were erected round the humbler quarters. The broad, almost impassable, thoroughfares were strewn with stones and sharp fragments of rock over which two steamrollers occasionally passed, and after them, to the surprise of the inhabitants, a brand new motor-driven water-cart. Strenuous and successful efforts were made by the police to clear the town of lepers, corpses, mutilated beggars, hyenas and other encumbrances which might give an impression of incomplete civilization. Attempts were even made at street lighting down the four main boulevards.

It must be remembered that Ethiopia had never before had to cope with any incursion of the present kind and though many of their attempts at hospitality were slightly ludicrous – such as the provision of a dozen new footballs for the recreation of the ambassadors – the remarkable thing was the degree of success more than the degree of failure of the proceedings. It is true that invitations to the official functions usually arrived a few minutes before, or on occasions a few hours after, the time when they were due to begin; that the luggage of the most distinguished guests was sometimes mislaid for long periods in its transit from station to palace; that most of the structural changes were quite unfinished by the date of the coronation. It would be easy but slightly ungracious to multiply instances of this sort almost indefinitely; but the fact remains that everything in the end did happen fairly smoothly.

The chief official functions were the unveiling of a gilt equestrian statue of the Emperor Menelik on 1 November; the coronation on 2 November; a procession on the 3rd, and a review of the troops on the 6th. Besides these, there were innumerable banquets and receptions at the palace and at the legations, a race meeting and the opening of a museum.

The coronation itself was very splendid and very exhausting. We assembled in the hall – a great pavilion specially built for the occasion – at seven in the morning. This entailed most of us rising at 5.30 to dress by lamp light in uniforms or morning coats. It was 12.30 before the ceremony was over. It seemed as though the clergy – realizing the predominating secular and military character of the other proceedings – had determined to make all they could of the one day that was unrestrictedly theirs. A choir of Coptic deacons sang almost incessantly throughout the five hours. The Emperor and Empress sat immovable on canopied divans; the chiefs of the foreign delegations sat near them on gilt arm-chairs, while the rest of the congregation wandered about, climbed on chairs, scrambled for medals, which were distributed on trays, sauntered out to smoke or dozed at the back of the hall. Photographers fought fiercely for positions of vantage. Outside, the six horses which were harnessed to the state coach became quite unmanageable and, after severely kicking one groom, had to be decreased to four.

For the rest, the week remains a somewhat confused medley of gold braid and lions' manes; black, fuzzy heads of slaves; the uniforms of European cavalry regiments; raw beef banquets for the populace, caviare and sweet champagne for the visitors; of native policemen engaged in a continual warfare with the people of the town, beating them into the side streets with whips and canes.

And of depressing western jealousies and intrigues about invitations to the legation receptions; of frantic pressmen attempting to get news from mute diplomats and unduly loquacious Armenians; of interminable, grossly expensive taxi drives over inconceivable roads; of gentle legation secretaries blinking miserably at this unwanted disturbance in the even, suburban life of their compounds; of the band of HMS *Effingham* marching from place to place, in obedience to repeatedly countermanded orders.

This smart and talented band deserves special mention; it formed a very peculiar feature of the proceedings. It was there by the Emperor's invitation to play at various functions during the week. Throughout their journey up, the men were given champagne to drink at every meal including breakfast; in Addis they were housed in a special requisitioned hotel, each in a separate bedroom furnished, among other luxuries, with brand new enamel spitoons and a pair of brushes. They all received medals and had the time of their lives.

I went to luncheon at the palace one day. It was a large party of eighty or a hundred guests. There was no plan of the tables. The Emperor sat down at once and we wandered round and round, for a quarter of an hour or twenty minutes, hunting for our places. No one had the effrontery to look at the cards on the right and left of the Emperor so that the most honoured guests were left standing until everyone else was seated. We had a fine luncheon of European food and wines. Suddenly, uninvited, a Syrian lady jumped to her feet, strode up to the Emperor and recited at great length and with lavish gestures a long complimenting ode composed by herself in Arabic, a language unintelligible to His Majesty. It was an odd party.

One incident, however, stands out most vividly in my memory and seems to embody the whole essence of modern Abyssinia. I was living in a kind of annexe at the back of my hotel; a stockade separated it from one of the clusters of native huts I have mentioned. Very late one night I had returned from a party at one of the legations. It was a magnificent night with a full moon and large, brilliant stars. I stood for some time outside the door of my room, dressed in the absurd white tie and tall hat of civilization. In one of the huts on the other side of the stockade a native party was going on. The door was open and I could see the interior dimly lit by a tiny oil flame; ten or a dozen people squatted round the walls; one of them had a little wooden drum covered with cowhide. They were clapping their hands and singing a nasal, infinitely monotonous tune. I think they were all drunk. It was probably a wedding or funeral party. At intervals throughout the night I woke up and heard the same chant going on. It seemed to me typical of the whole week; on one side the primitive song of unfathomable antiquity; on the other, the preposterously dressed European, with a stockade between them.

. ETHIOPIA TODAY
ROMANCE AND REALITY .
BEHIND THE SCENES AT ADDIS ABABA
(From our Special Correspondent)

Addis Ababa

There is perhaps no country in the world where it is so difficult to obtain accurate political information as in Ethiopia. Few statistics are available; the Abyssinians are constitutionally suspicious of inquiring strangers, and Europeans, even those who have spent most of their lives in the country in close touch with local officials, are often ignorant about the real state of affairs. Everyone is shy of talking politics in a country heavily policed by professional informers.

The Abyssinians will expand readily upon the history and achievements of their people in the past, but conversation becomes immediately difficult and cautious when any subject is mentioned subsequent to the death of Menelik II. The name of Lij Yasu – the deposed Emperor – will produce an uncomfortable silence in almost any room in Addis Ababa. Reservations must therefore be made before undertaking a survey of northern conditions. Efforts have been made to check every statement in the article with as good authority as possible. It aims at containing nothing but the truth, but it makes no claim to embody the whole truth.

The coronation of the Emperor Haile Selassie, which so captivated the imaginations of the European public at the beginning of November, was not a mere pageant of unusual splendour, but an event of first-rate importance in East African history, an event which had been very carefully prepared since the defeat and deposition of Lij Yasu in 1916. That movement, obscure in its details, may be summed up as representing the victory of the Church party in alliance with the northern Amharic nobles over the Moslems and pagans of the south. The explanation invariably given is that Lij Yasu had apostatized from Christianity, a report which was strengthened by the fact that his father was of Moslem origin. It is certain that he was not a zealous Christian, but the evidence for his conversion to Islam is extremely unconvincing. A photograph of him wearing a turban was widely circulated at the time of the rising as proof of his Moslem tendencies, but the prevailing opinion in responsible circles is that this piece of evidence was fabricated by an Armenian photographer in Addis Ababa.

The late Empress, who was remarkable for her orthodoxy and piety, strongly favoured the restoration of Lij Yasu. The only certain facts about the affair are that Lij Yasu was leading a life of extravagant dissipation which in no way reduced his popularity or prestige with his humbler subjects but which brought him into communication with many undesirable influences. He was in correspondence with the Mad Mullah in British Somaliland, and, when he allowed himself the opportunity for sober thought, he contemplated some sort of reorientation of his empire, with Harar as his capital, and its extension to the coast and absorption, under central European support, of Eritrea, French, British and Italian Somaliland. If he had been able to command the support of the Rases he might have proved a serious embarrassment to Allied interests in Africa, but he had personally alienated their respect by his indifference to their importance and his own grosser habits of life. He was defeated after a campaign marked by the most severe barbarities on either side and handed over to the keeping of Ras Kassa near Fiche, where he is said still to be living.

Ethiopia was left without an Emperor and without a constitution to deal with the situation. It must be borne in mind that although the country is now admitted to the League of Nations, it is still very far from having achieved the stage of unity assumed in the other parts of the world. The Ethiopian Empire, as it appears on the maps today, is barely fifty years old. It consists of the agglomeration of Menelik's conquests and includes many different races and creeds, Christians, Moslems, Jews and pagans, Negroes, Gallas, Somalis, in which the Abyssinians are a conquering minority, divided into large feudal provinces. The authority of the central government varies directly with the local ruler's personal opinion of the Emperor's capacity. It thus offers parallels with Old Testament history, France in the Middle Ages and Scotland in the time of Shakespeare's Macbeth. The principle of primogeniture has never been accepted there, and the question of hereditary right is complicated by the fact that little importance is attached to illegitimacy.

So far as Ethiopia can be said to have a constitution, the succession is regulated by royal proclamation, and there has rarely been a case of undisputed succession in recent Ethiopian history. The present Emperor has already had to fight two campaigns, that against Lij Yasu in alliance with the other races, and that in the spring of this year against Ras Gugsa, the divorced husband of the late Empress, and brother-in-law of the Emperor Menelik II, in which he appeared in the new light of the rightful monarch chastising a revolting vassal. Ras Kassa, who acted as host to the Duke of Gloucester during coronation week, seemed to be the natural successor to the Empress Zauditu by reason of his superior lineage, experience and great territorial possessions. There is little doubt that had he been ambitious of the throne, he might have attained it. He prefers, however, to devote his time to the management of his own estates and the performance of his religious duties.

Another important figure in Ethiopian politics is Ras Hailu, who rules in Gojjam. He is reputed to be the wealthiest man in the country, and is certainly a man of impressive appearance and personality. Each of these Rases, besides Ras Syonin and Sultan Abu Jaffar, has a large private army. In all feudal states it is the habit of the private soldier to look to his immediate overlord for allegiance, and not to the central government. The national army is the Emperor's force drawn from his own province. There is also the nucleus of an air force, which the Emperor carefully keeps under his own control. No private individual may own an aeroplane in Ethiopia, nor are aeroplanes allowed to land or leave the country except in rare circumstances.

The danger threatening Ethiopia after the death of Menelik was that the country would again split up into a group of petty kingdoms with the imperial title as a nominal suzerainty. In this condition the independence of the nation could scarcely have been preserved against European commercial interests. Ras Tafari had thus two separate problems to solve. He had to secure the recognition of his fellow Rases as the successor of the Empress Zauditu, and the recognition by the great powers of the integrity of Ethiopia. Every step in his foreign policy in the European capitals and at Geneva has had a correspond-ing influence in strengthening his position in his own country. Throughout the years between the fall of Lij Yasu and the death of the Empress, Ras Tafari worked for this end, and the spectacular celebrations in November were the culmination of this policy.

There were two main objects behind the pageantry and hospitality of the coronation. First, the Emperor wished to impress his own countrymen, and particularly the Rases, that he was accepted by the royal families in Europe. In this he succeeded. Secondly, the Emperor wished to impress his European visitors with the fact that Ethiopia was an up-to-date, civilized nation. In this he was only partially successful, for the Abyssinians are still so radically backward in culture and progress that evidence of the true state of things inevitably appeared from time to time. Enormous efforts had been made to prepare Addis Ababa for the European visitors, and if some of the improve-ments excited amusement, there was more to admire in the degree of success with which the authorities were able temporarily to disguise the nature of the people. Many of the visitors, however, availed themselves of the opportunity to see a little more of the country than was officially prepared for them, and these realized that the gold braid, brass bands and fine motor-cars of Addis Ababa, the caviare and sweet champagne, were a very superficial introduction to the national life.

It is absurd to pretend that Ethiopia is a civilized nation in any western sense of the word. Communications are still hopelessly bad. Except for a few miles outside Addis Ababa there is not a single motor road in the country. The railway from Djibouti to the capital does not pass through a single town except Dire Dawa, which sprang up on the line at the time of its construction. Harar, an important commercial centre, thirty-five miles from Dire Dawa, can only be reached by a two days' mule ride up the circuitous mountain caravan route. The cities of the north can only be reached by organizing a caravan and trekking to them. Ethiopian officials have yet to discover anything derogatory to their dignity in taking presents of money from strangers. The finances of the country are still rudimentary. Notes are issued by the Bank of Abyssinia against a silver deposit. The fall in price of silver has accordingly seriously upset the finance of the country, and the bank notes are useless in the country districts.

Even at Dire Dawa, two stations down the line from the capital, the local bank charges a 3 per cent discount in cashing its own notes. The Menelik dollar, the silver currency introduced by the government, has practically gone out of circulation because no one will accept it, though as a matter of fact it is of superior quality silver to the Maria Theresa dollar. This decorative but cumbrous coin is the only medium of exchange of practical value, and travellers going for a long trek are obliged to take several mule-loads of coin with them to pay their way. Intertribal raids and crimes of atrocious violence are common in the countryside. Public mutilations have been abolished from the penal system, but the conditions of the prisoners are greatly unhealthy, and deaths from typhus frequently follow imprisonment for trifling debts. Slavery is still universal, although many modifications are being made in the trade.

One could prolong the list of barbarities and anomalies to much greater length, but the object of its inclusion in this report is not to 'show up' Abyssinia, but to restore a correct balance of opinion. If Europeans, misled by descriptions of travellers who have confined their attention to what was officially shown them at Addis Ababa, go to Abyssinia with the impression that they are dealing with a fully civilized nation and that they will find there nothing but goodwill, co-operation and security for investments, there will inevitably be disappointments. Another generation of officials will have to grow up before the country will be suitable for commercial development on European lines; at present it is full of adventurers and frauds of every kind who embarrass the position of the respectable trader. Meanwhile, the Emperor's more romantic visitors are no doubt highly delighted to discover a country still so unmarked by tourists or speculators. The archaeology and anthropology of the country are practically unknown and it seems likely that it is in these directions that Ethiopia will excite more European attention during the next decade.

. LET US RETURN TO THE NINETIES .
BUT NOT TO OSCAR WILDE

There seems to be every indication that we are in for another of those revivalist movements to which European, and particularly English, taste is so fatally liable. This time it is to be the 1890s. The early Victorian tide in which, before luncheon, we paddled and splashed so gaily has washed up its wreckage and retreated, and all those glittering bits of shell and seaweed – the coloured glass paper-weights, wax fruit, Rex Whistler decorations, paper lace Valentines,

which we collected – have by late afternoon dried out very drab and disappointing and hardly discernible at all from the rest of the beach, while the enamelled
buckets, silver paper and banana skins of our own age still attract attention
among the sand castles. Nurse is exhorting us to tidy up our own territory
round the bathing tent, and even sets the example by digging in the confec-
tioner's box which held the buns for tea; but all eyes are fixed on the sea; the
tide has turned; the waves come tumbling up again with all manner of flotsam
and jetsam bobbing in the surf, and with shrill cries the children scamper down
to welcome the nineties.

These recurrent outbursts of enthusiasm for the fashions of bygone periods
are due to a very simple cause; the fact that it is a very arduous business to keep
up with one's own period. People talk about 'being modern' as though it were
simply a matter of buying a new dress, drinking some cocktails, putting on the
most recent gramophone record, and letting a mysterious 'spirit of the age' do
the rest. That way lie all the terrors of the pseudo. It takes as much serious
effort to be sincerely and completely modern as to swim the Channel – and it is
just about as profitable. There is an unhappy man in Paris called M. Cocteau
whose whole life is occupied in trying to be modern (and there are some people
in Bloomsbury with the same idea, but – whether because they started later, or
work less feverishly, I do not know – these poor Britons have never quite caught
up). There are many kind, rich ladies in London who think that they are
attaining this modernity, by inviting coloured people or the authors of the
latest best-sellers to luncheon; there are editors who imagine they are keeping
up to date by hiring very young people to write for them. But it is more
complicated than these people believe.

One great difficulty is that, individually, people become more modern as
they grow older. Undergraduates are absorbed in Rossetti and questions of
right and wrong, their own sex adventures, and ideas of liberty and justice; the
artists and writers who can justly claim to be thought avant-garde are almost
always middle-aged or quite elderly people – M. Picasso or Mr James Joyce. It
is as though it took an entire lifetime to bring oneself up to the spirit of one's
own age. More than this, there is the discouraging conclusion that by the time
one has really become modern, there is almost nothing to be said about it.
There was unlimited material for conversation in an Academy painting of
eighty years ago – what a sweet face the model had, and was the view from the
window done in Dorset or Wilts, and what was the doggy with the limpid eyes
really thinking about?

If one had learned the jargon there was quite a lot one could say about the
painting of ten years ago – 'recession', 'planes', 'significance', etc.; but before
a painting by M. Picasso in his latest manner, the most glib tongue is compelled to silence.

Now, it is the essence of fashion that it should be fluid. When it finds itself
dammed in one direction, it finds a new level elsewhere. Unable to go forward,
it goes back. Little rivulets find out paths for themselves and fall in sparkling

cascades – Mr Byron to Byzantium, Mr Sitwell to Baroque, M. Maritain to Aquinum, but the broad stream flows unimpeded. It is not to be wondered at if some of the nutshell boats, spinning in the eddies, lose their bearings a little, and one hears such odd judgments as I read recently that 'the nineties are the last word in modernity.'

It is perfectly natural that the fashionable flow should have come to temporary stagnation at that particular decade. Any period acquires a certain glamour after twenty-five years or so. Among simple minds the clothes of even a few years back excite derisive glee in theatre or cinematograph; to the more sophisticated the aesthetic and social codes of another generation are always instructive; but whereas almost any other period requires an acquaintance with Art and History far beyond the capacity of the young women who most eagerly follow the fashion, the nineties, or rather the fiction that has come to represent the nineties to the present generation, requires for its appreciation and imitation no sort of endowment of intellect or culture.

For the nineties have come to mean for us only one thing – the great, booby figure of Oscar Wilde. Even he was by no means as comic as his admirers have made him. He was overdressed, pompous, snobbish, sentimental and vain, but he had an undeniable *flair* for the possibilities of the contemporary, commercial theatre. He got himself into trouble, poor old thing, by the infringement of a very silly law, which was just as culpable and just as boring as an infringement of traffic or licensing regulations. For the rest of his life he became a professional sponge. But it is this unremarkable figure that has become the type to which the new fashion is tending. It is natural that one of the first signs of the new movement should have been the revival of his plays. No one can object to this, because they are in their own strictly limited way perfectly competent works. The sad thing for poor Wilde's reputation was that, in the grim social circles which he wished to penetrate, anything that was not Politics or Sport was Art. If he wore scent, or jewellery, or eccentric waistcoats, or collected knick-knacks of porcelain, or *chinoiserie* – it was all unusual and therefore was Art. If he lay a long time on a sofa in a silk dressing-gown – that was Art, too. Wilde went bowling all over the country to lecture about Art. He even persuaded himself that he suffered for Art.

It is no wonder that fashionable people in London look back wistfully to that happy decade. The word Art still has the same glamour. They long ardently to be artistic, but all the arts have withdrawn themselves far beyond their comprehension. How they have hungered for a time when a reputation for wit might be achieved through paradox and epigram – those monkey-tricks of the intellect. The revival of interest in the nineties is another – possibly a last – attempt of the amateurs and dilettanti to persuade themselves that they are cultured.

Well, we are in for this revival and we must put up with it as best we may; there seems to me only one way in which we can meet the rising flood. Let us, if we must, return to the nineties, but not to Oscar Wilde. There was much in those ten splendid years to which we can still look with approval. There was, for instance, the cult of the safety bicycle – that boon to postmen and university dons. Instead of sprawling about on divans, burning cheap joss sticks (or expensive ones for that matter) and fanning themselves with peacocks' feathers, I should like to see fashionable society pedalling out among the motor-cars for picnic lunches on Epping Common or Hampstead Heath.

While Beardsley and Condor were being admired in London, Cézanne, quite unknown to the aesthetes, was just entering upon the noblest phase of his art. We can thus be true to the nineties without denying the existence of responsible painting.

The truth is that the poor decadents were, less than anyone, in touch with their own age. All the time that they imagined themselves lapsing into over-civilized and slightly drugged repose, that apostle of over-civilization, Mr Edison, was hard at work devising the telephone bell which was to render the whole of the next generation permanently sleepless. While they talked about the earth slowing down at the *fin de siècle*, and of 'an age of inertia', the finishing touches were being put to the motor-car and plans were being made for heavier-than-air flying machines. While they vied with one another in exaggerating their moods and poses, the psychologists on the continent were developing a system of thought in which these conscious waves of emotion became the most negligible and valueless of human faculties. Let us by all means return to this splendid, fashionable decade – the decade of W. G. Grace and General Kitchener. In the words of that great laureate of the decadence, Mr Kipling,

> So it's knock out your pipes an' follow me!
> An' it's finish up your swipes an' follow me!
> Oh, 'ark to the big drum callin',
> Follow me – follow me 'ome!

. WHY GLORIFY YOUTH? .

Three years ago I was asked for the first time to write an article for a London paper. The subject set me was 'Give Youth a Chance'.[1] My heart sank, but I was in no position in those days to pick or choose among the chances that came my way of earning a few guineas.

I wrote the article, stuffing it with all the clichés I could remember and doing all I could by bombast and exaggeration to qualify it for the trade label of 'challenging'. I got my guineas and was grateful, but all the time I reflected what a fatuous subject it was. Now, three years later, I am invited to write on 'Why Glorify Youth?' – and it seems to me that this reversal of theme reveals a

Women's Journal, March 1932.
1 The article appeared as 'Too Young at Forty' (22 January 1929).

most salutary change of attitude, a cool wave of sanity that has swept public opinion during the intervening time, washing away the picnic litter of Youth-movement sentimentality.

Why Glorify Youth? Why, indeed? And it may be worth while pointing out at once that young people never – except in the way of business – evinced the smallest disposition to do so. The whole Glorious Youth legend was invented by the elderly and middle-aged. It took two main forms, according to the temperament of the particular worshipper. There was the Beauty of Youth Legend. This assured the success of such works as *Dusty Answer* and *Young Woodley*. Oh, lovely youths and maidens! Oh, bodies of classic grace and splendour! Rapturous calf love! Important doubts and disillusionments! Oh, grand apotheosis of pimply adolescence! The novels in their tens of thousands swirled and eddied like flood water through the circulating libraries: the curtains rose and fell to rapturous applause.

The Responsibility of Youth Legend took a soberer form. I hardly remember a single speech or sermon made to us at school which did not touch on this topic. 'You are the men of tomorrow,' they used to say to us. 'You are succeeding to the leadership of a broken and shaken world. The cure is in your hands,' etc., etc.

One or two people took this message seriously and have buried themselves in minor secretarial posts at Geneva, or forfeited their deposits regularly each general election, or are passing on the same clap-trap to university classes in remote parts of the globe. For the most part, however, the reply of my generation to all these glowing expectations was the period which will no doubt presently be known as the 'roaring twenties'. In the last year of that decade I wrote *Vile Bodies*, in which I attempted to summarize the chief features of those topsy-turvy years in which the younger generation succeeded in knocking the nonsense out of the attempts to sentimentalize them.

It is now abundantly clear that the 'roaring twenties' are over. The chief figures of the time have settled down to marriage and children, and others have become submerged completely. It seems clear enough that their successors have not the inclination to carry on the same tradition. The 'twenties' of this century will soon become a phrase like the 'nineties' of the last. But just as the 'nineties', odious as they now seem to us with their 'greenery-yallery' artiness, did do a valuable social service in finally breaking up British insular, bourgeois materialism, so the 'twenties' – futile, obstreperous, anarchic, vulgar, call them what you will – broke up post-war Rupert Brooke magnificently-unprepared-for-the-long-bitterness-of-life sentimentality, and made Youth openly and ludicrously inglorious.

It is, on the face of it, odd that such a decade should have been needed – fraught as it was with so much distress to parents, not to mention children – to emphasize what should be a self-evident truth. Who but the muddle-headed, mist-haunted races of northern Europe would ever commit the folly of glorifying incompleteness and immaturity? For what is Youth except a man or woman before it is ready or fit to be seen?

What could be more depressing or perverse than to imagine the whole active life of man as a gradual declivity from the perfection of 19, as those seedy old men must feel who once broke their public-school record for the hundred yards and have spent the succeeding fifty years or so of their lives reliving the event? And what a pathetic attainment to be proud of. If Youth is our most valuable possession, then we are every one of us poorer and more pitiable every moment of our lives from birth to death. Not everyone grows to be old but everyone has been younger than he now is.

No doubt much of this mistaken pessimism comes from the typically Teutonic confusion of general value with sex-appeal. As a race we are constitutionally so shy about sex that we are rarely prepared to praise anyone on those terms alone; we will insert some moral justification for our physical inclinations. Thus when people wish to say that they find youthfulness a desirable and exciting quality in a lover, they feel themselves obliged to set up a hymn of praise for the wholly contemptible concomitant qualities of mind and character.

But I am even sceptical of youth's supremacy in the very narrow field of physical attraction. Disembarrass the issue of all other considerations, refuse to attach importance to charm, wit, experience, prestige, and what have you left? A pretty small residue of puppyish, rubbery limb, clear skin, bright eyes, untidy hair; nothing to fall in love with, nothing to obsess one to the exclusion of other interests. Sex-appeal is made up of an infinite number of different stimuli, and in all but very few the woman of over 30 has the debutante hopelessly beaten.

Oh, how maddening after five minutes' conversation, those perky, fresh little faces, those bright blank eyes, those lips bubbling with senseless prattle. 'Oh, English girl, divine, demure,' how one longs to give you a marron glacé, a light kiss and put you under the chair, with the puppies and kittens who are your true associates.

The English debutante is fit only for the schoolroom, but it is our absurd custom to impose her on terms of social equality upon unfortunate young men ten years her senior. And here she is fighting on her own ground. Clumsy, gauche, ignorant and ill-dressed as she is, she is engaged in the contest in which the single weapon of Youth is of some value. In everything except sex-appeal Youth is a positive disadvantage.

A great mistake is made in confusing Youth with Modernity. One of the most sickening qualities of the young is that they are nearly always grossly old-fashioned. In the ordinary arts of civilization – eating, drinking, clothes, hospitality, furnishing – all fashions are set by people between the ages of 30 and 55. The reason why Sport is civilized while Athletics are not is that the sportsman profits almost indefinitely by experience, whereas the athlete has as a rule to retire from competition before his mind has begun to work at all. Still more with the Fine Arts of Literature, Music, Painting, the real 'moderns' are all men in late middle age. Undergraduates are still coquetting with the artistic fashions of 1910. It is many years before they begin to grow into their own age.

The 'moderns' are mature artists, such as Mr James Joyce and M. Picasso.

There seems to me to be in the Fine Arts no question of Youth and Age, but simply one of greater or less growth. An artist is not better through being old in years, but he has had the opportunity of being better. There is an antecedent improbability against any young man being a first-rate artist, because he has not had time to grow. Yet one constantly overhears silly old women pottering round art exhibitions saying, 'Only 22, my dear. I am all for Modernity. One wants new blood.' While if they only had the eyes to see it there is more advance in some invention or discovery of an elderly painter next door than in all the groping of the young genius.

How one wishes that the Arts had the same standards of age as Politics, where the 'promising' young men of the party are all 40 or 50, and the real hard work is left to those in the prime of life between 60 and 70. Why will literary critics not realize that Mr George Moore is every bit as 'promising' as Lady Eleanor Smith?

The Youth boom has been very convenient for young men like myself who have made a living out of it, but it seems to me time that criticism adopted some more significant standard.

. TOLERANCE .

Twenty-five years ago it was the fashion for those who considered themselves enlightened and progressive to cry out against intolerance as the one damning sin of their time.

The agitation was well founded and it resulted in the elimination from our social system of many elements that are cruel and unjust. But in the general revolution of opinion which followed, has not more been lost than gained?

It is better to be narrow-minded than to have no mind, to hold limited and rigid principles than none at all.

That is the danger which faces so many people today – to have no considered opinions on any subject, to put up with what is wasteful and harmful with the excuse that there is 'good in everything' – which in most cases means an inability to distinguish between good and bad.

There are still things which are worth fighting *against*.

Contribution to 'The Seven Deadly Sins of Today by Seven Famous Authors', *John Bull*, 2 April 1932, announcing the theme of a forthcoming story by Waugh, 'Too Much Tolerance'.

. THE CITADELS OF ETHIOPIA .

There is a common opinion among the untravelled that the whole world has now been 'discovered' and that *trains de luxe* and tourist agencies abound universally. In a very limited degree this is true. Certainly the greater part of the earth's surface is still inaccessible except through great discomfort and some danger; certainly there are numerous blank patches on the maps of Africa and South America; certainly both there and in central Asia there are vast areas about which our information is of a meagre and unsatisfactory kind, but it is possible to maintain that since the recent expeditions in southern Arabia there are no important territories which have not at some time in the last seventy years been traversed by responsible European observers and that for the future the important anthropological and geographical discoveries will come not so much from the mobile explorer as from the resident – the missionary and political officer making prolonged studies of small communities.

Mr Max Grühl, whose travel diary has just been translated from the German, is essentially an investigator of the old type. Complete with caravan, collecting boxes and notebooks, he tramps into a very unfrequented district and encounters a fine variety of dangers and delays; but after reading his book one is left with the impression that in spite of some spasmodic work with tape measure and callipers on the natives he meets, he has taken his scientific duties with a decent levity and has travelled more to divert himself than to enrich the world's knowledge. The route of his march lies through the Kafa and Jimma provinces of the Ethiopian Empire, north-west of Addis Ababa. It is rare enough to travel at all in Ethiopia; those who do so generally strike south-east from the Sudan or south-west from Eritrea, visiting the ancient Christian cities of Axum, Gondar and Lallibella. Mr Grühl is clearly a resourceful traveller; the trouble is that he is not a very good writer; that is to say, it is the defect that will inevitably restrict his public to that small circle, of which the present reviewer claims membership, who prefer all but the very worst travel books to all but the very best novels. Only two kinds of travel book claim attention outside this circle: books of specialized scientific interest and books such as M. André Gide's *Voyage au Congo*, in which a writer already established as a novelist elects to give his personal impressions of foreign places. In the later kind he may deal with the Mediterranean pleasure resorts or the monasteries of Athos – it is the writer's personality which is interesting, not his material. Very occasionally, of course, the supreme travel book appears – Doughty's *Arabia Deserta* for instance – which is both a work of science and of art. For the most part, however, the public expect and accept one or the other. *The Citadels of Ethiopia* is neither. But it has much to commend it. The illustrative photographs are all admirable and the narrative, though usually stilted and often sententious, still preserves the flavour of first-hand experience – for one reader at least an unmistakable and intoxicating flavour; the boys who cannot be made

Review of *The Citadels of Ethiopia*, by Max Grühl. *Spectator*, 9 April 1932.

to start on the appointed day and strike for higher wages in the bush; the death
of baggage animals; the interminable courtesies and suspicions of native notables; the exchanges of presents, livestock and provender on one side, European hardware on the other; the amateur clinic and the customary comedy of
medical advice wrongly understood; the impression produced on remote
peoples by cameras and gramophones; the bouts of fever and loss of mail – it is
all there, a mere whisper, uncouth, monotonous, but nevertheless the authentic voice that thunders through the mighty pages of *Arabia Deserta*.

. AN INDIAN COMEDY .

Mr J. R. Ackerley's Indian journal leaves the reviewer in some embarrassment
as to the terms in which he must praise it. For praise it certainly demands; the
difficulty is to control one's enthusiasm and to praise it temperately, for it is
certainly one of those books of rare occurrence which stand upon a superior and
totally distinct plane of artistic achievement above the ordinary trade-market,
high-grade competence of contemporary literature. The danger is one of
overstatement. It does not qualify for the epithets 'great', 'stupendous',
'epoch-making', &c., so generously flung about by critics, but it is a work of
high literary skill and very delicate aesthetic perception and it deals with a
character and a milieu which are novel and radiantly delightful. What more, in
an imperfect world, has one the right to expect?

It is in form a series of extracts from a private diary kept over a short period in
the court of one of the least important Indian maharajahs. Mr Ackerley went to
stay there in an ill-defined unofficial capacity: part companion, part prospective tutor. In reality he was there to fulfil His Highness's need for a sympathetic
friend; how warm, humorous and balanced that sympathy must have been is
clear from the portrait which he has given us in the diary. The picture, rich,
fantastic and solid, is built up for the most part with admirable dexterity in
snatches of dialogue. His Highness employs an exquisitely amusing diction full
of half-understood expressions. The word 'whimsical' has a somewhat opprobrious connotation, but it is difficult to find a substitute in describing the ruler's
capricious interest in metaphysics, his troubles with the inmates of his harem,
his superstitions and indecision; there is the boy Napoleon III whom he cannot
make up his mind to buy; there is the pilgrimage on which he cannot make up
his mind to start; the omens and religious practices which cause him capricious
alternation of reverence and ridicule; he is melancholy, romantic, eager,
listless, petulant, wistful, tender, dictatorial, vacillating – every entry in the
journal brings out some new surprising and usually lovable characteristic in the
complex little man. Even the repulsive Abdul, the type of all that Europeans
find unendurable in Indian character, becomes under Mr Ackerley's treatment

Review of *Hindoo Holiday*, by J. R. Ackerley. *Spectator*, 16 April 1932.

a humorous and therefore tolerable person; at times his reality becomes so formidable that he even eclipses the maharajah in importance.

Then there are the Europeans. So much fun has been made of the English in India, since Mr Kipling first brought them as raw material to the literary market, that it seems hardly conceivable that more can profitably be said. And yet Mr Ackerley succeeds in making them so wildly funny that the reader longs for their rare appearances in the story. Mrs Montgomery and Mrs Bristow are intoxicating characters and in them one sees personified a new idea about the British in India – not as vulgar and arrogant interlopers, not as heroic keepers of the King-Emperor's peace, not as liverish bores waiting for meagrely pensioned old age in Cheltenham, not as conquerors in any of the guises in which they have attracted satire, but as absurd, otherworldly, will-o'-the-wisps, floating in little misty companies about the landscape, futile, shy little creatures, half friendly, half suspicious, lurking like gnomes in their own bad places, a damp Celtic breath sighing in the powder-hot landscape of Asia.

. VENETIAN ADVENTURES .

My Dear H.   *Palazzo XYZ, Grand Canal, Venice.*
How I wish that you had come to Venice instead of trailing off drearily to Cannes. Quite half your friends are here; by far the more amusing half are all behaving in ways that would be a revelation to you. I shall never smell tuberoses again without envisaging queues of repentant young men apologizing after parties – however, that must all wait until we meet. I can't risk committing it to writing.

I must say your reasons for not coming made very little sense to me. They are what all the partisans of the Riviera always say. Mosquitoes? Yes, there are certainly plenty of them, but they disappear at dawn and as no one goes to bed much before that they are very little nuisance. One can get one's morning sleep unbroken. How much less boring than the horse-flies in the hills behind Grasse, where I fled this time last year from the traffic noises of the coast.

Smells? Yes, they can't be denied. Weaker some evenings than others but always heavy enough in the smaller canals. But the truth is I don't mind that particular smell – the sewage of garlic-eating countries – compared with those of the north. I smelled nothing in Venice to rival the smouldering cigarettes women leave under my nose at restaurants. And, anyway, it is pure affectation for anyone to complain of smells who keeps two spaniels. . . .

Scampi? I wonder how that delicious and salutary dish got its bad name. The English get ill through sprawling in the sun, as no sane southerner would dream of doing, and then say that they are poisoned with scampi. One thing at

Harper's Bazaar (London), October 1932.

least I know about them. It is pure legend that they are caught in the canals. I spent a night last week trawling in the Adriatic with one of the boats of the Chioggia fishing fleet, and watched netfuls of scampi being drawn in from the deep water for the Venice markets. We cooked them on a charcoal brazier and ate them in their shells at dawn – with cups of hideous coffee compounded, it seemed, of chicory, garlic and earth.

The Lido? That old charge of harbouring obese Germans and sand fleas? I admit its disadvantages. The warmth of the water removes half the stimulus from bathing; the only restaurant where one can lunch embodies all the views of monopoly; the expense is vast; the architecture of the Excelsior Hotel is the lowest in Europe; people do rattle backgammon boards when one wishes to sleep. But as far as a spectacle of beauty goes, its population this year seemed to me incomparable with that of any other *plage*. I don't think you can complain much of the appearance of a society where in one *coup* of the eye can be seen Diana Cooper, Diana Abdy, Bridget Parsons, Mary Lygon, Mrs Bryan Guinness, Doris Castlerosse, Anne Armstrong-Jones and Tilly Losch, not to mention (because I do not know their names) the beauties of five other nations. And, in its way, the very grubbiness of the beach has its charm, where one can immerse one's head in powder-dry sand and explore strata upon strata of débris, cigar ends, hairpins, playing cards, right down to the bits of rope and corroded iron bars of a genuine sea coast.

What do I like about Venice in August and September? I like the fact that it has a traditional culture against which many of our friends appear in an entirely new aspect. The French Riviera is the creation of its visitors – a barbarous strip of rocky shore on which foreign holidaymakers have perched hotels and bars and casinos. It has no history or nationality. It is morally the property of the sun-bathers and baccarat players who frequent it. And they are amply justified in behaving exactly how they like, and dressing how they like, and in swaggering about as though the place did, in fact, belong to them. Venice had the gay café life of the Piazza before the American colonists had learnt to speak with an accent and I enjoy very much the fact that they insist on their own standards of propriety. The Lido is the foreigners' property. People can dress how they like there. But if they wish to sit at Florian's in the evening they must dress as the Venetians think suitable. Young Englishmen who attempt to appear like gross schoolboys in shorts and vests present a very vulgar spectacle indeed under Venetian eyes.

As you know I am a confirmed heliophobe, and I like the fact that in Venice you can escape the sun in the cool depths of the churches and palaces. I like Venice at night, when it really becomes itself and we can drift quite silently, except for the gondoliers' cry at corners, on black water among the smells you condemn. I like the evening carnival, when all the poorer Venetians decorate their boats with lanterns and flow in processions down the Grand Canal, not to collect money or attract tourists, but simply because it is their idea of an agreeable evening. Most of my memories of Venice will be of its evenings; of a picnic on a monastic island and an absurd conversation in Latin with a friar who complained of *'Mulieres stridentes et vestitae immodestissime'* and my attempt to translate the advice, 'Tell him there are six English Members of Parliament here', into *'Hic sunt sex senatores Britannici . . .'* a laborious conversation happily ending in a donation to the monastery. I shall think, too, of a fragrant evening at Murano - a placid, English birthday party when glassblowers and gondoliers joined in and danced with the guests.

And I relish very much the compactness of Venetian life. On the Riviera there are so many villas, so many hotels, so many *plages* and casinos, so many miles of *corniche*. Here there are at the most about forty English or Americans, who know exactly what everyone is doing every minute of the day. They all meet every evening on the Piazza and discuss how they dined, and on the morning after a party I love to see the convergence of patinas, canoes and bathers, sometimes into a single Sargasso Sea of gossip, sometimes into rival camps with rare swimmers travelling between and fanning the dissension.

Well, this is an absurdly long letter and a useless one really, because everyone is leaving and it is too late now to persuade you to come. But perhaps it is not wasted if it induces you to think of joining us next year.

Love from

Evelyn.

. TRAVEL - AND ESCAPE FROM YOUR FRIENDS .

Voyage out; a week of severe cold and heavy seas in the North Atlantic; a week of increasing calm and warmth, as with the passing latitudes we changed from tweed to flannels and from flannels to white drill; a week pottering among the islands of the West Indies; at the end the forest and swamp and empty mountains of the Guianas. And throughout this voyage I have been wondering what it is that impels people - Anglo-Saxons and Teutons especially - to leave their native surroundings for distant and less civilized places.

When people ask me what I get out of it I say that I am looking for material for a book, but that is an explanation which holds very little water. The vast spate of the publishing season proves quite clearly that one has not got to go to the Equator to write books. Moreover, as is always being impressed on me by those who know the book trade, it is bad business. People would much sooner read about Mayfair than the jungle.[1]

Daily Mail, 16 January 1933.

1 See P. G. Wodehouse writing in 1934 about *A Handful of Dust*: 'What a snare this travelling business is to the young writer. He goes to some blasted jungle or other and imagines that everybody will be interested in it.' Quoted in Frances Donaldson, *P. G. Wodehouse* (London : Weidenfeld and Nicolson, 1982), p. 155.

Someone said to me before I left, 'You go off for six months on a lunatic expedition among cannibals and mosquitoes and then expect us to buy your travel books to pay the expenses.' Of course all an author's readers are engaged indirectly in supporting him, and why they should resent providing him with a canoe when they do not mind standing him supper at an expensive restaurant, I cannot imagine. But the fact remains that readers do feel like that, so that I cannot give my trade as an excuse for travel. The truth is that I am deeply interested in the jungle and only casually interested in Mayfair, and one has to write about what interests one. So we are back at the beginning of the argument. What do we travelmaniacs get out of it? Turning the question over in my mind during the few weeks' voyage, I have come to the following conclusions.

1. It is essential for people who practise no regular profession to take long holidays from their own lives. A man who goes regularly to work is in a strong position. From the moment he leaves his home in the morning until he returns there at night he is completely free from his domestic and social life. He is living among other men and business associates and absorbed in a pursuit quite alien to his family and personal interests. But men of leisure and writers are alike in this, that they never have a separation of interests. Their relationship with friends and relations and the routine of their day are invariable and interconnected. The more irritable have to get away or go off their heads.

2. Some measure of physical risk is as necessary to human well-being as physical exercise. I do not mean acts of reckless heroism which are reserved for a minority, and not always the most interesting, of men. But everyone instinctively needs an element of danger and uncertainty in his life. Some get this in the hunting field or climbing rocks or flying aeroplanes. It is one of the natural instincts of man and it is satisfied by travelling. I do not wish to pretend that we travellers are in a perpetual state of high courage, being ambushed by cannibals, pounced on by lions, hissed at by snakes, but that as soon as one leaves the ordinary highways of civilization there is a certain agreeable sense of danger never very far away.

3. If one is interested in one's fellow beings – and that after all is the first requisite of a novelist – one cannot neglect the study of human nature in unfamiliar surroundings; the aspects of character that are visible in civilized life give one material for only a superficial survey. The way in which people react to changes of conditions is valuable material.

4. But in the end the final, determining cause is always inquisitiveness about *places* themselves. A map, and particularly one with blank spaces and dotted rivers, can influence a travelmaniac as can no book or play. It is only those who have travelled a little who know how intensely different places can be. The stay-at-home vaguely imagines the world as being under calm European domination, peopled with peppery colonels and astute officials. But those who know the fantastic variety, even among British possessions, know that literally every place in the world is worth visiting, and treasures some peculiar gift for the traveller who goes there in decent humility.

. WAS HE RIGHT TO FREE THE SLAVES? .

The celebrations now being organized for the centenary of William Wilberforce are likely to command very tepid enthusiasm in the countries principally
affected by the philanthropist's work. On the one hand, the present generation
of negroes would sooner not be reminded of their antecedents, while the few
responsible whites are well aware that the emancipation of the slaves created a
series of economic, social and political problems that are no nearer solution
now than they were a hundred years ago.

If William Wilberforce could return to public life today and see the effects of
his work, the speeches shortly to be made in his honour would ring in his ears
with peculiar irony. None of the great movements of the nineteenth century is
more typical of its age than that for the freeing of the slaves. It depended on all
those fallacies that are being abandoned today: the idea of a perfectible
evolutionary man, of a responsible democratic voter, of the beneficial effect of
mechanization, and, above all, on sentimental belief in the basic sweetness of
human nature.

There are always honourable exceptions in any general racial condemnation,
and, heaven knows, the white people of the north have not made such a success
of their own civilization that they can afford any extravagance of phrase. But it
is not too much to say that in general character the descendants of the Negro
slaves in the British Empire are a thriftless and dissolute lot. It is an unexpected
development from the simple, woolly-headed, golden-hearted Bible-reading
old darky that was held up as an example to European subscribers – the good
old Uncle Tom who was to grow in the air of freedom into an educated, prudent
and pious family man and citizen. The sugar plantations have been ruined or
mechanized, and the Negroes, instead of following the example of the inden-
tured coolies and becoming small proprietors, working long hours in the
country, drift to the intermittent employment of the towns. They have proved
quite unfit for retail trade: they are clumsy mechanics, a superstitious and
excitable riff-raff hanging round the rum shops and staring listlessly at the
Chinese, Madeiran and East Indian immigrants, who outstrip them in every
branch of life.

In Liberia, where they have been put in political power, they have erected a
rigid racial bar between the immigrant and the aboriginal Negroes, and have
introduced a system of forced labour more onerous than the slavery from which
they were themselves freed. It was interesting, when the report on conditions in
Liberia was published, to notice the concern that it aroused. The greater part
of the British public had no idea that slavery existed anywhere in the world. We
had so often been told in school that the British people had stamped out slavery
that we had come to look on it as something wholly obsolete – as until a few

weeks back we imagined the persecution of Jews was obsolete. I have no first-hand experience of Liberia, but from all accounts I should say that slavery there exists in a far more offensive form than anywhere else, for it is the process of degrading a free people in their own country.

It is not the state of slavery so much as the process of enslavement that is intolerable: and it is worth noting that the European slave trade was principally for the transport of people already enslaved. That is to say, the traders purchased captives from the warrior tribes. Undoubtedly the trade stimulated the raiding, but free blacks first captured other free blacks and then sold them to the whites.

I have seen slave-owning communities in Abyssinia and Arabia and got the impression that the slaves are far better off than wage-earners in those countries. For one thing, there is no unemployment. In a country which is not socially organized on an industrial basis – that is to say, with old-age pensions, free hospitals, unemployment relief, etc. – the employer of free labour uses his workers on a subsistence wage for the best years of their life, and then turns them off without further obligation. In the houses I visited in Abyssinia the courtyards were full of decrepit old men and women, long past any useful service, who were fed regularly and sufficiently, and had no other duties than to prostrate themselves once or twice a day when their master went in or out. It is a matter of prestige to support a large household. In the old days of West Indian slavery the charge of ill-treating his slaves was one of the most odious that could be brought against a planter, and in many islands was tantamount to a challenge to a duel.

William Wilberforce was inflated by the true nineteenth-century arrogance of thinking a little local uplift could reverse the development of centuries. Slave raiding has from remotest times been the hobby of the warrior tribes of Africa: slave ownership has been one of the postulates of every civilization. British wealth and British sentiment were strong enough to upset a system which, like any other, had abuses but also many redeeming virtues, but British intelligence was not up to anticipating the problem it created.

. MR FLEMING IN BRAZIL .

Brazilian Adventure is an arresting and absorbing book. I want to make that clear before proceeding to criticism. It is the narrative of a highly exciting expedition written by a man with unusual literary gifts, an austere respect for accuracy, a clear mind in collating evidence and assessing probabilities, a sense of the dramatic, the beautiful and the comic. It is a story which must delight not only the specialized public who enjoy browsing in books of travel, but also

Review of *Brazilian Adventure*, by Peter Fleming. *Spectator*, 11 August 1933.

those with a taste for plot and detection and suspense. It deserves and, I am confident, will attain, a very wide success. I am putting it in a high class and the criticisms which follow must be understood as referring to high standards. Had it been less vital, the task of reviewing it would have been easier – a column of cordial commendation and gratitude – but as it stands there are several points for comment and regret.

It is an intensely self-conscious book. The trouble about all forms of writing is that one is working against a background of predecessors and contemporaries. It is the writer's duty to avoid embarrassment and here Mr Fleming has failed. There is scarcely a page on which he does not reveal his awareness that the spirit of adventure often results in literary trash. *The Boy's Own Paper*, *The Wide World Magazine*, the self-advertisements of female globe-trotters, the anecdotes of the club bore, haunt him all the time. To some extent this is inevitable. The larger one's humour and sensitiveness, the more readily does one's life slip into a habit of parody. Mr Fleming finds himself unable to use any of the ordinary phrases of sport and travel, such as 'making camp', without an implicit apology – as though he said, 'I know this is jargon and I am talking like that wizened old fraud at my club, but really I don't know any other way to express what happened.' When he was in very hard conditions, he tells us, one of his companions and he invented a parody language, speaking of water as the 'Precious Fluid' and so on. I can imagine exactly how enlivening that kind of joke was in Matto Grosso, but it expresses an attitude of mind that seriously cramps a work of literature. For the truth is that Mr Fleming has a really exciting story to tell, but he almost spoils it by going to the extreme limits of depreciation in his anxiety to avoid the pretentious.

The first chapters, before the expedition gets into the real jungle, are delightful, in the modern manner of Mr Robert Byron. And here I should like to call his bluff about this being the most truthful travel book ever written. On page 75 he quotes the notice, 'To Throw Stones at the Serpents is an Indication of Bad Character.' I suspect that the notice was in Portuguese and that Mr Fleming allowed himself the luxury of a literal and facetious translation.

Once the expedition gets moving and the characters of the members take shape, and the succession of obstacles assumes more and more formidable proportions, the story is enthralling. But Mr Fleming's shyness continually intrudes on the reader's enjoyment. He has, for instance, a fine instinct for natural beauty, a rich vocabulary and clear descriptive sense, but always he is afraid to let himself go; there is a tentative, luminous phrase followed by immediate recession. He is afraid of purple patches. That is all very well when one has little to describe, but Mr Fleming has an eyeful if he would only give it to us.

There is the same difficulty in his account of the living conditions. It is clear that during the land journey from the Tapirapé, Mr Fleming was the organizer of a genuinely heroic forlorn hope, that he and his companion were in constant danger and in discomfort well below the limit of tolerable living. The attempt to establish communication with the Indians and so work through to the Kuluene was a failure, but it was an act of high courage which none of Mr Fleming's underwriting can disguise.

The return journey, instead of forming an anticlimax as it well might, is the story of a chase as exciting as Jules Verne's *Round the World in Eighty Days*. It is hard to do justice to the skill with which Mr Fleming treats his relations with Major Pingle, the original leader of the expedition – the growing suspicion, the various attempts to bind him to a declaration of his intentions, the first antagonism and eventual detestation and open conflict when the Major confiscates his mail, his money and his revolvers. The suspense of the race is faultlessly preserved – as soon as an incident becomes definitely fantastic Mr Fleming is at his ease again – and I experienced vivid personal delight at its conclusion. But why did Mr Fleming not give us another chapter? I want to know what happened between the arrival of the steam launch and the departure of the ship for England; were there scenes at the consulate of mutual accusation? Were they able to stop Major Pingle's cheque? There was a hint that he prejudiced his position in Para by his wires to the shipping office and consulate – but how exactly did this occur? Where is Pingle now? One cannot get as absorbed as I was in that preposterous character and then see him disappear without a hint of his destination. Can we be sure that he will read Mr Fleming's book? It seems to me absolutely essential that he should, and I would willingly pursue him into Matto Grosso with a copy for the pleasure of watching him read it.

. GOSSIP .

In the early years of his career Waugh constantly appeared in gossip columns, and he often contributed to them. He was very popular with columnists and interviewers, probably because whether being funny or subversive he always said something quotable.

A CLERIHEW

On 8 May 1935 Mair Saklatvala, whose address was Brick Kiln Hill, submitted a clerihew to William Hickey's *Daily Express* column, 'These Names Make News':

> I've had more than enough
> Of Mr Waugh or Waugh.

On the following day Waugh replied by telegram:

Brick Kiln Hill holds a gala
On the rare appearance in print of the obscure name of Saklatvala.

MAIL FROM EVELYN WAUGH
RE *TABLET* ATTACK

On 8 September 1934 Ernest Oldmeadow, editor of the *Tablet*, wrote a full page review, 'The Pity of It', severely castigating *A Handful of Dust* on moral grounds. On 10 September William Hickey in the *Daily Express* reported the rift within the Catholic community. On 11 September Waugh published the following letter in Hickey's column. In explanation it should be said that Oldmeadow had claimed to be, and certainly was, speaking with Cardinal Bourne's approval when he had attacked *Black Mischief* in January 1933.

> Two aspects of *Tablet* article:–
> (a) an unfavourable criticism,
> (b) a moral lecture.
> The first is completely justifiable. A copy of my novel was sent to the *Tablet* for review, and the editor is therefore entitled to give his opinion of its literary quality in any terms he thinks suitable.
> In the second aspect he is in the position of a valet masquerading in his master's clothes. Long employment by a Prince of the Church has tempted him to ape his superiors, and, naturally enough, he gives an uncouth and impudent performance.

. DESERT AND FOREST .

Most modern travel books are the work, not of travellers who feel compelled to write, but of writers who feel compelled to travel. Of these some are ruminative intellectuals such as Mr Aldous Huxley who find in unfamiliar experiences the stimulus for reconsidering the familiar, who find in stunted forms and exotic overgrowths types which lead them to a new understanding of the forms of their own civilization; others, such as Mr Peter Fleming, are reporters whose main concern is selective, to find odd and exciting things abroad that can be purveyed for the amusement of readers at home. Both schools, typified by the exponents I have named, provide delightful reading, but pure travel literature is a narrower thing, narrower in its scope of both writer and reader. Mr Nesbitt's book is a fine example of this class. He is not a professional writer on a holiday, but an explorer whose adventures, of themselves, demand expression; and the proof of this is in the fact that during the course of his story he seems to be teaching himself to write. The last sections are greatly superior in ease and

Review of *Desert and Forest*, by L. M. Nesbitt. *Spectator*, 28 September 1934.

decision of style to the first. As the narrative becomes more direct, more austere, and abandons any attempt at reflection and comment, it becomes part of the journey itself, arid and exacting in places, as the very ground he covered, almost dull, but with the dead monotony of the trail, painful with the acute hardships his party suffered.

The journey was undertaken in 1928, from the Amharic plateau of Abyssinia, north to the Italian Red Sea-board, through the Danakil country, a great part of which had never before been crossed successfully by a white man. In his preface Mr Nesbitt expresses his gratitude that he was born in time to find a country so dangerous and obscure. He was only just in time. Already the establishment of Haile Selassie's empire is extending the radius of safe conduct; already his descriptions of Addis Ababa are slightly out of date. (By the way, surely, the city was founded by Menelik, not as Mr Nesbitt states, by the late Empress.) His descriptions of the less reputable European community are still accurate, but this is a type of writing at which Mr Fleming and the reporter school hold a pre-eminence not easily to be shaken. It is when Mr Nesbitt, none too soon, gets on the road that the vital part of the book begins. From then onwards it is admirable; the day-to-day record of hardship, danger and loss could not be improved by any amount of wit or fine writing; perhaps it is a book for a smaller public than *Beyond the Mexique Bay* or *One's Company*, but to the libraries of that small public who value pure travel books this will be a notable addition. It is worth adding that, unlike many recent books of the kind, *Desert and Forest* is supplied with a first-class map and index; the photographs are all interesting and the drawings eminently suitable matter-of-fact topographical statements without any arty pretensions.

. EAST AND SOUTH .

Mr Sacheverell Sitwell and his brother are two of the very few living Englishmen who can describe architecture; it is a very gracious gift, requiring a keen visual memory, discernment and enterprise in taste, a sense of social standards, delicate accuracy of expression, and, unobtrusive at the back, a full technical scholarship of date and name and material. Mr Sitwell has these gifts in a high degree, though in *Touching the Orient* he has not given himself scope for their free exercise. It is a slight and tantalizing work consisting of six sketches, three of which, in their sub-titles – 'a preface to an unpublished poem', 'the first pages of a book upon Morocco', 'from *The Three Indies*, an unfinished book' – give promise of more to come. In their present form the outstanding features are the essay on the mosques of Cairo and a gruesome description of beggars at Relizane; both brilliant pieces of writing in very different modes. I am impelled, by the way, to protest against Mr Sitwell's treatment of Fez, which he

Review of *Touching the Orient*, by Sacheverell Sitwell, *South to Cadiz*, by H. M. Tomlinson, and *Grand Tour*, by Patrick Balfour. *Spectator*, 7 December 1934.

compares to the poetical Hell of Dante. The Fazis as I know them are anything but 'the wicked who have all our sympathy . . . condemned for ever to live over and repeat their lives . . .' where punishment is 'not separation from each other, but just the hopelessness of any change in their lot.' Those serene old men whom he saw jogging along the streets become extremely optimistic over their dinner; they are much richer than Mr Sitwell or me, and they have the jolliest ideas of how to employ their leisure; they can outface any race in the world in commercial negotiation; every year or so they travel down to Tangier, change into bowler hats and black suits and embark on a profitable but slightly lugubrious journey to Manchester; they return with their business completed and eagerly change back into their white robes; at home a shabby, scarcely noticeable door in a high white wall opens into a courtyard of light tiles and running water, and beyond it, in a cool drawing-room furnished with brass bedsteads and cuckoo clocks, they can forget the inferno of western life of which they have had a glimpse.

It seems to me a pity that Mr Tomlinson chose Spain for his holidays; when the telephone 'whispered' to him (and who ever heard a telephone whisper?) he should surely have suggested a tramp in the Cotswolds or a cruise in the Norwegian fjords, for his ingenuous and whimsical mind, as revealed in *South to Cadiz*, was radically unsuited to deal with anything as alien as Spain; still less with Spain of the sixteenth century, which is inevitably the tourist's preoccupation. Of course, many entertaining travel books have resulted through their authors visiting unsuitable countries, but the trouble here is that Mr Tomlinson's bewilderment of impression has got into his writing. It is very difficult to believe that this book is the work of a mature and respected writer. The phrases are involved and slovenly, the metaphors mixed, the sentences in gross defiance of analysis. The Economic Congress in London, which was the alternative to this charabanc tour, is described as a 'new attempt to save the triumphs of industrial civilization from adding to the beauties of the hanging gardens of Babylon.' When a friend pushed some glasses away from him he 'retired our parade of tumblers two paces to the rear.' The driver of their bus 'poured it round the sharp bends of city streets as though the thing were an articulated reptile.' He describes the fortifications of Toledo as so secure that only birds could have got in and out 'when a righteous conviction was alert.' This of Toledo Cathedral: 'The piers are of granite, pale and emphasized in a dusk, and left to night'; of Seville: 'One is glad that among the animating chances in a lifetime that city was part of the luck.' There is a *gaucherie* which eventually becomes so painful that the book is barely readable.

Mr Balfour is refreshingly free from conceit or conceits. His *Grand Tour* is the diary of an extensive and highly amusing journey through Syria, Iraq, Persia, Afghanistan, India, Malaya and Siam. The first part was spent in a motor-car with a haphazard collection of companions, whose idiosyncrasies and adventures Mr Balfour describes with excellent wit. I admired the description of Miss Jumble, 'imperturbable as a tea-cosy'. Manfred, another companion, drove the car 'in and out and over the crossings with spectacular deftness and speed, like an expert needlewoman.' What a difference from Mr Tomlinson's driver pouring reptiles round corners. There is a lot about food in *Grand Tour*: too much for some readers, but not too much for me. I applaud the Persian's constitution who is awaked every morning by his servant squirting into his mouth a mixture of warm milk, whisky and honey so that 'his first conscious sensation each day is the taste of nectar.' I wish there was space for fuller quotation of the many enchanting observations: the melancholy consular clerk in Kandahar is unforgettable; as is the Andaman social custom 'by which relatives, on meeting, sit in one another's laps for a considerable time, first in silence and subsequently in floods of tears.' The book is full of excellent photographs, many of them taken in Nepal before the earthquake and presumably unique.

. AN AMERICAN SHOCKER .

In writing this new volume about the Rossettis the authoress has had access to no sources that are not already extensively known. A glance at the bibliography at the end shows that she has been content to jot down what is apparently a list of most of the books she has ever read (whether or no they have any direct bearing on her subject) and a few which, it is kinder to assume, she has not. The most notable omission is Miss Violet Hunt's life of Elizabeth Siddal, without a critical reading of which no survey of Rossetti's early years can be adequate. Miss Winwar, however, has made use of most of the stock authorities, and has followed the path made easy for her by numerous admirable predecessors, of reboiling the matter and dishing it up in saleable form. The book need not, therefore, be judged by any very high standard. All we look for in the authoress is a decent level of general culture, an agreeable style and a scrupulous honesty about facts. There is no need to go beyond the first chapter to see how far Miss Winwar comes up to our expectations.

General culture: the Pre-Raphaelites, as is well known, drew up a list of 'Immortals'. This included the name of the painter, Giovanni Bellini. Miss Winwar writes as follows: 'Bellini loomed big in solitude to represent the musicians.'

Style: Miss Winwar has chosen an attitude of the greatest familiarity with her subject. Everyone is spoken of by his or her Christian name, even Millais's mother; conversations are inserted some of which are quoted or misquoted from contemporary sources, while others are the invention of the authoress. There is no indication offered as to when she is quoting and when she is improvising. For example, she composes a hideously vulgar piece of stump oratory, which she puts into the mouth of Gabriel Rossetti:

Review of *The Rossettis and Their Circle*, by Frances Winwar. *Spectator*, 11 January 1935.

'We must protest against the intellectual emptiness of our so-called painters. We must protest in deed as well as in thought. Look at the stunners in the Campo Santo of Pisa. Have we anything like them now? No! It is for us to bring dignity and sincerity back to art; for us to strip art of conventionality.'

'But how can you –'

'– and to go back to Nature, not to what others have done before us! We must be sincere in our invention, truthful in our representation. We must be Early Christian – Pre Raphaelite!'

'Yea, Pre Raphaelite,' came the stirring chorus.

Honesty: Miss Winwar has decided to make Mrs Millais the main theme of the first chapter. She calls her Emily and affects to know exactly what was going on inside the lady's mind. She describes Mrs Millais's emotions and thoughts on the occasion when John Millais first locked his studio door against her, in order that he might work undisturbed, and introduces Rossetti to the reader at some length as the undesirable companion who has led Johnny to rebellion. This is all very well, and might perhaps be justified in the general looseness of American literary propriety, were it in accord with the facts. The truth, however, is that Millais locked out his parents in the early spring of 1848, and it was not until late summer that Hunt first brought Rossetti to his home at all.

In the same episode the authoress shows a further example of misuse of her facts. She writes: 'Emily listened anxiously, and pleaded to be let in. "I appeal to you, Hunt," she whimpered. "Is that the way for Johnny to treat his mother?"' The authority for this scene is Hunt himself, and a reference to his account shows that the words used were: 'Is that the way to treat parents?' Moreover, far from 'whimpering', Mrs Millais is described as 'full of fire'. Thus, in order to make the character ridiculous, Miss Winwar has deliberately falsified her evidence.

Later in the chapter, when Rossetti exhibits *The Girlhood of the Virgin* at the Free Exhibition instead of at the Academy, 'Emily murmured, and in her murmuring was the word "treason".' Then follows a speech put into Mrs Millais's mouth which is a paraphrase of her remarks actually made a year later, when 'treason' might very fairly be used, on the occasion of Rossetti revealing to Munro the meaning of the initials P.R.B.

All these faults occur in the first eight and a half pages of a longish book. None but the grossly uncharitable would wish to carry their examination further. But there is one particularly gloomy aspect which must be noted. On the wrapper of the book it is prominently announced that Miss Winwar has been awarded a £1,000 prize, and that this shocking work was selected from over 800 manuscripts. It is not revealed by whom the prize was offered or who made the selection. Perhaps the name was drawn out of a hat. But if, as it is reasonable to assume, this book was chosen for its superior merit, the mind reels at the thought of the unsuccessful 800.

. THE FIRST TIME I WENT TO THE NORTH .
FIASCO IN THE ARCTIC

As soon as we crossed the Arctic circle, it grew warmer. The sun streamed through the porthole all night, making sleep difficult. At Svalbad they were selling ice-cream on the quay. At Tromso, where we disembarked, it was hotter than at any place where we had stopped since Newcastle. Most of the little towns on the way north had been dry. At Tromso there were no bars or cafés, but we were able to buy a bottle of spirits, named '60%', which we took to our hotel. There were three of us. Hugh [Lygon] and I sat in our shirt-sleeves in his bedroom playing piquet and drinking '60%' while G.,[1] who was leader of the expedition, went to see a man about a boat. That evening we took the British Consul, who was a Norwegian, to the cinema.

Next day the government ship left for Spitzbergen. She is a minute, very clean little steamer. She makes the journey three times in the year. The captain gave us each a glass of Benedictine on the first evening, and the mate practised his English on us. 'I think your King has many children,' he said. 'Your Prince of Wales has no wife. The English people are greatly devoted to the monarchy.' He examined our maps and cameras and guns, our boat and our sledge which were lashed to the deck amidships. 'I think you will have a very interesting expedition,' he said. 'You are students of science or sportsmen?'

It was three days from Tromso to Spitzbergen, in heavy seas. There was some mail on board for the meteorological station on Bear Island, but it was too rough to put out a boat. When we reached Spitzbergen the sun was invisible behind low clouds. The cliffs were black, striped with snow like zebra-hide. We reached harbour at midnight; sunless, grey daylight; no one stirring; it was as cold as an English February, no worse.

There are two coal-mines on opposite sides of the bay; one belongs to Soviet Russia, the other to Norway. Apart from these the islands are uninhabited; trappers have a few cabins dotted about the coast which they visit from time to time during the winter. There are no police or government officials; the mining company administers law and social services. There are, in the Norwegian station, four or five hundred miners and thirty or forty women. They sign on for seven years. During that time they eat and sleep in barracks, and buy what they need from the company's store. During the winter it is dark all round the clock, the harbour is sealed up and they get no mail. There is a weekly cinema and weekly steam bath; a monthly bottle of whisky. They earn big wages and retire to Norway at the end of their seven years with substantial savings unless

Theodora Benson, ed., *The First Time I . . .* (London, 1935).
1 Sandy Glen, later Sir Alexander Glen, leader of the Oxford University Arctic Expedition, 1935-6. The trip described here was a preliminary to that expedition. See A. R. Glen, *Young Men in the Arctic: The Oxford University Arctic Expedition to Spitzbergen 1933* (London: Faber, 1935), p.227, where Glen comments on Waugh's inability to ski or to eat pemmican, and on his admirable endurance and unshakable pessimism.

they have lost them at poker. I met one man who had signed on three times running. He had no luck at cards. The women usually leave after three years; they make a bit too. There is an officer class of engineers who live in a comfortable mess.

But there was no one about when we landed. All we saw was an irregular street of timber buildings. It smelled a little. When we returned, after living on the ice, that was the first thing we noticed, the rank, fetid smell of human kind.

Generally speaking, there are two degrees of loneliness which affect the treatment of strangers. Communities that are fairly isolated are extravagantly pleased to see an outsider; those who are absolutely isolated find him a nuisance. We were a nuisance to the miners, but they treated us, nevertheless, with faultless courtesy.

G. had arranged for a sealer to take us up the coast to a bay on the west, where there were some huts erected by a prospecting company; they had been empty for twenty-five years, but were still in a fair state of preservation. Two previous expeditions had used them as base-store. There was still a length of rail connecting them with the beach and two or three rusty trolleys. The men from the sealer helped us land our stores and pull the boat up on to the shingle. We had provisions for about six weeks, a tent that had been used on the Everest expedition, the boat and a sledge. The plan was to work up a glacier and sledge across the inland ice to some unexplored territory on the north-east. Hugh and I were new to the north; G. had been there before.

The sealer chugged off. It was a desolate bit of shore, hung about with white fog, which sometimes lifted to reveal three or four big glaciers flowing down to the bay, between dark cliffs. We were on shingle, covered in places by moss, in places by snow. There was a small lake of fresh water behind the huts and a stream in front. It was a nesting-place for terns. The eggs lay all over the foreshore in shallow little pockets of gravel; some had already hatched out into flappers which tumbled about at our feet. It was difficult to avoid stepping on them; doubly difficult by reason of the assaults of the mother birds which kept our attention overhead. They hovered over us with shrill cries, lovely little white and grey birds with long tails that shut in a point and then flicked open in an attenuated V. They would drop suddenly on us, pecking the crowns of our balaclava helmets. Sometimes three or four would attack together, sweeping down in rapid succession and then wheeling off, high above us. It was not painful, but it was disconcerting. We found the best plan, when we went to draw water, was to carry an aluminium mess-tin on the end of a stick. This drew their attack while we stooped over the lake. The tins rang with the percussion of their beaks.

It was not particularly cold. G. tried to swim, but quickly scrambled out, blue and shuddering, saying that it had warmed him. We spent a day and a half repacking stores, lashing the sledge and waxing skis. G. had said that on the coast we could 'live on the country'. He and Hugh went out with their guns but came back empty-handed. There should have been duck and ptarmigan.

'Living on the country' and telling the time by the sun are common delusions of travellers. Late the second evening we set out in the boat and rowed for two or three hours across the bay, into another smaller bay where there was another derelict hut. Seals bobbed up in the water all round us; there were innumerable small icebergs, some white and fluffy, others deep green and blue like weathered copper, some opaque, some clear as glass, in preposterous shapes, with fragile, haphazard wings and feathers of ice, pierced by holes. The whole bay was filled with their music, sometimes a shrill cricket-cry, sometimes a sharp, almost regular metallic ticking, sometimes the low hum of a hive of bees, sometimes a sharp splintering, sometimes a resonant boom, coming from the shore where another crag of ice broke away from the underhung glaciers. The fog cleared about midnight, the sun lay on the horizon and in the superb Arctic light, that is both dawn and sunset, the ice face shone clear and blue to the white snow above it and the water was dense indigo.

The moraine of the glacier which we proposed to ascend was three miles from our landing-place; between us lay a mosquito-infested valley of mud and sharp stones over which we had to carry the stores on our backs. We made two journeys a day, taking between thirty and forty pounds in a load. It was beastly work. On the second night we had everything we needed at the foot of the moraine. Then followed some hours scrambling up and down over the precipitous wet gravel and rocks; at last everything was on the ice. We had been working twelve hours that day, because, in addition to the portering, we had spent most of the morning struggling to drag the boat clear of a possible high tide, with the aid of block and pulley and a series of stakes that would not hold in the loose shingle. Once on the ice, however, we felt that our worst labours were over; we wanted to make a start and camp out of sight of the bay and the atrocious mud valley. We loaded the sledge, spread the tarpaulin covers, lashed everything firm and prepared to start. Two of us went in front harnessed to ropes; a third stood behind holding the runners, to steer, push and see that none of the load worked loose. Tired, but light-hearted, we got into position; G. gave the word to start. We strained forward. The sledge stood immovable as rock. The two in front had ice axes. We bent down as though starting for a sprint, drove the axes in ahead of us to pull on; G., behind, heaved at the runners; the sledge moved six inches and again stuck. We changed the course, striking a traverse across the slope; we changed the traverse until it barely diverged from the horizontal. Then with the utmost labour we were able to get the thing along. We worked for two hours, tacking back and forward across the slope. At the end of that time we were spent. Our first camp lay a few hundred yards from the edge of the moraine. Next day we decided to relay the stores in two loads. In this way we travelled for a week, monotonously, working for ten hours a day and covering, on an average, about five miles.

Our difficulty, G. explained, was due to the exceptional thaw. There was never a moment when the sledge could run free. The ice was rough and hummocky, broken by rivulets, which sometimes overturned us, and sometimes necessitated unpacking, wading and repacking. The snow was soggy so that even on skis we sank in; much of the journey was over knee-deep *levé*, a kind of fine shingle of ice pebbles. At first G. promised us better conditions when we reached the northern slopes, but he was disappointed. It was now intensely cold; everything got wet, tent floor, clothes, bedding, and could not be dried. Most of the time we were enveloped in white mist which rendered our direction doubtful, but whenever it cleared the prospect was magnificent. We had two Primus stoves and ate twice a day – oatmeal, oranges, chocolate, tea, biscuits and pemmican. Pemmican derives its name from the dried reindeer flesh of the eskimos; now it is factory-made specially – and, I should imagine, exclusively – for Arctic and Antarctic expeditions. It is a very expensive, concentrated product of meat, fat and albumen. Its value, as revealed by chemical analysis, is stupendous. It is boiled in water; it remains suspended but undissolved, in a muddy broth; it must be constantly stirred to prevent its settling to the bottom; it leaves a coat of slime on spoons and dishes, which can be removed with industry. A noxious dish. Our stores also included three seven-pound tins of margarine. G. assured us that we should have a craving for fat as soon as we were on the ice. We did not find it so.

There were, however, some negative advantages of Arctic over tropical travel: the constant light, so that one was free from the anxiety of being overtaken at nightfall with one's camp unmade; so that instead of the twelve hours of black inactivity one could read and work without hindrance. Set against this was the fact that, however tired we were, sleep was very difficult in that bright, cold little tent. There was also the great cleanness of everything: cuts healed quickly; food remained fresh for weeks at a time; there were no insects, no microbes and no poisons, none of that unending warfare against corruption, the sterilizing and disinfecting, the iodine and the quinine, mosquito nets and snake boots, that impede one in the tropics.

The misfortune which ended the trip came quite suddenly. We had arrived at the foot of the glacier, known as the Martin Conway, up which we hoped to penetrate into the northern district; it proved to be so badly crevassed that ascent was impossible. Accordingly we turned west towards the shore, where, on the banks of Wijlde Bay, G. assured us, was a trappers' cabin and a boat left by his last expedition. In dense fog we began to descend a glacier. After a time we met a barrier of rock over which it was impossible to drag the sledge. We decided to push on to the hut, carrying on our backs our beds and provisions for a couple of days. We reached the shore and slept there, the fog being too thick for us to find the way. After a few hours it lifted. We pushed on, very tired, crossed a series of shallow streams, and about three miles further of rough going on the rocky shore brought us to a wide, shallow river and beyond it the cabin. It was smaller than G. had remembered it, the size of a *wagon lit* and extremely dirty. A single bunk gave accommodation for two lying feet to head; the third slept on the floor. In six or seven hours we awoke. A brief survey convinced us that G.'s boat was not there. We decided, however, to make the cabin our headquarters for the time and explore the surrounding hills, none of which had been mapped. Hugh and G. set off for the sledge to bring back further supplies, while I was left to get the cabin into order. I swept it clean of refuse, chopped up some driftwood that lay on the beach, cleaned the little stove, lay down on the furs that covered the bunk and fell asleep again. I was wakened by G., who was in a state of some agitation. Gradually, as we waded the river and tramped back up the bay, I gathered what had occurred. He and Hugh had got to the head of the bay, where they discovered that the series of little streams which we had crossed a few hours before had suddenly changed into a tearing flood. Hugh was a heavyweight boxer, of greatly superior physique to either G. or myself. He had managed to cross, but G. had been driven back. He had gone on to the sledge. It was certain he would not be able to get back to us, loaded, without assistance.

For half an hour before we reached it, we could hear the roar of the flood. When finally we stood on the bank the sound was so great that we could barely make ourselves heard, shouting in each other's ears. The flow was terrific, of no great depth as yet, and still divided by shingle banks into four or five streams, but running at a dizzy speed, full of boulders and blocks of ice, whirling down in it.

G. and I tied ourselves together round the waist. The climbing ropes were on the sledge, but we had found some tarred twine in the cabin which provided us with a treble length of about a dozen paces. First one of us waded in, the other paying him out from the shallow water. Half-way across the stream came to our middles and it was impossible to stand without the support of the cord; when the first was in shallow water, he pulled the other across; the cold was so intense that we did not feel the ice-blocks that pounded against us. In this way we reached the final channel. Hugh was already in sight with a laden pack. We threw him the string on a ski-stick and managed to drag him across. Then we began the return journey. At the last channel, after G. had got across, the twine broke in several places. Hugh and I were swept down, tumbled over and over. I had time to form the clear impression that we were both done for, when I found myself rolling in shallow water and was able to crawl ashore. Hugh was stuck on a small iceberg in midstream. There did not seem to be any way of helping him. We shouted to him to throw away his pack. But he got to his feet and came across, fully loaded. Uncertain memories of how we got back to the hut. At one time we seem to have rubbed one another with sand to get back our circulations. Our jaws were out of control, set tight with cold or chattering, so that we could not speak. Eventually we got into our sleeping-bags and slept. Our watches had been broken in the flood so that from now onwards we had no means of telling the time. We do not know how long we slept. When we awoke we found we could scarcely move from stiffness and bruises. Hugh had come off the worst with a badly swollen knee. For about twenty-four hours we lay in the cabin, two on the bunk, one on the floor, alternately dozing and investigating our injuries. Then we began to review our situation. G. said that the flood was temporary, due to the bursting of some ice-dam in the hills. When we felt better he and I hobbled up and found it deeper and stronger than before. It seemed clear that it would only cease with the thaw. Hugh could not possibly move for some days. We had pemmican and paraffin for three days' normal rations, enough to support life on for a fortnight or more. The trapper was not due at his hut for about a month, when he would probably arrive to revictual for the winter. There were three plans open to us: to attempt another crossing of the river to the sledge, to wait in semi-starvation for the return of the trapper, to abandon the sledge and tent and attempt a journey over the ice, behind the river to our original base, where we had left stores and the boat. All had abundant disadvantages. The decision depended largely upon Hugh's knee. We cut down rations to a subsistence basis and waited four days. Then he proclaimed himself able to walk. We took our beds and the remains of the provisions and tramped slowly to the river. It was worse than ever. We were still suffering from the effects of our previous crossing and weak from four days' under-feeding; with packs and without a line we should clearly never get across. G. maintained a pathetic belief in the abatement of the flood, but Hugh and I knew that this was its normal condition and that we had found it passable on the first morning only by reason of some ice-block higher up, forming a momentary dam. G. wished to build a turf cabin and wait for another occurrence of the same kind. Hugh and I voted for the mountain journey. I did not think it would be successful, but it seemed preferable to waiting. This essay might be called 'the first time I despaired of my life'. In fact, we did the journey in three days, without an adequate map, without tent, climbing rope, ice axes, crampons, with half a bowl of pemmican once a day as our only ration. I might also have called this article 'the first time that I felt really tired'.

4

. POLITICAL DECADE .

CORRESPONDENT, RIGHT-WING JOURNALIST, SOLDIER

FEBRUARY 1935 - JUNE 1945

I was not brought up to regard the evasion of the police as the prime aim of education, nor has my subsequent observation of the world given me any reason to think that either the wickedest men or even the worst citizens are to be found in prison. The real enemies of society are sitting snug behind typewriters and microphones pursuing their work of destruction amid popular applause.

From 'Religion in State Schools', *New Statesman and Nation*, 16 October 1943

. INTRODUCTION .

'I have never voted in a parliamentary election' ('Aspirations of a Mugwump', 2 October 1959).

'The greatest danger I went through in the Hitler war was that of becoming one of Churchill's young men, of getting a medal and standing for parliament; if things had gone as then seemed right . . . that is what I should be now' (*Diaries*, 7 May 1945).

The 'Pinfold' *persona* Waugh created in the 1950s and 1960s so overshadowed his former public selves that the first utterance came to typify him completely; while the second, when printed in 1976, struck most readers as grotesquely out of character. Yet at any time from 1935 to the early 1940s Waugh's style of life and writing was quite consistent with an ambition to sit in the House. It was the period when the formerly footloose author 'settled down'; when, having for several years owned 'no more than would fit on a porter's barrow', he decided, as he wrote to Alec, on 'marrying, procreating and purchasing property' (*Letters*, 1937). He also went into a political phase.

Having married, Waugh needed money badly. Four years separated *A Handful of Dust* (1934) from *Scoop* (1938), and *Scoop* from *Put Out More Flags* (1942), long intervals between novels that, while well regarded, were not yet gold mines. *Edmund Campion* (1935) was a gift to the Jesuits of Campion Hall; *Waugh in Abyssinia* (1936) and *Robbery Under Law* (1939) were only modestly profitable. By 1939 when the fighting broke out, Waugh was deep in debt. In the period from 1936, after his correspondentship in Abyssinia had ended, until 1939, when he joined the army, Waugh was eager for any journalism he could get. But jobs were scarce. A soldier has little opportunity for magazine work; and the success of *Put Out More Flags* in 1942 removed money worries, thus undermining a principal motive for writing articles.

The journalism of the period 1935–46 can therefore be all too easily summarized: covering the war in Abyssinia for the *Daily Mail* from August to November 1935; a dozen reviews in the *Tablet* intermittently from 1936; a book page in *Night and Day* from July to December 1937; a weekly review for the *Spectator* from March to July 1938, and others from time to time; a series of 'General Conversations', light weekly articles on subjects of Waugh's own choosing (what Waugh called a 'jam job'), from March 1937 in *Nash's Pall Mall Magazine* and drifting, after *Nash's* demise, into fairly regular articles for *Harper's Bazaar* until 1939. In addition there was a handful of assorted features and reviews, one of which, 'Commando Raid on Bardia' (17 November 1941), created a sensation. It is tempting to say that the outstanding journalism of the period was right-wing advocacy and Catholic polemic, because these were new to Waugh and characteristic of the period; but general reviewing also developed, for Waugh was now moved by the books he read to express a viewpoint on the issues they raised. Light articles altered least.

Society journalism follows the pattern Waugh had already established, and its few developments can be briefly noted. The implied author is no longer an *enfant terrible* or Bright Young Thing, but a householder or clubman. 'The New Rustics' (July 1939) and 'Well-Informed Circles – and How to Move in Them' (January 1939) most clearly exemplify the change. Many articles were light, mildly ironical pieces on the agonies of Christmas, or of wedding presents, such as countless English writers once produced effortlessly. Some 'articles', such as 'The Philistine Age of English Decoration' (March 1938) and 'A Call to the Orders' (26 February 1938) were in reality essays, revealing Waugh as very well read in the subjects that interested him. A few pieces, like 'Laying Down a Wine Cellar' (December 1937), betray a proclivity towards fine writing which was to come to full bloom in *Brideshead Revisited*. (So disliked was 'fine writing' in the 1930s that an American magazine's 'most hardened critic' claimed not to have been able 'to read thru' this article.)

Reviewing became clearly marked by the politics of the decade, by Waugh's growing involvement with his religion and, as has been said, by his new willingness to use reviews as the occasion for expressing a personal viewpoint on a wide variety of matters. Furthermore, not only are a high proportion of reviews opinionated, but the best opinionated writing is found·in reviews. *Night and Day* and the *Tablet* carried a number of criticisms of the prominent left-wing writers who, as Waugh often said, 'ganged up and captured the decade': typical are the examinations of Marxist belief in C. Day-Lewis's *The Mind in Chains*, and of obsessive anti-Fascism in Cyril Connolly's *Enemies of Promise*. An attack on Harold Laski's *Faith, Reason and Civilization* is one of the best examples of Waugh's destructive analyses. The most informative explanation of his stand on Abyssinia is found in a long review of Marshal de Bono's *Anno XIIII*. Many other topics arise: war and pacifism, Mass Observation and democracy; Mexico; suicide; and a non-Bellocian view of sixteenth-century England. Purely literary reviewing also advanced in insight and expression. Discussions of Edward Lear, Lewis Carroll and P. G. Wodehouse might throw some light on the workings of Waugh's own strain of fantasy. Among new writers, W. H. Auden and Aldous Huxley are regularly chastised; but most others, including prominent Marxists like Arthur Calder-Marshall and Christopher Isherwood, are dealt with appreciatively, notably Edith Sitwell, Georges Bernanos and Malcolm Muggeridge. Waugh was ahead of his time in enthusiastically welcoming David Jones's *In Parenthesis*.

Catholicism grew more influential in Waugh's life at this time, partly (we may presume) because of marriage into a Catholic family and because of deepening intimacy with the attractively religious Asquith family and their circle at Mells, but principally because what had been accepted as an intellectually satisfying explanation of the universe now took on personal importance. Certainly *Edmund Campion* (1935) marks a new level of religious commitment – and, less importantly, the wholesale adoption of what might, in shorthand, be called a Bellocian view of English history. Nevertheless, specifically religious journalism is still infrequent. A letter defending *Edmund Campion* and Desmond MacCarthy, who had favourably reviewed the biography over the BBC, against Protestant attacks forcefully amplifies the thesis of the book. A review of *Thomas Platter's Travels in Tudor England* recants *Campion*'s Bellocianism. The second of two reports about the Budapest Eucharistic Congress expresses a sympathy with common humanity not otherwise found outside *Helena*. Omitted here are two letters to the *New Statesman* defending religious schools against Marie Stopes (Marie Stopes had once written to the *Tablet* endorsing Ernest Oldmeadow's condemnation of *Black Mischief*); a letter to the *Tablet* questioning a 'miracle' reported by credulous clergy (*Letters*, 14 December 1937); and an account of Waugh's first visit to the Holy Land (with two letters defending his article against attacks in the *Tablet*), which is subsumed in 'The Defence of the Holy Places' (March 1952).

A very important development was forming a connection with the leading English Roman Catholic weekly, the *Tablet*. In the early 1930s the *Tablet* had been owned by the Catholic Primate of Great Britain and edited by Ernest Oldmeadow, a man liberal in political outlook but strictly puritanical about literature: he had sternly attacked *Black Mischief, A Handful of Dust* and Waugh's despatches to the *Daily Mail* from the Abyssinian front. In 1936 the paper was bought by a group of conservative laymen and the editorship given to Douglas Woodruff, one of Waugh's Oxford contemporaries. In Waugh's words the *Tablet*, which had shrunk to a 'narrowly sectarian and obscure position' under Oldmeadow, was raised by Woodruff to 'esteem and influence . . . as the most serious and trenchant Tory journalism surviving today' (3 April 1932). Waugh now had a civilized, welcoming medium – with a readership somewhat restricted to conservative Catholics – and he took advantage of it to express himself freely: more freely and sharply, indeed, than seemed prudent or charitable to the editor (see 'Judge and Jury Must Decide . . .', *Evelyn Waugh and His World*, ed. David Pryce Jones, London, 1973). Some of Waugh's most self-revealing work therefore appeared in the *Tablet*. As well, its correspondents who were in close touch with eastern Europe during and after the Second World War, and some of the profoundly intelligent conservatives who wrote for it on economic matters, may have influenced Waugh's political opinions.

Conservative politics and Roman Catholicism seriously entered Waugh's journalism together in the mid-1930s. In the years following many issues – the civil war in Spain, persecution of Catholics by the Marxist government of Mexico, the ceding of eastern Europe to Stalinist Russian hegemony – involved direct clashes between the Roman Catholic Church and Marxist regimes. Furthermore, educated Catholics then believed Christian theology and Marxist ideology to be involved in a war that far transcended in importance any localized dispute. Waugh loyally defended Catholics persecuted by Marxist governments and he attacked Marxism from a theistic viewpoint as when reviewing Harold Laski (22 April 1944). But he had been a conservative before he became a Roman Catholic, and his conservatism developed independently of his religion. The classic conservative thinkers were his political mentors. A significant difference between Waugh and most contemporary Catholics was that while they were much influenced by the popes' social encyclicals, he was not. It is incorrect, therefore, to treat his political attitudes, e.g. support for Italy against Abyssinia, as 'clerical–Fascist', or even as a simple extension of his Catholicism, for in this case the *Tablet* and the *Month* both strongly supported Abyssinia and the League of Nations. A conservative 'manifesto', taken from *Robbery Under Law* (1939), is appended to this introduction. It puts a specific meaning on a term which, undefined, is virtually meaningless, and states the principles assumed in most of Waugh's political writing.

The political journalism deals mainly with the Abyssinia crisis (Yugoslavia, and by implication the whole of eastern Europe, arises in 1945 but receives most attention after 1946) and with the ideologies of Marxism and anti-Fascism. Equally significant are some of Waugh's silences, about Spain by choice, and about Mexico because newspapers showed absolute non-interest in the subject. Firm opinions on a variety of other political matters, e.g. Fascism and democratic electoral processes, emerge, but only incidentally, in the course of more general discussions.

Early in 1935 increasing tension between Italy and Abyssinia was making war seem inevitable. As a popular novelist with Abyssinian experience, Waugh hoped for a correspondentship, and with it the chance of writing a really 'big' book about the conflict. 'Abyssinian Realities: We Can Applaud Italy' (13 February 1935), which was written at Waugh's suggestion and tailored to Lord Beaverbrook's policy (letter from Peters to Waugh, 25 January 1935), was probably intended to elicit an offer of work. But on 12 July 1935 Waugh was still asking Peters to 'get a correspondentship in Abyssinia for the coming war'. Shortly after that date the *Daily Mail* engaged Waugh (Lord Northcliffe having quarrelled with his paper's, and the journalistic profession's, brightest star, Sir Percival Phillips). Did Mrs Stitch jog Lord Copper's memory about *The Times*'s 'distinguished' reports of Haile Selassie's coronation? Perhaps, because Douglas Woodruff reports that what Waugh had written on that occasion 'caused him to be approached by the *Daily Mail*'. A large advance of £950 was now forthcoming, Longmans having outbid Rich and Cowan to secure the book. Everything seemed set for success. But over the coming months Waugh became a partisan of the unpopular side; more accurately, he set himself in opposition to British Government policies, misconceived (as he understood them) in response to the unreasoned indignation most Englishmen felt on Abyssinia's behalf. The result was bitter disappointment of every expectation.

Sixty cables appeared in the *Daily Mail* – and a few in the *Overseas Mail* – between 24 August and 20 November 1935. At first they were very prominently displayed. Later, when the agencies had better news than the special correspondents, who were held in Addis Ababa far from the fighting, Waugh's cables were used to support their stories. Later still, when Italian victory was imminent, news from the Italian side of the front took precedence over news from the Abyssinian side. Waugh's despatches generally read as well as most others. The second printed here is a spy story that should have been a scoop. Unhappily, when Waugh was away chasing it, news broke of vast oil and mineral concessions made to American interests, which could have had political consequences devastating to Italy. The concessions were the news story of the war, and they had been arranged by F. W. Rickett, an English businessman who shared Waugh's *pension*, and who had repeatedly promised him 'important news'. Believing further postponements of the news inevitable, Waugh had travelled to Harar in (successful) search of his spy. The next two despatches illustrate Waugh's habit of 'balancing' his stories with details damaging to the Abyssinians. This habit sometimes led to (what seemed to many) meanly petty anti-Abyssinian reports. The editor of the *Tablet* objected, for example, to Waugh's (apparent) ridiculing of rain-soaked Abyssinian school children at the Mascal ('End-of-Rains') Feast. Waugh had hard luck as a reporter. Famously, his advance news of the commencement of fighting was cabled in Latin to circumvent the opposition; the sub-editor could not recognize Latin, and Waugh was rebuked for a prank instead of being fêted for a scoop. But his failures as a news-gatherer – which Waugh greatly over-exaggerated – did him far less harm than did the ineptly hostile reports. They gained him a reputation for mere unintelligent prejudice, which endured. On his death in 1966 the *Guardian* still insisted that he had been in Ethiopia as a war correspondent 'with views that might have been more acceptable in a novelist than a reporter.'

Waugh in Abyssinia proves that judgment unfair, as does the journalism that followed it. The opening chapter, one of the most lucid and forceful essays of its time, is widely admitted to be an excellent exposition of the historical and political factors involved in the dispute. The closing chapter, which is based on a tour of Abyssinia from 18 August to 9 September 1936, when Waugh was the only notable English-speaking journalist in the country, is a unique view of the country immediately after Italian victory – and, it should be added, *before* savage Italian reprisals against Abyssinian resistance had begun. The concluding paragraphs of the book, the so-called 'hymn' to the stupendous road system being built across Abyssinia by the Italians, is very similar in sense to a letter by George Bernard Shaw, 'The Barbarians v. the Engineers', printed in *The Times* and reprinted in the *British–Italian Bulletin* on 27 December 1935. But *Waugh in Abyssinia* was too pro-Italian to sell well in England. To Waugh's intense annoyance, and despite strenuous efforts, it could not find a United States publisher at all, a Bobbs-Merril editor giving what was no doubt the real reason for many more polite refusals: 'Waugh seems to like the Italians and I don't and I don't imagine very many other people do – at least as regards their adventuring in Empire' (letter to Carol Hill, 11 December 1936). No newspaper would accept an article on Abyssinia, even after Waugh's second journey, when his material was unique.

Such journalism as did follow the book was a letter to *The Times* and reviews in the *Tablet* and in a low-paying quarterly. It had no chance of influencing opinion, but it does demonstrate the strength of Waugh's conviction, and usefully clarifies his thinking. Public opinion was preoccupied with two things: Abyssinia's right to protection as a member of the League of Nations, and detestation of Mussolini's Fascism. It seemed essential to uphold the authority of the League and to check a Fascist government's expansion. Catholic conservatives saw the situation differently. To them Mussolini appeared not so much the embodiment of Fascism, but Hitler's rival. Italian military strength, which then looked formidable, seemed the only barrier preventing Nazi Germany's annexing Catholic Austria. To oppose Italy's ambitions to empire on account of the League, or on account of generalized dislike of Fascism, seemed to them, and to Waugh, a course certain to have three results: to strengthen the war party in Italy and provoke military adventure; to encourage Abyssinia to endure appalling suffering fighting an unwinnable war; and to drive Mussolini into alliance with Hitler, with consequent sacrifice of Austria. All of these things did happen. Liberals believe other, graver evils resulted from England's not having opposed Mussolini more strongly. The argument will go on. But his journalism forbids the too easy assumption that Waugh adopted the position he did either out of blind anti-Abyssinian bigotry, or out of love of Fascism. When he wrote to Nancy Mitford on 16 March 1948, 'I am so weary about having been consistently right in all my political predictions for ten years', he was neither totally unserious, nor totally wrong.

'Appendix VIII' (28 February 1936), a statement about Abyssinian misuse of the Red Cross sign, was made by Waugh for inclusion in an Official Note addressed by the Italian Government to the League of Nations protesting against Abyssinian atrocities. It is the strongest published evidence against Waugh of having supported – as distinct from having understood the case of – Italy. To be fairly judged its drily factual words must be read in context, where they contrast with colourful accusations of mutilation, emasculation and skinning alive. The Statement was printed in the *British–Italian Bulletin*, a Soho Fascist paper, normally published in Italian, but brought out in English during the Abyssinia crisis.

The Spanish Civil War drew from Waugh neither article, nor review, nor letter, but only an answer to a questionnaire. In reply to the question, 'Are you for or against Franco and Fascism?' he replied coolly that he was 'not in the position of choosing between two evils' (1937). No issue since the French Revolution has excited and divided the British public so violently as the Spanish War. Educated opinion was overwhelmingly against Franco, whose victory, it was believed, would mean an unendurable extension of the evils of Italian and German Fascism. Catholic and many other conservatives, on the other hand, saw the results of a Republican victory as the setting up of a Soviet client state at the gateway to the Mediterranean, and the installation of a Marxist government dedicated to obliterating Christianity by the most savage means. It was from the extreme passion of the debate over Spain that organized Roman Catholic resistance movements against communism sprang. Waugh's silence about the war was resented by more conventional co-religionists. It would be reasonable to suppose that he was restrained by prudent consideration for his sales, for, having made himself unpopular over Abyssinia, he had taken care, when promoting the forthcoming *Scoop* in 1937, to promise 'No more Fascist propaganda.' But the truth is that he genuinely disliked Franco and Fascism, a dislike vividly expressed in the sour picture of Spanish government in *Scott-King's Modern Europe* (1947), and conclusively proved by his diary covering the visit on which the novel is based. The description of Franco and Fascism as 'the lesser of two evils' was not an evasion but a frank and exact statement.

In mid-1938 an English company with oil and agricultural interests in Mexico commissioned Waugh to write a book attacking the Mexican Government's expropriation of their holdings. *Robbery Under Law* came out in the following year. It is an eccentric book, in which political and economic argument of Macaulay-like force and clarity mingles with an apologia for the Roman Catholic Church in Mexico (then severely persecuted) and for the Spanish element in Mexican life. The dominating ethos of the work is conservative. Mexico's former prosperity and civilization is shown declining through a series of 'progressive' regimes into the poverty and chaos of the 1930s. England, it is suggested, will follow Mexico's example if conservative influence is excluded from the national life. Though Waugh tried very hard to sell articles about Mexico, going to the extent, unusual for him, of circulating summaries of his proposals, no editor could be induced to show interest. A review of Graham Greene's *The Lawless Roads* (10 March 1939) and a letter following it contain the germ of Waugh's thinking; apart from reprints from the book in the *Tablet*, these were the only writings on Mexico printed.

The war did not entirely put a stop to journalism. General reviews continued to appear, infrequently, in the *Spectator* and the *Tablet*. Moreover Waugh, as always, turned his experiences into literary profit. 'Commando Raid on Bardia' (17 November 1941), which tells the story of a raid in which Waugh took part, was a scoop. Until it appeared the new commando units had been strictly 'hush-hush', and Waugh's revelation of their activities created wide interest. Bungling by the War Office and the Ministry of Information also drew attention to the article. *Life* had commissioned it, and the *Evening Standard* had acquired exclusive English rights, with the full permission of the War Office. But after the first instalment had appeared in the *Standard*, the Ministry of Information issued the whole article as a press release. To the *Standard*'s intense annoyance, it was then widely printed – incidentally bringing Waugh a new kind of glamour. Beverley Nichols in the *Sunday Chronicle* of 23 November 1941 lauded him under the headline: 'Here is the Story of a "Bright Young Man" Who is One of the Toughest of Our Commando Troops.' The story began: 'The ex-dilettante writing exquisite froth between cocktails has proved one of the toughest . . .'

'R. M. Brigade' (April 1940) is a product of Waugh's service with the Royal Marines, when for a time he was brigade, then battalion, correspondent to the *Globe and Laurel*, the Marine journal. This reluctant correspondentship is entertainingly described in John St John's *To the War with Waugh* (London, 1974). To be fully savoured Waugh's piece must be read in its original surroundings, where reports tend to run, 'Still plodding along, our meeting on Saturday was its usual success, as also was the social. Now I just must remind members about their annual subscription.'

Two letters to *The Times* (23 May and 5 June 1945) begin a subject of real importance to Waugh's personal and artistic development and to his post-war journalism. When serving with the British Military Mission in Croatia, Waugh sought permission on 9 December 1944, through his Commanding Officer Brigadier (now Sir) Fitzroy Maclean, to investigate and report to the Foreign Office on the religious situation there. On 25 December 1944 Sir Fitzroy submitted his own report to the Foreign Office on Partisan Religious Policy. Waugh presented his report, 'Church and State in Liberated Croatia', in March 1945. As it accused the Partisans of suppressing the Catholic Church, and political opposition, by the methods of the police state, and argued that the British Government was bound to protect the victims of its client regime, it cut across official policy. Sir Fitzroy's report, it might appear, had been intended to refute Waugh's charges in advance. Now the British Ambassador in Belgrade was asked to comment, and he did so unfavourably to Waugh. Waugh was permitted to reveal the contents of his report privately to certain churchmen and Members of Parliament. A Member asked a question in the House on the basis of the report. The Foreign Minister's answer, prepared by his department, totally rejected the basis of the question. Officially the matter had ended.

Late in May 1945 Tito's Partisans occupied and laid claim to Trieste, a territory of mixed population also claimed by Italy and Austria. A debate began in *The Times* over the status of the territory, the issues being the constitution of the population and the economic significance of the port of Trieste to the region as a whole. Waugh's letters shifted the argument to the validity of Britain's allowing a violently anti-Catholic and tyrannous regime to rule a Roman Catholic population. The first letter dealt in general principles. After a letter of rebuttal, which Waugh wrongly attributed to Sir Fitzroy Maclean, Waugh wrote again, this time adding names and other details taken from his report. This letter was ignored. Waugh was defeated for the moment, but he was resilient; he returned to the attack many times in the post-war years. He had been witness of a tiny corner of a tragedy that had engulfed the whole of eastern and south-eastern Europe, a tragedy that would help shape his life and writings for many years to come. *Sword of Honour* is the final fruit of his meditation on that tragedy.

. CONSERVATIVE MANIFESTO .

Let me, then, warn the reader that I was a conservative when I went to Mexico and that everything I saw there strengthened my opinions. I believe that man is, by nature, an exile and will never be self-sufficient or complete on this earth; that his chances of happiness and virtue, here, remain more or less constant through the centuries and, generally speaking, are not much affected by the political and economic conditions in which he lives; that the balance of good and ill tends to revert to a norm; that sudden changes of physical condition are usually ill, and are advocated by the wrong people for the wrong reasons; that the intellectual communists of today have personal, irrelevant grounds for their antagonism to society, which they are trying to exploit. I believe in government; that men cannot live together without rules but that these should be kept at the bare minimum of safety; that there is no form of government ordained from God as being better than any other; that the anarchic elements in society are so strong that it is a whole-time task to keep the peace. I believe that inequalities of wealth and position are inevitable and that it is therefore meaningless to discuss the advantages of their elimination; that men naturally arrange themselves in a system of classes; that such a system is necessary for any form of co-operative work, more particularly the work of keeping a nation together. I believe in nationality; not in terms of race or of divine commissions for world conquest, but simply this: mankind inevitably organizes itself into communities according to its geographical distribution; these communities by sharing a common history develop common characteristics and inspire a local loyalty; the individual family develops most happily and fully when it accepts these natural limits. I do not think that British prosperity must necessarily be inimical to anyone else, but if, on occasions, it is, I want Britain to prosper and not her rivals. I believe that war and conquest are inevitable; that is how history has been made and that is how it will develop. I believe that Art is a natural function of man; it so happens that most of the greatest art has appeared under systems of political tyranny, but I do not think it has a connection with any particular system, least of all with representative government, as nowadays in England, America and France it seems popular to believe; . . .

A conservative is not merely an obstructionist who wishes to resist the introduction of novelties; nor is he, as was assumed by most nineteenth-century parliamentarians, a brake to frivolous experiment. He has positive work to do, whose value is particularly emphasized by the plight of Mexico. Civilization has no force of its own beyond what is given it from within. It is under constant assault and it takes most of the energies of civilized man to keep going at all. There are criminal ideas and a criminal class in every nation and the first action of every revolution, figuratively and literally, is to open the

From *Robbery Under Law*, pp. 16-17, 278-9.

prisons. Barbarism is never finally defeated; given propitious circumstances, men and women who seem quite orderly will commit every conceivable atrocity. The danger does not come merely from habitual hooligans; we are all potential recruits for anarchy. Unremitting effort is needed to keep men living together at peace; there is only a margin of energy left over for experiment however beneficent. Once the prisons of the mind have been opened, the orgy is on. There is no more agreeable position than that of dissident from a stable society. Theirs are all the solid advantages of other people's creation and preservation, and all the fun of detecting hypocrisies and inconsistencies. There are times when dissidents are not only enviable but valuable. The work of preserving society is sometimes onerous, sometimes almost effortless. The more elaborate the society, the more vulnerable it is to attack, and the more complete its collapse in case of defeat. At a time like the present it is notably precarious. If it falls we shall see not merely the dissolution of a few joint-stock corporations, but of the spiritual and material achievements of our history.

. WE CAN APPLAUD ITALY .

It is only necessary to study the atlas in order to appreciate the main features of the problem of Abyssinia.

It is a very large country entirely surrounded by the possessions of European powers, Britain, France and Italy. The British frontier is, in mileage, by far the greatest, but the French and Italian are the more important because it is by them that Abyssinia is cut off from the Red Sea. The only railway leads from the capital, Addis Ababa, to the French port of Djibouti, the main caravan trail from the northern provinces leads to the Italian port of Masawa. Practically all imports and exports pass through one or the other of these two places. The map, moreover, shows that in the whole, vast continent of Africa, Abyssinia, thus encircled, is the last survivor of independent, native rule. (Liberia is governed by immigrant Negroes who maintain as rigid a barrier against the original natives as the settlers of Kenya.)

The natural sympathy of anyone who knows no more of the country than is afforded by the occasional picturesque references to it in the European press is in favour of the Abyssinians. He sees photographs of their barbarous lion's-mane headdresses and the elaborate ritual of their ancient Church, and feels that it will be deplorable if all this is standardized and brought up to date; if European officials in pith helmets take the place of the romantic military governors, and metalled roads and motor-buses bring the remote villages into touch with European commercial development. The more adventurous globe-trotters resent the idea of yet another country being made safe and comfortable for them. But there is another side to all this. However exciting Abyssinia may

Evening Standard, 13 February 1935.

be for an occasional visit, it is intolerable as a permanent neighbour.

It is one of the facts of history that it is impossible for two peoples of widely different culture to live peaceably side by side. Sooner or later one must absorb the other. It is not necessarily the higher culture which survives. It is the more virile. Early history is full of the records of advanced and fine cultures being absorbed by barbarians. Lately – but only very lately, in the last two centuries – the tale has been reversed and we have seen, one by one, the lower civilizations falling to the higher. We have come to accept this as a universal law, when, in point of fact, it is due to the accident that our own civilization has taken the form, that invention has given new physical strength to counterbalance the loss in virility [*sic*].

But it is in the nature of civilization that it must be in constant conflict with barbarism. Very few empires have been the result of a deliberate ambition. They have grown, inevitably, because it has been found necessary to expand in order to preserve what is already held. The French had to annex Algiers because it was the only way in which the Mediterranean could be made safe from pirates. Empire moves in a series of 'incidents', and these 'incidents' mean that it is impossible for a country to live in isolation. Barbarism means constant provocation.

Now Abyssinia is still a barbarous country. By this I do not mean that it is simple. It is not merely a country where the inhabitants choose to live without cinemas and patent medicines and safety razors and motor-bicycles; nor even where they prefer to retain their natural wealth unexploited. I mean that it is capriciously and violently governed and that its own governmental machinery is not sufficient to cope with its own lawless elements. It is entertaining to find a country where the noblemen feast on raw beef, but less amusing when they enslave and castrate the villagers of neighbouring countries.

There is much to be said in favour of the institution of slavery; it is arguable that the lot of a man born in slavery in Abyssinia is on the whole preferable to that of a wage labourer in some gold mines of South Africa; but nothing can be said by any decent man in favour of the slave raids to which the natives of all Abyssinia's neighbours are liable.

Sentimentalists in Europe like to imagine a medieval, independent race living according to their own immemorial customs, just as they like to find villages where the people still dance round maypoles in their national costume, but the reality in Africa is more formidable. It is defensible enough for the Abyssinians to keep their mineral wealth hidden from European exploiters, but their commercial simplicity is less praiseworthy when one finds the peasant afraid to grow a full crop for fear of having it commandeered by local military governors.

'But,' the sentimentalist will complain, 'what *right* have Europeans to interfere? If people prefer to be badly governed by themselves, rather than well governed by foreigners, that is their business.' The answer is that throughout the greater part of the country the Abyssinians are just as much foreigners as the Italians. The proper title of Abyssinia is the Ethiopian Empire. It was taken by conquest a generation ago. The Emperor Menelik succeeded to a small hill kingdom and made himself master of a vast population differing absolutely from himself and his own people in race, religion and history. It was taken bloodily and is held, so far as it is held at all, by force of arms. In the matter of abstract justice, the Italians have as much right to govern; in the matter of practical politics, it is certain that their government would be for the benefit of the Ethiopian Empire and for the rest of Africa.

But it is another question whether, however desirable, Italian conquest is a possibility. The great defeat at Adowa in 1896 was, it is true, suffered against overwhelming odds and as the result of the misdirection from Rome. Italy has now a highly trained and equipped army, and it is probable that they could defeat any army sent against them; but military victory is not synonymous with conquest. There is, for example, Italy's overwhelming superiority in the air; but what are they going to bomb? The only town of any importance is Addis Ababa – a great village of tin huts inhabited for the most part by cosmopolitans – Greeks, Armenians, Indians and Jews. The Italians could presumably bomb any government into capitulation, but that would not concern the fierce Amharic highlanders, the Gallas, or the Danakils, who have very little respect for the government in any case. Every man in Abyssinia carries arms and knows how to use them. Only a prolonged and enormously expensive guerrilla warfare could reduce the provinces, and they would stay peaceable only so long as the garrisons remained in force.

For about fifteen centuries the Italians have never won an important battle. Whether their training of the last few years is enough to create a nation of soldiers remains to be seen. If it has done so, no greater triumph has been achieved by a single man, and no more severe test could have been chosen than the conquest of Abyssinia. It is an object which any patriotic European can applaud. Its accomplishment will be of service to the world, and, fortunately, the world may be allowed to play the part of spectator. It will be the supreme trial of Mussolini's regime. We can, with clear conscience, fold our hands and await the news on the wireless.

. IN QUEST OF THE PRE-WAR GEORGIAN .

An ornamental biscuit tin, the present of the grocer; a mug, the present of an aunt; a silver medal, which I vainly attempted to melt down – all bearing portraits of the new King and Queen; an album full of gilt and coloured pictures of the coronation ceremonies; an obscure seat in the flag-draped bow windows of my father's club, to see a procession – though whether it was King Edward's funeral or King George's coronation I cannot remember – probably the latter, for the atmosphere seemed to be festive; the appearance in my home

Harper's Bazaar (London), May 1935.

of a soldier uncle in the sensational full dress uniform of the Bengal Lancers; a bus ride with my nurse to Hendon to see a monoplane start on a record-breaking flight round England – we waited for hours, while mechanics gloomily swung the propeller, and left, eventually, before the machine could be induced to rise; these constitute my sole personal memories of the epoch 1910–11.

It is a period which, so far, has acquired singularly little flavour for most of us. It has not won a name of its own, but is referred to vaguely as 'pre-war'. We have clear enough impressions of other periods – whether they correspond at all to reality is another question; of the incandescent gas-light and camellias of the 'naughty nineties'; of the gross, plutocratic Edwardian era, with its whiff of cigar smoke and Turkish coffee, its yachts and racing stables and South African millionaires, its baccarat scandals and the discreet love affairs of the middle-aged; of the war, and our own 'roaring twenties'. But the pre-war Georgian era presents a blank, peopled only by the mild and misty characters of *Sinister Street*.

So I was led, first, to the library in quest of this elusive period and turned, as journalists habitually do in circumstances of this kind, to the bound volumes of *Punch*; but here for once I was disappointed, for the drawings and the inscriptions beneath them seemed less than a week old. Here was the same kind of joke I had just read at my hairdresser's, about disingenuous children, about urban sportsmen being rebuked for riding over hounds, about rich plebeians and poor aristocrats, about the changes in manners between Victorian and modern England. The clothes of the women, certainly, seemed a trifle odd, but not nearly so odd as those of 1935. At first it was a disappointment, but later I realized that I had learned one important fact. *Punch* as we know it today breathes the spirit of 1911.

The *Illustrated London News* was more directly helpful; then there were some books of reminiscences and some inquiries, not always welcome, addressed to my seniors. Gradually the quest was rewarded and the period began to acquire character. As I have said, it is doubtful how far our idea of 'period' ever resembles the reality, but for what they are worth, here are some impressions at second-hand of 1910–11.

It was the beginning of a time of far higher culture than the decade that had preceded it. It was, for instance, the high-summer of the Russian ballet, of Pavlova and Nijinsky, and fashionable London flocked to it with an unaffected enjoyment that they had never given to opera. After a lapse of two generations Society began to take cognizance of the Arts. The intrusion at the beginning of the century of the new millionaires, who supposed that the possession of racehorses and the provision of weekend entertainment was all that was required of them, had the effect, foreshadowed rather earlier in 'the Souls', of drawing the more cultured away from smartness. Now in 1911 the type of fashionable man changes; he is no longer the heavy 'swell' of Ouida novels, but the aesthetic 'Clovis' of 'Saki' Munro. For perhaps the last time in English history, our politics were led by two men of scholarship, Mr Asquith and Mr Balfour, who spent their leisure among connoisseurs and men of letters. It was now no longer necessary for painters to choose between the Bohemian obscurity of *Trilby* or the bourgeois obscurity of the great Pre-Raphaelites; they were accepted, almost on equal terms, among the ruling class. Russian novels began to be popular. The Post-Impressionist painters were being noticed and collected in London; the chief horrors of *art nouveau* were over; the pseudo-Elizabethan billiard-room ceased to be the centre of social life. Even among card-players there was some stirring of the new spirit, and auction bridge, a game which apparently requires intellect, began to usurp the popularity of the lunatic's delight, baccarat. Perhaps even the popular craze for jigsaw puzzles may be referred to the new interest in visual art.

One is naturally inclined to regard all periods but one's own as a conservative Utopia, where everything was tranquilly rooted in tradition, the rich respected, the poor contented, and everyone slept well and ate with a hearty appetite. Actually 1910–11 was a time of the wildest uncertainty and political ferment. True, those good old politicians who still figure in the cartoons were already with us, but in what different guise! Our die-hard Mr Winston Churchill was the radical Home Secretary; Mr Ramsay MacDonald was preaching class war with something very near to verbal coherence; Mr Lloyd George, whom frequent photographs have endeared to us as a benevolent landed proprietor, was inveighing against the privileges of the gentry in terms which might have been translated direct from Danton or Robespierre. The general rank and file of the Liberal majority contained more out-and-out revolutionaries than had been seen at Westminster since the Long Parliament of Charles I, or have ever been seen there since, while the Tories, like Cavaliers, were expressing their willingness to die for privilege with a recklessness which has no counterpart today. The ladies' gallery of the House of Commons was crowded by afternoon. Mr Redmond's Irish party held the balance in the great question, now shelved, of the abolition of the House of Lords; a question which divided the whole country so bitterly that the ladies of opposing parties found it impossible to be civil to one another in private life.

Outside the House frantic young women were constantly occupied in burning post-offices, spiking policemen with their hatpins, chaining themselves to railings, and knocking off their meals in Holloway Gaol, in the cause of woman's suffrage. There were constant strikes in the key industries, and the trade unions were claiming privileged immunity at law. General elections were fought with enormous gusto and a touching belief in the power for good or ill of the legislative chamber. Floodlighting was first employed to illuminate the statue of Gladstone in the 1910 election; cows were led about the streets painted like skeletons and labelled 'The Result of Free Trade'. Mr Hilaire Belloc, MP, was thundering against corruption in high places.

The appearance of Halley's comet, punctually on time, led the superstitious to predict world disturbances. There was revolution in Portugal and anarchist assassinations in Russia. President Roosevelt upset international propriety by a lecture tour in Europe. The Kaiser's visit to London was the occasion of a prodigious gala performance at Drury Lane, when the whole auditorium was stacked with hothouse flowers; the Crown Prince enjoyed a royal progress through India shooting tigers and antagonizing colonels, but there were frequent spy scares. It was rumoured that prosperous German families were laying down gun emplacements in the disguise of hard tennis courts. The serial stories in *Chums* were full of German invasion and the heroic exploits in repelling them performed by Boy Scouts – a phenomenon new in the countryside.

We all remember 1911 as a vintage year of champagne, but few are aware that it saw a huge outbreak of *jacquerie* in the wine-growing district when the peasants burnt down the houses of the growers, raided the cellars and at Aix alone destroyed six million bottles of champagne.

How did people amuse themselves during these disturbing times? The cinema was still a toy, the gramophone a torture; wireless was able to transmit messages only in the dots and dashes of the Morse code. Apart from these the general structure of fashionable amusement was almost identical with that of today. The classic features of the year – Ascot, Cowes, grouse, partridges, pheasants, foxes, the Courts and the big private balls, the opera, first nights at the theatre – have changed very little. There was less hotel and restaurant life. The Ritz and the Carlton were fashionable for luncheon and tea; the Savoy was supreme in the evenings for supper and dancing. The chaperone system was almost as rigid as it had ever been. Girls seldom lunched and never dined with young men; maids still sat up yawning and gossiping to drive back with their mistresses from parties. One famous and now immensely popular grill-room was then considered fast, and profound scandal was created when an elder brother took his débutante sister there for supper.

The great houses of London – Grosvenor House, Dorchester House, Lansdowne House – were still in private hands and all through the season there was frequent, often weekly, entertainment on a scale which is now seen only yearly. The Duchess of Sutherland at Stafford House and the Duchess of Rutland in Arlington Street were the undisputed leaders of social life. Then, as now, Hatfield was a centre of Conservatism and the Church of England. The great change in English social life began, not as is generally thought with the war, but with the season of 1914 and the new generation who came out in that spring. In 1911 there was, if not restraint, at least great discretion. Love affairs were known about, arranged for, but seldom mentioned except in extreme intimacy. Husbands and wives, who were known by all their friends to have other attachments, and who, in some cases, had not addressed a word to one another in private for ten or twenty years, still kept up a façade of agreement, appearing together in public, entertaining together in London and in the country. The great prominence given to the divorce cases which from time to time came into the courts testifies to their rarity. Divorced women were still exiled from most aristocratic houses.

The theatre occupied a far more important place than it does now. Today at a first night, unless it is of a new Cochran revue or of some sensational production such as *Cavalcade*, one sees for the most part an audience of strictly theatrical interests. Then it was a fashionable occasion. Acting was of a very high standard. Gerald du Maurier was playing juvenile leads. Tree was startling his audiences by more and more extravagant décor, more and more elaborate personal mannerisms. Now, the cinema has somewhat dulled our appetite for scenic effect; then, it was the producer's aim to present the most naturalistic woodland scenery with real rabbits hopping about blinded by the footlights, to bring aeroplanes on to the stage, and racehorses and chariots on moving boards, to have explosions and earthquakes and floods, to crowd on whole armies of soldiers. Miss Gladys Cooper was just becoming famous. Mrs Patrick Campbell and Miss Marie Tempest were reigning as tragic and comic muses. Miss Lily Elsie combined the talents and charm of Miss Gertrude Lawrence and Miss Evelyn Laye. Pelissier's Follies drew a regular set, who came night after night and made themselves part of the show as no audience has done between them and *Young England.* In 1910 Lord Yarmouth excited comment by appearing for a brief run as the principal boy in a musical comedy of his own composition. At the Empire in Leicester Square there was popular ballet; young guardsmen waited at the stage door and gallantly took chorus girls out to supper, an entertainment which often ended with breakfast at dawn on the terrace of the Star and Garter at Richmond; at the back of the circle was the famous 'promenade', the nearest approach to the continental *quartier toléré* which has been permitted in England since mid-Victorian days. Here it was that after going down from 'St Mary's', Michael Fane sought Lily. There were also discreet houses of entertainment in South Kensington whose addresses could be obtained from club hall-porters. Here young men in search of experience and old men in search of effortless recreation would travel by the new-fashioned taxi-cab. They rang the bell, offered a pseudonymous introduction, and were invited into a parlour where a kindly middle-aged lady entertained them to tea or whisky. After a few pleasantries the conversation would turn on to the subject of the lady's nieces. 'I wonder if you would care to look at the photographs,' she asked. The young men politely agreed and a vast family album would be produced, full of cabinet photographs of young women with soft smiles and a profusion of hair. The pages would be turned over until one or other of the pictures excited particular admiration.

'Yes,' the hostess would say, 'she is a *very* nice girl. It is interesting that you noticed her because, by an odd coincidence, she is coming to stay with me this evening. I wonder if you would care to meet her.'

Ten golden sovereigns exchanged hands and the young couple were introduced and left to their own amusement.

Motor-cars were expensive but not uncommon; the day was over when people would equip themselves with goggles, veils and fur coats for a pleasure drive. Cycling had ceased to be a sport, but bicycles were still in use in the country for short excursions of the kind for which people now employ two-seater cars. Tarmac was seldom seen and the high roads were still white and dusty. In 1911 the English press was able to boast that while the yearly street accidents from all causes in Paris numbered 68,552, the figure for London was 13,388 – 'a testimony to the supreme mechanical skill of the British and of their greater respect for law.'

Men's clubs still retained their importance; at all the most reputable there were waiting lists and, at some, keenly contested elections. The day of reduced and suspended entrance fees had not arrived. Bachelors still sat hour upon hour in their tall hats, gardenias in their buttonholes, gazing down from windows in St James's Street with evident distaste at the passers-by. A new phenomenon, however, appeared in the opening in 1911 of the RAC – the first club to offer service instead of companionship as the advantage of membership. Late hours were kept everywhere, but particularly in the card-rooms of White's and the St James's, where members would repair after parties in the early hours of the morning, for rubbers of bridge rendered more expensive by fines. Drinking was not particularly heavy; probably far lighter than in the twenties. Cocktails were just coming into use. 'Clovis', it will be remembered, invented one called the *Ella Wheeler Wilcox.*

A day in the life of a young lady of fashion in 1911 is not difficult to reconstruct. Unless she had been dancing late the night before, she would probably be expected downstairs for family breakfast; in many country houses there were family prayers. There would be a fair-sized correspondence by her plate, for though the telephone was installed everywhere, its use was still considered somewhat impolite and all invitations were confirmed in writing. Her mother would undoubtedly have glanced over the envelopes and studied the handwritings and postmarks. During breakfast her father would explain the enormities of the opposing political party. Her assignations with young men throughout the day were, for the most part, made at odd times and in places where they might have met accidentally, in the picture gallery, the park, or the circulating library. Shopping would occupy most of the morning, in shops which still kept to the commercial streets – Regent Street, Piccadilly, Bond Street – and had not yet begun to invade the residential squares. All but the most old-fashioned were allowed to shop without escort, but she would be careful to avoid the shady area of the Burlington Arcade. She carried a huge handbag under one arm, and possibly led one of the newly introduced Pekinese spaniels. Luncheon was at the same time as today, but was a more elaborate meal. She might go to one of four or five hotels, but could not lunch alone with a man without exciting some speculation. Or she might stay at home and play with a jigsaw puzzle, or read the latest novel – *Clayhanger* by Arnold Bennett, *At the Villa Rose* by Mr A. E. W. Mason; if she were reading Mr Wells's *Ann Veronica* she would have to hide it under a cushion when her mother entered the room.

At tea-time she might go roller-skating (having changed into a looser skirt) or to one of the tea dances that were becoming fashionable. She might go to sit for her portrait to Mr Sargent in his magnificent studio, or if her tastes were unusually modern, to Mr Augustus John, just becoming accepted by a slightly puzzled public. Home to dress for an early dinner before the theatre – the latest Barrie perhaps, or a Pinero, already a little old-fashioned. After the theatre, a ball, where she would gather up the threads of her day's intrigues. She no longer noted, as her eldest sister had done, the names of her partners in a programme or disguised them when necessary for fear her mother should look over it. They danced the two-step, and the valse, to the music of Strauss; once or twice in the evening the floor was cleared for lancers, danced with an abandon which occasionally led to twisted ankles. Quails, champagne – the traditional dance supper of England, untempered by the kippers and bacon and lager beer of a more genuinely epicurean generation. And so to bed, to reflect perhaps in the drowsy half-hour before she fell asleep on the handsome young guardsmen with whom she had been dancing, and to regret that they would never have the opportunity of proving their mettle, as soldiers used to do in the remote ages before Mr Asquith's enlightened government. Wars could never happen nowadays . . . and so she fell asleep.

. THE TOURIST'S MANUAL .

Very rarely does one meet anyone who admits to being a 'tourist'; throughout the English-speaking world, tourist is a term of contempt used about social inferiors of one's own race encountered abroad. The tourist is a vile and ludicrous figure; he is always wrong. It is he who debauches the simple hospitality of primitive peoples, who vulgarizes the great monuments of antiquity, littering cathedral squares with ice-cream stalls, the desert with luxury hotels. A comic figure, always inapt in his comments, incongruous in his appearance; romance withers before him, avarice and deceit attack him at every step; the shops that he patronizes are full of forgeries; the places of entertainment to which he is conducted, down dubious side-alleys after dinner, are shams conceived solely with the purpose of duping him.

But we need feel no scruple or twinge of uncertainty; *we* are travellers and cosmopolitans; the tourist is the other fellow, and below us in the graded ranks of those who leave their own country. The man who plans his own journey despises the man who works on a fixed itinerary and a book of coupons; he in turn despises the 'personally conducted party'; the traveller to Timbuctoo despises the tourist in Tangier; the explorer in Matto Grosso despises both; the lonely gold-prospector regards with amused tolerance the elaborate equipment of the explorer; and so on from unplumbed depths to cloud-wreathed heights.

Vogue (New York), 1 July 1935.

We can always be quite sure that whatever the hardships we endure, however remote and inaccessible the places we visit, there is somewhere someone who regards us as a mere tourist. Meanwhile, we observe the decencies of speech. 'I see you are a great traveller,' we say to the young lady who has shown some acquaintance with the Parthenon; not 'I see you are a great tourist.' All this is encouraging to the traveller, because it is a characteristic of all human action that it requires a certain amount of glamour, however shoddy; a little self-esteem is necessary to set the inert in motion.

The truth, of course, is apparent to anyone who cares to analyse the case fully; there are only two kinds of travellers: those who go abroad for pleasure and those who go for profit. The great travellers have been either missionaries or traders. Behind them come all the rest; they are the tourists, whether their peculiar tastes take them to Florence or Tibet or the North Pole; they are all in the same boat; a vast, diffuse, diverse World Pleasure Cruise; shipmates whose real life is lived in the countries of their origin, out for a little uplift and excitement, though their expedition may take them ten days or ten years. Writers of travel books and scientists are in an intermediate position; they live by retailing the experiences of travel to others.

It is curious that the tourists find most relish in their dangers and hardships; the main object of real travellers is to be as comfortable as they can be; discomfort is the result of bad organization or lack of foresight. If one's object is ascetic, it is far better to stay in London or Paris or New York; there is practically no extreme of heat or cold, physical risk, loneliness, hunger or thirst that cannot, with a little ingenuity, be conveniently achieved in the centres of civilization. This essay is intended for tourists who prefer to visit places which are outside the ordinary circuit of organized traffic, where the hotels are bad and the people unused to visitors of their kind, where communications are irregular and the tourist is obliged to act as his own guide and agent; it embodies a few precepts for preserving one's comfort and good temper.

First, there is the question of language, which always perplexes the untravelled. The answer is quite simple – disregard it altogether. As a tourist, one is always in the position of purchaser, and therefore superior. It is the aim of the inhabitant to equalize this advantage by playing on one's sense of helplessness, by embarrassing one and making one feel ill-mannered. If one attempts to speak his language, he can either humiliate one by pretending that he does not understand, or flatter one by pretending that he does; in either case, his game is half won. The secret is – throw away your phrase book and yellow-backed conversational guide and speak your own language; speak it fluently, colloquially, imperturbably, make no compromise with pidgin-English or simplified statements. Success is bound to follow, whether your object is to be polite or rude.

Suppose, for instance, you find yourself, as not infrequently happens, involved in a row; you are surrounded by a derisive and hostile crowd, a few criminal-looking policemen and some very irate opponents; the inexperienced tourist either repeats over and over again a few ineffective, ill-pronounced sentences, or, still worse, remains perfectly silent and leaves the talking to the other party – perhaps lamely interjecting 'Consulato Americano'. The man of experience gives himself up to a volume of argument and counter-abuse in his own tongue. People can seldom resist the fascination of listening to a foreign language (a principle well appreciated by the singers of drawing-room ballads). Moreover, if one is eloquent enough and profuse in gesture, it is more than likely that part of one's meaning will slip through, in a curious, telepathic, inexplicable way. This is still more the case when the occasion is polite and you wish to convey thanks, or mild apologies, or love; smile constantly, talk incessantly, and your meaning will be clear.

Remember that, however patient your study, you will never in adult life learn any language perfectly; the best you can hope for is to be a bore. Most people speaking even French or German are in the same position as a young girl at her first dinner party, watched from a corner of her mother's eye further up the table; her one anxiety is to appear constantly engaged in conversation; what she says is a minor consideration. There is no platitude so trite that a highly educated foreigner will not bring it out with pride. Also remember that in most parts of the world it is extremely chic to speak English; you will be flattering your acquaintances by pretending to understand them. The only thing that it is advisable to know in any language is the numerals; and even there, you can do a lot with the fingers.

This principle, properly applied, should save the tourist a great deal of exasperation and shame. The other mental anguish from which he is most likely to suffer is boredom. This is a thing one very quickly forgets on one's return; one remembers, in an agreeably exaggerated form, the pains and dangers; the boring days fade out, though in any expedition, they far out-number the exciting ones. They necessarily vary greatly with the individual. Some people tell me that they are never bored, but they are not the people who travel. Generally speaking, it is the people who suffer most from boredom who undertake the most ambitious journeys.

There is no universal cure. I can offer two tips; one is that any companion is better than none; though he may be grossly unsympathetic, a mass of nervous habits that throw one into a fever of irritation, it is better to have him there than to be alone.

The second is that only the lightest reading is tolerable in the wilds. Occasionally, there is a correspondence in the press about the books that the reader would choose to take with him to a desert island; people invariably select classics of tried worth, but they will be better off with the works of Mr Gilbert Frankau or Miss Ethel M. Dell. I often see people, in the first day of a voyage, settling themselves in their deck chairs with copies of Spengler's *Decline of the West*, or Marx's *Capital*, the collected speeches of Burke, or *The Golden Bough* – books they have long intended to read. Now, they think, with days of complete rest before them, is the opportunity to make up lost time. On the second or third day, they are hanging about before the library doors, waiting for the steward to unlock them, eager to find love-stories or detective novels. There is something about the condition of locomotion that makes serious reading impossible.

There is one other tip – that the best cure for boredom is some minor piece of skilled work – mending harness, packing stores, shaping an oar, building a fire. It is one of the saddest developments of travel that one is denied this in most parts of the world.

Then there are physical comforts. In some parts of the world, the managers of hotels are one's opponents in this quest. There is more than one method of approaching them. The conventional English school is 'make an arrangement'; that is to say that on arrival at the hotel, before your luggage is taken up, you embark upon elaborate negotiations with the manager, bargaining about the price of the room and about what services are included in that price, explaining to him in advance exactly what you will want to eat, how long you intend staying, what time you will want to be called, when you will want a bath, and so on. The disadvantage of this method is that it is apt to arouse antagonism between host and guest, and however circumspect you may be, it is certain that something will have been omitted from your concordat.

A second school is to work through the servants, ingratiate yourself with them by bribing and human sympathy, visit the cook in the kitchen and talk to him about his domestic worries, promise to find the barman a job in New York, and so on.

The third and regal method is often the most successful – that is to assume an air of very great grandeur and mild surprise when anything goes wrong. Do not ask about the price, make it apparent that you are accustomed to being cheated, accede to any extravagant suggestion, keep the entire staff and management wide-eyed at the prospect of gain; then, when the bill at length arrives, pay half and send a copy of it to the local head of police.

On board ship, the second method is the one to follow; a few cocktails and a little light conversation with the purser, a little personal interest in the ambitions of the head steward (it is safe to assume that everyone working at sea is looking for a job on shore) will generally ensure you a change of cabin and preferential treatment in the dining-saloon.

When at length you leave the last coastal ship, the last dusty railway carriage or lorry, the last hotel, and set out for the bush, or jungle, or pampas, or whatever the undeveloped country is called in the particular region of the globe you are visiting, no amount of bluff is any help to you, and your comfort depends entirely on your own judgment. According to the country, you will be travelling with porters, horses, oxen, mules, elephants or camels, but whatever the means of transport, your baggage is a nuisance to you. Unless you propose to make camp for several weeks at a time in one place, the secret of comfort is to take as little as possible with you. Whatever slight and precarious advantage one derives from the use of the collapsible furniture, the wireless receiving sets, india-rubber baths and ant-proof sugar boxes, which one sees for sale, is totally nullified by the delay and expense of carting them from place to place. A medicine-chest, beyond a handful of pills and a case of germicidal soap, is more than an encumbrance – it makes one the centre of pilgrimage for miles round of sick or malingering natives begging for medicine. A few explorers have been able to exploit the legend of the European's skill as a physician; it is now the white man's burden that primitive peoples of all races regard him as a dispenser; they come in clusters demanding pills to set broken legs and ointments to cure old age.

But when all is said and done, perhaps the most valuable commodity for the tourist, whether he is cruising along the French Riviera in a yacht or ploughing through unmapped areas of virgin forest, is alcohol. It is the universal language, the Esperanto, through which contact can be made with people of the most remote sympathies; it passes agreeably the leaden hours of waiting for trains and boats and mail; it gently obliterates one's rage at inefficient subordinates and soothes one's own exhaustion and irritation; it renders one oblivious to mosquitoes, calms one's apprehensions of being lost or catching fever; it gives glamour to the empty, steaming nights of the tropics. With a glass in his hand, the tourist can gaze out on the streets of Tangier, teeming with English governesses and retired colonels, and happily imagine himself a Marco Polo.

. WHITE TRASH .

Very occasionally it is worth while noticing a bad book at some length, if only to give hitherto reputable publishers a reminder that they must not be insolent in what they try and put over on a public already stupefied by literary over-production. Across the wrapper of Mlle Marcelle Prat's *White, Brown and Black*, and quite eclipsing its title in importance, has been placed a label bearing the legend: LEARN FROM THIS BOOK SOMETHING ABOUT ABYSSINIA, HER PEOPLE, THEIR CUSTOMS AND LIFE THERE TODAY. The propriety of this invitation may be judged from the facts that it is not until page 228 that the authoress crosses the frontier into Abyssinian territory, that on page 240 she is certainly back in the Sudan, and that of the intervening pages five deal with events which may have taken place in either the Sudan or Abyssinia, but with a strong probability from internal evidence in favour of the former. The reader who seeks for the information promised on the label may think seven pages expensive at seven and sixpence.

The greater part of the book deals with the United States and Mexico, but since the publishers regard the African section as the most important, it is fair to concentrate criticism upon that.

Review of *White, Brown and Black*, by Marcelle Prat. *Spectator*, 26 July 1935.

Mlle Prat is a French authoress who has written six books but, until the experiences here recorded, had not left her own country. She must, however, be a lady of prodigious aptitude for language, for within a few days of her arrival in Egypt she is able to carry on a prolonged conversation, presumably in Arabic, with an elderly witch. Alas, it is too often the case that linguistic and literary gifts do not exist together! Mlle Prat has chosen a method of narration which makes it painful to follow her movements. In Chapter X we find her trotting round the Pyramids; in Chapter XI she describes her first arrival at Alexandria. This confusion, tiresome enough when she is on the ordinary tourist route, becomes intolerable when she reaches more remote places.

She travels up the Nile and at Khartoum falls into the company of a stocky Italian who, residents warn her, is crazy and dishonest. From him she obtains most of the meagre supply of information which she henceforward retails.

The British authorities discourage trippers in the country round Rossaires, not as Mlle Prat seems to imagine, because the natives will harm them, but because they may harm the natives. Mlle Prat was able, however, without difficulty, to obtain permission for a camping excursion with her Italian escort. It was during this modest jaunt that they crossed the Abyssinian frontier. With the best will in the world and a good map – not provided in the book – it is impossible to follow their movements. They left the frontier post of Kurmuk and arrived at Senga, 200 miles NNE on the Blue Nile. It seems probable that they cut straight to the river, traversing a little bulge of Abyssinian territory about twenty miles in length, inhabited by the Shankallas, a race of uncircumcised Negroes universally derided throughout the Ethiopian Empire. The ruler, she tells us, was 'Sultan Ghogoli, a monster of cruelty'. The rest of the trip lay in British territory and away from Abyssinia.

She records four incidents in Abyssinia: (a) She was greeted by a village dancer, of the kind that is common throughout the country. Mlle Prat was horrified. 'Rakes, who have no thought beyond sexuality,' said the Italian. 'The organizer of orgies,' he called the leader. 'Giant black arms encircled the sweating bodies of gross Negresses. . . . Frenzies of joy shook them and until nightfall there would be room for nothing in the village but sexuality. Tomorrow it would begin again, and tomorrow's morrow.' What a scandal! Tut, Tut! Mlle Prat, you really should go out sometimes in the evening in your native Paris; (b) She heard the footsteps of a hippo; (c) She claims to have seen a slave caravan and describes it with all the stereotype details of chinking chains, goads and whips and kicks, expressionless masks of faces, sockets of eyes, gaping mouths. This procession, she says, passed quite near her bed; she even saw one of the slave-drivers 'bury the point of his lance' in the back of one of the captives. I wonder how common these caravans are; I imagine they are pretty rare; she was in luck to run across one. Chain gangs of convicts are much more common in every part of Africa; she was clever to know the difference. But her experience tallies so exactly with the observations of so many other lady travellers that we must credit them with a special vision in this kind of discovery; (*d*) She saw a slave women in a dirty hut turning a mill wheel. Again, it was clever of Mlle Prat to know she was a slave; anyone else might have taken her for an industrious housewife. Sometimes she turned the wheel with one hand, sometimes with the other – a very sensible expedient which Mlle Prat seems to regard as particularly gruesome. Has she ever seen a European wife mangling the family wash? 'For some days,' writes Mlle Prat, 'I prowled round this house and heard nothing beyond the grinding of the wheel, punctuated by cries of distress' – a callous male might have taken that for the involuntary grunts with which coloured people frequently accompany labour of any kind. Has she ever heard sailors pulling on a rope? – 'And one morning – nothing!' How the flesh creeps! Had someone come in and strangled her? I suggest that if Mlle Prat had looked into the hut instead of prowling round, she would have found that the old girl had finished her job and was taking a nap.

For the next incident there is no geographical identification, but it seems to have occurred in the Sudan. The Italian came to blows with one of the porters and Mlle Prat dispensed money to onlookers to separate them. Then for three days they camped 'near a mysterious village, whose name' she 'had better not mention.' Where was the mystery? A Greek storekeeper was buying some smuggled coffee with the minimum of caution. That was all.

Then the silly pair arrived at Senga, where the local magistrate took a small fine off them for fighting their porter. And then suddenly, but none too soon, this preposterous book comes to an end.

. EVELYN WAUGH'S VIVID
ADDIS ABABA CABLE .

3 MORE WEEKS OF
RAIN AND THEN –
WAR CERTAIN IN FEW WEEKS
From Evelyn Waugh, Our Special Correspondent

Addis Ababa, Friday.

From the Tigre uplands in the north-west to the province of Ogaden in the south-east a vast curtain of rain lies over Abyssinia. The lowlands are a steaming swamp and the highlands a network of torrents. It has rained since April, and will rain three more weeks.

No one here doubts that when the rains stop, talking will cease in Europe and war will begin.

I arrived expecting to find a menaced capital in a fever of preparation. Instead I find life following its traditional course. The usual succession of public holidays paralyses the activity of the city; the usual chattering crowds

Daily Mail, 24 August 1935.

are in the streets; and the police are attempting the old hopeless game of directing them into the gutters.

There is also the usual spectacle of a rural chief trotting on muleback, surrounded by running retainers.

There is nothing to suggest that in a few weeks the nation will be plunged in a desperate struggle. Indeed, with the exception of the Emperor and the handful of educated officials, no Abyssinians have the smallest conception of the gravity of the danger.

They are like children with noses pressed at the nursery window-pane longing for the rain to clear. They are absolutely confident of victory, and talk not only of maintaining their independence, but also of conquering the coastline.

When warned of gas, aeroplanes and other modern weapons of warfare, of which they have no experience, they reply by explaining the atrocities with which they will retaliate. They depreciate the courage of the Italian soldier and refer to the impenetrability of their own mountains.

Foreigners, however, are not so complacent. Every train takes a crowd of them to the coast. Englishwomen, however, are mostly staying with their husbands.

The present situation is particularly hard on the Dodecanese Greeks who made their homes in Abyssinia long before Italy took possession of their islands. I saw a dozen of these people at the Italian consulate awaiting passports. Homeless, they have no alternative but to be recruited in the army to fight against the country where they have lived most of their lives.

The Europeans who remain are a prey to constant scares and rumours. All newcomers are suspected spies, and there is little news, local or foreign.

There are few signs of soldiers of fortune. Many offers were received, but mostly from unemployed air pilots offering their services if the Abyssinians would provide machines. The Abyssinians say they are content with their own men. All they want from Europe are arms and munitions.

They regard the embargo on the export of arms as a hostile measure. Lighters are said to be lying off the Arabian coast with Polish arms awaiting permission to land.

The Turkish General Mehmet Vehib Pasha left Addis Ababa today to organize the Mohammedan tribes on the Ogaden front. Any fears of Mohammedan disloyalty, I am told, have been dispelled even in the recently disaffected Jimma district.

The Abyssinians claim that the whole of Ethiopia is wholeheartedly behind the Emperor. Indian Moslems have subscribed funds, as also have Coptic Egyptians. There is a report that a legion of 5,000 Egyptian volunteers has been formed.

Prayers for Abyssinian success offered in a mosque at Djibouti, French Somaliland, have been forbidden by the French authorities.

The American, Dr Torrance, has arrived to organize the Red Cross. This institution commands little popular sympathy, as the Abyssinians regard the wounded as the concern of their own women. The convention for treating enemy wounded is also highly repugnant.

Until recently Abyssinia refused to join the International Red Cross, but has now decided to do so, on condition, however, of the admission of the existence of a national unit. Dr Torrance's job is to organize this unit. If he is successful he will work in conjunction with a privately subscribed corps from England.

Dr Torrance has large stores of antiseptics and dressings at Marseilles awaiting shipment if his mission here succeeds.

. FRENCH COUNT'S ARREST IN ABYSSINIA .
CHARGED WITH WIFE AS A SPY
12 SUSPECTED NATIVES CAPTURED IN THE BUSH
From Evelyn Waugh, Our Special Correspondent

Jijiga, North-East Abyssinia, Sunday.
Count Maurice de Rocquefeuil du Bousquet and his wife are under close arrest here, suspected of espionage.

The Count settled at Jijiga three years ago, nominally as manager of an East African mineral company engaged in the exportation of mica. His manner of life excited suspicions, as he had many servants, entertained guests of all races, and seldom went out except to Mass on Sunday.

He is 56, with greying chestnut hair and moustache, and he has a scar under the right eye. He has been married only three months, and his wife, who was a widow, has one son.

An Abyssinian detective, Kebreth Astatkie, kept observation and detained an aged Somali woman, who was leaving the Count's house for Harar, about thirty miles distant. When he searched her he found a film tube under her left armpit containing, it is alleged, a photograph of a lorry corps with five pages of particulars concerning the defences of Jijiga. The document, it is stated, was addressed to the Italian Consul at Harar.

The detective then conducted a raid of the house, and discovered – the charges continue – an extensive correspondence with officers of Italian Somali-land.

When the Count and Countess were arrested, they were given the opportunity to communicate with the French Minister at Addis Ababa, but refused. The couple, who are in good health, occupy a large room in Government House. They have their own servants to cook their food. Guards with rifles are at the door and windows. Lion cubs, the pets of a local resident, are playing outside.

Daily Mail, 2 September 1935.

The Count and Countess will probably be conveyed to Harar tomorrow. It is a ten-hours journey over a waterlogged camel track.

Educated Abyssinians believe that the Count will be extradited, as there is no desire to provoke the French. The detective who made the arrest was educated in European police methods, and has visited England.

Twelve natives, whose names were discovered in the correspondence, resisted arrest and took to the bush. Half the Jijiga garrison turned out to hunt for them. Traffic was held up on the Harar road. Eventually the fugitives were captured and disarmed and brought to Jijiga through jeering crowds. The opinion in native quarters is that they will be hanged.

Much of the Count's information, it is stated, is inaccurate, and it is alleged that he had a network spy system all over the Ogaden and Somali district. Many arrests of natives will probably result.

The Count many years ago abandoned his houses in Paris and on the Riviera, and he sought fortune in South America. He came to Abyssinia nine years ago and has not visited Europe for four years.

Jijiga is a point of vital strategic importance. It is on the caravan and lorry route to Harar and the coast. Most of the inhabitants are Moslem, except the Abyssinian officials. It is, in fact, an outpost for the control of the savage Ogaden country.

It is a fortified, squalid town, with no European inhabitants except four Greeks and four Roman Catholic priests.

Count de Rocquefeuil, it is stated, constantly applied to become consular agent here, but his requests were refused.

Following the Jijiga arrests, spy fever has reached Harar. Several Armenians and Syrians under suspicion have had to undergo lengthy cross-examinations. My interpreter, who was arrested on suspicion, was released after the British Consul had visited the gaol.

. EMPEROR'S REVIEW IN STORM .
ABYSSINIAN CHIEFS' WAR DANCE
DELUGE AT 'END OF RAINS' CEREMONY

Addis Ababa, Friday.

Emperor Haile Selassie today held a spectacular military review in St George's Place – in the least unimposing quarter of Addis Ababa – to mark the public celebration of the Mascal (End-of-the-Rains) Feast.

The place is a circular space roughly laid with stones. In the centre concrete piers and iron railings enclose a garden which is normally unkempt, but where at the moment a brilliant disorder of flowers surrounds the grandiose gilt

Daily Mail, 28 September 1935.

equestrian statue of Menelik II, which was unveiled five years ago at the coronation of the present Emperor.

In a burst of last-minute activity labourers filled up the deepest crevices between the stones in a leisurely fashion.

In the background stands St George's Cathedral, within whose high octagonal stone walls stands a grove of olives.

CANOPIED THRONE

Immediately in front was a canopied throne and the imperial stand, garish with artificial silk draperies in the national colours – scarlet, mustard and emerald green – surmounted by a gilt crown and escutcheons, on which were rudely painted Lions of Judah.

The remaining scenery was typical of the ramshackle squalor of this city – tin shacks; large concrete offices, the erection of which was begun long ago, but has since been abandoned, and which are overgrown with high weeds; and tumbledown hutches, usually occupied by squatting vendors of handfuls of salt and red pepper, but today deserted.

The streets had been densely thronged since dawn for the celebration, which was marked by the heaviest storm seen here for years.

At 1.30 p.m. the Emperor, in military uniform, drove to the spot, escorted by soaking Lancers. He took his place on the throne, and sat waiting alone and immobile while the rain turned to hail.

LEAKING GRANDSTAND

It swept over the grandstand, burst through holes in the roof, and torrents of water ran down the streets. Priests arrayed in ceremonial vestments huddled together under cover while they waited for the Abuna (archbishop) to begin the celebration at the kind of maypole which had been erected.

The tedium was relieved by a constant losing battle waged by the police against a motley band of half-caste Levantine interlopers who invaded the diplomatic stand.

The delay was due to the natural reluctance of the Abuna – aged, infirm and born in a happier climate – to leave shelter and initiate the ceremony. Everything was at a standstill while he remained in shelter.

Eventually, at 3.15, the storm slackened. The old man ventured out, walked three times round the 'maypole', threw a wand bearing a bunch of yellow daisies to the foot of the pole, and hurried back to shelter.

The Emperor, accompanied by the Duke of Harar, also circled the pole and returned to the throne. The procession then began.

There was drizzle, intermittent heavy rain and thunder throughout the afternoon.

CHIEFS' GALA DRESS

The spectacle began with an hour's parade of chiefs and warriors, whose enthusiasm was unaffected by the weather.

The chiefs, mostly elderly greybeards, wore gala dress of a magnificence according to their wealth. They wore lion-mane headdresses and capes, carried elaborately ornamented shields and swords, and were mounted on mules or ponies. In many cases riderless horses were led in their retinue if they possessed more than one saddle deemed worthy of display.

Their followers ran round them endeavouring to maintain contact by touching the harness of the chiefs' mounts. Many carried wands and threw them on the rapidly growing pile round the 'maypole'.

Many chiefs dismounted, rushed on foot to the throne with drawn swords, and performed what seemed half a dance and half a sham-fight – capering, posturing, slashing the air and boasting loudly of their prowess in past battles and of the amount of blood – their own and others – which they proposed to shed in any coming war.

RAIN-SOAKED CHILDREN

Count Vinci and other members of the Italian Legation attended the ceremony with an air of polite interest.

The Emperor sat motionless, looking over the heads of the assembly as though oblivious of its presence.

A more sombre note was struck by the sudden appearance of a procession of sodden and shivering schoolchildren, singing a hymn in quavering tones.[1]

Occasional detachments of uniformed volunteers marched past in fours and presented arms.

The retinues of some chiefs included portions of antiquated artillery pieces picked up on the field of Adowa [where the Abyssinians defeated the Italians in 1896] and carried on mules.

The march-past also included the Imperial Guard – a mechanized army equipped with sixteen new anti-aircraft lorries, two field wireless vans and four Red Cross cars.

---

1 Ernest Oldmeadow, editor of the *Tablet*, attacked Waugh's correspondentship in Abyssinia, and this passage in particular, in 'News and Notes', *Tablet*, 12 October 1935, p. 451: 'The public interest . . . calls for a protest against the *Daily Mail*'s choice of a Correspondent . . . novelist who wrote a notorious book about a present-day Black Emperor . . . which the *Tablet* had to condemn for its gross coarseness . . . which is still being pushed and sold . . . while this unsuitable Correspondent thus indelicately stationed in Addis Ababa is sending home messages which chivalrous Englishmen resent. When he can taunt the Dark Emperor's incipient civilization he does it, as in his allusion to Addis Ababa's little children quavering out a hymn at the Maskal festival, after they had been drenched by a sudden rain storm.' Criticisms also appeared on 19 October 1935 and 8 February 1936.

. THROBBING DRUMS CALL
ABYSSINIANS TO WAR .
WARRIORS' WILD REJOICINGS AT
EMPEROR'S SUMMONS

Addis Ababa, Thursday.

The voice of M. Atto Lorenzo, confidential official to the Emperor, announcing the 'destruction' of Adowa, was drowned by the cheering of the crowds here this morning when general mobilization was proclaimed to a great concourse on the palace parade ground.

In the centre of the steps leading to the palace the drum of Menelik, which was last beaten on the field of Adowa in 1896 and stood between standards, throbbed with a slow rhythm like a tolling bell.

The crowds surged forward, shouting, to the foot of the steps. Then there was dead silence while M. Ligaba Tass, Grand Chamberlain of the Court, read the Emperor's proclamation, which stated:

'The hour is grave. Arise, each of you, take up arms, and rush to the defence of your country. Rally to your chiefs, obey them with single purpose, and repel the invader.

'FOR YOUR COUNTRY'

'May those who are unable because of weakness and infirmity to take an active part in this sacred quarrel help us with their prayers. The opinion of the world has been revolted by this aggression against us.

'All forward, for your Emperor and for your country.'

The proclamation was greeted with three formal bursts of clapping. Then there was a wild outburst of rejoicing. Swords were drawn and rifles brandished, and the crowd shouted and sang.

In its midst there appeared the little frock-coated figure of M. Lorenzo, who was once an Eritrean subject but left that colony because he was slighted by a European in a cinema. Since then he has nursed an undying grudge against the Italians.

EXCITED CROWDS

M. Lorenzo was seen attempting to draw Europeans aside and saying in French: 'Gentlemen, there is news of far graver importance.'

His voice, however, was inaudible among the delirious crowds. Eventually, however, in a corner of the palace, while the mob roared outside, he communicated, in a voice shaking with anger, Ras Seyum's message saying that Adowa had been bombed.

Daily Mail, 4 October 1935.

The allegations that four Italian war-planes this morning dropped seventy-eight bombs on the Adowa region, several of which fell on a hospital bearing the Red Cross emblem, were made in telegrams sent today by the Emperor to the League at Geneva.

One telegram stated that the Italian bombs had caused numerous victims among the civil population, including women and children, in the region of Adowa, and that hostilities had broken out in the province of Agame.

'These facts,' continued the telegram, 'occurring in Ethiopian territory, constitute violation of the frontier and a breach of the Covenant by Italian aggression.'

News of the mobilization order travelled fast and was greeted everywhere with rejoicing. Old soldiers began firing rifles into the air, but demonstrations were quickly repressed and the capital settled down calmly to its afternoon rest.

The only unusual feature was the heavy guard on the Italian Legation. Italians had been forbidden to appear in the streets without an escort of soldiers.

Anti-aircraft guns have been posted at the railway station in Menelik Square and at the palace to reassure the people. No air-raid, however, is feared while Europeans are still here.

The Emperor drove this morning to the new aerodrome at Jimma Road and inspected three new passenger aeroplanes – two French and the other Swiss, each capable of carrying eight people.

The machines, which arrived in May, have now been fitted up and painted with heraldic lions. They are intended for use on the lines of communication between the armies in the interior.

. EDMUND CAMPION .

I have never (except with singular lack of success in the Final Schools at Oxford) sought reputation as a historical scholar; if I did so, I do not think the fact of Mr Kensit's opposition would seriously imperil it; I do not care a hoot that Mr Kensit thinks my life of Edmund Campion a 'second-hand hearsay romance of the novelist'. But it *is* important that readers of the *Listener*, who lack the time and inclination for historical reading, should be left with the impression that new, damning evidence against Campion has lately come to light, reversing the judgment of previous history, and fouling a name which all of my Faith and countless others, who know the true marks of heroism and sanctity, hold in the highest honour.

Listener, 26 February 1936. Reply to J. A Kensit (*Listener*, 30 January, 12 February 1936) who had protested against Desmond MacCarthy's giving *Edmund Campion* a favourable review over the BBC. A long controversy developed. This has been collected in *The Campion–Parsons Invasion Plot, 1580* (London: Protestant Truth Society, 1936).

If Mr Kensit had had the patience to read my little book attentively, he would have found the topics he raises discussed in some detail; he would also have found listed in the bibliography the work upon which he mainly relies – Professor Meyer's *The English Catholics under Queen Elizabeth*. I knew all about the Cardinal of Como–Nuncio Sega correspondence. I did not mention it because it seemed to me irrelevant to the subject about which I was writing. Professor Meyer himself, summing up the case against Campion, says: 'The attempt to prove conspiracy failed entirely, and was bound to fail because the conspiracy had no existence'. Professor Pollard, reviewing the work, supported this view. These are first-class historians, non-Catholics, fully informed of the most recent documents. It is not surprising that Mr Kensit came to a different conclusion, but it must be made clear that the division is not one between historians who wrote prior to the publication of the Sega correspondence and those who wrote after it, but between the United Protestant Council and the massed wisdom and knowledge of European scholarship.

Of course there were English Catholics in Elizabeth's reign who saw in revolution and assassination the only cure for their ills. I constantly referred to them in my book. Elizabeth's legislation left the Catholics with the choice of three positions – apostasy, conspiracy or sacrifice. There was no place for legitimate opposition under the Tudors. The reason that we love Campion was that his teaching and example showed the way of sacrifice.

I cannot rewrite my book in the form of a letter.

I, too, was working from the *State Trials* used by Mr Kensit. Anyone who reads that account with an open mind *must* realize not only that the charges were unproved, but that they were made in bad faith. Mr Kensit slaps them down on the table as though the very fact of their having been made proved their truth. He assumes what he has to prove when he talks about 'Campion's Oath forms'. Personally, I think it very doubtful if they ever existed at all. What is certain is that no connection was ever established between them and Campion. They were not found in 'his lodgings', as Mr Kensit states. Campion had no lodgings; he was constantly on the move. They were not found in his saddle-bags. The most that his accusers dared say was that they were found in houses where Campion had visited. Mr Kensit has taken on himself the task of amplifying the evidence which even the perjurers and *agents provocateurs* of Cecil and Walsingham shrank from avowing.

Humphrey Ely was barely, if at all, known to Campion. He was a bitter opponent of Parsons and the Society of Jesus. Campion and Parsons were *not* 'inseparable companions'. They had not met before Campion was called to Rome for his journey to England; on the road to Rheims they seemed to have had little contact; they travelled to England separately and during their joint mission spent only a few days in one another's company.

At Lyford, in the sermon quoted, Campion was preaching to a congregation consisting mainly of pious old ladies. Does Mr Kensit really think he was exhorting them to armed rebellion and assassination?

There were certainly two other Jesuits in England at the same time as Campion and Parsons; they are named in my book. I am forced to the conclusion that Mr Kensit has not read it and that his rage is aroused, not that an inaccurate work should be unjustly commended, but that any book by a Catholic about a Catholic should be mentioned at all by anyone anywhere.

What a funny man he must be.

Evelyn Waugh

APPENDIX VIII TO THE
. OFFICIAL NOTE ADDRESSED BY THE ITALIAN GOVERNMENT TO THE LEAGUE OF NATIONS .

I was in Abyssinia from 20 August until 9 December 1935, acting as special correspondent for the *Daily Mail*. Movements of correspondents were rigidly restricted and I am only able to speak from personal experience of conditions in Addis Ababa, Harar province and Wallo province.

In Addis Ababa I saw no abuse of the Red Cross sign and I believe that its correct use is scrupulously observed. This is not true of the provinces. I was in Harar at the end of October. There were two old-established mission hospitals in the town – French and Swedish – but no Red Cross Ambulance unit. Certainly four – I think, but am not prepared to swear to more – government buildings bore the red cross. These were the Royal Palace (ghebbi), the Treasury, the Law Courts and an iron building attached to the headquarters of the Belgian military mission. There was also a red cross painted on the roof of the wireless station (old ghebbi) which had been lightly washed over. It would have been visible, I think, from the air, and in any case could have been scrubbed clear in a very short time. I was refused admission to all these buildings; inquiries made through my interpreter of the guards and citizens of the town revealed that none of the buildings mentioned above housed doctors, nurses or ambulance personnel, or contained any serious medical preparations. The house at the Belgian barracks was said to contain money subscribed for the Red Cross Fund.

I was at Dessye at the end of November. There were two properly constituted hospitals there: a French mission outside the town which was untouched in the subsequent bombardment, and the Adventist mission in, but at the extremity of, the town, where a ward was destroyed by fire. This lay next to the former Italian Consulate where a detachment of the Imperial Guards was stationed with two pieces of artillery and some anti-aircraft machine guns

'Appendix VIII' to the Official Note addressed by the Italian Government to the Secretary General of the League of Nations under date 28 February 1936. Reprinted in Supplement No. 3 of the *British–Italian Bulletin*, 11 April 1936.

mounted on lorries. A third building in the city flew the red cross; this was the Governor's private residence (not the Crown Prince's ghebbi). Two anti-aircraft guns were mounted on the verandah. An Irish transport officer quartered in this house, working for the Red Cross, protested about the presence of these guns and there was some talk of moving them. Whether it had been done before the attack on 6 December I cannot say.

On 28 November, at Dessye, I witnessed a review of troops leaving for the northern front. This included a native ambulance unit of which every man wore a Red Cross brassard on the arm and carried a brand-new rifle.

It may be noted that the Abyssinians have always regarded the red cross with great familiarity; it is the sign on brothels throughout the country; it is used as a charm on saddle-cloths (I have seen photographs in the European papers of military mules bearing this red cross described as ambulance transports); it is used on all pharmacies and chemist shops. Thus it is natural that it should have no sanctity in the Abyssinian mind.

. THE CONQUEST OF ABYSSINIA .

Sir, – The collapse of the Shoan monarchy in Ethiopia is now complete and apparent. The Abyssinians have murdered two of their most prominent benefactors[1] and the British public, which has constantly sneered at the Italian employment of native troops, is now rejoicing that the Sikh guard has been able to save the lives of the remaining white population of Addis Ababa. Until a few days ago correspondents in your columns, Englishmen safe in England, were exhorting the Abyssinians to further sacrifices. The soldiers and officials on the spot were less enthusiastic. We can only tell from fragmentary reports how great their sacrifices have been, but it is probable that they were enormous. It is natural to inquire whether they were not greatly increased by the utterances of uninstructed observers and the indecision of the governments of Europe.

In your leading article of 4 May you note 'a disposition to condemn the British government'. Resolute action on either side, you say, might have obviated an incalculable amount of suffering; nothing was done and 'the two charges obviously cancel each other out.' Is this an altogether candid conclusion? In December the two dominant powers in the League proposed a compromise which, if effected, would have saved countless lives.[2] This you describe as 'an unfortunate exception' to their policy of inaction.

Where did the British Government go wrong? It is possible to answer without incurring the charge of pretending to wisdom after the event. There has always

The Times, 19 May 1936.

1 Dr George Melly, Head of the British Red Cross Unit No. 1, and Dr Junod, Head of the International Red Cross in Abyssinia, were separately killed by Abyssinian rioters in the disturbances which followed the Emperor's flight.

2 The Hoare-Laval Agreement which would in effect have transferred Abyssinia's colonial territories to Italy, while leaving Abyssinia 'independent'.

been a small body of informed opinion in England which, however wrong its predictions of the military results of the war, has insisted upon the essential political problem. When Abyssinia applied for membership of the League, England opposed her admission, France and Italy supported it. Both parties realized that she did not constitute a homogeneous or orderly nation of the sort that could be admitted on equal terms to the councils of the world. The English believed that membership carried implications which no other country seriously considered. By 1923 the phraseology of the League Covenant already seemed archaic to the rest of the world.

In September of last year the Italians presented a fully documented case, which has never received proper attention, proving that Abyssinia had forfeited her rights to League membership. Two courses were open to the British government. We might maintain our high conception of the privileges and obligations of League membership and expel Abyssinia or we might, as most of the remaining members did, regard the Assembly at Geneva as a standing congress of minor practical convenience, whose machinery might be employed, occasionally, where it appeared expedient. Instead we kept Abyssinia in the League, asserted the inviolable sanctity of the writ of the Covenant, and encouraged what might have been a comparatively bloodless transition from a low to a higher form of imperialism to be effected with the maximum of immediate suffering and future bitterness.

I am, &c.,

Evelyn Waugh.

. SPANISH CIVIL WAR .

In 1937 Louis Aragon, Nancy Cunard and others sent a questionnaire to writers in the British Isles asking them to state their attitude towards the Spanish Civil War. The answers were printed in a pamphlet under the headings 'For the Government', 'Neutral?', and 'Against the Government'.

The question ran: 'Are you for, or against, the legal government and the people of republican Spain? Are you for, or against, Franco and Fascism? For it is impossible any longer to take no side.'

Waugh's reply, classified as 'Against the Government', was as follows:

I know Spain only as a tourist and a reader of the newspapers. I am no more impressed by the 'legality' of the Valencia government than are English Communists by the legality of the Crown, Lords and Commons. I believe it was a bad government, rapidly deteriorating. If I were a Spaniard I should be fighting for General Franco. As an Englishman I am not in the predicament of choosing between two evils. I am not a Fascist nor shall I become one unless it were the only alternative to Marxism. It is mischievous to suggest that such a choice is imminent.

Louis Aragon, ed., *Authors Take Sides on the Spanish War* (London, Left Review, 1937).

. A 'TIMES' CORRESPONDENT .

Mr George Steer was one of the first special correspondents to arrive in Addis Ababa in 1935, and one of the last to leave in 1936. He represented the most important newspaper in the world. He exhibited in a high degree the peculiar gifts required for that kind of journalism – keen curiosity of mind, a retentive memory, enterprise, a devotion to duty even at the expense of personal dignity and competitive zeal that was notable even in the international cut-throat rough and tumble of his colleagues. Those who knew him will be surprised to see that he couples himself with Captain Taylor, the military attaché, as 'good steady animals, the grizzly and opossum' of that menagerie. However much we liked and admired him, it was not in quite that way, but he did earn the affection and respect of many of us, and his book has been awaited impatiently.

It is the first work in English that has attempted to give a complete account of the affair. It is not Mr Steer's fault that the most valuable and exciting section has been contributed by another hand. Until the very end, when the Negus's government had collapsed, the journalists in Addis Ababa saw little for themselves. Whatever there was to see, Mr Steer saw. His sources of information were fuller and more reliable than any of his competitors'; but that, alas, is saying very little, and it is an almost fatal defect in his book that he does not give any reference for the majority of the facts he records, facts which could not be known to him by personal observation. His two main authorities appear to have been Mr Colson, the American adviser to the Negus, who, quite properly, for that was his job, issued the official propaganda, and Mr Holmes, the representative of the *Daily Worker*.

'I came young, I went away older,' says Mr Steer, 'I promised myself that I could never forget and never forgive.' Too credulous readers should remind themselves that a period of rapid adolescence is not the best time for accurate observation, nor a mood of personal resentment the best for a sober consideration of evidence. There are signs, too, that the book has been hastily put together; it has many avoidable slips; on one page the reader's attention is called to an illustration which is not there; the maps omit a great many of the place names mentioned in the text; there are gaucheries of style – characters mentioned without any explanatory introduction; Sir Sydney Barton is written of as 'Barton' throughout. In fact the only names accorded their proper prefixes are the Ethiopians' to whose titles of honour Mr Steer shows a scrupulous attention. He was almost unique among Europeans in admiring Amharic character. He had great sympathy, I think it is not unfair to say affinity, for those nimble-witted upstarts who formed the Negus's entourage, like himself African born, who had memorized so many of the facts of European education without ever participating in European culture. He genuinely liked them and it is to his credit that he now defends their memory. He was of

Review of *Caesar in Abyssinia*, by G. L. Steer. *Tablet*, 23 January 1937.

an age and disposition which needed a hero to worship. The Negus did not quite fill the role, but Mr Steer found one who did in Afewerk of the Ogaden, one of the very, very few Ethiopian leaders who fought loyally and fell at his post. *Caesar in Abyssinia* is in part dedicated to him.

It is one of Mr Steer's particular grievances that the decisive campaign was fought on the northern front. Like everyone else he started with the preconception that Graziani would advance immediately upon Harar. Unlike everyone else, Mr Steer took the trouble to acquaint himself fully with the Ogaden situation. It was wasted labour and no words are too intemperate for him to express his vexation. Intemperance is, in fact, everywhere apparent. Mr Steer can allow no credit to any single Italian. It is not enough that he thinks the war unjust. He will not even allow the Italians the credit of working their destructive machinery with any skill. Their airmen are individually cowardly and incompetent. When Biroli led a brilliant raid by Alpini and Blackshirts up the heights of Work Amba, to scatter hand-to-hand an immensely larger force – a feat comparable to General Wolfe's capture of Quebec – Mr Steer attributes his success to the fact that Ethiopian nerves had been frayed by aeroplanes. When the Italian generals followed the strategy of all successful generals and attacked in strength at weak places, Mr Steer accuses them of cowardice. He is, in fact, in something of a dilemma to explain how it was that the Italians won. He escapes with the magic word 'gas'.

There is no question that ypirite was used by the Italians on both fronts. Several cases were reported by European doctors of undoubted integrity. It was an action which all friends of Italy must deplore. Condemned to outlawry by the world, they allowed themselves to behave as outlaws. They could have won as quickly without it. No one knows – least of all the Italian fighting-men – how much ypirite was used. Its purpose seems to have been to make the bush on either side of the roads impenetrable to snipers. It is significant to note that it is nowhere mentioned in Colonel Konovaloff's eyewitness account of the battle of Mai Cio and the final rout. It was never used, as has been stated, on Harar. But it was used, and its use was inexcusable.

If for no other reason – and I hope that I have shown there are other reasons – Mr Steer's book is worth reading for the superb narrative of Colonel Konovaloff; a terrifying, almost stupefying account of the last days of the Negus's army. It is a frequent shock to professional writers to find how much better their work is done by amateurs. The Russian colonel's story, apart from its unique interest of subject, is a brilliant literary composition against which Mr Steer's careless prose shows up shabbily.

. GENERAL CONVERSATION:
MYSELF . . . .

A winter morning; a sombre and secluded library; leather-bound, unread, unreadable books lining the walls; below the windows, subdued, barely perceptible, like the hum of a mowing machine in summer on distant lawns, the sound of London traffic; overhead, in blue and white plaster, an elegant Adam ceiling; a huge heap of glowing coal in the marble fireplace; a leather-topped, mahogany writing-table; the pen poised indecisively above the foolscap – what more is needed to complete the picture of a leisured *littérateur* embarking upon his delicate labour?

Alas! too much. An elderly man has just entered, picked up a French novel and glanced at me resentfully. This is not my library. Nor, in the words of a French exercise, are these my pens, ink or paper. I am in my club, in the room set aside for silence and heavy after-luncheon sleep. It is three days past the date on which I promised delivery of copy. Leisured *littérateur* my foot.

'Eats well, sleeps well, but the moment he sees a job of work he comes over queer.' That is my trouble, an almost fanatical aversion from pens, ink or paper.

I keep seeing books – though not, I think, as often as I used – about young men who have literary souls and are thwarted and even made to go into the family business and become mere money-makers and breeders of children instead of great writers. My plight is the exact opposite. I was driven into writing because I found it was the only way a lazy and ill-educated man could make a decent living. I am not complaining about the wages. They always seem to me disproportionately high. What I mind so much is the work.

Of course, in my case, writing happens to be the family business; that takes away some of the glamour. My father is a literary critic and publisher. I think he can claim to have more books dedicated to him than any living man. They used to stand together on his shelves, among hundreds of inscribed copies from almost every English writer of eminence, until on one of my rather rare, recent visits to my home, I inadvertently set the house on fire, destroying the carefully garnered fruits of a lifetime of literary friendships.

I remember in childhood the Saturday morning hush over the home, when he was at work on his weekly article. I remember the numerous, patronizing literary elders who frequented our table.

My brother took to the trade without a moment's reluctance. He wrote a best-seller before he was 18 and has been at it uninterruptedly ever since. You can see his fingers twitching for a pen as he talks to you.

I held out until I was 24, swimming manfully against the tide; then I was sucked under. I tried everything I could think of first. After an inglorious career at the university I tried to be a painter, and went daily for some months to an art school crowded with young women in pinafores whose highest ambition was to design trade-marks for patent medicines. We stood at easels in a large, hideously overheated studio and drew from the nude from ten until four. Heavens, how badly I drew! The trouble about my upbringing was that whereas my family knew very well how badly I wrote, they had rosy illusions about my drawing. They could turn out a fine graphic picture in paper games, but none of them had drawn from the nude from ten till four, and they were fatally encouraging about my horrible, charcoal cartoons. It took me about three months to realize that I should not ever be up to designing a trade-mark. Meanwhile the annual deficit of expenditure over allowance had reached a formidable total and I looked for some way of making money – or, at any rate, of avoiding spending it.

There are only two sorts of job always open under the English social system – domestic service and education. However abominable one's record, though one may be fresh from prison or the lunatic asylum, one can always look after the silver or teach the young. I had not the right presence for a footman, so I chose the latter. For eighteen happy months I taught the young. I taught them almost everything – classics, history, modern languages, boxing, tennis and Rugby football – games I had never before played – the elements of religion, shooting and (believe it or not) drawing. At first the boys despised me, but I bought a motor-bicycle and from that moment was the idol of the school. I bribed them to behave well by letting them take down the engine. I thought the system was working well, but after the fourth term I got the sack.

My next plan was to be a carpenter, and for a winter I went regularly to classes in a government polytechnic. Those were delightful days, under the tuition of a brilliant and completely speechless little cabinet-maker who could explain nothing and demonstrate everything. To see him cutting concealed dovetails gave me the thrill which, I suppose, others get from seeing their favourite batsman at the wicket or bull fighter in the ring. It was a charming class too. There was one young woman who, during the whole time I was there, was engaged in sawing longways an immense log of teak. She worked and worked at it hour by hour and had cut about a yard when I left. I often wonder if she is still at it. There were two Egyptians who did veneering of exquisite skill and the most atrocious designs conceivable. I never got as far as veneering curved surfaces, but I made an indestructible mahogany bed-table, which I gave to my father, and which survived the fire.

It soon became apparent, however, that it would be many years before I should qualify for a wage, and then for a few shillings a week. That did not worry me, but I had an inclination to get married, so I looked for more remunerative work. Some dreary weeks followed during which, though I cannot claim to have trudged the streets without food, I certainly made a great number of fruitless and rather humiliating calls upon prospective employers.

Dickens held it against his parents that they tried to force him into a blacking factory instead of letting him write. The last firm at which I solicited a job was engaged, among other things, in the manufacture of blacking. I pleaded desperately. If I wasn't employed there I should be driven to Literature. But the manager was relentless. It was no use my thinking of blacking. That was not for the likes of me. I had better make up my mind and settle down to the humble rut which fate had ordained for me. I must write a book.

The value of writing books is that it gives one a market for articles. So here I am, pen poised indecisively over the foolscap, earning my living.

But I am not utterly enslaved. I still have dreams of shaking off the chains of creative endeavour. Rimbaud got away from it and became a gun runner. Vanbrugh gave up writing plays to build the most lovely houses in England. Disraeli and A. P. Herbert went into politics and did themselves proud. John Buchan is lording it in Quebec. Boulestin took to cooking. Perhaps there is a chance of freedom.

. THROUGH EUROPEAN EYES .

Anno XIIII is the year which those of us who still prefer to base our chronology upon a more remote but more glorious incident in the world's history than Signor Mussolini's assumption of rule in Rome know as AD 1935. It is a year which must always be a memory of bitter humiliation to Englishmen of every shade of political colour. Never, since the American War of Independence, has our prestige in the world fallen so low. The lessons of that year have been emphasized often enough; that popular sympathies have no place in diplomacy; that a private, ironically called a 'free' press, of the kind which flourishes in France, England and the United States – where no responsibility curbs its extravagances, where the news is merely a bait to attract attention to the advertisements – is the worst possible guide to popular sympathies; that law without force is no law at all; that justice capriciously applied is no justice. A detailed examination of the events of that year reveals every weakness in the present political situation. The results of English diplomacy are already apparent. Italy and Germany who in 1934 seemed irreconcilable opponents are now in close and formidable alliance and England is left to seek her friends among nations distracted to the point of impotence by internal dissension, dissensions which have been largely aggravated by the events themselves. We all see the result and are appalled; few trouble to probe farther and enquire into the false ideas which have exposed us to shame. We prefer to harbour a grievance and vent our rage in moral lessons to our neighbours, eagerly accepting any extravagant report which will confirm our belief that foreigners as usual have behaved like cads.

It is small wonder that, since our diplomacy is so little understood at home, it

Review of *Anno XIIII*, by Emilio de Bono. *London Mercury and Bookman*, June 1937.

should not at all be understood abroad. Marshal Emilio de Bono, in his book *Anno XIIII*, is only expressing the conviction, not only of every Italian, but of practically every European and Asiatic, when he assumes that our opposition to Italian aggrandizement in East Africa was directed solely from motives of imperial jealousy. Japan had been allowed to flout the League of Nations and still retained unchallenged the territories held by her under a League mandate. From that moment the League idea was dead everywhere except in the minds of the peace-balloters. The sudden revival of League machinery and League principles seemed to the world as malignant and capricious as a prosecution under the Lord's Day Observance Act. Marshal de Bono does not even bother to state this view; he assumes it and it is implicit in all his correspondence with Mussolini. England is their sole opponent; the only question at doubt is how far, in our disarmed state, we dare take our opposition. Marshal de Bono has nothing to tell about the political question; such interest as his book holds for us lies in the unusually frank account of the technical difficulties of the first stage of the campaign and the rather touching spectacle of a forgotten old man modestly claiming a share in his successor's triumph.

The Marshal owes no gratitude to the rendering in English. The rhetorical language naturally employed by the Latin races always sounds very near the ridiculous to English ears. Signor Gayda's turgid eloquence is habitually comic as it is translated in the English press. For a Fascist – or for that matter an Italian of any political party – the Marshal's style is unusually terse; he is even capable of touches of irony: 'the labourers . . . found it depressing to be so far from their homes and families . . . but they cheered up when they thought of the fine sum of money they would be able to put by for the near future. I was inflexible with mischief-makers and idlers and malingerers and the result of such behaviour was that the men always cheered me when I appeared.' But it would have needed very tactful translation to retain the dignity of the telegraphic correspondence between Signor Mussolini and his commander-in-chief.' ". . . *I am willing to commit a sin of excess but never a sin of deficiency*." I (de Bono) replied by telegraph raising no objections, and I had my reward in this telegram: "*I am glad to note that as always you will second my ideas with your intelligence, your experience, and above all your faith.*" ' Sometimes the translator seems to have misread a passage, 'The unruliness of the Rases may lead to a movement which will induce one or another of the stronger of them – even without the Emperor's wish – to rebel against the Emperor.' But generally speaking the book is a straightforward and rather dull account of great difficulties partially surmounted.

The conquest of Abyssinia was never, primarily, a military problem. Even had they been disposed to resist – and the majority were not – the Abyssinians could not in equipment or discipline offer a serious resistance. The problems were those of engineering, supply and hygiene, and in the solution of these problems the Italians astonished the world. They chose to pursue what any other imperial country would have treated as a minor colonial operation with the zeal and prodigality of – what in fact we had made it – a desperate national struggle for existence. The result staggered the military experts. It is true that in England we were very ill-advised of the true character of the Abyssinian – his venality, treachery, lack of patriotic consciousness, his bluster in victory and collapse in reverse; the true nature of the Abyssinian rout can only be read, at present, in the brilliant supplement by a Russian eyewitness to Mr Steer's *Caesar in Abyssinia*; but when all this is allowed for Badoglio's advance on Addis remains an enormous achievement. Marshal de Bono modestly claims attention for having prepared the way for that advance.

Attempts were made in the popular press, when *Anno XIIII* was first published in Rome last autumn, and again this spring when the translation appeared, to represent it as a book which sensationally exposed any claims which the Italians might have to a just cause of war. It is in fact possible to quote extracts which suggest that before the Wal-wal incident the annexation of Abyssinia was already decided, but this view, I think, will not bear close inspection.

Fascist policy is consistently and essentially opportunist. The party came into power without any very clear ideas about its policy. Signor Mussolini believed that the first thing was to establish a government, restore order, get the nation back to work and then see what was to be done with it. In foreign politics his natural enemy was Germany; he ruled a large German-speaking population; he had the natural contempt for Hitler which an original has for a counterfeit, a practical man of the world for a crank; his interests in Austria were directly opposed to Hitler's. The colonial question did not become pressing until the economic convulsion of 1930. His attention naturally turned to Abyssinia which had once been Italian in name, where there was an old disgrace to expiate, where the other powers consistently admitted Italian interests to be paramount. He wished to penetrate it peacefully, in the manner that USA penetrates her backward Latin neighbours. It seemed that by the Treaty of Friendship of 1928 this policy had triumphed. Tafari himself meanwhile was doing some more or less peaceful penetration and soon after his coronation was in a position to evade his obligations under the treaty. It seemed probable as early as 1933 that some show or threat of force would be needed if Italy was not to lose all the advantages she had gained. It is the work of a general staff to produce plans to meet various emergencies. It is the work of the diplomats and politicians to decide if and when the plans are to be used. Our own general staff has its plans for many operations which our rulers ardently hope never to employ. The Italian general staff were certainly engaged before the Wal-wal incident in investigating the chances of a successful invasion. That does not mean that Mussolini had made the decision to attack. It is natural that they would do their work with more zeal if they thought their labours were not wholly academic; it is natural that Marshal de Bono, now jostled from the limelight, should look back rather wistfully to the days when he enjoyed his chief's confidence; should read into the exchange of cordialities a greater confidence than perhaps existed. When de Bono left Italy in January 1935 to take up the post of High Commissioner in Eritrea, Mussolini's instructions were as follows:

> You leave with the olive bough in your pocket; we shall see how the Wal-wal affair turns out. If it suits us to accept the conditions offered us in consequence of the award you will inform the Emperor of your assumption of the post of High Commissioner, telling him that you have been sent out to clear up any misunderstandings and to collaborate in establishing friendly relations in the moral and material interests of the two states. In the meantime continue to make active preparations such as you would make in view of the more difficult and adverse outcome of the affair.

This passage has not been quoted in the English press, for it is the English press, combined with the vacillations at Geneva, and the genuine, muddled indignation of the English newspaper-public, and the illusion of support thus given to Tafari's more extreme advisers, which influenced this attitude and made it impossible for the Italian Government to withdraw and survive.

Now that the issue is decided it is easy to regard it as inevitable. At the time it was a very daring gamble. There was no popular enthusiasm in Italy for the war; there were grave doubts in high Fascist circles. Sanctions changed all that and reshuffled the political pack of Europe; in the re-deal we hold no trumps and very few honours.

. A MYSTIC IN THE TRENCHES .

Painters write well. They do most things, except choosing clothes, better than other people; they can sail boats and prune fruit trees and bandage cut fingers and work out sums in their heads. The truth is that far higher gifts are needed to paint even a bad picture than to write a good book. Mr David Jones's pictures are by no means bad and his first book, *In Parenthesis*, is admirable.

It is not easy to describe. It is certainly not a novel, for it lacks the two essentials of story and character; it is not what the publishers take it for, an epic poem, for it presents no complete human destiny. It is a piece of reporting interrupted by choruses. It reports a battle on the western front in the middle of the last European war; a private soldier leaves camp in England, crosses with his regiment to France, goes up the line, is hit in the leg and drags himself off leaving his rifle on the field. It is a book about battle rather than war; it is completely unsentimental and untendentious; it is not like *All Quiet*; it is not like *A Farewell to Arms*, though it might well have usurped that title; it is not the least like any other war book I have read. I can best describe it by saying that it is as though Mr T. S. Eliot had written *The Better 'Ole*.

The similarity to Mr Eliot's work is everywhere apparent, but it is by allusion rather than imitation. The sentry's password is 'Prickly Pear'. There

Review of *In Parenthesis*, by David Jones. *Night and Day*, 1 July 1937.

are the same defects of style – the statement in ponderous detail of simple physical facts – more common in the work of Mr Eliot's followers than in his own; the sentry setting his sights 'slid up the exact steel, the graduated leaf precisely angled to its bed'; on the officer's wrist 'the phosphorescent dial describes the equal seconds.' That way lie the extravagances of the Augustan tradition in decadence. There are also the too facile contrasts by juxtaposition of scholarly tags and modern slang – the standard fare of the parodist. There are whole passages which, out of the context, one might take for extracts from *The Waste Land*. 'You sensed him near you just now but that's more like a nettle to the touch; or on your left Joe Donkin walked, where only weeds stir to the night-gusts if you feel with your hands.' But there is an essential difference between *The Waste Land* and *In Parenthesis*. Mr Eliot in his great passage of the unknown intangible companion is writing metaphorically; he is seeking concrete images to express a psychological state. Mr Jones is describing an objective physical experience – the loss of contact with neighbouring files in a night attack. It is this painter's realism which lifts his work above any of Mr Eliot's followers and, in many places, above Mr Eliot himself. Moreover, he has a painter's *communicativeness*. The literary mind is a rat on a treadwheel; too many modern poetic writers employ a language which can be intelligible only to themselves; they relate experiences one to another inside themselves. Mr Jones is seldom obscure and never esoteric; he must be read with the attention of a surgeon, but there is not a sentence which on analysis lacks a precise meaning. Indeed he is at too great pains to explain himself. He would not, I think, like to pin an explanation to the frames of his pictures, and his writing is too lucid to need such adventitious contributions. For he writes with the respect of a stranger. He knows that he is practising an unfamiliar art, which has its own potentialities and limitations. As a painter he studies his subject for its visual qualities; now he is dealing with words, and his aim is to make a book about the verbal aspect of battle. For twenty years the rich components have been seeking their proper arrangements in his mind – the liturgical repetitions and variations of the drill sergeant's commands, the luminous phrases of Cockney and Welshman, the songs and trench-jokes – and he has at last got them into order, with remarkable felicity. That is his *rapportage*; in his choruses – as for want of a better word one can call the metaphysical reflections, often only a line in length – the reader is allowed the luxury of deducing his own conclusions.

It is always temerarious to attempt an explanation of a living writer's meaning. It seems to me that Mr Jones sees man in a dual rôle – as the individual soul, the exiled child of Eve, living, in a parenthesis, a Platonic shadow-life, two-dimensional, the Hollow Man; and man as the heir of his ancestors, the link in the continuous life-chain, the race-unit. Perhaps it is presumptuous to go further and suggest that the final, exquisitely written passages in which the hero abandons his weapons on the field – the ultimate reproach of the heroic age – are meant to show that the race-myth has been sloughed off, leaving only the stark alternatives of Heaven and Hell. That anyway is how I understand it.

. CIVILIZATION AND CULTURE .

Although *Stranger Wonders* is not in fact Mr Sykes's first book, one may greet him as a new writer. *Wassmuss* was of interest to a restricted public; *Stranger Wonders* will be a delight to all who have been waiting to see filled an enviable and essentially English place in letters by a successor in this generation to Mr Max Beerbohm. Years ago, when *Some People* appeared, it seemed that Mr Nicolson would succeed, but he has passed on to graver occupations. It is too early to predict how Mr Sykes will exploit his talents. It is enough to say that by one story in this book he excites the most eager anticipations. He, or his publishers, have collected eight pieces which differ greatly in form, temper, merit and, I should guess, in the date of their composition. In an enchanting introductory essay Mr Sykes claims for them a common hero, *le fou anglais*, but it is impossible to find this justified in 'Champagne and Mrs Chest' or 'The Wailing Wall'. Indeed I cannot see why Mr Sykes thought this latter sketch worth printing unless it was for the personal gratification of defining his attitude to a question of universal controversy.

The longest and cleverest part of the book is an admirable story called 'Invention'. Mr Garton, a prosperous novelist, visits a pseudo-Cypriot island, is entertained at the Residency, and finds inspiration there for a short story and a novel. Mr Garton's ghastly character and the horrors of his reception are brilliantly studied. The theme is the works by Mr Garton which spring from his visit. The novel arises from a story which he himself fabricates in a despairing effort to carry off a painful dinner; the short story, in an insubstantial, dream-like way, is derived from his actual experience. His host and hostess await its publication with obscene apprehension, and find the only passage taken directly from life:

> 'Have a drink. The women will be down in a minute.'
> Acklam pointed to a tray and began to read the papers. Presently there was a sound of finery and Mrs Acklam came into the room with her daughter.

The story within the story is given in full. It is first-class parody of the Maugham-*Nash's* school of fiction, full of ruthless and delectable touches of vulgar language and confused geography, but it is more than this; it is a penetrating study of the true springs of literary imagination. (There is a subtle by-plot when Mr Garton himself suffers from this imagination in overhearing a description of his own inglorious attempt at seduction.) In its precision and felicity and exquisite nicety of fancy, 'Invention' is comparable to the best of Mr Beerbohm's work. It has that rare, supremely delightful, barely detectable unreality – the inebriation of the first bottle.

'The Banquet and the Boy' is sound *rapportage* of the kind in which Mr Byron excels. Three little sketches deal delightfully with the interesting and

Reviews of *Stranger Wonders*, by Christopher Sykes and *The Road to Oxiana*, by Robert Byron. *Spectator*, 2 July 1937.

quite common phenomenon of the awful gulfs in social intercourse which make certain human beings totally unable to meet at all on the same plane of existence. 'The German Character' looked easy to write. Mr Sykes's drawings are expressive but very ugly on the page. I should have preferred the book without them.

It is perhaps invidious to compare Mr Sykes and Mr Byron. Each appears in the other's book. They have travelled together and shared many appalling experiences; they once collaborated on an unreadable novel. Mr Sykes is a new writer and to that extent an amateur; Mr Byron is an inveterate and indefatigable professional; he began writing before most of his generation and will, I hope, long flourish when the rest of them have given up. They have an almost identical sense of humour, but there is an essential difference between them which must be noted and can best be stated by saying that Mr Sykes is civilized and Mr Byron is cultured. Mr Sykes is at home in Europe. He sees England as an outlying province of a wide civilization; he is by education a member of Christendom. Mr Byron suffers from insularity run amok; he sees his home as a narrowly circumscribed, blessed plot beyond which lie vast tracts of alien territory, full of things for which he has no responsibility, to which he acknowledges no traditional tie; things to be visited and described and confidently judged. So he admits no limits to his insatiable aesthetic curiosity and no standards of judgment but his personal reactions. It is a grave handicap, but Mr Byron's gusto is so powerful that the reader can only applaud.

His latest book describes a strenuous search for architectural masterpieces in Persia and Afghanistan. He was richly rewarded, and is able to support his admirable photographs with copious verbal observations. These reports of ruins rapidly falling into worse decay should prove valuable to subsequent travellers who wish to appreciate the rate of dilapidation, but most of his readers will prefer the savage and pungent narrative of the actual events of his journey. He has chosen a form that is exceedingly difficult to handle – the selected journal – which presents two opposite dangers, that of over-artful revision and of discourteous take-it-or-leave-it, salt-on-the-tail, slap-dash jottings. Of the two, he is more liable to the second disaster and sometimes allows himself slip-shod phrases such as 'chloroformed with opium', but for the most part the writing is pointed and energetic. The scraps of conversation which he occasionally reports are of outstanding excellence.

. FOR SCHOOLBOYS ONLY .

It is not surprising to find that of the twelve socialists who have compiled *The Mind in Chains* the leading four are schoolmasters and ex-schoolmasters, and two others lecturers. There is a natural connection between the teaching profession and a taste for totalitarian government; prolonged association with

Review of *The Mind in Chains*, ed. C. Day-Lewis. *Night and Day*, 8 July 1937.

the immature – fanatical urchins competing for caps and blazers of distinguishing colours – the dangerous pleasures of over-simple exposition, the scars of
the endless losing battle for order and uniformity which rages in every class-
room, dispose even the most independent minds to shirt-dipping and saluting.

The twelve contributors, with perhaps one exception, are orthodox Marxists, but they are by no means of equal capacity – the editor, Mr Day-Lewis, is
lengths ahead; Mr Calder-Marshall and Mr Upward run neck-and-neck for
second place; the rest are bunched on the rails, nowhere, an indistinguishable
confusion of pounding hoofs and steaming horseflesh. Their aim is to state the
benefits which they expect in certain representative human activities from the
establishment of a Marxian state; each treats of his own topic in a single aspect
– the economic; they do it concisely and competently. 'Works of Art are
produced by artists,' Mr Blunt begins his essay; 'artists are men; men live in
society and are in a large measure formed by the society in which they live.
Therefore works of art cannot be considered historically except in human and
ultimately in social terms.' By 'social' Mr Blunt, as all his colleagues, means
'economic'. It would be equally true and equally fair to say 'Men live on the
earth, etc. Therefore works of art cannot be considered historically except in
geographical and ultimately in meteorological terms.' A metaphysician would
have little difficulty in demolishing Mr Upward's elementary statement of the
origin of life in a material universe. He jauntily skips every difficulty in his
theory of automatic evolution. His essay is of value, not as stating a theory of
aesthetics that can possibly interest an aesthetician, but as offering a rough and
ready system of class-room marking by which a certain number of capable
writers do in fact at the moment judge their own and other people's books. His
thesis, if I do not misunderstand him, is that the class struggle is the only topic
worth a writer's attention; his difficulty that this means relegating to insignifi-
cance almost the whole of the world's literature. He avoids but does not solve
the difficulty by assuming the social revolution to be so immediately imminent
that the writer's task is *now*, for the first time, radically different from what it
was in any other age. He cannot believe that there has ever been a time in
history when economic problems seemed as serious or that great writers were
willing to stand aloof. He contrasts Shakespeare's world with our own of 'class
struggle and crime and war' as though he really believed that *A Midsummer
Night's Dream* was the product of an age of arcadian innocence instead of an
escape from a world far more savage, far more unjust than ours, perplexed by a
loss of belief far wider and by social disturbance far more bitter than anything
we know.

. THE SOLDIERS SPEAK .

It is the natural inclination of any trade to provide the public with what it wants
rather than what it needs; in the sphere of economics this produces a recurrent

Review of *Vain Glory*, by Guy Chapman. *Night and Day*, 29 July 1937.

disastrous succession of slumps and booms. In matters of the mind exactly the same process is at work. It should be the proper function of an intelligentsia to correct popular sentiments and give the call to order in times of hysteria. Instead the editors and publishers, whose job it is to exploit the intelligence of others, see it as their interest to indulge and inflame popular emotion, so that the mind moves in feverish vacillation from one extreme to another instead of in calm and classical progress. People now use the phrase 'without contemporary significance' to express just those works which are of most immediate importance, works which eschew barbaric extremes and attempt to right the balance of civilization.

Mr Chapman's preface to *Vain Glory* raised the hope that he had produced one of those books; there are many sharp disappointments awaiting the reader and one moment at least of disgust, but in the end he is left with the belief that, in the present neurotic state of the general mind, this is as sane and valuable a book as could have been expected. I am sure it will have a wide popularity; it is a book that is badly needed almost everywhere but in England. Germans will not be allowed to read it, and I think the editor has made a great mistake and severely impaired the usefulness of his own work by yielding to the temptation to score points against the Nazi regime. We have no need in England to be reminded of the intolerable injustices of that regime; or have very little need to be reminded of the tedium and futility of war. There is, thank God, no considerable party in England which attempts to glorify war. Mr Chapman admirably states the traditional English attitude. The Englishman, he says, 'is the most serious fighter. He does not believe in war. In 1914 all the other combatants did. And the decline in their morale is the measure of their fallibility. The Englishman looked on it without enthusiasm as a dirty job to be carried out.' The danger in England today is that people will come to look on it as a dirty job to be evaded at all costs. But in Germany, and to a far less degree in all European countries, there is again the appalling danger of a generation growing up who look upon it as a glorious vocation to be followed for its own sake. Mr Chapman has made it absolutely impossible for his book to reach these wretched youths. Perhaps it could not have done so in any form, but it would have been better, surely, to leave the terrible responsibility of withholding the truth to the rulers themselves. So far as the abominable case of persecution with which he closes his narrative has any application to the history he is trying to relate, it is this: that by being defeated in battle one loses more than lives and land. I do not believe that the worst features of the Nazi regime could have appeared in a victorious nation. It is part of Mr Chapman's thesis that no one gains anything in war. This of course is true, absolutely. War is an absolute loss, but it admits of degrees; it is very bad to fight, but it is worse to lose. That was the realistic attitude of the British soldier which brought him to victory. Mr Chapman admits this important principle in his preface, but he seems to lose sight of it in the subsequent, often painfully pert, comments; it is a principle which, in general, Englishmen today are in grave danger of forgetting. *Vain Glory* would have been a more valuable book if it had been better emphasized.

But it is, nevertheless, a valuable book. It is almost entirely the work of soldiers, and, when soldiers speak, it is better for those of us who were too young to fight to keep silent. We are at liberty to quarrel with our contemporaries when they declare that nothing is worth defending, but we must avoid the vile impertinence of assuring our elders that fighting is on the whole rather fun. Mr Chapman has followed the course of the war in a series of extracts from the vast accumulation of documents at his disposal, with a preference for untendentious, unliterary, personal, transparently sincere narrative. He has chosen them, admittedly, to illustrate a theme – the effect of war upon the survivors. He is prepared to write off the obvious losses – the death and physical suffering – as irrelevant to his purpose. He has, generally speaking, avoided the temptation, ignobly exploited in a hundred war books, to make the flesh creep. He is occupied primarily with the spiritual consequences, the pollution of truth, the deterioration of human character in prolonged unnatural stress, the emergence of the bully and cad, the obliteration of chivalry. In his selection he has admitted occasional records of courage and adventure (among the flying-men for instance), but he has preferred those in which the temper is one of muddle and futility. Thus of the number of highly exciting successful escapes from German prison camps which he had at his disposal, he has chosen one in which the fugitives were recaptured. Zeebrugge and Jutland are the only naval engagements described; the first battle of Gaza is chosen to typify the Palestine campaign; a vulgar little incident outside Jerusalem is recorded instead of Allenby's noble entry; when Mr Chapman wishes to give an instance of the heroic tenacity of the French he chooses one which was magnificent but ineffectual – the defence of Fort Vaux. Almost every big battle is seen from the eyes of the defeated or of those units which muddled their objective. Each narrative is clearly truthful, but in combination they seem ill-proportioned; there are equally truthful accounts of the exultation of success, of neat ambushes and triumphant dashing raids; of endurance which was relieved in time, of self-sacrifice which bore fruit. Reading simply for information, as one who was not in the war asking those who were for a true account, one feels that one is not getting quite a straight deal.

From the literary point of view there are few complaints. The cross-headings are pointed enough; often too pointed; they smack of the 'This England' column in the *New Statesman*. One is foul: 'Gott mit uns' above Haig's sober and reverent statement of his sense of responsibility. 'Must not occur again', too, is shoddy; but one is given reason to hope that these are not from Mr Chapman's pen. There is a nasty atmosphere of *Cavalcade* in places – the extract from *The Times* for instance on page 8. But, taken altogether, the book has more sound unfamiliar narrative in it than I have met for a long time. And that is because it is not for the most part the work of professional writers.

. FOLKESTONE, FOR SHAME! .

Publishers' blurbs make easy game for the reviewer; it is easy to examine an author's work and damn it by reference to the praise impudently given it on the wrapper. Messrs Hutchinson make the intriguing claim for Miss Netta Muskett's *Middle Mist* that it is 'an intriguing Love Story'. Opening it at random, I found this stimulating sentence: 'To say that Sabine was angry at being abandoned in a strange hotel in Paris on her wedding night was grossly to understate the case.' Was I intrigued?

Miss Muskett's heroine is named Sabine Cliff; she is plain (until she smiles), of mature age, with black hair securely parted; she is a purposeful, ambitious and, it must be admitted, unscrupulous person; a new line in heroine; premonitory perhaps of a new type determined by a new historic figure? In chapter one we find her busy with the microscope; she is that formidable and forbidding character, more terrible in nature than in art, the female medical student; she has a friend Judith Day, who unhappily disappears from the story (one of its countless intriguing features). Miss Day had taken to medicine because Society life bored her. Not so Miss Cliff, who has already decided to be 'one of the greatest, if not the greatest' (difficult sentence, Miss Muskett) 'surgeon in the world', an ambition which is suddenly shaken by the beastly behaviour of her brother Eric. Eric is a fop and a libertine; he lives with his widowed mother in ignoble luxury at a Folkestone villa (Mrs Cliff 'had felt a little guilty herself about having Cora for all the time instead of just mornings . . . but really it was nice to have plenty of servants about'). Now, when Sabine is about to sit for, and carry off, the coveted Wainwrite Prize, Eric forges a cheque; Sabine's allowance ceases and back she comes to Folkestone. She finds herself 'inflexibly propelled towards that old life of clothes and bridge –' and worse. There is some excuse for Eric's moral inertia; his father is dead and Mrs Cliff lives in a 'drug-pervaded atmosphere'; this matter is treated with decent reticence; in a single phrase the edge of the curtain is raised, then dropped back into place. But now we know; we know why Cora had to sleep in; in a mad moment of revelation we see her, evening after evening, carrying her stupefied mistress to bed. No wonder that, after the austere regime of the hospital, Sabine revolts against Folkestone. Back she goes to London, this time as a typist at the office of Guyes and Co., chemical manufacturers.

For many many months she works at her desk, eating out her heart for the forceps and the kidney bowl; then comes love – an emotion to which her fellow students had supposed her impervious – hot passion for an unworthy clerk named Pip. Even from her drugged coma Mrs Cliff spotted that Pip was no good, but Sabine's awakening was ruder; she caught him out with Mardi – the fluffy type. Sabine is in despair, faced with the prospect of loveless years of ill-requited labour, when Fortune, hitherto unremittingly cruel, makes a

Review of *Middle Mist*, by Netta Muskett. *Night and Day*, 19 August 1937.

sensational *volte-face*. There are goings-on at Guyes and Co. Sinister strangers had been popping in and out. Absorbed in her thwarted passion, Sabine gave no heed, then one afternoon the solution fell into her hands; among the letters given her to copy, she finds one that was never intended for her eyes, one which exposed the whole horrible secret of the Guyes millions. Gas! And the sinister stranger, who was he? A foreign diplomat? an inscrutable oriental? an infamous international tout? a Russian agent? Not a bit of it. He was Traymar, His Majesty's Principal Secretary for Foreign Affairs. And that cryptic telephone message of the day before – that came from Mellor, also in the Cabinet. Ministers were in it up to the neck. Sabine, as we shall see, was later sworn to secrecy. It is not clear that even Miss Muskett knows the precise details of the plot. The reader remains for ever in darkness. My own belief is that Guyes, while supplying war materials to his own government, was, with the connivance of Traymar and Mellor – and who knows what other illustrious public men? – spending the profits in subsidising a German invasion. Miss Muskett has clearly been reading the papers and has formed a confused and terrifying view of world politics based on the Russian treason trials. 'War was already smouldering on the continent, ready to burst into flame' and here was the British government actively piling up war materials. What a story! And it is here that the Folkestone side of Sabine comes to the fore; forger-brother and dope-fiend mother, no father to guide her . . . who can blame the girl? Her plain duty is to rush to the *News Chronicle* office with the news. Instead she makes terms with the directors. And what terms! At a breathless board meeting she is offered a whacking big bribe, but she holds out for more. For what? I thought I had guessed. She is going back to the medical school, I thought, to the Wainwrite Prize; she will fulfil her early noble ambitions and turn the tainted gold of Guyes gas to the service of ophthalmology. But I was wrong. Before them all, wicked little Mr Galer, Lord Vosser, unworthy inheritor of an ancient name, Mr Lander, unobtrusive, vastly rich, 'a power in the land', and the supremely sinister Sir Jervis Guyes himself, she pronounces her terms: 'In only one capacity can I ever be safe to you, Sir Jervis.'

'And in what capacity is that?'

'As your wife.'

Thus it is that we find her abandoned on her wedding night in a strange Paris hotel. From then onwards, for another 150 pages, the tale follows its dizzy course to a happy climax. If there is no moment quite as sensational as the one I have quoted, there is a consistent high level of improbability that makes the book one of those 'which, once it has been picked up, cannot be put down'. Sabine, I am afraid, maintains her oblique sense of honour to the end. She teases the unworthy Pip unmercifully. She makes a bargain with Sir Jervis and fails to keep it, with consequences on page 201 which come very near to justifying Miss Muskett's ominous choice of name. Sir Jervis gives up gas but remains stinking rich and increasingly uxorious; he cannot, however, repress a taste for the company of Dictators and this gives rise to misunderstandings which are only cleared up by the death of his mother and his own temporary blindness; temporary, thanks to Sabine. During the years of separation, she purchases a hospital and practises surgery on the poor until she has reached such a degree of dexterity that she can cut up Sir Jervis himself; an operation from which even Krantzer of Vienna shrunk in awe. Eric, I am afraid, does not reform, for the moral welfare or exemplary punishment of her characters is no longer an essential care of the popular novelist, but one may think of him and Mrs Cliff, handsomely subsidized, building some softer and more vicious Folkestone in a remoter part of the Empire. A lovely book.

. ART FROM ANARCHY .

How hard it is, in literary criticism, to find words of praise. There are infinite gradations of blame, a thousand fresh and pungent metaphors for detraction, the epithets of dissatisfaction seem never to stale (perhaps that is why contemporary writings, and particularly contemporary essays, are usually noticeable only when they are abusive), but the moment one finds a work which genuinely impresses and delights, there seems no article of expression other than the clichés that grin at one from every publisher's advertisement. 'Promising', 'powerful', 'establishes his claim to a prominent place among the younger writers', 'authentic artist', 'meticulous craftsman', 'breadth of vision', 'variety of theme' . . . what is there left to say? *A Date With a Duchess* is a collection of short stories. The publication of such a book is a sticky business and one which publishers for the most part are reluctant to tackle. A single short story by a new (as, for that matter, by a very old) writer will often startle one when it is met in a magazine sandwiched between political lies or warnings against bad breath (according to the price of the magazine). Then one attempts to read half a dozen by the same writer and one finds how mechanical or jejune and bogus he really is. In the case of Mr Calder-Marshall the cumulative effect of the whole book is greater than of any part of it. It shows him as a thoroughly good writer with an admirably wide range of interests. The difficulty about praising a work justly is that any qualification appears condemnatory or patronizing. Mr Calder-Marshall is not within measurable distance of being a great writer, but I think that there are discernible elements of greatness in him. Whether they will ever mature is another matter. Mr William Gerhardi showed similar symptoms; so did the author of *The Young Visiters*. Mr Calder-Marshall's avowed aims, which he expanded at too great length in a book recently reviewed on this page,[1] strike at the whole integrity and decency of art. I approached this book prepared to see signs of deterioration, eager perhaps to point a moral against doctrinaire students. I find instead a book of fresh and vivid narratives, full of humour, penetration and acute observation. If this is Marxist fiction, I have no

Review of *A Date with a Duchess*, by Arthur Calder-Marshall. *Night and Day*, 16 September 1937.
1 *The Changing Scene*, reviewed 9 September 1937.

quarrel with it.

The eponymous story deals with repressed romance in the life of an hotel manageress. It is not the most important story and I suspect it has been given primacy simply because of its excellent title. Mr Calder-Marshall is so particularly attentive to vernacular propriety that I am surprised to find him using the abbreviation 'Guins'. Surely there is no precedent for this? 'One of the Leaders' is altogether admirable. I suppose it might be called proletarian in so far as it deals with a clash between strikers and police, but it is a thousand miles from the sanctimonious abstractions of Mr Calder-Marshall's colleagues in English politics. The mood of rebellion is brilliantly treated – the background of five weeks' boredom, of a nagging wife, of the camaraderie found only among fellow unfortunates, of the physical itch to hit something in an idle body accustomed to hewing coal. The whispered agitation before the outbreak of violence, the sudden sense of liberation in finding that bosses can be knocked about, that policemen's skulls can be cracked, the symbolism and futility of pushing the safe down the mine shaft, the exultance of manslaughter – all excellent. 'The Swan' shows another side of proletarian activity: the wanton destruction of something beautiful because it is felt to be alien and superior.

'Mr Thompson' is a delicious piece of satire on a hackneyed subject – the affection shown by old ladies and the sycophancy of the fortune-hunter. Nothing new there, but it is treated with an acidity that gives it a fine quality. 'Bulls' is enchanting: the story of a nightmare. Mr Wyndham Lewis tried something of the kind years ago in *Childermass*. In 'Bulls' there is no attempt to make the narrative anything but what it is – a straightforward document from the psychoanalyst; its madness is so prosaically and tersely stated that it is as pleasing as a painting by Dali.

'The Cat' is a little slice of life. Raw material but funny. 'Rosie' is almost whimsical, almost a *tour de force*, as though to show that the author can perform all the tricks if he cares to. But it has inimitable characteristics of its own.

'My Brother and I Were Walking' is the story of a scuffle in which a younger brother asserts his physical equality with his elder. It might give a slightly lubricious thrill to some spinsters; it left me cold.

'Bulge' is not much good and need not have been there. It doesn't make weight. The theme is old and for once Mr Calder-Marshall has been unable to infuse any new life into it. *Sugar in the Air* [by E. C. Large], which I reviewed some months ago [1 July 1937], did the same thing better.

'Pickle My Bones' is bound to be the most popular story in the book. It is about two youths who drink wood-alcohol. One dies and the other goes blind. The climax is skilfully managed. This isn't the first time a blind man in fiction or drama has called to have the light turned on, but it is always good for a few shivers and Mr Calder-Marshall does it as well as most of his predecessors. What I valued and admired the story for was the first seven pages which give one of the best drunk conversations I have ever read.

'A Pink Doll' is an echo of Katherine Mansfield with a hint of something rather vulgar out of *Good Housekeeping*; 'A Rich Man' another slice of raw material. 'The Password' is by far my favourite. A really memorable, irresistibly funny piece of *rapportage* about a polite lunatic. I don't see how an incident could be funnier or how it could have been better recounted. Really first-class. 'L'Enfant Posthume' is very grim and a little priggish: an anecdote of a barmaid who has seen better days, who has aspirations to liberty and taste and fecundity which all end in a little pet dog. Very horrible; a real shocker in no pleasurable sense. 'Terminus' gives a little touch of decorated Hemingway. In addition to these there are two stories showing the superiority of gypsies over refined Europeans, and two which I could not read, 'A Crime Against Cania' and 'The Smuggler's Wife'. Taken as a whole, the book justifies my sanguine judgments. It is the work of an anarchist, not a Marxist – and anarchy is the nearer to right order, for something that has not developed may reach the right end, while something which has fully developed wrongly cannot. I do not think any artist, certainly no writer, can be a genuine Marxist, for a writer's material must be the individual soul (which is the preconception of Christendom), while the Marxist can only think in classes and categories, and even in classes abhors variety. The disillusioned Marxist becomes a Fascist; the disillusioned anarchist, a Christian. A robust discontent, whether it be with joint stock banking or the World, Flesh and Devil, is good for a writer, and if that is all that Mr Calder-Marshall meant by his 'Left' politics, I am sorry I grumbled about them.

. A TEUTON IN TUDOR ENGLAND .

In natural revulsion from the exuberant and unscrupulous liberal historians of the last century, it has lately become fashionable to see the age of Elizabeth as a sombre and threatening time in English history: the old Queen, obscene, unprincipled and superstitious; a cut-throat court, extravagant and avaricious; an intelligentsia shrouded in the black despairs of Webster; a cranky and jealous bourgeoisie preparing the overthrow of the monarchy; a dispossessed and oppressed peasantry helpless under the upstart landowners – such in broad outlines has been the impression of the average Englishman educated during the last twenty years; such dissimilar impressarios as Lytton Strachey, Mr Hilaire Belloc and the 'Left Book' boys have conspired to fix this picture in our minds. No doubt there is more truth in it than in that of the Kingsley-Froude school. It needed emphasizing; now the time has come for more sober reflection and a book like Thomas Platter's travels provides many surprises which make one question the bases of one's assumptions. He was a foreigner who came to England in the year 1599 solely for recreation. That alone is surprising. We have been brought up to think of England as abruptly and

Review of *Thomas Platter's Travels in England*, ed. Clare Williams. *Night and Day*, 30 September 1937.

arbitrarily isolated from the rest of Europe. It is true that Platter came to England as to a foreign country, while his father's generation had come to an outlying province of Christendom. The Channel crossing was always disagreeable, and in the opinion of scholars hazardous, but when Erasmus had once landed he found himself in a place where Latin still ran and man thought in the same philosophical terms as himself. Platter found that in less than a century the language barrier had become almost insurmountable, but he also found the English hospitable and expansive and free apparently of the suspicions and patronage which later generations accord to continental visitors.

We know very little of Platter and what we do know is mostly gleaned from others. His book is almost ruthlessly objective. Writers of travel books today attempt primarily to interest the reader in themselves; then, having captivated him, they lead him about the world at their heels; his proper emotion is one of awe that such alarming events should occur to people so charming and witty. Not so Platter, whose interest is all in what he sees and hears. One reaches his narrative after 144 pages of admirable introduction written by the translator, who deserves our warmest thanks and congratulations upon every aspect of her work. She has – probably wisely – eschewed any attempt at Tudor-revival English and makes her translation in simple undated language.

So far as Platter's character emerges from the narrative at all, he seems to have been a stolid uncritical fellow, very much like those earthbound, value-for-money Teutons whom today one sees parading with equal zest the catacombs and the picture galleries and the casinos of Italy. He came amply provided with pocket-money and letters of introduction. He crossed from Calais to Dover, oddly enough on a French beer ship. The trade in French light wines is mentioned in any history book, but the importation of French beer to England is unexpected. He and his friends spent little over five weeks in England, but they surrendered themselves wholeheartedly to sightseeing. For a brief visit with difficulties of transport, their itinerary was excellently planned.

They went first to Canterbury where he found the cathedral clergy dressed exactly as in the Romanist countries. They seem to have kept him in ignorance of the total destruction of St Thomas's shrine or else he scamped this part of his sightseeing and made up his journal from the records of his predecessors, for he describes the cathedral as 'lavishly ornamented, where St Thomas the Scotchman lies interred'.

By easy stages they travelled to London 'so superior to other English towns that it is not said to be in England but rather England to be in London . . . so that he who sightsees London and the royal courts in its immediate vicinity may assert without impertinence that he is properly acquainted with England', a misconception that has baffled many well-meaning foreigners – Gunther and Co. – who attempt to understand the English. Platter was greatly impressed by the number of taverns and the prosperity; he cannot keep a note of surprise out of his rather pedestrian writing at finding such a wealth and variety of merchandise in a place so remote. English cooking had not then fallen into such evil repute and he is not superior to expressing his delight at a City dinner, though he mentions that the pastries were not to be compared for delicacy to the entrées. An Abyssinian note is set by the description of six captive lions at the Tower of London. That proved an expensive visit. He gave no less than seven separate tips. The first was of three shillings – a large sum in his day. He does not specify the later sums, but merely notes each occasion grimly; perhaps he grew more wary. Curiosity collecting was already an English characteristic and Platter visited several collections. It is interesting, by the way, to note the power with which Henry VIII seemed to dominate the imagination of Londoners of the time. Platter was constantly being shown objects which had belonged to him. Tyburn was one of the show places; he seems to have regarded the number of executions as remarkable, but there is no question in his mind of the fervent loyalty of the people to the Queen; so may an inquisitive stranger be impressed in any dictatorial regime, but it is certainly a happy and contented country which Platter draws.

At St Paul's he finds a service being conducted 'just as if they were celebrating Mass'. His impressions of the public school system lack the usual continental wonder. Of Eton: 'We did not see anything particular in this college except a number of clumsy scholars in long black gowns whose maintenance is amply provided by the Queen. . . . I could not discover a single student able to talk to me in Latin, they all pointed to their mouths with their fingers and shook their heads.' This passage is unusual for its criticism. Most of the time Platter merely records what he saw in the directest and simplest way. And a very readable account it makes.

. EDITH SITWELL'S FIRST NOVEL .

Some time ago I was privileged to hear a lady of modest private means and modest literary attainments talking about book-reviewing. She was describing how she had been sent a book for review by a weekly (of modest circulation). 'I had to send it back,' she said. 'I do not see how it is possible to give one's opinion on a book until one has read it twice with at least a month's interval between. I suppose the other wretched people do it for money.' At the time I felt unsympathetic; certainly we wretched people do it for money, but it has to be done quickly; there is just time to jot down a few points before the book fades from memory. The best we can hope to do is to give our readers some idea of a book's character so that they will know whether they are likely to want it. But now and then a book arrives which defies this cursory treatment. Miss Sitwell's novel is one of these. It is a book of delicacy and subtlety; but it is more than

Review of *I Live Under a Black Sun*, by Edith Sitwell. *Night and Day*, 21 October 1937.

that; it is a book of deep shadows, obscure, almost impenetrable at first; one's eyes must adjust themselves to the gloom before it is found to be richly peopled; these dark places lie next to brilliant points of lyrical light. One meets this vivid chiaroscuro often enough in modern fiction, but it is usually the black and white of the lino-cut; the blacks are flat dabs of ink, the white simple patches of plain paper. Miss Sitwell's book, or so it seems to me, is like a magnesium flame in a cavern, immediately and abundantly beautiful at first sight, provoking further boundless investigation. It is a book that must be read patiently, more than once, and it must be read. I say this in apology, for it is impossible in the limits of weekly journalism to do more than suggest its unique character. To say that it is a novel about Dean Swift, Stella and Vanessa translated into modern life is nonsense, but it is the best that I can find in a single sentence to describe it.

The date of the story is of no importance. Elsewhere Miss Sitwell has shown herself a master of 'period'. It is easy to imagine with what deft and significant touches she could, had she wished, have given us a historical background to the life of Swift; perhaps it is not impertinent to think that she may have begun with some such idea – a historical novel, the main theme set against a rich and various scene of court and café and lonely deanery. But the tragedy and the mystery of Swift were too potent for such treatment; she seems to have seen deep into his tortured soul, to horror lurking beneath horror, into a world where costume and décor become meaningless. It is a terrifying book.

. SAINT'S-EYE VIEW .

The *Journal d'un Curé de Campagne* which appeared in Paris last year was a difficult book for the English reader. Many laid it aside in the confidence that a book of such importance would sooner or later find a good translator; this has happened sooner than we dared hope, and Miss Morris's translation is admirable. It is still a difficult book because it deals with subjects as profound and complex as exist; I do not think it could have been made less obscure; indeed its very clarity makes it in places most puzzling.

The Diary of a Country Priest – what forebodings the title may raise! Forebodings little allayed by the muffled portrait of M. Bernanos on the wrapper. One thinks of some whimsical old cleric pottering about the walled gardens of his rectory distilling sweet little gobs of widsom from the wistaria; at the worst a dog-collared Beverley Nichols, at the best *The Provincial Lady Takes Holy Orders*. But 'the country' means something quite different to the French. We see it as a place for leisure – preferably opulent leisure among lakes and avenues, at the worst cosy with honeysuckle and thatch and clotted cream. To

Review of *The Diary of a Country Priest*, by Georges Bernanos. *Night and Day*, 28 October 1937.

the French 'the country' means the hardest possible manual labour, poverty, avarice and crime; M. Bernanos is not tempted to sentimentalize his village, still less to dramatize it. It is a very ordinary village and the sins of its inhabitants very ordinary sins, but they are seen through very exceptional eyes. M. Bernanos's hero is young, very ill, unscholarly, but he has the peculiar penetration and almost feverish sympathy that come from holiness. To him sin in its simplest forms is obscene and horrible, and through his eyes we see the family friction at the château and the silly viciousness of the village children as something monstrous. We live in a world of authors who try to make our flesh creep by elaborating more and more perverse and bloody crimes, but beside sin, as the saint sees it, these exploits are only the naughtiness of children, while the naughtiness of some children may cry to heaven for vengeance. It is this sense of sin which makes the book unique in temper; the incidents are managed with superb skill; the drama of the dialogue is tremendous both in its power and its grace. A really fine book.

. LAYING DOWN A WINE CELLAR .

An architect recently told me a very sad thing; that of the clients for whom he has built houses in the past twenty years, not one in a hundred has asked him to provide a wine cellar. He added something sadder still; that when called in to recondition an old house one of the most common tasks set him is to adapt the cellars to house boilers, gas plants and electric light engines. This means nothing less than the end of wine drinking, for just as a man may learn to ride tolerably well and enjoy a day's hunting on a hireling but can never understand horses until he has owned and stabled a horse himself, so he may learn to enjoy a good bottle of wine by touring the restaurants of France but can never hope to understand wine until he has owned and stocked a cellar. For – it cannot be said too often – wine is a living thing; a single good bottle bought and consumed in a moment of extravagance is to the wine lover no more than a bouquet of cut flowers to a gardener. Wine lives and dies; it has not only its hot youth, strong maturity and weary dotage but also its seasonal changes, its mysterious, almost mystical, link with its parent vine, so that when the sap is running in the wood on the middle slopes of the Côte d'Or, in a thousand cellars a thousand miles away the wine in its bottle quickens and responds. Only a man who has watched the growth of his wines, has sampled them at their various ages, has experimented with bottling and importing unusual vintages, has suffered bitter disappointments and enjoyed wildly happy surprises, can understand why the love of the vine is conterminous with civilization.

Like gardening, the keeping of wine is one of the noble pleasures which the

Harper's Bazaar (London), December 1937.

flat-dweller denies himself. For a cellar is essential; it may be quite small but it must be underground, free from vibration and change of temperature. Some people erroneously believe that the chill of a cellar is its desirable quality; wines die of cold as easily as of heat; what is needed is a constant temperature, winter and summer, of about 51°F. If you are beginning to lay down wine in a house you have lately acquired, or if you are not satisfied by the condition of wines you have inherited, check the temperature with a thermometer over the year; it may be that there is too much ventilation; revise and strengthen your system of doors; it may be that the cellar is only partly subterranean; to build a new one is an expensive business; it is the only real cure but you can do a great deal by binning in sawdust. Old butlers will say that it must be oak sawdust, but this is a refinement with which we need not bother ourselves; but it is absolutely essential to see that it is perfectly dry. It may be that a hot-water pipe runs near; in my own cellar a plumber of evil character laid one along the corridor of the cellar, but by insulating it very heavily and fixing stout doors at the entrance to the bins, I have found it possible to maintain a regular temperature. Of the two faults, I think that dampness, producing at times acute cold, is the more to be feared. At some restaurants they have the practice of coating the bottles of their more expensive ports and brandies with a kind of clammy black slime, which is evidence that, if they have come from a cellar at all, it is from an ill-conditioned one. There is sometimes a slight difference in temperature between the upper and lower bins; in this case it is said to be advisable to use the cooler places for champagnes or hocks, the middle for port, claret and burgundy and the top for sherry and madeira; but this is something of snobbery. Within rather narrow limits it is the constancy and not the degree of temperature which counts. Iron bins may be eschewed by all except the very rich. In any gentleman's house, built in the civilized ages, the brick or stone bins will be found more than adequate to the modern scale of consumption.

The questions of decanting and serving are of vital importance; nothing is easier than to ruin a really fine wine by careless handling, and in this case I have observed that the rubicund family retainer is often the worst offender. It is a very safe rule to decant all important wines oneself. A separate article – indeed a whole book – could be taken up with this subject. Suffice to say here that there are two schools; many first-rate judges – notably Mr Morton Shand – are anti-decanters, and I find myself ill at ease in being in disagreement with them. Certainly it is better not to decant than to do it inopportunely or clumsily.

The choice of wine is as wide as the choice of books for a library or plants for a garden. The traditional – though of rather recent tradition – pride of the English cellar is its port. If any further evidence were needed of the decadence of the age, it is the decrease of interest in port. There are several reasons for this. One is the Francophile folly. Most serious wine drinkers have received their education in France and they cannot reconcile themselves to any departure from French etiquette. Mr Shand once described port as a 'dubious heavy dragoon dago adventurer turned vulgar profiteer': such condemnation from so generous a lover of good wine suggests only one thing – a delicate digestion.

Port is unique among wines in that the better it is, the iller one can feel after drinking it heavily. A hangover should be unknown to the wine drinker, but half a bottle of vintage port has given many a man a queasy morning, and it is on such mornings as this that we feel most Francophile. But port responds sympathetically to the English climate and the English character – and still more to the Scottish, who were notable wine drinkers and still are (despite the constant advertisers' connection between tartans and whisky).

Port is essentially a wine for the home, and the restaurant habit is killing it. There are a hundred reasons why it is practically impossible to get good port at any restaurant or to enjoy it even if it were procurable. More than anything it is being killed by tobacco. It is *not* a fetish that you cannot smoke with or near port. If you do not believe this, take a glass of it, sip half, attentively, then light a cigarette and finish it. If you cannot taste the difference it is not worth your while ever talking or thinking about wine again. Stick to gin. But for the civilized Englishman port will always be a major interest. It is the wine most worth laying down. Some people are under the misapprehension that age alone confers merit. Take a bottle of 60 s. a dozen hunting port (a fine eleven-o'clock drink) and lay it down with all the care in the world; it may be slightly better in two years, it will be slightly worse in ten and undrinkable in twenty-five.

Port, as its enemies delight to emphasize, is a 'manufactured' wine. It is elaborately fortified; some is a blend of wines chosen to produce a required character drawn from different districts and different years and designed to be drunk within a year or two of its sale. But every few years the Douro vineyards produce a juice of notable quality able to stand alone and retain its peculiar qualities. These vintages are sugared and brandied and bottled early. The process is designed to arrest and prolong their growth so that it is at least fifteen years before they become drinkable and fifty before they are at their prime; some superlative vintages will live a century. It is these vintages which one should buy, as soon as they are shipped, and lay securely down for enjoyment in one's old age or for posterity. There is only one way of choosing them – trust a reputable shipper. No amateur can possibly tell by tasting a young vintage port how it is likely to mature. And no professional can tell exactly. Every wine of every year behaves slightly differently. Some come to an early ripeness. You must sample your wines from the time when you think they are getting drinkable, year by year, and judge for yourself how they are shaping. And your own palate is the true criterion. Some people avidly collect fifty-year-old champagne which most of us would discard.

Burgundies and clarets are the next consideration, and here the scope for scholarship is practically unlimited. Remember that the wine lists of even the best English restaurants are the worst possible guides. The best burgundy never, and the best claret rarely, comes to England. You must experiment in France. A good tip is to find a wine that is unknown in England but famous in Belgium – particularly in the case of burgundies. A good white claret is very rare in England. They are mostly sweet, and if you hear someone say, 'I only like dry wines,' it is pretty safe to assume that he does not like wine at all. Besides Yquem, which is of course tremendous, and so famous that it even appears on *our* wine lists, there are numerous châteaux of the Gironde – Filhot, Sudurian, La Rayne-Vigneau, etc. – which produce a rich dessert wine which makes a very fine substitute for port after champagne.

I knew a man who had drunk a great deal of good wine, who still believed that burgundy and claret were, like male and female in the animal kingdom, divisions into which all wines inevitably fell. (This is a folly encouraged by wine-merchants who cheerfully expose for sale – Spanish Burgundy, Cape Claret, etc.) It is well to remember that there are vast tracts of admirable vintage outside these areas, some of which will travel and others of which will not.

. MORE BARREN LEAVES .

Ends and Means performs what most of Mr Huxley's lighter work has recently promised – a full-dress parade of his multifarious studies and of his ruminations. I do not suppose that the author himself would claim any finality for his conclusions. Like all thinking beings, he is in motion – in his particular case a painful motion, so burdened is his mind with superfluous luggage. Now and then he pauses to report progress. There is no reason to suppose that in ten years' time he will hold any of the opinions he holds today; that is one of the great embarrassments of lonely and individual thinkers. No doubt it is convenient and clarifying for him to sum up now and then; but there is every mark of incompleteness and hesitation about Mr Huxley's present position. He has gone too far for the left-wing middlebrows, not far enough to be able to offer any more attractive goal than theirs. He eschews all the poetic–prophetic swoopings from point to point that have made the 'thinking aloud' school popular in the past. It is a dull book. One is often obliged to read dull books if one is to understand the world about one. Most of the great movements of history have been founded on dull books, but these have all, by their abstractions and syllogisms, led to sensational and world-shaking conclusions; Mr Huxley's exposition leads only to what Mr Huxley is thinking in 1937. It is a thesis which arouses few emotions except impatience; he knits away, taking now an objective, now a subjective point of view. As might be expected he refers casually to an enormous number of authors who are unknown to most readers – Kierkegaard, for instance. Now it so happens that I have a friend who has made a prolonged study of Kierkegaard, so that I have heard a good deal about him from time to time. I always thought that he was the peculiarity of my friend –

Review of *Ends and Means*, by Aldous Huxley. *Night and Day*, 23 December 1937.

indeed I sometimes suspected he was an invention; so that when, in his last book of essays, Mr Huxley began to quote him too, I displayed the passage as corroboration, which we all thought sadly needed, of Kierkegaard's historical existence. So far from being flattered, my friend exhibited the bitterest exasperation and said that Mr Huxley's acquaintance with the master must be of the slightest and his comprehension nil. I report this for what it is worth, as showing the dangers of being a know-all. There are very few subjects on which I can hope to dispute with anyone of Mr Huxley's voracious reading, but I must admit to impatience at all his very frequent references to the Catholic Church. On this subject he gives verdicts so silly that not only a recently instructed convert but the most lax and casual 'born Catholic' can expose him. When one finds an author at sea in subjects of which one has some acquaintance one is less inclined to accept him on those of which one is ignorant.

The disability lies deeper than imperfect knowledge. It is in Mr Huxley's machinery of thought.

'The human mind,' he says, 'has an invincible tendency to reduce the diverse to the identical. That which is given us, immediately, by our senses, is multitudinous and diverse. Our intellect, which hungers and thirsts after explanation, attempts to reduce this diversity to identity. . . . We derive a deep satisfaction from any doctrine which reduces irrational multiplicity to rational and comprehensible unity. To this fundamental psychological fact is due the existence of science, of philosophy, of theology. If we were not always trying to reduce diversity to identity, we should find it almost impossible to think at all.'

This seems to me the reverse of the truth. What our senses, unaided, perceive is far from multitudinous and diverse. We begin life in a world of practically uniform phenomena. A stretch of country to the Londoner, a street of houses to the Australian, a crowd of men and women to the book-worm, present no points of peculiarity; the trees and crops and lie of the land, the nature of the soil, require a long apprenticeship before they reveal their individual characters; a row of buildings may be a mere horizon of masonry or, to the instructed, an intricate narration of history. Men and women are only types – economic, physiological, what you will – until one knows them. The whole of thought and taste consists in distinguishing between similars. Mr Huxley carries his enthusiasm for reduction so far that he will claim identity between radically dissimilar things upon the strength of any common, or apparently common, feature. It is the old *Golden Bough* trouble at its worst.

. A CALL TO THE ORDERS .

How profusely they are strewn over England, the monuments of our Augustan age of architecture! They stand on all sides of us, rebuking, in their measured Johnsonian diction, their degenerate posterity. Even in London, that noble deer bayed and brought down and torn in pieces; the city of lamentations, ruled by Lilliputians and exploited by Yahoos,[1] whose splendid streets, once one of the splendours of Europe, are now fit only to serve as the promenades of pet dogs or as vast ashtrays for the stubs of a million typists – even in London, in by-ways and neglected places, a few buildings precariously survive in grace and decency.

Outside the stricken area one meets them at every turn of the road. They are in the towns, grouped as a rule round the market place or the church; solid and spacious houses of the bourgeoisie, with their regular rows of well-placed windows, their low stone steps spread out to the pavement, fanlight and pediment above the panelled doors, and behind them half an acre of walled garden, an old mulberry tree staining the grass, sometimes a statue; the coaching inn, rebuilt in Georgian times on a mediaeval plan, curving sympathetically to the line of the street, the porch, supported by pillars, surmounted by the sculptured sign of the house, the ample, three-centred arch of the stable entrance, and along the side of the courtyard the ballroom, built and decorated in the fashion of 1770, its walls encrusted with plaster sphinxes, garlands, goats, Muses and urns.

They are in the villages: the rectory, too large for the restricted progeny of the new incumbent, let, as often as not, to the local adjutant or to a businessman who keeps horses there for weekend hunting, but still eloquent of the gossip of Jane Austen's heroines and the rotund, prosaic sermons of happier clerics; and half a mile away the gentleman's house, 'standing,' as the houseagents say, 'in twenty acres of park-like grounds; three acres well matured gardens; entrance lodge, carriage drive, stabling for twelve and other outbuildings; may be had with or without additional 1,000 acre farmland at present let to long-established tenants; four recep., ten bed, usual offices, water by gravitation. Electric light available in near future. A feature of the property is the wealth of period decoration.' A lovely house where an aged colonel plays wireless music to an obese retriever.

And beyond these, dominating and completing the landscape, the great palaces of the Whig oligarchs, with their lakes and bridges and Grand Avenues, orangeries and follies, their immense façades and towering porticos, their colonnades and pavilions and terraces; those most commodious of all palaces,

Supplement to *Country Life*, 26 February 1938. After *Harper's Bazaar* refused this article, Waugh wrote to A. D. Peters on 30 November 1937: 'I think it is much the best thing I have written for Nash Harpers and ought to appear somewhere.'
1 Waugh wrote: 'ruled by hooligans and exploited by cads', but when the words were deemed actionable *Country Life* required a change. See letter from its editor to Peters, 25 January 1938.

planned to provide a sequestered family life; concealing beyond the saloons and galleries and state-apartments an intimate system of little breakfast-rooms and sun-lit studies; very homely palaces, even now when the cold light of electricity has cast its chill over rooms once warmed by a Christmas-tree blaze of tapers.

They are all over England, these models of civilized buildings, and of late years we have been turning to them again in our convalescence from the post-war Corbusier plague that has passed over us, leaving the face of England scarred and pitted, but still recognizable. For ten or fifteen years we all had the pest-mark scrawled across our doors and the watchman cried nightly: 'Bring out your dead!' From Tromso to Angora[1] the horrible little architects crept about – curly-headed, horn-spectacled, volubly explaining their 'machines for living'. Villas like sewage farms, mansions like half-submerged Channel steamers, offices like vast bee-hives and cucumber frames sprang up round their feet, furnished with electric fires that blistered the ankles, windows that blinded the eyes, patent 'sound-proof' partitions which resounded with the rattle of a hundred typewriters and the buzzing of a hundred telephones. In England we have an artistic constitution which can still put up a good fight; our own manifold diseases render us impervious to many microbes which work havoc upon the sounder but slighter races. We suffered less from the concrete-and-glass functional architecture than any country in Europe. In a few months our climate began to expose the imposture. The white flat walls that had looked as cheerful as a surgical sterilizing plant became mottled with damp; our east winds howled through the steel frames of the windows. The triumphs of the New Architecture began to assume the melancholy air of a deserted exhibition, almost before the tubular furniture within had become bent and tarnished. It has now become *par excellence* the style of the arterial highroads, the cinema studios, the face-cream factories, the tube stations of the farthest suburbs, the radio-ridden villas of the Sussex coast. We have had a fright – a period of high fever and delirium, a long depression, and now we are well on the way to recovery. We are again thinking of stone and brick and timber that will mellow and richen with age, and we have instinctively turned to the school in which our fathers excelled. The baroque has never had a place in England; its brief fashion was of short duration; it has been relegated to the holidays – a memory of the happy days in sun-glasses, washing away the dust of the southern roads with heady southern wines – and the fashion has returned for more austere models – that superb succession of masterpieces from Vanbrugh to Soane which are grouped, far too vaguely, under the absurdly insular title of 'Georgian'.

Now the trouble is all the other way; enthusiasm has outrun knowledge, and we are in danger of doing to the styles of the eighteenth century what our fathers and grandfathers did to Tudor and Jacobean. It is a serious danger,

1 Probably an old spelling for Ankara, Turkey, Waugh's intention being to indicate the extreme limits of Europe.

because imitation, if extensive enough, really does debauch one's taste for the genuine. It is almost impossible now to take any real delight in Elizabethan half-timber – logical and honourable as it is – because we are so sickened with the miles of shoddy imitation with which we are surrounded. We are now threatened with a new disorder, the first symptom of which is, usually, a formidable outcrop of urns; they are bristling up everywhere – on filling stations and cafés and cottage chimney-pieces. Now, there is nothing specifically beautiful about an urn as such – its value depends on its precise shape and where it is put. The builders of the eighteenth century used them liberally, but with clear purpose. Nowadays, we not only scatter them indiscriminately, but we seem to have lost the art of designing them – witness the ghastly jars that have been stuck up in Oxford along the St Aldates wall of the new gardens at Christ Church. And even where recent decorators have been to the trouble to buy up – only too easily, from the yards of the contractors who are demolishing London – genuine pieces of eighteenth-century work, they have often re-erected them with scant regard for architectural propriety. There is the Devil of Crazy Pavement constantly tugging at most English women. Crazy pavement itself, with Welsh dressers, warming-pans, fowling-pieces, and harness brasses, has disappeared from civilized life and can only be seen in the cottages of actresses and columnists; but the yearning for *bric-à-brac* persists. Eighteenth-century ornament is singularly ill-adapted for use as *bric-à-brac*; every piece of it has been designed for a specific purpose in accordance with a system of artistic law. I know of a house whose owner lately bought at an auction sale a pair of very fine columns; they are of fluted mahogany surmounted by graceful composite capitals, torn presumably from some dismantled library and sold apart from their surrounding panels and shelves. The happy purchaser has embedded them in the wall on either side of his fireplace; there they stand, supporting nothing. Of course, there is nothing remotely improper in using columns, like key-stones, in a purely decorative way – it has, in fact, been one of the main decorative devices of every great architect; but if you are having a sham column you must also have a sham architrave: the eye, with an instinctive understanding of the laws of physics, demands it.

There is a further trap into which the amateurs have sometimes fallen – the illusion that a design which looks pretty as a drawing will look equally pretty in stone. It is one of the arts of decorative draughtsmanship to exaggerate and accentuate; nothing looks more elegant, literally on paper, than the attenuated lines and fantasies of unimaginative buildings. People will sometimes think that they are saving themselves money by going to the local builder with a modish book-plate or programme-cover and asking him to copy it as a pavilion for their swimming pool or a porch to their garden. The result is almost always a gruesome failure. Gothic was made to be played with, and its misuse, like that of oriental styles, has often had the most enchanting effect; but classical architecture must be taken seriously if it is taken at all; in the great age, the classicists were full of jokes – Gothic, Indian, Chinese – but never classical jokes. They remained true to the Vitruvian canons, and it is to those canons that we must return. One of the difficulties is that during the last twenty years the architecture schools have been getting into the hands of a generation who do not understand the Orders; they can most of them do you a presentable reproduction of a Cotswold farm (for exactly ten times the cost of buying a genuine one), or they can advise you, with a flourish of scientific data, about the wearing qualities of different patent compositions for the kitchen floor; but very few of them have had that grinding, back-breaking apprenticeship with 'the Orders' about which the great architects of the past complained so bitterly and from which they profited so much. Very few Englishmen have read Vitruvius. It is rather discouraging to try. He is anything but the lucid grammarian of taste which those who have not attempted him imagine. In fact, when we say 'Vitruvius' we are really using a snob name for Palladio. While in England our forefathers were still building with gables and beams and mullioned windows, in Italy Palladio was evolving the style which was to come to us 150 years later, which we, with typical arrogance, were to rename after our line of kings. It was a style based on that of Imperial Rome and adapted to the changed habits of Renaissance noblemen. It was a style based on exact measurement and proportion; the relation of height to thickness in a column, the degree of its taper, the relation of capital to architrave, the particular ranges of ornament that were grouped together by convention. The whole thing was worked out, and the system was learnt by everyone who had any pretension to artistic interests – not only by the architect and his patron, but by the cabinet-maker. It is a highly significant thing that the first pages of the three great furniture albums of the eighteenth century all set out 'the Orders' – Tuscan, Doric, Ionic, Corinthian and Composite – in delicate introductory plates. It was by being drilled in these until the mind was conditioned to move automatically in the golden proportions that the designers were able to indulge the most exuberant fancies. By studying 'the Orders' you can produce Chippendale Chinese; by studying Chippendale Chinese you will produce nothing but magazine covers.

. THE PHILISTINE AGE OF ENGLISH DECORATION .

When William Morris married and set up house at the beginning of the sixties he found there was nothing for sale in the shops which he wanted to put in his home. He was almost unique in his dislike of the furniture of his decade. An aesthete as fastidious as Ruskin was perfectly content with his mother's drawing-room; he and the connoisseurs of the time took their pleasures in natural scenery and the fine arts; they no more expected Art in the drawing-

Harper's Bazaar (London), March 1938.

room chairs than we do today in our morning newspaper. When they had occasion to furnish a house they bought what they could afford from what was on show, new, varnished, straight from the workshop. Antique dealers did not exist except in mean streets and behind hawkers' barrows; scraps of fine furniture and china could be picked up cheaply as junk, but it was as unlikely that a mid-Victorian, who could afford anything new, would furnish at second-hand, as that a modern woman would dress herself at the cast-off-clothes-man's. It was typical of the sanguine spirit of his age that instead of becoming a collector, Morris became a designer; he designed every conceivable thing from printing type to commonwealths and changed the whole visible aspect of the English home; but it was ten years before his influence was felt outside his own circle, and the period between the Great Exhibition and the fall of the Second Empire remains a monument of what the plain Briton can do to his home when he is not badgered by his daughters into buying what he does not like.

Architecture, good or bad, cannot be said to have played much part in the formation of the Victorian home. It is, mostly, prosaic, nondescript and as slavishly functional as any 1920 theorist could demand. The mid-Victorian householder liked a large family well out of sight and sound; he liked numerous indoor servants who lived underground by day, high overhead by night, were crammed with food like poultry being fattened for the market and were seldom seen except before breakfast, in the dining-room, at family prayers; he did not want to entertain on any spectacular scale; he had no use for the communicating suites of state apartments beloved of his grandfather; he preferred a series of substantially constructed retreats. The hip-bath before the bedroom fire provided a luxurious predecessor of the chromium and decalite cubicals of his degenerate grandchildren. These requirements determined the plan of the house. For elevation he cared very little. He was not disposed to spend much on what was, after all, primarily for the enjoyment of strangers outside. Such ornament as he indulged was economical in material and, in form, bewilderingly eclectic. The nations of the world were coming to the City of London to borrow, and its citizens adorned their homes with motives arranged as capriciously as the unredeemed pledges in a pawnbroker's window – here a Venetian window, there a Gothic; over the door a terra-cotta plaque faintly reminiscent of the French Renaissance, round the porch columns which showed a perfunctory regard for the classics; a Swiss gable, a Moorish chimney. It is the only period of English architecture that cannot be said to have any style of any kind at all.

His garden was more expressive, if not more lavish; it can only be seen now in its reduced, shabby-genteel form, but, to judge by the water-colour drawings which were produced so plentifully by mid-Victorian debutantes, it was much the same in its prime. Its essential was privacy. The eighteenth-century gentleman liked to overlook the most extensive possible landscape, much of which he owned, most of which he ruled, and of all of which he regarded himself and his house as the principal ornaments. He liked to see and be seen.

The Victorian home was the retreat of the business man; he wanted something snug and private; he valued land, as most of us value it today, as a protection from being overlooked; hence his coniferous plantations and his shrubbery – especially the shrubbery; he was agoraphobic; he had no inclination to drive down enormous avenues lined with curtsying tenantry, but preferred to saunter unobserved, completely enclosed, in winding green tunnels of variegated laurel. When faced with a lawn he filled it with monkey-puzzles and Wellingtonias.

It is to the interior, the exclusive and domestic circle, that one must penetrate to appreciate the fine flower of the period. In those great days there was no doubt about an interior being an interior; none of the blaze of light and blast of fog-laden air that vex the modern flat-dweller. There was little need of open windows in rooms where no one smoked and a large coal fire maintained the continuous circulation of warm air; when a certain closeness of atmosphere was regarded as salubrious. The mid-Victorian home was a place of rest and retirement, indissolubly associated with Sunday afternoons, to be enjoyed to its full in the coma that comes of heavy eating. And yet, such was the national hardiness of body and conscience that our grandparents went to no extreme in search of physical ease. Eighteenth-century chairs were always accommodating; it takes a very righteous man to be comfortable in a chair of 1860. Nowadays we have to be coaxed into repose with every ingenuity of spring and padding; our grandparents lay stupefied on the most uncompromising horse-hair and on structures which outraged every principle of human anatomy. But in one matter of comfort they had the advantage of us. Their rooms were wonderfully dark. Great trees stood within a few yards of the plate-glass windows and touching them, dank and acrid ivy softened still further the gross daylight. Inside, double curtains of happily contrasted lace and plush induced a perpetual twilight. They were silent too. Oak boards and marble pavings were close covered with dense, machine-milled carpets. In the library-smoking-room – inviolable masculine sanctuary where the *pot de chambre* stood screened in the corner – morocco leather prevailed, but everywhere else materials were thick and woolly and deadening to sound.

It must not, however, be thought that the plain man had – or to this day has – any natural taste for plainness. Poor fellow, it has been drummed into him by a hundred experts, writing on what are ironically termed 'home pages', that ornament is vulgar, and today he endures blank slabs of concrete and bakelite, prisonlike bars of steel and aluminium; his only protest is to spend longer hours among the aspidistras of the bar parlour. Left to himself, in that golden age of philistinism, he ransacked the whole animal and vegetable kingdom and the realms of geometry for decorative notions. How few survive today of the rich suites that were turned out in their thousand! They are scattered and broken and maimed and burnt. But we need not despair. There was precious little Chippendale mahogany about until forty years ago when fashion set the forgers to work. The inevitable cycle of taste will restore all and more than all that was lost. Now is the time to form the collections of genuine pieces. One need not at present be on one's guard against counterfeit. What looks mid-Victorian today *is* mid-Victorian. The collector's art is to select what was most extravagantly representative of the period.

In this quest which has been zealously followed by a few for several years there is no better guide than Blackie's *Cabinet Makers' Assistant*, which is to the amateur of the sixties what Chippendale's and Sheraton's books are to the preceding century; whereas these cost £10 to £30 according to the address of the bookseller, Blackie can be got for five or ten shillings. These engravings, like their more famous predecessors, are idealized; they bear the same relation to the completed piece of furniture as do the illustrations in the seedman's catalogue to the growing plant; probably in the prosaic light of the workshop much of the detail was omitted or blunted; it is not by any means certain that all these designs were ever actually executed; doubtless they will be in future years – by the forger. Meanwhile where can they be sought? In the collections of the future a set of 'National Emblem Chairs' will be a magnificent possession. Where are those chairs today? There must be specimens of them loyally dusted by lonely spinsters in a dozen shady and secluded parlours. But where are the State Bedsteads? It seems only too probable that they have ceased to exist. They are too large for the homes which are now the chief guardians of the art of their age, unless perhaps a few still survive in the villas which adorn the grimy countryside round the industrial cities, habitations of widows of the commercial magnates of the past, mayors and provincial knights and pioneers of mechanization; proud, still affluent old ladies who never sought to cut a splash in the capital – they may still guard some treasures of their bridal days. These elaborate pieces of furniture can scarcely have been broken up for the manufacture of others; they are so veneered and chiselled that there is hardly a square foot of honest wood in them. The dining-room tables are going fast – those groaning boards of Dickensian hospitality; their legs have been sawn off, replaced by claw and ball cabrioles, and their massive mahogany tops shipped across the Atlantic as Chippendale. The wardrobes, too, are suffering daily, but the Canterbury Fire Screens must survive and the piano stools.

All these, however, are interesting only as showing the Victorian treatment of traditional types; the specialist will concentrate on collecting those peculiar articles of furniture which were devised by the Victorians for their own special uses, and died with them. What the Gout Stool is to the late Georgians, the What-not, the Umbrella Stand and the Chiffonier are to the mid-Victorians.

The What-not rose to popularity with the Photograph and is unique among mid-Victorian creations in its flimsiness. Blackie defines it rather loosely as 'a piece of furniture which serves occasional or incidental use and belongs indifferently to the dining-room, drawing-room or parlour.' It is a common error to regard the What-not as, essentially, a piece to put in the corner; examples exist which stand square to the wall and, even, isolated in the centre of the room. Its determining character is a series of trays set one above the other, usually of graduated sizes; the ornament is usually in fretwork and correspondingly fragile; perfect specimens are therefore exceedingly rare.

The mid-Victorian Hat and Umbrella Stand may still be found in use in provincial hotels; its chief defect is an unusual combination of weight and instability; if use is made of nearly all the pegs it offers, it tends to fall forwards upon the user. Its chief attraction is the almost infinite invention to which it gave scope. Elizabethan design was at this period considered most appropriate for the hall as being both sombre and aristocratic, and the best hat stands are ornamented with lozenges and frets boldly borrowed from Tudor stonework. A graceful but rather brittle kind has the form of a growing tree; there is an immense variety, but the collector will certainly seek the wheel pattern where the pegs are set in a single hoop which is crowned with geometrical scroll-work and supported on turned spirals.

The Chiffonier is perhaps the most enigmatic of all articles of furniture. It has nearly all the marks of the sideboard and is, in fact, often debased to this use in the lodging houses of Oxford and Cambridge. In its own day, however, it graced the drawing-room. Its essential feature is the pleated drapery in the panels behind latticework of metal or wood. It has been suggested that it was used for keeping novels in households where that type of reading was not publicly indulged.

The paintings of the period survive too plentifully to require description. In the age between the first Academicians and the Pre-Raphaelites picture-buying became the hobby of a class who were somewhat exacting in the matter of subject; classical subjects tended to the obscene, scriptural subjects to the popish; animals, therefore, living or dead, provided the most popular models. These in their sumptuous contemporary frames will form an important part of the collection.

. 'FASCIST'[1] .

Sir, – I am moved to write to you on a subject that has long been in my mind, by an anecdote I have just heard.

A friend of mine met someone who – I am sure, both you and he himself would readily admit – represents the highest strata of 'left-wing' culture. The conversation turned on the 'Mayfair' jewel robbers and the Socialist remarked that they exhibited 'typical Fascist mentality'. This seems to me an abuse of vocabulary so mischievous and so common that it is worth discussing.

New Statesman, 5 March 1938.

1 Waugh very much hoped to expand this letter into an article, but no editor could be interested in the proposal. 'Present Discontents' (3 December 1938) develops its theme that factitious and obsessive 'fear of Fascism' will lead to disaster.

There was a time in the early twenties when the word 'Bolshie' was current. It was used indiscriminately of refractory schoolchildren, employees who asked for a rise in wages, impertinent domestic servants, those who advocated an extension of the rights of property to the poor, and anything or anyone of whom the speaker disapproved. The only result was to impede reasonable discussion and clear thought.

I believe we are in danger of a similar, stultifying use of the word 'Fascist'. There was recently a petition sent to English writers (by a committee few, if any, of whom were English professional writers), asking them to subscribe themselves, categorically, as supporters of the Republican Party in Spain, or as 'Fascists'. When rioters are imprisoned it is described as a 'Fascist sentence'; the Means Test is Fascist; colonization is Fascist; military discipline is Fascist; patriotism is Fascist; Catholicism is Fascist; Buchmanism is Fascist; the ancient Japanese cult of their Emperor is Fascist; the Galla tribes' ancient detestation of theirs is Fascist; fox-hunting is Fascist. . . . Is it too late to call for order?

It is constantly said by those who observed the growth of Nazism, Fascism and other dictatorial systems (not, perhaps, excluding USSR) that they were engendered and nourished solely by Communism. I do not know how true that is, but I am inclined to believe it when I observe the pitiable stampede of the 'Left-Wing Intellectuals' in our own country. Only once was there anything like a Fascist movement in England; that was in 1926 when the middle class took over the public services; it now does not exist at all except as a form of anti-Semitism in the slums. Those of us who can afford to think without proclaiming ourselves 'intellectuals' do not want or expect a Fascist regime. But there is a highly nervous and highly vocal party who are busy creating a bogy; if they persist in throwing the epithet about it may begin to stick. They may one day find that there *is* a Fascist party which they have provoked. They will, of course, be the chief losers, but it is because I believe we shall all lose by such a development that I am addressing this through your columns.

Evelyn Waugh

. FELO DE SE .

It is inevitable that any treatise on suicide should resolve itself largely into a criticism of Christianity. Not only is it a problem on which the teaching of the Churches, Catholic and Protestant alike, has throughout their history been consistent and uncompromising; it is also one on which it cut straight across the highest pagan tradition. If one is ever tempted to suspect that the revived conception of 'Christendom' is a myth and a controversial device of Mr Hilaire

Review of *Suicide: A Social and Historical Study*, by Romilly Fedden. *Spectator*, 15 April 1938.

Belloc's one cannot find a more reassuring consideration than this. In classical times suicide, in circumstances of proper dignity, was one of the most honourable forms of death and, in the late Empire, one of the most convenient for the upper class. Cato and Brutus give types of the former, Seneca and Petronius of the latter death. Platonists found reasons to disapprove, but in general public opinion applauded the act.

Abruptly, with the triumph of Christianity, the practice ceases; for eleven centuries there are fewer notable suicides in Christian Europe than in a single year of the modern epoch; with the Renaissance it re-emerges in the theatre and in history; today when accurate figures are available the prevalence of suicide varies inversely with the hold of religion; even in the secularized regime of modern England a suicide is still at law a criminal or a criminal lunatic. The connection with Christianity is fundamental. The Church teaches that man is by nature an exile who in this world has no claims to an existence of uninterrupted bliss; moreover it lays particular emphasis on his final disposition; between the stirrup and the ground he can find eternal happiness or eternal damnation. 'There is something very niggard, very middle class, very nonconformist,' writes Mr Romilly Fedden, 'in judging life by its exodus.' Middle-class it may well be, but it is certainly not nonconformist; it conforms to the basic teaching of the Christian system.

The sentence quoted is typical of Mr Fedden's approach to his subject; he is aware, as anyone must be who has studied the subject at all, of the essential division, but his stoic distaste for Christianity in all its forms obliges him to adopt several rather disingenuous means to belittle it. For example he quotes the Albigensian and other mediaeval heresies as evidence that – to employ his modern jargon – the 'sadistic' legislation of the Church drove outsiders to death. The truth is that these semi-magical survivals of paganism – in particular the Catharists – abandoned Christianity largely on this very point; estimable as their lives were in other ways, they refused the responsibility of living and procreating.

Mr Fedden's study is full of fascinating anecdotes. To say that he has failed in his task is only to say that he has attempted what should have been the life-work of an exceptional scholar. His style of writing is usually agreeable, enlivened with numerous Gibbonesque sentences; at times he uses words like 'polydeism' and 'quieten', which his model would have eschewed; the sentence, 'The other [side of the picture] is the contempt for pain characteristic of the ancient world, and which we have met in an even greater degree among primitives,' may well be due to faulty proof-reading. In general the book is competently and even elegantly written, but when the publishers say that it is a book 'by no means purely for students', they say less than the truth. It is valueless to students. It has no index; Mr Fedden's Bibliographical Note consistently denies his authorities the courtesy of Christian names or initials; the dates given for them seem sometimes to refer to their publication, sometimes to their compilation – e.g., *Pepys: Diary, 1667*; although he claims to acknowledge sources whenever he quotes verbatim, this minimum decency is sometimes neglected, e.g., pp. 120 and 121; even had he been scrupulous in this the method would have been inadequate. The reader is left to ponder such surprising statements as that the numerous and intelligent Baganda nation (whom Mr Fedden describes as a 'tribe') 'have no knowledge of the real cause of pregnancy', or that St Athanasius 'approved' of suicide, without any textual reference to support them. He has, moreover, shirked a great deal of the work which a book of this kind demands. 'To discover how far the suicide laws were actually enforced during the eighteenth century is more difficult. It would be a lengthy business.' A work of scholarship must be a lengthy business. Again: 'The British Empire, and particularly our early history in India, would certainly yield many similar stories of native suicide. The subject is worth research, and results would throw a curious light on colonial expansion.' As he leaves the classics, where he seems at ease, and moves to mediaeval and modern history these imperfections become more irksome.

Moreover, he has encumbered his already ponderous task with irrelevances by including among suicides all examples of voluntarily accepted death, such as Falkland's and Raoul de Neele's, and also outbreaks of popular hysteria, such as the dancing mania in mediaeval France which occasionally resulted in death from exhaustion. Witchcraft, which is thoroughly apposite to his subject, he touches so clumsily that it had better been left alone. 'A frightened and toothless old hag trying in vain to combat local prejudice' is a description so inadequate that it smacks of wilful incomprehension. The delicate and interesting refinements of logic, in which Suarez excelled, are dismissed in a single footnote. He might well have taken these as his beginning and defined what he meant by suicide. The self-starvation of the Mayor of Cork is still almost of topical interest in Ireland, and is still debated by moral theologians. It has been maintained that a man trapped at the top of a burning building may jump to almost certain death without committing suicide, while he is guilty if he shoots himself rather than roast. Some rather narrow definition of Mr Fedden's subject would have kept the work nearer to his abilities and energy. He shows a typical obtuseness in dealing with the theory of Natural Law and its rationalizations among primitive people, accepting very uncritically their explanations of the repugnance to suicide as the origin of the feeling. He also accepts the old theory – which all his quoted examples tend to disprove – of the Renaissance as a vindication of human reason against authority instead of the more tenable view that it was a superstitious, sensual and romantic movement against the restrictions of Thomist logic.

These criticisms, however, only suggest that Mr Fedden is not qualified to write a survey of philosophical history; no one need be ashamed at having failed in such an ambitious task. He has at any rate succeeded in producing a very readable bed-book. The chapter on 'Epidemics and Eccentrics' is fascinating, and every page should furnish material for speakers in debating clubs when the motion, perennially popular among adolescents, is put to the sixth form, 'This

House considers suicide the most civilized form of death.' Many of us made our first public oration on this subject. We should all have done better if we had had Mr Fedden to draw from.

. THE HABITS OF THE ENGLISH .

The publication of its first Year Book brings to notice the rather surprising fact that the Mass Observation movement has been in existence for little over a year. It has already enrolled over 600 active members – some of them so active that they have given up their normal business and devoted their whole time to it. More than that it has come to mean something to the general public, and something very near the fact. The great speed of this establishment in the public consciousness is a sign that the promoters have already acquired an understanding of the way popular sympathies work and are worked which a professional publicity agent might envy; it also argues zealous efficiency in the office. On 2 January 1937 the scheme was first canvassed in the press; by Coronation Day a staff of observers had been organized; early in September the reports had been collected, edited, seen through the press and put on the market – a very remarkable feat.

By the publication of *May 12* they proved that whatever else they might be doing, they had certainly discovered a new way of writing a thoroughly exciting book, and it was on these terms that many of us welcomed it. Now, however, the movement shows signs of enlarging its claim to our attention.

As originally propounded, with an agreeable touch of levity, the intentions seemed purely objective and thus came in for a measure of praise which its authors now seem disposed to disclaim. The plan was to apply to the British Islanders the methods of scientific anthropological research which have hitherto been squandered on remote savages. Squads of observers were distributed about the country whose office was to make notes on the behaviour of their neighbours. The original manifesto and the first work, *May 12*, have already received 62,000 words of criticism which have been analysed. Many people were suspicious of its political trend; it was felt that it might easily provide a Devil's Handbook for the demagogue. It has lately been realized that those regimes prosper which stimulate enthusiasm more than those which appeal to reason and interest. The old idea that good government was the product of the board-school and the ballot-paper has been shocked by the spectacle of enthusiastic majorities voting away their constitutional rights. Democracy to some people presents the spectacle of a robot for whom the manufacturers' book of instructions has got mislaid; it is vitally important to

Review of *First Year's Work, 1937–38, by Mass Observation*, ed. C. Madge and T. Harrisson. *Spectator*, 15 April 1938.

discover the controls before it destroys itself. Mass Observation suggested an examination of the mechanism which would be dangerous in the wrong hands. Other criticisms more immediately apposite were that the categories into which the observed were divided – 'middle-aged', 'middle-class', &c. – were too vague to be valuable and that the observers in some cases became introspective and tried to define their own emotions. There was also a fear that the movement might degenerate into a 'trade inquiry' of the kind organized by sales-managers and advertising agents.

Of these dangers the one which seems most evident in the present programme is the last. An elaborate inquiry has been made into the smoking and drinking habits of the English; the motives and methods and times of their consumption, all of which may be of absorbing interest to the brewer and the tobacconist or to the prohibitionists of either of these trades, but are drab reading for those who hoped to see the movement found a literary school. It is sad, too, to find the editors subscribing to the distinctions of Left and Right which are now becoming as meaningless and mischievous as the circus colours of the Byzantine Empire. A paper which labels itself *Left Review* must not, I suppose, object to the principle, but to call the *Spectator*, with its long tradition of Liberalism, or the *Bystander*, whose one contributor to express any political views is vehemently Radical, 'Right', is profoundly silly.

The Year Book gives us no more than indications of what we may expect in book form in the coming months. Half a dozen whole-time observers settled in a northern industrial town to concentrate on an analysis of its social habits while at work, while a parallel survey was made at Blackpool of the same subjects at play. This latter theme will occupy a full volume which promises to be the most interesting of their forthcoming publications. An analysis of the subject matter of music-hall jokes gives the surprising result that the most risible references are to ill-health. A work of interest to 'reformers' should be the inquiry into the popularity of football pools.

An interesting feature of the Year Book is the analysis of the observers themselves. Those who presumed that they were predominantly elderly spinsters will be surprised to learn that of 412 analysed, 195 were bachelors, fifty-five married men and seventy married women; there are only five women over 60; in the age groups the great majority are males under 30, of whom no fewer than sixty are still in their teens. The motives are still more interesting. Ten per cent of the males did not know why they were doing it; 5 per cent of the females, 45 per cent of the males, worked in the cause of pure science; only 20 per cent[1] deluded themselves that they were improving social conditions as against 33 per cent females. Only 8 per cent of the total had any literary interest; another 8 per cent found it an 'emotional outlet', whatever that may mean.

But with these divergent motives the observers clearly take themselves

---

1 Presumably 'of the males' has been omitted here.

seriously. They are appealing for funds in the belief that theirs is a work of public importance, and the book concludes with a weighty section in which Professor Malinowski takes the movement under his wing in a somewhat enveloping manner. It is not clear how much the editors accept his guidance and how far they print it on the same terms as the other expressions of opinion they have collected. It is a sombre essay, which in contrast to the self-effacement of most of the observers, reads as painfully egotistical. Much of it is devoted to a eulogy of anthropology, and in particular to Professor Malinowski's contributions to the science. It is to these contributions, and to his invention of the convenient phrase 'functional method', that Professor Malinowski attributes the industry of the mass observers, and he sees possibilities in their work which no lay reader of *May 12* could have suspected. But first the movement must be purged of its lighter elements. The Professor chivalrously throws himself into its defence 'against the flippancy of the authors as much as against the criticism of the Press. The subject,' he says, 'is too important . . . too serious for mixing frivolities with argument or selling the birthright of the movement . . . for the acute but short-lived pleasure of irritating the academic bourgeois.'

The meaning of that is clear enough: no more funny footnotes. Those of us who were delighted that a new way had been discovered for providing us with enjoyable reading are to have no further pleasure. More than that, those of us who relished the impersonal, objective record of human inanities are to be disappointed too. That aloofness which is in reality more artistic than scientific is to be purged. The Professor sees Mass Observation as a convenient machinery not for studying but for instructing the islanders; as 'an organization which would make the masses better informed, more intelligent and better able to translate their opinion into effective expressive acts.' In fact, an organization for holding bigger and better house-to-house plebiscites and for coaching 'the masses' in the answers they should give.

Well, no doubt that will please the 26 per cent of the observers who are already actuated by the hope of improving social conditions and, English character being what it is, the 6 per cent who do not know why they are observing; but it seems to me that the other observers will find their 'field work' far less entertaining. It is a sharp change from counting stubs in the ashtrays of Bolton to canvassing Professor Malinowski's brand of pacifism from door to door. How will he quench the incorrigible levity of the five old ladies of sixty? And what will become of the sixty inquisitive little boys who have been having the time of their lives noting the idiosyncrasies of parents and schoolmasters? Are they to join in exhorting the masses 'to translate their opinion into effective expressive acts'?

Was Mass Observation perhaps too independent for an age that can only digest propaganda?

. THE IRISH BOURGEOISIE .

English visitors to Ireland, English readers of Irish novels, English audiences at Irish plays and, in particular, English recounters of funny Irish stories have evolved a picture of the country which is on the whole nearer the truth than most legends of national character, but they have confined themselves entirely to two classes, the Knoxes and the Murphies; the former a lovable race of squireens perpetually impoverished, hard riding, hard drinking, eccentric, extravagant, philistine; the peasants less lovable, poetic, whimsical, at times even prophetic; a world very closely resembling the Russia of Chekhov and Turgenev. It took two startling events, the publication of *Ulysses* and the establishment of an orderly and stable Free State, to wake England to the realization that there is, and for over a century has been, a very considerable Irish bourgeoisie. It was not altogether our fault that we ignored this community; Irish writers, whatever their origins, always elected to present themselves in London either as gentlemen of ancient family or as geniuses from the peat cabin. Miss O'Brien's hero, Matt Costello, on his first meeting with the actress who is to be his grand passion, tells her of his prison experiences but not of the substantial stud-farm where he was nurtured and where, erroneously as it turned out, he saw his destiny. This little incident, packed with implicit criticism, recorded unobtrusively, without comment, is typical of Miss O'Brien's art. Her observation is highly refined and it is for this that *Pray for the Wanderer* is chiefly valuable. She has drawn a picture of middle-class life in Ireland; of the farm-cattle now instead of horses, dinner instead of high tea, otherwise unchanged in twenty years; of the provincial town with its street of Georgian mansions; the sceptical, literary, argumentative, Rabelaisian attorney who knows his law and his clients, who invites the local Franciscan in for 'dialectical' evenings over the whiskey bottle, who has one sentimental attachment, and a number of amours lightly and practically regarded; the power of the Church and its local grimness and smugness, which are not specifically Irish or Catholic as Miss O'Brien seems to think, but merely plebeian, qualities common to all institutions managed by the book-learned poor.

The plot – or so, at least, the present reviewer feels – is a rather unsatisfactory rail on which to hang this fine piece of *genre* painting. Matt Costello revisits his old home, now the property of his brother and a delightful family, in the hope of finding relief from the rupture of a happy and passionate love affair. He is an exile from prosperous Bohemia in London; he is fretted with European politics. Ireland, though he has become *déraciné* and agnostic, still symbolizes stability and normality; Ireland in turn becomes symbolized by his brother's sister-in-law, to whom he proposes marriage. She is, in fact, a very fair symbol of the highest Irish character. She turns him down and he gives up the idea of finding solace in Mellick. The story fails because Miss O'Brien has attempted

Review of *Pray for the Wanderer*, by Kate O'Brien. *Spectator*, 29 April 1938.

two of the most difficult feats of fiction. She has tried to present a genius and – hardest of all – a literary genius. The reader is clearly expected to accept Matt Costello at his own valuation; to believe that there is more than personal importance in his successful play, his censored novels, his 'inspiration' and temperament. He is immensely life-like, but he is second-rate; one seems to have met him before, this moody, prosperous ex-gunman, with his forelock hanging on his face, his pride in his own virility, his Irish accent that has survived the cafés of Montparnasse; one knows him and he is a bore.

Miss O'Brien has also failed in what, perhaps, is an impossibility – to create a character of her own sex who is sexually attractive. Her heroine has every desirable quality of mind and spirit; her beauty and elegance are constantly commented on. And yet it is impossible to believe that Costello is really attracted to her.

One further criticism: there are moments, but rare ones, when Miss O'Brien seems in danger of one of the greatest faults the novelist can commit: of recording conversations for their general instead of their particular interest; because the views expressed would be interesting in a magazine article on the subject, not because a certain character is moved to express them at a certain time and place. Her views about modern Ireland are of first-class interest but they are best presented implicitly in the action of her book.

The final judgment, however, must be that this is a book of very high quality.

. A VICTORIAN ESCAPIST .

It may be from humility, it may be from a kind of arrogance, but, whatever the reason, it is notable that specialists tend to minimize the popularity of their studies, and I think that Mr Davidson does the educated Englishman an injustice by implying, as he does imply more than once in his admirable and wholly delightful biography, that Edward Lear is known only as the author of Nonsense. He was, in his day, a social lion of the gentlest sort; a man as discriminating and attentive in his friendships as only a bachelor has the time to be; he endeared himself to numerous quite distinct groups, to the Court, the Stanleys, the Barings, the Tennysons, the Holman Hunts and the cosmopolitan circles of Rome and Cannes; his name appears frequently in their published letters and journals, always with the respect due to a serious artist. Moreover he was so prolific in his career as a topographical draughtsman – he brought back 1,500 sketches from a rigorously curtailed trip to India – and enjoyed so wide a vogue – though greater perhaps among the givers of wedding presents than among collectors – that most of us at one time or another, in country house or cathedral lodgings or public gallery, must have been in the

Review of *Edward Lear*, by Angus Davidson. *Spectator*, 6 May 1938.

presence of examples of his work; perhaps we failed to recognize the identity of the name; perhaps – more likely – we did not pause to look; these drawings easily escape notice; they are so unemphatic in colour, merely tinted in symbolic way, they hung so unobtrusively on the walls, merging into their slightly foxed mounts, dusty gilt frames and faded wall-paper. But those who have had the curiosity to look closer, or have had their attention called to them by their owners, will have realized that though they are of no particular importance, they are immeasurably superior to the ordinary run of mid-Victorian album-landscape and that they excel in the very qualities which one would least have expected from the author of the nonsense poems. They are self-effacing, highly competent, accurate, prosaic. The oil paintings are less attractive – mere pompous restatements of the drawings – and Mr Davidson confirms what one suspected, that Lear was unhappy in the medium; he lived in an age when it was a matter of professional pride to exhibit oil paintings at the Royal Academy; that was the dividing line between the amateur and the real artist; and Lear, so complete an artist in his imaginative work, was, ironically enough, obliged painfully to struggle with an unsympathetic technique. That he succeeded as well as he did is evidence of robust moral stamina.

Most of us had formed an impression of Lear which approximates to that of all but the most intimate of his contemporaries – twinkling eyes behind gold-rimmed spectacles, a wistful smile behind the whiskers, a fund of puns and the art of pleasing children – but for those who cared to look deeper there was always an underlying problem; how was it that a man who possessed in a high degree the gifts of genuine poetic expression was content to limit them to nursery rhyming? Mr Davidson has provided an answer and at the same time the opportunity for recalling from disrepute a word which, if judiciously used, is of real value in criticism. A school of critics who see no reality except in the raw materials of civilization have popularized the jargon-word 'escapism' as a term to condemn all imaginative work; they hold that the only proper concern of man is buying, selling and manufacturing and the management of these activities in an equitable way; that anyone who interests himself in other things is trying to escape his obligations and his destiny. In consequence of this stultifying misuse a useful word is in danger of being lost as soon as it was born. For 'escapism' does represent a reality, and Lear gives a classic example.

His disability, now recorded for the first time, was not unique; it was the disability of feeling unique. His childhood was unfortunate. He was the youngest son of a huge family, brought up at first in affluence, suddenly struck with disgrace and poverty. As an impressionable little boy he saw his home broken up; his father imprisoned; his sisters suffering the equivalent of sale into slavery, being packed off as governesses where they wilted and died, four in four months; other sisters emigrating to the antipodes; a brother becoming a clergyman and marrying a Negress; he himself condemned to a lonely childhood in the care of a spinster sister who, alone, had a small subsistence. Worse than this he suffered all his life from slight, but very frequent, epileptic seizures. The loneliness engendered by this upbringing was accentuated by his later career. He had immense gifts of social charm but he made and kept his new friends as an oddity, someone delicious but altogether singular whom they petted and cosseted and enjoyed but always as someone essentially different from themselves. His emotions, too, became centred on friendships with other men which, in their nature, were inconclusive and disappointing. The friends liked him, lent him money, bought his pictures, asked him to stay, took him travelling, but they married and made careers for themselves and Lear was left constantly baffled and estranged. His feelings towards women were always tepid and the grave objections of his own ill-health and precarious fortune stood in the way of marriage. He was haunted, too, by a conviction, for which there seem to have been some grounds, that he was physically unprepossessing.

Social success was important in the career he had chosen; he sold his pictures largely on his personal popularity; so he drifted in a wide and frivolous social life while he yearned for privacy and intimacy. He escaped from his frustration in the company of children and in writing for their amusement poetry that is supremely aloof from his material life. *Alice* is prosaic in comparison to *Mrs Discobolos*. Without abandoning all intention of communication it would be impossible to remove oneself further. Mr Davidson's chapter on 'Lear as Poet and Painter' is, perhaps, the best part of a valuable book. It is hard to see how he could have done his work better. The biography is orderly and elegant; the illustrations are chosen tactfully – more than once with brilliance – the criticism, both explicit and implicit, sound and suggestive; an admirable book.

. DESERT ISLANDER .

Fifty years ago, to have said of a book – on a serious subject, by an experienced writer, under the imprint of a reputable firm – that it was grammatical would have been to damn it with faint praise; nowadays it is an extravagant expression of surprise and gratitude. There are, no doubt, many reasons for this general decay of literary decency – the popular heresy that resemblance constitutes identity; pernicious early association with teachers who, instead of knocking the elements of syntax into their pupils' pates, regard 'English' classes as an opportunity to inflame their imaginations; later, the habit of the typewriter and the stenographer; the final annulment of the long-estranged marriage of popular journalism and literature. Whatever the influences, Mr Muggeridge has escaped them, and it is a pleasure to welcome him into that very small company of writers whose work would escape the red ink of the Victorian governess. His new book gives the reader the hope that no two words mean exactly the same to him; the punctuation, though not always orthodox (commas before ands), is usually consistent; with the exception of three painful

Review of *In a Valley of This Restless Mind*, by Malcolm Muggeridge. *Spectator*, 27 May 1938.

conjunctival uses of 'like', there are no barbarities of grammar; there is an abundance of literary allusion and concealed quotation to flatter the reader's knowledge. It is, in fact, a highly unusual and welcome piece of workmanship.

The approval of the Victorian governess would, however, be rigidly limited to the book's style. Much of the subject matter would strike her as obscene and blasphemous and may even now offend the fastidious. That warning should be given before the book is commended without reserve. But it is a warning to the reader, not a criticism of the writer, because the indecent passages of the book are not blemishes; they are an organic part of it, necessary to its life.

It is not an easy book to describe. It has affinities, in form, with *Candide* and, in temper, with *Voyage au bout de la nuit*. It is a highly symbolized and stylized autobiography whose range includes satirical reportage and something very near prophecy.

'What are you interested in?' asks the literary editor.
I said I was interested in Lust and in Money and in God.
'I've seen a book lying about that might be suitable. Short notice if worth it.'

These three are the topics of Mr Muggeridge's inquiry. Several incidents – one very brilliantly and ruthlessly describes a passage with an intellectual and humane wanton – illustrate his attitude to lust, which is that of the surfeited and rather scared Calvinist. No one with an acute moral sense could take these passages for pornography; they will, however, be distasteful to those who shirk the theological implications of the word 'Lust'; to those, in particular, who like something 'spicy'. They are very dry and gloomy episodes reminiscent of the 'When lovely woman stoops to folly' passage in *The Waste Land*. In brief, what Mr Muggeridge has discovered and wishes to explain is the ancient piece of folk-wisdom that Lust and Love are antithetical and that Lust is boring.

His conclusions about money are that it has become the symbol in terms of which the greater part of mankind measure happiness and well-being; that it is in fact trash. The hero for a few delirious weeks enjoys the favours of Mammon, who is symbolized by a 'Sir John'; he is abandoned as capriciously as he has been adopted. He goes on a quest of money among his friends, finds a little and deliberately throws it away as worthless.

His quest for God, for 'Purity of Heart', does not take him very far. He meets an urbane archdeacon, a theatrical Anglo-Catholic monk, a revivalist, a psychoanalyst, an Indian theosophist, a rose-growing rector and finds that none of them are of any help to him. His is that particularly English loneliness of a religiously minded man suddenly made alive to the fact that he is outside Christendom.

The conclusions he reaches, indeed, are sound and topical; he has arrived at negative truths by a highly interesting process. Three other major characters move through the types which throng the book – the left-wing political journalist, the perverted novelist and a mysterious and horrible Mrs Angel; all these are drawn with a precision and confidence that suggest portraiture. Mrs

Angel, decaying, restless, tenacious of life, actuated by nothing except a futile curiosity, is the most remarkable of three triumphs of writing which, alone, would make the book valuable.

What has been written above may suggest the temper of the book; it gives little idea of the form. It is written in the first person but it makes no attempt at autobiography in the chronological or informative sense. The first words are, 'Looking for God, I sat in Westminster Abbey'; the last: 'I, a man, an atom of love, was soon to die, as every other man and beast and plant and stone, the very universe, must die.' Thus, in a sense, the whole order of the book has been turned topsy-turvy. Between these grave statements are included: a very good, brief letter describing a domestic holiday in Egypt, a dream of a dying wife, an analysis of newspaper reading, great gushes of rather Dickensian compassion quickly stifled; there is a scene of street-corner oratory which deserves extensive quotation:

> 'We are all in the same plight,' I shouted, 'all strangers in a strange land.'
> One or two gathered round . . . They were menacing. Someone gave me a push. 'You shut your mouth,' one or two of them grumbled.
> 'Ladies and gentlemen,' I began, to reassure them, 'I am here tonight to ask you to give your votes . . .'
> Now they were easier. They stood back.
> 'Comrades,' I began, 'you know what . . . hunger is . . . You have a Vote; cast it . . .'
> 'Hear, hear!' one or two shouted.
> 'May I suggest,' I went on, warming, 'that you become registered readers of the *Daily Express*. It's first with the news; . . . its motto is service; it costs only a penny.'
> I took off my hat and they began to feel in their pockets.

This passage, greatly compressed in quotation, is typical of the author's method; the sudden superb swoop into nonsense is, for the man of words, one of the bitterest denials possible; the denial that anything is more worth saying than anything else.

The book combines the sense of futility of the 'twenties' with the serious-mindedness and world-conscientiousness of the 'thirties'. I suggest that in the next ten years we shall see a number of imitators, as its spirit of disillusionment spreads among the ideologues. But it is too much to hope that we shall see many as well written.

. IMPRESSION OF SPLENDOUR AND GRACE .

The six days of the Eucharistic Congress were so crowded with incident that, probably, of all the immense multitude of pilgrims none had identical experi-

Catholic Herald, 3 June 1938.

ences or impressions. At every hour of the day something was going on, at every street corner there was something of interest to see, there were so many new associations formed, that each of us, looking back, will cherish some particular, personal memory. The general impression, however, must have been the same for all, an impression of splendour and grace.

For the great majority of us Budapest was unfamiliar and we arrived with heightened curiosity. It is hard to conceive of a city that could form a more fitting scene for a great spectacle. It lies in the heart of an agricultural country whose aspect has changed little since it was reconquered from the Turk. From whatever direction one comes the way lies through enormous, open tracts of arable and pasture; straight white roads bordered with trees, transected by unmetalled farm tracks, radiate from the capital; the fields run in long, unfenced strips, and the women were working in the plough, moving backward in line from furrow to furrow; little agricultural machinery is used, and the work is done by the traditional methods as old as the race; in the grass land were herds of swine, curious animals with long, matted hair which the uninformed would take for sheep. Presently the low horizon of the Danubian plain is broken by a hill which still retains its natural character of rock and wood, crossed with domes and spires, its slopes lined with gardens and terraces and houses of bright, rococo stucco work.

This is the city of Buda and below it, across the bridges, lies the modern city of Pest – modern, that is to say, in its symmetrical street plan, its hotels and cafés and smart cosmopolitan shops, but free from the harsher modernity of skyscrapers and traffic blocks; between the two cities, and typifying their life in its tranquil progress, flows the Danube, which, curiously enough, is at times nearly any colour but never blue. It is a city of broad streets and promenades, of a wide sky line, of countless open squares with chestnut and acacia trees, flower beds, and large, agreeable groups of patriotic sculpture. It has its fine buildings, of which it is justly proud, but it is not, primarily, a city for sightseers, so that we were free from the itch that besets the traveller in so many parts of the world, to embarrass his day with arduous cultural excursions into galleries and museums. We could devote ourselves wholeheartedly to enjoyment of the hospitality of the people and to participation in the diverse life of the Congress.

Without question the grandest spectacle was the procession of boats on Ascension Day evening. From dusk the river banks were thronged by expectant crowds. There was a reserved place for the pilgrims of each nationality; there was a special boat for the journalists, but to my great good fortune I got lost in the crowd and spent the evening standing on the embankment among the people of the town. I shall always be grateful for the confusion of tongues which landed me there. How often, at pageants of this kind, does one get the suspicion that it is a show put on for the visitors and that at their own national feasts the people themselves are being elbowed out by foreigners. At Budapest there was no suggestion of this. The Congress was international, but it was also the holy year of St Stephen, the ninth centenary of her royal patron saint. We were the welcome guests of the Hungarian people, but it was *their* celebration and they were enjoying it to the full. It was a lovely night, clear and starry, with a slight fresh breeze blowing upstream.

The people of Budapest have kept their river front clear of advertisements and night signs; on the opposite bank the solid, classical façade of the palace, the low white ramparts of the Turkish fort, and the Gothic pinnacles of the coronation church, symbolizing the three ages of Hungarian history, stood out, flood-lit, from the glow of the windows, while at the water's edge, reflected in the dark waters, ran a great line of torches; overhead, in the language of the people, loud-speakers led a continuous prayer; all around stood the people of the city of all ages and ranks – a girls' school in uniform, countrymen in their best clothes, city clerks – friendly and excited, full of eager expectation as each of the imposing dignitaries and his suite embarked below us. And when the rockets rose and broke to announce that the procession was starting, and the brilliant ships moved silently into mid-stream, they dropped on their knees with reverence that told of generations of heroic devotion.

For myself at any rate the other most moving event also took place at night – the midnight mass for men in the Heroes' Place. This square was the main centre of the Congress; a space larger, I should say, than Trafalgar Square had been converted into an immense open-air cathedral. High overhead on a platform stood the cardinals' thrones and an altar and baldichin copied from St Peter's at Rome; all round, backing on to the classical façades of the public buildings, were the tribunes; rows of benches filled the entire centre except for two great transecting aisles which, for the midnight Mass, were lined with torch-bearers; at hundreds of confessionals priests heard confessions in every language, while Cardinal Goma, attended by heroes of the Alcazar siege, said the low mass, and the priests moved down the lines of kneeling men giving communion while loud-speakers overhead led the devotions. For the English-speaking men Fr Martindale emphasized in a few incisive sentences what had, I think, in a more muddled way been in all our minds, that here alone, in a troubled world, lay a solution and a hope.

During the day there was a well-balanced programme of pageant, devotion, instruction and recreation. The Catholic Association arrangements worked with exemplary smoothness, and although at most hours of the day English pilgrims might be found in the office anxiously unfolding tales of alarm and uncertainty, their problems were all solved without mishap.

It was a week in which the life of the streets gave a continual entertainment. The Hungarians possess the gayest of uniforms and national costumes so that the many pilgrims who were making Budapest their first experience of foreign travel were confirmed in the hopes that had been aroused by films of Ruritanian glamour. In the course of half-an-hour's stroll in the late afternoon I counted (a) a cardinal and three prelates, (b) two Uniate Eastern priests with long black beards, stove pipe hats and their hair tied at the back in buns, (c) a company of peasants in national dress, (d) another cardinal attended by a nobleman in his national dress, (e) a coloured African priest, (f) a crocodile of schoolgirls in first-communion dress carrying banners, (g) a squadron of cavalry in full-dress uniform, (h) numberless monks and friars, and finally (i) the Regent himself driving at top speed through the town behind an escort of motor-cyclists. Those who, at home, delight in kissing the rings of high dignitaries found the game almost overwhelmingly abundant.

Nothing could have been more 'foreign' in the popular sense of the word (even the street names defied pronunciation) but I do not think that anyone could have felt a stranger, for the atmosphere was permeated through and through with Catholicism, and that, I think, was a most valuable part of the pilgrimage – to be living for a few days entirely surrounded by people leading a specifically Catholic life. In England we are always a minority, often a very small one. There is a danger that we look on ourselves as the exceptions, instead of in the true perspective of ourselves as normal and the irreligious as freaks. We may have been on other pilgrimages, to Lourdes, for example, where we meet specialized piety and devotion, or to Rome, where we see the Church as something so august as to be almost remote; but in Budapest we were mixing with fellow Catholics whose religion has taken on the gaiety and sweetness of their national character.

The Hungarian religious folk music has a unique lilt reminiscent of their dancing. The church set aside for our use – appropriately called the Church of the English Ladies – was decorated in delicate, feminine rococo. Those who think of religion as something heavy and cold should have seen the lightness and brightness that accompanied the reverence; those who think of crowds in terms of a hurrying and jostling competition should have seen the courtesy and patience with which the great masses of people assembled and dispersed. The Hungarians are renowned for their charm of manners and gentleness in all they do; this was accentuated in a week which everyone was devoting to their religion.

More than one person in England to whom I mentioned my intention of coming to Budapest remarked that though they were sure congresses of that kind were an excellent thing, they would themselves keep away because they had a horror of crowds. It was just these crowds, so diverse and so unified, which formed one of the most inspiring spectacles. One longed for them to be greater, to include all one's friends and relations and acquaintances and strangers.

The crowds were huge but there was room for more, and it would be dishonest to speak of the Congress without mentioning the shadow which lay over it; the empty places among the bishops' thrones, the empty benches in the square of the Heroes; the near neighbours abruptly and cruelly deprived of their primary human right of association in worship. Over a hundred thousand Austrians had made their preparations to come; none were allowed across the frontier. Of the whole great Teutonic Christian race only two were present in Budapest – tennis players competing in the early round of the Davis Cup championship. It was a sobering thought, never wholly forgotten either by guests or hosts. All over the world, men and women of every race and colour are looking to the Congress as a tangible sign of the Union of Christendom. Here, all too plainly, was another sign. At Budapest differences were being forgotten and ties strengthened; a few hours distant the conflict which dates from the fall of Adam still raged uncertainly. Europe was still divided. Here all was sunshine and warmth; there the sky was dark and a cold wind stirring. Who could say how long the good hours would last?

. PRESENT DISCONTENTS .

Generally speaking, the best literary criticism today is written either by amateurs – museum officials, clergymen, diplomats and so on – or by black-legs – people who normally engage in other kinds of writing and are too lazy to read, without inducement, the work of their contemporaries, who are moved to strong, personal feelings by what they read and like to give them expression; the worst is by the underworld of professional reviewers whose miseries and inevitable degradation Mr Connolly sympathetically expounds. But above this there is the rare Art of Criticism, with its own valuable and distinct literature, its own aspirations and achievements. The only man under 40 who shows any sign of reaching, or indeed of seeking, this altitude is Mr Cyril Connolly. It is therefore worth while inquiring, as he has inquired into the adverse conditions which beset a creative writer today, into those which seem to be holding him back from durable work.

'Creative' is an invidious term too often used at the expense of the critic. A better word, except that it would always involve explanation, would be 'architectural'. I believe that what makes a writer, as distinct from a clever and cultured man who can write, is an added energy and breadth of vision which enables him to conceive and complete a structure. Critics, so far as they are critics only, lack this; Mr Connolly very evidently, for his book, full as it is of phrase after phrase of lapidary form, of delicious exercises in parody, of good narrative, of luminous metaphors, and once at any rate – in the passages describing the nightmare of the man of promise – of haunting originality, is structurally jerry-built. It consists of the secondary stages of three separate books, an autobiography, an essay on the main division of modern literature between the esoteric (which he happily names the Mandarin School) and the popular, and a kind of Rogues Handbook of practical advice to an aspiring author. He comes very near to dishonesty in the way in which he fakes the transitions between these elements and attempts to pass them off as the expansion of a single theme.

Review of *Enemies of Promise*, by Cyril Connolly. *Tablet*, 3 December 1938.

Nor does he seem to be fully aware of this defect either in his own work or in those he examines; on page nine he recommends the habit of examining isolated passages, as a wine taster judges a vintage by rinsing a spoonful round his mouth; thus, says Mr Connolly, the style may be separated from the impure considerations of subject matter. But the style is the whole. Wine is a homogeneous substance: a spoonful and a Jeraboam have identical properties; writing is an art which exists in a time sequence; each sentence and each page is dependent on its predecessors and successors; a sentence which he admires may owe its significance to another fifty pages distant. I beg Mr Connolly to believe that even quite popular writers take great trouble sometimes in this matter.

Not only in general plan, but in detail, Mr Connolly shirks the extra effort which would have helped him to attain his avowed object of writing a durable book. There are numerous lapses into illiteracy – 'nobody has so squandered *their* gifts', 'Davy Jones' ' for 'David Jones's' (Mr Connolly's form is allowed by Fowler only in 'reverential contexts'), 'Nonsuch' for 'Nonesuch', 'Experiment and adventure *is* indicated' and so on. There are, as I have said, countless lapidary phrases but they lie jumbled up with the flattest clichés. Cliché hunting is a cruel and mischievous hobby – the badger digging of the literary blood sports – but it is one for which Mr Connolly himself shows a particular zest; he indulges it ruthlessly upon poor Mr Huxley and then proceeds to talk of 'the war-weary and disillusioned generation' and of the time when 'domestic happiness begins to cloy'.

Mr Connolly attempts to cover the whole field of the artist's relation to society; in particular his financial position in relation to his direct or indirect paymasters, and here, I think, he falls into an error in the character of the reading public. 'Most readers,' he says, 'live in London, they are run-down, querulous, constipated, soot-ridden, stained with asphalt and nicotine, and, as a result of sitting all day in a box and eating too fast, slightly mad and sufferers from indigestion.' A good description: newspaper editors have rightly taken this type as their public. But these are not the readers of novels. The London office-man reads, at the most, a book a month. The people who keep the literary market lively are the unemployed women, particularly in the provinces, and they particularly relish 'robust health' in their authors. But Mr Connolly is convinced that a writer cannot honourably earn a decent living; so much convinced that he falsifies an analysis of Mr Hemingway's *The Sun Also Rises*; Jake, he says (page fifty-four) suffers from 'economic inability to get enough to drink'; but Jake is a well-paid foreign correspondent, with a balance of $2,432 (page twenty-seven, Albatross edition), he is not only able to drink lashings himself, but lends freely to fellow dipsomaniacs.

But these are trivial complaints; they are, in fact, universal to his generation and his juniors'; they give that much-sought label of being 'contemporary'. *Enemies of Promise* is disappointing on wider grounds. Mr Connolly's belief in the value of art is unquestionable, and his defects like his virtues arise from the kind of art to which he inclines; he has fairly broad tastes, but in all he admires and all that strikes him as significant, whether for praise or blame, there is a single common quality – the lack of masculinity. Petronius, Gide, Firbank, Wilde . . . the names succeed one another of living and dead writers, all, or almost all, simpering and sidling across the stage with the gait of the great new British music-hall joke. He loyally says all that he conscientiously can for the left-wing school of writers, but he omits from his catalogue the name of Mr Calder-Marshall, whose faults are those of boisterousness and whose virtues virility and, unique among his fellows, enough self-sufficiency to be able to do his own work alone, without collaboration. It is from Mr Connolly's preference for the epicene – I use the word metaphorically, of their work only; I know nothing of their private characters – that his discontents spring, for the artists in whom he is interested have nearly all come to feel themselves outcasts and to transpose the antagonism, real or imagined, of society from themselves to their art. Now female authors like to live in jolly intimacy with their fellows; they rejoice in literary luncheons, publishers' teas and 'getting up' books together as if they were charades; male authors like to do their work in solitude and take their pleasure in the company that will distract them least from their serious business; but epicene authors like to huddle together and imagine plots and betrayals. So Mr Connolly sees recent literary history, not in terms of various people employing and exploring their talents in their own ways, but as a series of 'movements', sappings, bombings and encirclements, of party racketeering and jerrymandering. It is the Irish in him perhaps. Thus he sees his own career, which some of us might envy and all of us honour, as a struggle against intrigue and repression; for this reason he gives us, in the last section of his book, a closely documented history of his own adolescence. It is a Buchmanite exercise whose publication may fulfil some purgative requirement of his own; it is highly embarrassing to the reader and it is, in the last analysis, unnecessary, for there was nothing the least peculiar about Mr Connolly's early environment. Among his own family he saw something of rich and poor; he went to a typical private school and to Eton; there he was at great pains to secure election to a club for which he had not the proper qualifications of membership. Over a thousand boys had just the same education as Mr Connolly and none have grown up at all like him. He has temporarily fallen for the tedious old Pavlov mischief which has done so much to stultify his chief butt, Mr Aldous Huxley. Mr Connolly had an easy and agreeable upbringing as far as outward circumstances go; the fact that he was and is unhappy comes from other causes; and he is confident that everyone else is equally discontented.

He is divided in his mind. On one hand he sees English life as a secure, hierarchic organization, with, at the top, a glittering world where the artist should by right preen himself. An artist should have ease and appreciation; he should travel and dine well and be continuously in and out of love. On the other hand, he sees English life as rotten and tottering; the physical and moral dangers so imminent and appalling that the artist can only hope for a complete change for his life to be possible; a change which Mr Connolly inclines to think may be for the worse. He seems to have two peevish spirits whispering into either ear: one complaining that the bedroom in which he awakes is an ugly contrast to the splendid dining-room where he was entertained the previous evening; the other saying that the names have been made up for the firing squads; he must shoot first if he does not want to be shot. And it is into the claws of this latter bogy that Mr Connolly finally surrenders himself; the cold, dank pit of politics into which all his young friends have gone tobogganing; the fear of Fascism, that is the new fear of Hell to the new Quakers. It is indeed a sorry end to so much talent; the most insidious of all the enemies of promise. But it is reasonable to hope that it is not Mr Connolly's end; that one day he will escape from the café chatter, meet some of the people, whom he now fears as traitors, who are engaged in the practical work of government and think out for himself what Fascism means. It is a growth of certain peculiar soils; principally it needs two things – a frightened middle class who see themselves in danger of extinction in a proletarian state, and some indignant patriots who believe that their country, through internal dissension, is becoming bullied by the rest of the world. In England we had something like a Fascist movement in 1926, when the middle classes broke the General Strike. We have a middle class that is uniquely apt for strenuous physical adventures, amenable to discipline, bursting with *esprit de corps*, and a great fund of patriotism which has escaped serious indignation for some time only because it has been combined with incurious self-confidence. It is quite certain that England would become Fascist before it became Communist; it is quite unlikely to become either; but if anything is calculated to provoke the development which none desire, and Mr Connolly dreads almost neurotically, it is the behaviour of his hysterical young friends of the Communist Party.

. WELL-INFORMED CIRCLES . . . AND HOW TO MOVE IN THEM .

In the vocabulary of the daily press 'well-informed circles' have by now been relegated to a place of secondary importance. On those very frequent days when foreign and diplomatic correspondents find themselves without any credible information to report, it is their custom to appease their editors with modest forecasts of their own. On these occasions, it is usual to evoke as authority some anonymous source. If, for instance, they have heard something from the postman, they attribute it to 'a semi-official statement'; if they have fallen into conversation with a stranger at a bar, they can conscientiously describe him as 'a source that has hitherto proved unimpeachable'. It is only

Vogue (New York), 1 April 1939. First printed *Harper's Bazaar* (London), 19 January 1939.

when the journalist is reporting a whim of his own, and one to which he attaches minor importance, that he defines it as the opinion of 'well-informed circles'.

At home, however, in ordinary social intercourse, 'well-informed circles' still retain their prestige. It is significant of the diffidence with which we, as a nation, hold our opinions that the English for '*on dit*' is 'They say'. The Parisian reports what is being said at the café by his cronies and by himself; the Londoner pays homage to the enigmatic They – the people in the know. To be well-informed in England does not mean – as it used to in Germany and still does in the United States – to have studied the subject, written a thesis and earned a diploma. It means to be in constant, intimate association with the Great. Nothing is more helpful to a shy young man than to get this reputation. It is by no means difficult. Like all arts, it is simply a matter of the proper use of raw material.

The difficulty is not in meeting the Great – most of us from time to time find ourselves within measurable distance of them – but in making the proper use of our meetings. Suppose, for instance, you are asked to luncheon at the last moment by a harassed hostess and, on arrival, see in the distance a face which has long been familiar to you in newsreels and caricatures. You are introduced and drift away to a more obscure part of the room. At the table, he sits six places from you. You are dimly aware of his expressing a liking for porridge. He leaves immediately after luncheon. You wait until he is clear of the hall and then go, too. Nothing much there, you think, to qualify you for a member of the 'well-informed circles'.

'Mary had the Prime Minister to lunch today,' you report.

'Oh, how exciting. What did he say about Palestine?'

'I don't think he mentioned it.'

'Oh.'

No ice cut. But try it this way: 'I had luncheon with the Prime Minister today.'

'Oh, how exciting. What did he say about Palestine?'

'Mary was there, and, as you know, the PM never talks in front of her. He won't be saying anything about Palestine this week anyway. Ask me next Thursday, and I may be able to tell you something rather interesting.'

When celebrities fail, it is always possible to introduce quite unknown names with such an air of authority that no one dares challenge you. This is particularly useful when you meet a rival Well-Informed Man and are getting the worst of the encounter. You have asserted, for example, that the Paraguayan government is in the hands of a military clique; you have been caught on this by a sudden disclosure of superior knowledge. 'What about Hernandes, Cervantes and Alvarez?' you are suddenly asked. You have never heard of them; nor, in all probability, has your rival. Counter smartly with, 'You need not worry about them. Perhaps I ought not to say that. I got it only this morning from Henry Scudamore himself.' There is only one answer to this particular gambit. 'Ah yes. I suppose Scudamore was cutting your hair at the time?' It is conclusive, but it makes a lifelong enemy. Generally speaking, a certain reciprocal loyalty should be observed by 'well-informed men'.

Of these, there are two distinct schools, both of which enjoy wide popularity at the moment. Anyone who wishes to make a social career on these lines should decide early what school he wishes to belong to and follow it without deviation. His temperament must be the deciding factor.

The simpler, perhaps, is the Pseudo-Secret-Service. Those who seek admission to this honourable corps must have travelled a little in the Near East and, if possible, beyond. They must exhibit an interest in languages – a different and vastly easier thing than a knowledge of them. If, for instance, you are caught out by the menu, say blandly, 'I've never been able to pay much attention to Latin languages,' or, better still, 'the Romance Group'; and to such direct questions as, 'Do you speak Magyar?' answer, 'Not nearly as well as I ought.' It is good policy to introduce linguistic questions whenever possible; for instance, if someone says he has spent three weeks in Cairo, instead of asking about the hotels, say, 'Tell me, is much demotic Armenian spoken there now?', and if big-game hunting in Kenya is mentioned, say, 'I suppose one can muddle along with Swahili, Arabic and Kikuyu?' You must also be an expert on accents – '. . . she spoke Catalan with a strong Cretan accent . . .'

In appearance, the Pseudo-Secret-Service are conventional. From time to time, they must be seen in public with very queer company and, when asked about it, reply, 'Well in a way it's more or less my job.' They must have a keen memory for diplomatic appointments; not only our own, but the whole boiling. '. . . Going to Warsaw? Let's see, who have the Siamese got there now? . . .' You can also flatter your friends and enhance your own prestige by giving them little commissions to execute for you: 'Going to Paris? I wonder if you could find out something for me. I should very much like to know who owns a little weekly called *Le Faux Bonhomme* . . .' Or '. . . I wonder if you'd mind posting a letter for me in Budapest. I'd rather prefer the government not to have it through their hands . . .'

Above all, you must assume a mysterious compulsion behind all your movements. 'I may have to go abroad next week. Where? Well, I shan't really know until I reach Paris. It depends on what I hear when I get there. What shall I do? Well,' (with a knowing smile) 'I expect I shall play a little golf. I find it is a very good tip to take golf-clubs about with me abroad. They save one a lot of awkward questions.'

The strength of this school is that, as one of its prime objects is evasion, it is almost impossible to be shown up; the weakness is that it is very easy, in a confidential or convivial moment, to show oneself up. It also imposes restraints that often become irksome. For more boisterous and expansive spirits, the Bluff-and-Glory school is recommended.

Personal appearance counts for a lot here: an opulent and inartistic Bohemianism is the effect aimed at. The Pseudo-Secret-Service have affiliations with the Russian Ballet, Wiltshire and the fashionable weeklies; the Bluff-

and-Glory boys move about the Stock Exchange, Fleet Street and the House of Commons smoking-room. They have definite traces of City soot behind the ears, and they are usually too busy to visit the barber. They have hoarse and rather hectoring voices, a gangster vocabulary, effusive geniality. They eschew moderation and either drink to excess or not at all; they are boastful in love and pursue rather accessible quarry. They know the names of everyone with more than twenty thousand pounds a year and can furnish, unasked, exact details of the dispositions of their fortunes. 'Old So-and-so moved back one hundred thousand in Commodities,' they say, or, 'I will hand it to So-and-so, he made a very pretty clean-up last week in Oxides.' In Parliament, they know all the gossip from the lobbies and the Whips' offices. Cabinet secrets are no secrets to them, particularly in regard to personal dissensions. In spite of their ruggedness of appearance, they have a keen regard for personal comfort, and few of them have travelled further than Los Angeles and the Lido.

An essential quality is resilience in face of exposure. For example, you have been dominating the table for some time about the character of Catalan nationalism, and, towards the end of your discourse, you reveal the fact that you thought Bilbao and Guernica were in Catalonia. Do not be put out. Either say offensively, 'It's no use trying to talk reason to Communists' – or 'Fascists', at will; or shout, 'I'm not talking about Catalonia; I'm talking about the Basques,' or 'Who said anything about Bilbao? I'm talking about Barcelona,' or 'My dear fellow, look at the map. I'm not here to teach you elementary geography.' Any of these replies, or all of them in one fine peroration, should suffice to clear your reputation. Treat all discussion as though you were being heckled in a tough ward at an election. Rely on the impromptu statistic; e.g., someone says, 'All ships' engineers seem to be Scotsmen'; reply, 'The latest Mercantile Marine figures give the percentage at 78.4 recurring.' Attribute all facts of common knowledge to personal information; for instance, do not say, 'What a wet week it has been,' but, 'They tell me at Greenwich they have registered the highest rainfall for six weeks.' Instead of 'I see there have been a lot of jewel robberies lately,' say, 'The Chief Commissioner tells me that Scotland Yard is up against it.' Always refer to big-business concerns by the name of their chief magnate. 'Ashfield is making a new station,' 'Mond is putting up the price of pills,' 'Write to Astor about it.'

By following these simple instructions and studying the methods of those who have already made good in the job, you can assure yourself a glamorous youth, prosperous middle age, the title of Grand Old Man, and finally some laudatory obituaries.

. MACHIAVELLI AND UTOPIA –
REVISED VERSION .

Mr Wells's latest novel deals, like so many of its predecessors, with the immediate future. It traces the career from his birth to his death of the future World Dictator, who, it is to be presumed, is at this moment an undergraduate and will shortly begin hustling Mosleyite speakers off their stands in Hyde Park. It offers four possible directions of interest: a psychological study of the motives which lead a man to desire and achieve popular deification, a 'success-story' showing the steps by which he attains his object, a speculative curiosity as to whether any such series of events as Mr Wells describes is, in fact, likely to occur, and, closely allied to it, the curiosity as to why and how Mr Wells, in mature years, has retained the exuberant and almost bumptious optimism of his extreme youth. The more earnest the reader, the more likely he is to be disappointed in all four directions; the casual reader, with ruthless skipping, may get considerable enjoyment, for Mr Wells has still most of the instincts of a novelist, and when he has a story to tell, cannot tell it badly. But story-telling is very much more strenuous work than political dissertation, and Mr Wells shows an inclination to take longer and longer naps while his characters are left to take care of themselves and their disembodied voices drone on in a manner that must be easy to write but is almost impossible to read.

Rud – Mr Wells's hero – is an odious character. There have been many tales in the past of noble or potentially noble men depraved by power. Rud starts as a nasty little boy and grows into a nasty little man, of mean appearance and mediocre talents; even his oratory, to judge from the all too copious specimens provided, is completely commonplace. The qualities which lead him to eminence are selfishness and luck – the magic gift of being able to identify his own interests with those of the world and to accept the loyalty of others without gratitude, and the flair for choosing the right moment for his coups, the right phrase for his slogans. These are certainly the qualities which make millionaires; they might make a dictator. Mr Wells has gotten something there.

The 'success-story' has been badly shirked. It begins admirably. Rud's first flirtings with the various extreme parties, his choice of colleagues, his first violent push for popularity are well told. Then at the interesting stage – the transition from party leader to World Dictator – Mr Wells drops into generalizations and tells of his rise not as an intimate but as a remote historian – a historian of a loose and unscholarly kind – the author, in fact, of the *Outline of History*. There is the further grave disability that the minor characters are quite flat. Lord Horatio, the Leader of the Purple Shirts, offered grand opportunities for caricature which are neglected. The newspaper magnates are cyphers. There is also evidence that Mr Wells's association with the cinema has been deleterious. The 'shots' of Chiffan's domestic felicity are pure film

Review of *The Holy Terror*, by H. G. Wells. *Spectator*, 10 February 1939.

technique of the most hackneyed kind – not even Hollywood, Elstree – and the death of Rud might be the climax to 'Should a Doctor Tell?'

It is all too apparent that Mr Wells's interest lies in the diffuse political discussions which form the bulk of the book and that the story is incidental – comparable in fact to the sumptuous illustrations in the *Outline of History* – put there at some expense to make the work saleable. The idea is the familiar one, that Prosperity and Peace are Just Round the Corner. Mr Wells has believed this consistently for the best part of a lifetime; now when his liberal contemporaries are in panic, he refuses to budge. The glorious, egalitarian, sanitary, uninhibited world of applied popular science is still there; all that has been changed is the method of getting to it. Mr Wells sees that the fashion is now for gang rule and hero worship. Very well, here is the gang, here is a figurehead as contemptible as you can want – and yet in spite of – no, *because* of him the new world comes bouncing in like a football. It is Mr Wells's way of filling the gap that he himself made in his conception of human destiny. The widely accepted hypothesis of the Fall of Man and the Atonement – leaving aside the supernatural credentials on which they are held – did and still do explain the peculiar position of man in the universe. Remove them and, if you have a sanguine temperament, you must believe that only the most flimsy and artificial obstructions keep man from boundless physical well-being.

Mr Wells still sees these obstructions as those which afflicted him with claustrophobia in his youth – religion, nationality, monogamy, the Classics, gentility, general lack of general information. And here, too, in a way, he has gotten something. He refuses to be misled by the preposterous distinctions of Left and Right that make nonsense of contemporary politics. His hero Rud is able quite effortlessly to absorb both factions. There is, Mr Wells sees, a single proletarian movement aimed at the destruction of traditional culture; the fact that it is at the moment split only shows the puerile cussedness of people who have not learned chemistry; remove the sentimental obsessions – the schoolgirl 'crush' on the leader, the chivalrous concern for the under-dog – and there is basic agreement. Mr Wells has never been interested in foreigners; at least he has never believed they are foreign in anything but language; the vast heterogeneity of mankind and the rival systems of logic by which they reason have never perplexed him. Nor does he realize the vitality of the obstructionists. In fact he denies that there is any serious conflict at all. But at least he has done a service in clearing the issues as much as he has, and, if he can persuade the lower-middle-brow public for whom he writes that they are getting fussed about the wrong difficulty, this will be a highly salutary book; it is all the more regrettable that its intrinsic quality should be so meagre.

. THE TECHNICIAN .

It is often amusing when reading the book of an established writer to pretend to oneself that his name is unknown, and that one has casually picked up a first novel, and to ask whether, if one were a publisher's reader, one would recommend its acceptance without misgivings; if one were a critic, whether one would foretell its author's brilliant future. The result is sometimes illuminating. In the case of Mr Maugham, however, this kind of make-believe fails in the first page. One realizes immediately that one is dealing with the work of a highly experienced writer, and one reads it with a feeling of increasing respect for his mastery of his trade. One has the same delight as in watching a first-class cabinet-maker cutting dovetails; in the days of bakelite that is a rare and bewitching experience. In the days of dictated 'thinking-aloud' writing Mr Maugham's accomplishment is yearly more exhilarating. He is, I believe, the only living studio-master under whom one can study with profit. He has no marked idiosyncrasies which threaten the pupil with bad habits. His virtues of accuracy, economy and control are those most lacking today among his juniors.

For pure technical felicity I think his new novel is his best. It is the story of the Christmas holiday in Paris of a well-to-do, well-mannered, mildly cultured and quite exceptionally charming young Englishman. The important point about the hero is that he is not a prig. It is a common complaint that in modern novels there are too few likeable characters. Well, here is Charley. He goes to Paris for a few days' treat. The boy, Simon, who, until a year or two before, had been his best friend, is living there as a journalist. One of Charley's motives in coming is to renew their friendship. He finds a monomaniac. Simon had had an unhappy upbringing. Charley, in fact, was the sole being who had given him affection, and he had returned it fully. Now the perverse conditions of his childhood have reasserted their importance. He has developed a lust for power which takes the form of the ambition to be chief of the secret police under the political regime which he foresees in England – a regime to be established by communists, but in Simon's eyes bereft of all features except power.

To fit himself for this career he adopts a kind of satanic asceticism, physical and spiritual. No monk struggled more ruthlessly to expel sin than Simon struggles to expel goodness. His love for Charley is one of the things he is seeking to turn out of his life. Outrageous as this character is, and ludicrous as he would appear in other hands than Mr Maugham's, he is here completely convincing. Not unnaturally Charley finds the encounter an unhappy prelude to the good time he has promised himself. At a house of ill fame – whose sous-maîtresse deliciously says, 'Sometimes I think the life we lead is a little narrow' – he meets a Russian with whom, platonically and reluctantly, he spends the whole of his little holiday. She is the wife of a murderer, and she is working as a prostitute with the preposterous belief that she can thus expiate

Review of *Christmas Holiday*, by Somerset Maugham. *Spectator*, 17 February 1939.

her husband's crime – preposterous, but again absolutely convincing. Mr Maugham has elsewhere, more than once, given evidence of the belief that association with a Russian is a necessary part of an Englishman's adult education. Lydia teaches Charley to admire Chardin – at least, she teaches him by her own intense response to Chardin what it is to look at a picture. She tells him the story of her own disastrous marriage to a habitual criminal. This recitation occupies the greater part of the book. It is brilliantly done and needs studying closely in detail; the transitions from direct speech to stylized narrative, the change of narrator as Simon takes up part of the story, the suspense that is created even though the reader already knows what the climax will be, are models of technique. Charley meets in her company two returned convicts from Cayenne, one of whom has stayed on an extra two years in order to befriend his companion. He has some further conversations with Simon ending in a brutal parting. Then rather glumly he returns home. His family receive him with joy; his father with a kind of vicarious lubricity. The last sentence is this: 'Only one thing had happened to him, it was rather curious when you came to think of it, and he didn't just then quite know what to do about it: the bottom had fallen out of his world.'

But what has really happened is that the bottom has fallen out of Mr Maugham's book in this prodigious piece of bathos. All that inimitable artistry to end in this climax! For what does it amount to? Charley had led what is called a sheltered life, meeting mostly people who led the same kind of life or who accepted it as normal. In Paris he has been rather roughly introduced to some people with quite different ideas and habits. He must have known, intellectually, that they existed; he must have known that there were head-hunters in Borneo and monks in Tibet and lunatics in asylums who had totally different views of the universe. What was before an intellectual abstraction is now real and concrete to him. All he has learned is the heterogeneity of mankind. It is a valuable lesson; some people never learn it. But his own virtues of kindness and tolerance and humour and honesty are still virtues, his bed is still as comfortable and his dinner as satisfying, he has not received any compelling call, such as does apparently from time to time change people's lives, to any different destiny. He has lost a friend who, anyway, had not meant much to him in recent years; otherwise he has merely had an instructive and profitable holiday, and will be just the same kind of fellow in future with a slightly wider and wiser outlook.

. THE WASTE LAND .

I find it impossible to write of *The Lawless Roads* in any but personal terms, for I have been awaiting its publication with particular curiosity. It so happens that I

Review of *The Lawless Roads*, by Graham Greene. *Spectator*, 10 March 1939.

arrived in Mexico last summer with ulterior literary motives a few weeks after Mr Greene had left with his notebooks full. There was an element of anxiety in the interest with which I began to read the report of so immediate a predecessor. Before I finished it, moreover, I realized that the admiration it aroused had little that could not be shared by those who had no specialized interest in the subject. Here was a formidable rival.

Not only did our routes seldom coincide, but our circumstances were widely different. Mr Greene's was an heroic journey, mine was definitely homely; he had, besides, many reasons for distress which I had escaped – he was ill most of the time, I was tolerably well; he was alone, while I had delightful company; he was travelling as a poor man, I as a rich. There is a great difference there, particularly in a country like Mexico, where the divisions of rich and poor are sharply marked. In most countries the poor foreigner arouses distrust among natives and fellow-countrymen alike; in Mexico he also runs into very considerable dangers. There is a great deal to be said for travelling poor; one sees a different side of the country, and one is upheld in one's endurances by contempt for the 'tourist'; I have done a certain amount of that kind of travel and enjoyed it thoroughly in retrospect. The chief disadvantage is that the physical exhaustion incurred in merely getting from place to place often makes one abnormally unresponsive to their interest. Mr Greene, particularly, suffered from this. He makes no disguise of the fact that Mexico disgusted him.

In fairness, it must be added that England disgusts him, too. The Chiltern town from which his journey starts was, to him, the place where a boy and girl had lately been found headless on the railway line, where evening papers retail a sordid murder, where the popular game of 'Monopoly' epitomizes the ignoble ambitions of its people. Consciously or unconsciously, he slips into the imagery of *The Waste Land*, quoting the unidentified companion on Shackleton's last Antarctic trudge.

Mr Greene is, I think, an Augustinian Christian, a believer of the dark age of Mediterranean decadence when the barbarians were pressing along the frontiers and the City of God seemed yearly more remote and unattainable. He abominates the picturesque and the eccentric; earth is for the growing of food, houses for the rectitude of family life. Contemplation of the horrible ways in which men exercise their right of choice leads him into something very near a hatred of free-will. It is in this mood that he approaches Mexico, a country where the most buoyant feel crushed by the weight of sheer, hopeless wickedness. It is therefore not to be wondered at if his account at moments becomes savage.

He makes little attempt, except by occasional implication, to give the historical background of the tragedy. His book is a day-to-day account of his movements. He crossed the frontier from the United States at Laredo, travelled to Mexico City, stopping on the way to visit Cedillo, Cardenas's former friend, now shot to death in the mountains. Readers of the *Spectator* will remember the brilliant picture of that unhappy patriarch who wanted nothing more than to escape from politics and rule his own estates in his own compara-tively benevolent fashion. From Mexico City, Mr Greene set out into the wilds through the state of Tabasco, lately the scene of Garrido's atrocious rule, still officially Godless; from there through Chiapas, where the universal hopeless-ness seemed to brake all movement, back to the tourist route through Oaxaca and Puebla, and home among volunteers on their way to Spain. No responsible traveller has visited Tabasco and Chiapas lately, and Mr Greene's account is of great value in confirming the worst of the dark rumours one heard of them in the capital.

But it was not necessary to visit them to feel the sense of doom which lies over even the brightest places in the country. One essential difference between Mexico and other equally barbarous parts of the world is conscious decadence. In its colonial days it was prominent in culture in the New World; not only was it a land of magnificent architecture and prosperous industry, but of civil peace and high culture. Scarcely more than a hundred years ago, Humboldt, visiting it, criticized its institutions in European terms; in 1575, a century before the first printing press was set up in British America, books were printed in Mexico, not only in Spanish, but in twelve Indian languages; there were three universities there a century before the foundation of Harvard; anatomy with dissection was taught at the Royal and Pontifical University eighty-six years before William Hunter opened the first school in England; the Academy of Fine Arts, under Tolsa, was in the last years of Spanish power illustrious even in Europe; examples can be multiplied almost indefinitely.[1] Then, broken by the thirty-five years' dictatorship of Diaz, came a century of revolution and civil war, which has culminated in the present totalitarian-proletarian regime, whose work left Mr Greene and myself aghast. But this is no place to enter into an analysis of General Cardenas's manifest follies and iniquities. Mr Greene's cinematographic shots of present conditions provide ample evidence, the more damning because they are not linked by any political thesis. They are written with great pungency and a kind of grim humour. So far as the author had any particular purpose in his observations, it was to investigate the strength of the anti-religious policy of the governing gang. From this point of view, may I offer him one reflection? The Mexicans are not only the people who killed the martyrs; they are the people for whom the martyrs died. It is in that aspect alone that martyrdom is valuable.

---

[1] Other examples of Spanish-Mexican achievements are given in *Robbery Under Law* (1939), pp. 145–50. Waugh drew directly on Francis Clement Kelley, *Blood Drenched Altars* (Milwaukee, 1936) and indirectly on Alexander Von Humboldt, *Political Essay on the Kingdom of New Spain* (New York, 1811).

. MR ISHERWOOD AND FRIEND .

Journey to a War represents an experiment in publishing that should attract notice, and may set a fashion. Poetry has always been a worry to the trade; it will not sell; not only does an annual slim volume fail to support the author, it barely covers the modest expenses of its production. Hitherto poets have been credited with private means or alternative, prosaic occupations, and poetry, for the publisher, has been treated as a source of honourable loss, a form of conscience-money paid from less noble sources, the gangsters' wreath at the funeral of literature. Now, however, Messrs Faber and Faber have hit on a new dodge of incorporating the slim volume in a more solid and marketable work, and have attached forty-three pages of Mr Auden's verse to a substantial travel diary of Mr Isherwood's, nearly 200 pages in length. The mutual esteem of the two writers has apparently survived the vexations of hard travel, and – a far more severe test – they have, without dissension, been jointly fêted by their oriental admirers; so one may reasonably hope that this pantomime appearance as hind and front legs of a monster will not embarrass their happy relationship. It is impossible, however, to treat this publication as a single work; it is two books which for purposes of commercial convenience have been issued as one.

Mr Isherwood's diary covers the spring of 1938, and is for the most part in the form of a day-to-day record. He and Mr Auden travelled from Hong Kong to Canton, thence to Hankow and Chengchow, where the railway branches east and west to Suchow and Sian; here they visited the north battle-line; thence they returned to Shanghai, visiting the south front on their way. It is needless to say that their journey involved many inconveniences and some danger; at one stage they fell in with Mr Peter Fleming, and with him evacuated Meiki a few hours before the Japanese moved in. There are inevitably a few passages of the kind which begin: 'My feet now utterly collapsed', but the majority of the pages deal with sleeping-cars, mission-stations, consulates and universities. They travelled in a sensible way, accepting the comforts that were offered. These comforts have now become tolerably familiar to English readers; we have already shared the kindly domestic life that flourishes in the missions among bombs and bandits; we know that the papists will give you a drink, and the adventists will not; we have, vicariously, fumbled for adequate courtesies to exchange with Chinese officials.

There is only one portrait in Mr Isherwood's collection that does not recall a familiar type; that is the host of the Journey's End Hotel, Mr Charleton, and for the few pages of his appearance the narrative suddenly comes to life, and one is reminded that Mr Isherwood is not only the companion of Mr Auden, but the creator of Mr Norris and Miss Bowles. Not that his work ever falls below a high literary standard. It is admirable. The style is austerely respectable; not only does he seldom use a cliché, he never seems consciously to avoid

Review of *Journey to a War*, by W. H. Auden and Christopher Isherwood. *Spectator*, 24 March 1939.

one; a distinction due to a correct habit of thought. Anyone of decent education can revise his work finding alternatives for his clichés; a good writer is free from this drudgery; he thinks in other terms. Mr Isherwood writes a smooth and accurate kind of demotic language which is adequate for his needs; he never goes butterfly-hunting for a fine phrase. It is no fault of his technique that *Journey to a War* is rather flat; he is relating a flat experience, for he is far too individual an artist to be a satisfactory reporter. The essence of a journalist is enthusiasm; news must be something which excites him, not merely something he believes will excite someone else. Mr Isherwood – all honour to him for it – has no news sense. In particular, he is interested in people for other reasons than their notoriety. The quality which makes Americans and colonials excel in news-reporting is the ease with which they are impressed by fame. Mr Isherwood met nearly all the public characters in his district; he felt it his duty as a war correspondent to be interested in them. But they were bores – or rather the kind of contact a foreign journalist establishes with a public character is boring – and he is too honest a writer to disguise the fact. Nowhere in China did he seem to find the particular kind of stimulus that his writing requires.

Mr Auden contributes some good photographs and some verses. The English public has no particular use for a poet, but they believe they should have one or two about the place. There is an official laureate; there is also, always, an official young rebel. I do not know how he is chosen. At certain seasons the critics seem to set out piously together to find a reincarnation of Shelley, just as the lamas of Tibet search for their Dalai Lama. A year or two ago they proclaimed their success and exhibited Mr Auden. It is unfair to transfer to him the reproach that properly belongs to them. His work is awkward and dull, but it is no fault of his that he has become a public bore.[1]

. AN ANGELIC DOCTOR .
THE WORK OF MR P. G. WODEHOUSE

Oxford men – or, to employ the periphrasis which Doctor Buchman and the Board of Trade have now imposed on us, men who are or were members of the University – have in recent years suffered many strains on their loyalty. News of Oxford in the papers has been disquieting; personal experience has often been worse. Undergraduates drink milk and eat sweets in the day and, in the evening, to the strains of the ocarina, pass resolutions to exempt themselves from military service; the dons think and write like provincial school-mistresses; philosophy has become a parlour game of logical quibbles; the history school a conditioning process in tepid Marxism; the new Bodleian outrages one of the finest streets in Europe . . . all this may be true, but the

1 Stephen Spender strongly objected to this review, and Waugh replied. See *Spectator* 31 March and 21 April 1939. See also *Letters* at 21 April 1939.

Review of *Week-End Wodehouse*. *Tablet*, 17 June 1939.

University in conferring an honorary degree on Mr P. G. Wodehouse has suddenly exerted its failing strength in an action worthy of its tradition. It is speaking, as is one of its most splendid functions to speak, for the educated class of the country, in recognizing Mr Wodehouse's place in literature, not perhaps, as Mr Agate claims, as 'a little below Shakespeare's and any distance you like above anybody else's', but certainly as the equal among his contemporaries, as Sir Max Beerbohm and Mgr Knox, and high in the historic succession of the master-craftsmen of his trade.

At the same time there has appeared, with Mr Belloc's introduction, a somewhat daring volume under the title *Week-End Wodehouse*. The anonymous editor deserves both our thanks and our commiseration, for to make one's own selection from a writer as popular and as fertile as Mr Wodehouse is to invite the envy and recriminations of half the English-speaking world. We all have in our own hearts our own 'Week-End Wodehouse' and, inevitably, it differs widely from anyone else's. I cannot refrain from certain regrets about the present volume. First, its appearance. I do not like the type or the paper or the decorations. Secondly, its arrangement, which is far from scholarly; it will outrage the serious collector who treasures his *Gold Bat* of 1904 and the advertisement pages of 'Blacks' Boys and Girls Library' with which the master's earlier works appeared; it will, also, provide a difficulty to the younger student who is given no references for a great number of the quotations; the bibliography at the end is flagrantly inadequate, omitting as it does even some of the works (e.g. *The Man with Two Left Feet*) referred to in the text. Moreover, delicious as the passage is, I can see no reason why on page 366 there should be an extract which has already appeared earlier in the same volume in its proper context. Thirdly – but here we are in dispute about a matter of personal taste – I do not think the collection is fairly representative of Mr Wodehouse's versatility. The English public school, the English Church and Hollywood are important themes throughout Mr Wodehouse's work which are scarcely, if at all, represented here. No anthology, however small, should omit the scene from *Mike* when Mr Outwood enlists Psmith's help in tracing the painted boot. *Mike*, indeed, is one of the most important of Mr Wodehouse's books; it is there, half-way through, that the author of the *Tales of St Austin's* suddenly reveals the genius of his later work. *The Bishop's Move* might well have taken the place of one or other of the two Ukridge stories which are included. *Hollywood Interlude* should have been reinforced with the superb tale of the young man who went to retrieve his hat from a cinema magnate and found himself contracted to write dialogue. Moreover, for a tale of discomfort in a country house – though I agree in esteeming Sir Mortimer Prenbery very highly as an individual creation – I think *Goodbye to All Cats* falls short of *Strychnine in the Soup*.

Against these criticisms must be put admiration for an idea which might have escaped most of us – the inclusion of the prefaces and dedications; these provide a superb example of how to grow famous with perfect good manners.

On the whole it is as good a selection as one has the right to expect.

Mr Belloc's introduction is a model of correct and graceful approach. He does not expatiate on how funny Mr Wodehouse is, or adopt that patronizing bravado with which some critics express their praise. He treats him as he deserves, soberly and seriously, as a prose stylist and as the expression of a culture for the safety of which Mr Belloc feels anxiety. He emphasizes the important fact that Mr Wodehouse cannot be imitated; that every phrase is simple, exact and original. (To those he singles out for particular attention I would add one from the *Fiery Wooing of Mordred* – 'the acrid smell of burnt poetry'.) No one is better qualified than Mr Belloc to recognize distinction of writing. It would be an impertinence to add to his judicious and deliberate technical analysis. The final passage of the introduction, however, seems to me unduly pessimistic. He is dealing with Mr Wodehouse's prospect of lasting renown. There are reasons for uncertainty about this in the case of any humorous writer. Humour is the most ephemeral artistic quality. I never found anything really laughable in Aristophanes or Shakespeare; the kind of laugh which an audience gives to the classics is something quite different from the spontaneous, irresistible impulse that comes from even quite feeble contemporary jokes; moreover much of Mr Wodehouse's humour is allusive in a peculiarly subtle way; it depends on the differences between contemporary spoken English and his own version of it. A later generation may take Mr Wodehouse literally and suppose that his was merely the language of his day. For these reasons I think it possible that he will never give quite the same intoxicating delight to any generation after our own. But Mr Belloc's apprehensions are based on the belief that the upper class, and in particular its butlers, are a dying race. Although few have inveighed more pungently than he against the corruption and arrogance of the rich and their servants, Mr Belloc finds something regrettable in the change. But is the change inevitable? Or even probable? Supposing, as is still reasonable to suppose, that disparities of wealth are likely to continue, butling seems a trade certain to survive. Modern labour-saving devices have almost eliminated the housemaid, but the work of butler and cook remains essentially a handy-craft. It is true that much of the majesty of the butler rose from the fact that, although a servant in half of the house, he exercised despotic rights over a teeming population in the other half; that authority is likely to be reduced, but there is the compensating consideration that in the average modern household it is only the butler who understands the various switches and taps, the water softener, the fuse boxes, the ventilators and burglar traps which have taken the place of a large part of the domestic staff. Moreover Jeeves is no butler but a valet, and the more people live in hotels and temporary flats, the more valuable does a valet become as mediator and stabilizer between the individual and a mechanical universe.

I am confident that Mr Wodehouse's characters will live. It is the half-real characters of the ordinary popular novelist who disappear. Literary characters may survive either through being so real and round that they are true of any age and race, or through being so stylized that they carry their own world with them. Of the first group is the Pooter family, whose physical circumstances now correspond to those of no existing class; of the second are Mr Wodehouse's characters. They live in their own universe like the characters of a fairy story. 'Jeeves knows his place,' says Mr Wodehouse, in the introduction to the *Jeeves Omnibus*, 'and it is between the covers of a book.' That is his secret. Just as, say, the sculptured figures on the west front at Wells are patently sculptured figures, exciting a purely aesthetic interest – not a lot of real old ladies and gentlemen whose precarious position would move us to thoughts of calling out the fire escape and getting them down – so Mr Wodehouse's characters are purely and essentially *literary* characters. We do not concern ourselves with the economic implications of their position; we are not sceptical about their quite astonishing celibacy. We do not expect them to grow any older, like the Three Musketeers or the Forsytes. We are not interested in how they would 'react to changing social conditions' as publishers' blurbs invite us to be interested in other sagas. They are untroubled by wars (Jeeves first appeared, it should be noted, in 1917, and Bertie Wooster, then unquestionably of military age, was 'in the dreamless' at 11.30 a.m.). The 'Drones', with its piano, swimming baths, sugar throwing, and borrowing and lending of fivers, has no conceivable resemblance to any London club; its Beans and Crumpets even wear a distinguishing archaic costume of spats (like the Renaissance livery of the papal guard); their language has never been heard on human lips. Their desperate, transitory, romantic passions are unconnected with the hope or fear of procreation; age in their world is usually cantankerous, extreme youth, obnoxious; they all live, year after year, in their robust middle twenties; their only sickness is an occasional hangover. It is a world that cannot become dated because it has never existed. It may well be that in future generations Mr Wodehouse's public may shrink; the vast and grateful masses who now devour him and Mr Dornford Yates with equal relish will turn to other more topical entertainment, and Mr Wodehouse, the Honorary Doctor of Oxford University, will survive solely as an epicures' delight, the equivalent perhaps of Miss Compton-Burnett today. In a hundred years' time 'the kind of man who reads P. G. Wodehouse for pleasure' may become synonymous with an extravagantly fastidious taste. And that is indeed as it should be. What can be more enviable than to enjoy the rewards of limitless contemporary popularity with the confidence, in the distant years, when copyrights have lapsed and royalties lost their importance, of a serene ascent into a rarer atmosphere, a little above the clouds, away from the crush where only the keen and the noble can follow? It is pleasant to picture the shade of Mr Wodehouse in Olympian converse with his peers; the conversation turns upon the privations through which the immortals on earth attained their immortality; they tell their stories of garret and gutter; Mr Wodehouse remains silent and then, lightly improvising an anecdote from the life of Ukridge, leaves them all silent and abashed until he courteously puts them once more at their ease by turning the talk to the subject of academic honours.

. THE NEW RUSTICS .

As a nation we not only dislike our work, we have a peculiar aversion to our sources of income. This is puzzling for Americans, among whom trade statistics are the current coin of conversation. We treat the making of money as a rude physical function, an indiscreet subject. All that has changed in the last twenty years, you say. Has it? Ask yourself how much you really know about the employment of your friends; you can tell almost anything else about them – where they were at school, what love affairs they have had, their taste in furniture and food and books, the names of their dogs, you could draw a pretty accurate genealogical table of their families and make a fair guess at their bank balances and income-tax returns. When it comes to their work, however, in four cases out of five you will find yourself driven back to the hallowed euphemism, 'something in the City'. Making money is simply the boring antecedent to the interesting business of spending it. I believe that this national trait is largely responsible for the present change in the population of 'the country'.

A hundred years ago 'the country' was the source of income. People came to London to enjoy themselves, they retired to their estates to manage their business. Hence, except among misanthropes, one finds very little love of 'the country' in English letters. Nowadays London is the place where people go to earn their livings: consequently 'the country' is the social centre, and house-agents' business in small country houses is so brisk that, if one owns one, one is solicited to sell it on an average once a month. The small houses change hands like stocks and shares. There is a popular fallacy that it is the very large houses which are coming into the market. At any rate it is a fallacy as regards the only district with which I have close acquaintance. In the twenty-five-mile radius of my house there are three great houses: each is in the possession of the family which has held it for generations. On the other hand, there are not a dozen small houses whose occupants were brought up in them. The farms, cottages and local tradesmen have the names that one finds, centuries back, in the manor rolls and the churchyard, but there has been an almost clean sweep of the minor gentry. The reason is economic. One can no longer live in the manor house on the rent of a thousand acres. Nor, so far as I know, has any gentleman ever succeeded in farming his own estate at a profit. So the farms have been sold off, in many cases to banks, and the houses remain, with their gardens and twenty or thirty acres of protective meadowland, for the occupation of strangers who have other sources of income than agriculture.

These occupants are a new social class who form an innocuous and extremely happy community. It is composed from three sources so different as to give a delightful and rare variety to local entertainment.

First there are the 'retired' people. They have come from all parts of the world and all professions, services and trades. One way or another they have got

Harpers Bazaar (London), July 1939.

£1,200 a year or so. They arrive in late middle age and stay there till they die. They usually have a grandchild or two parked on them for indefinite periods. The husbands busy themselves with Boy Scouts and gas-masks, the wives with Women's Institutes and parochial bazaars. They seldom go out after seven in the evening. After dark they confine themselves to the radio, crosswords and visiting relatives. In their garden they specialize in alpine plants. They have no expectation that their sons will keep on the house after their death. There is a couple of this kind in practically every village in England; more often than not they are dignified by the cottagers, whatever their antecedents, by the title of 'Colonel'. A generation ago half of them would have made their homes in South Kensington or in some select seaside resort. But, alas, the English coast is now one limitless car-park, and as for London. . . .

It is the sack of London that is responsible for the other two groups. The first consists of what are known to the villagers as 'artists' and to sociologists as 'intellectuals'. There was a time when the arts and sciences were represented in the village by the vicar. Now, however, the Church of England has lost much of its old connection with the universities and with scholarship. When an archaeological find was made in the old days, it was almost always by the vicar. It was he who burrowed in the Roman encampments and wrote monographs, full of daring attributions, on the condition of his parish before the Norman conquest. It was he who explained the newspaper to the squire. That tradition seems to be lost, but the countryside is more full of learning and intellect than ever before, for people with individual work to do are leaving the cities in hundreds.

Especially those connected with the arts; a painter needs light and space for his work, a writer and, I presume, a composer, silence. All need peace of mind. And these necessary things are not to be found in London. They are necessary really for any kind of work, but artists alone are fortunate enough to be able to choose their own surroundings. I think every writer of any merit in England today lives, at any rate when he is working, in the country. This is very nice for them. But I think it is a bad thing for literature, for various reasons. For one, it means that writers very seldom meet one another. They are by nature misanthropic and mutually suspicious, but in the old days, when there was a genuine Bohemia in London, they did consort. Their squabbles have made some of the most readable pages in English literature, and their agreements have given rise to 'movements'. Criticism in most periodicals has now become a mere extension of the advertisement columns; writers work alone, each in his separate burrow, producing his annual book and taking his recreation among his poultry and his neighbours. There is no longer such a thing as an intellectual society. (This came to an end in the break up of 'Bloomsbury' ten years ago, when its second generation became obsessed with politics.) It weighs heavily, too, on London hostesses who, until now, have always been able to preserve something of the Holland House tradition by maintaining a sprinkling of intellect at their tables. They now have to give up the effort or content themselves with rather noisy substitutes. It also – and this is a thing which is not widely enough recognized – is killing good journalism. There used to be more than half a dozen highly intelligent weekly reviews, and many of the daily papers had respectable features. But it is absolutely essential for a good journalist to be on the spot. In particular weekly papers, to have character and point, must be the work of a clique. Editors and contributors must know one another well, meet constantly, share the same jokes and the same opinions. In the great days of weekly journalism they were in constant association, in public houses, clubs and in their homes. The paper grew out of their conversations. An assemblage of mailed contributions does not fill at all the same function.

But the most interesting section of the new rural population is of those who come to the country purely for fun. I do not mean those who come for sport, although they too are beginning to form a separate caste divorced from the traditional life of the countryside. Blood sports in England – particularly fox-hunting and pheasant-shooting – are organized in such an enormous and unnecessarily expensive manner that they are rapidly becoming purely a hobby for tired business men. A man who has only a few hours a week to spare for sport expects it to be on an intensive scale quite different from the man whose sport is part of his life. It is a commonplace that fox-hunting in England survives in most districts simply as the benefaction of the very rich; even so, the majority of the field in many hunts is made up of people who drive down for the night and lease only a stable and cottage in the country. But I do not refer to sport – I mean purely social fun.

This movement dates from the dissolution of 'the Bright Young People'. It is popularly supposed that they were killed by the slump. In fact they – or rather their successors, for few of the leading figures of the twenties can now claim to be very young or very bright – shifted their ground. London no longer offered a congenial background for that particular sort of exuberance. In the hands of the LCC and the speculative builder it was rapidly becoming what it is today – the ugliest capital city in the world. The exploits of the Bright Young People were all planned for effect; effects, either decorative or startling, became impossible against the drab background of demolition and still drabber rebuilding. Towards the end of that peculiar decade a gallant effort was made to find new scenes for the parties (perhaps we were feeling the loss of Wembley, which always used to provide a surrealist setting for an evening's fun). Parties were held in public swimming-baths and on stationary sailing ships, but at dawn there was always the gloomy revelation of London streets. How the hangovers of the twenties were embittered by those streets! Moreover London ceased to be shockable. Half the motive of the Bright Young People was *épater les bourgeois*. But London was no longer bourgeois; it was cosmopolitan and proletarian. The bourgeoisie were moving out into the country. Smart Bohemia began to follow.

There were other motives. The fall of the English pound and the rise of disciplinarian governments in Europe made going abroad less amusing. When the Bright Young People had thoroughly exhausted themselves, they used to go abroad and recuperate. In the thirties they have had to stay in England or behave less extravagantly when they travelled. There was also the question of dressing up. Fancy-dress, both for themselves and their houses, was their particular hobby. But you cannot do much with a modern flat except fill it with functional furniture; there is no pleasure in sitting in fancy dress in a traffic block. So the English countryside suddenly became gay and fashionable. Hitherto it had been smart to regard the country as irredeemably dim and hearty, a place full of draughts and sporting jargon, of interminable walks across plough and stubble, or dull neighbours and uneventful evenings. Now the gay world has suddenly taken up the county families. In the twenties they took up the rich and 'produced' them; they induced them to finance parties and in return flattered them into thinking themselves amusing. Now they are routing out bucolic landowners. The nondescript country house, with its porch and portico, its plain rows of sash windows, its stuffed bear in the hall, its spacious antique marbles and its four or five tolerable portraits, is now the height of fashion; if there is a Victorian fernery it becomes a show place and motor-loads of strangers in Tyrolean costume present themselves on Sunday afternoons. Two styles of architecture are admitted to exist: anything classical, from Inigo Jones to Smirke is saluted as 'Regency'; anything else is 'Gothic'; both styles excite squeals of appreciation.

For those who are subject to hay fever the social round has become a martyrdom. It has taken the place of gout as the penalty of social excess. The parties take place in marquees and hay fields. Houses round Salisbury, I am told, let for high rents during the 'season'. It is all a great deal brighter than the Bright Young People ever were.

What do the original inhabitants think of it all? I believe that most of them are highly delighted. English cottagers have a peculiar attitude to their superiors. Behind their feudal demeanour they have always cherished the belief that the gentry are exceedingly wicked. It has long been preached in every Bethel that the rich will go to Hell and it affords the utmost satisfaction to have such conspicuous confirmation of the fact. They bear endless malice to one another, but the rich, they feel, are in higher hands. If they make the most of their brief time of fun, who can blame them? And the surrounding squires, finding themselves subject to a battery of charming attention such as they have never known before, succumb in dozens. They have always been profoundly attached to their houses; they enjoy hearing them praised in ecstatic terms even when their admirers come in such disconcerting costumes and with such surprising frequency. The parties make food for reflection and discussion through the winter months when the gay visitors are away. But some of them remain. Some, who have come for the fun, gradually realize that there are all manner of other delights in the English country, besides fancy-dress balls. It is a realization which, when it comes, is likely to transcend fashion and become a permanent and delicious obsession.

. CARROLL AND DODGSON .

Of recent years the Nonesuch Press has set itself the modest but valuable work of providing a flat-dwellers' library of classic writers. The selection has been judicious, the form convenient, the price moderate. It is true that for the same sum the collector could in most cases have provided himself with a complete edition at second-hand, but the readers for whom the Nonesuch Press now caters have neither time to cultivate the bookshops nor space to accommodate their harvest. The Nonesuch Library is 'contemporary' in intention and achievement. In *The Complete Works of Lewis Carroll,* however, it is attempting something rather different. It is highly unlikely that a rival edition will appear in the near future; none but a half-dozen specialists possess, in any form, the greater part of the contents. The volume must be judged as a definitive edition and, as such, it exhibits certain easily avoidable defects. With regard to its form there is little cause of complaint; it is easier to handle and to read than most 'omnibus' books. It is regrettable that the beautiful illustrations of the *Hunting of the Snark* had to be omitted; Harry Furniss's drawings for *Sylvie and Bruno*, though deplorable, played, as the author's preface shows, a considerable part in the book's composition and deserved their place in the text. But judged by strictly contemporary standards the volume, physically, is satisfactory.

Its composition, however, is less happy. The editor effectively conceals both his identity and his intentions. 'Everything Lewis Carroll wrote appears in this volume,' he jauntily announces, ignoring a distinction which Dodgson himself was at constant pains to observe. For he includes in the volume not only the work published under the pseudonym of 'Lewis Carroll', but much which Dodgson wrote under his own name, anonymously, and under easily recognizable, transposed initials. The undeclared and untenable presupposition seems to be that whenever Dodgson was not being wholly professional, he was 'Lewis Carroll'; thus the most prosaic, donnish witticisms which he employed during his academic life are attributed to one of the most fantastic imaginations of the century. The task of editorship was, indeed, singularly complex. The only orderly solution would have been to confine all that was not published under the pseudonym 'Lewis Carroll' to an extensive appendix designed to illuminate the author's obscure character. What the Nonesuch editor has done is to comb a don's life work for anything likely to amuse – extracts from common-room memoranda, illustrations of logical forms, essays in academic controversy, light and serious, religious and political opinions – and lump them all together without preface or adequate notes, under the pseudonym which their author scrupulously preserved for a unique species of work.

Mr Alexander Woolcott takes no responsibility for the editorship, but contributes a chatty introduction which does, in fact, give the reader some consolation by steering his attention where he will be least disappointed.

Review of *The Complete Works of Lewis Carroll*. *Spectator*, 13 October 1939.

Dodgson's character constitutes a nice psychological problem, and this jumble of papers, rudely presented though it is, contains a multitude of significant data. (Incidentally, Mr Woolcott is at fault in declaring that *Alice in Wonderland* has not been subjected to psychoanalysis; it has been so treated, more than once, with highly painful results.) Dodgson is revealed as a man of precise and fastidious mind. As an academic wit he specialized in fanciful exaggeration and parody; Stephen Leacock and the authors of *1066 and All That* are in direct succession from him, and I do not know of any predecessors. In his serious moods, which seem to have predominated in his everyday life, Dodgson was deeply concerned with such questions as the cruelty of blood sports and vivisection, religious observance, and in particular with a morbidly scrupulous abhorrence of anything coarse or blasphemous. Bowdler's edition of Shakespeare disgusted him by its lewdness, and one of his dinner parties was ruined for him by a guest repeating the tale of a child's innocent irreverence. In all this he was an extreme but perfectly intelligible type of his age and class. The mystery is the transition by which Dodgson became 'Lewis Carroll', one of the great imaginative writers of the language. The most nutritious text for this study is *Sylvie and Bruno.*

It is easy to see why this book and its sequel failed to achieve the fame of *Alice*. They are wholly different in temper and only the explicit statements of the author's preface and of certain apostrophes in the text can convince the reader that they were ever intended for children. The main story, in which the fanciful passages are embedded, is a typical Victorian novel. An invalid narrator goes to stay with a friend who has for a long time nurtured an undeclared devotion for the daughter of a neighbouring earl; the devotion is undeclared because the lover is a poor country doctor; he inherits a fortune which makes him an eligible suitor but his diffidence persists and he is anticipated by a dashing but sceptical cousin. Lady Muriel at first inclines to the rival but his scepticism proves insurmountable and, after despairing, the doctor is accepted; on the day of his wedding duty calls him to a plague-stricken village where he is believed for a time to have perished – in the company of three religious ministers, Anglican, Wesleyan and Catholic. The cousin for the second time performs an act of heroism, rescues the doctor, restores him to Lady Muriel, and proclaims a partial conversion to the tenets of revealed religion, too late, however, to recover Lady Muriel's affections.

The peculiarity of the book lies in the fact that the narrator of this simple tale is intermittently haunted by two dream-children named Sylvie and Bruno. Sylvie has some undefined affinity to Lady Muriel, but Bruno, her junior, is a creation of unique horror, who babbles throughout in baby-talk, like the 'control' of a 'medium'. These children first appear as characters in a dream and are part of a Ruritanian state named Outland. Soon, however, Outland and its intrigues disappear, and the children pop up during the narrator's waking hours. They come to tea with the earl and puzzle him with a bunch of exotic flowers; Bruno becomes so concrete that only the rival lover's gallantry saves him from being run down by a railway train. Except for this single occasion, however, they play no part in the main story; they are not supernatural visitants of the type of *A Midsummer Night's Dream*, who appear in order to solve or complicate the affairs of the world, but aberrations of the narrator's mind which, one cannot help guessing, correspond to some psychological peculiarity of Dodgson's.

The construction of the book, and the author's elaborate and obfuscating analysis of it, deserve the closest scrutiny. There is only space in this article to suggest one explanation which occurred to one reader. It seems to me likely that Dodgson was tortured by religious scepticism; his abnormal tenderness of conscience with regard to blasphemy is explicable if we think of him as treasuring a religious faith so fragile that a child's prattle endangered it. He believed that the only way he could protect his faith was by escaping more and more from contemporary life – in his scholarship into remote and fanciful abstractions, in literature into nonsense. In order to keep his mind from rational speculation he cultivated a habit of day-dreaming and peopled his consciousness with fantastic characters. Children became for him the symbols of innocent faith and accordingly the only tolerable companions; converse with them gave his fantasies literary form. This, in the light of what we know of Victorian Oxford, seems to me a plausible explanation, or at least, a line of inquiry. It is, anyway, an absorbing topic and we may be grateful to the Nonesuch editor, shoddily as he has done his work, for providing the opportunity for its discussion.

. RM BRIGADE .

The profound secrecy which covers the activities of 'Churchill's Murder Gang' makes the duty of your correspondent a light one. We are still in England and still in training. The officers assembled for their tactical course from their various divisions at a house ingeniously chosen to defeat espionage; no spy could have suspected it as a possible rendezvous. There we learned the subtle arts of 'appreciating the situation', 'getting in and out of the picture' and 'receiving the bottle'.[1] There was also a notable outbreak of Marine language; temporary second lieutenants who, a few weeks earlier, had been something in the city, might be heard unblushingly expressing their intention of 'going ashore to see the madam', when they meant to visit their wives in Croydon. To those eager to pinpoint this locality it may be hinted that our walks on the pier were abruptly curtailed during our sojourn.

The *Globe and Laurel*, April 1940. Unsigned, but attributed to Waugh in the file copy of the *Globe and Laurel* at Royal Marine Barracks, Portsmouth. John St John describes the circumstances of composition in *To the War with Waugh* (London, 1974), p. 19.
1 'Receiving the bottle', 'collecting a bottle', etc. were Navy and Royal Marine slang for receiving a reprimand or 'rocket'.

At the end of the tactical course we moved to Brigade Headquarters, in a landscape of burned gorse and immature conifers, prettily embellished with spent cartridge cases. Here we joined our NCOs during the hobbies of stripping the Bren and guessing our pay; after dark some battalions are said to devote themselves primarily to the larger aspects of war, debating the effects of Roumanian policy upon the Anatolian jute industry, while others, more, or perhaps less, practical, wander through the marshes in darkness or threaten late visitors to the mess with fixed bayonets. The auspicious date of 1 April has been chosen for a wider extension of our training.

Moustaches are growing luxuriantly, coughs are on the decline; battle dress lends a menacing aspect to the most peaceable characters; Easter draws near, spirits are high.

. COMMANDO RAID ON BARDIA .

Remember the conditions in England in the days between Dunkirk and the first air battle of Britain? Half-trained battalions suddenly found themselves first line troops. The bulk of the regular Army was reorganizing and rearming. The Home Guard was untrained and short of equipment. Invasion was expected daily. In Poland, Norway and France we had found that one of the chief dangers to a defending force was the breakdown of communications between its large units. The need of the moment was for small bodies of picked fighting troops who, in the event of higher commands being paralysed, would be able to carry on independently and, without the machinery of full-scale operations, mount sharp little counter-attacks on their own. This was the original idea of the formation of commandos. They were literally picked men. First the commanders were chosen. They were all young men of an age when, normally, they would have had companies and squadrons. They were now given the task of raising their own forces.

My own commander, who eventually came to command the force put under him in the Middle East, was the commander *par excellence*. He had succeeded in combining life in the most fashionable cavalry regiment with a brilliant career at the Staff College, and such feats of toughness as sailing round the world as an ordinary seaman in a Finnish windjammer. An order was circulated in the Army asking for volunteers from officers and men for hazardous service. The supply greatly exceeded the demand. The commanders picked their officers and left them to pick their men.

There is a universal danger in all armies that, when volunteers are called to

Life (International), 17 November 1941. Also in modified form in *Evening Standard*: 'Commando Raid: The First Story of Britain's Hush-Hush Force in Action', 14 November; and ' "I Was in the Commando Raid": The Only Story of the Commando Raid by One Who Was There', 15 November. After the first but before the second instalment had appeared, the War Office released the whole article to the press. It was widely printed and publicized as a 'scoop' revelation of a hitherto 'hush-hush' force.

leave their regiments for special service, the worst get sent. No company commander wishes to lose good men; they all have some troublesome fellow they are glad to pass on. To avoid this our troop leaders visited the regimental depots, saw each man individually, looked up his records, talked to his former officers. The qualities they were seeking were simply the qualities of any good soldier – physical strength and endurance, fighting spirit, knowledge of his weapons, enterprise. There was nothing peculiar about our men. They were simply the best types of the regiments from which they came.

The officers were mostly from the Household Brigade. They got the reputation of being exclusively recruited from the very rich and very gay but there was a fair proportion of industrious professional soldiers to preserve the balance. I remember well my impression on first joining. The commando was at that time living in Scotland and the officers' mess was at a seaside hotel. I had come from the austerity and formality of the Royal Marines. In a Marine mess it is thought disgraceful to sit down before six in the evening; those who have nothing to do must pretend that they have. I found a young troop leader wearing a military tunic and corduroy trousers. He was reclining in a comfortable chair, a large cigar in his mouth. Then I noticed above the pocket of his coat the ribbon of the Military Cross, and later when I saw him with his troop I realized that his men would follow him anywhere. The names among our officers of Jellicoe, Keyes, Beatty and Churchill showed how the sons of the last war's leaders saw in the commandos the chance of reliving their fathers' achievements. There was something of the spirit which one reads in the letters and poetry of 1914. We had a more elastic system of discipline than is possible in an ordinary battalion. There was none of that daily succession of petty charges and petty punishments. If a man was a nuisance he was simply sent back to his regiment. All were volunteers and all proud of the additional rigours of their training. So as to cut down administration to a minimum and to have no one with us who was not a fighting man, we were simply paid a subsistence allowance and, ashore, left to find our own food and lodging. Troops were taught to live on the country and hunt for their food. A book could, and no doubt will be, written about the commandos in their aspect as an experiment in military organization. The object of this digression is merely to give an idea of the sort of force we were and the sort of work we meant to do.

We formed a pool from which detachments could be drawn when there was a special job for us. We had parties in Tobruk, in Crete, in Syria, and another detached for special reconnaissance with the Navy. We had our full share of medals and casualties. The following is an account of one small operation, a bloodless one, which was neatly planned and executed, typical of the special tasks for which we trained.

Bardia lies behind the enemy lines, between Salûm and Tobruk in Libya. It is a harbour and a small town. The supply road to Fort Capuzzo and the forward enemy troops runs through it. British GHQ wanted a raid there for several reasons. They wanted information – were the enemy garrisoning the town or encamped some distance away (i.e., was it worth while shelling and bombing it any more)? Were Germans or Italians there? Were there coast defence guns? Was it being used, as was reported, as a transport depot? More important than the information was the need to draw off enemy mechanized troops who were pressing uncomfortably on our front line. The enemy must be made to 'look over his shoulder' and withdraw men from the front to guard his lines of communication. If possible he must be made to think that a full-scale attack was being attempted in his rear and to rush large mechanized forces to Bardia that were needed elsewhere. As a minor consideration any damage we could do to roads, bridges or stores would be welcome. A single commando was chosen for the job. As things turned out, it could have been done by half the number, but we expected to find at least two battalions of enemy troops in possession of Bardia.

Our parent force had another job on that night – 250 men on a destroyer raiding farther up the Libyan coast. We could see them embarking at the quay opposite ours, while we stood waiting in the big, fast merchantman that had been fitted out for our purpose. The Bardia attacking party was under the command of its own colonel. We were guests at this assault. But we had been at work for a week on the details of the plan, gazing, until we squinted, at air photographs, checking and rechecking the timetable. We wanted to see our plan in action.

The secret had been well kept. I do not believe that a word of our intention got to the swarm of spies which infest Alexandria. Had the cat jumped out of the bag, our raid would not have gone as well as it did. We got away in cover of darkness, as we had to arrive at our station, four miles off the coast, at 11 p.m. Then we had to leave again in the darkness, with at least two hours' sailing time before dawn, for all the coast around Bardia was patrolled by enemy aircraft. This meant that allowing an hour each way between ship and beach we had just three hours ashore. It was not long but it was long enough if everything went right. Everyone understood that the timetable was inexorable, that if he was late on his beach, or if he went to the wrong beach, he must look out for himself. There was a sporting chance of being able later to get through the enemy line and join up with our troops near Salûm.

Bardia is on a small promontory where the cliffs rise up sharply from the seashore. There are four possible landing places where wadis (watercourses that are usually dry) break the face of the rocks and leave a little half circle of sand. A party was to land on each of these beaches simultaneously. Each troop had its own task. From the moment they left the ship until the moment they returned aboard, they would receive no further orders. Each had his objective. One unit was to hold the road against the arrival of enemy reinforcements. One unit was to cover each beach. Another was to blow a bridge on the road, while another unit destroyed stores and so on. Each troop had to tackle in its own way whatever opposition it found. These orders were kept entirely secret until we were at sea. The day's sailing was a blessing. It gave time to issue maps, photographs and written orders, for the troop leaders to master them and explain them fully to their men, so that everyone of them was capable of carrying on by himself if need be.

The only unhappy people on board were the half dozen or so who had been detailed to remain on board as rear party, the orderly room clerk, the quarter-master's batman, the rear signalling party, and so on. During the day each of them came to me and sought to be allowed to go ashore. I managed to fit most of them in under one excuse or another.

There was a suggestion that we should get some sleep between dusk and the time for manning the boats, but everyone was too cheerful to rest. They were sharpening bayonets, disposing grenades about their persons, blacking gym shoes. It reminded me of the scene in *The Wind in the Willows* where Badger prepares the attack on Toad Hall.

Toward evening the breeze began to freshen and we grew anxious for we had been turned home once before by bad weather. It is a ticklish business landing in the dark on a strange beach in any kind of surf. It is seldom really dark in the Mediterranean but tonight the stars were overcast. Standing to, on deck, we could barely see the guard rail or distinguish between the sea and sky. We were in position at our boat stations half an hour before the ship reached her destination. Then we heard the engine stop and we silently manned the boats. One sits in these boats in three lines, astride low seats. The bows have a ramp which lets down so that all three lines can pull out together. It takes less than half a minute for thirty men to clear the boat. The boats are comfortable enough in a calm sea for a short trip. But with four miles to go in rough water they are not so pleasant.

The boats were lowered, formed line abreast and made for the shore. Our heads were all below the level of the armoured sides. It was impossible to move a muscle. The man on my left was sick. The only movement he was capable of was to turn his head slightly toward me. Most of the men fell asleep, as the excitement had died down, and those of us who were awake thought about particular minor discomforts and looked forward to the beach for the chance to stretch.

At last a whisper passed back from the bow: 'Stand by to land' and we felt the bottom scrape on the shingle. The ramp went down. We pressed forward into knee-deep water and up the steep ledge of beach. Two men near me fell flat and got up dripping and cursing very quietly. There was a minute on the beach while the section leaders collected their men behind them. Then, without a word spoken, they were off to their objectives.

We could just discern the line of the escarpment ahead, slightly more solid than the starless sky. I had been busy with a watch and notebook checking the time of the boats beaching and disembarking. It had all gone off as smoothly as a training exercise. The boats hit the beach in line, emptied and reversed their engines. They were out of sight in one direction and the men out of sight in the other within a few seconds.

Something is wrong up front, however, and I go forward to find what it is. I find three parallel lines of men crossing a deep, waterlogged anti-tank ditch that had not been visible in any of the air photographs. No tank could conceivably climb the opposing wadi. It seems an odd place for a ditch, but there it is and crossing it costs us twenty minutes, for in the dark we cannot let men scatter as we would in daylight. They must keep within touch of one another, and the first must wait for the last to come up with them. It was a beast of a ditch.

After the ditch was crossed, the climb started. We had studied it in the spectroscope but comforted ourselves with the reflection that everything looks steeper than it is through this device. Our wadi was precipitous and composed of loose stones. All through our training we had practised moving at night, and on roads or solid rock we were almost noiseless as we wore rubber or rope-soled boots. Now, however, the din of 150 men scrambling up in the darkness seemed deafening. Stones came thudding down from above, gathering little avalanches as they came. Suddenly there were three rapid shots and bullets sang out overhead. The line paused for half a second and then pushed on. In the lull I thought: 'That's bitched it. They've let us get ashore and now they have caught us very nicely on the cliff face. We were not as clever as we thought at keeping the secret.' But when we pushed forward again there were no more shots and I thought, 'It was a single sentry. He's gone back to raise the garrison. But we shall be on the top by the time they are in position.'

In spite of hard training the climb took it out of us. We were rather behind our timetable. It was now a quarter to one and at a quarter past two we should begin withdrawal to the boats. That did not allow much time for delay, but the forward parties were already well on their way into the town. No sound came from them and we suddenly realized that the place was empty. Force HQ set up as an observation post near a great assembly of derelict motor-lorries. Behind us a troop was searching for a transport unit which had been reported there. In front another troop was entering the former Italian barracks. Further on again the other troops which had landed lower down were pushing up into the further side of the town. There was complete silence for about half an hour. We knew that the various parties were getting to their objectives and setting their demolition charges. Suddenly from all sides the detonations began. We were able to plot them pretty exactly: 'That's the coast defence battery on the hill'; 'That's the road bridge.' At the same time a splendid red fire mounted and curled half a mile away in the old barracks. They had found a store of new motor tyres – a precious thing in the desert – and it blazed gloriously.

There was still no sign of the enemy. At last a patrol of two motor-cycles, driving all out and without lights, came roaring down the main road. Everyone near had a shot at them with Tommy guns and grenades but they somehow got through. They were not an easy target. It was very lucky really that they did escape for it was through them that the enemy learned, as we particularly wanted them to learn, that a landing was taking place. Had they merely seen the blaze and heard the demolition charges from a distance they might have taken us for an air-raid. As it was, the impression which these men carried away was of a town strongly in enemy hands and it was due to their report that our major success was achieved. They did exactly what British higher command wanted and sent a strong detachment of tanks and armoured cars to repel the imagined invasion.

The work finished, we returned to our beaches. The way down was lighted by the burning stores, where flames now mounted high into the sky. The boats had been lying off and now came into the beaches. The wind had risen. There was a heavy surf pounding the shingle and washing over the ledges of sand. The naval party had a job to keep the boats head in to shore and one boat got her propeller screw fouled in the kedge anchor, broached to and was thrown up on to the shelf of sand. They destroyed her with a grenade in the petrol tank and the little bay was lit up by this second fire so that we should have made an easy target for an enemy on the heights above. But no enemy came. The sea was a great deal heavier than was healthy for these flat-bottomed, rather awkward craft and all had difficulties of one kind or another getting away. I was in one of the large MLCs. Her ramp got jammed and for half an hour we floated in the bay while all the other boats disappeared back to the ship. Finally two men cut through a steel cable with a bayonet and we eventually got her going and came alongside the ship just as they had despaired of us. One boat failed to find the rendezvous but sailed safely into Tobruk next day.

As we sailed we saw parachute flares dropping over the town from enemy reconnaissance planes. The timetable had worked out right to the minute, with nothing to spare. The only misadventure which marred the success of the night was the loss of a boatload of men who from the top of the escarpment took the wrong wadi and found themselves on a beach where there was no boat waiting. But we had made all our objectives.

. VICTORIAN TASTE .

Sir, – In time to come it is likely that we and our children will look back with increasing curiosity to the free and fecund life of Victorian England; may we therefore ask that the responsible officials will consider the inclusion of a few relics of the period among those they are protecting from the scrap heap? I refer in particular to the ornamental cast-iron work which was one of its unique achievements.

The Times, 3 March 1942. An editorial in the same issue of The Times, 'Taste in Transition', comments on Waugh's letter. Although neither Waugh nor The Times mentions Baldwin, Waugh might have been implying a protest against the apparently vindictive 'salvage' order placed on Stanley Baldwin's ornamental gates, which were finally preserved only by the direct order of Winston Churchill.

In the high mood of sacrifice with which so much is being broken and melted, it is possible to detect an undercurrent of satisfaction that national need should give the opportunity for removing what is now thought unsightly. There is always dead ground immediately in front of the lines of popular taste extending for the lives of two generations. It is only recently, still imperfectly and after heavy losses, that the work of the eighteenth century has been recognized as having aesthetic value. It is delightful that the best wrought-iron work of that time is being preserved. The phrase 'Victorian monstrosity' is common currency. Before it is too late, may we not consider that the rustic garden furniture, the Gothic gateposts and the Jubilee drinking fountains (often in the form of shrines with the seated figure of the Queen in the place of the saints of other countries), all in cast iron, gave keen pleasure at the time and therefore are almost certain to do so again?

The railings which adorned the homes of all classes were symbols of independence and privacy valued in an age which rated liberty above equality. The prevailing sentiment deprives them of this value and most of them are unremarkable in design. These can well be sacrificed, but here and there, particularly surrounding the larger villas in our provincial towns, one finds work of very elaborate classical and Gothic design. It would be pleasant to hear that some specimens are receiving serious consideration as worthy of preservation. Your obedient servant,

EVELYN WAUGH, Ty. A/Capt.

. A TRENCHANT TORY .

Mr Woodruff's notebook is not easy to review respectably. The temptation is to transcribe a series of extracts and leave the reader to judge from them whether the whole is to his taste, as was the literary habit of the popular press in the recent transition period between serious criticism and complete neglect. The book is itself a series of extracts, which might as happily have been entitled *Chosen at Random*, from the column which, for some years now, the editor has contributed regularly to the *Tablet*. That journal, under Mr Woodruff's editorship, has been raised from the narrowly sectarian and obscure position into which it had sunk to the esteem and influence it enjoyed eighty years ago, and is now studied abroad, and in circles wholly unconnected with the Church, as the most serious and trenchant Tory journalism surviving today. For this reason the editor's notebook deserves consideration for the illumination it gives on a rare and valuable mind.

It is essentially a personal compilation. Mr Woodruff has jotted down curious facts from his reading and observation, sometimes as the text for a witty

Review of *Talking at Random*, by Douglas Woodruff. *Spectator*, 3 April 1942.

paragraph of reflection, sometimes with no other comment than a heading. His reading is disconcertingly diverse – Aubrey's *Miscellanies*, the *Vegetarian Messenger*, Dale Carnegie's *How to Win Friends, Near Home or Europe Described*, 1850, *Pigs' Meat or Lessons for Swinish Multitude*, *The Feudal Manuals*, Isaac Taylor's *Natural History of Enthusiasm* are a few of the works casually referred to as though they were the normal currency of the literary market, and his observation is made in circles insufficiently explored by the educated classes – the *terra incognita* of the public banquet and the provincial study circle. From these voyages he returns deep-laden with curious lore. Now before you can have an acute sense of the curious you must also have a sense of normality, and here Mr Woodruff is almost unique among his contemporaries. We all tend to think in a historical way if left to ourselves, but our memories and habits of thought are now under constant battery from publicists to whom anything which existed before 1918 is intolerably antiquated and anything before about 1500 legendary and spurious. Mr Woodruff moves with great ease in the wide spaces of history. He sees the present in a vast perspective and yet maintains an interest in it, seeing modern follies in their most absurd light and yet remaining genial and hopeful.

He has a liking for all long-lived, slow-moving things, such as elephants, tortoises and clergymen, and the only form of vulgarity which really pains him is impatience. His heroines are the sisters of Brillat-Savarin, who lived to the ages of 98 and 99 and left their beds only for the two summer months when they entertained their brother. Americans, publishers, Nazis, go-getters excite him to the nearest he comes to asperity; but he can regard the steadier kinds of worldly ambition tolerantly, as a kind of immature naughtiness, as the juvenile courts nowadays regard the atrocious crimes that come before them.

A few extracts may be forgiven as illustrating the qualities I have tried to define:

'Newspapers, which resent the habit in other people, die exceedingly quietly themselves. If it was announced beforehand that the paper was stopping, the readers would feel free to pick and choose among other papers. This way the first they learn of any change is when another paper arrives incorporating the title of their own. Thus are masses of readers transferred, like the dumb beasts they are, with a minimum of loss.'

'The race between stupidity and extinction is one of the chief contests now going on in Britain. . . . While we shall all be mentally defective 3,000 years from now, we shall all be extinct less than 2,000 years hence. . . . The great consolation is that there are more ways than one of being mentally defective . . . but it is very disappointing for the people who rely upon posterity to admire their writings.'

'The Chinese presentation of *The Merry Widow* was given under the title "*He dead – she glad*".'

'It is high time that the aged were a little more truculent. They are soon going to be the great majority of the population, and by the quantitative fashions of the day, numerical majority will mean they are always right.'

. THE BRITISH CAMPAIGN IN ABYSSINIA .

The campaign in East Africa remains the only wholly successful British military operation of the war and, in many respects, the most obscure. The higher hopes and swift disappointments of Libya and the great objectives there distracted and still distract popular attention from the brilliant generalship and splendid fighting of a victory comparable to that of the Japanese in Malaya. So complete was the collapse of a vastly superior enemy force that we have even forgotten that that force, a few weeks before its dissolution, seemed to menace the whole Sudan and Egypt itself. We have come to think of it as a 'mopping-up' operation of an isolated garrison. Captain Steer's book does not pretend to give a full military history, but it tells us a great deal which never came into the newspapers, and tells it in a most readable manner.

At the outbreak of war with Italy, on the grounds that he had formed one of the motley horde of journalists who infested Addis Ababa in the war of 1935-6, Captain Steer was appointed G3 in Khartoum, in charge of propaganda. In this capacity he saw a great deal of the traffic in desertion which was called the 'patriot movement', and was in close touch with Col. Wingate's remarkable column of Sudanese and irregulars which kept disproportionately large enemy forces deployed in the disaffected north-western provinces and so greatly helped the Indian divisions in their decisive advance to Keren and Amba Alagi.

Most of those who interested themselves in the cause of the Emperor Haile Selassie in the years 1935-40 lacked either humour, knowledge or honesty. Captain Steer's humour is boundless, and his knowledge considerable. His honesty may best be judged from his own account (p. 130). 'Our next theme was to launch a personal attack on Lorenzini. He was a skunk and a coward. He had run away from Agordat and left his troops in the lurch . . . This of course was not true, for Lorenzini was a very brave man . . . (he) was killed at Keren. . . If I had thought that such a story could have passed a British censorship I would have announced that he had been shot in the back by a deserting Eritrean askari' (p. 164). 'The Emperor did not approve of the particularism of these sheets, and the imperial seal that I put on them was in fact a forgery.' The book is full of instances of this kind which Captain Steer records with evident relish. It must be remembered that he was opposed to an equally unscrupulous enemy. Whether it is prudent at this stage of the war to publish so very frank an account of a propaganda campaign, which on many occasions disgusted the fighting soldiers with whom he was associated, is a matter for the higher military authorities to decide. The lay reader may also make a note that this is how Captain Steer treats the truth when he is in a responsible official position. As a freelance journalist he has written of Abyssinia before, and of the civil war in Spain. We shall know in future how to take the author's statements when his sympathies are engaged.

Review of *Sealed and Delivered*, by G. L. Steer. *Tablet*, 26 September 1942.

Incidentally he gives a very interesting reason for his first disliking the Italians. A fellow traveller in an Italian train objected to his removing his boots in the carriage. Later he says that what endeared the Abyssinians to him was their beautiful manners. One sees a little light here.

But it would be a mistake to give the impression that this book is all bluster. It is full of witty narrative and sharp portraits. The author is never smug and, apart from the painful Charlie-Chaplin-like references to the Emperor as 'The Little Man' and an embarrassing sentence or two about his leave-taking from his wife, not intrinsically vulgar. He makes fine melodramatic figures out of men like Hailu, and does manage to create a Macbeth-like world in which their doings become sane. There is not overmuch self-pity in the final picture of himself left out in the rain, with his face pressed to the palace windows, watching the junketings within. There is even a kind of generosity visible here and there – never, it is true, to the defeated enemy – but to disappointing friends, which is perhaps the best generosity of all.

. DRAMA AND THE PEOPLE .

There seem to me only two ways in which you can properly write a very small book about a big subject. You may either take your readers on an equality, credit them with the same education and tastes as yourself, trust them to recognize your allusions and, in the main, to desire the same effects, and so throw out for their entertainment and subsequent discussion a number of personal opinions and theories; or, alternatively, you can play the schoolmaster and attempt to compress your own superior learning into a convenient and acceptable form. The scope of the 'Britain in Pictures' series – sumptuous little books that have attracted a diverse and distinguished company of writers – imposes the second method. These books are designed to interpret the British tradition to sympathetic but ignorant strangers both at home and overseas; the pictures, in the case of *British Dramatists* particularly well chosen, are meant to attract the attention of readers who would not sit down seriously with an encyclopaedia. Mr Greene has thus undertaken a slightly austere task for a writer of outstanding imaginative power. He fulfils it well, providing a great deal of valuable information lucidly and memorably. I am a little doubtful, however, whether this splendid novelist was a wholly tactful choice for this particular job.

My grounds for complaint are two. First, Mr Greene subscribes to the popular belief in 'the People'. An American statesman has announced that this is 'the century of the common man', and it is not to be wondered at that during the last ten years English writers have sought conspicuously to flatter the rising, and revile the falling, powers in the land, for they are by tradition a

Review of *British Dramatists*, by Graham Greene. *Spectator*, 6 November 1942.

sycophantic race. But allied to this normal exercise in personal protection has been an abnormal tendency to claim that not only this, but every, century has been 'of the common man'; in place of the old, simple belief of Christianity that differences of wealth and learning cannot affect the reality and ultimate importance of the individual, there has risen the new, complicated and stark crazy theory that only the poor are real and important and that the only live art is the art of the People. Now this preconception, which Mr Greene admits, is particularly unfortunate in regard to the theatre, which has been preeminently the art of the rich. Mr Greene is far too intelligent to ignore this and he is forced into the position of treating his subject as having died in infancy when drama moved from the tavern to the court – a death he ascribes to the Puritan revolution of the seventeenth century. From Congreve to Mr Maugham he sees British dramatists as 'unreal'; he is therefore out of sympathy with the greater part of his subject. Nor is he wholly honest in taking the historical division where he does, for the Elizabethan stage was very much the creation of the court and the nobility; the scenes between Hamlet and the players give a significant picture of the theatre's dependence on high patronage; great households maintained their own theatrical companies and great works of art were composed to celebrate fashionable weddings. If taverns and stews are represented it is because princes and noblemen were still interested in them, rather than because the People had any choice in the matter.

My second complaint is connected with the first. Mr Greene seems to ignore that a prime function of the theatre is to give pleasure. He traces the origin of drama to the Office of Holy Week and to mediaeval mystery plays. Deep roots, indeed, were struck in that soil, but also they were perpetually nourished by the pageants and buffoonery of chivalry and the shows of the merchant guilds. I have just been reading an account of the tournaments arranged by Henry VIII for the entertainment of Katharine of Aragon; there we have a rich source of comedy and of historical drama. In the progresses of Elizabeth about the country she was greeted with masques and plays by her hosts. If in later years the common man was not called in to share the revels, it was because he had killed a king and himself chosen to damn pleasure. In subsequent years the drama provided an escape from the tedium of court intrigue, politics and, later, from commerce. It is as a source of delight and escape that the theatre is today the most prosperous industry in the country.

. THE LAST HIGHBROW .

Channel Packet consists of forty essays, all but one in English, and all but two or three of the uniform size and style imposed by the limitations of weekly journalism. They range in subject from Anglican bishops to French symbol-

Review of *Channel Packet*, by Raymond Mortimer. *Tablet*, 20 February 1943.

ists, and cover, directly or by implication, all that might properly be expected of the cultural equipment of an early twentieth-century Englishman. In his essay on 'Beachcomber', Mr Mortimer remarks with surprise that Lord Beaverbrook should employ a jester expressly to outrage the principles of his own newspapers, but, in fact, there is great likeness here to Mr Mortimer's own position on the *New Statesman*; to turn the page from the peevish socialism of the main body of that paper to the urbane places where Mr Mortimer presides is to enter another world. No matter what conceivable truth may prevail in the socialist ascendancy or what artistic whims and aberrations may one day possess the victorious workers, it is quite certain that there will be no place for Mr Mortimer, who consciously and proudly represents the last encircled pocket of what was once known as 'Bloomsbury'. The artistic achievements of Mr Mortimer's friends are too splendid to need retelling, but it is more for their habits of life and thought that they are honoured by many such as myself, who had no personal acquaintance with them, and it is those habits which Mr Mortimer distils incongruously in the *New Statesman*. They could only exist in a world of prosperity, freedom, inequality and moral uprightness such as we shall not see again. They were Holland House gone shabby-genteel, but they maintained a tradition of the humanities which was perishing everywhere else. All honour to them – and yet why is it that there was always an element of opprobrium about the terms 'Bloomsbury' and 'highbrow'?

Mr Mortimer in his preface says, 'I am proud to consider myself a high-brow', by which he means 'one to whom the past and the present are equally significant and vivid' – a definition which might apply to senile decay. But I know what he means, and I think he is pointing to one of the main weaknesses of the 'highbrow', for not even the most exact scholar can know more than a fragment of the past; the most essential, structural facts of the best documented periods of history are lost in conjecture and controversy. So when Mr Mortimer speaks of finding the past as significant and vivid as the present, he only means that he has built up for himself a series of imaginative studio sets where he feels at ease. Sometimes this sense of ease with the past betrays him into folly, as in his essay on ancient Rome. Here he makes the singularly unhappy contrast between the Rome of Vitruvius and the Rome of Michelangelo. Vitruvius, as Mr Mortimer must once have known, was an ordnance officer of the time of Julius Caesar and Augustus, long before the great age of Roman architecture; he was concerned mostly with engines of war, and in old age composed a very obscure treatise on architecture, whose impor-tance derives solely and directly from the fact that it was made into a textbook in the age of Michelangelo. Mr Mortimer, wandering in this significant and vivid past of his, finds an affinity between ancient Rome and modern Fez. I used to know Fez well. Its predominant character to me was one of domestic privacy; a city of individuals who had no truck with affairs of state, and no public recreations. I cannot conceive how Mr Mortimer could inhabit ancient Rome for five minutes without finding himself disagreeably reminded that he was in a capital city, the seat of a prodigious civil service, with public processions at every corner and a system of mass entertainment provided by the state. This sudden, disconcerting silliness of highbrows – often in life, I believe, marked by a nervous giggle – is characteristic.

There is a further habit which Mr Mortimer exemplifies which I find personally antagonizing – the habit of assuming that the common quality discernible in good things is the whole of their goodness. For instance, Mr Mortimer enjoys both Poussin and Picasso. I enjoy Poussin and not Picasso. Mr Mortimer sees a common quality between the two paintings, and argues, 'It is affectation to pretend you like Poussin if you don't like Picasso. Their differences are superficial, their identity essential.' Thus, you might argue, it is affected to love one woman and be indifferent to another. The book is also typical in its abhorrence of physical pain and violence, in a degree which became common only with the decline of asceticism.

However, it is ungrateful to complain when there is no need to praise. The book is polite and consistently interesting. It may be noted that it is always respectful to, and often understanding of, the Catholic Church. Mr Mortimer may lack the scholarship and asperity needed to make him an Edmund Gosse, but he succeeds brilliantly in his own modest aspiration of being a highbrow journalist – the last of them.

. THE WRITING OF ENGLISH .

There are advantages in reviewing a book late; the chief of them is that more punctual critics help to define the contemporary background before which it must be studied.

Messrs Graves's and Hodge's *Handbook for Writers of English Prose* has attracted more attention than is healthy, for there is little in it that we did not know at the age of 18. But we live in an unhealthy age. What Mr Graves and Mr Hodge and I learned at school is no longer considered the rudimentary equipment of an educated man, nor is the educated man now considered as being better equipped than the uneducated for thinking and expressing his thoughts. There are numerous grounds for quarrel with the authors on matters of detail; what has annoyed the popular critics is the general scope and scheme of the book; they resent, not that the guidance offered is, in certain particulars, injudicious, but that there should be any guidance at all. This is further evidence of the present decay of literary decency that is abundantly apparent in many quarters. This is the century of the common man; let him write as he speaks and let him speak as he pleases. This is the deleterious opinion to which

Review of *The Reader Over Your Shoulder: A Handbook for Writers of English Prose*, by Robert Graves and Alan Hodge. *Tablet*, 3 July 1943.

The Reader Over Your Shoulder provides a welcome corrective; it ought not to be a particularly valuable work, but, in present conditions, it is.

Artists of all kinds – but writers more than others – face a problem which cannot long be left unsolved. Society is changing in a way which makes it increasingly difficult for them to live at their ease. A few potential artists will doubtless be found to submit to the new restraints and, as state functionaries, busy themselves in public relations offices and Ministries of Rest and Culture, popularizing the ideas of tomorrow and the undertakings which, in peace, will replace the Giant Salvage Drives of today. For the more vigorous, however, the choice lies in the two extremes of anarchic bohemianism and ascetic seclusion. Each provides a refuge from the state. The Bohemians will have a valuable function in teasing, it may be hoped to madness, the new bourgeoisie, but I believe it will be left to the ascetics to produce the works of art in which, if at all, English culture will survive.

In their own trade of writing, Messrs Graves and Hodge provide a useful indication of the needs of the new asceticism. Language must be preserved as a vehicle for accurate and graceful expression, and it is in danger of death from the decay of stratified society. Aristocracy saved the artist in many ways. By its patronage it offered him rewards more coveted than the mere cash value of its purchases; in its security it invited him to share its own personal freedom of thought and movement; it provided the leisured reader whom alone it is worth addressing; it curbed the vanity of the publicist and drew a sharp line between fame and notoriety; by its caprices it encouraged experiment; its scepticism exposed the humbug. These and countless other benefits are now forgotten or denied. Its particular service to literature was that it maintained the delicate and unstable balance between the spoken and the written word. Only a continuous tradition of gentle speech, with all its implications – the avoidance of boredom and vulgarity, the exchange of complicated ideas, the observance of subtle nuances of word and phrase – can preserve the written tongue from death, and lifelong habitude to such speech alone schools a man to write his own tongue. Today in England we are faced with writers who in their formative years learned the uncouth tongue of the pit and the factory and later, with effort, amassed a wider vocabulary of words they know only from books; in America the case is even worse, for vast sections of the population have learned English as a foreign language. The excruciating products of this education – when a man schooled to talk vaguely of his rudimentary needs finds himself desirous of expressing accurately abstract, delicate or complicated thoughts – are on every bookstall.

The Reader Over Your Shoulder is a call for order. The authors have not troubled to diagnose the ills of the moribund; they have rather pointed out hints of the frightful disease in the superficially robust, and have chosen for their case-histories the athletes and champions. These case-histories, which they call 'Examinations and Fair Copies', occupy rather more than half the book and are the more stimulating part. The 200 pages which form a preface to them comprise a history of English language and a statement of the principles of good writing. The first section might with profit be omitted. That kind of thing is still taught, I believe, between periods of 'citizenship' and 'dietetics' at all but the most experimental schools. The chapters on the principles of good writing – clarity and grace – are worth close attention; much is stated as axiomatic which is, in fact, highly speculative. I found myself in frequent disagreement, but this is no place to open a controversy on jots and tittles. The reviewer does his duty by telling the reader why a book is likely to be of use to him. In this case few people can afford to disregard the authors' warnings, and the fact of its stirring the mind to consider questions too long disregarded is itself immensely valuable even where the solutions are dubious. As a footnote I may add that as a result of having read *The Reader Over Your Shoulder* I have been haunted by this pest to a condition approaching persecution mania; I have taken about three times as long to write this review as is normal, and still dread committing it to print.

. MARXISM, THE OPIATE OF THE PEOPLE .

It is a sad reflection on our times that a man bearing the once honorific title of Professor should find it necessary to explain the inadequacy of his published work by pleading the conflicting claims of his duty as a citizen; sad, not that he should be preoccupied by his duties in this national crisis, but that he should think it better to write badly than not to write at all. For this is a deplorably shoddy piece of work; there is, I think, no literary vice that is not exemplified in it, and had we not the Professor's assurance that it is 'essentially an essay, nothing more', we might well take it for something much less – a hotch-potch of miscellaneous papers written at various times for various readers; only thus, it would have been charitable to think, could a writer of Professor Laski's long experience have produced a work so diffuse, repetitive and contradictory. It is a pity he did not take more trouble; six weeks' hard work could have put the thing into shape. Instead he lays himself open to the charge of being a literary Mrs Jellyby, who is too busy planning great economic changes to plan a pamphlet; so set on preaching the dignity of labour that he shirks his own work. And that is a pity because his argument is of some topical interest.

The argument, so far as I can claim to have followed it successfully through the hairpin bends and blind alleys in which it abounds, is this: Youth is being driven dumbly to the slaughter in a quarrel not of its making, for ends it does not understand; the rest of the community, on the other hand, is for the first time finding self-fulfilment in self-sacrifice for the common good. The unique

Review of *Faith, Reason and Civilization*, by Harold Laski. *Tablet*, 22 April 1944.

felicity of this situation we owe to the spread of an interest in the natural sciences. At this stage (chapter VI) there follows a train of reasoning which merits full analysis: all good comes from natural science, says the Professor; natural science must be taught; the state is the teacher; but mere instruction is not enough; the seed must fall on a prepared soil; the child from an impoverished home cannot hope to be a scientist; therefore it is the duty of the state to ensure a home for each of its subjects where science can flourish, i.e. one of physical comfort and security. But there is also something requisite besides refrigerators and pensions – 'values'; the 'values' of the past are dead; they are not to be found in art because Mr T. S. Eliot is not understood by manual labourers and James Joyce is understood by nobody. 'Values' can only be found now in Soviet Russia; the battle of Stalingrad proves it; all is not perfect in Russia, but there is no alternative source.

I do not think I am misinterpreting the Professor; if I am it is his own fault, for the argument has had to be traced through a multitude of digressions, which consist, for the most part, in a restatement of the conventional, socialist interpretation of history.

In a brief review it is best to disregard the digressions and concentrate on the argument. One may ask whether it is not odd that the spontaneous ebullition of self-fulfilment which the Professor finds on all sides should coincide with a system of legal compulsion unparalleled in English history; one may ask 'Is heroic military defence really conclusive evidence that the defenders have superior "values" to the attackers? If so, what about the Alcazar at Toledo, or the ruins of Cassino?'; one may ask 'Does religion not offer "values"?' and to this one gets an answer; in fact one gets two.

First, the Professor says religion is no good because it does not look like being immediately, universally acceptable. In his own sense that is a satisfactory answer. I, personally, do not believe that there will be universal peace and goodwill until the world is converted to Christianity and brought under Christ's Vicar; whether that ever comes about is not ordained, but depends on human free-will. It may well be that the Church will remain for ever an underground movement and that the Second Coming will find it still in a minority. Certainly I am one with the Professor in seeing no human probability of universal conversion in the next few thousand years. And the Professor must have a quick answer to reassure anxious pupils that they can safely concentrate on their books, and, if successful in attracting the notice of their superiors, expect influential positions, without the fear of being directed summarily into the mines or the Army Pay Corps. Looking about for a magic word to pacify the class, the Professor plumps for 'Stalin'.

But he does not leave it there. By a train of associations which does more credit to his zeal as a fire-watcher (or whatever citizen occupation has lately given him this self-fulfilment) than to his historical acumen, he traces Decay of civilization – Rome – rise of Christianity = Decay of capitalism – Russia – rise of Marxism; and throughout this book pursues the analogy until he almost seems seeking to convince us of an identity. It is therefore important to know what the Professor understands by this word, 'Christianity', which he uses with such assurance.

It was, he tells us, founded by a man whom the New Testament 'clearly' represents as 'one figure, however mighty, in the long record of Hebrew prophets, like Amos or Hosea'. This, it is notable, he has learned from the New Testament itself, not from one of Mr Gollancz's popular tracts. Now the claim of a man to be God is stupendous and, it may well seem, preposterous. Such a man might be a lunatic or a charlatan, or, just conceivably, God; what he could not be is a prophet like Amos or Hosea. This prophet, according to the Professor, 'protested passionately against the class-divisions of society', 'but had no very deep concern with a workaday world'. In that he conforms to a type that has become common enough in modern politics, but where does the Professor find him in the Gospels? Our Lord's reproaches to the scribes and pharisees were directed not at their privileged position but at their betrayal of the trust which justified the privileges, and as for the 'workaday world', what does he imagine was the life of the carpenter's shop at Nazareth? How could Our Lord show deeper concern for the workaday world than by living in it for half a normal lifetime, and then dying for it?

The religion founded by this stage creature of Professor Laski's musings over the stirrup-pump was confronted with a problem, and found an answer. 'The problem,' he writes – not even, it is worth remarking, 'one of the numerous problems' – but 'The problem that Christianity sought to solve was to reconcile the existence of the poverty of the poor with a state power which safeguarded the riches of the wealthy.' Whom did this problem obsess? Not the Fathers, if one can judge by their writings. Many highly complex and recondite problems seem to have vexed them, but this one, the one, scarcely at all. Who then? The answer is as surprising as anything else in Professor Laski's exposition of our Faith; it was the altar boys. 'A poor handful of brave acolytes' are cited as the original trustees of 'values'. How well one can see these precocious children clustered round the sacristy door. 'It's all very well for him to worry about the Dual Nature; what we want is to reconcile the existence of the poverty of the poor. . . .'

The question thus posed had already been answered. 'The central faith of the Gospels,' says the Professor – again note the pedagogic self-assurance; not 'an arguable corollary to the Faith', but the Central Faith of the Gospels – 'is' – guess what – 'that where the claim of son upon parents or brother upon brother is set in terms of the view that proximity of relationship means that one's property is proportionately available to one's kin also, the family becomes the nurse of avarice and narrowness, a hindrance, rather than a help, to fraternity in the commonwealth.'

Imagine the scene on that first Easter morning; the little group of dismayed disciples, in the upper room, behind the barred doors; day breaking; the messenger hot-foot from the sepulchre; 'Good news! Good news!'; they crowd round and there, for the first time, hear the great message that is to shake the earth, 'When the claim of son upon parents or brother upon brother is set in terms of the view . . .' Thomas can't believe it. Then the thing is confirmed in flesh and blood and fire, and the disciples set out to the uttermost parts of the earth to carry the good news and die for it. '. . . that proximity of relationship means that one's property is proportionately available . . .'

There we have Professor Laski's idea of our Church; there his portrait of its Founder; there the problem; there his somewhat disconcerting solution. And when we have learned all this the Professor lets us into another secret, suddenly and quite casually after we have puzzled our way through 117 pages. 'What it is not seriously open to a scholar to deny is that there is no more ground for accepting the validity of the postulates upon which the Churches build their rights than there is for accepting those of Mohammedanism and Buddhism.' Shake off the superfluous negatives, translate his horrible jargon into English, and read, 'Scholars have conclusively proved that the claims of Christianity are as false as those of Mohammedanism and Buddhism.'

Really, he might have told us this earlier. If the whole thing has been proved a fraud, it doesn't matter what it was all about – not enough anyway to compensate for the pain of reading Professor Laski's prose. It was all a fraud, it seems, put about by the rich Romans, as a means of keeping the poor in their place. Has the whole of our reading of this tract been wasted? Not entirely I think, for, although Professor Laski's views on Christianity are of no possible interest to Christians, he may yet be studied as a guide to contemporary politics. Perhaps there is a little kernel of wisdom hidden in the husk.

The Professor thinks there is an analogy between Christianity and Marxism. We see what he means by Christianity; what then does he think of Marxism? That it was once a secret whispered in upper rooms by humble, hopeful people; that it has become the official creed of a great empire; that an astute government has succeeded in so impressing a people with this creed that they willingly endure long toil, hard living, constant supervision, ruthless punishment, recurrent tragedy; that the latest imposture is more grossly impudent than its predecessor, Christianity, for the latter said, 'Ye will be happy hereafter,' and cannot be proved wrong (until Professor Laski's scholars get to work) while the former says, 'My dear comrades, you may not realize it, but you *are* happy at this moment'; that Marxism is the new opium of the people – is this what the Professor means? I doubt it, but it is what he comes very near saying in these muddled pages.

. A PILOT ALL AT SEA .

The Unquiet Grave is a curiosity, perhaps a portent. When it appeared last winter in a limited edition it was greeted as a potential 'classic' by Mr Desmond MacCarthy, Mr Raymond Mortimer, Miss Elizabeth Bowen and Mr V. S. Pritchett, none of whom is given to loose expressions of praise; when *Horizon* organized a questionnaire for the French, many young writers named it as the most important publication of the war years; for a year the literary ladies of the Dorchester Hotel have been talking about their 'Angst'. Now the book is issued to the general public. It is described as 'entirely revised and corrected', and the diligent reader may find several felicitous refinements of expression; 'the musty, golden orb of the sugar-melon' is more luscious, but many gross crudities remain which must therefore be accepted as part of the author's mind, not of a mood.

It is a book of *pensées*, the commonplaces of a year in the war-time life of a literary critic. The author retains his pseudonym, 'Palinurus', the drowned pilot of Virgil, thus austerely denying the reader a legitimate source of interest, for *obiter dicta* of this kind gain much in importance from knowledge of the speaker; suppose Goering had said '*L'art est sottise*,' and Rimbaud 'When I hear the word "Art" I feel for my pistol.' These notes are not, like *Trivia*, miniature essays; they are rather, like Samuel Butler's Note Books, the raw material of literature and it seems to me that a great deal of valuable matter has here been prematurely put in the killing-bottle and pinned on the setting-board; a writer, I believe, should be in no hurry to get his thoughts on paper; it is better to let half-remembered quotations and half-developed ideas ferment together; as soon as he expresses something he puts it out of his mind. 'Palinurus's' book suffers from the fact that his observations have not been able to influence each other and, faced with the heterogeneous and often contradictory nature of his jottings, he has sought a factitious unity by attempting an innocent and ingenious imposture, pretending to relate them to classical mythology to the great awe and perplexity of the literary ladies of the Dorchester Hotel.

We are invited to accept the book as a self-portrait; the prejudices and idiosyncrasies of any adult, firmly set out, are interesting; but here we seem to be in contact not with a single, complete personality but with three distinct characters. First, there is a middle-aged gentleman in reduced circumstances. He has hallowed memories of his better days, of scholarship, young love satisfied, holidays in the sun, fruit, wine and exotic pets; a disappointed hedonist who put his trust in fine weather and cannot face the storm; a wistful, fretful figure, hampered by minor ailments and small bills, who, in the fogs of bomb-ruined Bloomsbury, likes to imagine that in happier ages he would have been admitted to the intimacy of Petronius and Rochester. Secondly, his constant companion, always a few steps behind mocking and mimicking his master's gait, follows his disorderly Irish valet, a man of high comic abilities in

Review of *The Unquiet Grave*, by Cyril Connolly. *Tablet*, 10 November 1945.

whom high spirits alternate with black despair. His particular function, as of all buffoon-servants, is to deflate his master. '*O nimium coelo et pelago confise sereno*,' cries the gentleman; the man hoots back in gibberish, '*Saba dukkha, saba anatta, saba anikka*, your honour's worship' (a line whose translation – 'Sorrow is everywhere; in man is no abiding entity; in things no abiding reality' – sets a problem to the cryptologist. What does '*saba*' mean?). It is the valet who inspires the extremely funny, spoof epilogue, but he has his black hours when the Irishman's eschatology – the English gallows: Father O'Flynn's judgment: the USA: Hell, a densely crowded place where tribal enemies are tortured with the unslaked thirst of the drunkard – keens through the pages. The man drinks, too, and in his cups spits out some ugly blasphemies for which it were best to put his head under the stable pump. But in general master and man make a happy combination, direct descendants of many a classic pair. Unhappily they are not alone; a horrible third has attached herself to the party, the flushed and impetuous figure of a woman novelist. She is a terror, rattling with clichés from Freud and Frazer and Marx; she edits a column of advice to those suffering from what she calls 'the complexity of modern life'; she has a weakness for newly married couples. 'If we had all enjoyed a happy childhood,' she flutes, 'with happy parents, the prisons, barracks and asylums would be empty.' 'Why do we like war?' she asks: 'Is it that all men would revenge themselves for their betrayal by their mothers?' 'When the present slaughter terminates . . .' she begins, giving full rein to the tosh-horse whose hooves thunder through the penultimate passages.

But it is to the original, lovable, distressed gentleman that we return at the end. He writes with exquisite melody and precision; his lament for the lemurs and the final sentences of the book are as beautiful as any passages of modern English prose that I know; his occasional subdued, melancholy wit is enchanting. We leave the corpse of 'Palinurus', high and dry, briny and disfigured. What has been the cause of his tragedy? 'Too much trust in the calm of sky and sea,' he says. I think rather the reverse, too much trust in the weather reports forecasting storm. He has been duped and distracted by the chatter of psychoanalysts and socialists. His motto should have been 'Do not speak to the man at the wheel.'

. MARSHAL TITO'S REGIME – 1 .

Sir, – There is evident danger that the urgent and human problem of the disposition of the former Italian and Austrian territories claimed by Marshal Tito may be treated as an academic matter to be settled at leisure for ethnolo-

The Times, 23 May 1945. Contribution to a debate about Marshal Tito's occupation of, and claims to, Trieste which had been running in *The Times* since an editorial of 2 May 1945. Until Waugh's intervention the issues debated had been the regional economic significance of the port of Trieste and the constitution of her population.

gists, while, in fact, the Slav partisans are in effective possession, busily shooting and deporting people who are legally under our protection. It would be entirely inconsistent with our own histories if Great Britain and the United States were to accept the hypothesis that the ethnological issue is paramount. Just rule is needed there and everywhere, not any kind of rule so long as the rulers can claim common descent from the same remote and barbarous ancestors. The assertion of race as the sole bond between men was one of the more absurd and odious errors of our late enemies.

We have, in our thanksgiving for victory, reaffirmed the fact that we are a Christian nation and have solemnly and sincerely dedicated the peace to Christian principles. Within a few days of these ceremonies we are being invited to acquiesce in a gross extension of a spectacle which touched the conscience of our grandfathers – the subjection of the Christian people of the Balkans to non-Christian tyrannous rule. The peoples now overrun by the forces of Marshal Tito are predominantly Roman Catholic. The attitude of his regime to their Church is not a matter of conjecture: it has long been evident in Croatia; but the knowledge is confined to those who, owing it to official sources, may not speak. Has the time not come to proclaim the truth? During the German war it was thought convenient to attribute heroic virtues to any who shared our quarrel and to suppress all mention of their crimes. There can now be no honourable reason for further concealment.

If, when the truth is published, it is revealed that the regime of Marshal Tito has all the characteristics of Nazism – a secret, political police, an unscrupulous propaganda bureau, judicial murders of political opponents, the regimentation of children into fanatical, hero-worshipping gangs, the arrest and disappearance of civilians for no other reason than that they spoke English and had exchanged civilities with British troops, the kidnapping of political opponents on allied territory, the arrest and disappearance of a national leader who came under safe conduct to discuss co-operation; that, above all, the Church is subject to persecution aimed at its extinction, that great numbers of priests whose only offence was popular esteem have been done to death, religious houses closed and religious associations abolished; that the elaborate and violent machine of party propaganda is employed to vilify the religious and that no expression of opinion is possible outside the party machine – if these things are true, the nation will see where its duty lies towards people threatened with an extension of this regime.

We have been obliged to make many painful compromises with justice during the past ten years, some of which seem irreparable; here is a question where we have the power to do right.

I am, Sir, your obedient servant,

A British Soldier Lately in Yugoslavia

Sir, – In my letter in *The Times* of 23 May I made no claim to 'expert' knowledge of the Balkans. What I said was that Marshal Tito's record in Croatia – the only area where he has ruled any considerable number of Catholics for any considerable time – was beastly. Since my truthfulness seems in question, I beg room for a very few of 'the facts'.

The most popular party in Croatia was Dr Macek's Peasant Party. He resisted all inducements to serve the Germans. In September of last year he sent his vice-chairman, Dr Kosutic, to Topusko, to propose co-operation with the Communists against the invaders; the condition he proposed was that free elections should be held as soon as was feasible, and that the Peasant Party should go to the polls under their existing organization. The answer to this suggestion was the arrest and disappearance of Dr Kosutic. Since then the partisans join Dr Macek's name with Pavelic's as 'traitor', 'Fascist' and 'war criminal'.

These terms are used indiscriminately of anyone who refuses to accept Communist dictation. They are especially used of the clergy. It is true that a handful of clergy actively supported the Ustashe; it is also true that a handful – only one of whom was the least 'distinguished' – supported the partisans. The vast majority went on quietly with their parish duties. Their only offence was that, so far as they held any political opinions, they were anti-Communist.

I have 'studied the facts' of the treatment of this offence in a few dioceses. In Sibonik eight priests were killed, in Split ten, in Dubrovnik fourteen, in the Franciscan Province of the Redeemer twenty-three, in Mostar forty-five. These figures apply to a small area up to the end of February only.

A legally constituted government may, of course, try and punish traitors. In none of these executions was there any semblance of legality. Some of the victims were shot on their doorsteps; others were arraigned before partisan youths; the majority were carried off by Ozna (the secret police) and shot in secret.

All the Church schools have been closed; in the state schools the customary prayers are forbidden and the crosses and religious pictures removed to make

---

The Times, 5 June 1945. 'Another British Officer from Yugoslavia' (*not* Sir Fitzroy Maclean, as Waugh's diary suggests) answered Waugh's first letter in *The Times* on 26 May 1945. He claimed that Waugh had exhibited 'half-knowledge disguised as expert knowledge' and that he had not 'studied the facts'; that those executed by Tito, including priests, had 'intrigued with the enemy', but that 'many distinguished churchmen had supported and even led the national liberation movement'; that each federal unit of Yugoslavia 'guaranteed complete freedom for all religions'; and that Tito's forces had not 'overrun' the areas they occupied but 'inhabited' them.

Waugh's diary for 28 May 1945 reveals that he looked forward to a reply to his second letter 'with eagerness', but no reply appeared.

The general principles invoked in the first letter and the substantiating details in the second are drawn from 'Church and State in Liberated Croatia', a report written by Waugh and submitted to the Foreign Office through Brigadier Maclean on 30 March 1945: Foreign Office Registry Number R5927/1059/92; Public Record Office File FO 371 48910 6745, pp. 120–29.

room for 'wall newspapers', in which the children praise Russia and the Marshal. The order of the alphabet has even been changed in the spelling primers so that T, I, and O are now the first letters. 'Pioneers' are organized among the children on the Communist 'cell' principle with the purpose of undermining the influence of parents and priests. In spite of an overwhelming vote in its favour, religious instruction was abolished in the upper forms. The theological colleges have all been closed. In the agreement proposed at Split for the distribution of allied relief, 'private organizations' (by which is meant religious communities) were explicitly excluded from benefit.

Effective power emanates from the Marshal and is transmitted in a chain of command by commissars and party secretaries, independent of the 'governing' committees on which sit bemused bourgeois and peasants who lack all authority and knowledge of what is being planned. The gang that was terrorizing Dubrovnik in February was mainly drawn from Korcula and Split.

I wish I could share 'Another Officer's' hope that the federal autonomy promised to Slovenia will preserve the Church there. I believe that these federal units will have as much autonomy as the states of USSR; that the Ozna and the Communist Party will continue to transcend these frontiers; that in whatever territory the forces of the Marshal emerge, the future of the Church is precarious and, humanly speaking, hopeless.

I am, Sir, your obedient servant,

A British Soldier Lately in Yugoslavia

5

. CATHOLIC EPOCH .

CATHOLIC, STYLIST, CELEBRITY AND ENEMY OF THE 'MODERN WORLD'

APRIL 1946 – OCTOBER 1955

WARNING

When I wrote my first novel, sixteen years ago, my publishers advised me, and I readily agreed, to prefix the warning that it was 'meant to be funny'. The phrase proved a welcome gift to unsympathetic critics. Now, in a more sombre decade, I must provide them with another text, and, in honesty to the patrons who have supported me hitherto, state that *Brideshead Revisited* is *not* meant to be funny. There are passages of buffoonery, but the general theme is at once romantic and eschatological.

It is ambitious, perhaps intolerably presumptuous; nothing less than an attempt to trace the workings of the divine purpose in a pagan world, in the lives of an English Catholic family, half-paganized themselves, in the world of 1923–39. The story will be uncongenial alike to those who look back on that pagan world with unalloyed affection, and to those who see it as transitory, insignificant and, already, hopefully passed. Whom then can I hope to please? Perhaps those who have the leisure to read a book word by word for the interest of the writer's use of language; perhaps those who look to the future with black forebodings and need more solid comfort than rosy memories. For the latter I have given my hero, and them, if they will allow me, a hope, not, indeed, that anything but disaster lies ahead, but that the human spirit, redeemed, can survive all disasters.

'Warning' written by Waugh for the dust-jacket of the first edition of
Brideshead Revisited

. INTRODUCTION .

Brideshead Revisited (1945) signalled that Evelyn Waugh had undergone profound change. Only intense biographical investigation could fully explain why
the novel displayed such striking new absorption in Roman Catholicism, such
revulsion from the 'Modern World' and the 'Century of the Common Man',
and such 'orchidaceous luxury of bloom' in the writing. Beyond a brief
explanation of matters directly connected with journalism, no more is possible
here than to say that the change proved to be permanent, and that it resulted in
corresponding developments in the essays and articles of the post-war period.
Furthermore, the novel became a best-seller, making its author 'successful'
and (as Waugh over-optimistically put it) 'stinking rich'. This in turn had
marked effects on the practicalities of journalism, greatly increasing prices,
opportunities and freedom of subject and treatment. But the new financial
situation had less impact on Waugh's writing than did heightened feeling about
religion, politics, art and the condition of England. And while this owed
something to Arthur Waugh's death and Hubert Duggan's death-bed conversion in 1943, it sprang mainly from fierce loyalties and bitter disappointments
generated by the Second World War.

The war – or more exactly the social and political consequence of the
fighting and the personal disasters of army life – seems to have been most
immediately responsible for turning the soldier–novelist towards religious
commitment and artistic 'vocation', and for engendering deep hostility to
contemporary life. At the very least it dramatically accelerated existing tendencies. As we shall see, the social revolution broadly associated with the 'People's
War', and the shock of being compelled to resign from his brigade on the eve of
its going into action, had important effects. But outweighing every other cause
for concern was the ceding of large Roman Catholic populations in eastern and
south-eastern Europe to Stalinist governments which violently and systemati-
cally persecuted them. The feelings of Catholics who, like Waugh, were aware
of the situation, went far beyond angry disagreement with their government's
policies. Their experience was, and to some extent still is, foreign to the vast
majority of English and American men and women of good will. They were
overwhelmed by a sense of tragedy and national dishonour so deep as to be
profoundly personal in its consequences: such as American Jews might feel
today if their country, to serve its own interest, were to connive at Israel's being
annexed by Syria.

England's 'betrayal of Poland' was central to the conservative Catholic
experience. After centuries of partition Poland, whose cause had stirred generations of Bellocian Catholics, had been reunited in 1918 as an independent
Catholic state. When Hitler was threatening Polish integrity in 1939, England
guaranteed it. The direct results of the guarantee were the Ribbentrop–

Molotov Pact, German invasion of Poland from the west and Russian from the east, gallant Polish resistance on two fronts entailing enormous losses, and (with England prudently withholding all help) inevitable defeat. Germany and Russia treated Poland abominably, Russia in particular by brutal mass deportations. When the post-war settlements were being negotiated from 1943 onwards, Churchill forced the Polish Government into Russian arrangements designed to make Poland a Soviet client-state and a Stalinist dictatorship. Polish objections were officially represented as obstructive bickering.

These were the damning facts of the case – rendered doubly odious by the British Government's and the major newspapers' assurances of 'free and fair elections' even while terror was raging – as they appeared to a small group of untypical, mainly Catholic, Englishmen. A contemporary reviewer expressed their abhorrence of England's conduct: 'It is difficult to decide who were the greater villains: the Germans who first attacked, the Russians who exterminated the Poles in the most bestial ways, or ourselves who in the hour of victory not only deserted Poland but betrayed her to Russia.' There was no joy in victory. Instead of the almost universal acceptance of the war as a triumph of good over evil, to the few it seemed that England had sunk to the moral level of her enemies. There is a repeated accusing question in the Waugh diaries: 'Why did we betray Poland to Russia?' An exceedingly harsh, and still shocking, implied answer to that question can be found in *Scott-King's Modern Europe* (1947), which describes the war as 'a sweaty tug-of-war between teams of indistinguishable louts' (p. 5).

Historians will dispute the fairness, friends of Evelyn Waugh will regret the terms, of this judgment. It is set down here to illustrate the depth of bitterness he felt in the immediate post-war period. The moving threnodies for Poland in *Sword of Honour* – the unregarded frontier of Christendom from which trains carry their doomed loads east and west, while the Halberdiers sit bemused by wine and harmony – could not be written until time had softened that original bitterness.

Journalism after 1946 deals with a variety of subjects in a variety of styles. Some was literary or 'Society', in Waugh's established manner; most was distinctive because connected, whether directly or indirectly, with the changes wrought by the war. Four broad subjects have particular importance, though two tend to be present as themes in work on other topics rather than the overt matter of discussion. In order of occurrence the four subjects are: Yugoslavia under Marshal Tito, and by implication all of eastern Europe under Russian hegemony; the horror of the 'new Dark Age', which was the 'Modern World'; the new class structure in England; and Roman Catholicism. Two other issues arise: style, or the cultivation of 'fine writing', which involves Waugh's new-found sense of 'vocation' as an artist, and travel, which provided the greater part of the material for articles on Scandinavia, the United States, Hollywood and Goa. The motives, the inhibitions, governing journalism at this period will be enlarged on in connection with travel. It is sufficient to say here that the success of *Brideshead Revisited* gave Waugh a professional standing which brought him more numerous offers, at higher prices and from more prestigious quarters than he had before known. Thus he might now write an essay of 5,000 words for *Life* (which provided research assistance, office space and VIP treatment in meeting boats, trains, etc.), at a fee of $5,000, much of it in tax-free expenses; whereas previously he had been receiving £21 to £31.10 for 2,000–3,000 words from, say, *Harper's Bazaar* and $100 for the American reprinting in *Town and Country*. But ironically the high earnings from *Brideshead*, combined with confiscatory taxes, now removed the need for, and even the desirability of, additional income from journalism. The upshot was that Waugh now had freedom to select journalism according to taste and conviction, and even more confidence to write as he liked – 'to be as truthful as I like in the words I like' (letter to Peters, 19 November 1952). Thus he rejected an offer of regular work from the *Evening Standard*, but sought an 'understanding' that they would welcome articles 'from time to time when the subject particularly excites me' (letter to Peters, 12 November 1947). When a subject did excite him, like the theology of Graham Greene's *The Heart of the Matter*, he wrote to Peters: 'The money is of course of no importance. I simply want the review to reach the right public' (June 1948).

A dozen pieces about Yugoslavia are the journalism most overtly connected with the political outcome of the war. The introduction to Part 4 has described Waugh's report to the Foreign Office documenting persecution of the Catholic Church and suppression of non-Communist political activity in areas 'liberated' by Tito, and Waugh's subsequent letters on the subject to *The Times*. Both the report and the letters were quietly contradicted, then ignored. Waugh, though keen to do so, had no opportunity to take the matter further at the time. An excellent chance to re-open the issue came in early 1952 when Marshal Tito was invited by Winston Churchill and Anthony Eden to make a state visit to England. Waugh waited until November to launch a virulent attack in a prominent article in the *Sunday Express*, 'Our Guest of Dishonour' (30 November 1952). This drew loud protests from most of the English press, and protests from the Yugoslav embassies in London and Bonn. It has been called 'Beaverbrook journalism at its worst'. It is certainly oversimplified, rhetorical and deliberately insulting to Tito and Anthony Eden, but the underlying view of Tito's contribution to Allied victory and of the violent repression he instituted is in harmony with the report and at least arguable. During the four months before the visit took place Waugh wrote seven brief letters to editors, none of which warrants reprinting, and gave several speeches and interviews – for him a strenuous (and boring) campaign. More soberly expressed opinions about Yugoslavia are found in reviews of Major Rootham's book about Mihailovich (11 May 1946) and of President Tito's autobiography (April 1953), and most attractively in a preface to Christie Lawrence's *Irregular Adventure* (1947). It is instructive that Waugh refused several lucrative requests for denunciations similar in tone to 'Our Guest of Dishonour', which had advertised his talent for provoking uproar. Most notably, he countered an invitation to attack Khrushchev and Bulganin's state visit to England with a proposal that he explain why there was nothing objectionable in eating with *open* enemies (letter to Peters, 2 March 1956; quoted in full in *Letters* at 18 February 1953). One conclusion to be drawn from the refusals to provide vituperation for a fee is that the rhetoric of 'Our Guest of Dishonour' expresses totally genuine anger at the savage cruelties inflicted on fellow Catholics throughout eastern Europe, and at the bland indifference (or worse) of English officialdom to the terror their policies had, quite predictably, forwarded.

A less tangible product of the war than the direct anger expressed over Yugoslavia (but no less influential in Waugh's writing) was an indefinable disgust with England and despair of the Modern World. This arose out of the appalling suffering inflicted on large parts of post-war Europe. The vast majority of English-speaking men and women felt the reconstruction period to be one promising new equality, mitigation of poverty through welfare, and planned prosperity and full employment. It was a time of euphoria. Nancy Mitford wrote to Waugh using the phrase 'Heavenly 1948'. But to him 1948 was, as he replied, 'the blackest year in the world's history since 1793', because 'human misery and degradation [were] everywhere at [their] blackest' (10 and 17 January 1949). Like many other Catholics he had been made vividly aware for several years, through the *Tablet* in particular, of 'chaos and tyranny and sheer wickedness throughout two-thirds of Europe and all Asia' (*Letters*, 20 October 1945); of the forced repatriation of displaced persons, by British soldiers, to countries where they suffered appalling fates; of the terror inflicted on Christian populations from the Baltic to the Adriatic. The recent 'revelations' of Count Nicolas Tolstoi and Lord Bethell would have appeared to him, in their general outline, not as the unearthing of matters inherently secret, but as welcome recognition of facts that had been known at the time and studiously suppressed by governments and by the national press. These events produced a peculiar, inexplicable disgust with England:

> What is there to worry me here in Stinchcombe? . . . Apart from taxation and rationing, government interference is negligible . . . Why am I not at ease? Why is it I smell all the time wherever I turn the reek of the Displaced Persons' Camp? (*Diaries*, 10 November 1946.)

Furthermore the same terrible events shaped a profound despair about what Waugh now began to call 'the Modern World'. In 'Fan-Fare' (8 April 1946) and in the preface to *Elected Silence* (1949) the phrase suggests a barbarism and evil so complete as to be past human help. The Modern World is now the 'new Dark Age', to be redeemed only by 'heroic prayer'. The artist can hope for no more than to develop his own art, thus emulating ninth-century monks in creating 'little systems of order'. This was not mere rhetoric. Diary entries beginning on 18 April 1945 show Waugh discussing the tragic 'advance of Russia, heathenism' with various distinguished Catholics. He rejected their political solutions and 'recommended catacombs'. Waugh developed none of these concerns at length, but they are mentioned briefly several times and, more important, help make intelligible the bitterness which affects his thinking on many subjects, most notably on class.

A great deal too much has been made of Waugh's being snobbish, in the sense of his being a middle-class social climber fatuously in love with Birth and arrogantly contemptuous of his 'inferiors'. Plainly as a young man, like many other ambitious young men and women, he made efforts to advance himself socially, in his case among the smart and fashionable, not among the rich and powerful. Plainly he preferred to associate with the survivors of the aristocracy, and with the educated middle class, rather than with commercial magnates or industrial workers. This was, probably, a narrowness of social sympathy limiting in a novelist. But it does not begin to explain the bitter class-consciousness which first made its appearance in *Brideshead Revisited* in the portrait of Hooper, and which infected the journalism from 1945 onwards. The explanation of that bitterness lies in two directions: first in the extraordinary attacks launched against the upper class from 1939 until the mid-1950s, which Waugh resented; and secondly his keen awareness of the workings of the class system coupled with a rational (or rationalized?) conviction of its benefits.

The defence of the upper classes and the offensive against the lower which characterized Waugh's post-1945 career was in essence a reaction against the anti-upper-class campaign usually referred to as the 'People's War'. This is not to be confused with the lampooning of rich shirkers and profiteers, Colonel Bogus and the *Ritzkrieg;* nor with rhetoric to the effect that the war was being fought, as it was, by 'the People', i.e. by the whole population, civilian as well as military. The 'People's War', in the stricter sense, was a loose movement or tendency (comprising some small organizations with specific aims) which sought, with more or less deliberateness, to exploit the war situation in order to achieve social change (and in some cases, social revolution). It is to this tendency Waugh is referring in 'Anything Wrong with Priestley?' (13 September 1957) and in 'An Act of Homage and Reparation to P.G. Wodehouse' (July 1961), when he writes of 'men and women who sought to direct the struggle for national survival into proletarian revolution and to identify the enemy with their own upper classes.' The propaganda of the movement, as Waugh said, attempted to stigmatize the upper classes as pro-Fascist and potentially traitorous: 'The *Nouveau Riche* love the *Nouveau Reich*.' 'Anything Wrong with Priestley?' quotes J. B. Priestley's very famous expression of the Left's policy of attempting to eliminate the upper classes from the conduct of the war and from planning the peace: the country can win the war only 'by taking a firm grip on about 50,000 important, influential gentlemanly persons and telling them firmly to do nothing if they don't want to be put to doing some most unpleasant work.' This was the logical conclusion to be drawn from one of the Left's dominant myths of the 1930s, against which Waugh argued in 'Present Discontents' (3 December 1938), that the upper classes were conspiring to bring about Fascist revolution and alliance with the dictators. Some readers are surprised that Waugh, the arch-snob, should be critical of other writers' 'hypersensitiveness to class' (e.g. of Angus Wilson's in the review of *Hemlock and After*, October 1952). But it follows from his regarding egalitarians as aggressors in a class-war. The stridency of his own comments on class tends to match that of the attacks to which he is responding. And the bitter anger he felt at the People's War movement is an unspoken element in all of his pronouncements on class and classlessness.

In 'Mainly about Myself', written in 1898, George Bernard Shaw declared that 'equality' was 'the only possible permanent basis of social organization, discipline, subordination, good manners, and selection of fit persons for high functions.' Since then almost everyone has agreed with him, the Conservative Party having adopted the Classless Society as a major policy in the late 1950s. Evelyn Waugh, however, believed the precise opposite. To him it seemed that after 1945 the proletariat had become dominant in England, and that its dominance would hasten England's decline. A two-class state of proletariat and officials (to which he often refers) would eventuate:

> England as a great power is done for . . . the loss of possessions, the claim of the English proletariat to be a privileged race, sloth and envy, must produce increasing poverty . . . this time the cutting down will start at the top until only a proletariat and a bureaucracy survive. As a bachelor I could contemplate all this in a detached manner, but it is no country in which to bring up children. (*Diaries*, 9 November 1946.)

Writing soon after the Labour Party had swept into office with a majority which caused socialists to talk of a 'bloodless revolution', Waugh was no doubt inclined to exaggerate; but he believed that during the war power had decisively shifted from the upper to the lower classes. He also believed that England's prosperity and all the most attractive features of English life, had been created by the upper classes. 'What to Do with the Upper Classes: A Modest Proposal' (September 1946) expresses this viewpoint with Swiftian irony but with complete, literal conviction. Waugh, logically, also believed the converse, that proletarian dominance would make England poorer, law and administration less just and efficient, life disorderly and drab, and the arts dull. The benefits conferred by a flexible system of classes are expounded in the 'Commentary' to *The Private Man* (1962). A review of Graham Greene's *British Dramatists* (6 November 1942) and a letter defining the social status of Captain Cook and Clive of India (10 January 1965) reject the view that all worthwhile achievements have been the work of simple folk. But it is the relationship between language and class which most interested Waugh. 'Fan-Fare' (8 April 1946) maintains that the language has survived as a delicate instrument only through its connection with 'high civilized society' and a 'thin line of devotees'. The review of Alan Hodge and Robert Graves's *The Reader Over Your Shoulder* (3 July 1943) connects the 'tradition of gentle speech', and all artistic achievement, with the indirect influence of an aristocracy. No opinion could have been more at variance with received literary doctrine of the time; perhaps this accounts for some over-emphasis in Waugh's expression. But again a fear that traditional English culture could not survive in a new two-class society of officials and proletariat is an unspoken element prompting many seemingly irresponsible utterances and posturings about class.

The most overt development in Waugh's journalism after 1946 was a new preoccupation with Catholicism. All but one of the major essays ('Why Hollywood is a Term of Disparagement') are about Catholic subjects, or treat secular subjects (e.g. Forest Lawn cemetery) from a Catholic point of view. Furthermore the essays on the Catholic Church in America (19 September 1949), on the Holy Places (March 1952) and St Francis Xavier's festival at Goa (December 1953) were written at Waugh's suggestion, not, as has been suggested, at the prompting of *Life* or *Esquire*. Shorter pieces are mainly secular, though most, such as 'Fan-Fare' (8 April 1946), 'Palinurus in Never-Never Land' (27 July 1946) or 'A Progressive Game' (31 May 1951) make significant reference to religion. About a third of the reviews deal with Catholic writers or introduce a religious perspective into discussion. At least half the letters to editors are directly religious in subject, many of them combatively defending the Catholic Church against criticism. The explanation of the new emphasis on religion could be the simple professional one, that Catholic novelists are asked to write articles about Catholicism. But the true reason seems to be that Waugh had become more religious than he had been before.

In the immediate post-war period Waugh, as far as can be judged, sought to come to terms, personally and in a realistic way, with Roman Catholic doctrine and practice. In 1930 he had been a rather coldly intellectual, not very fervent convert. Since then he had been growing in knowledge and fervour, and the developments in the mid-1940s were arguably an extension of this growth. But in 1943 Arthur Waugh died, and in the same year at Hubert Duggan's death-bed Waugh played parts very similar to those of Bridey and Charles Ryder in *Brideshead Revisited*: like Bridey he introduced a priest against family opposition, and like Charles he waited for and saw 'a spark of gratitude for the love of God' (*Diaries*, 4–13 October 1943). These seem to have been crucial experiences. An important role must also be granted to inspiration from the savage persecution then being suffered by Catholics in eastern Europe, where, as the preface to the 1946 edition of *Edmund Campion* says, the Church was drawn underground in country after country, and where the saints subjected to cruelty and degradation were a 'pure light shining in darkness'. Many Catholics became more fervently religious at this time. On 7 April 1947 Waugh 'consulted a monk about welfare of my soul.' On 9 April he concluded, 'to aim at anything less than sanctity is not to aim at all. Oh for persecution.' And on 28 April he determined to give up cigars as a means of 'mortification' and of saving money, which he could then, in good conscience, give to charity.

On superficial acquaintance with his journalism, and particularly with some of his controversial exchanges, it is tempting to think of Waugh as having opinions rather than faith, of being interested in religion rather than religious.

Closer scrutiny, especially of some unobtrusive reviews, can lead to another view, that within the boundaries of Roman Catholic orthodoxy he had developed a religion of considerable personal character, which underlies his writings on less personal topics. The preface to the *Occasional Sermons of Ronald Knox* (1949) describes how an individual who accepts, as a whole, an all-embracing theological and moral system nevertheless develops a personal 'religion' as from time to time certain truths acquire urgent personal importance. 'Edith Stein' (December 1952) describes a young Jewish philosopher who owed her conversion to Catholicism to the application of sharp intelligence and to a disciplined will. This 'rationalistic' approach to faith was common – indeed almost normative – among educated Catholics of the time. When Waugh wrote to Nancy Mitford, 'I can never understand why everyone is not a Catholic' (24 August 1949), he meant, literally, that the case for Catholicism was logically compelling. In 'Felix Culpa?', a review of Graham Greene's *Heart of the Matter* (16 July 1948), Waugh describes himself as a 'logical, rule-of-thumb' Catholic and shows clear sympathy with cut-and-dried legalistic formulations when Greene, like almost every other Catholic novelist then writing, sought to transcend them. 'Mgr Knox at 4 a.m.' (December 1952) is about the mood of doubt and despair which periodically afflicts all Christians. Waugh, who was temperamentally hyper-sceptical, must have been subject to the '4 a.m. mood'. Was it, one wonders, his own acute sensitivity to logical flaws in the Christian case, his educated-Englishman's distaste for the unliterary harshness of Roman Catholic theological discussion, his awareness of the disparity between the moralists' pronouncements and what people actually did (see 'A Story with a Moral', 10 June 1956), and his constant temptation to fall into a state of apathy or despair – did these temperamental disinclinations to the Catholic Church lead Waugh to emphasize disciplined intelligence in the pursuit of truth, willed acceptance of unwelcome conclusions and adherence to the letter of official formulations of dogma?

Two less personal, more public tendencies also characterize Waugh's Catholicism: he was prone to bellicose controversy on behalf of his Church, and he was openly, indeed conspicuously, critical of the Church's clergy and outward aspect.

In 'Mgr Ronald Knox' (May 1948) Waugh writes: 'We are often embarrassed by the methods of doughty champions of our own side.' Few Catholic readers of Waugh's controversies will fail to see unconscious irony in this sentence. From one point of view Waugh could be said to have avoided the worst features of the textbook trained, non-literary Roman Catholic debaters of his day. But from another point of view his aggression, his tendency to make the premises of any argument the formulation of a dogma, or the Church's view of itself, current in the 1930s, left opponents unmoved and sympathizers uncomfortable. Historical debates with (the then) Professor Hugh Trevor-Roper (now Lord Dacre), who was quite as trenchant and quite as ready to argue 'for victory' as Waugh, were another matter altogether. The first of two bloody but well-informed battles with Professor Trevor-Roper has fortunately been reprinted in an appendix to the *Letters*. A very angry reply to an offensive aside in Professor Trevor-Roper's *The Last Days of Hitler*, which Waugh describes as 'manifestly absurd to anyone with a mind above a brute's' (28 June 1947); letters attacking the Bishop of Truro's plea for common prayer between Catholics and Protestants (21 and 28 May 1948); a defence of Thomas Merton and 'vocation' against V. S. Pritchett (20 August, 3, 10 and 17 September 1949); a rebuttal of Gerard Meath, OP's charge that he confused aristocracy and Catholicism (3 and 17 November 1951) – these are too much confined to quibble and detail to warrant reprinting. From July to October 1956 Waugh again engaged in continuous, acrimonious controversy in the *Spectator*, and in the *New Statesman* with Professor Trevor-Roper, over matters of doctrine and Church history.

Of Waugh's tendency to be critical of Catholic clergy, church buildings, 'superstitious' devotional practices and general vulgarity – criticisms to be found in 'The American Epoch in the Catholic Church' (19 September 1949) and in 'Come Inside' (1949) – nothing need be said except that such criticism, in print, was extremely rare in the 1940s and 1950s. When taken in conjunction with Waugh's opposition to censorship of films and books (see 'For Adult Audiences', 25 July 1930; 'Why Hollywood is a Term of Disparagement', 1 May 1947), and with his 'non-official' or 'semi-unorthodox' view that divorce legislation should suit the needs of a non-Christian population (see 'Tell the Truth about Marriage', *John Bull*, 23 August 1930; also 'Home Life is So Dull', 1 December 1935), Waugh's publicly critical attitude towards the clergy, and his willingness to quarrel with Church authorities in the press, marked him as liberal. His contributing to *Commonweal* in the 1940s and 1950s, when it was one of the very few 'progressive' Catholic periodicals in the English language, also marked him as ahead of his time. That the appearance of liberalism was superficial is proved, however, by two unobtrusive letters to *The Times* (21 and 25 May 1948) rebuking the Bishop of Truro's appeal for a very little, very simple common prayer between Catholics and Protestants. But English and American Progressives in 1960 had some reason for regarding Waugh as a former sympathizer lost to their cause.

Waugh's concept of 'vocation' is so clearly expounded in 'St Helena Empress' (January 1952) that it needs little comment. It warrants pointing out, however, because it plays a central part in both *Helena* and *Sword of Honour*, and in Waugh's career. Perhaps it is the one aspect of Christian belief Waugh developed into something approaching a personal philosophy. In his time it was customary for Catholics to think of achieving salvation in terms of satisfying the Examiner over the complete range of tests He had imposed. Waugh's emphasis on fulfilling a particular task, or tasks, 'which only we can do and for which we were each created', was novel. It was also personally important. Helena's task was to find the True Cross and direct the world's attention to the plain historical facts by which Christianity stands or falls; Guy Crouchback's was to marry the pregnant Virginia; Waugh's, after 1945, was to write.

Two tendencies explain the form taken by and the subject matter of much post-*Brideshead* journalism: the first was an impulse towards 'style', arguably a derivative of the newly acquired sense of 'vocation'; the second was a compulsion to travel.

After 1945 the journalism was always written with a deliberate intention of employing a richer vocabulary and more elaborate sentence structure than had previously served. The change could be explained as no more than the predictable development of existing tendencies. But it appears rather to have arisen from Waugh's determination to combat the drabness of contemporary prose styles, and from a quite new acceptance of writing as the true purpose of his life. This new sense of 'vocation' followed severe reverses in the army. Though Waugh was in debt in 1939 and ended the war rich owing to the success of *Put Out More Flags* (1942) and *Brideshead Revisited* (1945), in his terms he had a 'bad war'. Being told that he was 'so popular as to be unemployable as an officer' (*Diaries*, 23 March 1943), being compelled to resign from the Special Services Brigade on the eve of its seeing active service (*Diaries*, after 9 June 1943), were bitter blows. The second has been described by friends as having a shattering effect comparable to that inflicted by the breakdown of the first marriage. Waugh despaired: 'It [the war] has worked its cure with me . . . I don't want to influence opinions or events . . . or anything of that kind. I don't want to be of service to anyone or anything.' (*Diaries*, 29 August 1943.) The despair passed. Waugh would perform singular 'service' to Hubert Duggan and to the desperate in Yugoslavia. But the humiliation he had endured shocked him into recognizing that he was not a 'man of action'. For the first time in his life he found it 'pleasant to [be] writing . . . I thank God to find myself still a writer . . .' (*Diaries*, 6 May 1945). 'Fan-Fare' (8 April 1946) explains the development more formally: 'I have never until quite lately enjoyed writing . . . I wanted to be a man of the world and I took to writing as I might have taken to archaeology or diplomacy or any other profession . . . Now I see it as an end in itself.' The responsibilities of the new role were also set out in 'Fan-Fare': the first was to write about man in relation to God; the second was to cultivate 'style'.

The preface to the 1960 revision of *Brideshead Revisited* claims that the verbal extravagance of the original was a reaction against the bleakness of war-time conditions. But this was not a complete explanation. For one thing Waugh had always had a weakness for luxuriant prose, witness 'Laying down a Wine Cellar' (December 1937). Again Waugh was moved by disagreement with the then influential Marxist view of literature and by his own theoretical alternative. Reviewing Robert Graves and Alan Hodge's *The Reader Over Your Shoulder* (3 July 1943) he makes two relevant points. The first is that in the new society emerging at the time, artists would have only two choices: 'anarchic bohemianism' or 'ascetic seclusion': in the post-war period he chose a (much mitigated) 'ascetic seclusion' in order, as he explained, to provide 'works of art' which would assist 'English culture [to] survive'. If that were to be possible, 'language must be preserved as a vehicle for accurate and graceful expression.' In 'Fan-Fare' Waugh speaks of 'devotees' attempting to save the English language from extinction by employing its 'lavish and delicate' vocabulary, its subtle nuances of word and phrase, more fully than contemporary tastes allowed. The style of the post-war journalism reflects that ambition.

Travel became attractive to Waugh after 1945 for several reasons. Disgust with England – with Conservatives like Winston Churchill who had accomplished 'the dismemberment of Europe', with the socialists who had created the intellectual climate which made it inevitable – was more important, it seems, than mere petulance over a Labour Government, though Waugh did speak of the 'Attlee–Cripps terror' and of the socialists as an army of occupation. Shortages made life in England irksome, too. Overseas journalistic assignments were a means of escape, and a means of living luxuriously for a time on expenses. For 'The American Epoch in the Catholic Church' and for 'The Defence of the Holy Places' *Life* paid $5,000, 'up to $4,000 for expenses'. 'Spending money like a drunken sailor' while working on 'American Epoch' in New York, Waugh accumulated expenses of $4,665. As late as 1955, when attempting to secure a commission to write an article on St Francis of Assisi, he wrote to Peters: 'The important point for me is the tax-free expenses.' On the other hand the fees for a number of lucrative articles were paid directly to nominated charities. Travel, occasioned by a variety of needs, determined the subject matter, if not the themes, of a very large part of the post-war writings.

A brief conspectus of trips connected, or potentially connected, with journalism will best demonstrate how closely Waugh's writing depends on travel at this time. Nuremburg in April 1946 produced nothing. Spain in June 1946 gave only *Scott-King's Modern Europe* (1947). Hollywood in February–March 1947 gave an article on the Hollywood film industry, 'Why Hollywood is a Term of Disparagement' (30 April and 1 May 1947), which drew a reply from Sir Alexander Korda; an article on the cemetery of Forest Lawn and the work of the morticians there, 'Half in Love with Easeful Death' (18 October 1947); and 'The Man Hollywood Hates' (4 November 1947) an article defending Charlie Chaplin against anti-communist persecution and praising his latest film (Waugh met Chaplin and saw *Monsieur Verdoux* privately in Hollywood). Sweden, Norway and Denmark in August 1947 gave two articles on 'The Scandinavian Capitals' (11 and 13 November 1947) and an amusing sketch 'The Gentle Art of Being Interviewed' (1948–49). Five weeks in New York at *Life*'s expense around November 1948 produced 'American Epoch' (November 1949); January and February 1949 were spent lecturing throughout the United States. October 1950 was also spent in New York holidaying and lecturing. Each American visit produced a minor flurry caused by criticism of life in the United States. On 8 May 1948 Waugh had to write to the *Daily Mail*'s Don Iddon, who supplied a New York letter, to deny abuse of Hollywood hospitality. On 30 December 1948 his remarks on over-heated rooms, bubble gum, radios and the need for monasteries were quoted in the *Evening Standard*; on 12 January 1949 Don Iddon reported to the *Daily Mail* that Waugh was being 'kicked all the way down Main Street'. This time Waugh wrote 'Kicking against the Goad' (11 March 1949) to complain of misrepresentation. On 31 December 1950 the *New York Times* carried a story with a self-explanatory title, 'Waugh Scores Life in US'. January and February 1951 were spent in Palestine, Jordan and Turkey researching 'The Defence of the Holy Places' for *Life*. Goa in December 1952 and January 1953 led to an article for *Picture Post*, 'Farewell to a Saint' (24 January 1953), and to an expansion of that article, 'Goa: The Home of a Saint' (December 1953). These major trips were interspersed with many shorter visits: to Ireland house-hunting; to Paris, where close friends, Diana Cooper and Nancy Mitford, successively reigned in the British Embassy; to Italy, Belgium and Holland; to Colombo, on the 'Pinfold' journey; and to the West Indies where, having retreated from the Mediterranean, the tide of fashion was at the full.

. FAN-FARE .

Frequently, unobtrusively, in the last seventeen years I have had books published in the United States of America. No one noticed them. A parcel would appear on my breakfast table containing a familiar work with a strange wrapper and sometimes a strange title; an item would recur in my agent's accounts: 'Unearned advance on American edition', and that was the end of the matter. Now, unseasonably, like a shy water-fowl who has hatched out a dragon's egg, I find that I have written a 'best-seller'. 'Unseasonably', because the time has passed when the event brings any substantial reward. In a civilized age this unexpected moment of popularity would have endowed me with a competency for life. But perhaps in a civilized age I should not be so popular. As it is the politicians confiscate my earnings and I am left with the correspondence.

This is something new to me, for Englishwomen do not write letters to men they do not know; indeed they seldom write letters to anyone nowadays; they are too hard-driven at home. Even before the war English readers were seldom seen or heard. It is true that there are facilities for writers whose vanity so inclines them to join literary associations, make speeches and even expose themselves to view at public luncheons, but no one expects it of them or respects them for it. Instead of the Liberty, Equality and Fraternity of the Americas, Europe offers its artists Liberty, Diversity and Privacy. Perhaps it is for this that so many of the best American writers go abroad. But, as Hitler observed, there are no islands in the modern world. I have momentarily become an object of curiosity to Americans and I find that they believe that my friendship and confidence are included in the price of my book.

My father taught me that it was flagitious to leave a letter of any kind unanswered. (Indeed his courtesy was somewhat extravagant. He would write and thank people who wrote to thank him for wedding presents and when he encountered anyone as punctilious as himself the correspondence ended only with death.) I therefore eagerly accept this chance of answering collectively all the cordial inquiries I have received. Please believe me, dear ladies, it is not sloth or 'snootiness' that prevents my writing to you individually. It is simply that I cannot afford it. The royalty on your copy, by the time I have paid my taxes, literally does not leave me the price of a stamp.

You require to know what I look like? Well, I am 42 years of age, in good health, stockily built – no, I really cannot go on. Let me merely say that the tailors and hairdressers and hosiers of the small parish of St James's, London do all they can to render a naturally commonplace appearance completely inconspicuous. Stand on the pavement and scan the aquarium-faces which pass and gape and pass again in my club window; try and spot a novelist. You will not spot me. I once had an intellectual friend who complained that my appearance was noticeable in Bloomsbury. But I seldom leave St James's when I am in London, and I seldom go to London at all. I live in a shabby stone house in the country, where nothing is under a hundred years old except the plumbing and that does not work. I collect old books in an inexpensive, desultory way. I have a fast-emptying cellar of wine and gardens fast reverting to jungle. I am very contentedly married. I have numerous children whom I see once a day for ten, I hope, awe-inspiring minutes. In the first ten years of adult life I made a large number of friends. Now on the average I make one new one a year and lose two. It is all quite dull, you see: nothing here is worth the poke of a sightseer's sunshade.

It was not always thus with me. In youth I gadded about, and in those years and in the preposterous years of the Second World War I collected enough experience to last several lifetimes of novel-writing. If you hear a novelist say he needs to collect 'copy', be sure he is no good. Most of the great writers led very quiet lives; when, like Cervantes, they were adventurous, it was not for professional reasons. When I gadded, among savages and people of fashion and politicians and crazy generals, it was because I enjoyed them. I have settled down now because I ceased to enjoy them and because I have found a much more abiding interest – the English language. My father, who was a respected literary critic of his day, first imbued me with the desire to learn this language, of which he had a mastery. It is the most lavish and delicate which mankind has ever known. It is in perpetual danger of extinction and has survived so far by the combination of a high civilized society, where it was spoken and given its authority and sanctity, with a thin line of devotees who made its refinement and adornment their life's work. The first of these is being destroyed; if the thing is to be saved it will be by the second. I did not set out to be a writer. My first ambition was to paint. I had little talent but I enjoyed it as, I believe, many very bad writers enjoy writing. I spent some time at an art school which was not as wantonly wasted as it seemed then. Those hours with the plaster casts taught me to enjoy architecture, just as the hours with the Greek paradigms, now forgotten, taught me to enjoy reading English. I have never, until quite lately, enjoyed writing. I am lazy and it is intensely hard work. I wanted to be a man of the world and I took to writing as I might have taken to archaeology or diplomacy or any other profession as a means of coming to terms with the world. Now I see it as an end in itself. Most European writers suffer a climacteric at the age of 40. Youthful volubility carries them so far. After that they either become prophets or hacks or aesthetes. (American writers, I think, nearly all become hacks.) I am no prophet and, I hope, no hack.

That, I think, answers the second question so often put to me in the last few weeks: 'When can we expect another *Brideshead Revisited*?' Dear ladies, never. I can never hope to engage your attention again in quite the same way. I have already shaken off one of the American critics, Mr Edmund Wilson, who once professed a generous interest in me. He was outraged (quite legitimately by his standards) at finding God introduced into my story. I believe that you can only leave God out by making your characters pure abstractions. Countless admirable writers, perhaps some of the best in the world, succeed in this. Henry James was the last of them. The failure of modern novelists since and including James Joyce is one of presumption and exorbitance. They are not content with the artificial figures which hitherto passed so gracefully as men and women. They try to represent the whole human mind and soul and yet omit its determining character – that of being God's creature with a defined purpose.

So in my future books there will be two things to make them unpopular: a preoccupation with style and the attempt to represent man more fully, which, to me, means only one thing, man in his relation to God.

But before we part company there are other questions you ask which I will try to answer. A lady in Hempstead, NY asks me whether I consider my characters 'typical'. No, Mrs Schultz, I do not. It is horrible of you to ask. A novelist has no business with types; they are the property of economists and politicians and advertisers and the other professional bores of our period. The artist is interested only in individuals. The statesman who damned the age with the name 'the Century of the Common Man' neglected to notice the simple, historical fact that it is the artists, not the statesmen, who decide the character of a period. The Common Man does not exist. He is an abstraction invented by bores for bores. Even you, dear Mrs Schultz, are an individual. Do not ask yourself, when you read a story, 'Is this the behaviour common to such and such an age group, income group, psychologically conditioned group?' but, 'Why did these particular people behave in this particular way?' Otherwise you are wasting your time in reading works of imagination at all.

There is another more intelligent question more often asked: 'Are your characters drawn from life?' In the broadest sense, of course, they are. None except one or two negligible minor figures is a portrait; all the major characters are the result of numberless diverse observations fusing in the imagination into a single whole. My problem has been to distil comedy and sometimes tragedy from the knockabout farce of people's outward behaviour. Men and women as I see them would not be credible if they were literally transcribed; for instance the international journalists whom I met for a few delirious weeks in Addis Ababa, some of whose abandoned acts I tried to introduce into *Scoop*. Or there is the character Captain Grimes in *Decline and Fall*. I knew such a man. One of the more absurd escapades of my youth, the result of a debt-settlement conference with my father after which I undertook to make myself financially independent of him, was to take a job as master at a private school. There I met a man who made what has seemed to me the lapidary statement, 'This looks like being the first end of term I've seen, old boy, for two years.' But had I written anything like a full account of his iniquities, my publishers and I would have been in the police court.

As for the major characters, I really have very little control over them. I start them off with certain preconceived notions of what they will do and say in certain circumstances but I constantly find them moving another way. For example there was the heroine of *Put Out More Flags*, a Mrs Lyne. I had no idea until halfway through the book that she drank secretly. I could not understand why she behaved so oddly. Then when she sat down suddenly on the steps of the cinema I understood all and I had to go back and introduce a series of empty bottles into her flat. I was on board a troopship at the time. There is a young destroyer commander who sat next to me at table who can bear witness of this. He asked me one day at luncheon how my book was going. I said, 'Badly. I can't understand it at all,' and then quite suddenly, 'I know. Mrs Lyne has been drinking.'

A Handful of Dust, on the other hand, began at the end. I had written a short story about a man trapped in the jungle, ending his days reading Dickens aloud. The idea came quite naturally from the experience of visiting a lonely settler of that kind and reflecting how easily he could hold me prisoner. Then, after the short story was written and published, the idea kept working in my mind. I wanted to discover how the prisoner got there, and eventually the thing grew into a study of other sorts of savage at home and the civilized man's helpless plight among them.

People sometimes say to me, 'I met someone exactly like a character out of one of your books.' I meet them everywhere, not by choice but luck. I believe the world is populated by them. Before the war it was sometimes said that I must move in a very peculiar circle. Then I joined the army and served six years, mostly with regular soldiers who are reputed to be uniformly conventional. I found myself under the command and in the mess with one man of startling singularity after another. I have come to the conclusion that there is no such thing as normality. That is what makes story-telling such an absorbing task, the attempt to reduce to order the anarchic raw materials of life.

That leads to another question: 'Are your books meant to be satirical?' No.

Satire is a matter of period. It flourishes in a stable society and presupposes homogeneous moral standards – the early Roman Empire and eighteenth-century Europe. It is aimed at inconsistency and hypocrisy. It exposes polite cruelty and folly by exaggerating them. It seeks to produce shame. All this has no place in the Century of the Common Man where vice no longer pays lip service to virtue. The artist's only service to the disintegrated society of today is to create little independent systems of order of his own. I foresee in the dark age opening that the scribes may play the part of the monks after the first barbarian victories. They were not satirists.

A final question: 'Do you consider *Brideshead Revisited* your best book?' Yes. *A Handful of Dust,* my favourite hitherto, dealt entirely with behaviour. It was humanist and contained all I had to say about humanism. *Brideshead Revisited* is vastly more ambitious; perhaps less successful, but I am not deterred either by popular applause or critical blame from being rather proud of the attempt. In particular I am not the least worried about the charge of using clichés. I think to be oversensitive about clichés is like being oversensitive about table manners. It comes from keeping second-rate company. Professional reviewers read so many bad books in the course of duty that they get an unhealthy craving for arresting phrases. There are many occasions in writing when one needs an unobtrusive background to action, when the landscape *must* become conventionalized if the foreground is to have the right prominence. I do not believe that a serious writer has ever been shy of an expression because it has been used before. It is the writer of advertisements who is always straining to find bizarre epithets for commonplace objects.

Nor am I worried at the charge of snobbery. Class-consciousness, particularly in England, has been so much inflamed nowadays that to mention a nobleman is like mentioning a prostitute sixty years ago. The new prudes say, 'No doubt such people do exist but we would sooner not hear about them.' I reserve the right to deal with the kind of people I know best.

One criticism does deeply discourage me: a postcard from a man (my sole male correspondent) in Alexandria, Va. He says, 'Your *Brideshead Revisited* is a strange way to show that Catholicism is an answer to anything. Seems more like the kiss of Death.' I can only say: I am sorry, Mr McClose, I did my best. I am not quite clear what you mean by the 'kiss of Death' but I am sure it is gruesome. Is it something to do with halitosis? If so I have failed indeed and my characters have got wildly out of hand once more.

. A NEW HUMANISM .

The *Critical Essays* of Mr George Orwell comprise ten papers of varying length, written between 1939 and 1945, which together form a work of absorbing

Review of *Critical Essays*, by George Orwell. *Tablet*, 6 April 1946.

interest. They represent at its best the new humanism of the common man, of which Mass Observation is the lowest expression. It is a habit of mind rather than a school. Mr Edmund Wilson in the United States is an exponent and perhaps it is significant that two of Mr Orwell's ten subjects have been treated at length by him. The essential difference between this and previous critical habits is the abandonment of the hierarchic principle. It has hitherto been assumed that works of art exist in an order of precedence with the great masters, Virgil, Dante and their fellows, at the top and the popular novel of the season at the bottom. The critics' task has been primarily to preserve and adjust this classification. Their recreation has been to 'discover' recondite work and compete in securing honours each for his own protégé. This, I believe, is still the critic's essential task, but the work has fallen into decay lately through exorbitance. Critics of this popularly dubbed 'Mandarin' school must be kept under discipline by a civilized society whose servants they should be. For the past thirty years they have run wild and countenanced the cults of Picasso and Stein, and the new critics, of whom Mr Orwell is outstandingly the wisest, arrive opportunely to correct them. They begin their inquiry into a work of art by asking: 'What kind of man wrote or painted this? What were his motives, conscious or unconscious? What sort of people like his work? Why?' With the class distinctions the great colour-bar also disappears; that hitherto impassable gulf between what was 'Literature' and what was not. Vast territories are open for exploitation. Indeed the weakness of the new criticism lies there; that, whereas the 'Mandarins' failed by presumptuously attempting to insert cranks and charlatans into the ranks of the immortals, the new humanists tend to concentrate entirely on the base and ephemeral. Mr Orwell's three most delightful essays deal respectively with comic postcards, 'penny-dreadfuls' and Mr James Hadley Chase. He treats only once of a subject that is at all recondite, W. B. Yeats's philosophic system, and then, I think, not happily.

The longest essay is on Charles Dickens and is chiefly devoted to refuting the opinions of Chesterton and Mr T. A. Jackson. (In this connection Mr Orwell should note, what is often forgotten, that Chesterton became a Catholic late in life. Most of his best-known work was written while he was still groping for his faith, and though it bears the promise of future realization, contains opinions which cannot be blithely labelled 'Catholic'.) He is entirely successful in his refutation and he fills his argument with brilliantly chosen illustrations many of which are entirely new, at any rate to me. I had never before reflected on the profound fatuity of the future life of the characters implied in their 'happy ending'.

There follows an ingenious analysis of the *Gem* and *Magnet* magazines and their successors. At my private school these stories were contraband and I read them regularly with all the zeal of law-breaking. (The prohibition was on social, not moral grounds. *Chums*, *The Captain* and the *BOP* were permitted. These again were recognized as 'inferior' to *Bevis*, *Treasure Island* and such books, which my father read aloud to me. Thus was the hierarchic system early inculcated.) I think Mr Orwell talks nonsense when he suggests that the antiquated, conservative tone of these stories is deliberately maintained by capitalist newspaper proprietors in the interest of the class structure of society. A study of these noblemen's more important papers reveals a reckless disregard of any such obligation. Here, and elsewhere, Mr Orwell betrays the unreasoned animosity of a class-war in which he has not achieved neutrality.

The Art of Donald McGill is, perhaps, the masterpiece of the book, an analysis of the social assumptions of the vulgar postcard. This and *Raffles and Miss Blandish* exemplify the method in which the new school is supreme. Every essay in the book provokes and deserves comment as long as itself. Lack of space forbids anything more than notes. I think Mr Orwell has missed something in his *Defence of P. G. Wodehouse.* It is, of course, insane to speak of Mr Wodehouse as a 'fascist', and Mr Orwell finely exposes the motives and methods of the Bracken-sponsored abuse of this simple artist, but I do find in his work a notable strain of pacifism. It was in the dark spring of 1918 that Jeeves first 'shimmered in with the Bohea'. Of all Mr Wodehouse's characters Archie Moffam alone saw war service. Of the traditional aspects of English life the profession of arms alone is unmentioned; parsons, schoolmasters, doctors, merchants, squires abound, particularly parsons. Serving soldiers alone are absent, and this is the more remarkable since, so far as the members of the Drones Club correspond to anything in London life, they are officers of the Brigade of Guards. Moreover, it is not enough to say that Mr Wodehouse has not outgrown the loyalties of his old school. When Mr Orwell and I were at school, patriotism, the duties of an imperial caste, etc., were already slightly discredited; this was not so in Mr Wodehouse's schooldays, and I suggest that Mr Wodehouse did definitely reject this part of his upbringing.

The belief that Kipling 'sold out to the upper classes' which Mr Orwell shares with Mr Edmund Wilson, is not, I think, sound. What I know of Kipling's private life suggests that he had no social ambitions except so far as in his day the attention of the great was evidence of professional ability. The sinister thing about Kipling was his religion, a peculiar blend of Judaism, Mithraism and Mumbo-jumbo-masonry which Mr Orwell ignores. And here, I think, is found the one serious weakness of all his criticism. He has an unusually high moral sense and respect for justice and truth, but he seems never to have been touched at any point by a conception of religious thought and life. He allows himself, for instance, to use the very silly expression: 'Men are only as good' (morally) 'as their technical development allows them to be.' He frequently brings his argument to the point when having, with great acuteness, seen the falsity and internal contradiction of the humanist view of life, there seems no alternative but the acceptance of a revealed religion, and then stops short. This is particularly true of his criticism of M. Dali, where he presents the problem of a genuine artist genuinely willing to do evil and leaves it unexplained, and in his essay on Mr Koestler, where he reaches the brink of pessimism. I suspect he has never heard of Mgr Knox's *God and the Atom*, which begins where he ends and in an exquisitely balanced work of art offers what seems to me the only answer to the problem that vexes him. He says with unseemly jauntiness: 'Few thinking people now believe in life after death.' I can only answer that *all* the entirely sane, learned and logical men of my acquaintance, and more than half those of keen intelligence, do in fact sincerely and profoundly believe in it.

Mr Orwell seems as unaware of the existence of his Christian neighbours as is, say, Sir Max Beerbohm of the urban proletariat. He assumes that all his readers took Mr H. G. Wells as their guide in youth, and he repeatedly imputes to them prejudices and temptations of which we are innocent. It is this ignorance of Catholic life far more than his ignorance of the classic Catholic writers which renders Mr Orwell's criticism partial whenever he approaches the root of his matter.

It remains to say that Mr Orwell's writing is as readable as his thought is lucid. His style is conversational. Sometimes it lapses into the barrack-room slang of the class-war, as when he uses the word 'intellectual' to distinguish, merely, the man of general culture from the manual labourer instead of, as is more accurate, to distinguish the analytic, logical habit of mind from the romantic and aesthetic. It is a pity, I think, to desert the *lingua franca* of polite letters for the jargon of a coterie.

Perhaps in a journal largely read by the religious, it should be mentioned that one of the essays, 'Some Notes on Salvador Dali', was suppressed in a previous publication on grounds of obscenity. There and elsewhere Mr Orwell, when his theme requires it, does not shirk the use of coarse language. There is nothing in his writing that is inconsistent with high moral principles.

. FAILURE OF A MISSION .

In May 1943 Major Rootham was dropped by parachute in north-eastern Serbia with two other Englishmen, as one of the British Missions accredited to General Mihailovich's army of resistance. The object of these missions was to report to Middle East HQ the extent of the movement, to encourage it in offensive action against German communications, and to arrange for the reception of certain unspecified quantities of material help in the form of arms, explosives and medical supplies.

Each of these tasks requires elaboration. First, the Allied command had very meagre information about what was happening in Yugoslavia. There is, I believe, no authentic British villain in the melodrama. It is only in recent months that the situation of 1943 has become at all plain. It was more complex than Major Rootham, at the time of writing, seems to believe. The 'Bolshie

Review of *Miss Fire*, by Jasper Rootham. *Tablet*, 11 May 1946.

Bogy' was no creation of German propaganda. Tito had then only begun to be spoken of. His resistance movement was in fact purely Communist. Its leaders had spent the years before the war either in prison or in the International Brigade and in Comintern foreign service. To them the German invasion came as a great opportunity. They were out to achieve revolution, and their leaders knew that the greater the destruction of ordered life, the greater their chances of success. Reprisals meant nothing to them. When Italians, Germans or Ustashi burned villages, the partisans replied in kind, and the appalling devastation of the country they moved in is as much their doing as their enemies'. And this involves the second purpose of the British Missions; the Chetniks shrank from what seemed to them useless sacrifice. When Major Rootham's party fired on a boat in the Danube and killed one enemy, 150 Chetnik prisoners were executed. It did not seem to the Chetniks the way to protect their country. General Mihailovich believed in Allied victory. He knew that the mere withdrawal of the Germans was not an end in itself. He was a loyal soldier of his king, aiming at the restoration of the monarchy. Thirdly, he always supposed that 'liberation' would come by means of an English landing, not, as happened, by invasion by Russians and Bulgarians. The supplies made available for his army by ME HQ were pitiably inadequate. He could not believe that these were all a Great Power could spare, and believed always in a Grand Design which, in fact, did not exist. When help was sent in considerable quantities the decision had been taken to supply only his mortal enemies, the partisans. I can state with certainty that many of the British liaison officers with Tito's army were completely hoodwinked as to the true nature of the force they were supporting. There were sinister influences in London and Bari, and possibly at Casata, in 1944, but the individual British officers with the partisans were innocent and as baffled by the situation as those with the Chetniks.

Major Rootham spent a year in Serbia in circumstances which varied, but were usually of extreme privation and considerable danger. Many of his colleagues were captured, tortured and shot. His own account laudably understates his own initiative, patience and intrepidity. It is a most likeable record. He eschews all judgments outside his immediate experience, gives shrewd and graphic descriptions of the Serbs with whom he lived, describes without rancour the frustration which bad staff-work at Cairo inflicted on the man in the field. The notes of his narrative are candour, modesty and chivalry.

The mission, it can now be seen, was doomed to failure. Major Rootham traces its melancholy history from the first enthusiastic welcome, through the growing disappointment and suspicion, to the final days when, though it was plain that we were deserting them, the Chetniks observed unaltered comradeship-in-arms and personal consideration to the men they had grown to like. I think any honourable man who was involved in this small corner of the war feels a sense of guilt in the matter, and Major Rootham has written what may be read as an apology for all of them. Goodwill was not enough. I do not believe that British intervention in Yugoslavia was anywhere decisive. The tragedy was inevitable as soon as the Adriatic invasion was abandoned; but there can be no doubt that in the long memories of the people and in their brooding habit of mind, the British Missions to both sides will become a fixed idea of irresponsible betrayal.

I hope I have made it clear that Major Rootham's book is irresistibly readable. No simpler or more convincing picture can be needed of the week-by-week anxiety and bewilderment and the rare moments of exaltation of his mission.

. PALINURUS IN NEVER-NEVER LAND .
OR, THE *HORIZON* BLUE-PRINT OF CHAOS

Fitting neatly the pockets of battle-dress trousers and gas-mask haversack, read in tents and lorries and radio-haunted Nissen huts, passed from waif to waif in transit camps and field hospitals, the monthly magazine, *Horizon*, came to represent to countless soldiers the world of culture which they had left. Many of the contributions, it is true, were nonsensical, but of gentle, civilian nonsense which contrasted sweetly with the harsh nonsense of regimental orders and ABCA. With the armistice the influence of the magazine has spread abroad, where the intellectuals look to England, as in our troubles we English looked to Bloomsbury, as the still unliberated fortress of the mind. Some-where, we believed, in the minds of the editors of *Horizon* there existed a free and wise society of which we were all members.

Horizon seemed little concerned with politics, and it was not until the eve of the general election that its editor disconcerted his readers by suddenly exhort-ing them to vote Socialist. Now, in the June issue, he is more explicit and, under ten headings, offers us the first ground plans of the estate he has been preparing for us. It is a somewhat baffling document.

The first 'major indication of a civilized community' is the abolition of the death penalty. When I consider how small, even in the most savagely popular regimes, has been the actual number of people executed, and of that number how many have been the most illustrious of their time, and how painless, dignified and well-prepared is the gallows compared with the various forms in which death awaits us, it has, I confess, seemed to me one of the least of the terrors of the century of the common man.

That it is not mere squeamishness about the taking of life which makes Palinurus – if I may without offence so personify the mind of *Horizon* – put this first of his postulates, is shown by the next two: '2. Model prisons (criminals can be rehabilitated). 3. No slums. (The material conditions which produce crime need not exist.)' I think the implication of these three demands is plain.

Tablet, 27 July 1946. Response to 'Editor's Comment', *Horizon*, June 1946.

The civil government has no authority to *punish* at all. Human wickedness is predestined by economic conditions. Man is naturally virtuous and perfectible. It is the function of the State to perfect him. This is familiar ground. I would dispute his assumptions and conclusions in detail, but the purpose of this inquiry is merely to examine Palinurus's ideal world, not to oppose it with another. So far I do not think I misinterpret him, but his fourth 'major indication of a civilized community' does not admit such easy comprehension.

'4. Light and heat supplied free, like air and water. Clothing, nourishment, privacy and medical attention almost free. Transport as near as possible within the reach of all.' What is one to say to this? That air is not 'supplied' and that water is rarely free; that nothing is 'free' which requires the services of others and nothing is 'almost free' unless there is a depressed class who labour for almost nothing? That transport of all kinds has always, everywhere, been 'as near as possible' within the reach of all?

The basic question, I think, is: free for whom? For everyone or only for Palinurus and his friends? Is he proposing the creation of a privileged class of himself and 'Scottie' Wilson and other artists who should be warmed and illuminated by the rest of the community, whose tailors and doctors will delight to reduce their bills for the honour of serving them? If this is the suggestion I do not see how it differs from the wish to enjoy a large private fortune. It is probable, on the other hand, that he means 'free for all', in which case he is using 'free' in a very loose, modern way to mean that the amenities he claims should be distributed by the State without direct cash payment. In fact, of course, the price would not be lower, for the consumer would be purchasing these commodities indirectly with their cost enhanced by an increased service of middle-men. It would in theory be possible to create a society in which, instead of money, amenities were given to reward work, and it would be possible in such a State to allow literary critics special advantages. That Palinurus has some such ideal in mind, appears in his fifth, succinct demand: 'Vocations for all, not just work.'

If Palinurus believed, as he plainly does not, in an all-wise God who has a particular task for each individual soul, which the individual is free to accept or decline at will, and whose ultimate destiny is determined by his response to God's vocation, then this demand would be wholly intelligible. But, if not God, who is to do the calling? Plainly the State, and Palinurus is using a word of nobler antecedents to describe the modern principle of 'direction of labour'. Someone must be called or directed to stoke Palinurus's central heating, to run the electric light plant and to make him his new winter overcoat. But a tiny doubt rises; can Palinurus be absolutely sure that he would find himself 'called' to edit *Horizon*? It is just conceivable that he would find himself down a mine, and we should all be greatly the losers. It is to be noted, too, that the State given such enormous responsibilities has been disarmed from all disciplinary powers. Those who are deaf to its 'call' can only be 'rehabilitated' by psychiatrists, not punished. In the next, more diffuse, demand Palinurus goes further in condemning his functionaries to impotence.

'6. Full toleration of opinion. No censorship of written or spoken words, no tapping of telephones, opening of letters, compiling of dossiers. Special clinics for those who do compile them. No passports, identity cards or money-visas. All travel encouraged.' Wretched functionaries! They are forbidden to keep any record of the millions of men and women whom it is their duty to control. If they attempt to do so they are packed off to the clinical prisons, which, one way or another, it seems, will house half the population. Even there they cannot be sure of rehabilitation, for the psychiatrists 'called' to attend them are at the same time being encouraged to travel all over the place under assumed names.

The seventh demand is not worth quoting at length. It merely requires that there shall be no 'harsh and antiquated' punishments for offences against modesty and sexual morality. Since 'rehabilitation' has already been made the only penal sanction, this clause seems redundant. The eighth, however, is extremely odd and intriguing: '8. The acquisition of property to be recognized as an instinct which is, like the wish to excel, beneficial in moderation, but no one to own more property than he can see, nor the lives of other people, including children – and no children to be rich, which means also that no one would be the poorer for having them.'

With the best will in the world I cannot conceive that this means anything at all. Is it to be taken literally? That real estate is to be bounded by the horizon from some given viewpoint? Or does it mean that personal property can only exist in visible and tangible objects? That a man may own a mountain of gold but not the copyright of a novel? Does Palinurus merely forbid domestic slavery and the *patria potestas*, or does he also deny the authority of a ship's captain over his crew? And who is to own babies, if not their parents? Presumably State hostels, but are the matrons of these hostels to be sent to clinics if they keep dossiers of their little charges? Does he merely forbid minors the unrestricted use of their inheritance (as is the universal custom) or does he forbid parents the right to use their property, however plainly visible, for their children's welfare? May a man keep a mistress in luxury but not a daughter? Does Palinurus really suppose that parents will feel themselves the richer for having children over whom they have no authority and for whom they can provide no benefits?

'9. A passionate curiosity about art, science and the purpose of life . . . and a desire to preserve architecture, natural beauty and wild life.' This seems to me to smack more of the American women's lecture club than of the civilized community, but I can well believe that there might be some rather anxious curiosity about the purpose of life in Palinurus's Utopia. In passing, how does he propose to preserve wild life when he has stirred up the proletarian anthill and set everyone travelling everywhere? Presumably by the 'calling' of a vast army of game wardens. Bird's-nesters sent for rehabilitation to the model prisons.

Tenth, last and funniest: 'No discrimination against colour, race or creed.' These would have been encouraging words if they had come at the head. Unhappily we have read the preceding nine proposals. We live under a regime which not only discriminates against, but makes it an avowed purpose to exterminate, the nobility, gentry, yeomanry, burgesses and vagabonds, and to produce the modern two-class State of officials and proletariat. It would have been a heartening spectacle to see Palinurus, alone among the socialists, demanding the preservation of all the threatened classes, but he has given us a glimpse of his ideal State which makes this final cry of defiance sound hollow.

The significant feature of the Palinurus plan is that none of it makes any sense at all. It has been a hobby among literary men for centuries to describe ideal, theoretical States. There have been numberless ingenious contrivances, some so coherent that it seemed only pure mischance which made them remain mere works of reason and imagination without concrete form. It has been Palinurus's achievement to produce a plan so full of internal contradictions that it epitomizes the confusion of all his contemporaries. This plan is not the babbling of a secondary-school girl at a youth rally but the written words of the mature and respected leader of the English intellectuals. It is reassuring to know that the revelation came to him in what he, less than poetically, describes as 'a lyric contribution to the poetry of motion' – the new cocktail bar of the Golden Arrow train.

. WHAT TO DO WITH THE UPPER CLASSES .
A MODEST PROPOSAL

Until the grand climacteric of 1945 there existed in England an elaborate and flexible class structure which influenced, and often determined, all social and personal relations. It was the growth of centuries and so complex that no foreigner and few natives could completely comprehend it. There were recognizable a small, heterogeneous highest class and a lowest class scarcely larger or more homogeneous – the nomadic, destitute, outlawed. These classes occupied an entirely disproportionate place in our literature and, accordingly, in the impression of ourselves which we gave to the world. Between them lay an infinity of gradations so subtle and various that most Englishmen were aware only of the strata immediately below and above their own. Up and down through these delicate shades of superiority individuals and families were perpetually on the move, tending in general to oscillate about the line of origin, but sometimes making spectacular ascents or falls. The processes were described respectively as the stability of society, the career open to talent, and the punishment of folly.

Since the general election there is a group in power committed to the obliteration of these distinctions. It is plain to the unprejudiced observer that they will not at once succeed and that when they fall it will be to a group more vigorous than themselves in prosecuting this aim. It is also plain that they, in their turn, will find ancient habits hard to eradicate. The classless society, if and when it comes, will not be the fruit of purely English methods; it will come through foreign intervention and by the use of 'social engineering' of the sort that is prevalent in half of what was once Europe. The British state will have to be declared a danger to peace by UN and a punitive expedition sent to occupy the reactionary islands. Judicial murder, mass deportations and the 'psychological conditioning' of young children will be the means. They are not applicable this year or next year; they may even be delayed for a generation. Meanwhile we have the immediate problem of what to do with the upper classes.

They are, so far as the outside world is concerned, the sole, finished product of what is thought to be English culture. They created the English landscape, figuratively and literally; the whole national ingenuity has been organized to supply their peculiar needs. The foreigner, reading our history, supposes that they provided not only the statesmen and admirals and diplomats but also the cranks, aesthetes and revolutionaries; they formed our speech, they directed our artists and architects; they sent adventurous younger sons all over the world; they created and preserved our conceptions of justice and honour and forbearance; all mention of the middle and lower classes might be expunged from our record and leave only trifling gaps. That is what the foreigner thinks. We in England know – or we should know now, for the thing has been shrieked at us ever since Mr Bracken assumed direction of our minds – that all our past achievements were in fact the work of anonymous, common men. But in the eyes of the world we have been equalled and often surpassed by other peoples in most of the arts of peace and war; our sole, unique, historic creation is the English Gentleman. He still exists. Can he be made useful to the workers in the awkward interim period before his final extermination?

By common agreement we are in need of exports. Only by them can the worker be assured of the exotic luxuries he has learned to enjoy. Now in a thousand ways the English Gentleman was once one of our most valuable invisible exports. The market has shrunk since 1914 but it still exists. Wherever you find snobbery, you find English prestige stands high. Men's clothes are an example. London is the centre of the tailoring trade, not because Englishmen have any inherent, incommunicable secret of making clothes that fit, nor because they alone command stocks of durable stuff, but quite simply because large numbers of foreigners wish to look like English gentlemen. The Pasha waddling about his lush terraces in Alexandria, the jewelled Argentine on the links at Le Touquet, the patient Armenian at the baccarat table, each cherishes the innocent belief that the Savile Row label in his breast pocket makes him indistinguishable from a member of the Turf Club in London. In the ledgers of Savile Row the English upper class may appear mainly in columns of long overdue accounts, but eliminate them and the prestige of the street is gone for ever. The inscription in the Paris hosier's window, '*Très snob; très anglais; presque cad*' stands as the hallmark of a vast catalogue of exports whose value depends entirely on the legend that they are 'as supplied to the Royal Household and the Nobility'. As we let the cat out of the bag and reveal to the world that our upper class is in dissolution, there will be so many fewer cigarettes for the factory-girl and so much less Glorious Technicolor for the tired shop-steward.

English education, again, in the days before the politicians took it in hand, was highly esteemed abroad. Not only did boys and girls come from all over the world to our schools and universities, but a great army of governesses zealously performed all the more reputable functions of the British Council at no charge to the country; indeed at a modest gain, as their tiny savings were transferred each quarter to English securities. All this must be counted as lost, unless some modification, such as this essay proposes, is made in our immediate plans, for we must not hope to see world-wide popularity for our new training institutions for government clerks nor can foreign families be expected patiently to endure their products.

These, however, are imponderables. There is another great group of trades of acknowledged importance directly threatened by the class-war – Tourism. Our new rulers show eagerness to lure foreign travellers here. It is enormously to our advantage that they should come. But what have we to offer? It has been the experience of a middle-aged Englishman to be born into one of the most beautiful countries in the world and watch it change year by year into one of the ugliest. German bombs have made but a negligible addition to the sum of our own destructiveness. It is arguable that the entire process is traceable to the decay of aristocratic domination, but it is not the purpose of this essay to examine the causes; it is merely to state the plain fact that the proportion of beauty to ugliness in the aspect of our country has now so shifted that instead of there being a few unpleasant excrescences on a lovely scene, our surviving fine buildings and corners of landscape now only serve to accentuate the prevailing desolation. What will our visitors come into the desert to see? Why did we ourselves travel in the days when it was possible? Primarily to see native life.

And what did we mean by 'native life'? Chiefly what we had learned to expect from our reading and the tales of our fathers. In Morocco tourists crowded to see the antiquated Friday procession of the sultan to the mosque at Rabat; they thronged the bazaars of Marrakesh and the lanes of Fez. They did not show any concern with Lyautey's model plantations and medical services. It was a sore point with the late Italian Government that Englishmen and Americans preferred the historic pomp of the Vatican or the old-fashioned junketings of Sicilian peasants to the Foro Mussolini or the neat smallholdings on the Pontine Marshes. To Englishmen of the new age it is, of course, edifying to see the queues at the surgery door where teeth are pulled out at the public expense, or to know that colliers are spared the irksome toil of the mines by bulldozing park land and gardens. But will tourists share our pride? It is suggested that all will be well if we install better plumbing in provincial hotels. But can we seriously expect Americans to cross the Atlantic to have a bath? If they come, it will be to see 'native life', and by that they mean the traditional, doomed life of which the upper classes were the embodiment and the guardians; they mean meets of foxhounds, court balls, dandies in St James's Street, coaches at the Derby, inhabited castles. Anyone who has been taken round a historic house in a public party will have noticed that the questions put to the guide deal very little with history or architecture; they want to know where the earl sits after dinner. The house that has become a museum has lost nine-tenths of its popular charm.

It is thus expedient to preserve some semblance of the aristocracy; it is also humane. Until very recent times, few conquerors were so ruthless as not to leave some unwanted corners of their hunting grounds to the original owners of the soil, and it is in a system of 'native reservations' of the kind established in Africa and the USA that we must find our solution. The definition and elaboration of the system seems just such a task as our present rulers are well qualified to perform with the great bodies of 'planners' idle on their hands. The broad principle should be the provision of adequate living space for those whose upbringing and inclinations do not fit them for a useful place in the socialist state, where these forlorn survivals may live in the manner traditional to their people. The division should be temperamental rather than heraldic. No one, merely on the grounds of gentle birth, should be forced against his will into the reservations, while unprogressive people of the middle class should be encouraged to make their modest homes there. They could not, of course, be admitted to full citizenship, but should be 'protected persons' encouraged within their narrow boundaries to preserve intact their manner of life. Medical missions might be established under license from the Institute of Anthropology, but nothing should be done to disturb their simple beliefs and natural piety. They should have their own courts where such quaint tribal customs as the open administration of a known law, trial by jury, non-political judges, the admission of evidence for the defence and so on, should be observed. They would support life by agriculture and the arts, subsidized by the fees from tourist-visas paid by those who visit them. They would enjoy a monopoly of the 'luxury trades' and the less popular sports. On their great festivals such as Ascot Race Meeting, day-passes might be issued in large numbers for workers to visit the reservations.

A problem which at first sight seems difficult is the provision of the lower classes of the reservations, for, just as it takes a large ground-staff to put a single fighter-pilot in the air, so a gentleman needs extensive support from inferiors, and the 'direction' of workers from the socialist state to the reservations would be undesirable on many obvious grounds. This problem, however, is more apparent than real. Gentlemen have an inexplicable aptitude for endearing themselves to those under them and it may be expected that there will be an immediate response by volunteers from among elderly servants and estate labourers. These can be swollen indefinitely by foreigners who have had experience of the socialist state in their own countries, and it may be expected that, as the arduous nature of life in the socialist state becomes more evident, applications for entry to the reservations will exceed their capacity for absorption. Indeed, provision should be made in the reservation charter for a periodic revision of boundaries as the 'natives' multiply.

The boundaries can only be vaguely suggested at this stage. A casbah quarter, walled in and well guarded, must be created in London comprising most of St James's and Belgravia; perhaps many cities should have 'native towns' of this kind to house the craftsmen. One at least of our provincial towns, say Wells, should be surrendered entirely, one of our universities, presumably Oxford (this would entail the breaching of Magdalen Bridge), two or three public schools, and large tracts of the countryside. Whether it is best to reserve whole counties – Hereford, for example, Cumberland, and an oddly shaped Wessex – or to develop islands round each of the historic estates, is a matter for adjustment by the planners; probably a combination of both principles could be devised.

Other delicate problems are involved. Should gentlemen, for example, be allowed to bear arms? To deprive them of this right impairs their tribal tradition; on the other hand their presence in the army of the socialist state might provoke foreign intervention. Perhaps, as we recruit tribes outside British India, we might form native regiments under socialist senior officers, but there is the seed of trouble there. On the whole it may prove wisest to limit these forces to a Home Guard armed with pikes and sporting-guns.

Should gentlemen be allowed to travel abroad? Can new gentlemen ever be admitted? These and countless questions must be answered by experience. The important thing is that the principle of preservation be recognized while there is still something left to preserve. To the extreme advocates of total class-war the scheme should be acceptable as rendering all the more easy the eventual massacre.

. THE HOSPITALITY OF CAMPION HALL .

In the near future when books of reminiscence appear which cover the 1930s, and, opening them at the end, we search the index, as we used, for an indication of their character, how often and in what diverse company – between Caldey and Catholic Truth Society, perhaps, or Cabinet meeting and Camrose, or Café de Paris and Castlerosse, according to the tastes of the writer – we shall find the entry: 'Campion Hall, delightful evening at'.

Tablet, 26 October 1946.

We came from all quarters as guests of the house; fellows and undergraduates, gowned, from the neighbouring colleges, refugees from foreign tyranny, editors of Catholic papers from London, Under-Secretaries of State visiting the Chatham or the Canning, the President of the Royal Academy, the Spanish Ambassador, and men marked by no notoriety but distinguished by the high privilege of the Master's friendship. You never knew whom you would meet at Campion Hall but one thing was certain, that for a single evening at any rate they would all fit harmoniously into the social structure which the Master, without apparent effort, ingeniously contrived. Men you knew only by repute and, perhaps, had distrusted from afar, here revealed unsuspected points of sympathy; men you had seen at a disadvantage in other company shone here in the reflected light of the house's welcome; old friends seemed mysteriously to recover the engaging qualities which had attracted you in youth. And you yourself, growing daily in the outside world, it used to seem, narrower and duller, did you, too, not feel at Campion Hall an ease and receptiveness that you thought lost?

The building itself had a unique character, quintessentially of Oxford but without a counterpart. It was remarkable that the only house designed for religious in the University should appear less monastic than the secular colleges. The front door and doorbell opposite the lightless glass of Pembroke, the butler (seldom the same man as on your previous visit, but invariably starched and suave, a very remote kinsman of the traditional 'scout'), the carpeted entrance-hall, the broad staircase, the profusion of ornate furniture, the bedrooms with their tactful choice of bedside books, the prodigality and accessibility of hot water, all had the air of a private house rather than of a college; they charmed visitors from the grimmer cloisters of the continent and sometimes rather disconcerted the many newcomers for whom Campion Hall provided their first acquaintance with conventual life.

The evening had its own invariable and memorable rhythm. You dressed, if you were a Catholic, in time to slip into the back of the chapel for Benediction; then after an exchange of introductions in the ante-room, you were led to Hall. The entertainment began, as all good entertainment should, with some formality. Grace was expected but many an experienced diner-out, accustomed to open a light conversation as he unfolded his napkin, was taken unawares by the recital of the Martyrology. After a false start conversation began when the Master signed his thanks to the reader. Guests sat at High Table with the senior members; below them were the scholastics under the plaster flower in the ceiling, set there, Sir Edward Lutyens used to explain, so that they might talk *sub rosa*. Their turn came when the party adjourned to dessert in the library. Here we divided into groups and the scholastics were picked and distributed at the several small tables. They had an eagerness for discussion, born of long hours of silent study, that was exhilarating after the feebler talk of London; each had a topic he required to air. 'This is Mr So-and-so, who is reading Modern History. He is reading your last book and wants to ask you

. . .'; '. . . Mr So-and-so, who is much concerned by what you said in the House of Commons about secondary education. . .'; '. . . Mr So-and-so, who is writing a thesis on Egyptian cenobites and wants to know . . .' Thus they were led up to the guests and for half an hour subjected them to polite but penetrating cross-examination. Then they returned to their books and the nucleus of the party again adjourned, now to Micklem Hall, down the steps into the rosy light of the Senior Common Room.

I remember Micklem well in old days, now ingeniously incorporated with Campion Hall, then an undergraduate lodging-house which, generation after generation, maintained a tradition of high fashion. The inhabitants seemed never to wear other than hunting coats in winter and dressing-gowns in summer and to subsist on 'black velvet'. At most hours of the day or night it presented a *tableau vivant* of the first episode in Frith's *Road to Ruin*. Even today Nell Gwynne smiles enigmatically from its walls and beyond the french windows the pool survives which cooled many heated foreheads in the past.

The half circle of chairs in the Stuart Parlour was the setting for the culmination of the evening's hospitality. More often than not we were joined here by newcomers; Mgr Knox, perhaps, between whose lodging in the Old Palace and Campion Hall the lane was worn smooth by the feet of scholastic emissaries carrying telephone messages; or Lord David Cecil lured from the domestic fireside; or Mr Pakenham tousled from some unseasonable agitation in the purlieus of the Morris motor-works. Here in the single semicircle, while the Father Minister passed between us with decanter and cigar-box, the conversation was wide and free. I never knew anyone be a bore there; no one held forth; no one was ever intimidated by superior celebrity. Father D'Arcy has among his many gifts the supreme art of conducting a conversation, the rare, almost extinct craft that has today grossly descended to the 'question-masters' of the BBC. Sometimes he could be drawn into the defence of some romantic, anachronistic thesis; more often he was content to catch the ball and pass it, swift and spinning, to another hand. The topics are infinitely various; Mr Christopher Hollis maintaining that Roosevelt was recovering a lost province to Christendom; Mr Rothenstein attempting a Thomist version of the art-jargon of the Paris studios; Mr Scrymgeour-Wedderburn displaying immense scriptural knowledge on a point of exegesis; Sir Edward Lutyens riveting the attention with a series of Rabelaisian puns and pencilled diagrams. I hope someone has made notes of some of the conversations; they were the best I ever heard.

All too soon the time came to break up the party. The guests from outside went into the night. Those who were staying in the house sometimes continued the discussion upstairs in twos and threes. The Fathers retired to their own quarters, and if, waking in the night, you stood at your window to breathe the soft Oxford air and listen for the bells, you saw, all along the face of the building, lighted windows where the ceaseless industry of the place was being tirelessly pursued.

Hallowed memories of the few good things of a sad decade. But, unlike most else of the period, not inevitably lost. Not, indeed, lost at all. For Campion Hall still stands unchanged and unchanging, with new faces at table and in the Stuart Parlour, but the same warm and humane tradition tenderly guarded; in a few years it has become part of the stones of the place and part of the lives which are formed there; it will survive, pray God, until, with the succeeding generations, good things return once more to their proper place.

. WHEN LOYALTY NO HARM MEANT .

In 1937, a book of short stories, *Stranger Wonders*, excited the hope that in Mr Christopher Sykes a new writer had appeared who would maintain the threatened tradition of dandyism in English letters. Critics, among them the present reviewer, joyfully acclaimed a successor to 'Saki' Munro and Sir Max Beerbohm. There is a vast gulf between dandyism and dilettantism, and Mr Sykes alone among his contemporaries seemed to be on the right side. The subsequent nine years have not been favourable for the maturing of an original and polished humour. Mr Sykes's war was arduous and adventurous. As a writer he was silent save for an esoteric *roman à clef* named *High-Minded Murder*, in which fancy seemed to have run amok disastrously. Now, with *Four Studies in Loyalty*, Mr Sykes re-emerges as a writer for whom we must all be thankful.

'Loyalty' is not a happy word. It serves too conveniently to cover mere extensions of egotism – as when a man attributes false values to the associations to which he happens to belong – or a brutish tolerance of bores. 'Fidelity' is perhaps a better word for what Mr Sykes seeks to illustrate in his four studies. These comprise, first, his great-uncle, an Edwardian man of fashion; secondly, a Persian debauchee; thirdly, the late Robert Byron; fourthly, a number of men and women of the French Resistance.

As a literary work the first essay is incomparably the best in the book; it is indeed one of the very best English essays of recent years. The subject was the sad, beautiful, more than slightly absurd, man who was the intimate friend of Edward, Prince of Wales, and served as the butt for some of his vulgarest jokes. The Prince ruined him and eventually slew him, and too late made him the object of a burst of coarse, Teutonic remorse which itself turned to *fou rire* at the funeral. The tale is exquisitely told.

The Persian was faithful to a myth of his own creation; the demonstrably false statement that he had been educated at Balliol. So devoutly did the degraded old man hold this belief that he scornfully declined great material advantages offered by the Germans and returned to squalor rather than betray the land of his fictitious education.

Review of *Four Studies in Loyalty*, by Christopher Sykes. *Tablet*, 7 December 1946.

The last essay deals with a moving subject which is too near the author's immediate past to have been fully digested. Mr Sykes was one of a small and gallant force, many of whom perished horribly at the hands of the Gestapo, who landed by parachute behind the enemy's lines in France in 1945. He has written a vivid tribute to the French civilians who received and sheltered them and suffered rather than betray them. It may be read as first-hand, first-class journalism, with the hope that, recollected in tranquillity, these experiences may form the matter for the epic treatment they deserve.

The third, and by far the longest, section attempts a three-quarter-length portrait of Robert Byron, who after a life of enormous incident and variety was drowned at the age of 36, in 1941. Mr Sykes says: 'I have little doubt that had he lived he would have become one of the great names of our times,' and to support this judgment quotes extensively from Byron's published work. These extracts are pungent, bursting with life, exuberant, vehement in argument, rollicking in humour, like Byron himself. They express him completely, and for that reason will always be dear to the friends whose lives are left permanently empty by his death. Whether Byron's gifts were specifically literary, time would have shown. He was certainly a man of action, and it seemed as though in his last years he strove to express himself more in action than in art. Perhaps he did not recognize any clear distinction between the two. Mr Sykes's portrait will be studied differently by those who knew and did not know the sitter. The present reviewer knew him well and cannot put himself in the position of one who did not. Will such a reader gain from Mr Sykes a clear impression of a remarkably and much-loved man? *An* impression, certainly, for the portrait is highly skilful. But each of Byron's friends, as often appears in conversation, for his name is ever on their lips, had a different picture of him. For one, at least, the chief debt to Mr Sykes is his completely satisfactory explanation of the mood which possessed Byron in the last years of peace; a mood which arose from the sense of a personal, frustrated mission to arouse his fellow-countrymen to the imminence of war. It was a mood which accorded with an ugly period, and it is a matter of regret that some people are doomed to remember Byron chiefly, or even solely, as he was at the time of Munich. Mr Sykes puts this phase in its proper perspective and reminds us of the earlier, carefree aesthete and traveller.

There is a temptation, to which many critics have succumbed, to use Mr Sykes's book as an occasion to write about Robert Byron. Mr Sykes would be the last man to resent this, but a notice of his work must properly conclude by stating that *Four Studies in Loyalty* is one of the most admirable books of recent years.

. IRREGULAR ADVENTURE .

This is the record of the adventures of a young English officer from his capture in Crete in 1941 until his arrival in Belgrade almost exactly one year later. It is unique and romantic, and it is the plain truth.

I had the honour to serve, all too briefly, with its author in No. 8 Commando. That force, the first command of the officer who was later to become Chief of Combined Operations, deserves a place in literature, if not in military history. Through the misfortunes of war it never went into action as a single unit, but was dispersed in small groups, many of which performed some of the most surprising feats of war. Officers and men had volunteered because they sought service more adventurous than was offered at the time by normal regimental life; all were highly individualistic; none more so than Christie Lawrence, who as a junior subaltern was noticeable among his blander fellows for an appearance that was both bellicose and intellectual; of a type which was often recognizable later among the resistance movements of Europe. I last saw him in Crete at the end of May 1941, when communications and supplies had broken down and the island was being evacuated as quickly as possible. Hunger and exhaustion had by then produced a dream-night condition when people seemed to appear and disappear inconsequently and leave unconnected fragments of memory behind them. One of these fragments is my meeting Lawrence in a cave near Sphakia. He or I or both of us were slightly delirious. I remember his telling me a rambling story of his having run into a rock on a motor-bicycle. Then carrying two rifles he wandered off again, alone, in the direction of the enemy.

The book recalls in detail what befell him after the capitulation. It is typical of the spirit of No. 8 Commando that his first instinct after his first night's rest should be to escape from being 'one of the herd', and that, unsuccessful in his main object, he should be rewarded by driving to prison full of red wine and roast chicken. Later, as will appear, he escaped successfully; he alternately starved and feasted; he commanded a platoon of Chetniks, he indulged in a highly irregular politico-military intrigue, took the most startling risks in a land where all was anarchy save where the enemy had imposed their brutal law.

The story should bring encouragement to all who may be in danger of doubting whether knight-errantry is still possible in the conditions of modern war. No one could ask for a better thriller.

But the book has another importance. It will be of real value to the historian. Very little is known of the events in Yugoslavia which were unhappily described as her 'finding her soul'. Much that has been written has been deliberately false. It is gradually appearing now that whatever did happen there was of unsuspected importance in world history. At the time the country was treated by the Allied Command as a place of trivial interest for which a few aeroplanes

Introduction to *Irregular Adventure*, by Christie Lawrence. London, 1947.

and weapons were occasionally grudgingly spared; one whose people had no legitimate aims of their own but could be called upon to make the most appalling sacrifices in order to inconvenience the Germans. We now realize too late that the country is a vital fortress in political strategy.

Yugoslavia was the creation of the liberal peacemakers of the First World War, who light-heartedly placed the old Hapsburg dominions under the Karageorge dynasty. From the first years of the peace disruptive forces were apparent. Croats and Slovenes almost unanimously sought independence of the Serbs. Moreover outside the country three neighbours at least – Italy, Russia and Hungary – were training agents to exploit these disruptive forces at the first opportunity. This opportunity was provided by the English and French declaration of war on Germany. At the first pressure the country fell to pieces. Croats and Slovenes received their independence, at first gladly, then with growing resentment when they discovered that its price was the cession of territory to Italy and an Italian king. Serbia dissolved into bands whose leaders made their own policy in every degree of loyalty from stubborn resistance to open collaboration with the enemy. Lawrence's account gives the first authentic picture of this kaleidoscopic scene of villainy and heroism. It was in the long run a poor service to Mihailovich to proclaim him Minister of War, for it gave him responsibility for subordinates whom he could never fully control and with whom he could seldom communicate; and in the bitter end this responsibility made easy the task of the prosecution at his trial. The German system of reprisals stayed the offensive action of the Chetniks. They considered the price wholly out of proportion to the gain. The Communists were more ruthless. It was therefore easy for interested agents to represent them as the sole core of resistance. Communists, Chetniks, royalists, Croat peasants, all knew well that the Yugoslavs could not themselves defeat Germany or even seriously injure her. When liberation came it would come by invasion from outside. The black decision to abandon the Allied landings and to leave the decisive invasion to the Russians and Bulgarians meant the surrender of all who looked west for salvation to Communist domination and punishment.

Meanwhile the mock trials and the special pleading continue. It is invigorating to read this simple account of the observations of a single, unbiased, enterprising observer. Accounts such as this, pieced together, may one day serve to produce a true history of the Yugoslav disaster.

The end of this book raises the hope that there will be a sequel. Without self-assertion or introspection Lawrence has made himself into a literary character whose career cannot be left in suspense. I believe that I am only an early member of a great host of readers who will eagerly devour this book and impatiently await its successor.

. THE UNBEARABLE BASSINGTON .

'Saki' Munro was not a young man when the First World War ended his career as a writer and, at length, his life. His talent was mature. He left a large number of short stories, some horrific, the greater part humorous, and one novel, *The Unbearable Bassington*. It is for his short stories that he is most widely known and loved. He produced them year by year with apparently effortless invention and elegance. His one difficulty seems to have been length; perhaps he conformed too complacently to the requirements of the editors of his time; perhaps there was a defect in his exemplary literary tact. Whatever the reason, these stories too often have the air of being fancies and passing jests unduly expanded, or of dramatic themes unduly cramped. Occasionally, seven or eight times perhaps, the theme, by chance, it seems, exactly fits the prescribed dimensions and the result is a masterpiece. To have written seven or eight masterpieces is a notable achievement.

As a work of art *The Unbearable Bassington* is inferior to the best of the short stories; faults in construction, which are the more disconcerting by contrast with the high skill of the writing, betray the first novel. For example, the opening seems to presage a series of episodes, an *enfant terrible* repeatedly, in various ways, upsetting the plans of his mother; it is not until the fourth chapter that the story truly starts. There is an inexplicable interlude in chapter eight which only serves to arouse unfulfilled expectations in chapter fifteen. (Surely the mysterious Keriway will reappear in Vienna? But no.) The life of the book is lived within conventions more of the stage than of letters and already antiquated in 1912 – the complete exclusion of sex, for instance – which strain the apparatus of illusion. It is, however, with all its manifest defects a curiously interesting book.

Here, for the only time, 'Saki' offers, instead of the cut gardenia, the tree flowering in its pot, still the product of the hothouse, artificially nurtured, but a complete growth, leaf, stem, root, mould and all, and the rare object is found when in full view to be a sentimental tragedy; not, as a cursory reading might suggest, the tragedy of youth, but of the London drawing-room of a middle-aged lady.

The room, we are explicitly informed at the outset so that there shall be no mistaking it, is the lady's soul. It is also her life. It is one of countless similar drawing-rooms in the London of 1912, with its Bokhara rugs, buhl cabinets and Dresden figures; it is more precisely dated by the Frémiet bronze on the chimney-piece. It is dominated by an urbane battle-piece supposedly by Van der Meulen. In this room, by a tenure which is one of the frequent insupportable improbabilities of the story, surrounded by treasures and trophies, lives Francesca Bassington, once a beauty, still 'svelte', and at 40, one might suppose, still ripe for love. But her pleasures are limited to bridge, the theatre

Introduction to *The Unbearable Bassington*, by H. H. Munro ('Saki'). London, 1947.

and a succession of small luncheon and dinner parties. This life in and of her drawing-room is Francesca's entire life. It has no obvious attraction, for she has surrounded herself with what must, surely, be the dreariest people in London. With the single exception of Lady Caroline Benaresq, who is a Meredithian abstraction, a mere vehicle for the tart comments normally left unspoken, Francesca knows no one but bores. She has no particular liking for them and is often fretful in their company, but they are her world. With their talk of 'the dear archdeacon' and of bandicoots, they are caricatures from Cheltenham and Torquay. What are they doing at fashionable first nights? Why are they asked anywhere? 'Saki' endows them with titles and houses in Mayfair, but they remain obviously and hopelessly provincial. Among them Francesca has so atrophied that she is incapable of imagining any other life than they embody.

Of this life, threatened by penury, her son Comus may be either the saviour or the destroyer. He, the eponymous hero, exists for the reader only as he exists for his mother. We really know nothing of him. We are told he has friends, but he is not seen with them; at his last 'first night' he is alone; when he goes to his club we part company with him on the steps. We know about his extravagant tailor's bills and his modest losses at cards (two pounds down on the week). He exists only as a problem: how to use him in the service of the drawing-room. In real life, with the qualities ascribed to him, his future would be plain enough. A contemporary of Francesca's would take him in hand and educate him, but within the peculiar conventions in which the book is conceived, Comus must at once marry an heiress or perish. He perishes, of course. Heiresses are not captured by good-looking, self-centred boys fresh from school, but by men, of any age and appearance, who have learned from women the art of pleasing. So without more ado he is despatched to West Africa, where he dies, and the drawing-room is left in sole possession of Francesca. Then comes the catastrophe. The Van der Meulen, genuine or spurious, is not enough. This book, which is prefaced with the callow statement that it 'has no moral', discloses the ancient precept of the vanity of worldly goods, though 'Saki' chooses to translate it into his own less accurate idiom: 'What shall it profit a man if he save his soul and slay his heart in torment?'

The defects of the book have been remarked; its virtues are abundant and delectable. 'Saki' stands in succession between Wilde and Firbank in the extinct line of literary dandies. The wit is continuous and almost unfailing; there are phrases on every page which are as fresh and brilliant after thirty-four years (most cruel of all periods) as on the day they were written. 'Saki' has attempted and achieved a *tour de force* in limiting himself to the most commonplace material in its most commonplace aspect, in eschewing all the eccentrics which come so easily to English humorists, and the strong passions which are foundations of satire, and producing a work that is wholly brilliant.

It is impossible in reading *The Unbearable Bassington* at this date to avoid a prophetic and allegorical interpretation which cannot have been consciously present to the author. It was 1912. Comus had only to wait two years to find full employment for all his talents. He was cannon-fodder in a time of peace. And it is impossible, now, not to see Francesca as a type of the English civilization which sends its sons to death for a home whose chief ornament turns out, too late, to be spurious.

. WHY HOLLYWOOD IS A TERM OF DISPARAGEMENT .

It may seem both presumptuous and unkind to return from six weeks' generous entertainment abroad and at once to sit down and criticize one's hosts. In the case of Hollywood it is neither.

Not presumptuous: first, because a fortnight is ample time in which to appreciate the character of that remote community; there are no secrets under those unflickering floodlights; no undertones to which the stranger must attune his ear. All is loud, obvious and prosaic. Secondly, because Hollywood has made its business the business of half the world. Morally, intellectually, aesthetically, financially, Hollywood's entries are written huge in the household books of every nation outside the USSR; largest of all in those of America but, because of our common language, second only to them in our own.

Nor is it unkind, for one may say what one likes in perfect confidence that one is powerless to wound. No game licences are issued in the reserve where the great pachyderms of the film trade bask and browse complacently. They have no suspicion that in most of America and in the whole of Europe the word 'Hollywood' is pejorative.

Even in southern California the film community are a people apart. They are like monks in a desert oasis, their lives revolving about a few shrines – half a dozen immense studios, two hotels, one restaurant; their sacred texts are their own publicity and the local gossip columns. The only strangers they ever meet have come to seek their fortunes; refugees from central Europe for whom the ease and plenty and affability of the place, seen against the background of the concentration camp, appear as supreme goods, and astute renegades from the civilizations of the East who know that flattery is the first step to preferment. None of these will hold a mirror up to Caliban; all feel their own security threatened by a whisper of criticism. Artists and public men elsewhere live under a fusillade of detraction and derision; they accept it as a condition of their calling. Not so in Hollywood, where all is a continuous psalm of self-praise.

Place and people have the aspect of Philo's Alexandria; such, one thinks in one's first few days, must have been the life there in the great days of the

Daily Telegraph and Morning Post, 30 April 1947 and 1 May 1947. Sir Alexander Korda replied to Waugh with an article, 'Hollywood's Big Battalions', 14 May 1947. Correspondence, mainly favourable to Waugh, appeared on 5, 6, 12, 17, 23 and 26 May 1947.

Mouseion; some such withdrawal of the arts is necessary everywhere if culture is to survive the present century. But this is a whimsy. Things are not really like that. The seclusion of these hermits is purely one-sided. They live for and by the outer world of which they know nothing at first hand and whose needs they judge by gross quantitative standards. 'No film of ours is ever a failure,' an executive said to me. 'Some are greater successes than others, but we reckon to get our money back on everything we produce.'

There is the impasse, the insurmountable barrier of financial prosperity. Behold the endless succession of Hollywood films, the slick second-rateness of the best of them, the blank fatuity of the worst – and none of them failures! What goes on there?

Three groups are responsible for making a film, the technicians, the players and the writers. (Producers-directors bear the guilt of all three.)

Of these the least culpable are the technicians. It is they who make the studio the vast, enchanted toyshop which delights the visitors. In only two respects are the technicians guilty. It is their fault that the studios are there, 3,000 miles from the world's theatrical centre in New York, 6,000 miles from the intellectual centres of London and Paris. They came there because in the early days they needed the sun. Now almost all photography is done by artificial light. The sun serves only to enervate and stultify. But by now the thing has become too heavy to move. And the technicians are too enterprising. Their itch for invention keeps them always a move ahead of the producers.

Twenty years ago the silent film was just beginning to develop into a fine art; then talking apparatus set it back to its infancy. Technicolor is the present retarding revolution. Soon no doubt we shall have some trick of third-dimensional projection. Mr Charles Chaplin, abused everywhere as a 'progressive', is the one genuine conservative, artistically, in Hollywood. The others allow themselves no time to get at ease with their materials.

The technicians are almost anonymous. All the devices of publicity are employed to give exclusive prominence to a few leading players. They possess the popular imagination and excite the visitor's curiosity. What of them? Dramatic critics often ask whey the cinema has produced no actors comparable with the great figures of the stage, and point to the fact that in many 'documentaries' and continental films the best performances are given by unknown and untrained players. Even in Hollywood this year the highest Academy honours have gone to a man who was chosen simply because he had been maimed in the war. The wonder should be that so many stars are able to give as much as they do, for the conditions of their work are hostile to dramatic tradition. Certain disabilities seem to be inherent in the film; others are peculiar to Hollywood; all are exaggerated there.

There is an essential inhumanity about a film star's life. Compare it with that of a leading actress of fifty years ago. The latter worked in the capitals of the world; once her play was running smoothly her days were her own; she lived a life of leisure and fashion in an infinitely various society of her own choosing.

The company formed a corporate unit with its own intimacies, scandals and jokes; each performance was a separate artistic achievement; the play was conceived as an artistic whole which was nightly brought into existence in a sustained and cumulative emotional mood which is the essence of acting. The players were in direct contact with their audience. Each audience was different; the manager would nightly visit the dressing-rooms with news of who was 'in front'. Above all, acting was recognized as an art which it took a lifetime to learn. Almost all great plays were written for mature players; the 'juvenile lead' and the 'ingénue' were for youngsters learning their trade.

The Hollywood star lives in a remote suburb. She sees no one from one year's end to another except a handful of people all in the same trade as herself. She remains in purdah in the studio, inhabiting a tiny bathing-machine, surrounded by satellites who groom her and feed her until the technicians have finished with the 'stand-in' and require her presence on the set. When her work begins it consists of isolated fragments, chosen at the convenience of the technicians. It is rehearsal, hour after hour, for a few minutes of finished acting. At last in a Trilby-like trance she achieves the expression the director requires. She is 'shot', and they proceed to another, often unrelated fragment. And finally she has produced only the raw material for the 'cutter', who may nonchalantly discard the work of weeks or dovetail it into an entirely different situation.

And she must be young. Her life is as brief as a prize fighter's. By the time that she has become a finished actress she is relegated to 'supporting' roles. The work is physically exhausting and intellectually stultifying and there are no very great material rewards. A myth survives from past years that film stars live in Petronian luxury. The salary figures seem dazzling, and, indeed, she does often live in a degree of comfort very enviable by contemporary European measure. But it is no more than that. In fact her standard of life is precisely that of a moderately successful professional Englishman of fifty years ago. That is to say, she lives in a neat little villa with half an acre of garden; she has three servants, seldom more, very often fewer. Her antique furniture, collected at vast expense, would be commonplace in an English rectory. Her main time of entertainment is Sunday luncheon when she asks half a dozen professional friends to share her joint of beef. She has more clothes than her counterpart, but her menfolk are infinitely worse dressed. In only one substantial particular does she differ. She has a swimming pool which can be lit up at night. That is the mark of respectability, like the aspidistra in the cottage parlour.

And unlike her counterpart it is almost impossible for her to save money. If she attempted to live in simpler style she would lose 'face' and be rebuked by her studio. She cannot live more elaborately, for taxation intervenes. She can make this maximum in one film. After that for the rest of the time she is working for nothing. Consequently it is becoming increasingly hard to persuade her to do any work. Vanity is the sole inducement. She will therefore take no part in which she, and her male colleague, are anything less than the whole film. She must be on the stage all the time in a continuously alluring fashion. A play which depends on a team of various characters has no interest for her. A film must be her personal romantic adventures and nothing else. It is a short-sighted preference, for it means that when she is 50 there will be no adequate parts for her. But no one in Hollywood considers the possibility of growing up.

The infinite pains taken in Hollywood over all technical matters render all the more remarkable their nonchalance when it is a question of ideas. Go to the Art Research Department and they will tell you in a twinkling the kind of inkpot Dante used or the orders worn by the Duke of Wellington at Queen Victoria's coronation. Go on the set and hear the dozen or more experts wrangling round the 'stand-in' about light and sound; wait until the star appears and see how men with combs and clothes-brushes, women with elaborate catalogues, cluster round and perfect her. You will believe yourself present at one of the great achievements of human ingenuity and devotion. Then go to a 'story conference' and you find yourself in a world that is at once haphazard and banal.

It is not that they are wrong-headed, that in the interests of entertainment they deliberately choose to disregard certain human values and to distort others. It is not that, as is often suggested, they serve sinister interests aiming to preserve or destroy (according to choice) capitalist society and bourgeois morality, to advance American imperialism, Jewish internationalism, Catholicism, agnosticism or what you will. It is simply that they are empty-headed and quite without any purpose at all. Thus anyone interested in ideas is inevitably shocked by Hollywood according to his prejudices.

The novelist is shocked by their complete inability to follow a plain story. For in the cinema, he would think, is the perfect medium for presenting a straight plot. The effects at which he labours so painfully may here be achieved with ease. All descriptions are superfluous. Here you have narrative reduced to its essentials – dialogue and action. A great, simple art should have come into existence. But nothing of the kind has in fact occurred.

Literary considerations are as despised in the film studios as in those of modern painters. The producers, generally speaking, read nothing. They employ instead a staff of highly accomplished women who recite aloud, and with dramatic effects, the stories which filter down to them from a staff of readers. The producers sit round like children while the pseudo-nannie spins a tale, two or three in an afternoon – classical novels, Broadway comedies, the Book of the Month, popular biographies, anything. 'Bags I,' says the producer, when something takes his fancy. 'Daddy buy that.' Agents negotiate, a price is fixed. And from that moment the story belongs to the studio to deal with as they please.

Each of the books purchased has had some individual quality, good or bad, that has made it remarkable. It is the work of a staff of 'writers' to distinguish this quality, separate it and obliterate it. We all know frightful examples of favourite books we have seen thus sterilized. Perhaps of recent years the most notorious is Mr Somerset Maugham's *Christmas Holiday*, a brilliantly original story of an English schoolboy's awakening in Paris to some of the realities of life, eminently suitable for retelling in a film, which emerged from the mill as the adventure of an American airman with an escaped gangster. Why, one wonders, do they trouble to purchase rights? I cannot believe that any action for plagiarism would lie if they had produced that film without reference to Mr Maugham. It is simply, I think, that they like to have something to work on, and that the large sum paid to the author is an inconsiderable part of the total cost of production.

A film costs about $2,000,000. It must please 20,000,000 people. The film industry has accepted the great fallacy of the Century of the Common Man – epitomized recently in England by Dr Summerskill's condemnation of good cheese – that a thing can have no value for anyone which is not valued by all. In the old days a play which ran 100 nights was a success, a book which sold 5,000 copies might influence a generation. Even now a writer who sells more than 20,000 copies, instead of being elated, begins to wonder what has gone wrong with his work. But a film must please everyone.

The economics of this desperate situation illustrate the steps by which the Common Man is consolidating his victory. It is not the large sums paid to the stars and producers and authors (the greater part of which, incidentally, goes straight to the Common Man in taxes), but the overhead expenses of the studio which overweight the costs, and these are imposed by the trade unions and their system of redundant labour.

It would not be impossible to get together a team of first-class players and producers and writers who would work for a fraction of their present salaries if they could take genuine pride in their art and make a film which appealed only to a limited audience, but this would barely affect the cost of the film.

Situations which seem fantastic elsewhere are commonplace in Hollywood. I know a 'writer' who wished to put up a map on the wall of his room and asked for a hammer and four nails. He was told that all the carpenters would strike if he did the work himself. A trade unionist arrived with his tools and found that a small bookcase had to be moved to another wall. The writer took one side and invited the carpenter to take the other. But that was a breach of rules. Two furniture movers had to be called in. A special 'florist' has to be summoned if, in rearranging a 'set', the director wishes to move a vase of flowers from one table to another. The unions determine the numbers to be employed in any film. If a band of six instruments is required, a dozen men will arrive and half of them sit idle on full pay. Impositions of this kind, repeated hourly in a large studio, fix the exorbitant cost of a film. The capitalist at the head of the company is concerned solely with profits; the proletariat allow profits only to those who directly work for their pleasure; in this miniature class-war the artist vanishes.

The *reductio ad absurdum* of the principle of universal appeal is not in the intellectual or aesthetic sphere, but in the moral. The American censors observe no such fruitful distinction as exists in England between films suitable for children and for adults. Nor do most American parents enjoy the authority common in Europe over their children. They cannot prevent them going to the cinema; all they can hope to do is prevent the cinema showing films likely to corrupt them. In fact, no one really knows what will corrupt anyone else. There has been intense investigation of the question lately. It must be remembered that children seldom tell the truth to investigators, and that magistrates are usually sympathetic to the plea of the juvenile delinquent: 'I saw it done in the pictures.' Moreover, it is the spectacle rather than the theme which impresses a child. That is to say, a boy is excited by the use of firearms whether in the hands of a gangster or a soldier; an embrace is equally inflammatory whether between licit or illicit lovers. Americans are devoted to a conception of innocence which has little relation to life.

But when all this is said it remains broadly true that some films may be harmless to adults and harmful to children. This, with all the essential finer distinctions, the Americans ignore, and the function of the Hays Office is to enforce a code which forbids the production of any film which can be harmful to anyone, or offend any racial or religious susceptibility. No such code is feasible in a heterogeneous society. Logically applied it would condemn, for instance, almost the whole of Shakespeare. The unhappy compromise is evident in all Hollywood films except those of Mr Walt Disney. Every attempt is made by innuendo to pack as much lubricious material as possible into every story, while mature dramatic works intended for a morally stable, civilized audience have their essential structure hopelessly impaired.

The vagaries of the Hays Office may be quoted at indefinite length. One example must suffice here. A script was recently condemned as likely to undermine the conception of Christian marriage. The story was of an unhappy married man and woman who wished to divorce their respective partners and remarry one another. They institute proceedings, but in the end refrain from remarriage precisely because they come to realize that this would not constitute Christian marriage.[1] At the same time the excellent film *The Best Years of Our Lives* was being acclaimed as the embodiment of healthy American domesticity. That story depends for its happy end on the hero being deserted by his Bohemian wife and thus being free to marry the banker's innocent daughter. This was passed because it was never specifically stated that a divorce would have to intervene.

I have attempted to show some of the disabilities under which Hollywood works. Are they insuperable? I sincerely believe that they are. As far as the home of a living art is concerned, Hollywood has no importance. It may be a

---

1 This story strongly suggests *Brideshead Revisited*. Early in 1947 Waugh went to Hollywood to discuss its filming. On 15 March 1947 he telegraphed A. D. Peters, 'Censor forbids film of *Brideshead*.' Next day Peters's American partner, Carol Brandt, explained that the Johnston-Hays office refused to pass *Brideshead* without changes which Waugh would not accept.

useful laboratory for technical experiment. The great danger is that the European climate is becoming inclement for artists; they are notoriously comfort-loving people. The allurements of the modest luxury of Hollywood are strong. Will they be seduced there to their own extinction?

. HALF IN LOVE WITH EASEFUL DEATH .
AN EXAMINATION OF CALIFORNIAN BURIAL CUSTOMS

In a thousand years or so, when the first archaeologists from beyond the date-line unload their boat on the sands of southern California, they will find much the same scene as confronted the Franciscan missionaries. A dry landscape will extend from the ocean to the mountains. Bel Air and Beverly Hills will lie naked save for scrub and cactus, all their flimsy multitude of architectural styles turned long ago to dust, while the horned toad and the turkey buzzard leave their faint imprint on the dunes that will drift on Sunset Boulevard.

For Los Angeles, when its brief history comes to an end, will fall swiftly and silently. Too far dispersed for effective bombardment, too unimportant strategically for the use of expensive atomic devices, it will be destroyed by drought. Its water comes 250 miles from the Colorado River. A handful of parachutists or partisans anywhere along that vital aqueduct can make the coastal strip uninhabitable. Bones will whiten along the Santa Fé trail as the great recession struggles eastwards. Nature will reassert herself and the seasons gently obliterate the vast, deserted suburb. Its history will pass from memory to legend until, centuries later, as we have supposed, the archaeologists prick their ears at the cryptic references in the texts of the twentieth century to a cult which once flourished on this forgotten strand; of the idol Oscar – sexless image of infertility – of the great Star Goddesses who were once noisily worshipped there in a Holy Wood.

Without the testimony of tombs the science of archaeology could barely exist, and it will be a commonplace among the scholars of 2947 that the great cultural decline of the twentieth century was first evident in the graveyard. The wish to furnish the dead with magnificent habitations, to make an enduring record of their virtues and victories, to honour them and edify their descendants, raised all the great monuments of antiquity, the pyramids, the Taj Mahal, St Peter's at Rome, and was the mainspring of all the visual arts. It died, mysteriously and suddenly, at the end of the nineteenth century. England, once very rich in sepulchral statuary, commemorated her fallen soldiers of the First World War by a simple inscription in the floor of an abbey built nine centuries earlier to shelter the remains of a Saxon king. Rich patrons of art who, in an earlier century, would have spent the last decade of their lives in

Tablet, 18 October 1947; *Life*, 29 September 1947.

planning their own elaborate obsequies, deposed that their ashes should be broadcast from aeroplanes. The more practical Germans sent their corpses to the soap boiler. Only the primitive heathens of Russia observed a once-universal tradition in their shrine to Lenin.

All this will be a commonplace in the schools of 2947. The discoveries, therefore, of the Holy Wood Archaeological Expedition will be revolutionary, for when they have excavated and catalogued, and speculated hopelessly about the meaning of, a temple designed in the shape of a Derby hat and a concrete pavement covered with diverse monopedic prints, and have surveyed the featureless ruins of the great film studios, their steps will inevitably tend northward to what was once Glendale, and there they will encounter, on a gentle slope among embosoming hills, mellowed but still firm-rooted as the rocks, something to confound all the accepted generalizations, a necropolis of the age of the pharaohs, created in the middle of the impious twentieth century, the vast structure of Forest Lawn Memorial Park.

We can touch hands across the millennium with these discoveries, for it is in the same mood of incredulous awe that the visitor of our own age must approach this stupendous property. Visitors, indeed, flock there – in twice the numbers that frequent the Metropolitan Museum in New York – and with good reason, for there are many splendid collections of art elsewhere but Forest Lawn is entirely unique. Behind the largest wrought-iron gates in the world lie 300 acres of park-land, judiciously planted with evergreen (for no plant which sheds its leaf has a place there). The lawns, watered and drained by eighty miles of pipe, do not at first betray their solemn purpose. Even the names given to their various sections – Eventide, Babyland, Graceland, Inspiration Slope, Slumberland, Sweet Memories, Vesperland, Dawn of Tomorrow – are none of them specifically suggestive of the graveyard. The visitor is soothed by count-less radios concealed about the vegetation, which ceaselessly discourse the 'Hindu Lovesong'[1] and other popular melodies, and the amplified twittering of caged birds. It is only when he leaves the seven and a half miles of paved roadway that he becomes aware of the thousands of little bronze plates which lie in the grass. Commenting on this peculiarity in the *Art Guide of Forest Lawn with Interpretations* Mr Bruce Barton, author of *What can a man believe?*, says: 'The cemeteries of the world cry out man's utter hopelessness in the face of death. Their symbols are pagan and pessimistic . . . Here sorrow sees no ghastly monuments, but only life and hope.' The Christian visitor might here remark that by far the commonest feature of other graveyards is still the Cross, a symbol in which previous generations have found more Life and Hope than in the most elaborately watered evergreen shrub. This reproach will soon be

1 The *Life* text reads 'Indian Love Call', which Nelson Eddy and Jeannette MacDonald's *Rose-Marie* had made very popular in the 1940s. 'Hindu Lovesong' cannot be traced with certainty. The explanation of the different titles may be this. Waugh gave *Life* and the *Tablet* the same text. *Life* required cuts and changes, to which Waugh reluctantly agreed, and a *Life* editor possibly corrected Waugh's half-remembered title. The *Tablet* presumably printed the original copy.

removed in Forest Lawn's own grand way by a new acquisition, a prodigious canvas of the Crucifixion which took thirty years of the Polish painter, Jan Styka's life to complete; it will require a vast new building to house it. A miniature, 1/49th of the area of the original, now occupies one whole side of the largest hall in Forest Lawn and an explanatory speech has been recorded for the gramophone, identifying the hundreds of figures which in the original abound in life size. The canvas has had an unhappy history. Shipped to the USA in 1904 for the St Louis Exhibition, it was impounded for excise dues and sold, without profit to the artist, to its importer, who was, however, unable to find a pavilion large enough to house it. Since then it has lain about in warehouses, a prey to 'silver fish', and has been shown only once, in the Chicago Opera House, where it filled the entire stage and extended far into the auditorium. Soon it will form a suitable addition to the wonders of Forest Lawn.

These can be only briefly indicated in an essay of this length. There is the largest assembly of marble statuary in the United States, mostly secular in character, animals, children and even sculptured toys predominating; some of it erotic, and some of it enigmatically allegorical. There is also what is claimed to be the finest collection of stained glass in America, the glory of which is 'The Last Supper' in the Court of Honour; the original by Leonardo da Vinci has here, in the words of *Pictorial Forest Lawn*, been 'recreated in vibrant, glowing and indestructible colours'.

There are gardens and terraces, and a huge range of buildings, the most prominent of which is the rather Italian Mausoleum. There in marble-fronted tiers lie the coffins, gallery after gallery of them, surrounded by statuary and stained glass. Each niche bears a bronze plaque with the inmate's name, sometimes in magnified counterfeit of his signature. Each has a pair of bronze vases which a modest investment can keep perpetually replenished with fresh flowers. Adjacent lies the Columbarium, where stand urns of ashes from the Crematory. There is the Tudor-style Administration Building, the Mortuary (Tudor exterior, Georgian interior) and the more functional Crematory. All are designed to defy the operations of time; they are in 'Class A steel and concrete', proof against fire and earthquake. The Mausoleum alone, we are told, contains enough steel and concrete for a sixty-storey office building, and its foundations penetrate thirty-three feet into solid rock.

The Memorial Court of Honour is the crowning achievement of this group. 'Beneath the rare marbles of its floor are crypts which money cannot purchase, reserved as gifts of honoured interment for Americans whose lives shall have been crowned with genius.' There have so far been two recipients of this gift, Gutzon Borglum, the first sculptor in history to employ dynamite instead of the chisel, and Mrs Carrie Jacobs-Bond, author and composer of 'The End of a Perfect Day', at whose funeral last year, which cost $25,000, Dr Eaton, the Chairman of Forest Lawn, pronounced the solemn words: 'By the authority vested in me by the Council of Regents, I do herewith pronounce Carrie Jacobs-Bond an immortal of the Memorial Court of Honour.'

There is at the highest point a water-tower named 'The Tower of Legends', where at the dawn of Easter Sunday a number of white doves are liberated in the presence of a huge concourse whose singing is broadcast 'from coast to coast'. Of this building 'a noted art authority' has remarked: 'It depicts, more truly than any structure I have ever seen, real American architecture. It deserves the attention of the world' (*Art Guide*). But this precious edifice, alas, is due for demolition and will soon give place to the non-sectarian, Bishopless 'Cathedral' which is to house Jan Styka's masterpiece and provide in its shade fresh galleries of urns and coffins.

There are already three non-sectarian churches, 'The Little Church of the Flowers', 'The Wee Kirk o' the Heather' and 'The Church of the Recessional'. The first is, with modifications, a replica of Stoke Poges Church where Gray wrote his 'Elegy'; the second a reconstruction of the ruins of a chapel at Glencairn, Dumfriesshire where Annie Laurie worshipped; the third, again with modifications, is a replica of the parish church of Rottingdean in Sussex where Rudyard Kipling is claimed by Dr Eaton to have been inspired – by heaven knows what aberration of oratory from the pulpit so artlessly reproduced – to write *Kim*. The American visitor may well be surprised at the overwhelmingly British character of these places of worship in a state which has never enjoyed the blessings of British rule and is now inhabited by the most cosmopolitan people in the United States. The British visitor is surprised also at the modifications.

It is odd to find a church dedicated to Kipling, whose religion was highly idiosyncratic. The building is used not only for funerals but for weddings and christenings. Its courtyard is used for betrothals; there is a stone ring, named by Dr Eaton the Ring of Aldyth, through which the young lover is invited to clasp hands and swear fidelity to what Kipling described as 'a rag and a bone and hank of hair'. Round the courtyard are incised the texts of 'Recessional', 'If' and 'When earth's last picture is painted'. The interior of St Margaret's, Rottingdean, is not particularly remarkable among the many ancient parish churches of England, but the architects of Forest Lawn have used their ingenuity to enliven it. One aisle has been constructed of glass instead of stone, and filled with pot-plants and caged canaries; a chapel, hidden in what is no doubt thought to be devotional half-darkness, is illuminated by a spotlit painting of Bougereau's entitled *Song of the Angels*; in a kind of sacristry relics of the patron saint are exposed to veneration. They are not what ecclesiastics call 'major relics'; some photographs by the Topical Press, a rifle scoresheet signed by the poet, the photostatic copy of a letter to Sir Roderick Jones expressing Kipling's hope of attending a christening, a copy of Lady Jones's popular novel, *National Velvet*, an oleograph text from a nearby cottage; and so forth.

What will the archaeologists of 2947 make of all this and of the countless other rareties of the place? What webs of conjecture will be spun by the professors of comparative religion? We know with what confidence they define the intimate beliefs of remote ages. They flourished in the nineteenth century.

Then G. K. Chesterton, in a masterly book, sadly neglected in Europe but honoured in the USA – *The Everlasting Man* – gently exposed their fatuity. But they will flourish again, for it is a brand of scholarship well suited to dreamy natures who are not troubled by the itch of precise thought. What will the professors of the future make of Forest Lawn? What do we make of it ourselves? Here is the thing, under our noses, a first-class anthropological puzzle of our own period and neighbourhood. What does it mean?

First, of course, it is self-evidently a successful commercial undertaking. The works of sculpture enhance the value of the grave sites; the unification in a single business of all the allied crafts of undertaking is practical and, I believe, unique. But all this is the least interesting feature.

Secondly, the Park is a monument to local tradition. Europeans, whose traditions are measured in centuries, are wrong to suppose that American traditions, because they are a matter of decades, are the less powerful. They are a recent, swift and wiry growth. Southern California has developed a local character which is unique in the United States. The territory was won by military conquest less than a century ago. In the generations that followed the Spanish culture was obliterated, and survives today only in reconstructions. The main immigrations took place in living memory, and still continue. In 1930 it was calculated that of the million and a quarter inhabitants of Los Angeles half had arrived in the previous five years; only one tenth could claim longer than fifteen years' standing. In the last seventeen years the balance has changed still more in the newcomers' favour. Of this vast influx the rich came first. There was no pioneer period in which hungry young people won a living from the land. Elderly people from the East and Middle West brought their money with them to enjoy it in the sunshine, and they set up a tradition of leisure which is apparent today in the pathological sloth of the hotel servants and the aimless, genial coffee-house chatter which the film executives call 'conferences'.

It is not the leisure of Palm Beach and Monte Carlo where busy men go for a holiday. It is the leisure of those whose work is done. Here on the ultimate, sunset-shore they warm their old bodies and believe themselves alive, opening their scaly eyes two or three times a day to browse on salads and fruits. They have long forgotten the lands that gave them birth and the arts and trades they once practised. Here you find, forgetful and forgotten, men and women you supposed to be long dead, editors of defunct newspapers, playwrights and artists who were once the glory of long-demolished theatres, and round them congregate the priests of countless preposterous cults to soothe them into the cocoon-state in which they will slough their old bodies. The ideal is to shade off, so finely that it becomes imperceptible, the moment of transition, and it is to this process that Forest Lawn is the most conspicuous monument.

Dr Eaton has set up his Credo at the entrance. 'I believe in a happy Eternal Life,' he says. 'I believe those of us left behind should be glad in the certain belief that those gone before have entered into that happier Life.' This theme is repeated on Coleus Terrace: 'Be happy because they for whom you mourn are happy – far happier than ever before.' And again in Vesperland: ' . . . Happy because Forest Lawn has eradicated the old customs of Death and depicts Life not Death.'

The implication of these texts is clear. Forest Lawn has consciously turned its back on the 'old customs of death', the grim traditional alternatives of Heaven and Hell, and promises immediate eternal happiness for all its inmates. Similar claims are made for other holy places – the Ganges, Debra Lebanos in Abyssinia, and so on. Some of the simpler crusaders probably believed that they would go straight to Heaven if they died in the Holy Land. But there is a catch in most of these dispensations, a sincere repentance, sometimes an arduous pilgrimage, sometimes a monastic rule in the closing years. Dr Eaton is the first man to offer eternal salvation at an inclusive charge as part of his undertaking service.

There is a vital theological point on which Dr Eaton gives no *ex cathedra* definition. Does burial in Forest Lawn itself sanctify, or is sanctity the necessary qualification for admission? Discrimination is exercised. There is no room for the Negro or the Chinaman, however devout; avowed atheists are welcome, but notorious ill-doers are not. Al Capone, for example, had he applied, would have been excluded, although he died fortified by the last rites of his Church. 'Fatty' Arbuckle was refused burial, because, although acquitted by three juries of the crime imputed to him by rumour, he had been found guilty, twenty years or so earlier, of giving a rowdy party. Suicides, on the other hand, who, in 'the old customs of death' would lie at a crossroads, impaled, come in considerable numbers and, often, particularly in cases of hanging, present peculiar problems to the embalmer.

Embalming is so widely practised in California that many believe it to be a legal obligation. At Forest Lawn the bodies lie in state, sometimes on sofas, sometimes in open coffins, in apartments furnished like those of a luxurious hotel, and named 'Slumber Rooms'. Here the bereaved see them for the last time, fresh from the final beauty parlour, looking rather smaller than in life and much more dandified. There is a hint of the bassinet about these coffins, with their linings of quilted and padded satin and their frilled silk pillows. There is more than a hint, indeed, throughout Forest Lawn that death is a form of infancy, a Wordsworthian return to innocence. 'I am the Spirit of Forest Lawn,' wrote K. C. Beaton, in less than Wordsworthian phrase: 'I speak in the language of the Duck Baby,[1] happy childhood at play.' We are very far here from the traditional conception of an adult soul naked at the judgment seat and a body turning to corruption. There is usually a marble skeleton lurking somewhere among the marble draperies and quartered escutcheons of the tombs of the high Renaissance; often you find, gruesomely portrayed, the corpse half decayed with marble worms writhing in the marble adipocere.

---

1 A bronze figure by Edith Barrett Parsons representing a laughing nude child with poultry. It inspired Leo Robinson's poem 'After the lights went out'. E.W.

These macabre achievements were done with a simple moral purpose – to remind a highly civilized people that beauty was skin deep and pomp was mortal. In those realistic times Hell waited for the wicked and a long purgation for all but the saints, but Heaven, if at last attained, was a place of perfect knowledge. In Forest Lawn, as the builder claims, these old values are reversed. The body does not decay; it lives on, more chic in death than ever before, in its indestructible class A steel and concrete shelf; the soul goes straight from the Slumber Room to Paradise, where it enjoys an endless infancy – one of a great Caucasian nursery-party where Knights of Pythias toddle on chubby unsteady legs beside a Borglum whose baby-fingers could never direct a pneumatic drill and a Carrie Jacobs-Bond whose artless ditties are for the Duck Baby alone.

That, I think, is the message. To those of us too old-fashioned to listen respectfully, there is the hope that we may find ourselves, one day beyond time, standing at the balustrade of Heaven among the unrecognizably grown-up denizens of Forest Lawn, and, leaning there beside them, amicably gaze down on southern California, and share with them the huge joke of what the professors of anthropology will make of it all.

. THE MAN HOLLYWOOD HATES .

Charlie Chaplin is not merely unpopular in Hollywood. For many years he has been the victim of organized persecution.[1] A community whose morals are those of caged monkeys professes to be shocked by his domestic irregularities. He is accused, perhaps with some justice, of socialism and pacifism. He takes no part in the charitable causes to which the film world occasionally gives conspicuous support. Any stick is good enough to beat the man who has given more pure delight to millions than all the rest put together.

The simple truth is that he is hated because he is a great artist. Talent is sometimes forgiven in Hollywood, genius never. They smell it out and seek its death. As soon as it was known that Charlie had a work in progress, before anything had been seen outside his strictly guarded studio, the critics made ready to damn it. In America the abuse of his new film has been almost unanimous. Now it has come to Europe. I trust we shall give it a very different reception.

I saw it privately in Hollywood and went in a mood of sentimental anticipation, hoping to step back for an evening into the delights of boyhood. I found a startling and mature work of art. I do not mean that I found an acceptable 'message'. There is a 'message', and, I think, a deplorable one.

Review of *Monsieur Verdoux*, created by Charlie Chaplin. *Evening Standard*, 4 November 1947.
1 The American Legion had threatened to picket Chaplin's films, and some theatre circuits had cancelled arrangements to show them, as a protest against his being readmitted to the United States.

It is not possible for a European to live in that place of exile and retain the standards of civilization quite unpolluted. The nearest thing to intellectual society there consists of refugees from central Europe, and poor Charlie has picked up some rather shoddy ideas among them. But most men and women of genius have entertained preposterous opinions. The film is the essence of Charlie. He wrote it, produced it, directed it. He is on the screen almost continuously. It is the whole of him, preposterous opinions and all, and it is a really great piece of acting and story-telling.

The traditional tramp has gone. In his place is a dapper, old-fashioned French bourgeois, M. Verdoux, whose profession is to marry and kill his 'wives' for their money. He is strictly professional. He goes about his work with skill, without relish, and he returns after each coup to a tenderly idyllic home life in the provinces.

We meet him first in the rose garden; in the background a little column of smoke rises into the balmy air from the incinerator where he is disposing of his latest corpse. We part from him on the threshold of the guillotine, where, with a brilliant touch, the glass of rum which he has accepted because he 'never tasted it before', causes his delicate gait to become for the only time very slightly clumsy so that one is left by that departing figure with a single pure memory of all those previous, historic endings – the forlorn little waif waddling away to his unknown destiny.

Between these two scenes lies a series of dazzling inventions which only a spoil-sport would wish to disclose. It might be thought there was a danger of monotony in the single repeated theme of wife-murder. In fact it is continually fresh and surprising.

It is a long time since we have seen Charlie. Indeed, there must now be a large young cinema-going public who have never seen him at all. To them it will come as a revelation, to us it comes as an enchanting reminder, that we have, only now reaching maturity, one of the great actors of all time. The precision with which he performs every movement is the ballet dancer's. Watch him demonstrate with a turn of the foot the quality of the floor in the house he is trying to sell. Study him laying the breakfast table, first for two, then, as he suddenly remembers the successful murder of the preceding night, for one. Then compare these tiny, exquisite feats of acting with anything that is being done by any of the advertised stars and you will understand why he is resented. There is a scene in this film with the detective and a bottle of poisoned wine, which I will not spoil by telling. I wish merely to record that it is without qualification the finest piece of acting and dramatic construction I have ever seen.

There are, as I have said, moments of bogus philosophizing in the film. There are also moments of sentiment which I personally thought unseemly. But one cannot pick and choose with a work of art. *Monsieur Verdoux* is Charlie's individual creation. There are other members of the cast, all – with the exception of the prison chaplain – excellent, but they exist only as the expressions of Charlie's invention and the properties of his acting.

The success or failure of *Monsieur Verdoux* in England will be a test, not of Charlie, but of us. Have we been so drugged by Hollywood that we have lost the taste for the first-rate? I do not believe we have.

. THE SCANDINAVIAN CAPITALS: CONTRASTED POST-WAR MOODS .

In this third year of the Occupation[1] it is more bitter than sweet to read of the delights of travel, but it would be insincere and ungrateful to write of the problems of the Scandinavian countries without some mention of the beauty and ease which they offer the privileged visitor.

The politician, the journalist and the commercial traveller – most fortunate of modern Englishmen – may find in Stockholm and Copenhagen two of the most pleasant cities in the world: Stockholm, fatuously dubbed the 'Venice of the North' (it is as much like Rangoon), where in summer the low sun casts huge shadows before one and blinds the oncoming cyclists, where every street ends in a glitter of water, where the classic Mediterranean orders are crowned with eastern cupolas of green copper and rise amid funnels and rigging, where lovely women are still undefiled by the fashions of Hollywood, where the cooks are among the best in Europe and only the waiters are vile; Copenhagen, flat, open, clean, gay and decorous, encircled by palaces, where ancient quays and sailor-streets lead straight into spacious rococo squares, where Italian pantomime of the time of Bomba is still played nightly in the public gardens and unique cherry brandy is distilled in the original eighteenth-century mansion of the family who guard its secret; these cities leave memories to warm the tourist through many winters of discontent.

And Oslo – poor Oslo, one is inclined to think: all trams and shirt-sleeves and ice-cream cones, noisy, inelegant youngest sister – Oslo has not the least need of our compassion. She is radiant with civic pride and rapidly completing a prodigious town hall which, inside and out, promises to be the most hideous building in the world.

Very recent history has determined the mood of each of the Scandinavian capitals.

The Norwegians are conscious of having done well in the war. They fought and suffered and conquered, and in the process have been entirely cured of the inherited sense of inferiority which in the past sometimes rendered them less companionable than their neighbours. Their physical conditions are, of course, better than our own, but not vastly better. The difference is that they were very bad two years ago, have improved and are improving.

Alone among western peoples the Norwegians believe in progress, and this archaic illusion somewhat restricts mutual understanding, but their interest in English culture is boundless. In their bookshops, as in those of all Scandinavia,

Daily Telegraph and Morning Post, 11 November 1947.
1 Waugh's way of referring to England under the post-war Labour Government.

one can find the English books long rumoured to exist but quite forgotten rarities in their land of origin – poems, novels, manuals of child psychology, the fruit of a bloody and destructive decade. It is to us that the Norsemen look for culture. National pride swells at the display and then (dare one hint it?) suffers a deflation. So here they all are, those books we saw reviewed! This is what we were missing! Somehow we hoped it was rather more imposing.

It would be too much to say that Norwegian writers take the English as their models. They have grave troubles of their own, chief of which is their lack of any formal language. The battle of fifty years ago between the Danish-derived town-tongue and the rural folk-tongue resulted in no decision. It merely lost its fierceness. Now children return from school speaking a patois which is often strange to their parents. Most writers employ varieties of the town-language, pleasing themselves in their choice of spelling, grammar and vocabulary. The Norwegians await a genius to give their language definite shape. It is natural, therefore, that much of their exuberance for self-expression should take plastic and visual form. Vigeland, of whom hereafter, and Munch, the two masters, are lately dead, but under generous patronage by the state a new generation is painting acres of wall and carving tons of granite. It is perhaps not the adornment we should choose for our own ancient cities, but a good time is being had by all.

The Swedes, by contrast, seem a weary and cynical people, the children of endemic neutrality. The socialists order things better in Sweden, and at first glance they seem to have attained their paradise. The state is supreme, but humane; hereditary class distinctions barely exist, and taxation has brought the level of diminishing returns so low that the only serious labour problem is middle-class absenteeism. Domestic service has been abolished, and with it the private house. Almost everyone in Stockholm inhabits a tiny flat: the most conspicuously self-indulgent employ daily maids who decamp before dinner. Few have cars, many have sailing boats; nudists enjoy ample opportunities for their fun. Nothing except the changing of the royal guard is at all disorderly. At the universities technology is dominant; there are no debating societies.

I suppose that it was some such state as this which the English voter dimly aspired to create at the general election. And yet even here there are signs that physical well-being is not enough. The favourite authors of the young are Kafka and Sartre, there is a low birth-rate and a high suicide-rate, a thriving Communist Party and the most oppressive liquor restrictions in Europe.

For the Danes the war was a bitter experience. At first they suffered humiliation without tragedy. Normal life went on; the occupying forces were discreet. Oppression developed gradually; the Resistance was in the main conservative. It produced its heroes and martyrs, but the Danes lack, or seem to lack, that sense of a national war of liberation brought to a victorious end which characterizes the Norwegians. Their hatred of the Germans is unappeased. They are shocked by the stories of Anglo-German fraternization which reach them in distorted form from across their frontier. They do not respect what they know of American habits and resent their infiltration through films and magazines. But when all this is said they remain the most exhilarating people in Europe, for the reason that they are not obsessed by politics, national or international. More civilized than the Norwegians, more humorous and imaginative than the Swedes, they are a people for whom the Englishman feels a spontaneous, reciprocated sympathy.

The observer in passage who seeks a quick glimpse of Danish manners should visit the Tivoli gardens. Here in summer all Copenhagen has resorted for more than a century, children and elders, bourgeois and proletarian.

It costs a shilling to enter. There is a fun-fair, a concert hall, a little theatre, a circus, fireworks, beer gardens, cafés, restaurants; there are very few drunks and no hooligans; those who have an occasion to celebrate can dine luxuriously without arousing resentment. It is the microcosm of a happy urban community. Such a place could perhaps have prospered in London fifty years ago. Could it today?

. SCANDINAVIA PREFERS A BRIDGE TO AN EASTERN RAMPART .

Today it is not of art or cooking or domestic habits that the returning traveller is expected to give an account. There is one grim question set him: what about Russia? And it is particularly pertinent to the Scandinavian countries.

The Swedes are nearest to danger and the most scared. The destruction of the Baltic states and the conquest of Finland – lands intimately associated with them – impressed them more deeply than the spate of pro-Russian propaganda with which we sought to reassure them during the war. Now they see no advantage in being overrun in a third world war. Oblivious of the fact that it is usually in small countries that great wars begin, they behave like children at a party who do not wish to get involved in the rough games of the older boys.

A conservative Swede remarked to me that *I Chose Freedom* had enjoyed a record sale in Stockholm. 'It is a terrible thing,' he said.

'Why? Do you think it is false?'

'I know it to be quite true. But it will be a terrible thing if ill-feeling is aroused against Russia. Spiritually, of course, we belong to the West, but we must live in friendship with the East. We must be a bridge, not a rampart.'

I forebore to press the question which way he expected the traffic to flow on his bridge. The Swedes keep intent watch on Finland, where Russian tactics seem to differ greatly from the normal. Gen. Mannerheim, for example, lives unmolested, as would not happen in any other of Russia's recent conquests. Finnish industry works for Russia, but industrialists enjoy considerable freedom and privilege. Swedes can easily visit friends across the border. An

Daily Telegraph and Morning Post, 13 November 1947.

attempt was made this summer to make Helsinki a cultural centre. A congress of young northern writers was convened there which proved remarkable for a grave outbreak of typhus and a ferocious attack on the American *Reader's Digest* as the organ of international Facism.

Both in Norway and Sweden the Communist Party forms a vigorous minority among the dominant socialists. In Denmark it is losing prestige among manual labourers, but still attracts Bohemians. Nowhere in the world is Communist policy in doubt; nowhere does its numerical voting power indicate the feasibility of the policy. The test of any country's chance of survival is the awareness of those outside the party of the true character of the enemy. In this test both Norway and Sweden seem signally to fail.

The Swedes have made a trade agreement which makes them virtually a Russian workshop. They resent it, not because it ties them to the Soviet system, but because it does so on disadvantageous terms. Their own days of imperial ambition are so remote and proved so disastrous, their imagination is so dulled by long and lucrative neutrality, that they simply cannot conceive that anyone can be so silly as to inconvenience themselves for Glory or Power. 'Dollar diplomacy' they understand, or think they do. It seems reasonable enough to want money and they are easily convinced that America has sinister designs in her philanthropy. But the conception of a cosmic order to be imposed for its own sake and at all costs is meaningless to them. They believe very firmly in their own sanity. The word 'mad' is often on their lips, applied to individuals and peoples. They cover by this general charge most of the motive forces which history shows have in fact proved most potent for good and ill.

The tiny populations of Scandinavia can never hope to oppose aggression with physical force. If they are to survive it must be through spiritual strength, and there, alas, for all their charm and good humour and good sense, they are woefully enfeebled. When my friend said that 'spiritually' he belonged to the West, he meant, I am afraid, almost nothing except that he spoke perfect English, for Scandinavia has in the last century suffered a vast apostasy and no longer forms part of Christendom.[1] Foreign readers of Mass Observation's *Puzzled People* might be tempted to declare this of England also, but that penetrating and highly significant inquiry was made solely among English men and women who had been educated by the state. The report gave a devastating picture of the results of the system which the politicians seek to make universal, but there is in England a small but still influential body who had the good fortune to be taught by monks and nuns or to have spent their formative years at the public schools and older universities which are permeated by traditional Christianity.

No such society exists in Scandinavia. They are secularized from infancy by

---

[1] Letters denying these and subsequent assertions, and citing figures to show that Sweden was not only not irreligious but very much more religious than England, appeared from 15 to 21 November 1947. One protest came from the Swedish Embassy.

the omnicompetent state and as a result are unique in history in having no religion at all. A few eloquent pastors can attract congregations. Dr Buchman's 'Oxford' group has its adherents and, indeed, publishes a handsome magazine in Oslo. Each of the larger cities has a very small, very devout Roman Catholic community. But for the vast majority of Scandinavians, and in particular for the 'intellectuals' who throughout the West are now turning to formal Christianity in a degree unknown since the Renaissance, the religious conception of life, of man existing in relation to his Creator, of the world existing in relation to Heaven and Hell, is totally and, humanly speaking, irretrievably lost.

To find an expression of Scandinavian piety the seeker must visit Frogner Park in Oslo, where he will find a monument unique in Europe. Nearly twenty years ago the Oslo municipality decided that in Gustav Vigeland they had a genius comparable to Michelangelo. He was indeed a sculptor of high talent and boundless energy. They gave him what Michelangelo never enjoyed, complete *carte blanche* to develop his art. They built him a prodigious studio, gave him a large park to lay out and embellish; they provided all the assistants and workmen he asked for; they have spent up to date well over a million pounds on the project, and in exchange Vigeland worked year after year with ferocious energy. He saw no one except his masons and foundrymen. He showed no one what he was up to. In inviolable seclusion he worked and worked. The occupation and Quisling regime passed unnoticed in the studio, and it was during the war that his great work was finally revealed. It is a vast monolith, explicitly and uncompromisingly phallic, on which converge bridges and avenues lined with a multitudinous sub-human zoo in bronze and granite representing the cycles of life from embryo to skeleton. There are huge, bald, naked, bearded fleshy men wrestling and courting and kicking their children about like footballs; there are shrivelled old couples on the point of death; there is perhaps the only existing statue of a foetus.

It is a stupendous achievement, and in all that mass of writhing muscle there is no hint anywhere of any intellectual process or spiritual aspiration. I suppose it is the most depressing spectacle it is possible to encounter; something far more awful than the ruins of Hiroshima. And standing in that sunny park with the children splashing delightedly in the fountains I wondered what hope there was for the people who had made it.

. HONEYMOON TRAVEL .

Several contented and devoted wives have told me that not a day of the honeymoon passed without tears. No one has ever told me that it was the happiest time of her life. Brides expect too much. Everyone has conspired to

Joan Forbes, ed., *The Book for Brides* (London, 1948).

persuade them that the first month of marriage is a time of unshadowed bliss; when it proves to be full of ordinary annoyances they fall despondent and think:'If I am not deliriously happy now, when shall I ever be?' And later, when they find the married state pleasant enough, they blame their early disappointment on their husband's arrangements . . . We ought never to have gone to that awful hotel. No one told me how cold it could be at Antibes. We never had a moment alone. We never saw another soul. I was worn out walking through picture-galleries. There was absolutely nothing to do. He should never have let me eat *scampi* – I was never really well again until we got back to England . . . But it was not really the husband's fault; poor beast, he had his black moments, too, and if he did not actually weep (and it may be that he did) he thought very wistfully of his club at about six o'clock on most evenings. A honeymoon is a holiday; the first, one hopes, of many. It has certain unique features, but the more it is treated at the planning stage as something commonplace, the more enjoyable it is likely to be.

Once, not very long ago, it was regarded primarily as the period of the bride's initiation into the jollier Facts of Life. I am told educational reforms have changed all that, but for the purpose of this essay I shall assume that the young couple whom I am invited to advise are deeply in love and that this is their first adventure together. The weightiest counsel I can give is: avoid solitude. The endurances of the wedding are, today, less than they were. Once upon a time the fittings, the rehearsals, the arrangement of the presents, left the bride, as the bachelor celebrations left the bridegroom, in a state of prostration. It was natural then, and to a less degree it is still natural, for the weary couple to suppose that the world offers nothing more desirable than a shooting-box in the highlands, isolated amid miles of grouse moor from the agitations of social converse. That way lies stark melancholy. Love provides its own peculiar isolation in the densest crowd. It also, paradoxically, calls for ostentation. Each partner wants to show off to the other. Also – a simple thought rendered complex by the poverty of English syntax – each wants to show the other off to others. It is perhaps for this reason, rather than for its splendours of architecture and scenery, that the traditional ground for honeymoons has always been well inside the pinching belt. Venice, Porto Fino, Taormina, Brioni – at all these hallowed places the populace take the keenest relish in a bride and compete in marking their appreciation (marking indeed!) by sidling up to her in crowded public places and nipping her like lobsters.

Alas, the harsh laws under which we suffer have cut most of us from these simple pleasures. The question one would have asked ten years ago was: how much have you got to spend? The question now is: to what class do you belong? In the old days anyone through thrift or a lucky day at the races could qualify for a brief excursion among the rich. Now we live under brahminical rules of caste. The politician, the criminal, the commercial traveller, the journalist and Unesco (whatever Unesco may be) comprise the privileged classes to whom the world – a shrunken and battered world, maybe, but still a wide area – is open.

For the unprivileged there is the sterling area or the chance of a walking tour, healthy and informative no doubt, but unfitted to the sweets of love. It is hard to enter the magic circle of £10-a-day travellers. Perhaps Unesco is penetrable; who knows? But I urge the bridegroom not to attempt, unless he has had previous training, to set out as a crook. Even if he escapes prison he will suffer much in his male vanity, which must be paramount at this season, if in his first hours of married life he is stripped at the airport by economic police and robbed of his stamp collection. And, apropos of male vanity, a word of warning to the privileged: choose a country where you speak the language well. Nothing endows you with greater protective authority, nothing reduces human dignity more than the curse of Babel. You will fall heavily, perhaps permanently, in your bride's esteem if you lose her luggage and get involved in controversy. But for this I should advise Spain or Portugal. No one in either of these countries speaks a word of foreign language. Apart from that they offer almost all that the lover can desire. The physical comforts are not much greater than in England; the food is copious but excruciating; much of the wine is stultifying; but the aesthetic pleasures are supreme. Salamanca, Seville, Burgos, Valladolid, Ciudad Rodrigo, never much popularized, almost unvisited during the last fifteen years, quite undiscovered places for most of the young, are still as lovely as when the first lithographers recorded them a hundred years ago.

Of France and Italy it is impossible for the middle-aged to speak without prejudice. They are not the countries we knew and loved and when we go there now we tend churlishly to deplore what we miss instead of being grateful for what we still find. And, of course, there are splendours still incomparable; first vulgarized, now reduced, they are still the lands of the fine flowering of the human spirit; they are still there, in part, to rejoice the young; only the elderly need hold off.

For the privileged monoglot two cities have outstanding attractions – Copenhagen and New York. All Danes and most Americans speak excellent English. In New York, in any of the four or five prodigious hotels, you can enjoy all the solitude of the grouse moor. In contradistinction to Europe, it is a safe rule in America to go for the biggest in everything. These hotels provide many surprises – every time you ring the bell a different servant answers it; every time you touch the door handle there is a flash of blue lightning and you get a violent electric shock; there are only two sorts of food – tepid and iced – and all indistinguishable in taste whatever the name on the menu. But the beds are comfortable, the telephone girls are polite, and you have only to sit in the foyer to be endlessly amused and excited. You need never leave the hotel. Trade conventions are arriving and dispersing at every moment. You can wander through bazaars and cafés in every style of decoration. You can have your hair dyed and all your teeth pulled out. If you happen to die you can be embalmed and lie there in state.

Copenhagen has other attractions; small, leisurely, decorous, full of palaces and surrounded by a ring of Renaissance castles. There is everything to eat and drink except coffee. What is much more than these, the Danes think it quite proper for you to enjoy yourself. In New York, pleasure is compulsory; it is good for trade; it provides valuable 'contacts'; it refreshes you after work; it kills you at 50. But the Danes just go on quietly enjoying themselves and invite you to join them. Stockholm is the more beautiful city but the drink laws make it unsuitable for civilized visitors. In Copenhagen you can eat and drink all day long and it is thought quite inoffensive, as it is not in New York, to go to bed when you are sleepy.

But all this is advice for the privileged. What can be said to the humble? Don't cheat and don't cheese-pare: go where you are allowed and hope for better times. There is Ireland. Dublin with its quays and eighteenth-century squares has a close resemblance to Copenhagen. It is a dismal town in winter, particularly at the moment when there is no coal, but in summer and autumn it is full of light and beauty and a sort of grim, doleful humour. Some of the large Irish country houses have lately been turned into hotels and two or three of these are comfortable. Before booking rooms get an eyewitness account. Some are awful and travel in Ireland is more difficult than in England. There are the West Indies for the winter, varying enormously from island to island but everywhere delicious blue water and green bush and winding footpaths and ramshackle cottages and the smell of rum and molasses and bananas, the shuffling of bare feet and black laughter. Two warnings about the West Indies. Not everyone looks her best in great heat and not everyone enjoys the spectacle of abject poverty. There are two schools in both subjects. Sweat is said by psychologists to have a high erotic appeal and in films lately I have certainly seen some very shiny faces that were plainly intended to be alluring. Some gourmands in the past have kept starving prisoners in cages round the dining-room as an appetizer. So you may find the West Indies entirely congenial, but consider those points before embarking.

Finally, there is the cruising liner. This form of travel came in for a lot of derision in the old days when the word 'tourist' had an objectionable flavour and we all liked to think of ourselves as 'travellers'. But there is a great deal to be said for it. One is relieved of all anxiety and responsibility. You cannot lose your train or your luggage or run out of money, as you can when travelling on your own. You are not likely to be poisoned. There is a varied social life always accessible, in which you can take as little or as much part as you like. But again, two snags. I said above that a happy couple should be ostentatious, but there are limits to some of us. You may be quite sure that you will be recognized as a honeymoon couple as you come on board and that throughout the voyage you will be a subject of unusual attention – sentimental, lubricious, derisive, according to the natures of your fellow travellers. They will talk about you, incessantly, all of them. And the other matter is one of delicacy but must be mentioned. Beds. The bed plays a big part in the honeymoon and very few cabins in very few ships provide full scope for all your needs.

Reading this through I feel that most of my advice has been rather discouraging. Well, that is how I began the essay. Don't expect too much; and a very happy time to you both.

. MGR RONALD KNOX .

Many American universities take an annual vote to elect the student 'most likely to succeed'. Had this been the practice at Oxford in 1910, the choice would almost certainly have fallen on Ronald Knox, of Balliol. That age is now legendary. It is effortless to say as I have often heard said, that, had they grown to maturity, that heroic group loosely dubbed 'the Grenfells' would have developed the weaknesses of every other generation. All we know is that they died young leaving a unique reputation for brilliance, high-spirits and grace, and that a rich, determining tradition in English life seems to have withered and died with them. Ronald Knox as an undergraduate was an animating spirit of the innermost circle of this group. He was the most scholarly of them, the most nimble-witted and the most other-worldly. He came up from Eton with the lustre of a book already published and praised, verses in English, Latin and Greek of remarkable polish and ingenuity. All the coveted university distinctions – the Hertford, the Ireland, Presidency of the Union, a first in Greats – came to him as mere by-products of an intense and varied intellectual and social life. He took holy orders in the Church of England, was elected fellow of Trinity and made his rooms there the centre of the choicest spirits of the succeeding years.

He wrote brilliantly and copiously. The career predicted for him was, at the least ambitious, that of a great ecclesiastical wit, a Max Beerbohm in lawn sleeves; or, equally possible, that of an historic English churchman, a Cranmer or a Laud, who would gather up and redirect the faltering community, leaving his mark on the examination papers of the future – '"Archbishop Knox succeeded because he attempted too much" – Discuss this statement.'

There are numbers of men who enjoyed huge reputations as undergraduates, of whom we say: 'I wonder what happened to old So-and-so?' Everyone knows what happened to Ronald Knox. He became a Catholic priest. His office diverted him from the general stream of intellectual life of his country and with the years the separation has widened until, it may be, there are many readers who, ironically, think of him as a parodist and the writer of detective stories, and as nothing more.

The intention of this essay is secular, to introduce to the modern non-Catholic literary public the achievements of one of the most considerable living writers. It would not be seemly to treat here of his life as a priest, but some understanding of what that office means to him and to his fellow Catholics is essential to an understanding of his work. He is not, as many admirable

Horizon, May 1948.

Englishmen have been, a clergyman who finds recreation from his parochial duties in *belles-lettres*. As a matter of fact he has never been a parish-priest. Nor is he, like the many modern writers who support political or social causes, merely concerned to use his technical skill to insinuate extraneous dogmas. A Catholic priest is not a man who holds a certain set of opinions more strongly than his fellows; he regards himself, and is regarded by lay Catholics, as a man consecrated and set apart; not cleverer, or more learned or even more virtuous, but different, indelibly marked. His essential work is not in the study or the pulpit, but at the altar. He offers a daily sacrifice and everything else he does is an extension of this office. Mgr Knox has done what seems purely secular work but always, like the farm labour of a monk, as part of his priestly calling. (His detective stories were written to support the expenses of the Oxford University chaplaincy. The brilliant exercises in humorous scholarship by which he is most widely known – *The Studies in Sherlock Holmes* and so forth – were papers designed to enliven the stodgy fare of pious societies.)

There are those who, lacking other objects of reverence, now attribute a priest's, even a martyr's, sanctity to the artist. It is to them primarily that I wish to offer the spectacle of a man born with every aptitude and sensibility that make for literary eminence, who has without betrayal of that vocation subordinated it to, and harmonized it with, a higher.

Mgr Knox has written and published a great deal but I shall mention only the books which are most likely to interest the non-Christian reader. His work falls into certain easily recognizable categories.

First there is the controversial writing with which he originally became prominent. Some of the best was done before his conversion. He writes in *A Spiritual Aeneid* that he would have accepted the Roman obedience earlier if it had not been so obvious. The logical acrobatics of High Church apology were a delight to the mind which could demonstrate so felicitously that Queen Victoria wrote *In Memoriam*. *Absolute and Abitofhell*, *Some Loose Stones*, *Reunion all Round* are models of literary skill. But in 1914 came the realization that the verbal card-castles so delicately built in the Trinity common-room did not provide spiritual defence in the battle-fields where his friends were falling daily.

As a Catholic he has never sought adversaries. Editors and publishers have approached him from time to time with sheaves of press-cuttings and the demand: 'This needs answering.' Then, dutifully but without, I think, much relish, he has turned his old skill to the defence of his new, ancient faith. It is not, I am sure, simply because I am in agreement that I find him a master of controversy. (We are often embarrassed by the methods of doughty champions of our own side.) *Caliban in Grub Street*, 1930, was an examination of the slump-provoked interest in religion which was suddenly and absurdly exhibited by the daily press. But the best-sellers who were then hired to expound their beliefs were too inept to attract more than broad ridicule. In *Broadcast Minds*, 1932, he engaged more worthy opponents, H. G. Wells, Prof. Julian

Huxley, Lord Russell, Mencken, Mr Gerald Heard, Mr Langdon Davies, men who personify the sentiments of their time, whose influence can be discerned in countless odd corners today. At his hands these pundits became blundering, snorting animals, teased, baffled, pricked and finally left floundering in the sand. The most resolute modernist, if she is also a girl of genuine literary taste, must delight in the grace and precision of this series of *estocadas*. A rare quality in Mgr Knox's polemic is the fullness with which he accepts the meaning and implication of his opponents' point. Some modern Catholic controversialists assume an arrogant confidence in their cause and are content to turn aside a serious argument with a jolly verbal 'score'; Mgr Knox never. For all his wit he always engages the heart of the issue. Indeed he often summarizes his opponents' case far more lucidly and plausibly than they have done themselves. Once, in a correspondence published under the title of *Difficulties*, he had the rare experience of convincing his adversary, Mr Arnold Lunn. But in general these exhibitions of skill serve more to divert the faithful than convert the infidel. The meat is dragged out of the bull-ring but the *vacadas* still team with cattle. The old fallacies turn up again and again. It is not the priest's role to compete for applause. So, I think, in recent years Mgr Knox has wearied of these victories. No doubt if a great occasion arises in his lifetime we shall again see him toss his hat behind him. Meanwhile he tends to leave invitations from the bull-ring unanswered. He knows he is clever and he knows he is right and he has other things to do than demonstrate these facts weekly.

But there is one recent book that must be mentioned in connection with these works of controversy; *God and the Atom*, 1945. This swiftly written essay of less than 150 pages attracted little attention in the hubbub in which it appeared. It is in many ways the postscript to, and epitome of, all his controversial work. Twelve years before he had been in conflict with the jaunty materialistic optimism of Wells and Lord Russell. The destruction of Hiroshima provided a dramatic conclusion to the discussion and one of the greatnesses of this little book is that Mgr Knox is never content to say: 'I told you so.' He addresses equally the Christian tempted to *Schadenfreude* and the heathen tempted to despair.

To the practical warrior the atom bomb presented no particular moral or spiritual problem. We were engaged in destroying the enemy, civilians and combatants alike. We always assumed that destruction was roughly proportionate to the labour and material expended. Whether it was more convenient to destroy a city with one bomb or a hundred thousand depended on the relative costs of production. That is how the strategists saw it. But a sure popular instinct has made that bomb a symbol (a daily paper even adopted a new chronology and for a time dated its issues by 'Days of the Atomic Age'). The preliminary of Mgr Knox's examination is to show that the popular unquiet was based on the deepest philosophic grounds. The incident made a wound in the civilized mind and, significantly, Mgr Knox divides his essay into psychiatric sections – Trauma, Analysis, Adjustment and Sublimation.

There had been committed a triple outrage on Faith, Hope and Charity; on Faith in that the actual mechanics of the device, the discovery of 'an indeterminate element in the heart of things' (which atom will split?) seemed at first flush to cast doubt on the hypothesis of causality and the five classical Thomist proofs of the existence of God; on Hope, which I suspect has suffered the most widespread injury, in 'the prospect of an age in which the possibilities of evil are increased by an increase in the possibilities of destruction'; on Charity by 'the news that men fighting for a good cause have taken, at one particular moment of decision, the easier, not the nobler path'. He has gone, you see, right to the heart of the problem as he always did, though this time his adversary seemed to be, not a popular journalist, but the constitution of the Universe and the stream of History. And – or so it seems to me – just as he made rings round poor Mr Gerald Heard, he now makes rings round the Universe and History.

As one grows older one receives more frequent communications from strangers demanding peremptorily: 'Kindly state on the back of enclosed postcard the names of the books which have inspired you', and as one grows older it becomes harder to name one. *God and the Atom* inspired me; it came at a time of deflation and blew into me a clear breath of reason and wisdom. I believe it is a great book but the reader may well ask: 'Why have I not heard of it before? It was topical. The present day is all too apt for popularization. No doubt it had some particular, personal appeal to you. If it had been meant for me I should have found it in my hands before now.'

It is a valid point.

One reason, no doubt, is that there still survives from pre-emancipation days a definite, though barely conscious, discrimination on the part of librarians, literary editors and others against specifically Catholic books which does not extend to those which are specifically agnostic or atheist. For example, if I want a copy of any of Mgr Knox's works I have to go to a shop which specializes in rosaries and missals. It simply would not occur to the kindly ex-corporal who keeps the shop where I habitually deal that a book by a Monsignor called *God and the Atom* could be 'General Literature'.

But this is not the whole reason. There are certain limitations in the author himself which may always hamper his direct influence on his contemporaries.

First, in an age trained from infancy in inductive habits of thought, Mgr Knox has an instinctively deductive mind. Start him from scratch, as Mr Lunn did, and he will build you a very solid structure of philosophy. But in general he does not start every inquiry anew at scratch. He makes very large presuppositions and, confronted with an apparent anomaly, his method is not to question his principles but to examine the phenomenon to see how it can be reconciled with them. It is in no way a weakness but it weakens his appeal when he comes to address those with contrary principles or with no principles at all.

The second and graver limitation is one of language. Mgr Knox writes in an easy, conversational style but it is the conversation of pre-1914 Oxford when it was bad form to be pompous or overbearing or abstruse, but when a great deal of common ground was taken for granted. Many Englishmen learned this tongue in their homes and speak it naturally – indeed without being aware that there is any other means of human intercourse – but it is not at all natural to those educated, say, at the London School of Economics or at most American colleges. It presupposes, at the lowest, the sort of knowledge which enables one to solve *The Times* cross-word puzzle – a hotchpotch of half-forgotten fact and poetry and legend, chosen it may seem without much method but presenting a vague map of the world in which the Mediterranean is the centre. This was the equipment of the 'educated' man, a generation ago. Some had learned much more than others, but it was generally assumed that everyone had tried to learn the same sort of thing, and it is on this common fund of knowledge that Mgr Knox invariably draws when he seeks an apt illustration to his argument. Take, for example, this fine passage from *God and the Atom*, a book explicitly designed for 'the plain man': 'At the moment of victory a sign appeared in heaven; not the comforting Labarum of the Milvian Bridge, but the bright, evil cloud which hung over Hiroshima. In this sign we were to conquer'. How many members of the House of Commons today, how many editors or air marshals, know what the Labarum was? How many despondent American housewives? There may or may not be an intrinsic value in the content of traditional European education, but I do not see how a literary culture can survive at all without *some* corpus of common texts. One must be able to appeal to the known in order to explain the unknown. A traveller from Africa may describe a zebra as being like a striped pony and be understood in most parts of the world. Not, however, by an Eskimo, and to describe the zebra in terms of the walrus would be a delicate task. 'Humane Letters' once served the purpose of providing common ground. They do so no longer, and it has become difficult for men of opposed views to discuss their differences intelligibly.

There is, I think, little resentment today of superior information. People like to be told things. But Mgr Knox is the least didactic of savants. It is when he is trying to popularize, to make plain in untechnical terms a metaphysical question, that he draws on his superior knowledge, courteously assuming that we all remember our Virgil and Matthew Arnold. In doing so he reveals the existence of a society quite other than what he seeks to persuade, and the revelation, combined with his frequent, entirely unselfconscious references to nannies and gardeners and cross-Channel steamers and country-house visiting, and with his implicit assumption that a decent sufficiency of worldly goods is the normal lot of man, does, I think, carry a perceptible flavour of the class distinctions which are unmentionable today.

It was fashionable in the late thirties – and, for all I know, it is still fashionable – to assert that an artist must be 'contemporary'. Reflection shows that this obligation is quite illusory. Some very great artists have had this quality, many have not. The more learned and philosophic the man, the less likely he is to be 'contemporary', for he will know that most 'new' ideas are restatements of very old ones and that the latest events are in all essentials repetitions of what has happened before. Moreover, the nervous condition which induces a man to sit up late twiddling a wireless-set in order to hear the news before the morning paper does not, I think, conduce to high technical achievement in the Arts. But wise and great men – Thomas More for instance – *have* been 'contemporary' and Mgr Knox definitely is not.

I do not mean that he lives in a monkish and scholarly seclusion remote from the affairs of his neighbours. He knows what is going on about him – few better. But he lacks that zest for his own period which makes some men declare that however bloody and destructive the age, it is theirs and they would not have been born in any other. Perhaps Mgr Knox experienced that exhilaration in youth. He does not seek to recapture it now. The world for him is a place of exile and probation; it is impious to complain about it; it is fatuous to join Mr J. B. Priestley in representing it as entirely jolly. Most readers want to be assured that they live in stirring times, even if they are only stirred to horror. Mgr Knox refuses to play that game.

He has not often been happy in his choice of titles. I suspect that he allows editors and publishers – notoriously ineffectual guides – to choose them for him. *Let Dons Delight* is deplorably named. It suggests an academic squib, whereas the theme is a grave one, the cumulative, disastrous estrangement between Learning and Divinity as exemplified in nine conversations held in the same Oxford common-room at intervals of fifty years between 1588 and 1938. In *Absolute and Abitofhell* Mgr Knox had already shown a rare genius for pastiche and parody. In *Let Dons Delight* it is hard to distinguish where one ends and the other starts. He is ruthless with Mark Pattison (a man little read). In the rest of the writing – the Notes at the end of each chapter have much of the cream of it – the exaggerations are so delicate as to be barely peceptible. The distinctive flavour of each generation is precisely caught. One is there in the panelled room with them, hearing the dons talk.

Each conversation has the same pattern; the ageing provost, the go-ahead don, the guest, the subdued echo of the great events of the outside world, the misplaced confidence. The danger of such a method was, of course, monotony. Nine similar conversations must prove a strain on the invention; a strain which Mgr Knox supports with dazzling ingenuity. Each little scene is delicious in itself; the minor characters are all 'characters' – for example, in 1888, the awful young man who is being vetted for a fellowship. Of the major theme an indication is given in the sub-titles – 'Hannibal ad Portas: 1588', 'Cakes and Ale: 1638', 'The Pigeons Flutter: 1688', 'Lost Causes: 1738', 'The Unchanging World: 1788', 'False Dawn: 1838', 'A Rear-guard Action: 1888', 'Chaos: 1938'. The book contains the whole of the convert's criticism of the Church of England, that it was an improvisation which fortuitously assumed an aspect of permanence and then speedily came to nothing. It contains the philosopher's criticism of recent philosophic history – the factitious divorce of Reason from Revelation leading to the denial of both. It also contains the artist's most moving lament for the desolation of a loved city.

I believe that when Mgr Knox wrote *Let Dons Delight*, he did not know that he was leaving Oxford. If so, the work is strangely prophetic for there runs through it the thread of the dispossessed shepherd of the First Eclogue – *sitientes ibimus Afros* – the Elizabethan following the old faith to Douai and Tyburn, the scholar gypsy, the Tractarian preceding Newman into exile. And in fact *Let Dons Delight* proved to be Mgr Knox's own farewell to Oxford. In 1939 he was called from his thirteen-years' fruitful chaplaincy in the Old Palace in St Aldates to undertake his weightiest work, the translation of the Vulgate.

For a hundred years the loss of the majestic prose of the Jacobean Authorized Version has been a sentimental regret of Roman converts from the Church of England. The Douai version, roughly revised from time to time, carries a strong flavour of St Jerome's Latin but it is, as English, uncouth and abounds in such passages as:

> For the priesthood being translated, it is necessary that a translation also be made of the law. For he of whom these things are spoken is of another tribe, of which no one attended on the altar. For it is evident that our Lord sprang out of Juda; in which tribe Moses spoke nothing concerning priests. And it is yet far more evident: if according to the similitude of Melchisedec there ariseth another priest, who is made, not according to the law of a carnal commandment, but according to the power of an indissoluble life.

Since Newman's day the Catholic bishops have had it in mind to order a new translation. Newman was let slip. In Mgr Knox, they realized, they had been given a second chance. Here, among their clergy, was a scholar versed in all the ramifications of German Higher Criticism who was also an outstanding English stylist. Therefore ten years, at the height of his powers, were sequestered from Mgr Knox's life for this huge task. Some may feel that this was a high price, but Mgr Knox is a man under authority.

One must be precise about the terms of his duty. He had not to produce a new English Bible but a new translation of the Vulgate, the Latin version of the canonical scriptures compiled by St Jerome in the fourth century, and of the particular edition of that book issued in 1592 by Pope Clement VIII which has since been the official text of the Catholic Church. He was thus relieved of many of an editor's responsibilities in judging between various plausible readings; indeed, at first glance the work might appear to be one of mere drudgery for a Latinist of Mgr Knox's capacity.

One pictures a drowsy archiepiscopal schoolmaster and Knox quartus on to construe; 'Please sir, I couldn't find *seminiverbius*.' 'Well, what is it derived from?' '*Semen* and *Verbum*, sir?' 'Of course. I should render it "a sower of words".' 'But, please sir, that doesn't sound very good English, sir. I mean it doesn't seem to make sense. And if he meant that, why didn't he say *sator verborum*, sir?' 'Knox, do you not realize this is an Inspired Text? Get on, and don't ask irreverent questions.' A blue-bottle sails in at the class-room window.

But in fact the task set two problems of extreme delicacy. Every translator knows that it is very rare indeed to find in any two languages a pair of words which are invariably interchangeable. The Douai translators had merely set down what Jerome's Latin meant then to Englishmen in the sixteenth century. Mgr Knox's first problem was to enter the mind of a fourth-century Dalmatian ascetic and find what the original Greek and Hebrew texts had meant to *him*. The second problem was to put this meaning into the language of the twentieth century.

He was dealing, moreover, with a venerable book. I think that most Englishmen asked to explain the meaning of 'venerable', if they were not given time to think about its derivation, would suggest 'antiquity' as an essential connotation. To Mgr Knox the Scriptures are venerable, not because they are ancient, but on the contrary because they are of immediate topical importance. Custom ordains that at the altar he should wear the semblance of a sixth-century overcoat, but when he puts it off to read the Gospel and epistle in the common tongue he is charged with an entirely modern message. Add to this the further consideration that for practical purposes it is undesirable to have a fresh translation every decade; that he was required to produce a version which would be perfectly lucid throughout the English-speaking world for two or three hundred years; and the magnitude of the task appears.

He has accomplished it, alone, in ten years. It is the loneliness of the task which is especially impressive. A journalist on *Life* magazine has a whole team of 'researchers' running round for him when he sits down to produce an article. Mgr Knox settled down in Shropshire with a few dozen books of reference and day by day toiled at his typewriter, without any very lively encouragement from his friends or any very breathless expectancy from his superiors. As a result, the book has a unity and individuality which no other translation can claim.

It is unlikely that those who resort to the Bible for purely aesthetic pleasure will prefer Mgr Knox's translation. It was an ascetic exercise worthy of Jerome himself. No one could have done a more elegant pastiche; that was not his purpose. He has been grimly functional and has not scrupled to employ the driest periphrases in order to extract the fullest, most precise meaning from his original. The Epistles, in particular, which are often barely intelligible in either the Douai or the Authorized Version, here become modern and cogent. They are disquieting to those who from long familiarity have learned to enjoy the rhythms and august phrases without considering what they meant. The less the reader is concerned with the sense, the more he will resent their new form. But when one writes of 'familiarity' with the 'rhythm' of the Authorized Version, one is today betraying oneself as middle-aged. It is unquestioned that for the past three hundred years the Authorized Version has been the greatest single formative influence in English prose style. But that time is over. These 'rhythms and august phrases' were drummed into us and our ancestors, not for their beauty, but because they were universally accepted as the Word of God. They were read aloud daily at school, at the university and in many homes. People sat up in cottages conning them by candle light; they taught themselves to read with no other purpose. When the Bible ceases, as it is ceasing, to be accepted as a sacred text it will not long survive for its fine writing. It will take place beside the *Anatomy of Melancholy* and *Urn Burial* as a book to be read by very few at very rare occasions. It seems to me probable that in a hundred years' time the only Englishmen who know their Bibles will be Catholic. And they will know it in Mgr Knox's version. *Sitientes ibimus Afros*. The incised rock of this desert exile may well be his most lasting monument.

Lastly (for I do not mean to write here of the detective stories) there are the sermons, a category likely to provoke alarm even among church-goers. It is notorious that this is a new and un-English prejudice. Dr Johnson could weigh all the prominent preachers of his day. '. . . South is one of the best if you except his peculiarities and his violence and sometimes coarseness of language. Seed has a very fine style . . . Sherlock's style, too, is very elegant though he has not made it his principal study – and you may add Smalridge . . . I should like to read all that Ogden has written . . .' and so on through all the catalogue of sonorous, forgotten names, until in the pause rendered doubly famous by Sir Max Beerbohm, the small, doomed voice, piped up: 'Were not Dodd's sermons addressed to the passions?'

Mgr Knox's sermons are very definitely not addressed to the passions. There are several books of them and a great number still unpublished. Heard or read they are quiet in tone without oratorical effects, emotional appeal or trenchant argument. They are addressed primarily to the imagination. The reader who wishes to sample their peculiar flavour might well dip into *The Mystery of the Kingdom*, 1937, though there is no representative in that collection of a *genre* in which Mgr Knox stands in his age alone – the formal panegyric.

On certain great occasions – the centenary, for example, of Newman's conversion – Mgr Knox is often invited to preach before a select audience and in these set-pieces he allows himself some ornament and elaboration. Most of them have to be sought in the back-numbers of the *Tablet* and I hope that one day we shall see them collected in a fine quarto volume. The sermons which have so far appeared in book-form are mostly in series – conferences to undergraduates, courses for retreats. They are very pure and symmetrical in form, consisting for the most part of the examination of some familiar text or parable, the unfolding of it to reveal deeper meaning, and the application of it to a problem in the spiritual life. Were there not abundant evidence that they appeal to a great diversity of hearers I should say that they were specifically literary, for in each of them there is that sudden flash and fusion of ideas and observed fact which corresponds exactly to the process known as literary 'creation'.

Mgr Knox is now in his sixtieth year. His long labour on the Vulgate is drawing to a close. He has already achieved a body of work which will ensure his lasting renown among specialists. Will his place in English Literature be a Challoner's or a Newman's?

It depends I think purely on outside circumstances. He is at the height of his powers but it is not in his priestly vocation to pursue personal fame. Newman, whose career has so many similarities with Mgr Knox's, remained almost forgotten by the world until at the age of 64, he suddenly stepped into glory with the work of a few weeks – the *Apologia*. Should the propitious moment come, we may well see Mgr Knox emerge from his seclusion in the Mendips and quietly take his place among the most illustrious, beside Pascal and Bossuet; but neither he nor his friends search for a portent in the skies with any anxiety. That is in other hands.

. THE GENTLE ART OF BEING INTERVIEWED .

Was it a peculiarity of my own, or do you, Gentle Reader, as I once did, keep a black list of public characters? Mine grew longer every year. It comprised men and women, quite unknown to me except through the newspapers, for whom, nevertheless, I had a sharp personal dislike.

In a few cases, no doubt, the trouble was visual – a smirk in the photographer's flashlamp, a jaunty step in the news-reel, a hat; sometimes it was aural – adenoids at the microphone; but the vast majority of the people, at any rate on *my* list, were there for intellectual offences. It was something they were reported to have said to the press.

I refer, of course, to those utterances which seem to gush out spontaneously, washing away the patient camouflage of years in a great cataract of self-revelation. These people are kind in the home, good at their jobs, but when there are reporters about something comes over them, and it is then that they make their atrocious, unforgettable utterances – or so I used to think, when I watched them chatting to the men with the notebooks, posing for the men with the cameras.

The classic ground for the sport is a liner arriving in New York. New Yorkers still retain a friendly curiosity about their foreign visitors – indeed, believe it or not, a bulletin is printed and daily pushed under your door in the chief hotels, telling you just what celebrities are in town, where they are staying, and nominating a Celebrity of the Day, an introduction to whom is often included among the prizes in radio competitions.

To satisfy this human appetite, the reporters come on board with the first officials and have ample time before the ship finally berths to prosecute their quest. They are not got-up to please. Indeed, their appearance is rather like Poe's Red Death – a stark reminder of real life after five days during which one has seen no one who was not either elegantly dressed or neatly uniformed. American papers have at their command most prepossessing creatures of both sexes, but they choose only those who look like murderers to greet visitors. They are elderly and, one supposes, embittered men. They have not advanced far in their profession and their business is exclusively with the successful. Their revenge is a ruthless professionalism. They look the passengers over and make their choice, like fish-brokers at market. One of their number, the grimmest, stalks into the lounge, breaks into a distinguished group, taps an ambassador on the arm and says: 'The boys want a word with you outside.'

I have often watched the process and decided that the fox, on the whole, rather enjoyed it. Eminent people get the feeling of moving everywhere among flashlamps and questions, and miss them if they are not there, as dog-lovers like to be greeted by a hairy, dribbling, barking herd whenever they enter their own house. I suppose it is like being an officer in the army. One's first day in uniform one was embarrassed at being saluted; after a short time one expected it. Anyway, I used to think, as I saw the distinguished goats segregated from the sheep and hustled away so brusquely, that they would greatly have resented being left out, and I read the results with stony heart. How they gave themselves away, I thought.

But I have become altogether a softer man in this matter since last year when, for one ghastly afternoon, I found myself one of the victims – not, I need hardly say, in the open competition of the first-class deck of a Cunarder, but in far more modest but equally disturbing circumstances.

It was shortly before it became a criminal offence to travel abroad. I made a last-minute rush to a country which I will call 'Happiland'; a small, friendly country never much visited by the English, and last summer quite deserted by them, so that my arrival was, to that extent, remarkable.

I came by air. We landed at what should have been lunch-time, at what indeed *was* lunch-time for the various officials whose consent was necessary for our entry. This is no season in which to expect a sympathetic hearing of vexations of travel. We will all go through hell cheerfully nowadays to get abroad. I did not repine, but I was weary when at length some hours later I reached my hotel. It was a stuffy afternoon; Happilandic trams rattled below the window. I shut out their sound, and with it every breath of fresh air. I lay down on the bed, lit a cigar, and before I had smoked half an inch was asleep. It was still in my fingers when I awoke at dusk; there was ash all over me, a hole in the top sheet and a smell of tobacco and burned linen. There was a strange figure in my room. It turned on the light and revealed itself as a young woman dressed as though for sport – not 'le sport' of Mr Michael Arlen; athletics, putting the weight, most likely.

'Good night, Mr Wog,' said this apparition. 'Excuse please, I must make a reportage of you.'

I sat up and began slowly to remember where I was; much more slowly than in detective stories the heroine comes round from chloroform.

'I am of . . .' said my visitor, uttering some deep Happilandic gutturals, 'our great liberal newspaper.'

'Do sit down.' I waved to the armchair; then noticed that it was full of my clothes. 'I am sorry to receive you like this.'

'How you are sorry to receive me? I represent all anti-Fascist intellectual activities.'

'Ah, well; do you smoke?'

'Not too much.'

She sat on my clothes and looked at me for some time without noticeable interest.

'Well,' I said at length, 'I suppose this is really worse for you than for me.'

'Excuse please?'

'I simply said this was worse for you than for me.'

'In what directions, please?'

'Well, perhaps it isn't really.'

'I am not understanding what is worse, Mr Wog.'

'No, it meant nothing.'

'So.'

There was another pause in which I began slowly to regain my self-possession It was a game of snakes and ladders. The next throw set me back six squares.

'Mr Wog, you are a great satyr.'

'I assure you not.'

'My editor says you have satirized the English nobility. It is for this he has sent me to make a reportage. You are the famous Wog, are you not?'

'Well, I'd hardly say that. Some of my books have been fairly popular . . . a very ordinary Wog, you know.'

'I know, like the great Priestley.'

'No, much more ordinary. Quite different.'

'How different, Mr Wog? You have said "Fairly", "Popular", "Ordinary". I have those words written down. I understand well. You believe in social justice, you write for the people, yes? You represent the ordinary man? That is why you satirize the nobility. They abuse you?'

'Yes, come to think of it, some of them do.'

'Of course. In Happiland we are having many such proletarian writers. But since we have no nobility, they must satirize the secretaries of the trades unions. Do you also satirize the secretaries?'

'No, I can't say I do. You see, I've never met one.'

'They are high people?'

'Yes, very high.'

'So. I find you are a timid man, Mr Wog, to be afraid of the secretaries. In Happiland are many jokes about them.'

She seemed cast down by her memories of Happilandic humour and sat silent for some time. When she next spoke it was in the *plume de ma tante* tradition.

'Mr Wog, how are your pens?'

I did not try. I simply said, 'Very well, thank you.'

'Here are many pens. I am not a pen. My editor has been an international pen in Swissland. Were you an international pen, Mr Wog?'

Light broke. 'The Pen Club? I'm afraid I am not a member, myself.'

'How can that be? In Happiland all the great authors are pens. There is much jealousy to belong. Some say the elections are by intrigue, but it is not so. It is all by merit. Is it not so in England?'

'Yes, I am sure it is.'

'How then, please, are you not a pen? Do the great English writers scorn you?'

'That's exactly it.'

'Because you are a proletarian?'

'I expect so.'

'Oh, Mr Wog, how I will satirize them in my reportage! It will enrage my editor. He will protest to the International Committee of Pens.'

'Jolly decent of him,' I said, perhaps rather weakly.

She wrote busily, in longhand, covering several leaves of her notebook. Then she said: 'Mr Wog, you have come here to satirize Happiland?'

'Certainly not.'

'Why then have you come?'

'Oh, just for the change.'

'That is interesting me very much. You think Happiland is greatly changed?'

'I mean for myself.'

'In what directions, please, do you wish to change?'

'In all directions.'

'So. And you come to Happiland for these changes? Because of the new Age-Spirit?'

That was a long snake, leading me back half-way down the board. 'Yes,' I said, contemptibly.

'And your school? That will change too?'

'Oh, I expect so. All the schools are changing every day, I'm told. . . . I know what you're going to ask; in what directions? Well, not so much classics, you know, modern languages, more stinks.'

This seemed a ladder.

'I am not understanding stinks, Mr Wog.'

'That's what we used to call science at my school.'

'Yes, yes, now I understand you. It is an American idiom. Science stinks, yes? You suffer the cosmic despair because of the atom bomb. You antagonize the sciences. In Happiland we are having many such desperate intellectuals. And to express this world-sorrow you are leading your school of proletarian satyrs to new language-forms away from the classics. Mr Wog, this will be a fine reportage.[1] I must go with it to my editor.'

[1] Waugh's diary for 19 August 1947 describes an interview with a 'dull young woman, fat', and goes on: 'when the interview appeared it was headed "Huxley's Ape makes hobby of graveyards".' An interview titled 'Kyrkogård hobby för Huxley's apa: här par besök' appeared in Dagens Nyheter (Stockholm), 20 August 1947, p. 11.

She was gone, and as I lay back among the singed bed-clothes I felt deep gratitude that none of my friends read Happilandic and deep compunction for the injustice which for years I had been doing a number of suffering fellow humans.

Think of this more or less true story, Gentle Reader, when you next feel moved to intolerance. It may be your turn next.

. FELIX CULPA? .

Of Mr Graham Greene alone among contemporary writers one can say without affectation that his breaking silence with a new serious novel is a literary 'event'. It is eight years since the publication of *The Power and the Glory*. During that time he has remained inconspicuous and his reputation has grown huge. We have had leisure to reread his earlier books and to appreciate the gravity and intensity which underlie their severe modern surface. More than this, the spirit of the time has begun to catch up with them.

The artist, however aloof he holds himself, is always and specially the creature of the *Zeitgeist*; however formally antique his tastes, he is in spite of himself in the advance guard. Men of affairs stumble far behind.

In the last twenty-five years the artist's interest has moved from sociology to eschatology. Out of hearing, out of sight, politicians and journalists and popular preachers exhort him to sing the splendours of high wages and sanitation. His eyes are on the Four Last Things, and so mountainous are the disappointments of recent history that there are already signs of a popular breakaway to join him, of a stampede to the heights.

I find the question most commonly asked by the agnostic is not: 'Do you believe in the authenticity of the Holy House at Loreto?' or 'Do you think an individual can justly inherit a right to the labour of another?' but 'Do you believe in Hell?'

Mr Greene has long shown an absorbing curiosity in the subject. In *Brighton Rock* he ingeniously gave life to a theological abstraction. We are often told: 'The Church does not teach that any man is damned. We only know that Hell exists for those who deserve it. Perhaps it is now empty and will remain so for all eternity.' This was not the sentiment of earlier and healthier ages. The Last Judgment above the mediaeval door showed the lost and the saved as fairly equally divided; the path to salvation as exceedingly narrow and beset with booby-traps; the reek of brimstone was everywhere. Mr Greene challenged the soft modern mood by creating a completely damnable youth. Pinkie of *Brighton Rock* is the ideal examinee for entry to Hell. He gets a pure alpha on every paper. His story is a brilliant and appalling imaginative achievement but falls

Review of *The Heart of the Matter*, by Graham Greene. *Commonweal*, 16 July 1948.

short of the real hell-fire sermon by its very completeness. We leave our seats edified but smug. However vile we are, we are better than Pinkie. The warning of the preacher was that one unrepented slip obliterated the accumulated merits of a lifetime's struggle to be good. *Brighton Rock* might be taken to mean that one has to be as wicked as Pinkie before one runs into serious danger.

Mr Greene's latest book, *The Heart of the Matter*, should be read as the complement of *Brighton Rock*. It poses a vastly more subtle problem. Its hero speaks of the Church as 'knowing all the answers', but his life and death comprise a problem to which the answer is in the mind of God alone, the reconciliation of perfect justice with perfect mercy. It is a book which only a Catholic could write and only a Catholic can understand. I mean that only a Catholic can understand the nature of the problem. Many Catholics, I am sure, will gravely misunderstand it, particularly in the United States of America, where its selection as the Book of the Month will bring it to a much larger public than can profitably read it. There are loyal Catholics here and in America who think it the function of the Catholic writer to produce only advertising brochures setting out in attractive terms the advantages of Church membership. To them this profoundly reverent book will seem a scandal. For it not only portrays Catholics as unlikeable human beings but shows them as tortured by their Faith. It will be the object of controversy and perhaps even of condemnation. Thousands of heathen will read it with innocent excitement, quite unaware that they are intruding among the innermost mysteries of faith. There is a third class who will see what this book intends and yet be troubled by doubt of its theological propriety.

Mr Greene divides his fiction into 'Novels' and 'Entertainments'. Superficially there is no great difference between the two categories. There is no Ruth Draper switch from comic to pathetic. 'Novels' and 'Entertainments' are both written in the same grim style, both deal mainly with charmless characters, both have a structure of sound, exciting plot. You cannot tell from the skeleton whether the man was baptized or not. And that is the difference; the 'Novels' have been baptized, held deep under in the waters of life. The author has said: 'These characters are not my creation but God's. They have an eternal destiny. They are not merely playing a part for the reader's amusement. They are souls whom Christ died to save.' This, I think, explains his preoccupation with the charmless. The children of Adam are not a race of noble savages who need only a divine spark to perfect them. They are aboriginally corrupt. Their tiny relative advantages of intelligence and taste and good looks and good manners are quite insignificant. The compassion and condescension of the Word becoming flesh are glorified in the depths.

As I have said above, the style of writing is grim. It is not a specifically literary style at all. The words are functional, devoid of sensuous attraction, of ancestry and of independent life. Literary stylists regard language as intrinsically precious and its proper use as a worthy and pleasant task. A polyglot could read Mr Greene, lay him aside, retain a sharp memory of all he said and yet, I think, entirely forget what tongue he was using. The words are simply mathematical signs for his thought. Moreover, no relation is established between writer and reader. The reader has not had a conversation with a third party such as he enjoys with Sterne or Thackeray. Nor is there within the structure of the story an observer through whom the events are recorded and the emotions transmitted. It is as though out of an infinite length of film, sequences had been cut which, assembled, comprise an experience which is the reader's alone, without any correspondence to the experience of the protagonists. The writer has become director and producer. Indeed, the affinity to the film is everywhere apparent. It is the camera's eye which moves from the hotel balcony to the street below, picks out the policeman, follows him to his office, moves about the room from the handcuffs on the wall to the broken rosary in the drawer, recording significant detail. It is the modern way of telling a story. In Elizabethan drama one can usually discern an artistic sense formed on the dumb-show and the masque. In Henry James's novels scene after scene evolves as though on the stage of a drawing-room comedy. Now it is the cinema which has taught a new habit of narrative. Perhaps it is the only contribution the cinema is destined to make to the arts.

There is no technical trick about good story-telling in this or any other manner. All depends on the natural qualities of the narrator's mind, whether or no he sees events in a necessary sequence. Mr Greene is a story-teller of genius. Born in another age, he would still be spinning yarns. His particular habits are accidental. The plot of *The Heart of the Matter* might well have been used by M. Simenon or Mr Somerset Maugham.

The scene is a West African port in war-time. It has affinities with the Brighton of *Brighton Rock*, parasitic, cosmopolitan, corrupt. The population are all strangers, British officials, detribalized natives, immigrant West Indian Negroes, Asiatics, Syrians. There are poisonous gossip at the club and voodoo bottles on the wharf, intrigues for administrative posts, intrigues to monopolize the illicit diamond trade. The hero, Scobie, is deputy-commissioner of police, one of the oldest inhabitants among the white officials; he has a compassionate liking for the place and the people. He is honest and unpopular and, when the story begins, he has been passed over for promotion. His wife Louise is also unpopular, for other reasons. She is neurotic and pretentious. Their only child died at school in England. Both are Catholic. His failure to get made commissioner is the final humiliation. She whines and nags to escape to South Africa. Two hundred pounds are needed to send her. Husband and wife are found together in the depths of distress.

The illegal export of diamonds is prevalent, both as industrial stones for the benefit of the enemy and gems for private investment. Scobie's police are entirely ineffective in stopping it, although it is notorious that two Syrians, Tallit and Yusef, are competitors for the monopoly. A police spy is sent from England to investigate. He falls in love with Louise. Scobie, in order to fulfil his promise to get Louise out of the country, borrows money from Yusef. As a result of this association he is involved in an attempt to 'frame' Tallit. The police spy animated by hate and jealousy is on his heels. Meanwhile survivors from a torpedoed ship are brought across from French territory, among them an English bride widowed in the sinking. She and Scobie fall in love and she becomes his mistress. Yusef secures evidence of the intrigue and blackmails Scobie into definitely criminal participation in his trade. His association with Yusef culminates in the murder of Ali, Scobie's supposedly devoted native servant, whom he now suspects of giving information to the police spy. Louise returns. Unable to abandon either woman, inextricably involved in crime, hunted by his enemy, Scobie takes poison; his women become listlessly acquiescent to other suitors.

These are the bare bones of the story, the ground plan on which almost any kind of building might be erected. The art of story-telling has little to do with the choice of plot. One can imagine the dreariest kind of film (Miss Bacall's pretty head lolling on the stretcher) accurately constructed to these specifications. Mr Greene, as his admirers would expect, makes of his material a precise and plausible drama. His technical mastery has never been better manifested than in his statement of the scene – the sweat and infection, the ill-built town, which is beautiful for a few minutes at sundown, the brothel where all men are equal, the vultures, the priest who, when he laughed 'swung his great empty-sounding bell to and fro, Ho, ho, ho, like a leper proclaiming his misery', the snobbery of the second-class public schools, the law which all can evade, the ever-present haunting underworld of gossip, spying, bribery, violence and betrayal. There are incidents of the highest imaginative power – Scobie at the bedside of a dying child, improvising his tale of the Bantus. It is so well done that one forgets the doer. The characters are real people whose moral and spiritual predicament is our own because they are part of our personal experience.

As I have suggested above, Scobie is the complement of Pinkie. Both believe in damnation and believe themselves damned. Both die in mortal sin as defined by moral theologians. The conclusion of the book is the reflection that no one knows the secrets of the human heart or the nature of God's mercy. It is improper to speculate on another's damnation. Nevertheless the reader is haunted by the question: Is Scobie damned? One does not really worry very much about whether Becky Sharp or Fagin is damned. It is the central question of *The Heart of the Matter*. I believe that Mr Greene thinks him a saint. Perhaps I am wrong in this, but in any case Mr Greene's opinion on that matter is of no more value than the reader's. Scobie is not Mr Greene's creature, devised to illustrate a thesis. He is a man of independent soul.[1] Can one separate his moral from his spiritual state? Both are complex and ambiguous.

First, there is his professional delinquency. In the first pages he appears as

1 In a letter dated 11 August 1948 about a proposed translation of this review, Waugh asked A. D. Peters to delete the passage, 'I believe that Mr Greene thinks him a saint . . . a man of independent soul', and to substitute for it, 'Several critics have taken Scobie to be a saint.' Waugh continued: 'You might make a note of this correction in case anyone else wants to reprint the review – as I should very much like them to do.' A letter to the *Tablet*, 17 July 1948, p. 41, makes the same correction.

an Aristides, disliked for his rectitude; by the end of the book he has become a criminal. There is nothing inevitable in his decline. He compromises himself first in order to get his wife's passage money. She is in a deplorable nervous condition; perhaps, even, her reason is in danger. He is full of compassion. But she is making his own life intolerable; he wants her out of the way for his own peace. As things turn out the trip to South Africa was quite unnecessary. Providence had its own cure ready if he had only waited. He gets the commissionership in the end, which was ostensibly all that Louise wanted. But behind that again lies the deeper cause of her melancholy, that Scobie no longer loves her in the way that would gratify her vanity. And behind the betrayal of his official trust lies the futility of his official position. The law he administers has little connection with morals or justice. It is all a matter of regulations – a Portuguese sea-captain's right to correspond with his daughter in Germany, the right of a tenant to divide and sub-let her hut, the right of a merchant to provide out of his own property for the security of his family. He knows that his subordinates are corrupt and can do nothing about it. Whom or what has he in fact betrayed, except his own pride?

Secondly, there is his adultery. His affection for the waif cast up on the beach is at first compassionate and protective; it becomes carnal. Why? He is an elderly man long schooled in chastity. There is another suitor of Helen Rolt, Bagster the Air Force philanderer. It is Bagster's prowling round the bungalow which precipitates the change of relationship. It is Bagster in the background who makes him persevere in adultery when his wife's return affords a convenient occasion for parting. Bagster is a promiscuous cad. Helen must be saved from Bagster. Why? Scobie arrogates to himself the prerogatives of providence. He presumes that an illicit relation with himself is better than an illicit relation with Bagster. But why, in fact, need it have been illicit? She might marry Bagster.

Thirdly, there is the murder of Ali. We do not know whether Ali was betraying him. If he had not been a smuggler and an adulterer there would have been nothing to betray. Ali dies to emphasize the culpability of these sins.

Fourthly, there are the sacrilegious communions which Louise forces upon him; and fifthly, his suicide, a restatement of that blasphemy in other terms. He dies believing himself damned but also in an obscure way – at least in a way that is obscure to me – believing that he is offering his damnation as a loving sacrifice for others.

We are told that he is actuated throughout by the love of God. A love, it is true, that falls short of trust, but a love, we must suppose, which sanctifies his sins. That is the heart of the matter. Is such a sacrifice feasible? To me the idea is totally unintelligible, but it is not unfamiliar. Did the Quietists not speak in something like these terms? I ask in all humility whether nowadays logical rule-of-thumb Catholics are not a little too humble towards the mystics. We are inclined to say: 'Ah, that is mysticism. I'm quite out of my depth there,' as though the subject were higher mathematics, while in fact our whole Faith is essentially mystical. We may well fight shy of discussing ecstatic states of prayer with which we have no acquaintance, but sacrilege and suicide are acts of which we are perfectly capable. To me the idea of willing my own damnation for the love of God is either a very loose poetical expression or a mad blasphemy, for the God who accepted that sacrifice could be neither just nor lovable.

Mr Greene has put a quotation from Péguy at the beginning of the book: '*Le pécheur est au coeur même de chrétienté . . . Nul n'est aussi compétent que le pécheur en matière de chrétienté. Nul, si ce n'est le saint,*' and it seems to me probable that it was in his mind to illustrate the '*Nouveau Théologien*' from which it is taken, just as in *Brighton Rock* he illustrates the Penny Catechism. The theme of that remarkable essay is that Christianity is a city to which a bad citizen belongs and the good stranger does not. Péguy describes the Church, very beautifully, as a chain of saints and sinners with clasped fingers, pulling one another up to Jesus. But there are also passages which, if read literally, are grossly exorbitant. Péguy was not three years a convert when he wrote it, and he was not in communion with the Church. He daily saw men and women, who seemed to him lacking his own intense spirituality, trooping up to the altar rails while he was obliged to stay in his place excommunicate. The '*Nouveau Théologien*' is his meditation on his predicament. He feels there is a city of which he is a true citizen, but it is not the community of conventional practising Catholics, who are not, in his odd, often repeated phrase, '*compétent en matière de chrétienté*'. He feels a kinship with the saints that these conventional church-goers do not know and in his strange, narrow, brooding mind he makes the preposterous deduction that this very true and strong bond is made, not by his faith and love, but by his sins. '*Littéralement*,' he writes, '*celui qui est pécheur, celui qui commet un péché est déjà chrétien, est en cela même chrétien. On pourrait presque dire est un bon chrétien*.' '*Littéralement*'?: what is the precise force of that passage? Much depends on it. Does 'literally' mean that any and every sinner is by virtue of his sin a Christian? Was Yusef a sinner and therefore Christian? No, because Péguy has already stated that strangers outside the chain of clasped hands cannot commit sin at all. Is Yusef damned? Can a sinner by this definition never be damned? The argument works in a circle of undefined terms. And what of the '*presque*'? How does one 'almost' say something? Is one prevented by the fear of shocking others or the realization at the last moment that what one was going to say does not in fact make sense? In that case why record it? Why 'almost' say it? This is not a matter of quibbling. If Péguy is saying anything at all, he is saying something very startling and something which people seem to find increasingly important. Mr Greene has removed the argument from Péguy's mumbled version and restated it in brilliantly plain human terms; and it is there, at the heart of the matter, that the literary critic must resign his judgment to the theologian.

. COME INSIDE .

I was born in England in 1903 with a strong hereditary predisposition toward the Established Church. My family tree burgeons on every twig with Anglican clergymen. My father was what was called a 'sound churchman'; that is to say, he attended church regularly and led an exemplary life. He had no interest in theology. He had no interest in politics but always voted Tory as his father and grandfather had done. In the same spirit he was punctilious in his religious duties.

At the age of 10 I composed a long and tedious poem about Purgatory in the metre of *Hiawatha* and to the dismay of my parents, who held a just estimate of my character, expressed my intention of becoming a clergyman. The enthusiasm which my little school-fellows devoted to birds' eggs and model trains I turned on church affairs and spoke glibly of chasubles and Erastianism. I was accordingly sent to the school which was reputed to have the strongest ecclesiastical bent. At the age of 16 I formally notified the school chaplain that there was no God. At the age of 26 I was received into the Catholic Church to which all subsequent experience has served to confirm my loyalty.

I am now invited to explain these vagaries.

First, of my early religiosity. I am reluctant to deny all reality to that precocious enthusiasm, but it was in the main a hobby like the birds' eggs and model trains of my school-fellows. The appeal was part hereditary and part aesthetic. Many are drawn in this way throughout their lives. In my case it was a concomitant of puberty. But those of my readers outside England should understand that the aesthetic appeal of the Church of England is unique and peculiar to those islands. Elsewhere a first interest in the Catholic Church is often kindled in the convert's imagination by the splendours of her worship in contrast with the bleakness and meanness of the Protestant sects. In England the pull is all the other way. The mediaeval cathedrals and churches, the rich ceremonies that surround the monarchy, the historic titles of Canterbury and York, the social organization of the country parishes, the traditional culture of Oxford and Cambridge, the liturgy composed in the heyday of English prose style – all these are the property of the Church of England, while Catholics meet in modern buildings, often of deplorable design, and are usually served by simple Irish missionaries.

The shallowness of my early piety is shown by the ease with which I abandoned it. There are, of course, countless Catholics who, for a part of their lives at least, lose their faith, but it is always after a bitter struggle – usually a moral struggle. I shed my inherited faith as lightheartedly as though it had been an outgrown coat. The circumstances were these: during the First World War many university dons patriotically volunteered to release young school-

The Road to Damascus, ed. John A. O'Brien. New York and London, 1949.

masters to serve in the army. Among these there came to my school a leading Oxford theologian, now a bishop. This learned and devout man inadvertently made me an atheist.[1] He explained to his divinity class that none of the books of the Bible were by their supposed authors; he invited us to speculate, in the manner of the fourth century, on the nature of Christ. When he had removed the inherited axioms of my faith I found myself quite unable to follow him in the higher flights of logic by which he reconciled his own scepticism with his position as a clergyman.

At the same time I read Pope's *Essay on Man*; the notes led me to Leibnitz and I began an unguided and half-comprehended study of metaphysics. I advanced far enough to be thoroughly muddled about the nature of cognition. It seemed simplest to abandon the quest and assume that man was incapable of knowing anything. I have no doubt I was a prig and a bore but I think that if I had been a Catholic boy at a Catholic school I should have found among its teaching orders someone patient enough to examine with me my callow presumption. Also, if I had been fortified by the sacraments, I should have valued my faith too highly to abandon it so capriciously. At my school I was quite correctly regarded as 'going through a phase' normal to all clever boys, and left to find my own way home.

The next ten years of my life are material more suitable to the novelist than the essayist. Those who have read my works will perhaps understand the character of the world into which I exuberantly launched myself. Ten years of that world sufficed to show me that life there, or anywhere, was unintelligible and unendurable without God. The conclusion was obvious; the question now arises: why Rome? A Catholic who loses his faith and rediscovers the need of it returns inevitably to the Church he left. Why did not I?

Here, I think, the European has some slight advantage in particular over the American. It is possible, I conceive, for a man to grow up in parts of the United States without ever being really aware of the Church's unique position. He sees Catholics as one out of a number of admirable societies, each claiming his allegiance. That is not possible for a European. England was Catholic for nine hundred years, then Protestant for three hundred, then agnostic for a century. The Catholic structure still lies lightly buried beneath every phase of English life; history, topography, law, archaeology everywhere reveal Catholic origins. Foreign travel anywhere reveals the local, temporary character of the heresies and schisms and the universal, eternal character of the Church. It was self-evident to me that no heresy or schism could be right and the Church wrong. It was possible that all were wrong, that the whole Christian revelation was an imposture or a misconception. But if the Christian revelation was true, then the Church was the society founded by Christ and all other bodies were only good so far as they had salvaged something from the wrecks of the Great

1 Waugh's diary of 4 March 1956 records his meeting 'the Bishop of Derby . . . Mr Rawlinson who came to Lancing in 1918 as a fiery young don from the House, a modernist, one of the authors of 'Foundations' . . . whose agnosticism first unsettled my childish faith . . .'

Schism and the Reformation. This proposition seemed so plain to me that it admitted of no discussion. It only remained to examine the historical and philosophic grounds for supposing the Christian revelation to be genuine. I was fortunate enough to be introduced to a brilliant and holy priest who undertook to prove this to me, and so on firm intellectual conviction but with little emotion I was admitted into the Church.

My life since then has been an endless delighted tour of discovery in the huge territory of which I was made free. I have heard it said that some converts in later life look back rather wistfully to the fervour of their first months of faith. With me it is quite the opposite. I look back aghast at the presumption with which I thought myself suitable for reception and with wonder at the trust of the priest who saw the possibility of growth in such a dry soul.

From time to time friends outside the Church consult me. They are attracted by certain features, repelled or puzzled by others. To them I can only say, from my own experience: 'Come inside. You cannot know what the Church is like from outside. However learned you are in theology, nothing you know amounts to anything in comparison with the knowledge of the simplest actual member of the Communion of Saints.'

. ELECTED SILENCE .

This very remarkable autobiography has, under the title of *The Seven Storey Mountain*, enjoyed prodigious success in the USA. The present text has been renamed and very slightly abridged in order to adapt it to European tastes. Nothing has been cut out except certain passages which seemed to be of purely local interest.[1] It remains essentially American. Despite a cosmopolitan childhood, 'Thomas Merton' – Father Louis, as he is now named – is typical of what is newest and best in his country. Columbia not Cambridge formed his literary style. His spirituality, though French in discipline, is a flower of the Catholic life of the New World. Americans no longer become expatriates in their quest for full cultural development. They are learning to draw away from what is distracting in their own civilization while remaining in their own borders.

Here in fresh, simple, colloquial American is the record of a soul experiencing, first, disgust with the modern world, then Faith, then a clear vocation to the way in which Faith may be applied to the modern world. The word 'prodigious' is used with full intent. It is a prodigy of the new spirit of the New World that this book should have been read by hundreds of thousands. For several generations American Catholics have abounded in works of corporate charity such as still flourish everywhere, and in recent years have produced

Foreword to *Elected Silence*, by Thomas Merton. London, 1949.
1 Waugh edited Merton's text for the English market, cutting about one third and rewriting much of what remained. See R. M. Davis, 'How Waugh Cut Merton', *Month*, April 1973, pp. 150–53.

such typically contemporary enterprises as Friendship House in Harlem and the House of Hospitality in Mott Street. The contemplative life has until very lately drawn few in proportion to the numbers. Now Carmelite convents can barely cope with the press of postulants, and the Trappists are opening new houses in the Deep South and in the hills of Utah. But the life of these communities is by its nature unostentatious, and *The Seven Storey Mountain* came as a startling revelation to most non-Catholic Americans who were quite unaware of the existence in their midst of institutions which seemed a denial of the American 'way of life'. The book suddenly made remote people conscious of warmth silently generated in these furnaces of devotion. To one observer at least it seems probable that the USA will shortly be the scene of a great monastic revival. There is an ascetic tradition deep in the American heart which has sometimes taken odd and unlovable forms. Here in the historic Rules of the Church lies its proper fulfilment.

In the natural order the modern world is rapidly being made uninhabitable by the scientists and politicians. We are back in the age of Gregory, Augustine and Boniface, and in compensation the Devil is being disarmed of many of his former enchantments. Power is all he can offer now; the temptations of wealth and elegance no longer assail us. As in the Dark Ages the cloister offers the sanest and most civilized way of life.

And in the supernatural order the times require more than a tepid and dutiful piety. Prayer must become heroic. That is the theme of this book which should take its place among the classic records of spiritual experience.

. THE OCCASIONAL SERMONS OF MGR RONALD KNOX .

Of the eleven sermons here presented, one only, now entitled 'Success', has previously appeared in a book, *Captive Flames*, to whose publishers, Messrs Burns and Oates, thanks are due for permission to include it. Some have been printed from time to time in the *Tablet*; others are now published for the first. A few very small changes have been made to adapt the spoken to the written word; otherwise they are exactly as they were originally delivered on the occasions indicated.

There is some excuse for the intrusion of the editor's name on the title page of this book for it comprises a purely personal selection. It makes no attempt to illustrate the full scope of the author's talents; still less to provide a conspectus of his thought. One admirer, merely, has taken it on himself to name what he thinks the most notable of Mgr Knox's achievements in a single field of his art.

Preface to *A Selection from the Occasional Sermons of the Rt Reverend Monsignor Ronald Arbuthnott Knox . . .*, ed. Evelyn Waugh. (London, 1949.)

Mgr Knox has been a priest for more than thirty years and almost every week of that time he has illumined with a delicate and original composition, storing up a unique emporium of varied material – the fine linen of his devotional conferences; the durable tweed of his instruction at the Old Palace (stuff of traditional pattern fit to make for a young man a coat that will last him to the grave); fresh little lace handkerchiefs for the schoolgirls at Aldenham; rich carpets spread for the feet of prelates and scholars. It is from this last range that the present collection is chiefly made; some are more intimate, some more formal, but all have it in common that they were designed for single specific occasions.

It has not been a propitious age for the fame of a preacher. Microphone and magazine have largely usurped the place of the pulpit, but the sermon remains a classic literary form, long anterior to the essay or the novel. The libraries of our grandparents bear witness to the esteem in which they – indeed in which every previous age – held it. Mgr Knox is almost alone today as the scion of this long and illustrious descent.

One plain difference is apparent between him and his great predecessors – his brevity. With a humility which does greater honour to themselves than to the laity, the clergy of today seem to believe that twenty minutes is the extreme span of patient attention, so that the panegyric, the form most apt for grand architectural plan and enrichment, is in danger of following the masque and the epic into obsolescence. For this reason the orations here splendidly printed have a literary importance independent of the religious sympathies which they presuppose.

Delicacy and originality have been predicated of them – neither a quality common in the pulpit; least of all, perhaps, in the Church which proclaims an orthodox and complete theological system. For generation after generation the same lessons have to be hammered home and the preacher may well be counted successful who is content merely to restate them and render them memorable in topical and arresting phrases. Year after year the solemn festivals recur; thirty Easters, thirty Pentecosts – and a new thought for each!

There is a further straitening of the preacher's case; the proverbial half-truth that he is addressing himself to the converted whose presence in the pew is evidence of agreement. Mgr Knox is not, in the ordinary sense, a missionary and the crowds who flock to hear him are, in general, better instructed and more attentive to the claims of their religion than the average parochial congregation. It might seem not only bold but superfluous to preach to the assembled Hierarchy.

But this is far from the full truth, for to every man, however learned or devout, there come occasions when he hears a familiar dogma or precept as though for the first time. Many – perhaps most – Catholics cultivate widely scattered small-holdings in the great territory of their faith. A few truths seem self-evident and of practical importance. The rest we take on trust and if, as sometimes happens, we learn on authority that we have got the wrong end of the stick in some philosophical question, we reverse our opinion without being greatly disconcerted. But to a wider view Right is homogeneous and indivisible, Wrong something foreign, eternally at war with the Truth, eternally unassimilable, and it is only through the existence of shadowy districts in the soul that it can ever reside there undetected. Faith expands year by year as some formulary, long implicitly accepted, suddenly takes life and becomes a matter of urgent personal importance. To strike these lights in the mind is the preacher's highest gift. Sometimes it is done, humanly speaking, by telepathy. There are great preachers whose recorded sermons make unimpressive reading. Once they overwhelmed multitudes; today the man himself is lacking. He had to be there himself, visible and audible, communicating his own faith in some fashion that was independent of his words. Mgr Knox's message owes nothing to these preternatural gifts. It survives entire in black and white, as compelling in print as in his quiet, scholar's voice. His ideas, complex and seemingly incongruous, come together, fuse, and become simple, permanent and luminous. That, rather than his abounding verbal felicity, is what makes his art notable. Those are the occasions.

. KICKING AGAINST THE GOAD .

I have just read in a London newspaper the following paragraph: 'Evelyn Waugh is in trouble. He's being quoted from coast to coast (of USA) as saying that Americans heat their rooms to 75 degrees, nail down the windows, chew coloured bubble gum, keep their radios on all day and talk too much – poor Waugh is being kicked all the way down Main Street.'[1]

No man of honour patiently submits to kicking, but I cannot pretend that at my own fireside, 3,000 miles from Main Street, I have found the experience unendurable. Moreover, I am very sure that the countless Americans whose friendship I value took no part in the outrage. I should not, therefore, protest were it not that the incident seems to me a tiny window opening upon very wide prospects of general misunderstanding.

First, as regards the incident. Certain trades and classes seek personal publicity; not so respectable writers, for their entire vocation is one of self-expression and it seems obvious to them that if they cannot make themselves understood in years of laborious writing, they will not succeed in a few minutes of conversation. So when we see interviewers advancing, we fly. But on the last day of a recent, happy visit to the USA, I was caught by a very young lady and talked earnestly to her for nearly an hour. She asked what had impressed me most in America. I said the Trappist Monastery in Kentucky. It transpired

Commonweal, 11 March 1949.
1 'Don Iddon's Diary: New York, Tuesday'. Daily Mail, 12 January 1949, p. 4.

that the wretched girl was as ignorant of the simplest truths of Christianity as Topsy in *Uncle Tom's Cabin*. My apostolic zeal was roused, and, frankly, I preached to her. In particular, I told her about monasticism. It is a subject I have at heart because I believe that we are returning to a stage when on the supernatural plane only heroic prayer can save us and when, on the natural plane, the cloister offers a saner and more civilized life than 'the world'. There was little need to expatiate on this latter point in regard to Europe and Asia, where oppression, anarchy, famine and massacre are commonplaces, but when I found her bewildered by the physical austerities of the Trappist rule, I did point out that her own way of life had its painful features – overheated rooms, radio and so forth.

The puzzled catechumen then cabled to London some fragments of her instruction. There a sub-editor plied his hideous trade. What he left was picked up by correspondents in London and cabled back to sub-editors in New York, so that eventually these few trite and irrelevant comments were all that emerged from my unaccustomed and well meant flow of eloquence. It was my own fault. I should have known better than to give tongue. It is not of the least importance that one foreign visitor should have been made a fool of, but it is important that the process is being repeated hourly in hundreds of similar cases, with the result that incalculable volumes of malice and misunderstanding are being constantly generated. And that is a bad thing for all of us.

A second alarming thought follows; one affecting the whole relationship of the public to a writer, and especially to a foreign writer. It is plain to me from the comments on this interview that the general reader believes he is doing the writer a great personal kindness in buying his books.

Now when I buy a new hat, I do so because I need one. I go to a hatter who, I believe, knows his job. If the hat disintegrated in the first fall of rain, I should make a row about it. But I do not assume that because I have bought a hat from him the hatter is in honour bound to think my head an object of reverence. Nor do I suppose I am entitled to a photograph of the hatter's mother and to an itemized account of his private life. I do not expect the hatter to love me. And yet hats are more costly than books and, in some cases, of less permanent value. But readers, even when they have not bought a book at all but merely borrowed it, do apparently sincerely believe that a writer is bound to them by ties of the most tender affection and gratitude.

It so happens that I like visiting America, love and respect countless Americans, and, knowing their peculiar sensitiveness, take pains not to make the kind of criticisms of them that I should freely make of any other nation, most of all my own. But there are many European writers who have, perhaps, not been so fortunate as I have in the Americans they have met, and therefore strongly dislike the country and strongly say so. At once the whine goes up. 'Boohoo, the beast! We buy his books, and yet he does not love us. He only loves our dollars.' But that is the precise nature of the transaction. The writer sweats to write well; the reader sweats to make dollars; writer and reader exchange books for dollars.

And this raises the most curious point of all. There does seem to be in modern industrial society a popular belief that when an exchange takes place of goods and money, the party who pays the money has, somehow, conferred a benefit on the party who delivers the goods. This is a mercantile system gone stark crazy, for money is quite valueless except as the symbol of the goods for which it can be exchanged. When I walk out of my hatter's, I have on my head an object which he has been at great pains to make, and I have chosen as fulfilling my need, an object which will retain its character and usefulness for years to come. I leave him with some bits of paper which may in an hour, through a whim of the government, become quite valueless. Money is only useful when you get rid of it. It is like the odd card in 'Old Maid'; the player who is finally left with it has lost. That is a thought which should vex the garrison at Fort Knox.

. PIONEER! O PIONEER! .

'Here is a selection of stories,' writes Mr Lehmann, the publisher, 'that will delight those who are weary both of the tough background and the sentimental approach so characteristic of much modern fiction.'

'Boom!' writes Mr Powers, the author thus commended. 'Clyde hits Banjo twice in the chin and mouth quick and drops him like a handkerchief. Banjo is all over the floor and his mouth is hanging open like a spring is busted and blood is leaking out the one side and he has got some bridgework loose.

' "Hand me the nine, Roy," Clyde says to me. I get the nine ball and give it to Clyde. He shoves it way into Banjo's mouth that is hanging open and bleeding good.

'Then Clyde lets him have one more across the jaw and you can hear the nine ball rattle inside Banjo's mouth.'

One is curious to know what Mr Lehmann keeps under the counter for those who are *not* 'weary of the tough background'. Indeed Mr Lehmann seems, with singular fatuity, to have picked out for praise the only two serious defects in Mr Powers's art. For this otherwise admirable young writer is sentimental also – unexceptionally – in his gentle account of the death of an old friar in 'Lions, harts, leaping does'; less agreeably in 'The Old Bird; a love story'. The shadows of Hemingway and Steinbeck lie over the work but not so heavily as to obscure the brilliant and determining quality which Mr Lehmann does not choose to notice. The book is Catholic. Mr Powers has a full philosophy with which to oppose the follies of his age and nation.

This is very much more remarkable in the USA than in Europe. Here, what is infelicitously dubbed 'the Catholic Intellectual' is a commonplace; there he is scarcely known. Indeed the nation has a dismal record of 'intellectual'

Review of *Prince of Darkness*, by J. F. Powers. *Month*, March 1949.

apostasies. In England we should be somewhat disconcerted to see a man described as a 'leading Baptist novelist' or a 'notable recruit to the younger school of Presbyterian poets'. In rather the same way Americans know the Catholic Church for countless solid virtues but not as the parent or nurse of the Arts. Many American Catholics are becoming aware of this anomaly and discuss it freely and anxiously. This is not the place to examine it, but merely to note that Mr Powers's position is lonely. Fr Thomas Merton's Trappist calling removes him from the general traffic of literary life; Mr Harry Sylvester betrays at moments an all too fierce impatience with the restraints of orthodoxy; Mr Powers is almost unique in his country as a lay writer who is at ease in the Church; whose whole art, moreover, is everywhere infused and directed by his Faith.

This is not to say either that he is a propagandist or that he here deals, like Bernanos, with high supernatural problems. He is concerned with the natural order as a pure story-teller; matter and manner are topical and local; base-ball, jazz, the Negro problem, usury, the search for a living, the daily round of the presbytery – these are his subjects but all are seen in true perspective. Man has a purpose and a proper place in creation in Mr Powers's stories as he has not in those which superficially resemble them – the *New Yorker* school. It is perhaps the tales of the presbytery which will most delight the English reader as being at the same time the most novel and the most intelligible. Here we see the Middle West Irish priest – chaste, philistine, prosaic, energetic in youth, run rather to fat in age – who provides the strength and the limitations of the American Church.

The most remarkable of these stories is the one which gives its name to the book. 'Prince of Darkness' is a magnificent study of sloth – a sin which has not attracted much attention of late and which, perhaps, is the besetting sin of the age. Catholic novelists have dealt at length with lust, blasphemy, cruelty and greed – these provide obvious dramatic possibilities. We have been inclined to wink at sloth; even, in a world of go-getters, almost to praise it. An imaginative writer has advantages over the preacher and Mr Powers exposes this almost forgotten, widely practised, capital sin, in a way which brought an alarming whiff of brimstone to the nostrils of at least one reader.

. ROSSETTI REVISITED .
PRE-RAPHAELISM AND RELIGION

D. G. Rossetti died at the age of 54, after spending the last ten years of his life in seclusion. Thus very few who had known him were alive in 1928 to celebrate the centenary of his birth. Much was written on that occasion. Writers had two

Review of *Dante Gabriel Rossetti*, by Helen Rossetti Angeli. *Tablet*, 16 July 1949.

bodies of material to work on. There were the established authorities – the publications of William Rossetti and the autobiographies and official biographies of eminent contemporaries – and there was a large accumulation of hearsay, some of it in print, from less reputable sources. It was a time when interest in Rossetti's painting was slight, both among critics and collectors; how slight his niece and latest biographer, Mrs Angeli, does not perhaps fully realize. Writers therefore tended to concentrate more upon their subject's private life, which had many rather macabre features. Ironically, it has been largely this curiosity about the man which has in recent years led to a re-examination and wider popularity of his art. 1928 was a year when irreverence in biography was highly fashionable. Mrs Angeli uses altogether too strong a term when she describes this mood as one of 'denigration', but it is true that a student of that date in perusing his texts was likely to have his eye caught by the less pleasant items. There was an abundance of these in Rossetti's life. There were also a number of more agreeable elements which Mrs Angeli believes were not sufficiently emphasized. Her dutiful aim in writing her book has been to redress the balance.

Her advantages for the task are a keen sense of mission, a lively style and, of course, her family connections. She did not know her uncle but she knew many of the survivors of his generation. In the main she has had to rely on the same established authorities as her predecessors. Her father's editorship of the family papers was scrupulous and unusually candid – so candid indeed as to incur the censure of Edmund Gosse. Most of Mrs Angeli's quotations are from published sources. She has followed the same method, with contrary aim, as the biographers she rebukes. She has patiently collected all that was amiable about her uncle. She has also exposed a number of misstatements which have gained currency. In this she has done her uncle's memory some service. But does the book succeed in its avowed intention of presenting an authentic and admirable character in place of what she wrongly supposes to be malicious travesty? With all respect to her *pietas* the answer, for one reader at least, is: no.

Consider for example the circumstances of Elizabeth Siddal's suicide, upon which she very properly directs close scrutiny. Violet Hunt declared that the note pinned to the nightgown comprised the words: 'My life is so miserable I wish for no more of it.' When challenged she gave a very unsatisfactory account of the authority for her statement. It seems probable, in fact, that she was entirely mistaken about that and other incidents of the evening. Mrs Angeli successfully convicts Violet Hunt of wild irresponsibility, but this does nothing to exculpate Rossetti. Presumably every suicide finds life so miserable as to wish for no more of it. When the victim is a young woman two years married, is it very uncharitable to suggest that her husband's behaviour towards her had something to do with it? We shall never know the full story, but we know that Rossetti had made the acquaintance of both the women who most affected his life – Fanny Cornforth and Janey Morris – before his wife's death; we know his wife killed herself; we know he was periodically obsessed by guilt ever afterwards.

Mrs Angeli deeply resents the imputation that her uncle was sharp about money and stoutly maintains that an artist is fully justified in selling his work for the highest possible price. Of course he is, and no one ever blamed Rossetti on that score. What his critics complain of is that he painted too much with an eye to the market, as Millais did and as Holman Hunt and Burne-Jones did not, and further that his methods of sale should have made him particularly scrupulous; he did not exhibit and let his pictures find their just market price. He dealt personally with most of his patrons, profiting by the mystical awe which surrounded an artist in their simple mercantile minds; when the bargain was struck a new process often began of postponement and substitution. His honour was involved in these intricate transactions whose records leave the reader in no doubt as to which party he would sooner have dealings with.

Sloth is the kindest excuse for his repeated evasion of his obligations. But Mrs Angeli stops this earth by claiming for him 'exemplary diligence'. She has wrestled bravely and won a few falls, particularly about Rossetti's alleged quarrelsomeness. Many of his old friends prove as testy as he. But she is out of her weight. She floors some of his frailer critics, but, when the dust settles, Rossetti emerges very much as he was before – a haunted and haunting figure of unfulfilled promise.

Near the close of her book Mrs Angeli suggests an explanation. He was, she writes, 'by innate tendency as religious-minded as his sisters.'

How does anybody maintain health of mind outside the Church? It becomes increasingly rare as more chinks appear in the iron curtain of invincible ignorance. In 1760 many educated Englishmen were safe in its shelter; in 1860 far fewer. In particular the Pre-Raphaelites knew too much about the Church to thrive outside it. In each of them, Ruskin especially, one sees the large gaps of his want of faith, but most of all in the Rossettis, who were implicated in recent apostasy on both sides of their family and had no patriotic tradition to take the place of their lost loyalty. On the question of her forebears' loss of faith, Mrs Angeli is less than frank. 'They may *almost*' (my italics), she writes, 'be termed *dissenters* from the Church. Neither of them actually repudiated the Faith of their forefathers.' In fact Gabriele Rossetti was a prominent and active Freemason. 'His religious opinions,' according to William, 'progressed into very fierce opposition to Papal dogma' and the sacramental system; his writings 'often developed the anti-Christian views of other authors' until late in his life when a new coterie formed round him, of 'disfrocked priests and semi-Waldensian semi-simpletons' who drew him into their association to convert Italy to Protestantism.

It has been customary to treat Gabriele lightly on the supposition that foreign revolutionaries are always funny. In the last thirty years Englishmen have had to revise that opinion. It may well be that Gabriele was up to much more public mischief than appeared. Certainly he did a huge injury to Gabriel in depriving him of his faith. Gabriel's was not a logical mind that could work its way to the truth without strong sentimental pressure; and his sentiments were peculiarly wayward. Once at least he expressed a desire for Penance, his primal need. If he had been schooled in the habit, once firmly attached to that invisible thread of Chesterton's, his moral failure, which at every point frustrated his genius, would have been saved.

Deprived of the sacraments, imaginative minds invent all kinds of fetishes for themselves. Woman for Rossetti assumed a transcendental and magical significance. Nothing could be more inept than Buchanan's charge that he exalted 'fleshliness'. His fault was quite the contrary, and Mrs Angeli shows she is aware of this. Cheated of the knowledge and love of the Mother of God, Rossetti fell into the vague idolatry of ideal womanhood, incarnate in certain pathetically inadequate types. This aberration spoiled him as a man and as an artist. And for this the political passion of his father was largely responsible.

. THE AMERICAN EPOCH IN THE CATHOLIC CHURCH .

'AD or BC?' How often among the monuments of the Old World, the dazed sightseer asks this question, interrupting the guide's flow of dates! How often he wearily leaves it unasked! AD 100 or 100 BC; a span of two centuries; what does that matter, one way or the other, compared with the huge, crowded interval between then and now?

For most people the birth of Christ is a chronological device, used beyond the bounds of Christendom in Delhi and Tel Aviv and Moscow; a date-line as arbitrary as the meridian of Greenwich. It is not even accurate, for Christ was born four or five years before the traditional date. From time to time politicians have sought to impose an exploit of their own – the first French Republic, the Fascist March on Rome – as a more notable event from which to number the years. The old calendar came back for reasons of convenience rather than piety. But the Christian, when he dates his letters from the Year of Our Lord, is affirming his Faith. He is placing the Incarnation where for him it must always stand, in the centre of human history. Before that Year of Grace man lived in the mists, haunted by ancestral memories of a lost Eden, taught enigmatically by hints and portents, punished by awful dooms. The Incarnation restored order. In place of his bloody guilt-offerings man was given a single, complete expiytion; in place of his magic, the sacramental system, a regular service of communication with the supernatural; in place of his mystery-cults, an open, divinely constituted human society in which to live and multiply. All his history from then onwards, seen through Christian eyes, all the migrations of peoples and the rise and fall of empires, comprise merely a succession of moods and phases in the life of that society, the Church Christ founded.

Month, November 1949. First printed *Life* (Chicago), 19 September 1949.

In this deep perspective it seems that in every age some one branch of the Church, racial, cultural or national, bears peculiar responsibilities towards the whole. Vitality mysteriously waxes and wanes among the peoples. Again and again Christianity seems dying at its centre. Always Providence has another people quietly maturing to relieve the decadent of their burden. To a Christian of the fourth century the seat of authority at Rome must have seemed almost on the frontier; France, Spain and Germany were crude, missionary countries while all that was subtle and gracious in the Faith flourished in the southern and eastern Mediterranean. For him it was barely possible to conceive of a Church which had lost Constantinople, Alexandria and Carthage. To Louis XIV the Faith of those places belonged to remote history. He could not think of Christendom without France. Yet in less than a century France was officially atheist. Challoner, the saintly Catholic leader of eighteenth-century England, would have thought it a preposterous forecast that the grandchildren of his dim, disheartened little flock would see the bishops restored and the religious orders flourishing in every county. So the battle continues, one that can never be lost and may never be won until the Last Trump. No loss is impossible, no loss irretrievable, no loss – not Rome itself – mortal. It may well be that Catholics of today, in their own lifetime, may have to make enormous adjustments in their conception of the temporal nature of the Church. Many indeed are already doing so, and in the process turning their regard with hope and curiosity to the New World, where, it seems, Providence is schooling and strengthening a people for the historic destiny long borne by Europe.

Hope and curiosity. At first sight hope is subdued by many features of American history and psychology. Indeed, it could be quite plausibly argued that the people of the United States were resolutely anti-Catholic. Although most of the great adventures of exploration in the new continent were made by Catholic missionaries, the first colonists (everywhere except in Maryland) were Protestants whose chief complaint against their mother country was that she retained too much traditional character in her Established Church. School textbooks do not make much of the fact, which research abundantly proves, that it was the Quebec Act tolerating Popery in Canada, quite as much as the Stamp Act and the Tea Duties, which rendered George III intolerable to the colonists. The Constitution-makers little thought that in separating Church and State they were laying their country open to the prodigious Catholic growth of the nineteenth century, and in recent months the Supreme Court has shown in the McCollum case,[1] that the phrase may be interpreted to the Church's injury. In foreign policy, when religious questions were involved, America has usually supported the anti-Catholic side, particularly where she is most powerful, in Mexico. President Wilson did nothing to oppose the disastrous anti-Catholic prejudices of the peace-makers of 1919.

Moreover the individual qualities that are regarded as particularly charac-

1 Mrs Vashti McCollum sued to have religious instruction discontinued in public schools attended by her son. The Supreme Court ruled in her favour in 1948.

teristic of Americans, their endemic revolt against traditional authority, their respect for success and sheer activity, their belief that progress is beneficent, their welcome of novelties, their suspicion of titles and uniforms and cere- monies, their dislike of dogmas that divide good citizens and their love of the generalities which unite them, their resentment of discipline – all these and others are unsympathetic to the habits of the Church. Mr Geoffrey Gorer has discerned deep in the American soul a psychopathic antagonism to paternity and all its symbols;[1] Catholics call both their priests and their God 'Father'. The language of the Church is largely that of the court; her liturgy was composed in lands where the honorific titles of royalty were accepted naturally and it abounds in phrases which sound strange on republican and democratic lips. Many pages could be filled with instances of this kind, proving on paper very cogently that America can never play an important part in the life of the Church. It would be a fatuous exercise, for already at this moment Catholics are the largest religious body in the United States, the richest and in certain ways the most lively branch of the Catholic Church in the world.

Fifty years ago it even looked as though America might soon become predominantly Catholic. That hope, or fear, is now remote. Immigration from Catholic Europe has dwindled, peasant stock has lost its fertility in the cities, conversions barely keep pace with apostasies. Humanly speaking it is now certain that the Church is stabilized as a minority, the most important in the country, but subject to both the advantages and disadvantages of an unprivileged position. There is a paradox inherent in all her history that the Church, designed in her nature to be universal, remains everywhere a minor- ity. We are inclined to think that from the age of Constantine to that of Luther there was a single, consistently triumphant, universally respected authority and to wonder why, in fact, she made such poor use of her opportunities. In fact, of course, the Church has always been at grips with enemies inside or outside her body, has never enjoyed that serene rule her constitution expects, has repeatedly suffered disasters from which it seemed barely possible she would recover. Her position in America cannot be understood unless her previous history is kept always in mind. From time to time, from place to place she has been in hiding; and she has been on the throne. In America her problems are less simple. There she is firmly grounded in a neutral, secular state.

The United States does not form part of Christendom in the traditional sense of the word. She is the child of late eighteenth-century 'enlightenment' and the liberalism of her founders has persisted through all the changes of her history and penetrated into every part of her life. Separation of Church and State was an essential dogma. Government, whatever its form, was looked upon as the captain of a liner, whose concern is purely with navigation. He holds his command ultimately from the passengers. Under his immediate authority the

---

1 Geoffrey Gorer, a cultural anthropologist, wrote *American People: A Study in National Character* (New York, 1948).

public rooms of his ship are used for religious assemblies of all kinds, while in the bar anyone may quietly blaspheme. That is the ideal relationship between ruler and ruled, between the individual *qua* citizen and the individual *qua* immortal soul, as conceived by doctrinaire liberals of the period when the United States was founded. Men required and tolerated very little from their government. The realm of 'private life' was large and inviolable. And the division of Church and State is feasible only under those conditions. Today in most nations the analogy between State and ship has broken down. In some places the captain has developed the mentality of Bligh of the *Bounty*; in others the passengers have been more or less willingly pressed into the crew; all are continuously occupied in keeping the ship running; the voyage is no longer a means to an end but an end in itself. As the State, whether it consist of the will of the majority or the power of a clique, usurps more and more of the individual's 'private life', the more prominent become the discrepancies between the secular and the religious philosophies, for many things are convenient to the ruler which are not healthy for the soul.

The tragic fate of Europe is witness to the failure of secular States. But America through the unique circumstances of her growth has so far been proof against this decay and is thus the centre of hope even for those who are most critical of her idiosyncrasies.

These idiosyncrasies are now the object of boundless curiosity. A generation ago they caused mild amusement as the eccentricities of a likeable but remote people. Today they are studied as portents of the development of the whole western world. Catholics in particular study them, for it is a necessary consequence of the universality of the Church that she should develop marked superficial variations in her different branches. The Mass as offered in, say, St Patrick's in New York or in a Tyrolean village or a Franciscan mission in Africa, is barely recognizable by the uninitiated as the same sacrifice. Mr Aldous Huxley, no fool, writes in *Ends and Means*: 'Christianity, like Hinduism or Buddhism, is not one religion but several. A Christian Church in southern Spain or Mexico or Sicily is singularly like a Hindu temple. The eye is delighted by the same gaudy colours, the same tripe-like decorations, the same gesticulatory statues; the nose inhales the same intoxicating smells; the ear and, along with it, the understanding are lulled by the drone of the same incomprehensible incantations, roused by the same loud impressive music. At the other end of the scale, consider the chapel of a Cistercian monastery and the meditation hall of a community of Zen Buddhists. They are equally bare. . . . Here are two distinct religions for two distinct kinds of human beings.' Only a very learned man can be quite as hopelessly and articulately wrong as that. Any altar-boy could tell him that the 'incantations' of the Mass are identical whether in Guadelupe or Gethsemani, Ky, and are comprehensible or not simply so far as one understands Latin. Cistercian incense smells the same as Jesuit. There is high farce in his picture of a home-sick Andalusian in India frequenting the rites of Juggernaut in preference to the more severe devotions of the mission church. But it is palpably true that each culture gives an idiosyncratic local flavour to its Church.

We differ most, perhaps, in our notions of reverence. I have seen a procession of the Blessed Sacrament in Spain which the people applauded by exploding fire-crackers under the feet of the clergy. It was done with genuine devotion, but to a northern mind the effect was disconcerting. In the same way it strikes Europeans as odd that Americans find the voices of film stars on the radio an aid to saying the rosary. American manufacturers of 'religious goods' offer many ingenious novelties, including a 'rosary aid', which records each 'Ave' on a dial with a sharp click, and a plastic crucifix which, I was assured, had the advantage that you could 'throw it on the ground and stamp on it'. But I remembered that in France I had seen children eating ginger-bread Madonnas. All these observations add to the charm of travel. But there is also 'flavour' of a more philosophic kind.

Europeans are very anxious to catch the American flavour for they believe that for two or three generations it will predominate. They ask countless questions about it and get some very misleading answers, for one can find instances to give colour to almost any generalization. I saw both in London and Chicago the Italian film *Paisan*, one incident of which portrays, with fewer anomalies than usual, the life of a small Franciscan community in a remote mountain district. Three American chaplains arrive there and are warmly welcomed. It transpires that only one is Catholic, the other two being respectively a Protestant and a Jew. The friars are disconcerted and impose a fast on themselves for the conversion of their two non-Catholic guests. In London the audience was mainly non-Catholic, but its sympathy was plainly with the friars. In Chicago the audience was composed mainly of Italian speakers, presumably Catholics of a sort, and to them the friars seemed purely comic. It would be easy to generalize from this contrast that American Catholics care little for doctrinal niceties or the ascetic life; that they exalt the natural virtues above the supernatural, and consider good fellowship and material generosity the true ends of man. That is, in fact, just the kind of generalization which is current in Europe. Yet at that very time Boston was being torn by theological controversy, a contumacious Irish priest proclaiming damnation on all heretics[1] and the authorities reaffirming the possibility of salvation outside the Church in the orthodox terms, which are generous but strict. And all over the country monks and nuns were quietly going about their business of the Opus Dei, singing their office and living by mediaeval rules, in just the fashion which excited laughter in a Chicago theatre.

The two chief impressions which I brought home from America were, first, that there is as great variety there between the outward forms of Catholicism as can be found in Europe, and secondly that Catholicism is not something alien

---

1 Father Leonard Feeney, SJ, insisted that genuine Catholic doctrine excluded the possibility of salvation outside the Church. He and four followers had been dismissed from Boston College and formally ordered to return to the Church, which they refused to do.

and opposed to the American spirit but an essential part of it.

To enlarge on these two propositions. In vast areas of what is now the United States Catholicism was in colonial times the established religion. It was loosely established and in most of those areas now survives mainly in picturesque, ruined or restored, missions. Only two states can be said to have a strong, continuous Catholic tradition – Louisiana and Maryland. In the first of these the Church has never known persecution or even discouragement, and over a length of time that is not an entirely healthy condition. Catholics need to be reminded every few generations that theirs is a challenging creed. In no European country have the faithful been subject to so enervating a toleration as have the inhabitants of New Orleans. It is therefore not surprising that they take their faith easily and sentimentally, with some scepticism among the rich and some superstition among the poor, of the kind that was found in France before the Revolution. It is one of the Devil's devices to persuade people that their religion is so much 'in their bones' that they do not have to bother; that it is in rather poor taste to talk too much about it. Marital confusions, the material advantages of secular education, the mere lassitude induced by the climate, keep many from practising their religion. There is a strange shrine there, unrecognized by the clergy, where the decoration and forms of prayer are Catholic, to which the coloured people resort for cures and favours. There is witchcraft in New Orleans, as there was at the court of Mme de Montespan. Yet it was there that I saw one of the most moving sights of my tour. Ash Wednesday; warm rain falling in streets unsightly with the draggled survivals of carnival. The Roosevelt Hotel overflowing with crapulous tourists planning their return journeys. How many of them knew anything about Lent? But across the way the Jesuit Church was teeming with life all day long; a continuous, dense crowd of all colours and conditions moving up to the altar rails and returning with their foreheads signed with ash. And the old grim message was being repeated over each penitent: 'Dust thou art and unto dust shalt thou return.' One grows parched for that straight style of speech in the desert of modern euphemisms, where the halt and lame are dubbed 'handicapped'; the hungry, 'under-privileged'; the mad, 'emotionally disturbed'. Here it was, plainly stated, quietly accepted, and all that day, all over that light-hearted city, one encountered the little black smudge on the forehead which sealed us members of a great brotherhood who can both rejoice and recognize the limits of rejoicing.

The history of Maryland has been different. Catholicism was never established there as an official religion as it was in the French and Spanish colonies. The state was founded by Catholics as a place where they could practise their religion in peace, side by side with Protestants. The peace was soon broken and the Church persecuted and subdued. But it survived and emerged at the Declaration of Independence in much the same temper as in England at the Catholic Emancipation Act. The old Catholic families of Baltimore have much in common with the old Catholic families of Lancashire. The countryside round Leonardstown has the same tradition of Jesuit missionaries moving in disguise from family to family, celebrating Mass in remote plantations, inculcating the same austere devotional habits, the same tenacious, unobtrusive fidelity. That peninsula between Chesapeake Bay and the Potomac is one of the most fascinating areas for the Catholic visitor, and one of the things which inspires him most is the heroic fidelity of the Negro Catholics. The Church has not always been a kind mother to them. Everywhere in the South Catholic planters brought their slaves to the sacraments, but in the bitter years after the Reconstruction few whites, priests or laity, recognized any special obligation towards them. Often they could only practise their religion at the cost of much humiliation. Some drifted from the Church to preposterous sects or reverted to paganism, but many families remained steadfast. Theirs was a sharper test than the white Catholics had earlier undergone, for here the persecutors were fellow-members in the Household of the Faith. But, supernaturally, they knew the character of the Church better than their clergy. Today all this is fast changing. Catholics are everywhere leading the movement to make amends and in another generation, no doubt, those scandals will seem to belong to the distant past. But in the effort to forget them, honour must never be neglected to those thousands of coloured Catholics who so accurately traced their Master's road amid insult and injury.

Except in Louisiana and Maryland Catholics form a negligible part of the *haute bourgeoisie* of the country clubs and social registers. Most of them, Irish apart, grew up to the sound of foreign languages spoken by parents or grandparents in the home. Some, in the south-west, are survivors of Spanish colonization; most descend from the great waves of immigration from central and southern Europe. To the newly arrived immigrant his church is especially dear. It unites him in prayer and association with the home he has left; it is a social centre where he meets his own kind; it is a refuge full of familiar things in a bewildering new world. But the second and third generations have no tender memories of Europe. They have been reared on tales of the oppression and squalor from which their parents courageously rescued them. They want to be purely American and they develop a raw and rather guilty resentment against the Old World which, I think, explains the loud Sicilian laughter I heard in the Chicago cinema. There is a temptation to identify the Church with their inferior station; to associate it with the smell of garlic and olive oil and grandfather muttering over the foreign-language newspaper; to think of it as something to be discarded, as they rise in the social scale, as they discard their accents and surnames. Some, of course, do so. It is rare to find formal apostates, but occasionally parents who have ceased to care about their religion have their children brought up by Episcopalian or Baptist, in the belief that it gives them a better start in life and that, anyway, it is the child's business to choose for himself later on. But not often: it is one of the prime achievements of the American Catholic clergy that they have reconciled those first stirrings of a new loyalty with the ancestral faith, and Europeans should remember the problem that had to be solved before they look askance at the cruder expressions of nationalism which get quoted.

The Irish, on the other hand, present a precisely contrasting problem. They have never suffered a prick of shame in avowing their origins. Indeed, the further they move in time and place from their homeland the louder they sing about it. Should they ever return they would be shocked by the cynicism of their Dublin cousins. The problem with the Irish is to guard them from the huge presumption of treating the Universal Church as a friendly association of their own, and that problem has not been solved. In New York on St Patrick's Day, among the green carnations first invented by the Irishman, Oscar Wilde, for quite another significance; in Boston on any day of the year; the stranger might well suppose that Catholicism was a tribal cult. Only when he comes to study American hagiology does he learn that other races have their share in Pentecost. To the European it seems that the Irish have been led to betray their manifest historical destiny. When Englishmen in the last century founded a review which was to be for Catholics what the *Edinburgh Review* was for rationalists, they called it the *Dublin Review*. When there was a project for a national Catholic university, Newman went to Ireland. Had Ireland remained in the United Kingdom, Dublin would today be one of the great religious capitals of the world where Catholics from all over the British Empire resorted for education and leadership. That splendid hope was defeated by the politicians. What Europe lost, America has gained. The historic destiny of the Irish is being fulfilled on the other side of the Atlantic, where they have settled in their millions, bringing with them all their ancient grudges and the melancholy of the bogs, but, also, their hard, ancient wisdom. They alone of the newcomers are never for a moment taken in by the multifarious frauds of modernity. They have been changed from peasants and soldiers into townsmen. They have learned some of the superficial habits of 'good citizenship', but at heart they remain the same adroit and joyless race that broke the hearts of all who ever tried to help them.

It is one of the functions of an upper class to remind the clergy of the true balance between their spiritual and their temporal positions.[1] In most Catholic communities in the United States, so far as there is an upper class at all, the clergy themselves comprise it. From one year to another they never meet anyone better informed or more elegant than themselves. The deference with which they are treated on purely social occasions would tend to spoil all but the most heroic humility.

The presbyteries of Mr Harry Sylvester's *Moon Gaffney* and Mr J. F. Powers's *Prince of Darkness* are not mere literary inventions. Reading those admirable stories one can understand why there is often a distinct whiff of anti-clericalism where Irish priests are in power. They are faithful and chaste

1, 2 Waugh's MS reads, 'It is one of the functions of an upper class to see that the clergy do not get above themselves . . .' and 'they have lost their peasant simplicity without acquiring a modest carriage of their rather modest learning . . .'.

and, in youth at any rate, industrious, but many live out their lives in a painful state of transition; they have lost their ancestral simplicity without yet acquiring a modest carriage of their superior learning[2] or, more important, delicacy in their human relations, or imagination, or agility of mind. To them, however, and to the Germans, must go the main credit for the construction of the Church in America. Without them the more sensitive Latins and Slavs would have at first huddled together in obscure congregations, then dispersed and perhaps have been lost to the Faith. The Irish with their truculence and practical good sense have built and paid for the churches, opening new parishes as fast as the population grew; they have staffed the active religious orders and have created a national system of Catholic education.

This last achievement is, indeed, something entirely unique. Without help from the State – indeed in direct competition with it – the poor of the nation have covered their land with schools, colleges and universities, boldly asserting the principle that nothing less than an entire Christian education is necessary to produce Christians. For the Faith is not a mere matter of learning a few prayers and pious stories in the home. It is a complete culture infusing all human knowledge. It is no doubt true that some branches of specialized scholarship can best be learned in the vastly richer, secular institutions. The Catholic colleges do not set themselves the aims of Harvard or Oxford or the Sorbonne. Their object is to transform a proletariat into a bourgeoisie; to produce a faithful laity, qualified to take its part in the general life of the nation; and in this way they are manifestly successful. Their students are not, in the main, drawn from scholarly homes. Many of them handle the English language uneasily. The teaching faculties are still dependent on European recruits for many of the refinements of learning. But, when all this is said, the Englishman, who can boast no single institution of higher Catholic education and is obliged to frequent universities that are Anglican in formation and agnostic in temper, can only applaud what American Catholics have done in the last hundred years. It is a very great thing that young men who are going out to be dentists or salesmen should have a grounding of formal logic and Christian ethics. 'Prove syllogistically that natural rights exist': 'Give the fundamental reason why usury is wrong': 'What is the difference between soul and mind?': 'Give and explain a definition of Sacrifice': these are questions chosen almost at random from the examination papers of a Jesuit college. I have heard it said that American adolescents tend to 'learn the answers' parrotwise without much speculation. This was not the impression I formed in talking with them, but even if it were so, they have learned something which most Europeans ignore. It is a great gain, while the memory is active, to store up formulas. Experience will give them life and later, when he is confronted with a problem, phrases from his college days will come into a man's mind with sudden vivid importance. I noticed this enormous advantage which religiously educated American adults enjoy over their more learned fellows from the secular universities. With the latter, when discussion became general, one got the impression that outside their particular subjects everything was shapeless and meaningless. Nuclear fission threatens material progress; they apprehend this and are at once in despair. What are they here for if not to participate in a benevolent scheme of evolution? It is a question which only the God-fearing can answer. The Catholic remembers the phrases of his youth, which at the time, perhaps, seemed a mere combination of words to be memorized for the satisfaction of an examiner, and suddenly the words have topical significance. He can tap at will the inexhaustible sources of theology.

This fine work of education is, at the moment, somewhat precarious. In America, as elsewhere, the independent schools are in the position of a poker-player among men much richer than himself who are continually raising the stakes. The apparatus of education is becoming exorbitantly expensive. The Catholic colleges cannot long hope to compete with the State in providing the engines of modern physical science. There is, moreover, a powerful group in the nation who openly aspire to uniformity as to something good in itself. I met many anxious Catholic educationists, but I left with confidence that those who have achieved such stupendous feats in the recent past will somehow triumph over their enemies.

There is no doubt that the Catholic colleges maintain a remarkably high standard of duty and piety. The holy places of Notre Dame are crowded before a football match. The number and frequency of communions are startling to a European and dispose of the charge of Jansenism often loosely preferred against the Irish clergy. The habit thus inculcated often continues through life as any visitor to any church can recognize. The quantity is there. No one can judge the quality. Every soul in his traffic with God has his own secrets. A youth who is inarticulate in conversation may well be eloquent in prayer. It would be an intolerable impertinence to attempt to judge. What is plain to the observer is that throughout the nation the altar rails are everywhere crowded. It is normally from just such a deep soil of popular devotion that the fine flowers of the Faith grow. The Church does not exist in order to produce elegant preachers or imaginative writers or artists or philosophers. It exists to produce saints. God alone knows his own. Without doubt lives of deep unobtrusive sanctity are being lived in all parts of the United States, but it is true that the American Church up to the present time has produced few illustrious heroes or heroines. Archbishop Cicognani in his *Sanctity in America* lately collected thirty-five brief biographies of men and women of eminent holiness who worked in the United States. Of these, thirty-one were foreign-born and foreign-educated. Of the four natives none, it may be noted, were of Irish extraction. Two, Catherine Tekakwitha, the Indian, and Mother Elizabeth Ann Seton, the Foundress of the Sisters of Charity, were converts. Bishop Richard Miles, the Dominican of Tennessee, was a zealous and devoted pastor and administrator. Sister Miriam Teresa Demjanovich was training to be a teacher. None were pure contemplatives.

The contemplative life is, of course, only one form of the Christian life. It is a matter of observation, however, that the health of religion in any place and age may be fairly judged by the number of contemplative vocations. Until recent years America has a poor record in this matter, but lately there are signs of change. The case of Thomas Merton has aroused wide interest but he is merely one, unusually articulate, representative of a wide and healthy movement. New Trappist houses are being established, postulants for Carmel exceed the accommodation. Man is made for the knowledge of God and for no other purpose. Where that purpose is recognized there will always be found many who seek Him in the cloisters, from which Grace spreads to an entire people.

The Church and the world need monks and nuns more than they need writers. These merely decorate. The Church can get along very well without them. If they appear, it is a natural growth. They are not much in evidence in America at the moment, and the well-meant attempts to produce them artificially by special courses of study seem to me unlikely to succeed. A more fruitful source of such luxuries is the variety of interests which Catholics have quite recently developed – the small magazines devoted to the liturgy, to social studies, to the translation and explanation of foreign literature and so forth; the works, for example, of John and Mary Ryan in Boston, of John Pick in Milwaukee, of *Commonweal* in New York, of the Sheil School in Chicago. There is a fermentation everywhere.

I mentioned a second conclusion: that Catholicism is part of the American spirit. I do not mean that it lacks enemies. Recently there was an attempt, which very nearly succeeded, to ban specifically Christian Christmas carols from the state schools in New York. The shops all over the country seek to substitute Santa Claus and his reindeer for the Christ Child. I witnessed, early in Lent, the arrival at a railway station of an 'Easter Bunny', attended by brass band and a posse of police. Just as the early Christians adopted the pagan festivals and consecrated them, so everywhere, but particularly in the United States, pagan commerce is seeking to adopt and desecrate the feasts of the Church. And wherever the matter is one for public authority, the State is 'neutral' – a euphemism for 'unchristian'.

I mean that 'Americanism' is the complex of what all Americans consider the good life and that in this complex Christianity, and pre-eminently Catholicism, is the redeeming part. Unhappily 'Americanism' has come to mean for most of the world what a few, very vociferous, far from typical, Americans wish to make it. The peoples of other continents look to America half in hope and half in alarm. They see that their own future is inextricably involved with it and their judgment is based on what they see in the cinema, what they read in the popular magazines, what they hear from the loudest advertiser. Gratitude for the enormous material benefits received is tempered with distaste for what they believe is the spiritual poverty of the benefactor. It is only when one travels in America that one realizes that most Americans either share this distaste or are genuinely unaware of the kind of false impression which interested parties have conspired to spread.

The Christian believes that he was created to know, love and serve God in this world and to be happy with Him in the next. That is the sole reason for his existence. 'Good citizenship', properly understood, is a necessary by-product of this essential task, but more and more the phrase has come to mean mere amenability to the demands of the government. At present the State makes few exorbitant demands in America, but there are many Americans, resolutely opposed to the mechanisms of Communism and Fascism, who yet exalt this limited conception of 'good citizenship' as the highest virtue, and regard the creation of a homogeneous society as the first end of statesmanship. In this popular, neutral opinion Catholics, Protestants, Jews, atheists, theosophists and all the strange sects of the nation differ only in the rites they practise, or do not practise, in certain buildings for an hour or two a week. This is pure make-believe. They differ hugely in morals, social custom and philosophy of life – in fact in all the things they value most highly. The neutral, secular State can only function justly by keeping itself within strict limits. It is not for a foreigner to predict how long the government of the United States will resist the prevalent temptation to encroachment. He merely notes admiringly and gratefully that hitherto the temptations have been largely resisted, and also that the constitutional separation of Church and State does not, when temptation offers, guarantee the continued welfare of any particular, minority, religious body.

The Catholic holds certain territories that he can never surrender to the temporal power. He hopes that in his time there will be no invasion, but he knows that the history of his Church is one of conflict. If his rulers force him to choose between them and his Faith, in the last resort he must choose his Faith. And because in his heart he knows this, he tends to be conspicuously loyal whenever he can be so with a clear conscience. Bossuet could write without embarrassment: *'Le Roi, Jésus-Christ et l'Eglise, Dieu en ces trois noms'.* Similarly many American prelates speak as though they believed that representative, majority government were of divine institution, and the lay American Catholic insists more emphatically on his 'Americanism' than do Protestants or atheists of, perhaps, longer American ancestry.

There is a purely American 'way of life' led by every good American Christian that is point-for-point opposed to the publicized and largely fictitious 'way of life' dreaded in Europe and Asia. And that, by the Grace of God, is the 'way of life' that will prevail.

. AN ADMIRABLE NOVEL .

Miss Antonia White's *Frost in May*, published in 1933, was a minor masterpiece. In itself it was completely successful, but it was the kind of book which is

Review of *The Lost Traveller*, by Antonia White. *Tablet*, 22 April 1950.

written every now and then by people who never write again; a story of childhood in a life to which adolescence brought no further deep experience. One had begun to fear that Miss White might be such a writer. Now, seventeen years later, she gives us *The Lost Traveller* and establishes herself as one of the very best novelists of the day. Her place is beside Miss Elizabeth Bowen and Miss Compton-Burnett, almost their equal in technical ability, their superior in scope and in certain depths of perception.

I compare her only to women writers, for her work is essentially female. Sex-character shows in the novelist more than in any other artist. A man could not possibly have written *The Lost Traveller*, not because the main character is an adolescent girl, but because the father is seen with the penetration of which only a woman is capable.

There are three characters, a father, a mother and daughter, and the story is of their relationship from the girl's fifteenth to her eighteenth year, before and during the First World War. It begins and ends with a death; the grandfather's and a child's, whom the daughter has charge of. In the course of the story the daughter changes school, from a fashionable convent to a London day school, makes new friends, becomes engaged to be married. The mother falls in love. The plot is admirable, compact and symmetrical. The writing is graceful. All the actors are seen in the round, even the least important. The three protagonists are portrayed with exquisite sympathy.

As every truthful account of the English must be, this story is vividly class-conscious. The father is of plebeian origin, the descendant of what approximates in this country to a peasantry. Classical education has brought him into a different and rather inferior world. His roots and affections are in his Sussex village. The mother is born of dreary gentlepeople, and very conscious of it. She has no aspirations to mix with a higher world – and when she falls in love it is with someone entirely Bohemian – but she nurses her sensitiveness in an unhealthy way. The daughter has her father's brains, and her conception of aristocracy, sharpened by the *ancien régime* of her convent, is deeply romantic. At first one's sympathies are all with the father, but when the crisis comes – a disaster in which the girl is barely culpable – it is the basic village artisan in the man who comes to the fore and quite overmasters the aesthete. He thinks of his job when the mother thinks of her daughter.

In all this matter Miss White is simply an admirable novelist telling an admirable story; one of perhaps a dozen contemporary writers. Where she stands apart from and excels her rivals is in her superior vision of the nature of human life. She knows that man is in the world for quite another purpose than teaching Greek or winning the war or marrying well or even writing admirable novels. He is here to love and serve God, and any portrayal of him which neglects this primary function must be superficial. Sexual love, prosperity, culture may determine numberless decisions but they do not explain a purpose. The more novelists try to squeeze an explanation out of them, the more they are betraying their duty. In this sense *No Orchids for Miss Blandish* is a better book than *Howard's End*. You can show man bereft of God and therefore hopeless as Macbeth and Miss Blandish, but you must not flatter his pretensions to self-sufficiency.

Miss White's characters are all infused with the Catholic faith. God is the supreme influence to whom everything returns in their lives. They have in fact made sacrifices for their faith. The father would be headmaster but for his conversion. The mother weakens herself with repeated pregnancies. When she falls in love she resists temptation. When disaster threatens they all turn to prayer. Their religion is their life although superficially they are occupied with other things. There is no question of 'dragging religion in'. It is there all the time at the centre of the story.

Discussion groups all over the country are debating: 'What is the Catholic novel?' Many have begun to doubt whether there is such a thing. Well, here they can find it in a complete and very beautiful form.

. THE HAPPY CRITIC .

In this volume Miss Bowen has assembled the best of her large and very good literary by-products of nearly twenty years. It is journalism at its highest; as, indeed, it exists in no other country today. With one or two exceptions the component pieces were written from week to week without research or deep reflection. They represent an active and discerning mind healthily and happily at work. Their scope is as wide as the publishers' lists. Miss Bowen is unassumingly at ease with the whole of European literature and with most of English and Irish social life. One general impression is that, unlike most of her colleagues, she likes books. She has always been an outstandingly kind critic in a period of extreme bitterness. Most reviewers seem not only to dislike reading but to dislike writing, even when the task they set themselves is merely to express their disgust. Miss Bowen is happy in her work.

To her reviews and light essays she has added 'Two pieces from *Orion*' and five prefaces which do more than record the immediate response to current literary events. They come near to defining her own aims in her own writing. And here lies the importance of the entire collection, in the fact that it is by Miss Bowen. She is one of the few good moralists at work today, and therefore anything she says has particular value, quite apart from the subject she discusses. When we talk to those we love we are entranced by their views on proportional representation or capital punishment, not for any light they throw on these tedious topics, but for the light on the speaker. So with Miss Bowen. We are absorbed by her description of school life because it was that schooling

Review of *Collected Impressions*, by Elizabeth Bowen. *Tablet*, 24 June 1950.

which produced the novelist. We are disturbed by her taste for D. H. Lawrence because we know that somewhere, somehow that negligible writer must have contributed to her art. For she is a writer very much influenced by others. One can sometimes guess from page to page of her beautiful novels what novelist she has been reading last – Miss Compton-Burnett here, Henry James there. Most imaginative writers, I think, are immune to literary influence after adolescence. They read the encyclopaedias, the dictionary, the daily papers; they reread their own work and a few old favourites. But they are not at all interested in what their fellows are doing. Miss Bowen's life seems full and rich with fresh literary excitements. It is admirable and enviable, and perhaps explains her continuous artistic growth. For this reason all devotees of her novels should study her *Collected Impressions* with a double zeal.

. WINNER TAKE NOTHING .

Mr Ernest Hemingway's long-expected novel has been out for some weeks, and has already been conspicuously reviewed by all the leading critics. It is now impossible to approach it without some prejudice either against the book itself or against its critics, for their disapproval has been unanimous. They have been smug, condescending, derisive, some with unconcealed glee, some with an affectation of pity; all are agreed that there is a great failure to celebrate. It is the culmination of a whispering campaign of some years' duration, that 'Hemingway is finished.'

I read the reviews before I read the book, and I was in the mood to make the best of it. Mr Hemingway is one of the most original and powerful of living writers. Even if he had written a completely fatuous book, this was not the way to treat it. What, in fact, he has done is to write a story entirely characteristic of himself, not his best book, perhaps his worst, but still something very much better than most of the work to which the same critics give their tepid applause.

It is the story of the death of an old soldier. He knows he is mortally ill, and he chooses to spend his last days in and near Venice, shooting and making love. The book is largely a monologue. The veteran ruminates bitterly over old battles. He exults in his young mistress. And all is written in that pungent vernacular which Mr Hemingway should have patented.

It may be conceded at once that the hero is not an attractive character. He is a boor and a bore, jocular, humourless, self-centred, arrogant; he rose to command a brigade, but he is consumed by the under-dog's resentment of his superiors both in the army and elsewhere; the last man, in fact, to choose as one's companion in Venice. But these reviewers have been telling us for years that we must not judge novels by the amiability of their characters, any more

Review of *Across the River and into the Trees*, by Ernest Hemingway. *Tablet*, 30 September 1950.

than we must judge pictures by the beauty of their subjects. Mr Hemingway makes a full, strong portrait of his obnoxious hero.

The heroine, a very young Venetian, is strangely unchaperoned. If social conventions have indeed relaxed so much since I was last in that city, this young lady's behaviour provides ample evidence that the traditional, rigid code was highly desirable. But are our reviewers the right people to complain of her goings-on? I think it is the troubadour in Mr Hemingway which impels him to ennoble his heroines. He did the same thing in his first, startlingly brilliant *Fiesta*. There is a strong affinity between that book and this. How it delighted and impressed us a quarter of a century ago! How flatly we accept the same gifts today!

Of course, between then and now there have been the shoals of imitators. It was so easy. You have to be an accomplished writer to imitate Henry James. Any journalist can produce a not quite passable imitation of Mr Hemingway. But it was not only the inventions in technique that impressed us in *Fiesta*. It was the mood. English literature is peculiarly rich in first-class Philistine novelists – Surtees and Mr P. G. Wodehouse, for example. But their characters were always happy. Mr Hemingway has melancholy, a sense of doom. His men and women are as sad as those huge, soulless apes that huddle in their cages at the zoo. And that mood is still with us.

Across the River and into the Trees is the nemesis of the Philistine. The hero is 51 years of age, when the civilized man is just beginning the most fruitful period of his life. But the Philistine is done for, a 'beat-up old bastard', as he expresses it. He has lived for sport and drink and love-making and professional success, and now there is nothing left for him. He has to be decorated with a physical, mortal illness as with a medal. In accentuation of the pathos of his position, he regards himself as rather cultured and sophisticated. He has been places. He is one with that baffled, bibulous crew of *Fiesta* who thought they were plunging deep into the heart of Europe by getting on friendly terms with barmen; who thought their café pick-ups the flower of decadent European aristocracy. He believes he is the sort of guy for whom the Old Masters painted, and to hell with the art experts.

All the faults of this latest book were abundantly present in the first; and most of the merits of the first are here again. Why has there been this concerted attack on Mr Hemingway?

It began a few months ago with a softening-up blitz in the *New Yorker*. That widely read paper attached a female reporter to Mr Hemingway to study him while he was on a holiday in New York. She ate and drank, went shopping and visited art galleries with him, and took careful note of every silly or vulgar thing he said or did during his spree. One might suppose that only a megalomaniac or a simpleton would expose himself to such an ordeal. She made a complete ass of him, of course; not altogether a lovable ass, either. I have never met Mr Hemingway, but I think it probable that his own boisterous manners have contributed to his present unpopularity.

He has really done almost everything to render himself a 'beat-up old bastard'. His reputation was unassailable in 1936. Then, with much trumpeting, he went to Madrid and Barcelona. Here was something greater than bull-fights and *bistros*. The greatest modern writer was devoting his art to the greatest modern theme. Picasso had painted Guernica; Messrs Auden and Spender had written something or other; now the great warrior-artist of the New World was going to write the Modern Epic. But it did not turn out like that. *For Whom the Bell Tolls* was not at all what the socialists wanted. They had been busy denying atrocities; Mr Hemingway described them in detail with relish. They had denied the presence of Russians; Mr Hemingway led us straight into the front door of the Gaylord Hotel. He made Marty and la Passionaria as comic as any *New Yorker* correspondent could have done. From then on he was on the wrong side of the barricades for the socialists, while his pounding revolutionary heart still drove him from civilization.

His sense of superiority to Americans combined with his sense of inferiority to Europeans to give him the sort of patriotism which pleased no one. He could not abide the urban commercial development of his own country; he supposed, rather rightly, that the English were snooty about him, and the French wanted only his dollars. He had a Kiplingesque delight in the technicalities of every trade but his own. He remained, of course, an admirable technician, but, while he could talk for nights to fishermen about their tackle, he was nauseated by the jargon of other writers. Indeed, in this book he uses an American novelist as the typic contrast to his hero; a seedy, industrious fellow in the same hotel, sober, with no young mistress and no scars of battle, and no rollicking jokes with the servants.

When the second war came Mr Hemingway could not be a soldier, and he despised war correspondents; he became a war correspondent. There is plenty to account for the bitterness and frustration of his present work. But our critics thrive on bitterness and frustration. They have forgotten that they once raised clenched fists to the red flag in Barcelona. Not more than a handful have been physically assaulted by the man. Why do they all hate him so?

I believe the truth is that they have detected in him something they find quite unforgivable – Decent Feeling. Behind all the bluster and cursing and fisticuffs he has an elementary sense of chivalry – respect for women, pity of the weak, love of honour – which keeps breaking in. There is a form of high, supercilious caddishness which is all the rage nowadays in literary circles. That is what the critics seek in vain in this book, and that is why their complaints are so loud and confident.

. TWO UNQUIET LIVES .

It is a commonplace that while in the last ten years of the last century England was full of vigorous and original writers, the phrase 'the nineties' means, and always will mean, Ernest Dowson and the decadence. In the same way 'the thirties' of this century mean a particular group which by no means comprised the best of the period. Messrs Graham Greene, John Betjeman, Henry Green, Anthony Powell, among others, were then all in the first phase of their careers; a dozen or more of their elders were in full fruit; but each worked alone in quiet self-sufficiency. Certain young men ganged up and captured the decade. These were by no means untalented. Among many interesting writers there was one of bright accomplishment, Mr Christopher Isherwood. There was also the enigmatic Mr Auden. It seems one had to know Mr Auden to appreciate him. Nothing in his written work explains the dominating position he held. There was something, apparently, in the tone of his voice reading his and his friends' work, which greatly excited his hearers. (After all, it was the age of Hitler.) To this group Mr Stephen Spender early attached himself with ardent hero-worship.

The obvious common characteristic of the group was their Marxist philosophy, and they profited hugely by it, having at their disposal all the publicity-machine of the Left Book Club; hitting the jackpot of popular enthusiasm for the losing causes in Spain and also of the equally prevalent mean panic at the prospect of bombs and gas. But their politics were not their most interesting characteristic. What made them unlike any writers in English history except the early Pre-Raphaelites was their chumminess. They clung together. They collaborated. It seemed always to take at least two of them to generate any literary work however modest. They praised one another tirelessly and an unfavourable review anywhere raised a babble of protest from the authors' young friends. Mr Spender describes how he was moved to fury by a criticism of Mr Isherwood's first novel before he had read the book or even met the author. And these young cards convinced half the reading public, not only that they were very clever fellows, but that they represented all that was noble and beautiful and unworldly, that they alone inherited the glories of the past, that the future was theirs alone and that anyone who differed from them was either a blackguard or a freak.

At the time it all seemed a bit too sharp; but the nuisance is past. At the first squeak of an air-raid warning the gang dispersed. One can look back now with simple curiosity. How was the trick worked? Mr Spender offers himself as a guide to the ruins and one opens his book with pleasant anticipation. Here, perhaps, is the William Rossetti or the Theodore Watts-Dunton of the movement. But, alas, something is lacking. At his christening the fairy godparents showered on Mr Spender all the fashionable neuroses but they quite forgot the

Review of *World within World*, by Stephen Spender and *Saints and Parachutes*, by John Miller. *Tablet*, 5 May 1951.

gift of literary skill.

At one stage of his life Mr Spender took to painting and, he naïvely tells us, then learned the great lesson that 'it is possible entirely to lack talent in an art where one believes oneself to have creative feeling.' It is odd that this never occurred to him while he was writing, for to see him fumbling with our rich and delicate language is to experience all the horror of seeing a Sèvres vase in the hands of a chimpanzee. 'When I write prose,' he blandly admits, 'I am impatient with that side of writing which consists in balancing a sentence, choosing the exact word, writing grammatically even.' It would, therefore, be idle to risk Mr Spender's impatience by exposing in detail his numerous, manifest failures in 'that side' of his work. Only when he imputes his own illiteracy to others must the critic protest. He really should not represent Dr Edith Sitwell as saying: 'The ghost brings extreme misfortune to whomever sees it.'

One is reminded of the Anglican bishop who remarked that 'the spiritual side of the job' did not greatly appeal to him. Why, one asks, does Mr Spender write at all? The answer seems to be that he early fell in love with The Literary Life. When he met Mr T. S. Eliot he confessed the desire 'to be a poet'.

'I can understand your wanting to write poems,' replied the Master. 'But I don't know what you mean by "being a poet".'

Mr Spender knew very well. He meant going to literary luncheons, addressing youth rallies and summer schools, saluting the great and 'discovering' the young, adding his name to letters to *The Times*, flitting about the world to cultural congresses. All the penalties of eminence which real writers shirk Mr Spender pays with enthusiasm and they may very well be grateful to him. In middle age he forms a valuable dummy who draws off the bores while they get on with their work.

Nevertheless, it is a great pity that he did not hire one of them as a 'ghost' to put his reminiscences into shape for he has a number of interesting things to tell. He has led a various and even adventurous life. Even he, with all his natural disadvantages, is far from tedious when describing Mr Auden at Oxford recruiting his gang or the homosexuals of pre-Hitler Hamburg, or the quest for a deserter in communist Spain.

Was there no one among all the illustrious acquaintances whom Mr Spender names in the preface as his advisers, who would say to him: 'Climb down. Don't call your book *The Autobiography of Stephen Spender*. Write instead: "*An Autobiography by* . . ." Don't hold up your parents to contempt. After all, you are their son and it is just possible that you may take after them. Don't give your opinions about Art and the Purpose of Life. They are of little interest and, anyway, you can't express them. Don't analyse yourself. Give the relevant facts and let your readers make their own judgments. Stick to your story. It is not the most important subject in history but it is one about which you are uniquely qualified to speak. Here and there you show a gift for pertinent anecdote. Exploit that and you may produce a permanently interesting little book'?

It would be very convenient for the reviewer if he could make a point by point contrast between Mr Spender and Mr Miller. There are many marked dissimilarities. Mr Miller comes of Tory, Anglican, landed stock and learned the classics at Rugby. While Mr Spender was feasting in Valencia, Mr Miller was working philanthropically among the English unemployed. In the war he joined the hazardous naval Land Incident Section and won the George Cross. He is now, he says, a Catholic. The 'Parachutes' of his title are the horrific objects popularly known as 'land mines'. Mr Miller dismantled fifteen of these single-handed and half his book consists of modest and cheerful anecdotes of his own service. The publishers speak of this work as 'desperately dangerous'. It certainly required steady nerves and resourcefulness but 'desperately dangerous' is too strong. There were in fact only eleven deaths in this Force as against seventy-two decorations.

Even in this section there is a note of gush. He describes the sailor who worked with him as, 'without qualification, the finest fellow who ever put in eighteen years' service with the Royal Navy'. Mr Miller cannot possibly know that. For no very clear reason he has chosen to alternate the two halves of his book chapter by chapter. The second half, the 'Saints' of his title, is his spiritual record and it makes perplexing reading.

Mr Miller is a year or two older than Mr Spender but despite their differences of upbringing, they seem to have fallen under much the same early influences – psychoanalysis, socialism, modern painting, agnosticism. Mr Miller made a quick recovery; his curiosity aroused by Pringle-Pattison's *Scottish Philosophy*, he, at Oxford, decided to test the truth of Christianity 'by practical methods'. 'Church services were alleged to be the normal means of getting into touch with God and I determined to make a trial and see what would happen.' So he went to the University Church where 'I met God in five days and fell in love with him. It was simply a love affair . . . in the sense that one could love a girl.' From then onwards 'the presence of God never left me and I simply lived in it.'

These are big claims; God forbid that one should frivolously discount them; but his subsequent development was distinctly rum. Five months later he was walking up St Giles's when he glanced upward. 'I saw a man wearing a top-hat coming down the street in the front seat of the upper deck of a bus . . . and suddenly my world gave way. The life by which I was surrounded collapsed. . . . As I hope I have made plain, I had been struggling for four years with a growing sense of the unreality of life as I knew it. That a man should actually be moving along in a top-hat . . . was at that stage too much. The horror never left me for five years.'

Well, well. Top-hats were certainly rare in Oxford at that date. Who was this apocalyptic figure? A mourner or reveller presumably, of modest means returning from a funeral or a wedding in North Oxford. We are never told what significance he had; merely that he plunged Mr Miller from the heights to the depths of spiritual life.

In despair he sought the Norfolk Broads and in an hotel picked up a life of St Teresa of Jesus. At once Mr Miller recognized his symptoms. The depression started by the top-hat was merely the Dark Night of the Soul. It is impossible to quote without irreverence the chapter he devotes to mystical prayer. Everything which is mysterious to the devoted religious seems plain to Mr Miller; everything which the simple Catholic hesitates to mention is part of his common intercourse. 'It is difficult to understand,' he says, 'why these important things are so completely unknown to the average educated Englishman.' But he suggests a reason. 'Christian mystical writing, in long patches, is extremely dismal. . . . St Teresa, St John of the Cross, St Catherine of Genoa, all in their own ways present an appalling picture of the type of mental life which in the past has been associated with Christian mysticism. Yet,' he politely adds, 'when they throw aside everything but their experience of the love of God, their writings are entrancing.'

Later in this embarrassing chapter he says: 'It is surely important that they' (the clergy) 'should frankly state that this experience' (the union with God) 'is something which is separable from the profession of Christianity.' And he curiously appends: 'The theory that Christianity is the prerequisite of religion is still carried to such extremes in English life that it is impossible to proceed to the higher degrees of Freemasonry without first professing belief in it.'

However, Mr Miller then went to a theological college to prepare for Anglican ordination. He was then, he tells us, an Anglo-Catholic. To one who has never, in adult life, known the charms of Anglo-Catholicism, the mood in which Mr Miller approached the ministry is unintelligible. He did not believe in the historic truth of the Incarnation. He and his fiancée approved of the communal sexual life they found in a settlement of cranks. But he was readily accepted as a candidate for Anglican Orders.

What is more puzzling is that he seems to have been received without any 'conversation on controversial matters' into the Catholic Church. This is all the more odd on account of the nature of the revelation which led him to the presbytery. He has a strong belief in 'that very horrid thing': private divine revelation. While he was puzzling where his allegiance lay between Rome and Canterbury, he prayed for guidance to the Holy Ghost and got an immediate reply 'like a clap of thunder' . . . 'They are both wrong.'

'In a few moments I was laughing. . . . The thing about God's remarks is that they do settle an argument. . . . The nineteenth Article of the Church of England states that the Church of Rome hath erred. It was delicious to discover that God heartily agreed with my fellow-Anglicans.'

One is accustomed to find converts come to the Church from the most unlikely quarters professing the oddest reasons for seeking admission. Once in, it is usual for them to settle down comfortably, disavow their former aberrations or at the least keep silent about them. It would be agreeable but not entirely candid to conclude this review by saying that Mr Miller had done this.

Perhaps he needs another vision. Somewhere round the corner another bus is approaching bearing another man in some other kind of hat. He will look up amazed and all will be well. The first revelation seems to have gone off half-cock.

. A PROGRESSIVE GAME .

The National Book League do not claim to be an academy establishing the prestige of one writer, rebuking the licence of another. They simply, frankly and quite laudably wish to establish the prestige of books in general. Their motto might be taken from George Orwell's original farm: 'All the animals are equal'. But this year, in order to contribute to the gaiety of the present festivities, they have added 'but some animals are more equal than others', and charged a committee to select from the publications of the last thirty years one hundred which they thought specially notable. Although the judges explicitly repudiate the claim, this list has inevitably been dubbed 'the hundred best books'.

The hundred best books would, of course, consist of an average of four or five books from twenty or twenty-five writers. The Book League have decided that there shall be one book by each writer chosen; they might, one would think, have allowed two exhibits to those who have written both prose and poetry, and several more to those versatile minds such as Mr Aldous Huxley and Mgr Ronald Knox, who are equally eminent in three or four quite distinct branches of literature. However, the rule was made and has been strictly kept, and the resulting catalogue is a document which provides high entertainment. I say 'the catalogue', for the exhibition itself is not extravagantly exciting. Last year the Dutch organized something of the kind at The Hague. They invited modern writers to send objects expressive of their personalities. One British novelist sent a patchwork cushion cover, while another sent his sword. There are no such treats in Albemarle Street. Here there are only a hundred broody faces, and a hundred heaps of manuscript. Go there by all means to see the charming examples of printing and book design, which are also on view, but, dear ladies and gentlemen of the Third Programme, if you wish to preserve the Festival spirit, shun the hundred best authors. Just slip in, purchase a catalogue and take it home with you. It is itself the product of a laborious paper game, and it can be used in a number of diverting ways.

Let us begin by marking ourselves. These books, let us assume, constitute the minimum essential furniture of any civilized home. They represent an annual expenditure of less than two pounds. How many are on your shelves? How many have you read? The system of marking I suggest is: one for each book and author you have heard of. You must have heard of both to score. It is

Listener, 31 May 1951. Talk delivered over BBC Radio Third Programme.

no good claiming that you have heard the name Lehmann and connect it with literature. You must be able to answer correctly: Who wrote *The Ballad and the Source*? Two marks for each book we either possess or have read: three for each we both possess and have read. The maximum score, of course, is 300. I suppose that if it were a list of the best books of 1820-50, we should all score about 250. For our own times, surely, any score under 200 is a disgrace. I have tried it on several friends. An Oxford don, himself an exhibit, scored just 200. One of the judges, I am reliably informed, scored 201. Since he or she must have read all the works selected, this can only mean he or she possesses only one. Which one, I wonder? I myself scored 171. The highest score so far is 216 by Mr Graham Greene; the lowest, 142, by Mr Henry Green, both of them, of course, exhibits themselves. The average score, I find, for normally well-read people – the kind of people for whom authors write and to whom they look for their living – is well under 150. It is a rather disturbing conclusion. Writers cannot support life by buying one another's books. How do we expect literature to survive, still less to flourish, if we are so indifferent to it?

But before we accuse ourselves too harshly, let us consider two possible explanations. It may be that we have just lived through a particularly barren period in which contemporary books were not desirable acquisitions; in which, in fact, we got better value for our money from gin and films. Or it may be that this list is too narrow or too recondite, and that we possess, know and love a hundred better books.

It would be absurd to pretend that we have progressed beyond the splendours of the period 1820–50, but when I confidently say we should all score highly on that period, I am thinking of books rather than writers. We can effortlessly rattle off twenty or thirty names of that period – among them the very greatest in our history. Then we have to think, and can with an effort produce, say, another twenty. After that most of us, I think, would stick. A hundred swans and no geese is altogether too much to ask of any thirty years of any nation. Certainly we cannot accuse the judges of narrowing their field. They have extended it almost too far. This is the *National* Book League celebrating the Festival of *Britain*. A certain insularity would have been excusable. This list is compiled from the wide world. They have drawn on the Empire, as I suppose they have good right to do. There are the expatriates, fugitives from Welfare who live abroad and mean to stay there. They are a formidable part of the list. No doubt they are technically British, but they are scarcely the names to display from the Skylon advertising our way of life. And how about the Irish? James Joyce's *Ulysses* is among the exhibits. He was born and brought up in what is now alien soil. He lived and died on the continent. *Ulysses* was published in Paris, and for many years it was a criminal offence to introduce a copy into this kingdom. Can we really claim him as a national hero?

And how about naturalized Americans? Surely we can either claim Logan Pearsall Smith and Mr T. S. Eliot, or Mr Auden? Can we claim all three? The judges do. It would be a very thin list indeed if it had been strictly patriotic.

Even so it is pretty thin. A hundred was too many to ask for. The result is that no one can feel the least elated at being included, while almost anyone can feel justifiably aggrieved if he is left out. The judges seem chiefly conscious of this latter consideration, and have contrived a curiously enigmatic apology. 'The Committee,' they say in their preface, 'regards each author as being the delegate on behalf of others who have been excluded because of the limits of the Exhibition's space.' Now what on earth does that mean? It is the practice of the army when a unit has fought exceptionally well to decorate the commanding officer. Both he and his men fully realize that the honour is shared by all. But writers do not advance in troops and squadrons. Each works alone producing a separate self-sufficient object. We must, I suppose, imagine a judge being haunted by the ghost of Hugh Walpole. He placates the troubled spirit by saying: 'Sweet Sir Hugh, rest in peace. You have a delegate. The Order of Knights is represented by Sir Maurice Bowra.'

It is not to be expected or desired that our choice shall coincide everywhere with the judges'. They tell us that some writers refused to join. That may account for some odd omissions among the living, but it cannot explain the absence of G. K. Chesterton, Maurice Baring and Ford Madox Ford. A very good game can be played by drawing up lists of books none of which is included. Would your own list be much better? Try and see. My own impression is that, granted certain pre-existing limitations of taste, the judges have done well, and that makes all the sadder what candour compels one to admit: that the general impression of the Exhibition is depressing. One can but sum up three-quarters of it as 'dreariness relieved by frivolity'. There is plenty of competence, plenty of fun, a remarkable absence of imposture and bluster. But there is a woeful absence of glory, and also – what one would not expect – a complete divorce from life. For the absence of glory we cannot blame our judges. There are no towering geniuses whom they have jealously ignored. The really great come and go unpredictably. We happen now to have struck a bad patch. That is all. But the separation of life and art argues either an unhealthy civilization or some obscurity of judgment in the committee.

At Christmas time, literary editors often solicit eminent men and women – and I don't mean film stars and pugilists; I mean just the kind of people who form the basis of the critical, informed reading public – to name their favourite book of the year. Nine times out of ten, you will find that they choose something which is not by a professional writer at all. Now our judges at this Exhibition have been loyally professional. They want to encourage the whole-time writer, with the result that even the book-reviewers, if they have themselves written a book, get a place. There is just a whiff of trade-unionism about their preferences. But this is not the heart of the matter. It accounts for some of the dreariness, but not for the frivolity of their taste. When I say 'divorce from life' I do not primarily mean from lively autobiographies and accounts of adventures. I mean the moments when a writer believes he has something of value to say. Let us take two examples – D. H. Lawrence and Mr Huxley. Both are known everywhere abroad as prophets and messengers. Personally, I consider their messages erroneous. That is not the point. It is for this that they are known. In each case the judges have represented them by a minor literary exercise.

Let us for a moment examine the judges themselves: Miss Rose Macaulay, Mr Pritchett and Professor Day-Lewis. They need, as chairmen say, no introduction. Their attainments seem to be wide apart. But there clearly must be sympathy in any committee, otherwise its consultations become fruitless wrangles like a meeting of foreign ministers. What have these three in common? I think one can find the answer quite simply in the lowest common denominator. There is only one piece of plain trash in the Exhibition, and that is H. G. Wells's *Outline of History*. Miss Macaulay is not a lady of ungovernable political passion, but she will not, I am sure, think it either impolite or inaccurate if I describe her as 'progressive'. Mr Pritchett is closely associated with the leading socialist weekly. Professor Lewis was a leading member of the Marxist school of writers in the late thirties. All, in varying degrees, are what foreigners call of 'the Left'. H. G. Wells's cosmology is their meeting ground, but having established this by its inclusion, they then go to great lengths to avoid partiality. Politicians are represented by Mr Winston Churchill and Sir Duff Cooper, not by Mr John Strachey; clergymen by Archbishop Mathew, not by the Dean of Canterbury. At least half their chosen authors are traditional Tories, or else possessed by some idiosyncrasy which progressives call 'cannibalism'. The judges seem, at a glance, to have triumphed over their prejudices. But it is not quite as simple as that. What they have done is to fall back on the arid standards of pure literary taste, in order to suppress anything tendentious unless the tendency is 'progressive'.

Professor Lewis set forth his aesthetic in his preface to *The Mind in Chains*. This is a frustrated artistic epoch, he says, because we live under such peculiar social conditions that it is possible for a man to work for his own profit. The only hope for the artist is to identify himself with the proletariat. Well, there is very little proletarian inspiration in this eminently genteel Exhibition, but then there is very little inspiration. As though deliberately to illustrate the frustration of man, the judges show an odd preference for the first or very early publications of writers whose powers have widened and deepened. If it had happened once, twice, three times, one might have accepted the tragic fact of early promise unfulfilled, but it happens again and again. It is partly, perhaps, the boredom of the reviewer whose sad lot is now and then brightened by a discovery, but more often depressed by the need to find something new to say about an established writer. But it is also the voice of the progressive saying: 'Look at her; killed by capitalism.'

But there is a further and deeper cause for the dreariness and frivolity of the Wells view of life – its atheism. This feature is curiously illuminated in the Exhibition's 'Preface'. In a staggering verdict the three judges write: 'It sometimes happens that important books, especially of criticism, are badly written.

There are examples in our selection. Important books have been written on economics, divinity and science, but they are specialized and unless the authors are remarkably good writers, they are not considered eligible.'

There we have the progressive cat, a great brute of an animal, clear out of the bag. One would have supposed that there are few drearier spectacles than a critic who could not write. But like a trade union official who has lost productive dexterity, he must be accepted as part of the industry. But Divinity, the Queen of Sciences, the mainspring and deep abiding channel of human thought; the branch of writing which, at its lowest, is first in the English tradition from the start of our tongue until the death of our grandparents, which filled our libraries with homilies and controversy, and occupied the sharpest minds of every age, which even today is second, I believe, for quantity in all branches of publishing, and for quality commands the deepest intellects and the sharpest wits; the science which deals with the purpose and destination of the spirit of man – that, compared with a literary critic who can't express himself, is merely something 'specialized'. Dear ladies and gentlemen of the Third Programme, words fail me.

. NANCY MITFORD .

In a world where almost everything becomes daily more uniform and more drab, it is a joy to contemplate the recent metamorphosis of Miss Nancy Mitford. Visit her today. You cross the Seine and penetrate into the very heart of the fashionable quarter of Paris, the Faubourg St Germain. You go to a quiet side street, so exclusively aristocratic that few taxi-drivers know its name, and ring at a great, white, shabby door which in due time opens, revealing a courtyard surrounded on three sides by low buildings of the period of the restored Bourbon monarchy. Straight in front, on the ground floor, with its glass doors opening into a garden behind, lie the apartments of Miss Mitford. She greets you in a Dior dress, her waist so small that one fears it may snap at any moment. This is the only waspish thing about her; all else is sweetness, happiness and inexpressible levity. She leads you to her salon, full of the exquisite *bibelots* she has amassed, and talks, prattles, giggles – of what? Gossip, outrageous, incredible, entirely funny; of the art of the three great Louis, scholarly, precise, discriminating; of France, with schoolgirlish enthusiasm. Miss Mitford has a crush on France and everything French. You may not even remark in her presence that the matches are bad. She is expecting friends. Whom? Either formidable dowagers of the very *gratin* of French society, or the most discredited Bohemians from across the Channel. On each she showers an equal, loving regard, but she does not mix them. She is too wise

Book-of-the-Month-Club News, September 1951.

a bird for that. She will talk of everything – of politics idiotically, of all except her beloved *grand siècle* barbarously – but she speaks little of her own works. You would not know that she has a comedy, adapted by herself from the French, running to enthusiastic audiences in London and New York and that her works are daily reaching a wider and more appreciative public.

How did this delicious creature come into being? Cast back to her home. She is the first of the long line of daughters of Lord Redesdale, a retiring but violent nobleman who is still happily with us. Suffice to say that the portrait of 'Uncle Matthew' in *The Pursuit of Love* is thought, by those who know the family best, to resemble him. All the Mitford daughters are beautiful and wildly individual. They include a member of an American left-wing party, an English duchess and a lady who spent most of the war in prison on unspecified charges of Nazi sympathies. The upbringing of these enchanting objects might be expected to have produced eccentric results. Their mother imposed the Mosaic diet upon them under the belief that Jews never suffered from cancer. It was a common spectacle for guests at the Mitford breakfast table to observe the fair, blue-eyed, long-legged future duchess tucking pork sausages up her knickers to consume in secret. Their father forbade them paint, powder and publicity. Awful storms shook the house when he detected scent on their persons or found their photographs in the *Tatler*. Nancy received no education at all except in horsemanship and French. Liverish critics may sometimes detect traces of this defect in her work. But she wrote and read continually and has in the end achieved a patchy but bright culture and a way of writing so light and personal that it can almost be called a 'style'.

She married the Hon. Peter Rodd, the second son of Lord Rennell, an ambassador best known for his early friendship with Oscar Wilde. Peter is a man of conspicuous versatility, an explorer, linguist, seaman, boon-companion and heaven knows what else, of startling good looks. With not much money between them Peter and Nancy settled in London in the criminal quarter behind Paddington Station, where their house was much frequented by homeless drunks and socialists. The Rennells had one or two houses in Italy and when the London slums became oppressive the young couple would slip away to the sun. Nancy at intervals wrote her early works, full of private, evanescent jokes, which never enjoyed much success outside the circle of her own friends.

Then came 1939. Peter, of course, went off immediately with the army. Nancy remained in London revelling in the comic incidents of the blitz. Entirely fearless, entirely frivolous, she giggled among the falling bombs, working at the same time tirelessly as Air Raid Warden for her *louche* district. When the dust cleared from the first heavy bombardments, she found herself penniless and took work in a Mayfair bookshop, which she quickly made a centre for all that was left of fashionable and intellectual London. When we came on leave, we always made straight for Nancy's shop, confident of finding a circle of old friends who had become dependent on their daily dose of Nancy's gaiety. There is at least one American sergeant who will remember those long, laughing sessions among the buzz-bombs.

Then came peace and welfare. Most of us settled down glumly to the drab world about us. Not so Nancy, who, having voted socialist and so done her best to make England uninhabitable, broke from her chrysalis, took wing and settled lightly in the heart of Paris where we find her today. Her present, glittering book gives a picture of what she finds there.

. THE POINT OF DEPARTURE .

No one but Mr Graham Greene could have written his latest novel *The End of the Affair*; his unique personality is apparent on every page. All the qualities which we think of as being particularly his own are here in abundance; his dark and tender acceptance of the inevitability of suffering; his conviction, which lies at the root of all morality, that the consequences of every human act for good or ill are an endless progression, and that human beings, especially men and women in their sexual relationship, are ceaselessly working on one another, reforming or corrupting; the deliberately contrived squalor of all the scenery and stage effects – in this book 'onions' are made, perhaps in conscious allusion, to perform precisely the same function in the lovers' talk as 'cattleyas' did for Swann and Odette; the rich idiosyncrasy of phrase – 'misery's graduate', 'fellow strangers', 'I remember. That is what hope feels like.' All these qualities are here. Nevertheless, the book differs sharply from its predecessors in method and material.

Hitherto Mr Greene's characteristic achievement has been to take the contemporary form of melodrama and to transfuse it with spiritual life. His books have been tense, fast stories with the minimum of comment and the maximum of incident, his characters unreflective, unaesthetic, unintelligent, his villains have been vile and his heroines subhuman; all have inhabited a violent social no-man's-land. Every book has ended with death and a sense of finality. Whatever speculations were aroused, the reader felt that as far as the author was concerned the job was done. He had been told all that was needed.

In *The End of the Affair*, Mr Greene has chosen another contemporary form, domestic, romantic drama of the type of *Brief Encounter*, and has transformed that in his own inimitable way. The characters are industrious professional people of respectable appearance and settled habits. The pursuing detective, previously a figure of terror, is here a clown. But the great change in this new adventure is the method of telling. For the first time there is a narrator; everything is seen through his eyes and with his limitations. Instead of an omniscient and impersonal recorder we have the chief character giving his

Review of *The End of the Affair*, by Graham Greene. *Month*, 6 September 1951.

distorted version; a narrator who is himself in course of evolution, whose real story is only beginning at the conclusion of the book, who is himself unaware of the fate we can dimly foresee for him. *The End of the Affair* is an ironic title; the affair has not yet reached its climax when the record ceases.

It is the tale of a suburban adultery. A competent, fairly successful novelist wishes to write about a civil servant. In order to learn the authentic details of his life he seeks the acquaintance of a neighbour's wife, falls deeply in love with her and she with him. Their affair prospers, although he is tortured by jealousy and the sense that their happiness is necessarily impermanent, until after a bomb narrowly misses killing him, the mistress suddenly and inexplicably breaks relations with him. Two or three years go by of complete separation. Then the husband, who has never suspected his wife at the time of her infidelity, consults the former lover; he thinks she is now deceiving him. The lover is more jealous than the husband. It is he who engages a detective to investigate the third man. This Third Man turns out to be God. Throughout the love affair the quality in the heroine that has been stressed is her abandonment. She learns the true object of abandonment and dies in the knowledge. After her death she, now in Heaven, begins, in a way that is slightly reminiscent of Maurice Baring's characters, to work on those with whom she was involved on earth. We leave the narrator-lover still tormented by uncomprehending hate but with the certainty in our own minds that her love will reach and heal him.

That, very baldly, is the story, a singularly beautiful and moving one. This *précis* gives no indication of the variety and precision of the craftsmanship. The relationship of lover to husband with its crazy mutations of pity, hate, comradeship, jealousy and contempt is superbly described. For the first time in Mr Greene's work there is humour. The heroine is consistently lovable. Again and again Mr Greene has entered fully into a scene of high emotion which anyone else would have shirked. Instead of pistol-shots there are tears.

The story deals extensively with sexual relations and here any writer, however skilful, is gravely handicapped by the lack of suitable words. Our language took form during the centuries when the subject was not plainly handled with the result that we have no vocabulary for the sexual acts which is not quaintly antiquated, scientific, or grossly colloquial. To say that lovers 'sleep together' is an absurdity in describing the hasty incidents of passion which occur in this book. Mr Greene often uses the term 'make love' to describe sexual intercourse. Normally that is an inoffensive euphemism, but here, where love is as often used in its high spiritual sense, there is an ironical twist in the phrase which frustrates the writer's aim. It is an artistic trap from which, once it closes, there is no escape. One must simply walk circumspectly round it.

The heroine, after her death, begins to work miracles. We are not left, as we often are by Maurice Baring, with a sense of brooding gracious sweetness; there is active beneficent supernatural interference. This is a brave invention of Mr Greene's. His voice is listened to in many dark places and this defiant assertion of the supernatural is entirely admirable. His earlier books have tended to show Catholics to themselves and set them puzzling. *The End of the Affair* is addressed to the Gentiles. It shows them the Church as something in their midst, mysterious and triumphant and working for their good. One might even say that in places it is too emphatically sectarian. It transpires, for instance, after the heroine's death that she was baptized by a Catholic priest. There is some speculation as to whether 'it took'; whether it was an infection caught in infancy, and so on. But Mr Greene knows very well that she would have been as surely baptized by the local vicar. It would be a pity if he gave an impression of the Catholic Church as a secret society, as Mr T. S. Eliot did of his Church in *The Cocktail Party*. Clearly that is not Mr Greene's intention nor can it be justly read into his words, but in the dark places where his apostolate lies I can imagine some passages carrying a whiff of occultism.

One further criticism, a matter of plausibility. The heroine is robbed of an intimate journal. Would this not have been noticed at once with consternation? Mr Greene is usually so scrupulous in detail that it is surprising to find this overlooked. But this is a trifle.

To conclude, Mr Greene is to be congratulated on a fresh achievement. He shows that in middle life his mind is suppler and his interests wider than in youth; that he is a writer of real stamina. He has triumphantly passed the dangerous climacteric where so many talents fail. We need have no anxiety about his development, only cheerful curiosity.

. EDINBURGH RECTORIAL ELECTION .
MR WAUGH'S APPEAL[1]

When I come to itemize my claims to your suffrage, I find them mostly negative. I have never gone into public life. Most of the ills we suffer are caused by people going into public life. I have never voted in a parliamentary election. I believe a man's chief civic duty consists in fighting for his king when the men in public life have put the realm in danger. That I have done. I have raised a family and paid such taxes as I find unavoidable. I have learned and practised a very difficult trade with some fair success.

It seems to me essential to your repute among the great universities of Christendom that you should choose a man connected with the arts. I am opposed by a poet. If he writes better than I, please vote for him. But do not, I beg, choose anyone connected with commerce or with the fabrication of noisy, dangerous or quite ephemeral machinery. Do not choose a man in public life. Do not choose a pure clown. That is not in keeping with your great history.

The Times, 8 November 1951.
1 Waugh stood for the rectorship of Edinburgh University at the invitation of Bruce Cooper, an Edinburgh student (see *Letters*, 17 October 1951). Sir Alexander Fleming won the election.

. ST HELENA EMPRESS .

We are advised to meditate on the lives of the saints, but this precept originated in the ages when meditation was a more precise and arduous activity than we are tempted to think it today. Heavy apparatus has been at work in the last hundred years to enervate and stultify the imaginative faculties. First, realistic novels and plays, then the cinema have made the urban mentality increasingly subject to suggestion so that it now lapses effortlessly into a trance-like escape from its condition. It is said that great popularity in fiction and film is only attained by works into which readers and audience can transpose themselves and be vicariously endangered, loved and applauded. This kind of reverie is not meditation, even when its objects are worthy of high devotion. It may do little harm, perhaps even some little good, to fall day-dreaming and play the parts of Sir Thomas More, King Lewis IX or Father Damien. There are evident dangers in identifying ourselves with St Francis or St John of the Cross. We can invoke the help of the saints and study the workings of God in them, but if we delude ourselves that we are walking in their shoes, seeing through their eyes and thinking with their minds, we lose sight of the one certain course of our salvation. There is only one saint that Bridget Hogan can actually become, St Bridget Hogan, and that saint she *must* become, here or in the fires of purgatory, if she is to enter heaven. She cannot slip through in fancy-dress, made up as Joan of Arc.

For this reason it is well to pay particular attention to the saints about whom our information is incomplete. There are names in the calendar about which we know nothing at all except those names, and then sometimes in a form that would puzzle their contemporaries. There are others about whom, humanly speaking, we know almost everything, who have left us a conspectus of their minds in their own writings, who were accompanied through life by pious biographers recording every movement and saying, who were conspicuous in the history of their times so that we can see them from all sides as they impressed friends and opponents. And midway between these two groups are the saints who are remembered for a single act. To this class Helena eminently belongs. In extreme old age, as Empress Dowager, she made a journey into one part of her son's immense dominions, to Jerusalem. From that journey spring the relics of the True Cross that are venerated everywhere in Christendom. That is what we know; most else is surmise.

Helena was at a time, literally, the most important woman in the world, yet we know next to nothing about her. Two places claim to be her birthplace: Colchester in England and Drepanum, a seaside resort, now quite vanished, in Turkey. The evidence for neither is so strong that Englishman or Turk need abandon his pretension. She was probably of modest rank, not servile, not illustrious. Constantius married her early in his rise to power and abandoned

Month, January 1952. Talk delivered over BBC Radio: Bristol and Third Programme.

her later for a royal match. She may have been brought up at one of the post-stables on an imperial trunk road and have there attracted Constantius's attention on one of his official journeys. Or she may, conceivably, have been what legend makes her, the daughter of a British chief. She bore one son, Constantine the Great, probably at Nish in Serbia. After her divorce she settled at Trier (Trèves) where the Cathedral probably stands on the foundations of her palace. Almost certainly it was there that she became Christian. Lactantius, who was tutor to her grandson Crispus, may have helped instruct her. At the very end of her life she suddenly emerged for her great adventure. She died at Constantinople and her body was thereupon or later moved to Rome. Her tomb never became a great centre of pilgrimage. She, herself, seems never to have attracted great personal devotion; but she was a popular saint. Numberless churches are dedicated to her; numberless girls baptized with her name; she appears everywhere in painting, sculpture and mosaic. She has fitted, in a homely and substantial way, into the family life of Christendom.

There is little of heroism or genius in any of this. We can assume that she was devout, chaste, munificent; a thoroughly good woman in an age when palaces were mostly occupied by the wicked; but she lived grandly and comfortably whereas most of the saints in every age have accepted poverty as the condition of their calling. We know of no suffering of hers, physical, spiritual or mental, beyond the normal bereavements, disappointments and infirmities which we all expect to bear. Yet she lived in an age when Christians had often to choose between flight, apostasy or brutal punishment. Where, one may ask, lies her sanctity? Where the particular lesson for us who live in such very different circumstances?

For the world of Constantine, as we catch glimpses of it, is utterly remote from ours. There are certain superficial similarities. Poetry was dead and prose dying. Architecture had lapsed into the horny hands of engineers. Sculpture had fallen so low that in all his empire Constantine could not find a mason capable of decorating his triumphal arch and preferred instead to rob the 200-year-old arch of Trajan. An enormous bureaucracy was virtually sovereign, controlling taxation on the sources of wealth, for the pleasure of city mobs and for the defence of frontiers more and more dangerously pressed by barbarians from the East. The civilized world was obliged to find a new capital. All this seems familiar but for the event of supreme importance, the victory of Christianity, we can find no counterpart in contemporary history. We cannot by any effort of the imagination share the emotions of Lactantius or Macarius. Helena, more than anyone, stands in the heart of that mystery.

She might claim, like that other, less prudent queen: 'In my end is my beginning.' But for her final, triumphant journey, she would have no fame. We should think of her, if at all, as we think of Constantine; someone who neatly made the best of both worlds. The strong purpose of her pilgrimage shed a new and happier light on the long years of uneventful retirement showing us that it was by an act of will, grounded in patience and humility, that she accepted her position. Or rather, her positions. We do not know in exactly what state Constantius found her. She certainly did not choose him for his hopes of power. Those hopes, indeed, proved her undoing and dismissed her, divorced, into exile. In a court full of intrigue and murder she formed no party, took no steps against her rival, but quietly accepted her disgrace. Constantine rose to power, proclaimed her empress, struck coins in her honour, opened the whole imperial treasury for her use. And she accepted that too. Only in her religious practices did she maintain her private station, slipping in to Mass at Rome among the crowd, helping with the housework at the convent on Mount Sion. She accepted the fact that God had His own use for her. Others faced the lions in the circus; others lived in caves in the desert. She was to be St Helena Empress, not St Helena Martyr or St Helena Anchorite. She accepted a state of life full of dangers to the soul in which many foundered, and she remained fixed in her purpose until at last it seemed God had no other need of her except to continue to the end, a kind old lady. Then came her call to a single peculiar act of service, something unattempted before and unrepeatable – the finding of the True Cross.

We have no absolute certainty that she found it. The old sneer, that there was enough 'wood of the cross' to build a ship, though still repeated, has long been nullified. All the splinters and shavings venerated everywhere have been patiently measured and found to comprise a volume far short of a cross. We know that most of these fragments have a plain pedigree back to the early fourth century. But there is no guarantee, which would satisfy an antiquary, of the authenticity of Helena's discovery. If she found the True Cross, it was by direct supernatural aid, not by archaeological reasoning. That, from the first, was its patent of title. There are certain elements about the surviving relics which are so odd that they seem to preclude the possibility of imposture. The 'Label', for example – the inscription *Jesus of Nazareth, King of the Jews* – now preserved in Santa Croce seems the most unlikely product of a forger's art. And who would have tried to cheat her? Not St Macarius certainly. But it *is* nevertheless possible that Helena was tricked, or that she and her companions mistook casual baulks of timber, builders' waste long buried, for the wood they sought; that the Label, somehow, got added to her treasure later. Even so her enterprise was something life-bringing.

It is not fantastic to claim that her discovery entitles her to a place in the Doctorate of the Church, for she was not merely adding one more stupendous trophy to the hoard of relics which were everywhere being unearthed and enshrined. She was asserting in sensational form a dogma that was in danger of neglect. Power was shifting. In the academies of the eastern and south-eastern Mediterranean sharp, sly minds were everywhere looking for phrases and analogies to reconcile the new, blunt creed for which men had died, with the ancient speculations which had beguiled their minds, and with the occult rites which had for generations spiced their logic.

Another phase of existence which select souls enjoyed when the body was shed; a priesthood; a sacramental system, even in certain details of eating, anointing and washing – all these had already a shadowy place in fashionable thought. Everything about the new religion was capable of interpretation, could be refined and diminished; everything except the unreasonable assertion that God became man and died on the Cross; not a myth or an allegory; true God, truly incarnate, tortured to death at a particular moment in time, at a particular geographical place, as a matter of plain historical fact. This was the stumbling block in Carthage, Alexandria, Ephesus and Athens, and at this all the talents of the time went to work, to reduce, hide and eliminate.

Constantine was no match for them. Schooled on battle-fields and in diplomatic conferences, where retreat was often the highest strategy, where truth was a compromise between irreconcilable opposites; busy with all the affairs of state; unused to the technical terms of philosophy; Constantine not yet baptized, still fuddled perhaps by dreams of Alexander, not quite sure that he was not himself divine, not himself the incarnation of the Supreme Being of whom Jove and Jehovah were alike imperfect emanations; Constantine was quite out of his depth. The situation of the Church was more perilous, though few saw it, than in the days of persecution. And at that crisis suddenly emerged God-sent from luxurious retirement in the far north a lonely, resolute old woman with a single concrete, practical task clear before her; to turn the eyes of the world back to the planks of wood on which their salvation hung.

That was Helena's achievement, and for us who, whatever our difficulties, are no longer troubled by those particular philosophic confusions that clouded the fourth century, it has the refreshing quality that we cannot hope to imitate it. The Cross is very plain for us today; plainer perhaps than for many centuries. What we can learn from Helena is something about the workings of God; that He wants a different thing from each of us, laborious or easy, conspicuous or quite private, but something which only we can do and for which we were each created.

. THE DEFENCE OF THE HOLY PLACES .

On one side a people possessed by implacable resentment, on the other by limitless ambition; between them a haphazard frontier determined by the accidents of battle and still, in spite of the truce, the scene of recurrent acts of atrocity and revenge; on that line and cut through by it, the most sacred city in the world.

Publicists and politicians have conspired to forget and to make forgotten this open wound in international honour. On 11 December 1948, the General Assembly of the United Nations proclaimed Jerusalem unique and granted it international status under United Nations control which neither then nor later was made effective. Now by a double act of aggression as flagrant as the

Life, 24 December 1951; Month, March 1952; The Holy Places (London, 1952; New York 1953). See textual note p. 420.

invasion of South Korea, the city has become a battle-ground temporarily divided between two irreconcilable enemies. One voice only is heard reproaching the nations with their betrayal – the Pope's; but he speaks as always in terms of generations and centuries. When he says that internationalization is the only proper solution of the problem he does not mean that it is expedient to evict the usurpers immediately. The great opportunity has been lost. It will come back one day on the tide of history. Meanwhile the Holy City stands as a chilly monument to the moral confusion of our rulers.

It was typical of this confusion that even at the time when it seemed as though the international politicians were ready to protect Jerusalem, they spoke of it as being 'sacred to three great world religions', suggesting that the rights and claims of Christian, Mohammedan and Jew were similar and equal. In fact there are decisive theological and historical differences. Christianity and Mohammedanism may both reasonably be called 'world religions' in that each offers a cosmic system of the relations of all mankind to God. Judaism is the religion of a particular people, a system of rites and social habits which united and distinguished a nation once dispersed, now partly reassembled in a national state. The Temple of Jerusalem was once the sole focus of Jewish worship. There alone a priestly order sacrificed to the national deity. When the Temple was destroyed by Titus in AD 70 the Jewish religion was profoundly changed. Since then there has been no priesthood and no sacrifice. In AD 363 the Emperor Julian the Apostate ordered the restoration of the Temple and of its worship but the work was interrupted by a cataclasm which contemporary witnesses accepted as a divine judgment. Since then no responsible Jew has advocated the rebuilding of the Temple. The meat shortage alone would make the ancient sacrifices impossible. The orthodox Jews, who form some 18 per cent of the population of Israel, believe that the work can only be undertaken when there is an unmistakable, apocalyptic summons. The 10 per cent of dogmatic atheists, of course, expect no such event. The majority of Zionists are being encouraged to see the fulfilment of the Prophecies in the establishment of the State of Israel. For the first time no Jew has access to the Wailing Wall, but it is not in the temper of the new state to lament past glories but instead to exalt present achievements. There is a strong movement to divert the national disposition for mourning into more topical channels. A shrine has been erected under the walls of the old city where the ashes of Jews murdered by the Germans are unceasingly venerated. It is probable that this will take the place of the Wailing Wall in the minds of the next generation.

The Mohammedans were late-comers. Jerusalem had been the sacred city of Christendom for 600 years before it fell to Omar. He himself entered with all reverence and chivalrously refrained from entering the Holy Sepulchre, an act commemorated in the neighbouring mosque. It is probable that the Prophet passed through Jerusalem on his way to Damascus. It is certain that he picked up a great respect for the place in the garbled versions of Christianity and Judaism which formed the basis of his meditations. At one time he turned towards Jerusalem to pray. But in the end he left his bones in Medina and appointed Mecca as the prime centre of pilgrimage and devotion. Jerusalem comes third to the Mohammedan and only one spot there is of supreme importance, the rock over which the great Dome stands, reputed to be the altar on which Abraham prepared to sacrifice Isaac; the foundation of the altar is both the Jewish Holy of Holies and the taking-off place of the Prophet's visionary visit to Paradise. It was a Christian church for three hundred years before Omar and again for a century under the Crusaders, but it is now recognized by all as an inalienable Mohammedan possession. It lies on its great platform on the east of the city with access through the Golden Gate to the Kingdom of Jordan. The barrier of its walls makes a clear frontier between it and the rest of the city and when internationalization comes, it will be easy to separate it from the zone and make it an integral part of the Arab Kingdom.

The rest of the ancient city comprises a dense constellation of Christian Holy Places. This term can be used loosely to include all properties belonging to various Christian bodies – convents, hostels, churches – many of which sprang up in the Holy Land during the last century of Turkish rule; strictly it should mean only those places which were venerated before the Mohammedan invasion as the sites of Christian history. It is to those that the pilgrims flocked, and it was the chief of these that became the subject of the intricate system of *Status Quo* which was elaborated by the *firmans* of successive sultans, recognized by international treaty and by the British during their thirty years of rule. Of Holy Places in this strict sense there are some forty in the walled city of Jerusalem and on the Mount of Olives; seven in the adjoining village of Bethany and sixteen in and around Bethlehem, which is five miles distant by the old road, now cut by a Jewish salient. All these lie in the *de facto* authority of the Hashemite Kingdom of Jordan. In the State of Israel lie the Church of the Dormition and the Cenacle under the walls of the old city, three Holy Places at Ein Karim, one at Emmaus, nine at Nazareth, five on the Sea of Galilee, three at Cana, one at Carmel. The most important of these is Nazareth, which stands in a peculiar position in Israel. Elsewhere the Jews were able to stampede the inhabitants (who now live in destitution, some half million in the wastes of Jordan alone), and hastily fill their homes with Jewish immigrants. But at Nazareth the Arabs, mostly Christians, remained. They now live under restraint, forbidden to travel outside their area or go to work, as they used, in Haifa. Special police passes are required by foreigners to enter the district. The inhabitants are naturally entirely unsympathetic to the State of Israel and would welcome internationalization.

To move from one part of the Holy Land to the other is almost impossible for a subject of either part. For the foreign pilgrim it is difficult but possible. He must possess duplicate passports, he must be ferried across the line at a prearranged time, normally by the kind offices of his consul; once across there is no return by that route. He must fly out from Amman or drive up to Syria and Lebanon. It may be added that the fictitious rate of exchange makes travel in Israel more costly than anywhere else in the world. That is the trick by which a modern government exacts the dues which were considered intolerably oppressive in the Middle Ages. Indeed the conditions which provoked the First Crusade were scarcely more offensive to the pilgrim than those existing today.

But we should not protest too much. It is in the nature of a pilgrimage to be uncomfortable. Often they are undertaken as penance and early rules for pilgrims enjoin bare feet and uncombed hair as essential features. St Patrick's Purgatory in Ireland is today the only place in the world which maintains the full discipline of the primitive Church, though even there the brush and comb are permitted, and it is thronged with penitents.

The pilgrim's instinct is deep-set in the human heart. It is indeed an affair of the heart rather than of the head. Reason tells us that Christ is as fully present in one church as in another, but we know by experience that some churches have what we most inadequately call an 'atmosphere' in which we pray easily, while others do not. How much more is this true of the spots marked by great events and by the devotion of the saints. Stern moralists of the Middle Ages were constantly exhorting their flocks to stay at home and warning them that the spiritual dangers of the wanderer might quite undo the benefits. But the tide was not to be stayed. It flowed ceaselessly to Compostela and Canterbury and Rome and Cologne and to countless shrines all over the ancient world. As soon as one place was desecrated by Mohammedan and Reformer, other places sprang up. In the last hundred years Lourdes and Fatima have taken rank with the great centres of mediaeval devotion. Restlessness and mere curiosity no doubt have a part (the motives of human action are inextricably mixed), but far above these is the empty human imagination seeking an object for its attention. In this most natural quest the Holy Land has for the Christian a primacy which Rome itself cannot approach.

Nevertheless it is a fact that many visitors are disconcerted by what they see there. Those who come fresh from the towering splendours of Catholic Europe find architecture which is often ramshackle, often meanly modern. Those who come from the light, spacious, plain conventicles of Protestant worship find murky caves cluttered with shabby ornament and echoing with exotic liturgies. Those whose imaginations have been filled from childhood by bright biblical illustrations and such hymns as Mrs Alexander's 'There is a green hill far away' find a confusing topography in which the Way of the Cross runs through an oriental bazaar. A little girl remarked at Calvary: 'I never knew Our Lord was crucified indoors'; she was expressing an uneasiness that troubles many minds; that troubled General Gordon so much that he was impelled to seek the tomb elsewhere and to find it in a site – archaeologically preposterous – which has comforted many bewildered Nordics. 'The Garden Tomb' is what their Sunday school teachers led them to expect, not the Graeco-Russian kiosk of 1809 which now sadly crowns the site unearthed by St Macarius in 326.

This confusion of mind was expounded in the English House of Lords when they debated the antiquities of Jerusalem at the end of the mandate. Their

Lordships were then comforted by the suggestion that since there was some doubt in some minds about their authenticity, the Holy Places did not greatly matter. Perhaps most Americans and Englishmen who have not studied the matter have a vague impression that there has been a good deal of conscious imposture. Certainly no one accepts as *de fide* the authenticity of all.

What I suppose is plain to anyone who accepts the truth of the Gospels is that Galilee and the district in and around Jerusalem are sacred to the incidents of Our Lord's life, death, resurrection and ascension. It is, moreover, certain that the vast majority of the spots venerated today were those identified by a living tradition in the fourth century and have been continuously recognized ever since. Whether this living tradition erred occasionally and precise spots were over-enthusiastically accepted where a rather vague memory survived, we cannot know. Recent excavations, for example those at the Lithostrotos of Pilate's Judgment Hall, have confirmed tradition. We now know that our forefathers were wrong in supposing that the Ecce Homo Arch was the building from which Christ was exposed to the people. We do know, however, that deep below the present Via Dolorosa there does lie the actual path He trod to Calvary. We cannot know whether the Stations are the exact sites of the various incidents. The Holy Places indeed comprise the whole gamut of credibility from the 'Tomb of Adam' – a fantasy, surely; the fruit of ancient prosaic minds seeking a concrete form for the poetic imagery used of the Atonement – to the rock of Calvary which no one but an ill-informed bigot would attempt to discredit. Between these two extremes the other shrines could be arranged in a rough order of probability, but the question is primarily antiquarian rather than religious. Suppose – though there is no particular reason to do so – that the place of John the Baptist's birth were not where we think, but a few yards away, in another street, even, of the same village, the devotion of centuries has made the traditional site a Holy Place in fact.

This last may be taken as typical of the minor shrines and of the surprises that await the pilgrim. He has come to Ein Karim to see the home of the Baptist. He finds a handsome modern church in the Spanish style. He is led down a precipitous staircase into a small cave where he is invited to kiss a marble boss. This, he is told, is the birthplace of St John. His guide is a bearded Franciscan. If they have a language in common, and even perhaps if they have not, the pilgrim will be told at length the stories of St Elizabeth and of Zachary. He may be shown some pottery of Herod's time found on the spot and the mosaic remains of two Byzantine chapels. But the Franciscans of the Custody are seldom archaeologists and never aesthetes. Their first characteristic is tenacity. They inherited the flag of the Crusades in 1291. When the knights and barons retreated, the friars remained. They have stayed on for more than 600 years with absolute singleness of purpose, undisturbed by theological and artistic fashions, holding fast to the Gospel and to the stony places where it was enacted. Their struggle has swayed back and forth. They have often been cheated and brutally dispossessed of their property; they have time received fine benefactions. They have more than once in all their under-takings seen the full revolution of the cycle, decay, destruction, restoration, and have learned to avoid undue attachment to their own transient structures. Indeed they seem positively to relish the demolition of buildings which any-where else would be patiently preserved. Give them the chance to put up something brand new, strong and convenient, and the Franciscans of the Custody jump to it. They have no sentiment except the highest. No association later than the Apostles interests them. There is only one 'period' for them: the years of Our Lord. It is not for us to look askance. They have had small help from art connoisseurs during their age-long, lonely sentry-duty.

But the cave, too, is not what we might have expected. These sacred grottoes are everywhere; here, at Nazareth, at Bethlehem, on the Mount of Olives, as far away as the Old Christian quarter beyond the walls of Cairo. The early painters loved to elaborate them and the poetic imagination may leap delight-edly from these places to the catacombs, to St Anthony's cell and St Jerome's, and again to Lourdes; but, by prosaic Franciscan lights, it does seem remark-ably odd that St Elizabeth should go down to the cellar for her *accouchement*. The explanation, I think, is that she did nothing of the kind. The houses of this district mostly stand over honeycombs of natural and hewn cisterns and store-rooms. These remain when the houses fall or burn. In identifying a site in the fourth century villagers would say: 'Here, our fathers have told us, John was born.' Nothing is more natural than that a confusion should occur and the cave usurp the history of the former house. We may explain in the same way such objects of veneration as the block of stone from which Our Lord is said to have mounted the ass for his entry into Jerusalem. It is probable that the stone was first put there simply to mark the spot and that later generations made it a participant in the actual drama. Concessions such as these are all that need be made to the sceptic. We may admit, too, that the sites of the Dormition and Our Lady's Tomb have strong rivals at Ephesus. But when all these small debts to plausibility have been paid in full, the residual wealth of the Holy Land in authentic gilt-edged association is incomparably large. The supreme treasury is, of course, the great Church of the Holy Sepulchre in Jerusalem.

And here, as one might expect, one finds exemplified and accentuated all the peculiarities of the Holy Land. The first impression, as one enters the court-yard, is that one has come inopportunely. The steps by which one approaches are arched over with a structure of steel girders and wood props; the fine, twelfth-century façade and entrance is entirely obscured by scaffolding. Inside, as one's eyes become accustomed to the gloom, one finds that all the arches of choir and rotunda are reinforced with a dense armature of timber, that everywhere a forest of beams and struts spreads between the ancient columns, and that the walls are bound like a clumsily wrapped parcel with a tangle of steel ties. There has been some recent mishap or some defect has suddenly become apparent, the visitor supposes. Work must be in progress; the men are just on holiday. But such is not the case. The disturbance took place in 1927. Grave danger to the whole fabric was apparent seven years later and these girders and baulks of timber are the hasty improvisations of local British engineers, a first-aid treatment while the ecclesiastical authorities were deciding on a plan. In 1942 further dangers were discerned and further temporary measures taken by the same engineers. Now they have gone away; nothing is being done. The dead hand of the old Ottoman *firmans* and the Treaty of Berlin of 1878 render the ecclesiastical authorities powerless. They are merely waiting for the inevitable collapse, perhaps in their time, perhaps in the time of their successors, when the Christian world will be obliged to turn its attention to its principal shrine.

Meanwhile one wanders backward through history. One notices first the work of the English sappers, next the reconstruction of the Greek builders of 1810; then, if one has an eye for architecture, one sees that all these encumbrances stand in a great Transitional-Norman Cathedral, still almost intact; then one may find tucked away underground all that is left of the original buildings of Constantine and Helena. That great assembly of buildings was destroyed by the Persians before the Mohammedan invasions, by Chosroes in 614, who carried off the True Cross. The Emperor Heraclius was the first true Crusader. Solemnly dedicating his arms he invaded Persia eight years later and brought the relic home in triumph, while the monk Modestus travelled throughout the empire raising funds for the rebuilding. The fortunes of the shrine were inextricably interlocked with the history of that land of earthquake, invasion and civil riot. Damage, restoration, damage, succeed one another through the centuries. Certain events are of determining importance. This destruction by Chosroes and rebuilding by Modestus and Heraclius is one of them; next, very soon after, the surrender of the city to the Caliph Omar in 637. His Mohammedan successors did not emulate his chivalry. In 1009 the Caliph Hakim, an Egyptian, tried to extirpate Christianity in his dominions. He was probably insane. He reversed his policy later but not before the Church of Modestus had been demolished and the Sepulchre itself, which until then had preserved its original rock-hewn form, had lost roof and walls so that nothing now remains except the floor and the slab upon which Our Lord's body lay. Succeeding *edicules* have been masonry. It was not until forty years later that the local Christians with the help of the Emperor Monomachus were able to complete a rebuilding which lacked most of the splendour of its predecessors and left half the former shrine in ruins. Hakim's persecution shocked Christendom. It was thought intolerable that the Holy City should be at the mercy of the caprices of Mohammedan potentates.

The Emperor of the East had become a reduced and localized power scarcely able to maintain himself at Constantinople, still less to reconquer Palestine. The crusade was preached in the West. In 1099 a Christian army recaptured Jerusalem and established a Latin kingdom there which survived for barely a century. Under this rule was built the church which stands today enclosing under a single roof the sites of the Crucifixion and the Resurrection. But meanwhile the Great Schism had occurred. On 16 July 1054, the bickerings of 200 years took violent form in the excommunication by the Papal Legates of the Patriarch of Constantinople in his own cathedral. The Patriarchs of Alexandria, Antioch and Jerusalem followed him into schism. This was an event quite different from any of the previous outbreaks of heresy. From time to time in the preceding centuries individuals representing every aberration of theology had broken from the Universal Church, taking with them numbers of adherents. Most of these bodies disappeared in a generation unless kept alive by particular racial loyalties. But the separation of four historic orthodox patriarchates, on personal and political grounds chiefly, was a disaster from which Christendom still terribly suffers today. It was recognized as something unnatural and deplorable even when tempers were most exacerbated. There were continual attempts at reconciliation. In 1439 at the Council of Florence peace was made, but by that time the Greek clergy had become crassly sectarian and they repudiated their leaders. When Constantinople fell in 1453 St Sophia was again a Catholic church as it had been in its first days. The last Emperor of the East died a Catholic, gallantly fighting on the walls. Congregations all over the Levant remained loyal to Rome and survive prosperously today. But, as the whole of Eastern Christendom fell under the Turk, an iron curtain descended between it and the West behind which the great majority of Orthodox Christians was caught at an unpropitious moment. Their schism became the badge of their loyalty. Untouched by humanism, by the stimulating controversy of the fifteenth century, by the great revitalizing power of the Counter-Reformation, cut off from the sap of Christian fellowship, the Eastern Churches dried up and hardened.

Thus were born the disputes over the Holy Places which in their turn produced the *Status Quo*. As the Turkish power matured and softened the administration relied more and more upon the clever subject peoples for its courtiers and civil servants. Persecution alternated with appeasement in the policy towards Greeks, Armenians and Copts. The cheapest form of appeasement is always to pay with the property of others, and throughout the eighteenth century, as the mind of Europe grew less religious and the sovereigns fought for colonies in the New World and Russia gradually emerged as a great Orthodox Christian power, the sultans granted more and more licences to the Eastern clergy for encroachment on the rights of the Latins, until by 1757 an immensely complex code was evolved defining precisely how many lamps each cult might hang and on how many feet of ground they might worship at each holy place. France had been the recognized protector of the Catholics in the East. At the Revolution France became atheist. At the height of the Napoleonic regime a fire took place in the Church of the Sepulchre. While the West was indifferent and preoccupied, the Greeks acted, swept away the tombs of the Latin kings and the Latin choir and reconstructed all they could in their own characteristic style. That is the Church we see today. The Treaties of Paris of 1855, and of Berlin in 1878, reaffirmed the *Status Quo* of 1757.

The principle of the *Status Quo* was that property belonged to whoever could prove that he had last exercised the right of repairing it. While certain places were subdivided, others were left as common property of the Catholics, Greeks and Armenians. Nothing can be done to common property, which includes the general fabric of the Church of the Holy Sepulchre, without the consent and participation of all. There is thus a complete *impasse* in which the place is visibly falling to pieces. It may be noted in passing that when a small fire recently occurred in the dome, King Abdullah patched it up without consulting anyone and without anyone minding. He also broke with Turkish precedent in appointing, on 5 January 1951, an official of his own as Curator of the Holy Places. No one seems to know what this official's duties are. He offers no explanation. What is certain is that the Kingdom of Jordan has not the means to effect the huge repairs that are urgently needed.

In this situation a totally new plan has been produced under the patronage of the Apostolic Delegate in Jerusalem. It is one of total demolition and rebuilding. Two Italian architects – Barluzzi and Marangoni – have produced a pretty album of their designs – *Il Santo Sepolchro di Gerusalemme: Splendori – Miserie – Speranze* – at the Institute of Art at Bergamo, in which is envisaged a scheme of town clearance, demanding a whole quarter of the densely populated city, demolishing two mosques including the historic site of Omar's prayer, and the ancient convents that now cluster round the basilica, and planting in the centre of this space a huge brand-new edifice where Calvary and the Sepulchre would stand, as they did under Constantine, as separate buildings in an open court. Centred in this court would stand the churches of all the rites which have claims in the existing building and also of the Anglican Church which does not.

No one, I think, regards this undertaking as practicable; few as desirable. Apart from any aesthetic objection – and there are many – there is the supreme objection that this immense erection would be in effect a monument to the divisions of the Church. These divisions are so much a part of the tradition and daily lives of the Franciscans of the Custody that it is small wonder if they have come to accept them as normal and permanent. But there is all the difference between a quarrelsome family who still share one home and jostle one another on the stairs, and one which has coldly split up into separate, inaccessible households. The extreme animosities of the past have subsided, but it is not impossible that they should break out anew. The clergy of the different rites treat one another with courtesy, but they are constantly vigilant; no quarrels have recently occurred because the *Status Quo* has been rigidly observed. Any infringement of it would provide immediate protest and, perhaps, retaliation. It is, of course, all very unseemly and unedifying. But so also is the division of the Church. Under the proposed reconstruction there would be no fear of friction. It would be a great deal more convenient for everyone concerned. But ease would have been bought by the formal perpetuation of a disgrace.

What is needed, surely, is not the grandiose Franciscan plan, but a patient restoration of the building as it stood in 1800? This, indeed, would be no small task, but no greater than the restoration of Rheims Cathedral after the First World War and of far wider significance. If the funds and the direction came from some source quite unconnected with any of the rival religious bodies, their consent would doubtless be obtainable. It is a task for which the United Nations are eminently suited. They owe a heavy debt to the Holy City. This might form a token payment. But even in its decrepit and defaced condition the great church is an inspiration, for the whole history of Christendom is there to be read by those who trouble to study it. Even the superstitions of early science have their monument there in the stone called 'the centre of the earth'. Every degree of pilgrim and tourist pass and repass all day long, with every degree of piety and insolence, but at night the place really comes to life.

There is only one door now. It shuts at sundown. Just before that hour an Arab soldier clears the darkening aisles of the last penitents and sightseers. The Arab doorkeeper, whose family have held the office since the time of Suleiman the Magnificent – since Omar, some will tell you – climbs a ladder and turns the locks from outside, passes the ladder in through a square trap which a priest locks from his side. The windows fade and disappear, the roof is lost. There is no light except from the oil lamps which glow on Calvary, before the Sepulchre and over the Stone of Unction. Absolute silence falls. The air becomes close and chilly, with the faintest smell of oil and candle wax and incense. The place seems quite empty. But, in fact, there are thirty or more sleeping men tucked away out of sight in various dens and galleries, like bats in a sunless cave. Nothing happens for hours. Some of the oil lamps begin to burn out. You can sit on the doorman's divan and think yourself at the bottom of the sea.

And then, a little before eleven o'clock, lights begin to appear and move in unsuspected apertures and galleries. There is a snuffling and shuffling and from their various lairs – the Greek from a balcony above the rock of Calvary, the Franciscan from a tunnel in the wall beyond the Latin Chapel, the Armenian down an iron fire-escape above the spot of the Stabat Mater – three bearded sacristans appear and begin filling and trimming the lamps. Soon after this there is a sound of door-knocking, knuckles, wooden hammers, a little electric bell somewhere; a yawning and muttering and coughing and rustling. At 11.30 something like a jungle war-drum starts up. That is the Greeks. Then a great irregular banging together of planks. That is the Armenians. Then two vested thurifers appear and proceed by opposite routes round the whole building, censing every altar with a chinking of brass and clouds of aromatic smoke. Then here and there raw little electric bulbs flash on. The monks and friars assemble in their choirs and just before midnight the night offices start, the severe monotone of the Latins contrasting with the exuberant gaiety of the Armenians who are out of sight, up their iron staircase in their own bright vault, but whose music sounds like a distant village festival of folk-dancing and peasant ballads.

The Latin Office is the most brief. The friars file out into their tunnel. The Greeks and Armenians sing on. And then something new, unexpected and quite delicious stirs the drowsy senses – the sweet, unmistakable smell of new-baked bread. It is the Easterns cooking the Hosts for their Masses. Mass is said daily in the tomb by the three chief rites. On some days the Copts celebrate at an altar built against the outer wall. On Sunday morning the Syrians, too, have their service. And daily on the roof, in the sad little African hovels to which they were driven by the rich Armenians, the Monophysite Abyssinians perform their own ancient liturgy.

The Greek Mass is the first, followed by the Armenian. There is room only for priest and server in the inner chamber of the Sepulchre. Two or three more may kneel in the outer room. The remainder of the choir stand outside. While the Armenian Mass is going on the Catholics may be heard not far off in their chapel intoning another office. By 3.30 the *edicule* is clear of the Armenians and the Franciscan sacristan busies himself with a portable altar and the Mass furniture of the West. At four o'clock the door is opened. A servant of the Judeh family brings the key, which for convenience he now hangs in the Greek convent on the north of the courtyard, and hands it to the representative of the Musedi family. A monk opens the trapdoor and pushes out the ladder. With a squeak and a clang the locks are turned and the door swings open. The monks and the gate-keepers salaam and the gate-keepers shuffle back to bed.

At 4.30 the Catholic Mass is said in the Sepulchre, followed by others through all the early hours of the morning on Calvary, in the Chapel of the Franks and in the Latin Chapel. And at dawn as one steps out into the courtyard after one's vigil one is met by the cry of the muezzin from the minaret of Omar's prayer, proclaiming that there is no God but Allah and Mohammed is his Prophet.

One has been in the core of one's religion. It is all there, with all its human faults and its superhuman triumphs, and one fully realizes, perhaps for the first time, that Christianity did not strike its first root at Rome or Canterbury or Geneva or Maynooth, but here in the Levant where everything is inextricably mixed and nothing is assimilated. In the Levant there works an alchemy the very reverse of the American melting-pot. Different races and creeds jostle one another for centuries and their diversity becomes only the more accentuated. Our Lord was born into a fiercely divided civilization and so it has remained. But our hope must always be for unity, and as long as the Church of the Sepulchre remains a single building, however subdivided, it forms a memorial to that essential hope.

Waugh found thirty-nine 'misprints . . . mostly my mistakes' in *The Holy Places* (London: Queen Anne Press, 1952), which reprinted the *Month* text of this essay (letters to Peters, 27 January–2 February 1953). Queen Anne Press subsequently made changes in its New York edition (1953), most of which are adopted here. *Month*'s version is fuller than *Life*'s.

. A CLEAN SWEEP .

The reviewer who comes late to his task is at great advantage for he joins the debate after the question has been defined. All interested in novels may now be presumed to have read *Hemlock and After* or to have read enough about it to have decided that the book is not for them. The temptation of the late critic is to deal only with his predecessors, the least intelligent of whom were those of the BBC. These savants, who discuss books and things on Sunday morning, sought a way out of their puzzlement by saying that the book could be treated 'on two levels' as though it comprised two complementary cellophane tracings, ignoring the fact that any book worth discussing at length exists in three dimensions, a solid thing which can be viewed from any angle and cut in any section. Most good novels vary in mood and method – satire, comedy, drama, allegory, analysis, description, comment and criticism, all have their part.

Hemlock and After is a singularly rich, compact and intricate artifact, and the first thing any critic should make clear is that whatever its defects, it is a thing to rejoice over. In England, in any branch of literature from detective stories to theology, we are reading precisely the same writers as we were reading eighteen years ago. Here at last is someone new. Mr Wilson has already shown himself to be incomparably the cleverest and most skilful story-teller since the brief passage across our skies of Mr Christopher Isherwood. Now he has produced a novel which in less precise hands might have run to three times its length. Indeed almost the only just complaint that can be made of his craftsmanship is that it puts a considerable strain on the reader. Let the mind slacken for the length of a line and you will miss something important.

Thus the plot defies adequate summary. The 'Hemlock' of the title is, of course, an allusion to the death of Socrates. The central theme is the tragedy of an elderly man of letters, a liberal-humanist. He desires to crown his life's work by the establishment of a Home for young poets. The test of his prestige is his success or failure in enlisting the support of all the political and scholarly bodies who can make his conception practicable. He triumphs. For the Inauguration Mr Wilson provides all the traditional comic effects of an English function – the drunk servants, the gate-crashers, the bores and snobs and frauds, the incompetent and insolent workmen. But there is a deep personal tragedy in the personal life of the hero of the day, which causes him to deliver a message of despair instead of one of hope. His wife is out of her mind and he, Mr Sands, the great man, has in advanced years developed and indulged homosexual tendencies, which have attached him successively to two contrasted youths, a pert young cad and the feeble, retarded victim of a 'graciously living' American mother. More than this, there has established herself at his gates (he lives in Metroland) a formidable woman named Mrs Curry, a procuress, who carries on her trade in a rose-embowered cottage. Almost

Review of *Hemlock and After*, by Angus Wilson. *Month*, October 1952.

unanimously the critics have condemned this character as preposterous. The present writer was able, at a pinch, to accept her, but he found her methods of trading quite incredible. It would not be surprising to learn that she had in fact been drawn quite accurately from life. That is often the case with the least plausible characters in fiction and when it happens it marks an artistic failure on the part of the writer. Mrs Curry's horrible *ménage* forms a caricature of the secret life of Mr Sands. When she plans a particularly nasty service for one of her neighbours, Mr Sands is disgusted and determines to intervene. But he has nothing except his disgust. His liberal-humanism has been invoked to justify his own vices. He has silenced his conscience by professing that his interest in his catamites is benevolent. By what standard are he and his set the superiors of Mrs Curry and hers? He acts, but dies in an agony of mind. It is left to Mrs Sands, who comes to her senses in the crisis, to complete the work of purgation.

First and last it is the story of a 'bad conscience', though the scene is so densely thronged with minor but essential characters that it needs hard reading to follow it. The characters are 'unpleasant' and this is a fact which the reviewers have firmly grasped. The broadcasting critics found the characters so odious as to forfeit all interest. But the case is odder than that. There is a superfluity of the outrageously wicked certainly, but there is almost an equal number of people who under other eyes than Mr Wilson's might be quite likeable. Mr Wilson is unique in his detestation of all of his creatures; their most innocent hobbies are as reprehensible as their vices. The facts that they wear certain clothes or decorate their rooms in certain ways or speak with certain mannerisms are noted as damning evidence – of what?

There seem two prepossessions of Mr Wilson's which greatly detract from his power as an artist. Perhaps they are Marxist in origin. One is his hypersensitiveness to class. Nowhere, except perhaps in parts of Asia, is the class structure as subtle and elaborate as in England. Everyone in England has a precise and particular place in the social scale and constantly manifests the fact in habit and word. Many writers have found a rich source in this national idiosyncrasy. Few writers have a sharper nose for class than Mr Wilson. But when he defines he seems to condemn. It is as though he found something obscene in the mere fact of class membership. Can he be troubled by remote dreams of The Classless Society?

The other characteristic may spring from the same indoctrination. He appears to believe that revolution is just around the corner. This apocalyptic sense puts all his creation in a dubious light. If his characters are really the products of economic forces and if those forces are about to cease; if his whole story is simply a flickering shadow on a screen which, any moment, will rise on Real Life; if there are no abiding consequences to anything they do; if there is no heaven or hell for them – then indeed the broadcasters are right in saying that they are devoid of interest or meaning.

But Mr Wilson is too true an artist to be a victim for long of these fatuous views – if indeed he holds them at all. When he is really wholeheartedly engaged with his characters, however obscure, he *knows* they matter, and the reader knows too.

And there is another aspect from which the book can be read. A writer's relation with his symbols is on the whole a private concern. A reader is entitled to find his own allegory. For this reader, at any rate, there was great significance in the return to sanity of Mrs Sands. It was as though she had been the Conscience of the book, atrophied at first, then stirring and coming to action, and triumphantly and serenely making a great clean sweep. All that is lacking in a work elsewhere so full of fine definition is the name of the new life-giving power.

. URBANE ENJOYMENT PERSONIFIED: SIR OSBERT SITWELL .

The physical profile is familiar. The bland, patrician features have been cast in brass by Frank Dobson and exquisitely limned by Sir Max Beerbohm; they have been photographed by Mr Beaton and snapped by a host of camera men. The tall, well-dressed figure, the courteous manner (Mr Turveydrop ameliorates the stern carriage of Sir Leicester Dedlock in this baronet) might, at first glance, belong to any well-to-do, cultivated English bachelor of a passing generation. Closer scrutiny reveals a hint of alertness and menace, as though a rattlesnake may be expected round the next corner and the nice conduct of the clouded cane might any minute require a good whack. There is little to indicate the transition that has occurred in the last fifteen years between the *enfant terrible* and the Grand Old Man of English Letters.

For that, beyond dispute, is Sir Osbert's present position. He is not our only one. We are fairly free with the title; less so than the French; more, I think, than Americans. It comes in the end to all genuine talent which has not been prematurely extinguished. It comes sometimes to men who have ceased writing for twenty years or more. The interest of Sir Osbert's fame is that it rests on a lifetime of uninterrupted development and enrichment. His natural growth has continued into late middle age so that his latest book has always been his best. He acquired his reputation first, then seriously settled down to earn it.

In my youth, when Sir Osbert's literary achievement was still very small, the English scene was full of august figures – Hardy, Yeats, Bridges – but there was little doubt in any of our minds as to whom we aspired to know. Already it was the Sitwells, for they radiated an aura of high spirit, elegance, impudence, unpredictability; above all of sheer enjoyment. Most writers are best known in their work. They are dull dogs to meet and only come alive at their desks pen in hand. Sir Osbert is a full, rich, singular personality first, and a shelf of books

New York Times Magazine, 30 November 1952.

second. His achievement is to have mastered the art of recording and communicating his personality. There has never, I think, been a writer who has had at the same time so great an influence and so few imitators. Mr Hemingway pre-eminently, to a less degree D. H. Lawrence, Virginia Woolf and Mr Eliot, are all overcast and tainted by the crop of disciples they have sowed.

There is no identifiable school of Sitwell. Three of them was enough.

No one sought to ape their escapades. They spread no infectious literary rash. We simply basked in the warmth they generated and went back to our several tasks exhilarated. But their influence permeates all that remains of civilized English life.

It is best defined I think as pure enjoyment – of people and places, art and absurdity, the latest thing and the oldest; an equal zest for battle and for placid contemplation.

Sir Osbert was a regular soldier before the First World War. He belongs to a generation most of whom were killed or fatally embittered. He emerged from the war with some bitterness too, but this he extruded in his satirical writing. It never appeared in his life, which was unfailingly gay even in his rages. A great waste of time had been forced on him in stables and trenches. He was determined to make up for it. Where others sought mere distraction, he and his brother found real enjoyment.

They declared war on dullness. The British bourgeoisie were no longer fair game. Their self-complacency had gone with their power during the war. The Sitwells attacked from within that still-depressing section of the upper class that devoted itself solely to sport and politics. By 1939 English society had been revolutionized, lightened and brightened, very largely through the Sitwell influence. They taught the grandees to enjoy their possessions while they still had them. They made the bore recognized and abhorred as the prime social sinner.

They attacked from without the professional worlds of art and literature, where a new and insidious philistinism was being preached. Mud from the fields, where 'conscientious objectors' had played at farming, bespattered everything. There was a shrinking from the rare and lovely and elaborate, and a welcome for the commonplace. Scrawls from the Infant School were as 'significant' as the finest draftsmanship. Vocabularies were purged of all but their drabbest epithets. A decade later all this bilge was canalized by the Marxists. Then it had half London and Paris awash. The Sitwells careered like Indians round these covered wagons, loosing their flaming arrows into the Bible readings.

Sir Osbert and his brother Sacheverell had a well-bred disdain for the conventions of good taste. They revelled in publicity. Most English writers genuinely shrink from it. Others have a guilty vanity that makes them woo it in secret. The Sitwells left their press cuttings in bowls on the drawing-room table. Popular newspapers with all their absurd vulgarity were just a part of the exciting contemporary world in which the Sitwells romped. They were weapons in the total warfare against dullness.

The Sitwells were frankly and recklessly resolved to be conspicuous. Others produced slim volumes of verse and waited timidly for the reviews. Miss Edith Sitwell's poems were recited through a megaphone from behind a screen. I vividly remember the first night of 'Façade'. My memory differs slightly from Sir Osbert's. He was aware of hostile demonstrators among an audience which seemed to me uniformly enthusiastic. No one could mistake the subsequent swish and smack of the tomahawks when a critical head showed itself.

The world is united now in its deference toward Sir Osbert. In those days he saw it – perhaps with exaggeration – as divided into opposed camps of his friends and enemies. Toward his enemies he was implacable and deadly. No one was too trivial or too august to escape savage retaliation for an insult. Most writers, in the course of their careers, become thick-skinned and learn to accept vituperation, which in any other profession would be unimaginably offensive, as a healthy counterpoise to unintelligent praise. Not so the Sitwells. If those bowlfuls of press cuttings survive – and I suspect that they do, somewhere among the archives of Renishaw – they will make a rich store of material for future biographers; controversies on every conceivable subject, appalling snubs, sledge-hammer blows on thick skulls and frail insects alike. At one time indeed, these ferocious campaigns threatened to undo their own work of publicity, for editors and critics alike became timid of mentioning Sir Osbert at all for fear of the consequences.

And meanwhile Sir Osbert continued to enjoy things. He has three enchanting houses but no one has got more than he out of travel. Like all good travellers, he rejected accustomed amenities and sought in every place what is idiosyncratic of it. In America, for instance, where the friendliest visitors tend to wilt in the central heating, Sir Osbert finds the fierce temperature highly stimulating, just as in China he rejoiced at the whistling pigeons. Books will no doubt multiply about Sir Osbert's social and artistic adventures.

One quality, perhaps because it lends itself least to the raconteur, is seldom emphasized; that is Sir Osbert's continuous kindness to other artists. Many of his battles have been fought in defence of others. And he has been recklessly liberal in the role of patron. There can be few painters or writers or musicians of his period who are not bound to him with gratitude. Two instances come to my mind, for they involve acquaintances. A penniless undergraduate, thought at the time a promising poet, was sent down from Oxford. He was immediately invited to make Renishaw his home until he had found his feet. Another young man, now a fine novelist, then unknown, worked in the publishing office which produced Sir Osbert's earlier books. He seemed lonely and dispirited. Sir Osbert invited him to give a dinner party for his friends at his London house.

Throughout his life, too, Sir Osbert has shown the far rarer generosity of encouraging the successful.

And all the time that Sir Osbert was enjoying himself, 'going everywhere', as they used to say, 'and knowing everyone', he was hard at work mastering his difficult art. His life and his writing are indivisible. It is fitting that his masterpiece should be the five lucid, opulent volumes of his autobiography.

These calm, leisurely pages were written during the stresses of the Second World War. Sir Osbert refused to be hurried; refused to modify his idiosyncratic attitude to life in deference to the debased standards of the time. He knew he had a valuable message to deliver – one of urbane enjoyment. He knew he had an artistic creation to perfect – his portrait of his own father. He knew he had a uniquely rich experience to develop – a lifetime lived in and for the arts. Those five volumes have given him a secure place in English literature.

. OUR GUEST OF DISHONOUR .

Mr Eden has invited his great new friend Broz to stay with us. We shall be expected to line the streets and foot the bill for the triumphal progress.

Who is this man? He will come under the latest, and perhaps the last, of many aliases as Marshal Tito, the name and title conferred on him by the Russians. 'Tito' was simply his Comintern code-word. Marshal was a rank of the Red Army unknown in Yugoslavia. He held Stalin's commission and Stalin sent him his marshal's cap. I well remember the day Tito first wore it on the Island of Vis, where in August 1944 he was living under the protection of our Fleet and Air Force. It was not a well-made cap by English standards. It was not becoming by any standard. But Tito waddled about the island as proud as a dog with two tails because it came like a halo from his Russian heaven.

He was busy then, as now, in the work for which he has a peculiar aptitude – hoodwinking the British. The Germans were then in retreat from the Balkans. Their only use for Yugoslavia was an escape route. The partisans lurked in the hills and forests and left the main roads to the Germans. They had two civil wars on their hands – against the Serbian royalists and the Croat nationalists. Tito's job was to persuade us to arm him for these wars under pretence of fighting the Germans. He succeeded.

As soon as the Red Army invaded from Bulgaria he flew to join it without a word to our headquarters. Thenceforward he refused all co-operation with the West and set himself to impose on his decimated and distracted people a Communist regime with all the familiar, sickening concomitants of secret police and judicial murder. Now he is at it again, and again he is succeeding. The only difference between the Tito of 1944 and 1952 is that he has sought to postpone the fate which devours each Communist hero in turn, by the desperate step of quarrelling with Stalin.

Politicians cannot be squeamish about their business associates. We do not look to them for an example of fastidious moral rectitude. All we ask is

Sunday Express, 30 November 1952.

commonsense experience of the world. Do they really suppose that Tito, who has betrayed in turn emperor, king, friends, and finally his one consistent loyalty to Stalin, will prove a trustworthy friend to *them*? Apparently, in their naïve vanity, they do. They are sending him huge subsidies. It is our money, but it is their political reputations that are at hazard.

We might have rested content to watch the gamble and penalize the losers, but they go too far in bringing him here as an honoured guest because, though the politicians seem oblivious of the fact, there is a loyal multitude of Her Majesty's subjects who recognize in him one of the six or seven most deadly and most powerful enemies of all they hold holy. Tito is seeking to extirpate Christianity in Yugoslavia. Make no mistake about it. He is not squabbling with the Vatican about rights and privileges. Orthodox as well as Catholics are doomed if his rule continues. He has not, except in early days when partisan bands roamed the country murdering priests at will, used the same sensational violence as his Hungarian neighbours. But the aim is identical, as logically it must be in a regime which boasts itself as the only true-model Leninist state.

Some churches are still open and some priests are still at their altars. A few old peasants may be allowed to die in peace. But the younger generation are being driven from their faith with all the specialized mechanism of modern statesmanship. Details of the persecution have been reported from time to time, not very prominently, in the national press. They follow the pattern – prohibition of religious teaching in schools, compulsory anti-religious teach-ing, prohibition of religious teaching in the home and in church, except during the actual Mass, crushing financial levies, closing the seminaries and theologi-cal faculties at the universities and so on. In the last few weeks a new resolution has been written into the constitution forbidding any member of the governing party to practise any religion at all.

The significant feature of the story is that these measures have been inten-sified during the last three months, the very period of English Conservative courtship. The government must suppose that their supporters are ignorant of all this – or are they really unaware that England is still largely a Christian country? In hundreds of thousands of homes the fully documented history of the persecution has been followed with anger in the religious press. It is not merely the 10 per cent Roman Catholic population of the country who are outraged at the prospect of Tito's visit, but zealous churchmen of every denomination.

Our leaders are properly cautious of offending religious and racial minorities. Mr Eden would not invite the country to feast and flatter a notorious Jew-baiter. Only when Christianity is at stake do our leaders show bland indifference. If they are really indifferent let them shorten their speeches and say frankly: 'We see nothing abhorrent in the methods and aims of Communist rule. It is only Russia we are scared of. We will make every effort to strengthen any Communist dictator and arm him to impose his tyranny, provided only that he is temporarily estranged from Stalin. We welcome the transformation of great territories of Christendom into atheist police states. We despise the Christian peoples who look to us for sympathy and we despise the Christian voters at home, who, anyway, break about even at the polls.'

Is that really what is in their minds?

No doubt, if Tito comes, a crowd will assemble, as it will for any notoriety, and no doubt there will be some cheering. But let Mr Eden not think that his guest is welcome. We are not given to breaking windows and throwing stink-bombs, we English Christians. We refuse to learn the ugly modern lesson that nothing succeeds except conspiracy and violence. No doubt the deplorable event will pass off without Mr Eden's guest being aware that numberless heads are bowed in national dishonour and in prayer for the frustration of all his ambitions.

. MR BETJEMAN DESPAIRS .

In the small, shrinking, perhaps vanishing society which honours beauty and humour, Mr Betjeman is literally a household word. His name has passed into the vernacular as surely as Spooner and Banting. 'A Betjeman character', 'a Betjeman house', have plain meanings. His poems are the best remembered, the most quoted, of any writer's save Mr Belloc. Are there circles where after-dinner revellers leap to their feet uninvited and declaim Mr Stephen Spender's verses for the sheer delight of hearing them again? Perhaps. But the present writer suspects that such entertainments are rarer and vastly less exhilarating than the continuous, almost liturgical recitation of Mr Betjeman's office.

'Betjemanism' is a mood of the moment like existentialism. His following is among the gayest element of his contemporaries. Some make a good thing out of it, gleaning where he has so profusely sowed. Many hundreds of devotees enjoy a vicarious intimacy with the ladies to whom many of his finest poems were addressed. One of these charming muses has now come forward as the editress of his prose writings. Under the title *First and Last Loves*, Mrs Piper, the immortal 'Myfanwy', presents thirty-two pieces – there is no other word for them. She would have put us more deeply in her debt had she dated each and given the reference for its first publication. Thirteen pieces were admittedly composed for broadcasting. It seems probable that certain others have the same origin. The collection does not show Mr Betjeman at the top of his form. He is, first and last, a poet – one of high technical ability – and prose does not become him. A poet writing prose often has something of the uneasiness of an actor asked to a party after his performance. There are traces of grease paint behind the ears; the manner is either too vivacious or betrays a

Review of *First and Last Loves*, by John Betjeman. *Month*, December 1952.

studied normality. The broadcast pieces were popular and no doubt there are many who will wish to be reminded of them. The present writer attempted to listen on several occasions and each time turned off the machine in embarrassment. Now, printed, they still bear the awful stains of their birth – the jauntiness, the intrusive, false intimacy, the sentimentality – which seem inseparable from this medium. Other essays are informative and satirical, designed for a graver audience. But many of Mr Betjeman's disciples write this kind of thing as well as he. Connoisseurs will value this collection less as a work of art than as a conspectus of 'Betjemanism'.

Mr Betjeman's principal themes are architectural, amorous (these essays have no example of this interest) and ecclesiastical. He celebrates the odd and the obscure. He is exclusively insular. A large part of his vogue springs from the recent embargo on foreign travel. Denied their traditional hunting grounds, aesthetes have had to make good with odds and ends at home. The normal process of Betjemanizing is first the undesired stop in a provincial English town, then the 'discovery' there of a rather peculiar police station, *circa* 1880; the enquiry and identification of its architect. Further research reveals that a Methodist chapel in another town is by the same hand. Then the hunt is up. More buildings are identified. The obscure name is uttered with reverence befitting Bernini. The senile master is found to be alive, in distressed circumstances in a northern suburb of London. He is a 'character'; he has vague, personal memories of other long dead, equally revered contemporaries. In his last years he is either rejuvenated or else driven mad to find himself the object of pilgrimage. It is all very beguiling and beside it there flourishes a genuine, sound love of the simpler sorts of craftsmanship.

Mr Betjeman's religious interests are everywhere apparent. Theology is totally closed to him, but he has sung hymns in every kind of Protestant conventicle and acquired an *expertise* in Anglican deviations. Show him the hassocks in a country church and he will know unerringly whether the incumbent was educated at Cambridge or Durham; one glance at the lectern and he will tell you the hours of Sunday services. And the services are a deep source to him of excitement and sentiment. *First and Last Loves* has an instructive chapter on Nonconformist Architecture. It is regrettable that he omits from this category that vigorous Nonconformist body, the Catholic Church. One day perhaps he will turn his attention towards it. He will find English Catholic history of the last two centuries a territory rich in potential 'discoveries'.

There are several ingenious drawings by Mr Piper in this book; other illustrations suffer from modern methods of reproduction. It would be a suitable Christmas book, nothing more, were it not for the inclusion of an introduction which is highly significant. 'Love is dead' Mr Betjeman warns us. All that follows is the record of a game which the principal player is tired of. He has reached a conclusion which was predicted for him some years ago. In one of the editorial 'Comments' in *Horizon*, Mr Connolly imagined a benevolent dictator of England who would seek to clean the country of all its hideousness and leave only the old and the beautiful. Methodically his airmen set to work, but before the sound of their engines had died away the inhabitants had crept out of their burrows and were busy re-erecting all that was beastly. That is the point Mr Betjeman has reached. No prospect pleases because man himself is vile. He is not troubled by the cosmic despair of George Orwell. He thinks it probable that the politicians and planners will succeed in their task. He thinks security is just round the corner. He looks about him and despairs. There is nothing to look forward to except mediocrity, forcibly imposed, infidelity and vulgarity. The game is up. He is not greatly concerned with the future. The present is hell.

Who can fail to sympathize? 'Why was I born when I was?' An heroic past, an idyllic future – those are the alternatives, according to temperament, of the unhappy artist in any age. Never jam today. All the agonies and annoyances of growing up, which may last a lifetime, spring from the slow, necessary realization of the truth of the fall of Adam, and of the exiled condition of his progeny. Mr Betjeman has kept himself going – and given great delight to others in the process – with a series of distractions. Now the game is up.

One must sympathize, but it would be becoming in Mr Betjeman to show more penitence and less condemnation in his palinode. Who is to blame? If there were an *épuration* of those who had collaborated with the destroying forces, Mr Betjeman's friends, the present writer among them, would compete for the privilege of rescuing and hiding him. But his name would be on the list of guilty men.

In January 1938 there was an architectural exhibition in London of all that Mr Betjeman now deplores. The exhibitors called themselves the MARS group. Their catalogue had a preface by Bernard Shaw exulting over the destruction of Adelphi Terrace. The introduction hailed Le Corbusier as the liberator of architecture. And in the group beside Arup, Gropius, Chermayeff, Lubetkin and Zweigenthal stands the name of Mr Betjeman.

He rants against state control, but he is a member of the Church of England. In the face of that prodigious state usurpation laments about the colour of nationalized railway engines lose their poignancy.

He denounces suburban mediocrity, while he himself has been the leader and sole instigator of the fashionable flight from Greatness, away from the traditional hierarchy of classic genius, away from the library to the threepenny-box of the second-hand bookseller, away from the Mediterranean to the Isle of Man, away from the Universal Church into odd sects and schisms, away from historic palaces into odd corners of Aberdeen. All very diverting but the second-rate is not enough, and it is not for Mr Betjeman to scold anyone but himself when he discovers it. He has been trying to subsist on a very low, though spicy, diet, and is wilting with malnutrition.

. MGR KNOX AT 4 A.M. .

Most mature writers employ a single idiosyncratic recognizable style. Not so Mgr Knox. If one had to name the single characteristic of his genius that sets him furthest apart, it would not be his humour or wit or scholarship, or subtlety – though of course he has all these qualities in pre-eminent abundance – but his versatility. In his translation of the Vulgate he exhibits a vast variety; compare his treatment of narrative, poetry and exhortation. Look beyond that great work and compare *Let Dons Delight*, *Broadcast Minds*, *The Mass in Slow Motion*, *Enthusiasm*; each a notable literary achievement in an entirely distinct *genre*. No major writer in our history has ever shown such an extent of accomplishment. Certain minor writers with little to say have shown skill in pastiche, but here we are dealing with a profound, learned and original mind. Is there anywhere in all this dazzling display a quintessential Knox? One can only offer a personal opinion. One admirer at least finds him in the quiet little Oxford conferences, begun when he was chaplain and continued since then as a regular guest.

The Oxford of Mgr Knox's chaplaincy was the perplexed generation of the 1930s. Logical Positivism and Communism were the fashion. In that decade two great men living within a few yards of one another, Father Martin D'Arcy, SJ, and Mgr Knox, were providentially raised as defenders of the Faith. There is quite a different University today with quite different problems which are being bravely handled by their successors. It is neither invidious nor sentimental to look back on that decade as a golden age of Oxford Catholicism.

Mgr Knox's purpose in these sermons was not primarily to attract converts or to awaken the adolescent conscience. He speaks to young people who have grown up in Catholic homes and at Catholic schools and have, most of them, had little previous contact with unbelievers. His task is to equip them to meet arguments against the Faith which they have never heard before and to ensure that the simple dogmatic and apologetic instruction of their youth keeps pace with the Philosophy and History Schools which are mostly directed by unsympathetic minds.

In *In Soft Garments*, the previous series, he took his charges methodically through the curriculum of Faith restating and revivifying the definitions in colloquial terms, with brilliantly apt local illustrations.

In *The Hidden Stream* he follows something of the same plan but in this series he has come closer to his hearers. Although a visitor from outside he seems to be more intimate than before. He is sharing his own difficulties – the fidgeting doubts that disturb the early hours of the light sleeper – and explaining how he allays them until dawn comes and with it the daily sacrifice that dispels them. The group of problems to which he reverts so often that they can be said to comprise a central theme, deals with the inexplicable interdependence of mind

Review of *The Hidden Stream*, by Ronald Knox. *Duckett's Register*, December 1952.

and matter, body and soul. Do modern undergraduates worry much about these deep mysteries? If not, they should. Outwardly their preoccupations today seem largely practical – good works, social order, participation in the politics of the time, the observance of the moral law, resistance to Communism, the cultivation of tolerance. All necessary and admirable. But perhaps more of them than appears have their black moments when the enthusiasm of the rally has worn off, when the phrase 'social justice' seems estranged from the salvation of the soul. In what Mgr Knox calls 'the 4 a.m. mood' a sense of futility creeps in, a suspicion that the Christian system does not really hang together, that there are flaws in the logic, and adroit shifting about between natural causes, revelation and authority, that there are too many unresolved contradictions. And there are some, perhaps many, to whom it is nearly always 4 a.m. To this mood with its temptation to despair, Mgr Knox talks with unfailing kindness and solace. He is not concerned here to demolish, as he has so brilliantly done in the past, false opinions. He is restoring and creating confidence.

Fortunate young people to hear that comforting voice! But it is not for them alone. Those who have left their formal education far behind them will find huge solace in reading and rereading this book. It should be at every bedside, ready to be opened at 4 a.m.

. EDITH STEIN .

Last year a little book named *Waiting on God* attracted great attention inside and outside the Church. It comprised a selection from the writings of a young, highly intelligent French Jewess, Simone Weil, who died in England in 1943. The most interesting pages were taken from her letters to a French Dominican priest, whose answers are lacking. In them Mlle Weil professes an ardent love for the proletariat and a zeal for self-sacrifice, which she attempted to put into action by taking employment first in a factory and later at the Headquarters of the Free French in London; she was consumptive and hastened her death by going short of food in sympathy for her countrymen under the occupation. She seemed to accept the main truths of Christianity, but died unbaptized leaving a copious apologia which can be reduced to two themes: a distaste for the exclusive and authoritative tone of the Church and for the unworthiness of some of its members and a conviction that God would tell her as He had St Paul in an unmistakable and personal way when He required her submission. Some

Review of *Waiting on God*, by Simone Weil and *Edith Stein*, by Sister Teresia de Spiritu Sancto, ODC (Posselt). *Catholic Mother*, Christmas 1952. Lady Lothian, who edited the *Catholic Mother* in 1952, writes: 'Evelyn Waugh wrote the enclosed at my request to help *me* pursue research into the attitudes towards Christianity of women who were highly respected as philosophers. I asked if I might publish it. He was kind enough to agree although it had been written for private information only.'

readers, among them the present writer, are unable to silence the suspicion that this apologia could be starkly summarized: 'The Church isn't quite good enough for *me*, but, of course, if God really insists . . .'

At almost the same time there appeared another book, *Edith Stein* by Sister Teresia de Spiritu Sancto, ODC. It is the biography, or rather the first sketch for a biography, of a highly intelligent German Jewess, who was known for the last eight years of her life as Sister Teresia Benedicta a Cruce, ODC. It has been admirably compiled from her own and her friends' accounts and reveals a life which has remarkable similarities to Mlle Weil's and still more remarkable contrasts. It might be a useful exercise to make a line-for-line comparison between the two women, but it is an ungracious habit to praise one thing while disparaging another. Suffice to say that those who have been dismayed by the vogue of Mlle Weil may find a prompt restorative in Edith Stein.

She was born at Breslau on 12 October 1891, the youngest of seven children who were left fatherless when Edith was three years old. Thenceforward the mother assumed control of the family and the family business – the masculine occupation of timber merchant – and managed it prosperously until the early thirties when industry was breaking down throughout Germany. The matriarch was devoutly and rigidly orthodox in religion. The children were in various degrees infected by the scepticism of their period, Edith most of all. From the moment she began to think until her twenty-second year she was dogmatically atheist. There was nothing recognizably Jewish in her appearance but she was Jewish at heart and even after her conversion to Christianity she could happily pray beside her mother in the synagogue.

The early chapters of the book give a charming picture of German Jewry in its heyday under the Empire, the period of Edith's adolescence. The Steins were well-to-do, living in solid, unostentatious comfort, patriotic – indeed thoroughly Prussian – in sympathies, highly respectful of the *Kultur* which their race had done so much to establish. They associated only with Jews, chiefly with their own kin, but they regarded themselves as being as German as the Junkers. They were a distinct part of the nation, Jewish Germans rather than German Jews, with little sympathy for Zionism or international socialism; the antithesis of the Nazi bogy. This was the world, now vanished without trace, in which Edith grew up.

She was a bright, pretty, affectionate child; the only fault imputed to her was excessive ambition. German education under the Kaiser was formidably efficient. She set all her precocious intellect and energies into surmounting its various grades and was brilliantly successful. At adolescence she was possessed by what is described as a thirst for knowledge, but which is perhaps better called a thirst for truth. All her intellectual force was early canalized into philosophy and she began her search of the universities for a master who would show her the way of truth; the quest which found its final satisfaction in Carmel.

At Göttingen she found a group of students and teachers gathered round

Edmund Husserl, whose writing she already knew. Their philosophical system is called the Phenomenological School. Edith soon established herself in the inner circle of disciples both by her quick comprehension and her original speculations, and in 1916 when he was appointed Professor at Freiburg, the master summoned Edith to be his personal assistant. In order to accept this post she left the Red Cross in which she had devotedly served since the outbreak of war. But first she had another task. At Göttingen Husserl had for his colleague Adolph Reinach, an apostate Lutheran who returned to his faith while in the army. Reinach was killed and Edith accepted the task of arranging his manuscript writings. She was now 26 years old but had never given any thought to Christianity. The phenomenologists had broken down her crude rationalism; many of them had begun to move towards Catholicism, but it had not occurred to Edith to examine the credentials of the Church. Reinach had stated shortly before his death that he would teach philosophy in future only as a means of leading men to God. No doubt among the papers which Edith now perused, there were indications of this change of heart, but what impressed her was the behaviour of his widow. Edith could see nothing but absolute loss in the premature end of a brilliant academic career. Frau Reinach (who later became a Catholic) accepted it with resignation and hope and for the first time Edith encountered Christian Faith in action; she noted the phenomenon in her accurate mind.

After the war, in a vastly changed world, the German universities made an attempt to re-establish the old life. Edith became 'Fräulein Doktor' with a growing reputation as a philosopher but the slim, simple appearance of a young girl; she wrote a thesis on the Soul which was a plain acknowledgement of the religious basis of life. Some of her friends supposed her to be already a Christian. But her conversion was delayed until she chose at random from the shelf of a friend St Teresa of Avila's *Life* of herself. Edith read the book straight through and concluded: 'That is the Truth.' She then set about instructing herself in the practical, thorough way in which she did everything. She bought a catechism and a missal and studied them. Then for the first time in her life she went to Mass and understood every phrase and gesture. After Mass she followed the priest to the presbytery and asked for baptism.

'Who has instructed you and for how long?' 'Test my knowledge.' The subsequent discussion ranged over the whole field of Catholic theology. Edith's answers were satisfactory and she was baptized on New Year's Day, 1922. There can have been few conversions so cool and impersonal. Contrast it with Pascal's. But this was no mere intellectual acceptance of a philosophical system. It was the start of a new life of devotion and prayer.

The effects of this huge change on Edith's mother, sisters and friends, the transition of the popular lecturer to Carmelite nun with the first turbulence of the German disaster in the background, are briefly but beautifully told. As the Nazis came to power, Edith was moved, as was hoped for her safety, to a sister house in Holland. The Nazis came there too. Sister Teresia Benedicta a Cruce went calmly about her duties. Permission was sought, and obtained too late, to transfer her to safety to Switzerland.

On Sunday 26 July 1942, the Archbishop of Utrecht issued a pastoral condemning the persecution of the Jews. Retribution was immediate. All Catholic priests and religious with Jewish connections were rounded up by the SS. On 1 August Edith was arrested and driven off with the other victims of the Terror; somewhere, quite soon probably, she was killed in one of the extermination camps in the east. Attempts have been made to sift the various conflicting reports of people who saw her or thought they saw her during her last journey. Nothing is certain except the fact of her death. She disappeared bodily in the total, hellish darkness.

Her spirit shines out, very clear and lonely; a brilliant intelligence; a pure, disciplined will; a single motive power, the Grace of God. The circumstances of her death touch us for they lie at the heart of contemporary disaster. The aimless, impersonal wickedness which could drag a victim from the holy silence of Carmel and drive her, stripped and crowded, to the gas chamber and the furnace, still lurks in the darkness. But Edith's death is perhaps an irrelevant horror. Her life was completed in Carmel. She did not sit, waiting on God. She went out alone and by the God-given light of her intelligence and strength of purpose, she found Him.

. THE VOICE OF TITO .

President Tito's apologia, *Tito*, is not designed to placate. It is conceived in a mood of deep self-satisfaction and defiance. Tito has got out of a number of scrapes, he is surrounded by hero-worshippers, and he believes he is now sufficiently secure in a position which few cool observers envy him, to issue a pronouncement to the world.

It is to be hoped that his Tory admirers will read this book patiently. Unhappily considerable patience is required. Inevitably it abounds in technical terms of Communist philosophy and organization which make it hard going for the lay reader. The writing is devoid of literary distinction. (No translator's name is given.) The construction is uncouth. Tito begins the task himself but wearies after ninety-one pages (this 'Worker', as is shown in the text, regarded every job as an invitation to down tools) and hands it over to Mr Dedijer, an intimate, to finish. Mr Dedijer also employs the first person singular, at the same time incorporating large extracts from Tito's draft preserving the original 'I'. It is therefore not a book to dip into. Far too much of the ample space is given to Tito's public statements, far too little to the narrative of his personal

Review of *Tito* (New York), by Vladimir Dedijer. *Commonweal*, 8 May 1953. First printed *Month*, April 1953.

adventures. All this is regrettable because at the core of the work there lies an exciting and significant story.

Tito was brought up in the 'bad home' of the typical delinquent. His father drank, brothers and sisters sickened and died, his uncle stole his boots. Later he worked as a locksmith, acquired some skill in general metalwork and drifted about Europe fomenting ill-feeling against his various employers. After an inglorious army career in the First World War (he was saved from court martial only by perjury) he was wounded in the back and taken for the first time to Russia as a prisoner of war. He returned home to the newly created Kingdom of Yugoslavia, resumed his vocation of agitator and in 1923 joined the Communist Party.

From then until 1941 Tito's life followed the course that has lately become familiar from countless popular narratives. He moved all over Europe with forged papers and under aliases so numerous that on one occasion he found himself unable to remember the name on the particular passport he was carrying. He did time in prison and waxes naïvely indignant about the 'Terror' of the royal regime. Since assassination has always been a feature of Balkan public life and was successfully employed by his comrades on more than one occasion, and since he admits that one of his tasks was to prepare for an uprising with secret stores of arms, one is amazed at the leniency of his treatment.

The Yugoslav police were vigilant and (in comparison with the courts) cruel and by 1938 the Party was almost extinct. Its controlling members lived in Vienna and Moscow. Tito had two important achievements at this period. He successfully sent 1,500 compatriots underground to the International Brigade. Of these 300 survived to join him in Yugoslavia and to play a decisive part in his war effort. Of the second achievement he is more reticent. The head of the Yugoslav Party at this time was an emigré named Gorkic, who was put over his head, much to his chagrin, by the authorities in Moscow. Tito obediently submitted although, he now states, he then believed him to be a police informer. In 1937 Gorkic was suddenly arrested in Moscow (and presumably murdered) on the usual charges of treachery. Who denounced him? Tito stepped into his shoes and returned home to purge and reorganize what was left of the Party. He boldly carried out the policy he had advocated: that the head of the Party must stay on the spot. By 1941 he had re-established a number of cells in various parts of the country.

From April 1941 when the Germans invaded until July 1943 when Mr Deakin, a most gallant English soldier, dropped in to establish the British Military Mission, Yugoslav history remains dark.

Mr Deakin found in existence a Resistance Movement which could without absurdity be called an army. This force began its activity in June 1941 when Russia was attacked. Tito ingenuously asks his readers to believe that the coincidence was fortuitous. On the day when, in a phrase which Mr Churchill would now perhaps like to forget, 'Yugoslavia found her soul,' Tito was absent.

The army Mr Deakin found was scattered physically but under unified Communist control. It comprised four elements: the veterans from Spain everywhere in key positions; the very young who had left their classrooms and for two years lived in conditions of savagery; a large number of non-political patriots who had enrolled in the nearest organization that offered resistance to the invaders; and conscripts from the 'liberated' areas. Of these, those who were not caught and shot deserting quickly caught the enthusiasm of their fellows. The losses of this force, largely from privation and disease, had been great. Those who survived were united in a formidable *esprit de corps*.

What happened in those two years? We shall never know. Those who could have told us are dead. Tito had two aims: to cause as much annoyance as possible to the invaders in order to relieve the pressure on Russia and exterminate the two sections of his countrymen, Croat separatists and Serbian royalists, who envisaged a different regime from his in the event of victory. Loyalty to Russia was the overriding emotion. The young partisans, as he describes, died with the name of Stalin on their lips.

Since British troops have been in conflict with guerrillas in Malaya we are disposed to take a less romantic view than formerly of his type of warfare. Tito speaks of 'offensives', and of 'brigades' and 'divisions' breaking through. We must rather think of periodic punitive 'sweeps' in a terrain well suited to the escape of small unencumbered bands; of a country brutally plundered and victimized by all sides; of betrayals and reprisals and devastation on an appalling scale. The people who survived the anarchy were in no position to pick and choose among their rulers; anything for a stable rule.

The book under review tells very little of the unhappy history of the British Military Mission. The best comment is Himmler's, like calling to like across embattled Europe: 'I wish we had a dozen Titos in Germany,' he said in September 1944. 'The man had nothing, nothing at all. He was between the Russians, the British and the Americans, and had the nerve actually to fool and humiliate the British and Americans in the most comical way.'

Party ideologues are now disputing the question: 'Who liberated Yugoslavia?' Russians and partisans claim exclusive honours. There was good reason for Allied ineffectiveness: Tito's consistent hostility. With frankness that must be disconcerting to many, he admits that he would have regarded an Allied landing as a hostile invasion. He describes in detail the precautions he took to keep secret from those who thought themselves his friends his flight from Vis to Moscow in the summer of 1944. The people of Split and Dubrovnik were aghast to see the crew of a British cruiser and a brigade group ostentatiously insulted by gangs of prematurely adult boys and girls armed with British tommy-guns. And all the time Allied propaganda was churning out misinformation about Tito's aims and character.

Considerable space is given to the manoeuvres by which Tito achieved recognition for his Communist regime after the war. Whatever face was saved for the Allies by the compromise, they immediately lost. In 1946 Yugoslavia settled down as part of the Russian hegemony. The main substance and central theme of this book is Tito's subsequent dismissal and survival. This is the story Tito has been longing to tell and here the interest of the western reader is likely to flag unless he (or more probably she) suffers from the prevalent monomania which makes reading a form of rumination. These readers will devour any and every book which feeds their obsession, savouring every repetition. More sophisticated readers may well be bored. There are 200 pages of it, all no doubt of titivating novelty in Belgrade but sad stuff to us who have been glutted with the confessions of repentant dupes and liars. It is no news to us that Stalin was a blackguard and his rule intolerable. For nearly 250 pages we have borne with Tito's monotonous denunciation of everyone who crossed his path as a traitor and a spy. Now the nozzle is directed at him; he squirts back. The exchange is less than enthralling.

Tito's simple thesis is that the whole Communist world is out of step except himself; that Stalin had 'deviated' from the pure doctrine of Marx and Lenin and that Belgrade is the New Rome. But Mr Dedijer is not quite up to the very special pleading required to make his case plausible. The truth peeps through everywhere that there is no real difference in philosophy or policy. It is purely a matter of personalities.

Stalin decided to destroy Tito and for a variety of reasons did not succeed. The method of destruction first chosen was ingenious. There are many good reasons for the federation of Bulgaria and Yugoslavia. Tito would not object to being their joint president. But the government of Bulgaria is purely a Soviet creation imposed on a defeated nation. The NKVD reigns there supreme. Tito had his own secret police and the efforts of the NKVD to establish itself in Yugoslavia had not been entirely successful. Once Tito's solid little gang of war-time comrades had been diluted with Bulgarians, he could have been dispatched in the regular way.

But Tito had observed and assisted in too many 'purges' to be caught so easily. He knew that by breaking with Russia he would be increasing the destitution of his unhappy country which was completely dependent on Russia for her welfare and development. Once before he had been faced with a similar less drastic choice. In 1944 UNRRA came with help to his starving people. As in every other country they stipulated that their own officials should distribute supplies. This would have meant that at the crucial time when Tito was consolidating his power there would be independent observers to see his manner of doing so. It would have meant, too, that relief would go impartially to all in need. Tito had drawn up a scale of precedence which insured that only those he favoured would benefit. (The present writer saw a copy of this scale.) Rather than allow UNRRA its essential right, Tito repudiated all relief. Better the people should starve than that he should suffer any diminution of authority. But his bluff succeeded and he got the provisions on his own terms.

In March 1948 it was not a fraction of authority that was at stake but his very existence; it scarcely seemed possible that the West, once duped, would trust him a second time. But Tito did not hesitate for long. His little gang, all save two, stood by him, and incalculably the western powers began to shower him with subsidies and offers of friendship.

Why did the Russians wish to dispense with him? This kind of cannibalism is, of course, endemic in the Communist system. Moreover there seems everywhere (as shown by the electorate in France and Britain) a disposition to overthrow war-leaders at the height of their triumph. But in Tito's case there was a further personal cause. He plainly bored them all unendurably by his boasting.

The British title of this book, *Tito Speaks*, suggests the eagerly awaited breaking of a long silence, as though by an eastern mystic after years of solitary contemplation. In fact Tito has never ceased speaking. Again and again in the latter chapters of this book we are told that Tito, addressing some congress, began by rehearsing the history and triumphs of the Yugoslav Army of Liberation. It seems to be his normal warming-up before any utterance and no doubt it was extremely tedious to comrades like Bierut who have no such achievements to proclaim.

The book ends as it began with what is plainly meant to be an appealing human portrait. We hear of Tito's love of his dog, the warmth and gentleness of his blue eyes, his simple plebeian tastes. We are told he is much in demand as godfather to infants. It is not stated whether he attends the service and vicariously demands Faith. There is little in the book (beyond the stock, often refuted, accusations against Cardinal Stepinac) about the Church. Tito ascribes his theological vacuum to an early cuffing from a priest whom he had served at the altar. There is, however, another recorded memory. Tito was a very greedy little boy and he grudged the small alms which his mother occasionally gave to the friars. It is significant that although portly himself Tito seldom mentions a priest without the pejorative epithet 'fat'. No doubt psychologists could explain much of his zest for starving out religious by the early horror of seeing good food going to a good cause.

Tito never allows himself the pleasure of a single chivalrous word about an opponent. Even Stalin, no Bayard, was shocked by his grossness in this matter. There is, however, an evident attempt in this book to change the myth of the bandit chief for that of the 'Big Brother' of George Orwell's *1984*. His present position is precarious. It would be ironical if we found ourselves involved in World War III in his defence.

Is there any further danger in 'Titoism'? There is indeed. Everywhere except in the bazaars and jungles of Asia and Africa Communists are losing faith in Russia. Russia is the one land in which a whole generation has grown up without knowledge of God and the humanities. Power politics and 'purges' are the sickening fruit of the process. Man without God is less than Man. But there is an evident danger that the true sequence of cause and effect may be neglected. Observers point out that Stalin was merely the old Czar writ large; that there is something in Russian character naturally sympathetic to tyranny;

that there is nothing wrong with Communism, merely with Russia. Such a view is acceptable alike to Tory opportunists and to sentimental Marxists. That way lies the promise of further disaster.

. MR WAUGH REPLIES .

Some of my earliest memories are of book-reviewing. My father wrote a weekly literary article for the *Daily Telegraph*. He was also the head of a publishing firm and it is significant of the high standards of the day that no one, so far as I know, ever thought the combination odd or suspected that he might use his position to push his own wares or discriminate against rivals. He greatly enjoyed this work, would read the book under review attentively and discuss it at table. Then on Saturday mornings a hush fell on the house while he wrote his article.

My own first regular literary employment was reviewing for the *Observer* in the late twenties. I too enjoyed it. The world seemed full of exciting new books and Miss Garvin's office a free bookshop. We used to assemble among the piles of bright wrappers and each make his choice. The pay was low and we supplemented it by selling copies at half-price. There were usually one or two expensive 'Art Books' and these would be surreptitiously shifted from pile to pile in the course of the afternoon. Since then, off and on, I have done a good deal of such work, always with pleasure.

In the mid thirties it became fashionable for reviewers to complain that they were ill-used. Their minds, they said, were being bruised, their creative faculties numbed, their styles corrupted by the battery of inferior minds. It is notable that the best reviewing of this time – such as Mr Cyril Connolly's in the *New Statesman* – was hostile and derisive.

Since the war there has been some further deterioration. Few reviewers are now able to recapitulate a plot with accuracy. But perhaps the deterioration among the books has been more noticeable. I suspect that nowadays the best criticism is never seen in print. All over the country clever and learned men and women are lecturing to university students. I do not know whether our universities, like those of America, give degrees in 'Creative Writing', but it is plain from the letters I get that modern books are being seriously examined and that discourses of the kind which used to fill the pages of the quarterly reviews now vanish in the Biro scribbles of students' notebooks.

In no periodical have we now anyone approaching a Grand Cham. The subtlest critics, such as Mr Raymond Mortimer and Mr Connolly, are starved of space so that they can only throw out a few luminous hints, a few charmingly written paragraphs, as it were from *Trivia*. Many of the papers with the largest circulations do not notice the Arts at all. The most influential among book buyers and librarians are said to be: *The Times Literary Supplement*, the *New Statesman*, the *Spectator*, *Time and Tide*, the *Listener*, the *Observer*, the *Sunday Times*, and of daily papers *The Times* and the *Telegraph*. The *Daily Mail* alone of the popular papers has some literary prestige. Mr Quennell is a widely read, fastidious critic and a competent writer. One may be sure that, if it were not his job, he would not spend ten minutes on nine out of ten of the books he commends. He tells his readers week by week, with self-effacement and high competence, what books are likely to interest them. He writes the most useful, if not the most exhilarating, literary journalism today but I am told that even he, with his great circulation, has little influence on the market and that his laurel wreath of the 'Book of the Month' is barely worth £25 to the author, unless of a first book. Reviewers can greatly encourage or cruelly wound a young writer; perhaps also a very old one, fearful of failing powers. They do not much concern the middle-aged. For this reason I can, I hope, without rancour or egotism, examine the work of the modern reviewer in the single light of my own latest book which has been pretty generally condemned.

It is a brief, very prettily produced fantasy about life in the near future with certain obvious defects. It was begun as a longer work three years ago, abandoned, and resumed with the realization that the characters lacked substance for more than a short story. As it stands it is designed purely to amuse and is therefore subject to a snap verdict, yes or no. Either it comes off or it fails. It was an easy job for the reviewer in contrast, say, to a new work by Mr David Jones. I may add that I myself live in seclusion. I do not attend gatherings of the PEN or Foyle's lunches or literary cocktail parties (if such things really exist), so that I cannot have incurred personal enmity in my profession. Despite its reception this book is selling in numbers which seem to satisfy its publishers.

If we take the snap-decision of the periodicals listed above, we find: *Times Literary Supplement*; yes, 'we laugh helplessly.' *New Statesman*; yes, 'wit crackles drily on every page.' *Spectator*; no, 'his satire has ceased to be a laughing matter. . . . Not in the same class as *The Loved One*. . . . He is left more or less speechless.' *Time and Tide*; yes and no, 'this isn't vintage Waugh.' The *Listener*; yes, 'pre-Brideshead Waugh.' *Observer*; no, modified, 'it would be amusing if it were by a beginner.' *Sunday Times*; yes, 'delight and pleasure.' *Times*; yes, modified, 'bland satirical extravagance raises more smiles than laughter.' *Telegraph*; yes, modified. *Daily Mail*; yes, modified, 'the joke is a little too complicated – and possibly a little too bitter.'

All this seems to amount to an audible chuckle, if not a hearty laugh. No funny man should expect more every time he attempts a joke. There is a general mild tone of regret that it disappoints expectations, though there is no unanimity as to the exact moment of my decline; some put it eight, some twenty-five years ago, some this month. It is when we come to the less influential papers that the criticism becomes uniformly adverse and oddly violent.

Where the reviewers of even the well-mannered papers seem to have deteriorated, in a way my father would have thought intolerable, is in their tendency to write about the author rather than the book and in assuming a personal intimacy with him which in fact they do not enjoy. The young lady, for instance, who says many kind things about me in the *New Statesman* ventures to question my good faith in religion and imputes to me lack of compassion for the poor. No doubt she has no conception of the deadliness of her accusation. If at all true, it would be a matter for my confessor not for her. Others equally unknown to me impute a hankering for the eighteenth century. It was Mr Clive Bell, the champion of Post-Impressionism, who wrote of 'the adorable century', not I, whose preferences are for the thirteenth or the fourth. But it is in the Beaverbrook press that I find the most curious claims to intimacy.

Mr George Malcolm Thomson of the *Evening Standard* seems to have studied some file of gossip paragraphs and to have transcribed all the most offensive, inaccurate and irrelevant. He reports that I do not like oysters, that I advocate slavery, that I am sensitive about my low stature.[1] Mr Thomson, alas, is a cypher to me (no doubt he is a fine gangling fellow), but I have some acquaintance with Lord Beaverbrook. Over the years I have heard him give tongue on a great variety of topics but it never occurred to me until now to speculate whether he suffered from humiliation at being slightly shorter than myself. How does Mr Thomson know my height? It is not recorded in any book of reference. How can he possibly know whether I am sensitive about it? Has he seen me tripping about Shoe Lane on stilts? Has he had an eye to the keyhole of a gymnasium where I was engaged in stretching exercises? And, really, what has it got to do with my writing? Are my plots a continual retelling of the story of David and Goliath, where evil giants are overcome by heroic pigmies?

Mr Shulman of the *Sunday Express* accuses me of snobbery. He goes further and predicts that 'in future' only snobs will enjoy my books.[2] This seems very odd since the book under review is the only novel I have ever written in which there appears no member of the upper class, either as buffoon or heroine.

The critic of the *Daily Express* merely says he yawned and yawned and yawned, without indicating the time of day or night when he attempted to read it, or even whether he is adept at reading at all.[3]

This unanimity of the Beaverbrook press is striking. All abuse, not so much my little book, as me, in terms which, used of a coal-miner, would precipitate a general strike. Now it so happens that quite recently my solitude has been disturbed on several occasions by appeals for help from their office. One of

---

1 'Why So Gloomy, Mr Waugh?' *Evening Standard*, 3 June 1953, p. 10. It is clear from his review-profile that Thomson drew on the *Daily Express*'s Waugh file, now in the British Library. The piece is curiously jumbled. Some of the jibes are more offensive than those Waugh reports, e.g. that Waugh had been said to look like 'an indignant White Leghorn'.

2 'What a Wet Squib, Mr Waugh'. *Sunday Express*, 31 May 1953, p. 8.

3 Nancy Spain, 'Nancy Spain Reads in Rome a Book That Takes Her into the Vatican: So I Yawned. . .', *Daily Express*, 29 May 1953, p. 4. A review of three books, including *Love among the Ruins*, all by overtly Roman Catholic authors. Two books are highly praised, *Love among the Ruins* is panned.

their gossip writers politely asked me for information I was unwilling to give. The *Sunday Express* offered me a seat in the Abbey for the Coronation. The *Evening Standard* suggested my going abroad to interview a royal person (not, I hasten to say, the ex-King of Egypt). If I am such a bad writer why do they solicit my work? For different good reasons I was obliged to refuse these flattering offers. I know these Beaverbrook men to be busy. I was brief with them. Did I seem curt? Can it be that I gave offence and that those fiery, independent spirits, the arbiters of literary taste of millions, are influenced by other than purely artistic considerations?[1]

. RUSKIN AND KATHLEEN OLANDER .

In all Ruskin's personal relationships, particularly in his romantic relationships with women and young girls, there appear three quests: Abelard in search of an Héloïse, Svengali in search of a Trilby, and a lonely little boy in search of a playmate. There was also, intermittently and somewhat ambiguously, the search of a man for his mate. E. T. Cook used his discretion seriously in treating of his subject's loves. Had Ruskin not himself made public in *Praeterita* so much of the story of Rose La Touche, it may be doubted whether she would have figured at all in the official biography. The name of Kathleen Olander was totally suppressed and it is only now, sixty-five years after they were written, that his love letters to her are printed and her poignant predicament revealed.

Kathleen Olander, now Mrs Prynne, was an art student of 20 when she met Ruskin, then aged 68. Their correspondence, of which Ruskin's part alone is preserved, lasted less than a year. It developed rapidly from playful patronage to a serious proposal of marriage. It was cut short by the girl's parents on one side and by Mrs Severn on the other. Three letters were destroyed because they spoke critically of Mrs Severn. The remainder were confiscated by Mr Olander and restored (to the husband) on his daughter's subsequent marriage. She did not marry until Ruskin's death and maintained a steadfast devotion to him which shines through her brief, candid and dignified notes to this volume. Her wish was to help him in whatever way he wished. She thought of becoming his housekeeper or secretary or adopted daughter. The prospect of marriage at first dismayed her, but she was ready to accept it, if that was what he needed.

---

1 The publication of *Love among the Ruins*, a bitter satire on post-war England, coincided with the coronation of Queen Elizabeth II. As this was a time of euphoria, when Englishmen generally were welcoming 'the new Elizabethan Age', the book struck a discordant note. Mr Milton Shulman was not aware of any directive from Lord Beaverbrook, or of any collusion among the Beaverbrook reviewers, to attack Waugh. On the other hand George Malcolm Thomson was generally believed to reflect Beaverbrook's opinions fairly accurately.

Review of *The Gulf of the Years: Love Letters from John Ruskin to Kathleen Olander*, ed. Rayner Unwin. *Spectator*, 17 July 1953.

She aspired to being much more than a pretty toy, or a nurse, or a helpmeet in his still large activities. She sought to reclaim him to Christianity and there were hints that she partly succeeded.

Ruskin often speaks of her as having been 'sent to him' by 'Rosie'. Except in their piety there was little resemblance between the two girls. Rose La Touche was the shadow of a wraith, pampered, immature, morbid, barely capable, it appeared, of love. She made a gracious contrast to that other woman in Ruskin's life, Euphemia Gray, whose every recorded utterance smacks of the Misses Steele in *Sense and Sensibility*, but she had nothing to give Ruskin in her brief, troubled existence between the nursery and the sick-bed. Kathleen Olander was healthy, generous and capable, unhappy in her severe, philistine home, deeply appreciative of Ruskin's genius. If only, one speculates, she had been born a generation earlier . . . ? But the case is not quite as simple as that. There was something in Ruskin's brilliant horoscope which predisposed him to unhappiness. It is not given to one man to enjoy domestic content and also the transports of aesthetic delight to which he was moved by rock-formations and sunsets. Imagine him the father of a family, and he becomes absurd. And he knew it.

Much has been blamed on his upbringing. It is true that he was that rare phenomenon of the period, an only child, and that the great weight of Victorian patriarchal authority was designed to be borne on many young shoulders. But we cannot credit his parents with his exquisite sensibility or his stupendous mastery of language. Why should they be blamed for his weaknesses?

It remains to say that Mr Rayner Unwin's preface and notes are exemplary. The book is one which every library *must* possess, if it seeks to provide a complete picture of Ruskin. More than that, it is a delight to read, in spite of the sorrow of the theme, for the reflection it gives of a lovable and admirable girl, and for the illumination of a great writer in his last days of hope.

. APOTHEOSIS OF AN UNHAPPY HYPOCRITE .

The latest study of Charles Dickens has already been published in the USA. It comes to us with very high claims to our attention: 'Unquestionably the definitive life,' Mr Lionel Trilling. 'Not only the definitive biography; it is a landmark in Dickens criticism,' *New York Herald Tribune*. 'Unquestionably the most comprehensive and authoritative life,' the publishers. There are over 1,000 pages of text and some 250 pages of notes and index, more than 100 illustrations. The price is £3 10s. for the two volumes. It is therefore right to judge it by a high standard and to expect an unusual propriety of arrangement and format.

Such expectations are not wholly realized. It is, for example, odd to find

Review of *Charles Dickens*, by Edgar Johnson. *Spectator*, 2 October 1953.

within the covers of the book itself (not on the wrapper) a page of 'blurb' in praise of the author, Professor Edgar Johnson, telling us among other things that his family consists of 'Judy and Laurie'.

'The illustrations,' we are told, 'are particularly interesting.' It is not apparent that any particular interest attaches to an imaginary sketch of Maria Beadnell, described as 'from the *Sphere*, February 20th, 1909'. These illustrations, moreover, are mostly collected into two sections, in the manner of the 'rotogravure supplement' of an American Sunday newspaper, and are printed two or three to the page in sizes seldom larger than $2\frac{1}{2}$ inches square.

The apparatus of reference is not the most convenient. The book is divided into ten parts and each part into anything from five to nine chapters numbered anew in each part. The reference numbers start anew in each chapter. Thus, if he wishes to check the authority for a statement, the reader has first to turn back to find the number of the chapter he is reading, then back again to find the number of the part. Only then can he identify the required note – say 'Hall, *Retrospect*' – and must then turn on again to the end of the second volume, to find 'Hall, Samuel Carter. *Retrospect of a Long Life*'. Some trouble could be spared if the notes were printed after each chapter, and if each volume had its bibliography and index.

This work, in spite of the assertion that it 'swept' Mr Henry Morton Robinson 'along on a compelling tide', can only be of interest to a patient and devoted reader. A cursory reviewer must take on trust the Professor's claims to laborious and exact research, merely remarking that in many passages dealing with English social and political history, the author's naïveté verges on silliness and that several glaring solecisms – for example, the description of the 'Five Sisters' window at York as 'gorgeously hued' – have escaped correction. An enormous number of facts have certainly been accumulated, many of them – for example the name of the man who married the maid-of-all-work in one of Dickens's boyhood homes – of absolute unimportance. It is unlikely that much further information will transpire; all that is available is recorded. In this sense Professor Johnson's work may be said to be definitive.

The lives of writers, and especially of abnormally industrious writers, are seldom of great interest. Dickens wrote and wrote and wrote. His recreation was with a set of cronies, thinned by frequent quarrels, with whom he enjoyed boisterous games. He presided at countless public banquets. He joined the Athenaeum Club by ordinary election thereby winning, according to the Professor, 'one of England's most coveted distinctions'. He appeared now and then, clothed in an unsuitable imitation of Count d'Orsay, at Lady Blessington's. He travelled a little, but always cloaked in impermeable insular smugness. He had better have stuck to Broadstairs.

There were, and no doubt still are, ardent 'Dickensians' who made a hobby of the Master, without any particular appreciation of his genius, just as certain scholars have made a hobby of Bradshaw's *Railway Guide*. These gentle souls have made Dickens a symbol of family affection, benevolence and good-cheer.

Perhaps they should stop reading biographical studies after Chesterton's for – the pity of it – the more we know of Dickens, the less we like him.

His conduct to his wife and particularly his announcement of the separation were deplorable. His treatment in middle age of Maria Beadnell was even worse. His benefactions to his family were grudging and ungracious. Faults which would be excusable in other men become odious in the light of Dickens's writing. He frequented the *demi-monde* with Wilkie Collins. He probably seduced and certainly kept the young actress Ellen Ternan, to whom he left £1,000 in his will, thereby putting her name in disrepute while at the same time leaving her miserably provided. All this is very ugly in the creator of Little Emily and Martha. He claimed a spurious pedigree and used an illicit crest – a simple weakness in anyone except himself who vehemently denounced the importance attached to gentle birth. In success he was intolerably boastful, in the smallest reverse abject with self-pity. He was domineering and dishonourable in his treatment of his publishers. He was, in fact, a thumping cad. Here is all the evidence set out in tedious detail.

The reader familiar with the work of Mr Erle Stanley Gardner will constantly find himself crying out in the tones of the District Attorney: 'I object, your honour. This is incompetent, irrelevant and immaterial.' But he will also find himself like Perry Mason crying: 'Objection. This is merely a conclusion of the witness's.' And in each case he will answer from the bench, 'Objection sustained.' For interspersed in the narrative is a series of chapters of criticism. It would have been seemly in Professor Johnson to have forbidden the rather lavish use of the word 'definitive' of a book containing so much of his own personal opinions and conjectures. Professor Johnson has a theme and a silly one: that Dickens gradually realized the vices of contemporary capitalism, more and more devoted himself to their denunciation, and became the proto-martyr (through overwork) of the Welfare State. In each novel he claims to discern a widening spirit of revolution.

Now Dickens, as everyone knows, was a Radical and an anti-clerical and he was what, in Professor Johnson's country, is called a 'tear jerker' about the sufferings of the poor. He also gave some time to the service of Miss Coutts (Baroness Burdett-Coutts) in her philanthropic activities. He received incidentally several material advantages, including the education of one of his sons, from this association. But the truth is that violent radical advocacy was a highly remunerative and popular activity in his time. Dickens was ready enough to introduce rhetorical passages about social reform into his stories, just as he celebrated Christmas – indeed appointed himself the special patron of the feast – while privately proclaiming disbelief in the event which it commemorates. He did on one occasion, in Professor Johnson's curious but characteristic phrase, 'tear off a molten pamphlet' against Sir Andrew Agnew's proposal to tighten the law against Sabbath breaking, but he carefully provided a cosy Sunday-at-home ethos for all the magazines he edited. The mission he preached on his first visit to the USA had nothing to do with slavery or the exploitation of immigrant labour; it was a complaint about his own financial losses through the lack of an international copyright law. He promised on his return to devote himself to 'hammer blows' on the social system in England. He had the opportunity for one such blow in an article commissioned by the *Edinburgh Review* on the 'ragged schools'. He got up the facts but never wrote the essay, turning instead to the more profitable *Christmas Carol*, a work of peculiar fatuity to economist and sociologist. He gave some public readings for charity. As soon as he realized their potentialities, he took to giving them for his own profit. Apropos of protests that the issue of *Pickwick* in cheap monthly parts was undignified, Professor Johnson writes: 'He [Dickens] valued the laughter and tears of the poor as much as he did the acclaim of the rich.'

This verdict occurs six pages after he has quoted a letter of Dickens's referring to his contributions to the *Carlton Chronicle*: 'The circulation is a small one . . . It is all among the nobs too – Better still. They'll buy the book.' By Professor Johnson's own showing it is impossible to represent Dickens as a figure of Charity. It is significant that he excelled in the portrayal of hypocrites.

The height of absurdity is reached when the Professor discerns in *Edwin Drood* a subtle exposure of British imperialism in the East and 'the whole vainglorious gospel of backward races and the white man's burden'. We must leave the Professor with his hobby-horse. Everyone, provided he does not dub it 'definitive', is entitled to his own interpretation of Dickens's complex genius. Almost every critic has at one time or another attempted to elucidate its mystery. The novelist was literally and metaphorically a mesmerist. He 'magnetized' Mme de la Rue when the poor lady was 'an insensible ball', only finding her head 'by following her long hair to its source'. He magnetized the audiences at his readings to a condition approaching hysteria. And he magnetizes still.

The happiest comparison perhaps is to Mr Charles Chaplin, in particular to the film *City Lights*. There we have scenes of appalling sentimentality and unreality; we have a slight undercurrent of proletarian animosity; but we have a unique genius in full exuberance. The theme, it will be remembered, is the relationship of a tramp and a rich drunkard. The reader of Dickens often finds himself cast in the latter, unamiable role. In his cups the rich man embraces the tramp as a brother; crapulous, he rejects him. We all have our moods when Dickens sickens us. In a lighter, looser and perhaps higher mood we fall victim to his 'magnetism'. Like Mme de la Rue we unroll from our insensible ball and do what the Master orders. It is this constantly changing mood of appreciation that makes everyone's fingers itch for the pen at the mention of his name.

. GOA: THE HOME OF A SAINT .

Diu, Daman, Goa, Maké, Karikal, Pondicherry, Yanam – how odd these places, strung out along the coast of India, used to look in the school atlas; as though small, alien teeth had been nibbling at the edges of the huge vermilion expanse of British India.

'Couldn't we turn them out, Sir?'

'Of course. Any time we wanted to.'

'Then why don't we, Sir?'

And we were told that these quaint survivals were a part of history, of the remote days when France and Portugal competed with us for empire: furthermore that their neglected condition provided a salutary example to any Indian who was crass enough to doubt the benevolence of the British Raj.

'Are there really Indians like that, Sir?'

'A few Bengali babus.'

That was how the geography lesson ran nearly forty years ago.

> The tumult and the shouting dies
> The captains and the kings depart . . .

Today, after all the pageantry of British surrender, these places remain the solitary outposts of European authority.

I had long wanted to visit them; Goa especially, for I had been endeared to many Goans in many parts of the world; I had read travellers' tales of the Golden City that had once been the capital and emporium of all the widespread Portuguese empire of the East, and now stood quite deserted; I had seen prints and photographs of the great baroque buildings engulfed in jungle, and lately I had read Father James Brodrick's biography of St Francis Xavier, whose body is Goa's greatest treasure. December 1952 was the saint's particular month, the 400th anniversary of his death, when his relics were to be exposed to veneration for the last time in their long and strange history. It was then or never to make the pilgrimage.

Goa can be reached by sea from Bombay or overland from Belgaum, a straggling cantonment on the air-route to the south. The bus at Belgaum was full of pilgrims. A polite youth distributed printed warnings of the brutality of the 'Fascist' regime ahead of us. He was one of the dissident Goans, a small organized group of whom exists in Bombay. This was my introduction to the threat which hangs over the European territories. Covetous eyes are on them in Delhi where the Congress politicians are more ambitious than their predecessors in power, the British imperialists. Even in happy Goa, at the time of the British withdrawal, many Hindus and some Christians were excited by the jubilation beyond their frontiers. A dozen agitators were deported and now live in Portugal in complete freedom, subject to a ban on their returning home to

Month, December 1953; *Esquire*, December 1953.

resume their activities. A small section only of the population is interested in public affairs. The wisest of these have patiently compared the new Republic of India with their own, giving particular attention to the state of order, the purity of the financial administration, the welfare of the poorest classes, the penal system and the respect shown to minority communities such as the Eurasians. In none of these respects have they found reason for envy. There are very few European officials in the territory. Goans have strong local patriotism but they are, in fact, Portuguese. They are not a subject or 'protected' people. They enjoy full and equal citizenship with the descendants of the Conquistadors and can rise to any position in the republic. There is no exclusive club. In one thing only are they deficient in comparison with the Indians. Politics are the cocaine of the people and this unhealthy stimulant is little used in Goa. Wherever he goes in India, the western visitor is beset by begging students. At first, remembering, perhaps, Ignatius Loyola at the University of Paris, he is warmed with sympathy at the traditional spectacle of poverty in pursuit of knowledge. Then he asks: what subject are they studying? What profession do they aspire to practise? And often the chilling answers are: politics, politicians. The ambitions of Indian youth are no longer confined to a clerkship and a pension. There are larger prizes very remote but very brilliant, at Delhi and in the Indian embassies.

For a few Goan youths it may seem sad to grow up deprived of the mass oratory and demonstrations, overturned buses, tear-gas and *lathi*-charges which enrich the frugal life of the Indian student. These, if they go to Bombay for their education, become recruits for the Congress Party. The more experienced value their Portuguese citizenship for the privileges it confers. There is little extravagant devotion to Lisbon. Portuguese rule was violent in its early days, neglectful later; only in the present generation has it begun to redeem its past. Goans of Brahman descent never fail to announce the fact, while those of mixed blood are silent on the subject. Patriotism at home and among the diaspora – the thousands of Goans in Africa, Bombay, and along the trade routes of British shipping – is Goan. But, paradoxically, the only guarantee of local integrity is Portuguese nationality.

These are the impressions of several subsequent weeks of inquiry and discussion. On that first morning there was barely time to glance at the Congress leaflet before the bus started and all attention was devoted to the hard work of travel. This was called a 'luxury coach' and later acquaintance with the normal service confirmed its claim to certain superior amenities. The number of passengers was limited to the number of seats. These, that morning, were all Goans visiting their homes for the festival, all in western dress, all very polite and in the best of spirits except when, rather often, they were being sick. Clinging to the hard, narrow seats we bounced and banged our way to the frontier in a brown dust-storm of our own making.

In two hours we reached the Indian road-block.

Smuggling is said to be well organized and profitable. Most things are cheaper in Goa but the main illicit export is whisky, for the state of Bombay, like most of southern India, has used its new-found freedom to decree prohibition – an ineffective piece of bigotry and an odd one, for there is nothing in Hindu religion or tradition to discourage fermented liquors. The smugglers do not follow the highway or use public transport; the traffic goes one way only, but even in our exodus the Indian officials were tediously vigilant. The festival of St Francis Xavier was not officially popular in India. Indeed, the Indians were then staging what looked rather like a specially contrived counter-attraction – a festival at Ernakulam to celebrate the 1,900th anniversary of the arrival there of St Thomas the Apostle. St Thomas is the patron of sceptics. He will not, I think, condemn the doubt of his ever having reached India at all; still less of his having done so in December '52. But Indians rejoice in festivals and both occasions were enthusiastically thronged.

We changed into a more comfortable vehicle and half an hour later reached the Goan frontier-post, where easy-going cordiality prevailed. A booth sold beer and wine and most of the male passengers celebrated their return to civilized ways. Then we began our headlong descent through scenery quite unlike what we had passed hitherto. It is a countryside of enchanting natural beauty; our dust-cloud turned to powdered chocolate from the deep red-brown earth and rock in which the road is cut. High on one side, deep on the other rose and fell dense green plantations of indigenous palm and plantain and the sturdy little cashew trees which the Portuguese brought from Brazil. The watery depths of the valley were brilliant with young rice. The whole landscape tilted forward before us to where the two fine rivers break into a jumble of islands and streams and broad creeks, with beyond them the open sea.

Goa, particularly in the 'Old Conquests', is better populated than appears from the road. Neat homesteads are hidden everywhere in the trees. There are half a million inhabitants, most of whom eschew the towns. In our descent we were passing through the 'New Conquests'. There is a considerable difference between the two areas. The 'Old Conquests' were Albuquerque's territory. He took them from Mohammedan invaders. To the Portuguese of that period all Mohammedans were the hated Moors. Albuquerque exterminated the males and gave the women as wives to his men. Hindus he treated with greater clemency but in effect they were given the choice of emigration or baptism. Within a generation almost all his subjects bore Portuguese names, professed the Christian faith and were the ancestors of the most devout and moral people in India. He destroyed all the temples, many of which are reputed to have been splendid works of art. In extenuation of this aesthetic outrage it may be said that Hindu art probably struck him and his contemporaries as being not only expressive of an erroneous theology, but also preposterously obscene. The 'Old Conquests' preserve their ancient egalitarian system of land tenure; each man, however far he travels, is bound to his ancestral village by his share in the common lands; each village committee preserves the list of its community and relieves its poor.

The 'New Conquests' were added in 1795, an age of 'enlightenment'. There are many temples, not very ancient but gracious and commodious, still served by the dancing-girls whose role has been abolished in most parts of India. We passed one near Ponda, a glimpse at the end of a fine avenue quickly obliterated by our cloud of dust. There is a child Raja living without ostentation beside the temple of Sunda and farther south a feudal nobleman, a gunner officer in the Indian Army. The villages and farms of the 'New Conquests' are shabbier than the old, for the wealthier Hindus congregate in the towns where most of the shops are in their hands. There are plenty of Hindus among the Christians and some Christians among the Hindus, living independently but amicably side by side. In general, however, the old frontier holds and divides two distinct cultures.

We crossed it at the bridge over the Combarjua and almost at once were skirting Old Goa, another glimpse through the dust – white cupolas, an arch, laterite walls hairy as coconuts with dry weed – then a metalled road beside the river Mandovi, a great stretch of tidal water full of small sails, with wooded hills beyond; and so to New Goa or Pangim, the modern capital.

There is nothing outstandingly modern in Pangim except the hotel, which is so new that it was still being loudly built during the festival month which it had been designed to serve. That alone breaks the charm of the water-front, whose remarkable features are the fine, placid old Government House and a wildly vivacious new statue of the Abbé Farias, a Goan mesmerist of the Napoleonic era, mentioned by Dumas and caught here in hot bronze at the climax of an experiment, rampant over an entranced female.

Pangim makes no pretensions to gaiety. The transient Portuguese officials are economical, the Goan residents home-loving. Weekend tourists from Bombay have grown in numbers since prohibition. These alone, in normal times, disturb the tranquillity of the town. In honour of the festival loud-speakers had been set up in the main squares. In one of these was a neat little Industrial Exhibition and a temporary café. There was also an exhibition of modern art which deserved more attention than it got. All other activity was on the quay and at the bus station, for Pangim, that month, was purely a place of passage for Old Goa, eight miles upstream.

There are many vivid accounts of Old Goa both in its prosperity and its ruin. Its prosperity lasted barely 150 years. Its ruin was swift, caused by Dutch rivalry and the sheer lack of Portuguese manpower, and accelerated by plague and fever. Most travellers reached it after a voyage of great privation and danger. Perhaps they tended to exaggerate the splendours they found. There was treasure certainly and warehouses full of expensive eastern merchandise; but there was little that could be called 'civilization', either Asiatic or European. The masons built solidly but they followed without imagination a limited range of models. Most of the portraits of viceroys and patriarchs are of historical interest only. In population it equalled Elizabethan London but most were servile, and the social life, even of the prosperous and important, sounds devoid of charm. Those sweltering, swaggering *fidalgos* and their sickly womenfolk, with their palanquins and sweets and scents and retinues of handmaids, were not real ladies and gentlemen but the riff-raff of Portugal over-dressed and over-privileged. The Church alone sustained what there was of culture and the Church alone displays some of its former grandeur today.

The city was abandoned in 1759. Its palaces and colleges were used as quarries. The jungle closed in, thrusting roots between the laterite blocks. Vaults and façades crumbled into the steep streets. A hundred years later Richard Burton, a subaltern then on sick-leave from Bombay, found only the huge Convent of St Monica inhabited. He did not know it – he was too busy listening to scandalous stories to inquire – but there were barely a dozen nuns living there at the time of his impertinent visit. The last of them survived alone into the late seventies, when the illustrious foundation came to end. The vast, buttressed walls stood firm but the paintings flaked away in the cloisters and the odorous, enclosed garden ran all to weed. It had enjoyed a remarkable history, guarding its strict and secret piety among the gaming-houses and brothels, receiving splendid benefactions, passing through the little revolving hatch that was its access to the world of commerce, special sweetmeats for sale and delicate pieces of needlework; sheltering once a stigmatic German sister and a crucifix which is said to have rebuked a mitigation of rule with fresh-flowing blood.

It was the last religious house to survive the legislation of the anti-clerical faction in Portugal. When Santa Monica stood empty the soul of Old Goa seemed finally to have departed. Memories of fever and plague haunted it. No one cared to stay there after sunset. The Canons of the Cathedral came punctually to their stalls and sang their daily office but returned to Pangim to sleep. Like Gibbon ruminating on the steps of Ara Coeli, many romantic trippers in the last hundred years have stood under the Arch of the Viceroys, considered the vanity of earthly empire and indulged in forebodings of the future of British India. The last of these was Robert Byron who, unaccountably and quite without foundation, put it on record that the Cathedral housed a mechanical organ.

In the last two years there has been a stir in the city's sleep. Officials have exterminated the mosquitoes. Vegetation and rubble have been cleared so that the four great remaining churches stand in an open space. Several of the chapels that lie around them are being repaired. There is a plan to use Santa Monica as the archdiocesan seminary. But during the festival month the whole area was temporarily transformed into a fair-ground and bivouac. The pilgrims were everywhere in possession, a constantly changing population of some 50,000 men, women and children.

The papal delegation and high officers had been there for the opening ceremonies and were gone before I arrived. Day after day I watched the changing parade of Christian India with inexhaustible fascination. Sometimes a wealthy family or an official from the government of India would arrive in a private car, enter privately ahead of the queue, pay their homage and turn straight home. One day half a village community of black little aboriginals were led in by the priest who had just converted them. They had never before left their ancestral forest and had no idea that the world contained so many other Christians.

There were prosperous Goan parishes marching in procession, men and women apart, carrying wands and banners, singing litanies and wearing the insignia of pious sodalities. For these a whole bazaar had been constructed selling souvenirs and rosaries and beer. But the traders were not doing quite as well as they had hoped. At last, after 200 years, the Jesuits were again in charge and everything was more efficiently ordered than on previous occasions. There was less waiting about. And the overwhelming majority of pilgrims were very poor people who had pinched and saved and borrowed to raise their fares. They carried bundles of provisions and when they were not praying they were cooking and eating. They prayed long and often with rapt devotion, resolutely visiting all the altars and all the statues, kissing the stones; and they ate long and often, squatting in groups over the wood smoke and spicy steam, chattering in half a dozen languages.

When a bishop passed – and prelates were plentiful there all that month – they would rise and dart to kiss his ring, brilliant, swift and unanimous as a shoal of carnivorous fish. They came from all over India and Ceylon but mostly from the southern coast between Bombay and Madras which had heard the preaching of St Francis Xavier. They were the descendants of his converts. Always, from before dawn until late evening, patient queues formed and moved slowly forward to the side-door of the Cathedral. Hitherto the relics had been exposed in the Jesuit church of Bom Jesus. Now for the first and last time they stood in the transept of the Cathedral. They were the goal of the pilgrimage. Three-quarters of a million Indians were coming to thank a Spaniard, who had died far away, just 400 years ago, for their gift of Faith.

Francis Xavier is no figure of tradition and legend. We know more about him, in more authentic detail, than about many contemporary celebrities. Generations of patient scholars, culminating in Father Georg Schurhammer, SJ, have patiently collected and collated the evidence. Last year the fruit of their work was set before English readers in the lively narrative of Father James Brodrick, SJ. 'Lively' is the right word, not merely for the vivacious humour of the writing, but for the whole image he has created, a study 'from the life', complete in the round, seeming palpable. Francis Xavier lived in an age of great adventurers. In England we incline to regard our Elizabethan sea-dogs as unique national heroes. The Portuguese went first and went farther, and among those fierce and fearless men, Francis Xavier was pre-eminent in daring and endurance. In him renaissance exuberance coexisted with mediaeval faith – faith like a meteorite, compact, impermeable, incorruptible. But there was another component which belongs to no period in time – an insatiable love for his fellow men. Love raised him to the altars of the Church and love keeps him alive in the hearts of his devotees today. He believed that those who died in the darkness of heathenism were in danger of eternal damnation. The most perfect gift Love could bring was Christian Truth. That was the single, irresistible motive force that drove him across seas wide open to piracy, through forts seething with disease and sin, along bare inland tracks devoid of food and shelter, to wherever he could find a foothold and a hearing.

Ten years were the total span of his stupendous mission. He came to the East under obedience, a Jesuit priest, one of the earliest companions of St Ignatius Loyola. The King of Portugal required Jesuits in his eastern empire. There were few to choose from then. Even so Francis Xavier was a second choice. He came almost by chance. Had a colleague not fallen ill he might have completed his life in a European university.

Goa was his base. There he began his work and there, three times, he returned to re-equip himself for his great journeys and to attend to local ecclesiastical affairs. His mission lay wherever there were souls to be saved. The colonists, their slaves and prisoners, the newly converted Indians, the heathen – all were in his charge, and his methods were as diverse as the peoples. He walked the streets of Goa with a handbell calling all and sundry to prayer. He dined with the luxurious and laughed them out of their excesses. He lay night-long beside the dying in the crowded and stifling hospitals hearing confessions and whispering comfort. He stood among the fishing boats and taught through an interpreter the simple prayers that are used there today. Basque was his mother tongue to which he reverted as he lay dying. His Portuguese, as appears in his letters, was imperfect. Of the numberless languages of Asia he had a bare smattering, but nowhere, except among the Japanese, did he meet with misunderstanding. He had the gift of tongues which springs from love and burns its way into the mind without the intermediary of words. He was possessed by the Word. He covered, in his ten years, all that was known of Asia, he penetrated unknown Japan and fell at last with his dying eyes on China, quite worn out at the age of 46 and still yearning for further conquests.

During his lifetime he was recognized as a saint. When the news of his death reached Malacca his bones were sent for, from where he had been buried in lime on the island of Sancian. Thus was first observed the phenomenon whose strangeness caught the imagination of East and West alike. After ten weeks he was found as fresh and supple and flushed as on the day he died. The body was taken to Malacca and reburied there, bent double and pressed down under the floor of the church. There it remained until news of his death reached Goa. The capital of the Indies required it, and five months later it was again dug up and again found incorrupt and quite unchanged except for some wounds caused by its clumsy burial.

The body, now acclaimed as miraculous, was borne to Goa and rapturously welcomed. It was also carefully examined by doctors and pronounced to be untouched by any embalmer. On several subsequent occasions it was re-examined by critical foreigners and found in a state of preternatural preservation. An elaborate silver casket was made for it and later mounted on a monument of Tuscan marble. There it stands today in the old Jesuit church of Bom Jesus.

For 150 years it defied corruption though much mishandled by the curious and the pious. One over-pious lady bit off a toe and smuggled it away in triumph to Lisbon. The Pope sent for an arm. On both occasions there was a flow of fresh blood. In the late sixteenth century the face was so lifelike and warmly coloured that the merchant seaman Alexander Hamilton, seeing it from four yards distance, took it for waxwork.

But some signs of desiccation had already appeared. Early in the eighteenth century the Jesuits submitted that the spectacle had ceased to be edifying, and should be decently abandoned. The King of Portugal ordered that the casket should be opened only at the command of the Viceroy. Then in 1757 Pombal, the anti-clerical minister of the King of Portugal, had the Jesuits expelled from the King's dominions and a horrified whisper ran round the bazaars that they had taken the saint's body away with them. The rumour grew instead of subsiding. Christian India clamoured for a sight of its saint. Pombal fell in 1777, and in 1782 the casket was once more laid open to the lips of the people. The body was by then quite dry and stiff. Since then there has been an exposition every ten years.

The body is now officially spoken of merely as 'the relics' of the saint. At their final exposition the face, an arm and a foot were all that appeared from the sumptuous vestments. The panels in the side of the casket were removed affording a clear view; the open coffin was pulled out a few inches to allow the pilgrims to kiss the withered foot. This was what they had come for; not to see a miracle but say thank you and to seek protection. Hour after hour they filed past paying their inherited debt of love. The festival was planned to close on 3 January. They begged for an extension. Three more days were granted. Still they asked for longer. There were people far away who had not made their arrangements in time; seamen were coming on leave. But the powers of the organizers had been stretched to the utmost. The hygienic authorities were anxious. On 6 January the casket was carried back to Bom Jesus, its panels replaced, its doors locked, and the saint's restless bones at last found peace, not to be touched or seen again until the Day of Judgment.

His beloved Goans stand guard over him and he over them. He is their single renowned possession. India is littered with prodigious monuments – Buddhist, Jain, Hindu, Mohammedan and the Anglo-Saxon engineer have responded to the vast wealth of the place, expanded and sought to perpetuate themselves.

Goa has St Francis Xavier and his spirit can be recognized in every face; not his exuberance, perhaps, though Goans are great travellers, but his faith and love. Goans have a peculiar, pervading, unobtrusive benignity which is not found anywhere except in deeply Christian places. They had a special place in his story. They made a home for him. They were his beginning, not the remote unattainable end of his striving. To them he returned to take stock and recuperate. To them finally he was borne in triumph. And they are making a congenial home for him still.

. HERE'S RICHNESS .

Hilaire Belloc's death last summer came at the end of nearly fifteen years during which he had written nothing and made no public appearance. Most of his books were out of print. The weekly paper to which he had devoted himself so prodigally had ceased publication. And yet at his Requiem Mass the great nave of Westminster Cathedral was thronged and by a congregation the greater part of whom, it seemed to one observer, were drawn by Belloc's fame rather than by personal acquaintance. It was not a literary occasion. Belloc was strictly, perhaps even ruthlessly, professional as a writer, but he made his life among men of action and women of society. Younger writers were often disconcerted when they discerned behind his massive courtesy an absolute ignorance of who they were and what they had written. There were friends in plenty in the Cathedral that August morning, men and women whose wide variety gave witness of the fullness of the man they were commemorating. (Belloc has been spoken of as a bigot and it is worth noting that of his close friends not more than half shared his religious faith and very few, if any, his political opinions.) But mingling with them and outnumbering them were people of all kinds and ages who may never have set eyes on Belloc but loved him in his work.

Those are Belloc's prime characters as a man and as a writer, his breadth of scope and the love he inspires. His poetry is quintessential of him. He himself recognized this fact most clearly. His prose works are copious, always lucid, often rising to fine passages of rhetoric, often memorable in their sharp definition of word, but they are for the most part the work of a craftsman, often a craftsman hired for an imposed task. His poetry is his art, something he kept quite distinct from literary commerce, to which he gave his full concentrated attention, into which he distilled all the noble essences which made him unique as a man, in which he confided as his warranty of lasting fame. Most of it was written before 1914, none after 1939. But in his years of leisure and rumination he never undertook the task of collection and collation. That, he was confident, would come later and here, very punctually, we have it; a most welcome and worthy book. Mr Roughead is an editor of Scottish prudence and precision; Sir Francis Meynell, a publisher of unwearied charm. The arrangement, the rare notes, the apparatus of reference are admirably convenient. The verses are set in the fine, clear italic of the Romulus fount and printed on paper which it is

Review of *The Verses of Hilaire Belloc*, ed. W. N. Roughead. *Spectator*, 21 May 1954.

a pleasure to handle. One thousand six hundred and fifty copies have so far been printed. It is to be hoped that an unlimited popular edition will follow.

In only one particular can fault be found with this admirable pair, editor and publisher. Mr Roughead states: 'This book contains what I believe to be the whole of Hilaire Belloc's poetry, except for a few manuscript verses and printed fragments too slight to be worth including and some oral-tradition verses vague as to text and over-sharp in intention.' It is not quite clear how many categories of exception Mr Roughead here intends. Are all the manuscript verses not included held to be too slight? Are the 'over-sharp' verses all also vague in text? What is certain is that, for fear of offence, some of Belloc's wittiest and most characteristic verses have been omitted. The second Lord Devonport has set an example of truly noble magnanimity in giving his approval to the publication of 'The grocer Hudson Kearley'. Lords Swaythling, Wimborne and Rothschild and Mr Edward James seem, with some reason, to have been less accommodating. Could not a few blank leaves have been included at the end of the volume on which owners might transcribe their favourite *expurgata*?

There are more than 370 items in the collection, ranging in size and dignity from:

> I said to Heart, 'How goes it?' Heart replied:
> 'Right as a Ribstone Pippin!' But it lied.

to the sonorous ode on wine. The children's rhymes, almost every syllable of them a familiar quotation, are here reprinted without the illustrations which seemed an inalienable part of them. It is remarkable how well they stand alone. The order of the original books of verses has been broken and the various poems felicitously regrouped under their forms as sonnets, songs, epigrams, ballades and so on. There are eleven items never before printed, thirteen that were privately printed, and forty-six that have not appeared in any previous collection. Now that all is gathered in, it can be seen how small a part of Belloc's work was 'Bellocian' in the vulgar usage.

> May all good fellows that here agree
> Drink Audit Ale in heaven with me,
> And may all my enemies go to hell!
> Noël! Noël! Noël! Noël!

Early lines, interpolations in a prose fantasy, far from typical, but meat for the parodist; the ebullience of a brief mood. Belloc's verse is by turn humorous, comic, tender, witty, angry, melancholy, formal; very seldom jolly. It is in large the complete expression of a man's soul – and a great soul. His themes are the stuff of common life as he knew it in a warmer age; strenuous male companionship, romantic love of woman, the sea, the seasons, the transience of earthly beauty, the unremitting benevolent watchfulness of Our Lady and the angels, the innocence of childhood, the absurdity of pedantry and ambition, the wickedness and stark danger of power. His diction and prosody are the fruit of classical schooling. He was a Christian Shropshire Lad and, by that enrichment, immeasurably Housman's superior. He needs no critical interpretation. He is here to be enjoyed. For that reason there were few articles about him in the literary reviews and many mourners at his obsequies.

He had an idiosyncratic conspectus, formed early, which seemed not to vary from 1912 until the day of his death. In his opinions, he was a traditionalist and a revolutionary. It will be the gracious task of Mr Robert Speaight, his biographer, to count the components of his intellectual structure and trace the origins of those seemingly discordant convictions which coexisted harmoniously in him. The reviewer of his *Verses* has an easier task, to express wonder at their variety and richness.

For satire:

> Distinguish carefully between these two,
> This thing is yours, that other thing is mine.
> You have a shirt, a brimless hat, a shoe
> And half a coat. I am the Lord benign
> Of fifty hundred acres . . .
> . . . I do not envy you your hat, your shoe,
> Why should you envy me my small estate?

And the 'Verses to a Lord who, in the House of Lords, said that those who opposed the South African adventure confused soldiers with money-grubbers.'

For humour:

> Sir! you have disappointed us!
> We had intended you to be
> The next Prime Minister but three:
> The stocks were sold: the Press was squared;
> The Middle Class was quite prepared.
> But as it is! My language fails!
> Go out and govern New South Wales.

For sustained classic dignity, the 'Heroic Poem on Wine'.
For pure lyric beauty the lyric beginning:

> O my companion, O my sister Sleep,
> The valley is all before us. . . .

But it is tedious to call attention to such established landmarks. Lines of Belloc's sing a multitude of memories. The wonder is, in finding them all collected, how profuse and how pure a genius is here displayed.

. AGE OF UNREST .

The Baroque came late to England and left early. It was never a very easy guest. The climate proved uncongenial. Even at the brief height of the vogue there were scoffers. When it fell from favour it fell into contempt and loathing, which persisted for 200 years. English taste does not normally run to invention and display. We like, in our dwellings, dignity, repose and elegance. The Adams gave us just what Dr Johnson ordered. In our more fanciful, poetic moods we turn naturally to Gothic. Higher excitements are the reward of travel, very enjoyable in their proper place. For one generation only, in the spring of the eighteenth century, the Baroque satisfied a restless temper; the period – dramatic and dangerous by contrast to the succeeding two centuries – of a disputed succession, gross ambitions, precarious prosperity, of Marlborough's victories and the South Sea Bubble. We dub this generation 'the Age of Vanbrugh'.

Little enough remains of his work, nothing precisely as he planned it. Claremont and Eastbury are quite gone, Seaton Delaval a ruin, Castle Howard sadly disfigured; his gardens never grew to maturity; Blenheim and Grimsthorpe are his chief monuments. No great architect except Soane has been so ill-used by posterity. But his name has been a magnet to which attributions have stuck, and one of Mr Whistler's aims in his present work has been to redistribute the credit among his brilliant but less illustrious contemporaries.

It is natural that Vanbrugh should have engrossed the period. He was the inspired amateur – soldier, prisoner in the Bastille, playwright, herald and, until late in life, convivial bachelor. Many must feel that they could build better than the professional architects given the chance. Vanbrugh, through personal charm, got the chance in his first enormous commission from Lord Carlisle. He moved easily among the first Whig magnates who were, perhaps unconsciously, eager to overlay the guilt of treason with prodigal ostentation. He treated his patrons with sympathy, good humour and independence. The Duchess of Marlborough alone failed to respond and came near ruining him. But his was a happy and brilliant life.

Mr Whistler's *Sir John Vanbrugh, Architect and Dramatist*, published in 1938, is now scarce. The first glance at *The Imagination of Vanbrugh* raises the expectation that here is a glorified reissue. It is both less and more than that. It is a collection of highly specialized studies. There is little direct biographical narrative, no continuous argument. There are fifty-eight sections and three appendices, which print for the first time letters and documents of prime value to the serious student. The authenticity of the sketches in the W. J. Smith scrap-book in the Victoria and Albert Museum is carefully examined. Vanbrugh's associates, some of them unknown to the general reader, are rewarded with recognition for their very considerable contributions. Hawksmoor, in

Review of *The Imagination of Vanbrugh and His Fellow Artists*, by Laurence Whistler. *Observer*, 6 June 1954.

particular, emerges with his credit much enhanced. There are 140 plates and six illustrations in the text, which include Rex Whistler's charming drawing of the Satyr Gate at Castle Howard. The engraved glass of the author's and his fine cover design add to the attractions of an entirely attractive book.

. MR BETJEMAN'S BOUQUET .

Mr John Betjeman is a happy example of consistent fertility. He is not one of those poets who, like athletes who broke records in early youth, become eminent spectators in middle age; nor does he, like so many of his juniors, complain that it is impossible to write poetry when burdened with the duty of earning his living. Despite multifarious other activities he continues to produce a book of new verses every five years or so. His 1954 volume is longer than either *New Bats in Old Belfries* or *Old Lights for New Chancels*, and is fully their equal in quality. It comprises, the publishers state, poems written since 1948. There is some discrepancy here. One of them, 'Christmas', was quoted by the Warden of All Souls in his introduction to the *Selected Poems* of that year. This is more than a mere point for the thesis-writer because the poem in question has an affinity with the recent 'House of Rest', which might lead the unwary to think that Mr Betjeman was developing a new, purely devotional interest, which in fact has been present fitfully for many years.

Most, if not all, of these poems have appeared already and will be familiar to the host of admirers who hurry out to purchase any periodical to which they are told he has contributed. (Mr Betjeman, it may be noted, still observes the pleasant old-world custom of thanking editors for the permission to reprint which they have no right to withhold.) It is a keen pleasure to have them now collected in a book. Gone are the days of the extravagant production of *Mount Zion* and *Continual Dew*. The present volume is uniform with its immediate predecessors in a good taste which their author earlier might have condemned as 'ghastly'.

He has named it *A Few Late Chrysanthemums*. At first glance those mid-Victorian exotics, heavy and haunting in scent, rich in autumnal colours, might seem a happy epithet. But those ragged mops of petal? – no, in form Mr Betjeman's poems have the crisp precision of the iris. A dashing young critic has lately proclaimed: 'Saying something in verse and writing a poem are two different things. The better you are at the first, the more unlikely it is that you will do well at the second.' By this rule Mr Betjeman is certainly among the goats with Tennyson, Browning, Keats, Wordsworth, Milton and Shakespeare, not among the sheep with – with whomever the young critic had in mind. For two characteristics of his writing are, first, that he 'says something'; his poems consist of grammatical, translatable English sentences; and secondly

Review of *A Few Late Chrysanthemums*, by John Betjeman. *Sunday Times*, 11 July 1954.

that he exhibits a startling metrical dexterity. Poetry is a flower that breaks, or a bird that nests, in the delicate branches of his verse. It is this constant blossoming, or bird-song, of pure poetry which raises him above, say, Calverley or Praed, who excelled him in technical ingenuity.

Mr Betjeman has no element of satire in him, and when he comes nearest to attempting it, he comes nearest to failure. Scorn is the essence of satire. Mr Betjeman is moved sometimes to vexation, more often to sorrow, by the nastiness all around him, of which he is intensely conscious. This large difference of temper apart, there is a close affinity between Mr Betjeman and Hilaire Belloc. Both are true poets. The reputation of each stands in the same danger of vulgarization. Just as there is a habit of mind dubbed pejoratively 'Bellocian', which was in fact expressed in a very small part of his verses, so there is now a cant use of the word 'Betjemanian', which may deter a later generation from full enjoyment.

It was new and gay in Edwardian days, when Rand millionaires did deals over the champagne with agnostic Liberals, to sing of pubs and the open road and the Old Faith. It was new and gay between the wars, when Regency and the Baroque were all the vogue, to sing of Surrey villas and dripping evergreens and the parish church. This predilection of Mr Betjeman's shows dangerous signs of catching on. A new generation may find his wistful Anglicanism as distasteful as some modern readers find Belloc's rumbustious Romanism.

The loss will be theirs, for Mr Betjeman primarily uses his idiosyncratic apparatus as a series of symbols to evoke childhood. It seems to have been his unique experience to be born and brought up in every county and town in England. The entire Ordnance Survey speaks to him in the language of adolescence. Little that happens between preparatory school and the churchyard is of much significance to him. Death obtrudes, particularly in this volume, where the best, the epitaph to Walter Ramsden, and the worst, 'Late Flowering Lust', are both *mementos mori*. Baldness discloses the skull, and it is notable that in this book, I think for the first time, Mr Betjeman repeatedly commends the beauties of thatch. Miss Hunter-Dunn is no longer responsive. Her ghost reappears in forbidding shape in 'The Olympic Girl'. There is certainly a more consistent melancholy in this collection than in its predecessors. But the voice of authentic poetry speaks through the deepening gloom, sweeter and clearer than ever.

. DROPMORE PRESS MAKES GOOD .

The Dropmore Press and the closely allied Queen Anne Press have in recent years produced a number of enterprising, experimental little books and one massive monument of frivolity in the reproduction of postage stamps. Now at

Review of *The Holkham Bible Picture Book*, ed. W. O. Hassall. *Spectator*, 16 July 1954.

last they have done what their well-wishers have always hoped for them and have created a work of art. *The Holkham Bible Picture Book* is in this reviewer's experience the most beautiful piece of book-making to appear anywhere since the war and one of the finest of the century. It comes at the right time when the decay of craftsmanship is being everywhere deplored. Future historians will have to qualify their generalizations. 1954 cannot be such a bleak year as is generally supposed.

'Bible Picture Book' is a convenient but not very accurate name for the manuscript here reproduced. It is a series of drawings, made probably in London in about 1325, under Dominican patronage. The forty-two parchment leaves were taken out of the country, presumably at the Reformation, purchased abroad for £30 in 1816 on behalf of Thomas William Coke of Holkham – the celebrated 'Coke of Norfolk' who was later created Earl of Leicester – and remained in the possession of the family until the famous library was denuded by death duties in 1952. They are now in the British Museum. This is not an illuminated manuscript. The drawings are not intended as an embellishment of the text: the text, in Anglo-Norman, is explanatory of the drawings and fitted into the page where the artist allows. The pictures are not merely illustrative of the bible narrative. More than a quarter of them portray subjects which lack scriptural authority and all are enriched with details, legendary, traditional, symbolic and, it seems, occasionally purely imaginative. This is a theological tract in pictorial form dealing with man's creation, fall, redemption and final judgment. It is also plainly intended as an aid to meditation. It is addressed, the editor argues, to city burgesses rather than to the court or the convent.

The drawings are in pen and ink. The colouring is by another, less accomplished hand. Indeed there must have been a great temptation to the publishers to disregard the painting entirely and with the searching technique of modern photography to reproduce the original line alone. A beautiful series of plates would have resulted for the drawing is brilliant, elegant, vigorous and versatile. The drowned woman in the Deluge is of arresting beauty. It has been plausibly suggested that these were cartoons for mural decorations.

For the mediaevalist this is clearly a source of prime importance. The present reviewer is not qualified to give any opinion on this specialized topic beyond remarking that to the layman Mr W. O. Hassall's introduction and notes seem to provide all that the scholar will demand. It is a matter for sorrow that even in this vineyard of four years' loving labour the snake of imperfect proof-reading rears his ugly head; on page 12, line 19, '15v' should read '15'.

The volume is very moderately priced at £12 12s. and will doubtless appreciate in value. The Roxburghe *Sherborne Missal* of 1920 for example, a less sumptuous work, usually sells today for about £35. The *Grimani Breviary*, about twelve times its size, sells for £275. Perhaps it is ungracious for the reviewer who has received this splendid work as a gift to suggest that a few shillings added to the price and a gilt top-edge might have been an advantage.

The binding is excellent. The back and fore edges of the covers are of niger morocco, the sides of parchment with a fine blind stamp of Regency Gothic design on the top-side and a dove of more modern aspect on the back-side. Paper and typography are entirely admirable. The eighty-four plates are in collotype, eight in colour, the remainder in monochrome. The character of the original is particularly apt for 'facsimile'. There is no gilding, always the snag in reproduction. The paint, though more opaque than one could wish, has not the solidity of most mediaeval manuscripts. This solidity, so brilliantly and arduously counterfeited early in the last century by the hand-colouring of Henry Shaw and the lithography of Owen Jones, was quite lost in the photographic, three-colour process at the beginning of this century. The collotypes here displayed, the work of the Oxford University Press, are models of fidelity. One can distinguish the hairside from the inside in the grain of the parchment. Only the wide margins destroy the illusion of identity.

The planners of this noble volume are all too modest. Only the editor's name is given. One would have welcomed a list of 'credits' in the manner of the cinema. Credit is indeed due to everyone from the magnate who financed the undertaking to the journeyman in the workshop; more than credit; joyous gratitude that an object of such rare beauty should have taken shape among us.

. ANOTHER AND BETTER RUSKIN .

Like actors wanting to play Hamlet, English writers all want to have their say about Ruskin. The story is familiar and perennially fascinating. Each feels that some nuance has been lost, some essential ingredient neglected, by his predecessors. Forty years ago when Mr Clive Bell published *Art*, such a turn of taste would have been unimaginable. It is ironical that Ruskin should have been restored to upper-middle brow sympathies by Proust. Now we have come to realize that in his life and his art Ruskin sets a series of rudimentary puzzles which can keep us guessing for a lifetime.

The latest attempt at a summary and a conspectus comes from a lady well qualified to help. Like Ruskin Miss Evans has taken for her subject objects of beauty anywhere which excite her appetites. No age is alien to her which produced works of art. But, like Ruskin, she has found an especial delight in the European Middle Ages. She is well disciplined in the habits of research and one has the confidence in all her work which comes from the knowledge that whatever she undertakes has been begun and completed with disinterested enthusiasm. Not for her the speculation of the weary professional: 'Fifteen years since the last assessment of So-and-so. Perhaps the time is come for another.' Thus she produces a work on Ruskin at the end of a rather brisk

Review of *John Ruskin*, by Joan Evans. *Spectator*, 17 September 1954.

succession of competitors. One may say 'at the end' because it seems unlikely that much unpublished material will now come to light and because Miss Evans has handled all that was previously available and some valuable new matter lucidly and wisely. She has in fact succeeded where her predecessors have just failed and produced what should for all general purposes prove to be the standard brief life.

Miss Evans's claim to this title, besides her own personal distinction, is her position as joint editor with Mr J. Howard Whitehouse of Ruskin's diaries which are to appear next year from the Clarendon Press. She has drawn liberally on this exciting new source particularly from the middle, crucial years of Ruskin's life. It is revealing particularly in showing the egotism of the subject. Because he was munificent and without personal gross ambitions, he has acquired a reputation for generosity and selflessness which, it is a shock to discover, was little deserved.

This is the stage in a review when the reviewer is tempted to leave his proper subject and begin an essay of his own. This would be no service to reader or author. Perhaps a few notes are permissible on what, in reading Ruskin's story once more, immediately impresses. First, as mentioned above, Ruskin's self-ishness. Then his precocity; the first volume of *Modern Painters* was written when he was 23; that work was finished, the *Stones of Venice* and the *Seven Lamps* begun and ended, in the next ten years. His chief life-work was then accomplished by the age of 33. That would not be remarkable in a poet and, in truth, Ruskin was a poet, pure and simple. His ideas were mostly preposterous and inconsistent. As a thinker, aesthetically, politically or theologically, there is an awful frivolity about him – as there was, indeed, about Tennyson. He was gifted with a superb organ-voice which ennobled everything he said. It is not that he had a trick of making the fatuous impressive, but that the fatuous became filled with his own genius.

Of recent years a slightly prurient importance has been attached to the failure of Ruskin's marriage and of his subsequent romantic aspirations. Miss Evans tactfully and firmly sets these incidents in their proper place. She is interested in him primarily as an artist. She has studied his written work with an attention not given to it, perhaps, by any of his recent biographers. He never, it seems, held an intellectual conviction. He was all sensibility. He was brilliantly devoid of snobbery, ingenuously ignorant so that he came fresh to anything ready to be swept up or rebuffed by the mood of the moment, quite content to join Tintoretto and Mulready and Kate Greenaway in the same circle of felicity, stubbing his toe hard when he came on Catholicism or Marxism or any of the solid elements of his century, so confident in his discordant judgments that intellectual disintegration was inevitable.

Again the fever of writing about Ruskin has taken hold of the reviewer. Let him end strictly by repeating that Miss Evans's study is the most complete and trustworthy that has yet appeared or is likely to appear for the convenience of the 'general reader'.

. THOSE HAPPY HOMES .

Some weeks ago this journal published the photograph of a stark 'contemporary' interior with some apt comments by Mr Robert Harling. I reflected then that of the many horrors and annoyances of contemporary life this at least had been spared me. This style of furnishing has been going on longer than Mr Harling seems to think. It must be more than a quarter of a century since Curtis Moffat filled his showrooms in Fitzroy Square with it. And yet never once in this country have I found my nose in a private dwelling so furnished, although I enjoy a reasonably wide acquaintance with young and old, rich and poor, aesthetic and philistine. This age seems the first in which the activities of professional designers and instructors in schools of art have left no trace in the homes of the people. We are in no position to feel superior to even the most bizarre and banal of our grandparents' tastes.

In the reign of Queen Victoria, until the Jubilee certainly and to some extent beyond, taste developed from cycle to cycle as it had done for two centuries. Craftsmanship was ingenious, invention exuberant. Those who cannot appreciate the furniture of the fifties and sixties incline to say that money was then in the hands of Podsnaps and Veneerings, a barbarous mercantile class who cared only for display and bulk. In fact, the fashions were set, as always, by the aristocracy, richer then than ever before: men and women far better educated and better mannered than ourselves who everywhere had their Kent and Chippendale carried to the attics to give place to what was new. It is also misleading to say, as is said, that the new furniture was shoddily mass-produced. Ways had been found, it is true, to make inexpensive copies, but the masterpieces, such as were exhibited in 1851 and 1862, were as brilliantly executed as those of a century earlier. Ruskin lived at ease among contemporary decorations.

Victorians furnished their homes for their own delight and their homes were of predominant importance. There was no great breaking up of class distinctions in that age. There was rather a great multiplication of classes. Where at the start of the century there were five or six social categories of Englishmen there were at the close fifty or sixty, so that it was only among their own kin that people felt entirely at ease.

The vision of listless oppressed families languishing year in year out beyond the tall stucco façades in Bayswater is a nightmare of modern London journalists. In that happy age the roots of almost all families lay deep in the countryside. It was to the country that men retired from work and in the country, as far as possible, that children were brought up. This was a vital condition not only of the great families with ancestral seats but of the professional and merchant classes who had grandparents and uncles, gentle, clerical or yeoman, living close to the soil. Kensington, like Calcutta, was a place of exile.

Review of *The Victorian Home*, by Ralph Dutton. *Sunday Times*, 28 November 1954.

The huge euphoria of the Victorian home may be attributed directly to the abundance of ornament. How much of the neurotic boredom of today comes from the hygienic blankness of offices, aerodrome waiting-rooms, hospitals? The human mind requires constant minor occupations to put it at rest. The eye must be caught and held before the brain will work. The reason, I am sure, why cooks require constant wireless-noises is the lack of ornament in modern kitchens.

The foregoing observations are provoked by the title and ostensible aim of Mr Ralph Dutton's *The Victorian Home*, a book which cannot be wholeheartedly commended to any class of reader. As a popular picture-book it can hardly, at the price of 30s., hope to rival Mr Laver's *Victorian Vista* at 25s. The illustrations, though numerous and well chosen, are very poorly reproduced. The text is trite and patronizing. With little space at his disposal Mr Dutton has chosen to attempt a general conspectus of English social history in the nineteenth century which is tedious even to the moderately well-informed. In the matter of aesthetic fashions the information is seldom recondite and often inaccurate.

Indeed, the only readers likely to derive enjoyment from it are those who indulge in the badger-digging of literary blood sports, the exposure of error. A few howlers leapt to my own far from scholarly eye.

Pugin did not die 'insane in Bedlam' but lucid and cheerful in his own house at Ramsgate. 'Deluges of rain' did not occur 'almost without intermission' for the three days of the Eglinton Tournament. The afternoon of the second day and the whole of the third day were fine. The contemporary estimate of the cost given in the authorized brochure is £20,000, not £40,000. Rossetti spent years collecting 'blue and white' china and was an early connoisseur of it. His collection was one of the most coveted in England. This is oddly described by Mr Dutton as: 'Rossetti added a number of Japanese objects to the extremely catholic collection which filled his house.' More preposterous is the statement ' "Bubbles" brought an equal renown to the artist and to Pears' Soap.' At the time when Millais, with a grandfather's doting, painted this least remarkable of his works he was already the most renowned painter in England. The copyright of its reproduction was sold without his previous knowledge to Pears by the original purchasers, *The Illustrated London News*, and the transaction was injurious to Millais's reputation.

The painting reproduced on page 64 over the title, ' "Visiting the Great Exhibition." From a contemporary painting', is by William Maw Egley. It quite certainly does not represent the Great Exhibition. I am pretty sure it is the Kensington Exhibition of 1862. Mr Dutton is welcome to examine the original in my drawing-room if he is interested.

. WILLIAM WESTON .

There is no Independence Day in the English calendar. The determining events in our history are, two of them, conquests and one betrayal. It may seem to us now that for the fullest development of our national genius we required a third conquest, by Philip of Spain. Instead of him we got, just a hundred years later, William of Orange. The Elizabethans could not have foreseen that, and it is plain that, except for a few *émigrés*, they were all of them, Catholic and Protestant alike, infected with the spirit of nationalism which had been gnawing at the vitals of Europe for three generations. Thus we have the strange complex of plots, so modern in character, and the astute confusion, by its instigators, of the conspiracy to extirpate the Catholic faith with the cause of insular independence.

These plots and that confusion cast a shadow over many noble lives, William Weston's among them. We can understand the temper of the Elizabethan age better than our grandparents could. Its modernity is partly of Germany – there are many Goerings strutting about the court and the glimpse of more than one Himmler. But there was no Hitler. Where did the power reside? It is in Russia and her dependencies that one finds the closer analogy. Hitler's bloody acts were irrational dooms. Who ruled in Elizabeth's time had a philosophy and a policy. There were efforts to persuade and to extort confessions. There were plots in which it is even now impossible to extricate the genuine from the fabricated. How much of the indictment did the judges and the prosecutors believe? How much did they care?

One by one the lives of the Catholics are being disinterred from scholarly and sectarian works and presented to the general public. Father Caraman who has already served John Gerard so well now gives us a very different character in William Weston. Here the work of editing is of even greater importance, for the gentle, self-effacing little narrative that forms the core of the book tells us little of the hero. With Gerard we are reading Buchan. Here it is Bernanos; one the unambiguous man of action; the other the mystic beset with the mystic's devils, drawn to the desperate; contemporaries of the same Society, pursuing the same ends and the same dangers, but distinct from one another by all the breadth of Catholicity. If any is tempted to suppose that the discipline of Ignatius produces a uniform type, he will find assurance in the careers of these two holy and heroic men.

Foreword to *William Weston: The Autobiography of an Elizabethan*, trans. and ed. by Philip Caraman, SJ (London, 1955).

. AWAKE MY SOUL! IT IS A LORD[1] .

'I'm not on business. I'm a member of the House of Lords.' These moving and rather mysterious words were uttered on my doorstep the other evening and recorded by the leading literary critic of the Beaverbrook press. They have haunted me, waking and sleeping, ever since. I am sometimes accused of a partiality for lords; whatever touches them, it is hinted, vicariously touches me. Certainly the nobleman who tried to insinuate himself into my house half an hour before dinner that evening has become a nine days' obsession.

Does anyone, I wonder, remember *Young England*, the drama of more than twenty years ago, which was taken up as an esoteric joke, soon became a popular saturnalia, but never failed to enchant? Here across the years came an authentic echo of that production; and the speaker, too, bald and overgrown though he was, had all the artless bearing of that inimitable troop of Boy Scouts.

But to explain his presence. The popular papers, I conceive, are fitfully and uneasily aware that there are spheres of English life in which they hold a negligible influence. The fifty or sixty thousand people in this country who alone support the Arts do not go to Lord Beaverbrook's critics for guidance. So it is that artists of all kinds form part of the battle-training of green reporters. 'Don't lounge about the office, lad,' the editors say, 'sit up and insult an artist.' Rather frequently writers, among others, are troubled by the telephone asking for interviews. When these are refused, the journalist goes to what in a news-paper office is lightly called 'the library', takes the file of his predecessors' misstatements, copies it out, adds a few of his own, and no one suffers except the readers of the popular press, who must, I should think, be getting bored with the recitation of old, false anecdotes.[2] That is the normal routine – unless there is a lord handy, who is not subject to the conventions of the trade.

On the morning of the visit my wife said: 'An *Express* reporter and a lord wanted to come and see you this afternoon.'

'You told them not to?'

'Of course.'

'What lord?'

'Noel someone.'

'Has Noël Coward got a peerage? I'd like to see him.'

'No, it wasn't anyone I had heard of.'

There, I supposed, the matter ended. But that evening, just as I was going to prepare myself for dinner, I heard an altercation at the front door. My poor

Spectator, 8 July 1955.

1 Waugh unintentionally conflated the opening lines of two hymns, 'Awake my soul and with the sun' and 'Hark my soul it is the Lord'. See *Letters*, 14 July 1955.

2 See 'Mr Waugh Replies' (3 July 1953) with the note describing George Malcolm Thomson's 'Why So Gloomy Mr Waugh?' That profile was the opening shot in the war between Beaverbrook and Waugh, which ended in Waugh's winning £5,000 in damages from two libel suits.

wife, weary from the hay-field, was being kept from her bath by a forbidding pair.

The lady of the party, Miss Spain, has recorded in two columns their day's doings. They were on what she called a 'pilgrimage'.[1] This took them, uninvited, to tea with the Poet Laureate. 'Lord Noel-Buxton just walked into the house,' she writes, while she trampled the hay. The poet was 'silent, dreaming back in the past,' thinking, no doubt, that in all his years before the mast he had never met such tough customers. He gave them oat-cake. Then he brightened, 'his blue eyes danced'. The old 'darling' had thought of a way out. He urged them on to me. '"See you? Of course he'll see you."' On they came to the village where I live which, curiously, they found to be a 'straggly collection of prefabricated houses' (there is not one in the place), and entered the pub, where they got into talk with its rustic patrons. I have since made inquiries and learn that they somehow gave the impression that they were touts for television. Members of the village band sought to interest them in their music, and the cordiality, thus mistakenly engendered, emboldened the two pilgrims. They attempted to effect an entry into my house and wrangled until I dismissed them in terms intelligible even to them.

Lord Noel-Buxton seems to have been unaware of having done anything odd. 'Oh, Nancy, do stop!' he is said to have cried, when I went out to see that they were not slipping round to suck up to the cook. 'He's coming to apologize.'

A faulty appreciation.

What, I have been asking myself ever since, was Lord Noel-Buxton's part in the escapade? He is not, I have established, on the pay-roll of the *Daily Express*. All he seems to have got out of it is a jaunt in a motor-car, an oat-cake and a novel he can hardly hope to understand.[2] Who, in the popular phrase, does he think he is?

Well, I looked him up and find that he is the second generation of one of Ramsay MacDonald's creation. To the student of social stratification this is significant. Is there, in our midst, unregarded, a new social sub-class? The men who bought peerages from Lloyd George believed they were founding aristocratic houses, and there was, indeed, then a reasonable supposition that a

1 'My Pilgrimage to See Mr Waugh', *Daily Express*, 23 June 1953, p. 6. This article was part of a series called 'A Cool Look at the Loved Ones', which aimed at 'reappraising the famous in the light of their achievements'. 'Who are the lionized idols of the land? . . . But how far will these "loved ones" survive a cooler look?' Evelyn Waugh, Sir Malcolm Sargent, J. B. Priestley and the Oliviers were listed as subjects for reappraisal. The Oliviers and Sir Malcolm Sargent had been dealt with before Waugh was approached for an interview.

2 'We stopped at Oxford [on the way from John Masefield to Waugh] to buy Lord Noel-Buxton a copy of a novel by Mr Waugh so that he could mug it up.' According to Nancy Spain's article, Lord Noel-Buxton had never read a Waugh novel – indeed he seems not to have known the *sort* of book he wrote, or even his reputation for fierceness. The nobleman's part in Nancy Spain's attempt 'to gatecrash my idol' remains mysterious.

generation or two of inherited wealth might refine the descendants of the gross originators. But the men who were put into ermine by MacDonald believed that the order they were entering was doomed. That statesman's bizarre appointments in the Church of England are eliminated by time, but the Upper House stands and the peerages he created survive. Are there, I wonder, many such orphans of the storm which blew itself out? Here, at any rate, was one specimen in full plumage on my doorstep.

I asked a secretarial agency, who sometimes helps me, to find out something about him. All they could say was that he is not strong, poor fellow, and was invalided out of the Territorial Army at the beginning of the war. Now, when he is not on a literary pilgrimage, he appears to spend much time paddling in rivers.

He clearly cannot have met many other lords. Students of *Punch* know that from the eighties of the past century until the thirties of this there was a standing joke about the distressed descendants of Crusaders who were reduced to retail trade. Now the thing is commonplace; not perhaps at the Co-operative Stores where, presumably, Lord Noel-Buxton does his shopping; but it is hard to believe that nowhere in the purlieus of the Upper House has he ever been approached with an advantageous offer of wine or clothing. But we must believe it. 'I'm not on business. I'm a member of the House of Lords.' The two ideas, in the mind of this naïve nobleman, are axiomatically irreconcilable.

We have many sorts of lord in our country: lords haughty, who think that commoners all seek their acquaintance and must be kept at a distance; lords affable, who like mixing with their fellow-men of all degrees and know the conventions of good society by which introductions are effected; lords lavish and leisurely; and dead-broke lords eager to earn an honest living. In Lord Noel-Buxton we see the lord predatory. He appears to think that his barony gives him the right to a seat at the dinner-table in any private house in the kingdom.

Fear of this lord is clearly the beginning of wisdom.

. YOUTH AT THE HELM AND PLEASURE AT THE PROW .

Not everyone in 1923, not I for one, knew without recourse to the dictionary that a 'hey' or 'hay' was a country jig. As we sped from Blackwell's with our eagerly awaited copies of Mr Aldous Huxley's second novel, its title suggested a neglected stable and, strange to recall, as we read it in that fragrant age, the tale did smack a little sour. To be quite accurate in reminiscence I got my own copy second-hand from the present literary critic of the *Daily Mail*[1] – a young

Part of a critical symposium on Aldous Huxley, *London Magazine*, August 1955.
1 Peter Quennell

man already plainly destined for high position – and he passed it to me (for a financial consideration) saying I should find it 'dreary'. *Dreary!* Reread now after all that has happened, after all that has been written, after all Mr Huxley has written, the book has the lilt of Old Vienna.

It is placed in London in springtime. The weather, page after page, is warm and airy and brilliant. Did we ever enjoy quite such a delightful climate? We certainly do not find it in modern fiction. And London is still in 1923 eminently habitable, a city of private houses and private lives, leisurely, not too full even in the season, all leafy squares and stucco façades and Piranesan mewses. The pavements of Bond Street are 'perfumed', the shops are full of desirable goods. All one needs is a little money – not much; £300 a year is a competence, £5,000 is wealth – and that little is easily acquired by some whimsical invention such as a pair of pneumatic trousers. Regent Street is doomed but Verrey's is still open, open after luncheon until it is time to go out to tea. A few miles out in Surrey and Sussex an arcadian countryside is opening to the never-failing sun. Although all the inhabitants of this delicious city have been everywhere and speak every language they are thoroughly English, at home in their own capital. No character in *Antic Hay* ever uses the telephone. They write letters, they telegraph, they call, and there are always suitable servants to say 'not at home' to bores. It is Henry James's London possessed by carnival. A chain of brilliant young people linked and interlaced winds past the burnished front doors in pursuit of happiness. Happiness is growing wild for anyone to pick, only the perverse miss it. There has been the single unpredictable, inexplicable, unrepeatable calamity of 'the Great War'. It has left broken hearts – Mrs Viveash's among them – but the other characters are newly liberated from their comfortable refuges of Conscientious Objection, to run wild through the streets.

The central theme of the book is the study of two falterers 'more or less' in their 'great task of happiness', Mrs Viveash and Theodore Gumbril. Everyone else, if young, has a good time. Two clowns, Lypiatt and Shearwater, get knocked about, but that is the clown's *métier*. Rosie is happy in her pink underclothes and her daze of romantic fantasy, picked up, rolled over, passed on, giving and gaining pleasure and all the time astutely learning the nuances of cultural advancement. Coleman is happy, uproariously blaspheming. Men rather like him turn up later in Mr Huxley's works, miserable men, haunted and damned. Coleman is boisterously happy, a sort of diabolic Belloc. And Mercaptan is happy, unambitious, sensual, accomplished, radiantly second-rate. He is a period piece, still in his twenties with the tastes and pretentions of ripe middle age. They do not come like that today. Today one knows quite certainly that a young bachelor with a *penchant* for white satin sofas and *bibelots* would not be running after girls and, moreover, that though he might drop into idiomatic French, he would be quite incapable of writing grammatical English.

Mrs Viveash and Gumbril are the falterers in the Great Task and their situation is not quite desperate. She has her classic, dignified bereavement. Promiscuous sexual relations bore her. But she has, we are told, almost limitless power, power which, I must confess, has never much impressed me. She was 25 when I was 20. She seemed then appallingly mature. The girls I knew did not whisper in 'expiring' voices and 'smile agonizingly' from their 'death-beds'. They grinned from ear to ear and yelled one's head off. And now thirty years on, when women of 25 seem to me moody children, I still cannot weep for Mrs Viveash's tragic emptiness.

Gumbril rejects the chance of a *Happy Hypocrite* idyll, of love, literally, in a cottage. But it would never have done. He is a clever, zestful cad. He would have been hideously bored in a week. He is off abroad to a wide, smiling continent full of wine and pictures and loose young women. He will be all right.

The story is told richly and elegantly with few of the interruptions which, despite their intrinsic interest, mar so much of Mr Huxley's story-telling. The disquisition on Wren's London should be in a book of essays but the parody of the night-club play is so funny that one welcomes its intrusion. The 'novel of ideas' raises its ugly head twice only, in the scenes with the tailor and the financier, crashing bores both of them but mere spectators at the dance. They do not hold up the fun for long.

And there is another delicious quality. The city is not always James's London. Sometimes it becomes Mediterranean, central to the live tradition. The dance winds through piazzas and alleys, under arches, round fountains and everywhere are the embellishments of the old religion. An ancient pagan feast, long christianized in name, is being celebrated in a Christian city. The story begins in a school chapel, Domenichino's *Jerome* hangs by Rosie's bed, Coleman quotes the Fathers. There is an insistent undertone, audible through the carnival music, saying all the time, not in Mrs Viveash's 'expiring' voice, that happiness is a reality.

Since 1923 Mr Huxley has travelled far. He has done more than change climate and diet. I miss that undertone in his later work. It was because he was then so near the essentials of the human condition that he could write a book that is frivolous and sentimental and perennially delightful.

. BELLOC ANADYOMENOS[1] .

Hilaire Belloc had a strong dislike of personal publicity and of all forms of written gossip. During the last twenty years of his life he made few, if any, new friends. In his last ten years he lived in seclusion. The men who were boys when he was a boy died. A generation has grown up wholly ignorant of the private character of the great man who until lately was alive among them. Now the time has come to display that unique personality.

Review of *The Cruise of the 'Nona'*, by Hilaire Belloc. *Spectator*, 26 August 1955.

1 The title appeared as 'Belloc Anadyomene'. Waugh corrected the slip in the next issue of the *Spectator*.

We have already had an admirable study by Mr John Morton. We are promised a full biography by Mr Robert Speaight. Meanwhile Lord Stanley of Alderley has written a sound, shipshape introduction, full of new material, to the new edition of *The Cruise of the 'Nona'*.

Mr Morton wrote as a devoted and worthy disciple who shared most of his master's opinions and tastes, and knew intimately his hard life as a journalist. Lord Stanley is a younger, more independent man. His father gave Belloc the *Nona* in 1914. The son often sailed with him and to know Belloc at sea was to know him at his most light-hearted and free-minded, far from the telephone and the writing-table, in brief terms of liberty during which he could expatiate and speculate to the full. For Belloc was never at sea for longer than a week or two at a stretch. The title *The Cruise of the 'Nona'* is somewhat misleading. It is a literary composition comprising records of ten years' intermittent voyaging round the coast of Great Britain and the reminiscences of two-thirds of a lifetime.

Lord Stanley adds a new and endearing portrait to the collection that is being assembled. He also makes his own apt criticisms and appreciation of the book he introduces. He divides his essay into sections: the Catholic, the Historian, the Politician, the Sailor, the Poet, the Man and Companion. The first is remarkable for its understanding of a Faith which he does not share. Lord Stanley, with Belloc's authority, compares it to the furniture of his mind. In later life it became the entire structure. In early youth personal piety, orthodoxy and a rigid morality coexisted with the disconcerting revolutionary enthusiasm which prompted such rash lines as:

> The cause of all the poor in '93,
> The cause of all the world at Waterloo.

Later he emphasized the traditional and cultural aspect of the Church, coming near to identifying it with the continent of Europe. But as the attachments of youth faded and its hopes were disappointed he was more and more absorbed in the faith which alone upheld him in his last silent years.

The Cruise of the 'Nona' was written in middle life at the full maturity of his power. It is richer and wiser than the more popular *Path to Rome*. Like that early work it was done to his own plan in his own time. If any one book could be claimed as quintessential of him, this is it. Descriptions of the sea, of the land seen from it, of the art of seamanship, all superbly fresh, racy and decisive, so that they can be read with delight by landsmen, form about half of the matter. For the rest he ranges at will over his favourite topics which were, indeed, no foibles, but the basic themes of humanity – the history of man, his destiny in the next world, the organization of his life with his fellows on earth, his temporary achievements in art and knowledge.

He has lived through the First World War – the Great War, as it was dubbed – and he is still adjusting himself to its enormous consequences. One profound effect it had had on him. It had taken the lustre from battle. In the long and often ignoble peace into which he was born, it was tempting to exalt the seemingly decadent martial virtues. His dislike of the Boer War was that it was the wrong kind of war, fought by the strong against the weak for the benefit of men who were not risking their own skins. But both he and Chesterton before 1914 could be accused with some justice of Fleet Street sabre-rattling. Neither did so after they had seen war close.

He was writing in the mid-twenties – an impossible date for the political prophet. Many of his predictions proved false. He gives little attention to the Communist revolution in Russia. He then regarded the Russians as barbarians who had never had any business in European affairs, who had lapsed into chaos and impotence, and good riddance to them. He saw Prussia as the essential enemy of Christendom. It did not occur to him – how could it? – that when Germany next emerged as a danger it would be under the leadership of apostates from the Catholic south. He saw Mussolini, as did many lesser men (the present reviewer among them) as a hopeful portent. No one could then foresee that Italy would be jerked into alliance with Germany but we should, perhaps, have seen that public respect for Christian things was not enough and that only a Christian is fit to rule a Christian nation. Belloc believed in the permanence of Poland as an independent nation and of the French colonization of North Africa. He believed in the permanence of the English plutocracy. He saw men everywhere doomed to something near slavery but supposed they would become the property of a few rich men, upstart, atheist, cosmopolitan Liberals of the kind he had learned to loathe. Within his own lifetime these rich men were swept away as effortlessly as the British Raj in India, but it is doubtful whether he ever appreciated the character of that revolution. He believed that corruption – the use of political power to acquire private wealth – was rooted in the English parliamentary system whereas, since 1922, that particular, rather small evil has diminished almost to extinction in a way unknown in France or the United States. Our politicians are, many of them, unprincipled, vain and mischievous, but they have had to curb their avarice.

All these errors, splendidly enunciated, are to be found in *The Cruise of the 'Nona'*, intermingled with much more that is eternally wise. One does not read a work of literature to discover whether its author was lucky in his guesses. One does not read it primarily to discover what kind of man the author was. *The Cruise of the 'Nona'* is a work of art. Belloc himself might be a little impatient of that claim. He distrusted Henry James. But just as now we can without offence indulge some curiosity about his personal life and habit, so we can honour him in terms which he might in his lifetime have repudiated. He liked to call himself a journalist and a versifier. We salute an illustrious artist.

. TITUS WITH A GRAIN OF SALT .

From the extremity of the circle, which at Stratford-on-Avon is politely misnamed a 'box', every face in the audience can be plainly seen. Dense, devout, heterogeneous, Americans, Negroes and orientals, little girls and grandfathers, they extended without a gap from wall to wall and from roof to floor. The English were dressed, it seemed, for the beach at Broadstairs, the exotics more respectably. How many, I wondered, were there by habit? How many, like myself, had been brought into Warwickshire that day by other business, had booked their tickets blind and had learned with something like chagrin that the play to be presented was *Titus Andronicus*? How many had planned their visit in expectation of a great treat?

Curiosity was the emotion proper to the evening. Producer and players were engaged on the creation of an original work out of what had been for centuries absolute void. There is no tradition of *Titus Andronicus*; only the established faith that it is unactable. Reread on the eve of the performance, the unfamiliar text seemed to hold no potentiality save of burlesque. Its notorious horrors, repellent to gentler generations, seemed drab today, consisting as they do of plain butchery devoid of evil or pity. There is no plausible character, still less a likeable one. There is no line of poetry, hardly a dozen lines of memorable rhetoric. There are three scenes of gross absurdity: where Lavinia reveals the identity of her ravishers, where the distracted Titus looses flights of arrows to the Gods, and where Tamora disguises herself as the Spirit of Revenge. How could even the masterly Mr Peter Brook and all his eminent company make anything of this preposterous composition? One brief great scene there was, waiting to catch the discerning eye – where Aaron receives his blackamoor child and defends it against the Gothic princes – but it needed an expert to spot it, and an unusually zealous actor to convey it to the layman.

So we assembled and waited with no very high expectations until the lights came up on the stage and we rather suddenly realized that we were in for something of rare quality.

The revelation was not immediate. The author's opening is, I suppose, irredeemable – a trite wrangle before a background of solid but unidentified classical architecture. Dire foreboding seemed to be confirmed. But it was brief. The actors got through it somehow and very soon we had Sir Laurence Olivier on the stage, full of experience and authority, and with him Miss Maxine Audley as a flashy Tamora, more Ptolemy than Goth. The first corpses came too with their attendant mutes. What seemed the plinth of a column opened ponderously to disgorge glowing priests of Babylonish aspect. It was a very pretty spectacle but still the words dragged until Sir Laurence reached the abysmal line: 'O sacred receptacle of my joys.' He boldly gave us 'rēcĕp/tāclĕ'. Here was panache. Here, or so I took it, was the first hint, a broad

Review of *Titus Andronicus*, produced by Peter Brook. *Spectrum: A Spectator Miscellany* (London, 1956). First printed *Spectator*, 2 September 1955.

wink, telling us: 'This is not a hallowed text. We have a great lump of almost intractable raw material on our hands. Just wait and see what we make of it.' All that in a freak of prosody.

Mr Brook's problem was to avoid the ludicrous. The one sure armour against ridicule is humour. If he had treated the whole work as sublime, making Titus a minor Lear; if he had treated it as simple melodrama, a thing of plot and passion – do Stratford audiences, I wonder, ever laugh in the wrong places? My 'box' offered none of the conventional privacies. If Mr Brook had handled the play in any other way than he did, I fear that I at least must have disgraced myself. But he resolved his problems by treating them, as literary dons say, at various levels. Each scene was played for all it was worth and no more. There was a consistent unifying dignity of spectacle. The supers were superb. The costumes audaciously various, with no attempt at historical propriety. Fourteenth-century justices and fourth-century legionaries mingled felicitously with visions from Bakst ballet. The stage carpentry was just adequate. The doors and aperture in the plinth had to work overtime – opulent changes of scene are least of the casualties in the war of attrition waged everywhere by the artisan against the artist. But the full burden of holding the piece together fell on Sir Laurence himself and was triumphantly borne.

Titus is an arduous part. He is on the stage almost continuously as heroic veteran, stoic parent, implacable devotee of barbarous pieties, crazy victim, adroit avenger. Sir Laurence is a *great* impersonator. He is the one actor who, on the stage, is never himself. He has a vitality which never flags and a keen intelligence. It is this intelligence I think which comes between him and poetry. That and the age he lives in. Elderly persons have long suspected that the idiosyncrasies of many writers now acclaimed as poets spring quite simply from defective ear, and lately a youngish critic, more shameless than his fellows, has proclaimed as 'moribund' the belief that 'the vowel and consonantal sounds' of a poem have any part in its power. Sir Laurence can be trusted to get the deepest meaning out of all he has to say. In Shakespeare he excels in the prose passages. His film of *Hamlet* touched greatness once – in the words never, I think, previously illumined: 'Father and mother is man and wife, man and wife is one flesh, and so, my mother.' For the full organ-notes and delicate melody of Shakespeare's poetry we look to him in vain; but, as I said above, there is no poetry in *Titus Andronicus*, so here for the first time in Shakespearean drama we could see all his talents fully extended and applaud them without reservation.

What is more, this absence of poetry helped the play by maintaining the momentum which is its prime virtue. In the great works we sit, as it were, crunching the nuts and waiting for the decanter to come round bringing the vintage of the famous speeches. . . . 'Not quite up to the Gielgud '38.' 'Ah, but you're too young to remember the Forbes-Robinson '08.' *Titus Andronicus* was all novelty and there are fewer superfluities in it than in any play of the period. It comes as though straight from the cutting room. Mr Brook had to make few adjustments of the text. To compensate little Lucius for missing the cannibal feast, he was given a fly to squash. One critic, I notice, complained of the omission of 'Baked in that pie.' I thought I heard it spoken. It should have been there, certainly. The only complaint that could be made against Mr Brook was of squeamishness. He did well, I think, to have the Gothic princes executed off-stage and to strangle the midwife rather than stab her, but I should have liked to see the severed hands – gloves full of plasticine perhaps – properly displayed. And why moble the heads of Martius and Quintus? Livid masks would have looked well in the cages. The corpses that accumulated about the stage were very elegant, particularly the ladies. I don't suppose the stalls could see them well. They played to the gallery, lying gracefully disposed, all unlike the real debris of carnage.

Mr Quayle has been fully and justly praised for his performance of Aaron. It is a rich part and he exploited it splendidly. Praise is also due to the Gothic villains. They maintained a revolting rubbery exuberance, nimble as PT instructors, amoral and sub-human.

Miss Vivien Leigh, as Lavinia, celebrated a private rite of enchantment. It is an empty part; she filled it with humour and made it a delicious little work of art. (I am not in her confidence in this matter. Heaven forfend a gaffe!) When she left us to collect a basin full of blood she mimed a demure Victorian bride. When she mewed over the bookshelves, when she raised her paws to enumerate her ravishers, she just hinted an affinity with Dick Whittington's cat. She wrote in the sand with endearing nonchalance. When she was dragged off to her horrible fate she ventured a tiny impudent, barely perceptible, roll of the eyes, as who should say: 'My word! What next?' She established complete confidence between the audience and the production. 'We aren't trying to take you in,' she seemed to say. 'You're too clever, and we are too clever. Just enjoy yourselves.' It was the grain of salt which gave savour to the whole rich stew.

. LITERARY STYLE IN ENGLAND AND AMERICA .

From the middle of the eighteenth century until the middle of the nineteenth there was published in England a series of architectural designs for the use of provincial builders and private patrons. The plates display buildings of varying sizes, from gate-lodges to mansions, decorated in various 'styles', Palladian, Greek, Gothic, even Chinese. The ground plans are identical, the 'style' consists of surface enrichment. At the end of this period it was even possible for very important works such as the Houses of Parliament in London to be the work of two hands, Barry designing the structure, Pugin overlaying it with mediaeval ornament. And the result is not to be despised. In the present half century we have seen architects abandon all attempt at 'style' and our eyes are everywhere sickened with boredom at the blank, unlovely, unlovable façades which have arisen from Constantinople to Los Angeles. But this use of style is literally superficial. Properly understood style is not a seductive decoration added to a functional structure; it is of the essence of a work of art.

This is unconsciously recognized by popular usage. When anyone speaks of 'literary style' the probability is that he is thinking of prose. A poem is dimly recognized as existing in its form. There are no poetic ideas; only poetic utterances and, as Wordsworth pointed out, the true antithesis is not between prose and poetry, but between prose and metre. Now that poets have largely abandoned metre, the distinction has become so vague as to be hardly recognizable. Instead of two separate bodies of writing, we must see a series of innumerable gradations from the melodious and mystical to the scientific.

Literature is the right use of language irrespective of the subject or reason of the utterance. A political speech may be, and sometimes is, literature; a sonnet to the moon may be, and often is, trash. Style is what distinguishes literature from trash. Nevertheless in certain quarters the appellation 'stylist' bears a pejorative sense. Logan Pearsall Smith, that splendid American, is dismissed fretfully while D. H. Lawrence, who wrote squalidly, is accepted as an artist because his themes were of wider and deeper interest. This is a paradox which academic critics, to whom one would look to correct popular misconceptions, do little to resolve. Many indeed aggravate it, for there is a lurking puritanism at Cambridge (England) and in many parts of the New World, which is ever ready to condemn pleasure even in its purest form. If this seems doubtful consider the case of James Joyce. There was a writer possessed by style. His later work lost almost all faculty of communication, so intimate, allusive and idiosyncratic did it become, so obsessed by euphony and nuance. But because he was obscure and can only be read with intense intellectual effort – and therefore without easy pleasure – he is admitted into the academic canon. But it is just in this task of communication that Joyce's style fails, for the necessary elements of style are lucidity, elegance, individuality; these three qualities combine to form a preservative which ensures the nearest approximation to permanence in the fugitive art of letters.

Lucidity does not imply universal intelligibility. Henry James is the most lucid of writers, but not the simplest. The simplest statements in law or philosophy are usually those which, in application, require the greatest weight of commentary and provoke the longest debate. A great deal of what is most worth saying must always remain unintelligible to most readers. The test of lucidity is whether the statement can be read as meaning anything other than what it intends. Military orders should be, and often are, models of lucidity. The correspondence of businessmen abounds in ambiguities.

Elegance is the quality in a work of art which imparts direct pleasure; again not universal pleasure. There is a huge, envious world to whom elegance is positively offensive. English is incomparably the richest of languages, dead or living. One can devote one's life to learning it and die without achieving mastery. No two words are identical in meaning, sound and connotation. The majority of English speakers muddle through with a minute vocabulary. To them any words not in vulgar use are 'fancy' and it is, perhaps, in ignoble deference to their susceptibilities that there has been a notable flight from magnificence in English writing. Sixty years ago, when 'jewelled prose' was all the rage, there were some pretentious efforts at fine writing which excited great ridicule. There was an inevitable reaction, but surveying the bleak prospect today, one can recognize that those absurdities are a small price to pay for the magnificence of the preceding masters. When I hear the word 'tawdry', I suspect the puritan. The man who can enjoy the flimsy and fantastic decorations of Naples is much more likely to appreciate the grandeur of Roman baroque than the prig who demands Michelangelo or nothing. It is a matter for thankfulness that the modern school of critics are unable or unwilling to compose a pleasurable sentence. It greatly limits the harm they do.

Individuality needs little explanation. It is the hand-writing, the tone of voice, that makes a work recognizable as being by a particular artist (or in rare decades of highly homogeneous culture, by one of a particular set).

Permanence is the result of the foregoing. Style is what makes a work memorable and unmistakable. We remember the false judgments of Voltaire and Gibbon and Lytton Strachey long after they have been corrected, because of their sharp, polished form and because of the sensual pleasure of dwelling on them. They come to one, not merely as printed words, but as a lively experience, with the full force of another human being personally encountered – that is to say because they are lucid, elegant and individual.

Among living writers of English prose there are few who attempt magnificence. Sir Osbert Sitwell's great five-volume autobiography and Sir Winston Churchill's historical studies stand almost alone and the latter, though highly creditable for a man with so much else to occupy him, do not really survive close attention. He can seldom offer the keen, unmistakable aesthetic pleasure of the genuine artist. Elegance in the present century tends to be modest. We have no organ voice to rival Sir Thomas Browne's, but we have a volume of exquisite and haunting music. Sir Max Beerbohm and Mgr Ronald Knox; each stands at the summit of his own art. They differ in scope. Where they attempt the same tasks, in parody, they are equal and supreme over all competitors. Sir Max has confined himself to the arts; Mgr Knox goes higher, to the loftiest regions of the human spirit. His *Enthusiasm* should be recognized as the greatest work of literary art of the century. Below these two masters there is an honourable company of very fine craftsmen, none, it must be admitted, in their first youth. Mr E. M. Forster, particularly in the first half of *Pharos and Pharillon*, set a model of lucidity and individuality in which the elegance is so unobtrusive as to pass some readers unnoticed. Curiously enough it is not in the universities that one finds fine writing; Sir Maurice Bowra is learned and lucid, but dull; Lord David Cecil has grace but no grammar; Mr Isaiah Berlin is diffuse and voluble; Mr Trevor-Roper vulgar. Among critics in the press the standard is higher. Mr Raymond Mortimer never fails. Mr Cyril Connolly has fitfully achieved some lovely effects. Among novelists Mr Anthony Powell, Mr Graham Greene, Miss Compton-Burnett, Mr Henry Green all have intensely personal and beautiful styles. One could never mistake a page of their writing for anyone else's.

It will be noticed that all these examples are drawn from England. Logan Pearsall Smith wrote:

> And America, the land of my birth, America! . . . Youth has its dreams, its longings for distinction; among all the eager young men and women of that vast country . . . in not one of those resounding cities or multitudinous universities, does the thought never come to anyone, I ask myself, that the instrument of speech which they make use of all day long has resonances within it of unimaginable beauty? . . . The golden sceptre of style gilds everything it touches, and can make immortal those who grasp it: to not one of those aspiring youths does the thought ever suggest itself that it might be an adventure among adventures to try to wield that wand? . . . From the point of view of Style that whole Continent could sink beneath the sea and never leave a ripple.

That was written in 1934. Can we today qualify the severe judgment? There is Mr Hemingway. He is lucid and individual and euphonious. He has imposed limits on his powers which only a master can survive. He has won mastery, but at the cost of a sad brood of imitators. Mr Faulkner has individuality but nothing else. Perhaps the languages of the two continents have grown so separate that it is impossible for an Englishman to catch the nuances of American diction. From this great distance it seems that there are editorial styles only – a rather good, dry style in *The New Yorker*, a very poor style in *Time* – and one sometimes suspects that austerity has been imposed on the contributors so that they shall not distract attention from the more luxurious wording of the advertisements. American critics, I believe, are impatient of the airs and graces of English writers. It is one of the great gulfs between our two civilizations that each finds the other effeminate. To the American, English writers are like prim spinsters fidgeting with the china, punctilious about good taste, and inwardly full of thwarted, tepid and perverse passions. We see the Americans as gushing adolescents, repetitive and slangy, rather nasty sometimes in their zest for violence and bad language. The difference, I think, is this. All English boys, of the kind who are now writers, learned Latin from the age of nine. Very few girls did. The boys did not become ripe scholars, but they acquired a basic sense of the structure of language which never left them; they learned to scan quite elaborate metres; they learned to compose Latin verses of a kind themselves. Little girls learned French and were praised for idiomatic volubility. When they grew up they wrote as though they were babbling down the telephone – often very prettily, like Miss Nancy Mitford. We regard this sort of writing as womanly and that is the quality we find in American male writers, who, I believe, learn Latin late and thoroughly in a few cases but often not at all. But in the Protestant schools in England, Latin is no longer universally taught. It may be that in the next generation only the boys from Jesuit and Benedictine schools will carry on the tradition of English prose. That is by the way.

One thing I hold as certain, that a writer, if he is to develop, must concern himself more and more with Style. He cannot hope to interest the majority of his readers in his progress. It is his own interest that is at stake. Style alone can keep him from being bored with his own work. In youth high spirits carry one over a book or two. The world is full of discoveries that demand expression. Later a writer must face the choice of becoming an artist or a prophet. He can shut himself up at his desk and selfishly seek pleasure in the perfecting of his own skill or he can pace about, dictating dooms and exhortations on the topics of the day. The recluse at the desk has a bare chance of giving abiding pleasure to others; the publicist has none at all.

6

. CONTRA MUNDUM .

ARBITER ELEGANTIARUM,
ECCLESIASTICAL DIE-HARD

1955 – APRIL 1966

Women smoking in the streets should be placed under close arrest.

From the MS of 'Manners and Morals'

. . .the experiences of each succeeding year confirmed [Mr Pinfold] in his scepticism of all other philosophic systems [than the Roman Catholic]; he felt an increasing loyalty towards a body which he had joined on very slight acquaintance; more than this he became increasingly aware of the process operating without conscious effort of his own, drawing him outside himself into a communion which owned a remote cousinship to the prayers of the holy.

Adapted from the MS of *The Ordeal of Gilbert Pinfold*

The Abbot goes on to say: 'Is not attack the best form of defence?' That certainly was the belief of her champions. *'Les païens ont tort.'*

From 'The Council: Phase One', *Tablet*, 7 September 1963

. INTRODUCTION .

Although no national or personal crisis and no new subject divides the journalism of Waugh's final decade from that of the immediate post-war period, much occasional work done from the mid-1950s onwards is unique. Whether it is merely more offensive to liberal consciences than anything Waugh had published earlier, or whether it is fascinating in a new way, are teasing questions. The truth is that while Waugh's late work is unmistakable, its qualities are elusive. Furthermore understanding is still hindered by the currency of grotesquely distorted versions of his utterances. A reasonable view – and it is still overly ambitious when considering Waugh to aspire beyond reasonable approximation – must take into account several related matters. The most important of these are reduced income and limited opportunities for journalism, incessant hostile criticism provoking a defiant reaction, creation of a striking public 'front', and the triumph of liberalism, even in the Roman Catholic Church.

By 1955 Waugh's income from fiction was much reduced and still falling. The earnings of *Brideshead Revisited* had been long exhausted, and sales since *The Loved One* (1948) only moderate. A financial crisis entailing severe economies had struck as early as January 1950. Six children would impose an increasing burden for most of Waugh's remaining working life. Between 1955 and 1966 A. D. Peters received a number of appeals from Waugh of which the following is typical: 'I shall be hard up soon. Please give anxious thought to my future' (14 December 1959).

Journalism was the obvious answer to the problem, but it presented difficulties. First *Ronald Knox* (1959) made excessive demands on time, and then Waugh felt the need, as he explained to Peters, of continuing to write novels as long as he had any 'inventive strength left' and 'any capacity left for original work' (18 April 1958). More importantly, declining popularity (the 'fall from fame' to be discussed a little later) reduced normal opportunities. It must also be said that Waugh had recklessly thrown away the goodwill gained by earlier success, for example by insulting the well-disposed Henry and Clare Luce of *Life* magazine; and that though he was normally brisk in literary business, Waugh's misgivings about the 'commissions' offered by American editors led to correspondence of Byzantine complexity and to reluctance on the editors' part to employ him. The days of occasionally selecting offers as conviction or pleasure dictated (fees to charity) were over.

Of course editors still approached Waugh and he successfully approached editors. Examples of suggestions made to him – some bizarre, some highly attractive – include small books on Palestine (1953), on a 'City of on Enchantment' (February 1958) and on Teilhard de Chardin (1963); and articles on the Queen (August 1957), the Royal Academy Exhibition (April 1958), St Bernadette (January 1959), South Africa (April 1959), children's reading and 'Are We Becoming too Americanized?' (October 1959), a series to be called 'A Space Man's Report on Us' (March 1960), and a 'Great Blunder of the Twentieth Century' (November 1962). On the other hand many of Waugh's proposals and even commissioned pieces were rejected, a symptom of the sharp discrepancy between Waugh's view of what he had to offer newspapers and their views of what they wanted from him.

Essentially Waugh considered himself a thinker – a stylist too, but above all a 'strong, deep' thinker – to the extent that he despised as muddled and illogical articles which most other people considered sage and important. Thus of John Kobler's series 'Adventures of the Mind', which included such writers as J. Robert Oppenheimer, Aldous Huxley, Fred Hoyle and Bertrand Russell, he wrote: 'Have you seen Kobler's series . . . ? They are drivel. I will try and drivel too' (5 April 1960). Newspapers such as the *Daily Mail*, however, thought of Waugh as a writer who by brilliance and nerve could make snobbery and prejudice compellingly readable. In this difference of estimates probably lies the root cause of Waugh's and the newspapers' finding themselves at cross-purposes, and the explanations of each party for rejecting work or for refusing to compromise over payments or conditions tend to sound hollow. In 1955 Waugh failed to reach agreement with *Life* over essays about St Francis of Assisi and about Christianity in India, a project still being canvassed with the *Sunday Times* and other papers in the 1960s. In September 1957 the *Daily Mail* invited and paid for, but did not use, a 'strongly expressed Catholic viewpoint' for its series 'What Do You Believe?' although Waugh had welcomed the job most eagerly. In November 1960 a contribution to a debate in the *Daily Mail* over *Lady Chatterley's Lover* was again paid for but not used. A comment on Dr Fisher, the Archbishop of Canterbury's, meeting with Pope John XXIII, though urgently sought by the *Sunday Dispatch*, was relegated to the North, Midlands and Ireland editions on account of 'pressure of space'. Seemingly unaware of how trivial and mischievous his article might appear to others, Waugh protested that 'a good workman, even if paid, does not like to see his work wasted' (7 November 1960). But Waugh's relationship with the *Mail*, and incidentally with the quality papers, is best illustrated by the related histories of three articles, 'Here They Are, the English Lotus-Eaters' (20 March 1962), 'Manners and Morals' (12–13 April 1962) and ' Eldorado Revisited' (12 August 1962). In the first place it should be said that the editor of the *Mail*, Walter Hayes, had been (as Waugh gratefully reported to Peters) outstand- ingly 'civil and accommodating', and had regarded it as 'a tremendous triumph when we had got him back into journalism' – with 'I see nothing but bore- dom . . . everywhere' (28 December 1959) and with the 'Passport into Spring' series (28–31 March 1960). There was therefore no lack of goodwill when late in 1960 Waugh began looking for an assignment to give him a 'change of scene'. After negotiations with the *Sunday Telegraph* and *Sunday Times* over articles on Algeria, places of pilgrimage and the ever-fascinating India had foundered, the

Daily Mail agreed to send Waugh to British Guiana, then on the eve of independence, 'to retrace my steps of 29 years ago . . . and note changes'. Five articles were to be written for £2,000. Waugh's diaries reveal that he took the trip seriously, interviewing politicians and investigating economic conditions. The subsequent evolution of the articles is too complicated to relate, but the outcome is instructive. In the event the *Daily Mail* published only one article, on cruising and tipping ('Here They Are, the English Lotus-Eaters'). It cut Waugh's serious account of the country so savagely that he felt compelled to transfer it to the *Sunday Times* where, after rewriting, it appeared in its present form as 'Return to Eldorado'. In lieu of the articles on Guiana which the *Daily Mail* had commissioned, Waugh gave them 'Manners and Morals'. Ostensibly a review of the *Pan Book of Etiquette*, this was in reality a 'hard-hitting' attack on English slovenliness and egalitarian ways. It was not a 'congenial' task for Waugh; he would have preferred a 'serious study for a serious paper'. And yet the *Mail* were delighted with what they were given. Perhaps they felt, and were right to feel, that while numberless journalists could compile reports of distressed dependencies, only Waugh could readably denounce the English as a race of 'slatterns and louts'. Of course 'Manners and Morals' does much more than that, for Waugh's flourishing extravagances always cling to a solid core of talent and intelligence. But its arresting idiosyncrasy is not at all easy to define as a purely literary phenomenon: it depends too much on the exploitation of an assumed authorial personality, or 'front', gained over many years of public notoriety.

Mr Pinfold's creation of a 'front of pomposity mitigated by indiscretion, that was bright and antiquated as a cuirass', or, alternatively, of a 'character of burlesque', reflects one of Waugh's most remarkable achievements in the post-war period. He turned himself into a sharply defined national figure, often detested but always brilliantly recognizable, often ridiculed but always curiously formidable. Without trespassing on the biographer's territory, an editor might remark that writings gain much of their significance from knowledge of the author: suppose (as Waugh remarked) Goering had said '*L'art est sottise*,' and Rimbaud, 'When I hear the word "Art" I reach for my pistol.' Reputation and notoriety, 'front' and 'character of burlesque', are, then, essential ingredients of Waugh's most idiosyncratic forays. And they originate, principally, in Waugh's refusal 'to go flopping along with the times', and in his fierce Old Testament policy of reprisals against the criticism which his stand incurred.

The mood of post-war England – at least as it appeared to a principled conservative – was overwhelmingly liberal and modern. Democracy and equality had acquired almost religious sanction in six years of People's War. By the late 1950s the Tory party was competitively promoting the Welfare State and the Classless Society. And by the 1960s the influential organs of opinion – the quality newspapers and weeklies, the more successful publishers, the BBC and the universities – were so far liberal as virtually not to recognize any other ethos as significant. No periodical with pretensions to articulacy or flair welcomed conservative opinion as does the *Spectator* today. No prominent journalist or academic economist worked publicly from a defined conservative viewpoint. The *Observer* critic who wrote, 'Like most reviewers, I am of a conventionally liberal turn of mind; and the problem with which Mr Waugh confronts us, is how to do him justice in spite of his views,' was smug but almost uniquely self-aware. (Despite his stated concern for justice, however, and despite his declared subject being the author's 'mind and attitudes', this same critic went on to describe *Unconditional Surrender* as 'misanthropic', 'lunatic McCarthy-ism?', 'painfully gushing and vulgar', 'fantastically confused in values', and 'appealing in the same way as the *Queen* magazine', without once recognizing the existence of, let alone confronting, the novel's themes or the historical viewpoint on which it is based.)

From where Waugh stood, therefore, liberalism looked totally victorious, and conservatism less rejected than relegated to oblivion. Realistically he admitted in 'Aspirations of a Mugwump' (2 October 1959) that 'expectation of [change] in my lifetime is pure fantasy'. On the other hand he knew that anything which had appealed to large numbers of intelligent people in the past would, with the inevitable swing of public opinion, appeal again. In the meantime he had to adopt an attitude. His knowledge of how public opinion worked was sophisticated. He knew that point by point opposition to liberal initiatives at the height of a liberal epoch would be futile, and would condemn the opposer to dimmest obscurity. Strategically he had only one choice. If he were to be effective, if he were to be *heard*, he must startle an intellectually self-satisfied audience into self-doubt by total intransigence. He must create the enemy he was to attack. It was a strategy he was well-equipped to carry out. He had once explained it, only half facetiously, in 'Take Your Home into Your Own Hands' (16 January 1929). That article advised unwilling slaves of fashion to state their true, unfashionable tastes with 'absolute complacency', so as to cause 'profound shock'. This would embolden them to defy the tyrannous voice of fashion and would eventually persuade others to do the same, however timorously.

Waugh was also aggressively bent on trouble-making, and inclined to respond to opposition by redoubling his provocations. When *The Loved One* (1948) had restored his reputation in intellectual circles (as he had ensured it would, by publishing it in *Horizon*), he wrote to Nancy Mitford: 'They think my heart is in the right place. I'll show them' (16 March 1948). Jealous of his reputation for fierceness, he wrote in 1952: 'Talk about my becoming nicer. You couldn't write an obscene phrase like that except to offend.' When added to innate pugnacity, a compulsion to revenge insults, a tendency to turbulent excess – to outbursts of affection, to outbursts of rage – and an unquenchable proclivity to mix up jokes in every subject, the policy of 'I'll show them' resulted in some of the most startling utterances in recent English literature.

Three short pieces illustrate the combined effect of the strategy and the temperament just outlined. The foreword to William Weston's *Autobiography* (1955) remarks, as though stating a truism, that for 'the fullest development of the national genius' England 'required a third conquest, by Philip of Spain'. To the vast majority of Englishmen who, regardless of denomination, looked on the defeat of the Spanish Armada as a great national victory, Waugh's regret at its defeat was almost unbelievably preposterous. Perhaps it was healthy for them to contemplate a different possibility. But the motive for Waugh's utterance was not a mere desire to shock. Since writing *Edmund Campion* in 1935 he had held an eccentric view of the Counter-Reformation, equating it less with the imposition of orthodoxy and discipline than with the gallantry of the English Jesuit martyrs and with the intellectual and spiritual resurgence expressed, for him, in Baroque architecture. He seriously believed that England had lost by being cut off from it; a contentious point of view, but not one necessarily implying retrospective desire for conquest by Spain. Some months before the foreword was written, however, Hugh Trevor-Roper had published a highly offensive attack in the *New Statesman* (5 December 1953) on the Counter-Reformation ('mumbo-jumbo multiplied'), on the Jesuit missionaries ('landed in England to organize the fifth column'), on modern priestly biographies of the recusants ('empty them of their intellectual contents . . . restore them as mascots') and on Waugh ('follow me, says Mr Evelyn Waugh, for in the intellectual emptiness of modern English Catholicism only the snob-appeal is left . . . '). Thus sorely provoked, when Waugh wrote the foreword to the Jesuit missionary William Weston's autobiography, edited by Philip Caraman, SJ, he began it defiantly by going to the quite new extreme of regretting the failure of the Armada.

The hazards of popular election are pointed out in 'Aspirations of a Mugwump' (2 October 1959), a contribution to a symposium of pre-general election comments:

> Great Britain is not a democracy. All authority emanates from the Crown. Judges . . . and especially ministers exist by the royal will. In the last 300 years, especially in the last hundred, the Crown has adopted what seems to me a very hazardous method of choosing advisers: popular election. Many great evils have resulted . . . I do not aspire to advise my sovereign in her choice of servants.

The *Guardian* handsomely said of the often-quoted sentence ('I do not aspire to advise my sovereign . . . ') that 'No other contemporary would have been capable of a comic line of that stature' (11 April 1966). This was a well-deserved tribute to a dead-pan joke conceived on a massive scale. But since democracy in the sense of government by popular election commands universal, almost religious respect in the English-speaking world, the joke might easily be interpreted as anarchic and irresponsible. The truth is that it grew out of very serious concerns. Since the 1930s Waugh had argued that obsession with politics distracted citizens from more productive activities: 'In the sixteenth century,' he wrote in *Robbery under Law* (1939), 'human life was disordered and talent stultified by obsession of theology; today we are plague-stricken by politics' (p. 3). He was also acutely conscious of the ways in which mass electorates responded to the professional manipulation of public opinion. As a conservative he placed more importance on 'good government' than on nationalist or ideological aspirations. But in the intellectual climate of 1959 he saw no point in advancing these arguments except in striking comic form.

Objections to Roman Catholicism, an informatively titled book of essays written by Progressive Roman Catholics, was published in 1964. It created a sensation, not least because some of the opinions expressed were thought heretical by traditionalists. Waugh was invited to its launching, a Foyle's literary lunch. His refusal was printed in the *Evening Standard*: 'I would gladly attend an auto-da-fé at which your guests were incinerated. But I will certainly not sit down to a social meal in their company.' The joke, if it was a joke, turned on 'social meal', a jargon term employed by Progressives who were arguing that the Mass should have less the character of a sacrifice and more the sense of a shared meal. Waugh seriously believed that the Church authorities had been remiss in not controverting what he believed heretical Progressive opinion. Whether his postcard was an attempt at humour and self-parody (considering his well-established reputation as England's 'leading ecclesiastical Die-hard', the invitation was a very funny one), or a provocative way of making heard in a totally liberal atmosphere the point that heresy should be combated (by argument), is not at all easy to say. The one thing certain is that this 'joke' causes revulsion rather than shock. It illustrates how easily an 'I'll show them' policy can go wrong.

A provocative stance is successful if it provokes. In these terms Waugh's stance was so successful that it brought on him and on his work a torrent of abuse. By 1947 Waugh was complaining to Nancy Mitford that the reviews of *Scott-King's Modern Europe* 'instead of being about the book, have been about me saying that I am ill-tempered and self-infatuated . . . It hurts.' Each year reviews grew steadily less literary and attacked Waugh more personally. In 1953 he was 'much upset', as he wrote to Christopher Sykes, by 'violent and inaccurate abuse' in a review-profile of *Love among the Ruins* written by George Malcolm Thomson, a Beaverbrook journalist widely believed to reflect his employer's opinions. The 'violence and inaccuracy' of the abuse cannot be fully learned from the quotations in 'Mr Waugh Replies' (3 July 1953), because Waugh omitted mention of jibes, such as that an ancestor had resigned from the Church of Scotland when it softened its policy on witches, and that he (Waugh) resembled 'an indignant White Leghorn'. The motive for the attack is also unclear, but it may have been indignation at Waugh's publishing a bitter satire on contemporary England to coincide with Elizabeth II's coronation, an occasion of widespread euphoria about a New Elizabethan Age. But Thomson's profile was notable only because its abuse was so crude, and because it would in time be avenged in the courts. Many other profiles and gossip paragraphs, and particularly those written pseudonymously by friends, or friends of friends, were more damaging. Cyril Connolly's in *Time*, an associate of Randolph Churchill, Alan Brien's in *Truth* (1954), and Tom Driberg's in the *New Statesman* (1961), though amusing and in part appreciative, fixed the terms in which Waugh would be discussed – snobbery, social climbing, brutality and bigotry – for many years to come. Academic criticism of the novels became obsessed with snobbery after Conor Cruise O'Brien in 1946 published a brilliant piece of invective, 'The Pieties of Evelyn Waugh'. From the early 1950s, when the 'anti-Establishment' group sometimes referred to as Angry Young Men – Kingsley Amis, John Wain, John Braine, John Osborne – became influential in the *Spectator* and the *Observer*, Waugh was roughly handled in territory which had once been friendly. In 1955 Cyril Connolly, in the *Sunday Times*, dismissed *Officers and Gentlemen* as more or less negligible and dull. Subsequently, reviews of the fiction in all the quality papers, and particularly Philip Toynbee's in the *Observer*, became increasingly hostile and contemptuous.

When the Crown Prince of Prussia walked out of a performance of *Androcles and the Lion*, George Bernard Shaw praised his intelligence, confirmed his logic and expressed pleasure at being so well understood. It may be thought that Waugh, having attacked his contemporaries so vigorously, would have welcomed their retaliation as a sign of success. He did not. He disliked criticism. By 1952 he was 'harassed with unpopularity catching me up at last' (letter to Clarissa Churchill, 8 January 1952). 'I am awfully encouraged that you like *Officers and Gentlemen*,' he wrote to Sir Maurice Bowra in 1955. 'The reviewers don't, fuck them.' His resentment was increased by knowing that the reviews printed in the influential Sunday literary pages and weeklies were affecting a dull disappointment that would hurt sales. He was sure of the quality of his writing, and angered by criticism of it. When he could retaliate directly he did; sometimes he struck back obliquely.

The most overt counter-attack was a series of three related court cases involving the Beaverbrook press. It seems plain that in going to law Waugh was primarily punishing George Malcolm Thomson's profile, which he had seen as part of a Beaverbrook 'conspiracy' to discredit him. 'Mr Waugh Replies' (3 July 1953) was the first shot in the counter-offensive. Then in July 1955 Nancy Spain, the chief literary critic of the Beaverbrook press, in company with Lord Noel-Buxton, attempted to 'gatecrash my idol', Waugh, in order to get copy for an article in a debunking series titled 'A Cool Look at the Loved Ones'. Both Nancy Spain and Waugh wrote amusing accounts of the incident. Waugh's, 'Awake My Soul! It is a Lord' (8 July 1955), was cruel as well as funny and captured a lot of attention. Early in the following year John Wain reviewed P. G. Wodehouse's *French Leave* unkindly in the *Observer*. Waugh replied with 'Dr Wodehouse and Mr Wain' in the *Spectator* (24 February 1956). His article, which is concerned only with John Wain and 'the new state-educated graduates' (letter to Terence Kilmartin, 12 February 1956), not with Nancy Spain, begins by quoting a survey showing that the quality papers alone had influence on the book trade, while the popular press had none. Nancy Spain replied crossly in the *Daily Express* by claiming that her review of *Island in the Sun* had brought Alec Waugh sales far higher than any Evelyn had achieved. It was an intemperate paragraph, not personally insulting, but grossly inaccurate and technically libellous. Waugh sued. Before the case came to court, Anthony Hern, another Beaverbrook journalist, libelled Waugh and Graham Greene, freely quoting the 1956 Pan Books reissue of Rebecca West's *The Meaning of Treason*. Waugh launched two new proceedings. In the event all three actions were successful. *The Meaning of Treason* was withdrawn from sale (13 December 1956), and Waugh won £2,000 from Nancy Spain and the Beaverbrook press (20 February 1957) and £3,000 from Anthony Hern and the Beaverbrook press (4 April 1957).

Literary counter-offensives were more problematic because Waugh's temperament led him to ill-judged extremes. Understandably Waugh resented the treatment he received from what he called in private the 'Braine-Wain-Ames' or the 'Teddy-Boy' school of young writers. But his response brought more obloquy on his own head than on theirs. As they were of lower-middle-class origin and had (he believed) attended university under the provisions of the post-war Butler Education Act ('for the free distribution of university degrees to the deserving poor'), he habitually referred to them, for example in *A Little Learning* (1964), as 'state-trained'. 'An Open Letter to the Honble Mrs Peter Rodd' (December 1955) also begins with a longish attack on these 'sour young people coming off the assembly lines in their hundreds every year and finding employment as critics, even as poets and novelists.' The novelists, Waugh continued, knew nothing of a 'more expensive' world than their own other than 'loose women who take taxis, crooks in silk shirts'. As this abuse was irrelevant to the subject of the 'Open Letter', and since Waugh gave no hint of what occasioned his outburst, the passage reads like gratuitous snobbery. The more likely explanation is that Waugh was provoked by criticism into expressing disproportionate contempt. Teased, he ridiculed his opponents clumsily and offensively.

The prose style adopted during these last years is a happy modification of the more 'rhetorical and ornamental' one which had characterized the immediate post-war years. The 1960 revision of *Brideshead Revisited* is the clearest evidence of how 'distasteful' the earlier manner had become to Waugh. 'Sinking, Shadowed and Sad – the Last Glory of Europe' (30 March 1960), a tribute to Venice, is a good example of the new way of writing adapted to popular journalism. Waugh still sometimes consciously aimed at 'elegance' – as when writing about champagne, or when writing an introduction to a sumptuous edition of *The Man of Property* – but it was a drier, more ironic elegance than he had previously affected.

Three essays of the period stand out as centrally significant. 'An Open Letter to the Honble Mrs Peter Rodd' (December 1955) is marred by an ill-executed assault on literary enemies, and is a subversion of, rather than a contribution to, the U and Non-U debate. But it is a thoughtful comment on the English class system, justifying Andrew Sinclair's tribute to Waugh in *The Last of the Best: The Aristocracy of Europe in the Twentieth Century* (London: 1969), as 'the most perfect observer of English social gradations in this century.' The intricacy of the class system is one of Waugh's constant themes. 'An Act of Homage and Reparation to P. G. Wodehouse' (16 July 1961) was, as the *Guardian* editorialized, 'one of the most imaginative and helpful . . . finely thought-out acts of one writer towards another.' It also states Waugh's understanding of the attempts made between 1939 and 1945 to convert the Second World War into an opportunity for social revolution. Read in conjunction with 'Anything Wrong with Priestley?' (13 September 1957) the 'Act of Homage' explains much of Waugh's hostility to post-war English society. 'Sloth' (January 1962) condemned the slackness and easy-going ways which had caused such marked decline in qualitative standards in England (a life-long theme). But its importance lies in its principal definition of 'sloth' as 'refusal to take the proper means of salvation because the apparatus [causes] tedium and disgust.' The sentence holds one of the keys to Waugh's uniqueness. In spite of the 'tedium and disgust' he felt with the 'apparatus of salvation' (or institutional religion) he would not be deterred from taking 'the proper means of salvation'. Hence the stress on disciplined intelligence and will in 'Edith Stein' (Christmas, 1952). Hence, too, Waugh's support in 'The Same Again, Please' (23 November 1962) of the Roman Catholic Church as impersonal dispenser of grace and truth for the 'middle rank' of Catholics.

Waugh's opposition to the Roman Catholic Church's *aggiornamento*, or 'Change' as it will be called here, was the most distinctive feature of the journalism of his last years. Between March 1963 and January 1966 he wrote seventeen very combative letters to the *Tablet*, the *Catholic Herald* and *Commonweal*. He also wrote a major essay, originally published in the *Spectator* and since widely reprinted, 'The Same Again, Please' (23 November 1962). The essay and letters raise much the same issues, so much so that it was unnecessary to reprint here more than the essay and one fairly comprehensive letter, 'Changes in the Church' (7 August 1964) – which has the additional advantage of being written in Waugh's idiosyncratic fighting style. Two other pieces not reprinted here are relevant to Waugh's attitudes to Change. His obituary of Pius XII (12 October 1958) gives only an impression of a magnetic personality. This was a significantly incomplete picture of a man who had prided himself on being, and had been generally regarded as, a thinker, teacher and innovator. Waugh, however, disliked his liturgical reforms and always blamed Pius XII, rather than John XXIII alone, for the most troublesome aspects of the *aggiornamento*. 'An Appreciation of Pope John' (27 July 1963) is remarkable for what it does not say. It portrays a lovable, learned conservative whose policies may, or may not, turn out to have been wise; in hinting doubt and disapproval when the whole world seemed to be applauding John's summoning of the Second Vatican Council Waugh's obituary was uniquely tentative.

The significance of Waugh's contribution to the debate over Change is not to be judged by the content of his criticisms. They were inadequate in various ways, but certainly no more so than a great deal of Progressive afflatus then current. Their importance lies in the fact of their being made at all. The liberal euphoria of the Council days was totally overwhelming. Furthermore the Pope himself, the Second Vatican Council and the English hierarchy were officially sponsoring policies on vernacular liturgy, ecumenism and the like, which the vast majority of lay Catholics either welcomed or accepted. Almost without exception Conservatives, trained in obedience to Church authority, remained silent. Waugh, like Athanasius, was *contra mundum* .

. AN OPEN LETTER TO THE HONBLE MRS PETER RODD (NANCY MITFORD) ON A VERY SERIOUS SUBJECT .

Dearest Nancy,

Were you surprised that your article on the English aristocracy caused such a to-do? I wasn't. I have long revered you as an agitator – agitatrix, *agitateuse*? – of genius. You have only to publish a few cool reflections on eighteenth-century furniture to set gangs on the prowl through the Faubourg St Germain splashing the walls with 'Nancy, go home'.[1] In England class distinctions have always roused higher feelings than national honour; they have always been the subject of feverish but very private debate. So, when you brought them into the open, of course everyone talked, of course the columnists quoted you and corrected you. Letters poured in to the various editors, many of them, I am told, unprintably violent. You were the subject of a literary competition (which produced very sad entries) and now here am I, late but implacable, chipping in too.

Should delicacy have restrained you? your friends anxiously ask. There are subjects too intimate for print. Surely class is one? The vast and elaborate structure grew up almost in secret. Now it shows alarming signs of delapidation. Is this the moment to throw it open to the heavy-footed public? Yes, I think it is, and particularly, as you have done, to the literary public. My reproach is that, in doing so, you have in your skittish way bamboozled a great number of needy young persons. Have you ever heard of the 'Butler Education Act'? I suppose not, although it happened in the days when you still lived among us. It was one of the things that politicians did when no one was looking, towards the end of the war. It has nothing at all to do with training male indoor-servants nor with instructing the designer of the 'Unknown Political Prisoner' in the intricacies of his craft. The name derives from the Mr Butler

---

In *Noblesse Oblige* ed. N. Mitford (London, 1956). First printed *Encounter*, December 1955.

1 When living in the fashionable Faubourg Saint-Germain Nancy Mitford criticized Marie Antoinette in an article and was reportedly ostracized by the *gratin* of French society. See *Letters*, 23 July 1955.

who at the time of writing has just knocked a few shillings off the price of my trousers. Clearly he is a generous fellow. In his Education Act he provided for the free distribution of university degrees to the deserving poor. Very handy for splitting atoms and that kind of thing, you will say. But many of Mr Butler's protégés choose, or are directed into, 'Literature'. I could make your flesh creep by telling you about the new wave of philistinism with which we are threatened by these sour young people who are coming off the assembly lines in their hundreds every year and finding employment as critics, even as poets and novelists. L'École de Butler are the primal men and women of the classless society. Their novelists seem to be aware of the existence of a rather more expensive world than their own – bars in which spirits are regularly drunk in preference to beer, loose women who take taxis, crooks in silk shirts – but of the ramifications of the social order which have obsessed some of the acutest minds of the last 150 years, they know less than of the castes of India. What can their critics hope to make of the undertones and innuendoes, the evocative, reminiscent epithets of, say, Tony Powell or Leslie Hartley?

It was a worthy project to take them through a rudimentary course of social map-reading and no one should have been better qualified for the task than you with your host of friends in every class.

Nor was L'École de Butler your only source of pupils. Consider the cinema trade, the immigrant producers from God knows where who perhaps have never set foot in a private house in the kingdom. Their solecisms glare at us in blazing colour and shriek at us from amplifiers. At the BBC, a hive of addicts to the deplorable 'Dear Nancy Mitford' form of address, a huge mission field was white for your sickle. Eager, appealing eyes were turned to you through the cigarette smoke. Was it kind, dear Nancy, to pull their legs?

II

You very properly steer clear of the royal family and start your exposition with the peerage. You remark, correctly, that a title in England has a precise legal significance, as it has scarcely anywhere else, and that, partly from our system of primogeniture, titled people do not constitute a separate caste. But you go on to say that a man 'becomes an aristocrat as soon as he receives a title', ' . . . his outlook from now on will be the outlook of an aristocrat'. You know jolly well that that isn't true.

The relationship between aristocracy and nobility in England is certainly baffling. I do not suppose you could find any two people in complete agreement about it. My own estimate would be that about half the nobility are aristocrats and about two-thirds of the aristocracy are noble (in which catalogue I loosely include baronets and people descended in the male line from peers, whether or no they are themselves titled). There is no greater degree of social uniformity in the Upper House of Parliament than in the Commons. The official order of precedence is, of course, quite irrelevant in determining true social position. Ancestry, possessions, achievements, even humour and good looks, have their part in deciding real precedence.

You say: 'Ancestry has never counted much in England.' As a guide to human character, pedigrees are, I suppose, about as valuable as horoscopes. Some of the world's greatest men have resorted to astrologers and millions of subtle Asiatics direct their lives by them today. Learned opinion may change. It may be decided that there was something in the stars after all. My own scepticism about theories of inherited characteristics is based on the impossibility of identifying the real fathers in the ages when adultery was very common and divorce very rare. Whenever there is a scandal elderly persons will remark, 'Ah, that is the Fortinbras blood coming out', and explain that all their mothers' generation were irregularly conceived. But undoubtedly most of our fellow-countrymen attach great importance to ancestry. Take a look at the shelves marked 'Genealogy' in any large second-hand bookshop. You will find displayed at modest prices hundreds of volumes expensively produced, mostly during the last hundred years, for the sole purpose of exalting their authors' families. Genealogy is still as thriving a trade as it was in the days of Elizabeth I, when the Officers of Arms began fabricating the great pedigrees that link the despoilers of the Church with the age of chivalry. People in the last century have been caught filling their parish churches with bogus tombs. Scholars such as Round and Barron spent their lives in exposing fraudulent pedigrees and many who are not scholars, but who, like myself, cherish the delusion that we possess a 'historical sense', have felt the fascination of this sonorous and decorative pursuit.

However, you give us some genealogical figures. Are you sure you have got them right? I know you went to high authority for them, but I can't help wondering how much the present Officers of Arms regard themselves as bound in honour to support the decisions of their less scrupulous predecessors. You say that 382 peers have arms granted before 1485 *and have inherited them in the male line*. My italics, as they say; for the statement staggers me. Neither of us is an expert. We can only look about us and go by rough personal impressions. It seems to me that a remarkably large number of our ancient families have the entry 'assumed by royal licence the name and arms' somewhere in their pedigrees. Look at the Fortinbrases. Sly Ned Fartingbrass who got the estate at the Dissolution was known to all. It was for his grandson that the Heralds invented a link with the extinct crusaders, Fortinbras. The peerage was granted by Charles I and failed in the male line in 1722 when Mr Binks married the heiress and sat in the Commons as Mr Fortinbras-Binks, exercising the full political influence of his wife's family. His son, who called himself Mr Binks-Fortinbras, married well, could return two members; he was rewarded by a peerage; Fortinbras, in the second creation. From that time Binks was dropped and the stolen coat of Fortinbras moved across, with the connivance of the College of Heralds, to the first quarter.

You say that sixty-five existing baronies were created before 1711. Do you include the quaint house of Strabolgi?

Noble families die out almost as fast as new ones are created. I have just taken a sample from Burke's *Peerage and Baronetage 1949* and compared it with the issue for 1885. The volumes fall open, need I say it? at Redesdale. Of the succeeding dozen names only one (and that, incidentally, a family of foreign origin) is to be found in the earlier edition; and of the twelve families who followed Redesdale in 1885, six are already extinct. That is a big turnover in two generations. Perhaps you will argue that it is the new families who die out, since the older the family, the further you can cast back for an heir. Well, looking round, the feudal overlords in the district where I live were the Berkeleys. That earldom has lately become extinct. And their next-door neighbours, who bear a mediaeval name and arms, have borne and changed no less than five surnames in the last eight generations as the property devolved on female heirs. I think you should have questioned your pursuivant more closely before accepting his figures.[1]

III

The Fortinbrases are a delicious vignette, typical of your fictions. I find one fault only. Surely they should have more children? Impotence and sodomy are socially OK but birth control is flagrantly middle-class. But you invented them, I know, to illustrate your theme that aristocrats can't or won't make money. I could remind you of half a dozen prosperous and industrious City men of impeccable origins but I should have to admit that they have not worn well. The acceptance of high living and leisure as part of the natural order is a prerequisite of the aristocratic qualities and achievements. The debonair duke living by his wits, so popular on the stage, soon grows to resemble the plebeian crook. His brother who goes into business and sticks to it and makes good is soon indistinguishable from his neighbours in Sunningdale. You should have said, not that aristocrats can't make money in commerce, but that when they do, they become middle-class.

It is here that we reach the topic that has caused the pother – the supposed gulf between what you inelegantly describe as 'U and non-U'.

This gulf exists in every English mind. What has shocked your critics is that you fix it where you do, definitely, arbitrarily and, some would say, capriciously. There is an unwholesome contemporary appetite – the product, perhaps, of psychiatry and the civil service – for categories of all kinds. People seem to be comforted instead of outraged when they are told that their eccentricities entitle them to membership in a class of 'psychological types'. They are inured to filling in forms which require a 'description' of themselves and their houses. So they have fastened with avidity on the section of your comprehensive essay which pretends to provide the mechanism for grading themselves and their friends.

Everything turns on 'the grand old name of gentleman'. We have no equival-

1 Sir Iain Moncrieffe. See *U and Non-U Revisited* (London, 1978), pp. 101–3.

ent phrase in English to *'noblesse oblige'*. All precepts of manners and morals define the proper conduct of 'gentlemen'. Lord Curzon, a paragon of aristocratic usage, when, as Chancellor of the University, he was shown the menu of a proposed entertainment of the King at Balliol, remarked succinctly: 'No gentleman has soup at luncheon'; he did not say: 'No monarch . . .' or 'No marquis . . .' He appealed above the standards of court or castle to the most elusive standard in the world.

When I was last in Palestine I asked a Zionist how he defined a Jew. Immigrants from every climate from China to Peru were jostling round us. There were atheist Slavs, orthodox Semites from the ghettoes of Morocco and Negroes from the Upper Nile who are reputed to eat snakes. It seemed a pertinent question. He answered: 'Everyone who thinks he is a Jew is one.'

In the same way, the basic principle of English social life is that *everyone* (everyone, that is to say, who comes to the front door) *thinks he is a gentleman*. There is a second principle of almost equal importance: *everyone draws the line of demarcation immediately below his own heels*. The professions rule out the trades; the services, the professions; the Household Brigade, the line regiments; squires, squireens; landed families who had London houses ruled out those who spent all the year at home; and so on, in an infinite number of degrees and in secret, the line is, or was, drawn. It is essentially a process of ruling *out*. If you examine the accumulated code of precepts which define 'the gentleman' you will find that almost all are negative.

Few well-bred people are aware, still less observant, of more than a small fraction of this code. Most people have a handful of taboos, acquired quite at random. Usually at an impressionable age someone has delivered a judgment which has taken root. The lack of reason in these dooms makes them the more memorable, and no subsequent experience mitigates their authority.

For example, there is a cousin of yours, a jolly, badly dressed baron. He and I were talking one day when there passed an acquaintance, a grandee, a member of the Jockey Club, your cousin's superior and *a fortiori* mine. Your cousin, not a very serious man normally, regarded this sleek, russet figure with aversion and said, with deep seriousness: 'My father told me that no gentleman ever wore a brown suit.'

Another cousin of yours, of more august descent, is a man notorious for the grossness of his vocabulary. He has only to hear a piece of *argot* from the Bowery to adopt it as his own. But once, in early youth, he was sharply corrected for calling a kinsman his 'relative' or 'relation'. He cannot remember which, but both words have become anathema. Of all the sage advice poured out on him by schoolmasters and clergymen and dons and commanding officers, that alone remains, and if either word is used in his hearing, he starts as though stung and, being what he is, he rounds on the speaker with abuse.

All nannies and many governesses, when pouring out tea, put the milk in first. (It is said by tea-fanciers to produce a richer mixture.) Sharp children notice that this is not normally done in the drawing-room. To some this revelation becomes symbolic. We have a friend you may remember, far from conventional in other ways, who makes it her touchstone. 'Rather MIF, darling,' she says in condemnation.

There is the question of ichthyotomy. Some years ago a friend of mine, in a novel, described the wife of a Master of Hounds as using a fish-knife. I warned him that this would cause offence and, sure enough, the wife of a neighbouring MFH got as far as this passage and threw the book from her, crying: 'The fellow can't even write like a gentleman,' while all the time, higher in the social scale, at some (I am told at many) of the really august stately homes fish-knives have been in continuous use for nearly a hundred years.

They were a Victorian invention in pretty general use in polite society in the sixties. Certain old-fashioned people, of the kind who today eschew the tele-phone, derided the gadgets, which soon began to appear among the wedding presents of professional persons. The old-fashioned people scratched away with two forks and also picked their teeth at table, which was considered low by smart Londoners. The old-fashioned people won through an odd alliance with the aesthetes. When people began moving their Chippendale chairs down from the attics, they began denuding their tables of Victorian silver. In our lifetime we have seen few fish-knives in private houses and many toothpicks. But it has all been a matter of fashion not of class.

I could multiply examples almost without end. There is practically no human activity or form of expression which, at one time or another in one place or another, I have not heard confidently condemned as plebeian, for genera-tions of English have used the epithets 'common' and 'middle-class' as general pejoratives to describe anything which gets on their nerves.

It is natural to the literary mind to be unduly observant of the choice of words. Logan Pearsall Smith was the classical case. I met him once only. He did not speak to me until we stood on the doorstep leaving. He then said: 'Tell me, how would you describe the garment you are wearing? A greatcoat? An overcoat? A topcoat?' I replied: 'Overcoat.' 'Ah, would you? Yes. Most interest-ing. And, tell me, would that also be the usage of an armigerous admiral?'

That way lay madness and I fear that if you are taken too seriously you and Professor Ross may well drive your readers into the bin. When in your novel you made 'Uncle Matthew' utter his catalogue of irrational prohibitions, you were accurately recording a typical conversational extravagance. When you emerge *in propria persona* as the guide to Doric youth, you are more mischiev-ous. Of course, it is broadly true that twenty-five or thirty years ago the phrases you dub 'U' came more naturally to most ladies and gentlemen than those you condemn. Traces of that lingo survive today here and there among well-brought-up young people. But fashionable usage was even then in constant transition. Every family and every set always had its private vocabulary and syntax and still has. I know people whose terms of condemnation are quite simply NLU and NLO ('not like us' and 'not like one'). Everyone has always regarded any usage but his own as either barbarous or pedantic. Phrases that were originally adopted facetiously, in inverted commas as it were, pass into habitual use; the chic jargon of one decade – Philip Sassoon's 'I couldn't like it more', for instance – becomes the vulgarism of the next; words once abhorred, like 'weekend', become polite. Consider the influence of the USA. There are few families without American connections today and American polite vocabulary is very different from ours. We fight shy of abbreviations and euphemisms. They rejoice in them. The blind and maimed are called 'handicapped', the destitute, 'underprivileged'. 'Toilet' is pure American (but remember that our 'lavatory' is equally a euphemism). Remember too that the American vocabulary is pulverized between two stones, refinement and overstatement. *'O let me not be mentally ill, not mentally ill, sweet heaven'* sounds odd, but in the USA 'mad' merely means 'cross'. If Professor Ross's Finns or your literary disciples wander out into the English world armed with your lexicon, seeking to identify the classes they encounter, they will drop many bricks. For habits of speech are not a matter of class but of society and on the whole English people do not congregate exclusively or by preference with their social equals.

Look back twenty-five years to the time when there was still a fairly firm aristocratic structure and the country was still divided into spheres of influence among hereditary magnates. My memory is that the grandees avoided one another unless they were closely related. They met on state occasions and on the race-course. They did not frequent one another's houses. You might find almost anyone in a ducal castle – convalescent, penurious cousins, advisory experts, sycophants, gigolos and plain blackmailers. The one thing you could be sure of not finding was a concourse of other dukes. English society, it seemed to me, was a complex of tribes, each with its chief and elders and witch-doctors and braves, each with its own dialect and deity, each strongly xenophobic.

Dons by habit mark everything α, β, γ. They speak of 'upper, middle and lower classes'. Socialists speak of 'capitalists, bourgeois, intellectuals, workers'. But these simple categories do not apply in England. Here there is very little horizontal stratification apart from the single, variable, great divide specified above. There is instead precedence, a single wholly imaginary line (a Platonic idea) extending from Windsor to Wormwood Scrubs, of separate individuals each justly and precisely graded. In the matter of talking together, eating together, sleeping together, this mysterious line makes little difference, but every Englishman is sharply aware of its existence, and this awareness often spices these associations very pleasantly.

I V

It is when we come to the last part of your article, much the most important part, which has nevertheless attracted least notice, that my amusement at your prank becomes a little strained.

'The English lord is a wily old bird' you take as your text, and your theme is that he is enormously rich. He pays neither taxes nor death duties. He 'glories' in turning his house into a public museum. He has given up London simply because he is not witty enough to keep a salon. He sells his pictures because he does not appreciate them. He prefers herbaceous borders and flowering shrubs to the formal parterres which require two dozen gardeners. His reduced circumstances are all a hoax. He is biding his time until the present craze for equality has passed, when he will re-emerge in all his finery to claim all his privileges, to ravish village brides and transport poachers to Botany Bay.

Can you really believe any of this, even living, as you do, so remote from the scene you describe? Not long ago an American cutie, married to a Labour politician, published a book propounding the same argument. Everyone tolerantly asked: 'What can an American cutie married to a Labour politician hope to know of such things? Ask her to dinner and let her see for herself.' But what are we to say now when Nancy, Queen of the Hons, comes out with the same malicious errors? The English, you should remember, have a way of making jokes about their disasters, but you would find, if you lived here, that the loudest jokes about opening stately homes are made by the wives who have recent and perhaps direful associations with them, rather than by the husbands. Half Bowood, you should know, is being demolished because its owner prefers privacy. I am not familiar with the household accounts of the few magnates who still preserve a recognizable ghost of their former establishments, but I am pretty sure something has to be sold every year to keep going. But instead of expostulating with you let me turn to your dupes and tell them two facts, which you have never attempted to hide, bless you, but which are not well known.

The first is rather endearing. You were at the vital age of twelve when your father succeeded to his peerage, and until less than a year before there was little likelihood of his ever succeeding. It was a great day for 'Hons' when you and your merry sisters acquired that prefix of nobility. Hitherto it had been the most shadowy of titles, never spoken, and rarely written. You brought it to light, emphasized and aspirated, and made a glory of it. And with that magic vocable came (very briefly it is true) a sensational change of fortune. If your uncle had not been killed in action, if your posthumous cousin had been a boy, all you enchanting children would have been whisked away to a ranch in Canada or a sheep-run in New Zealand. It is fascinating to speculate what your careers would then have been. Anyway, at that impressionable age an indelible impression was made; Hons were unique and lords were rich.

The other fact is not nice. You are a socialist, as devoted and as old-fashioned as the American cutie. As you confess in your article, you regard Lloyd George as a great man (and, we must suppose, as a great aristocrat too in his last days). You are dedicated to the class-war. Has the whisper reached you from our bleak island, as you recline in elegant seclusion, that the cause of 'Social Justice' is now being pleaded by the Hons? Alertly studied, your novels reveal themselves as revolutionary tracts and here, in your essay, you speak out boldly: 'Hear me, comrades. I come from the heart of the enemy's camp. You think they have lost heart for the fight. I have sat with them round their camp fires and heard them laughing. They are laughing at *you*. They are not beaten yet, comrades. Up and at them again.'

Is that what you are really saying, Nancy? I hope you are just teasing, as I am. I hope. I wonder.

Fondest love,
EVELYN

. THE FORERUNNER .

It is notorious that Great Britain, as compared with Italy, France, Spain and the Netherlands, has made a meagre contribution to the visual arts. We had a brief period of fine landscape, some sound portraits, but in what elsewhere were the highest achievements, in religious devotion and in secular magnificence, our painters and sculptors are negligible. In only one branch of painting, and that not the most honoured even in our own country, did we produce a unique, idiosyncratic national school. That is the school of narrative composition founded by Hogarth and perfected a hundred years later. It would be absurd to claim a place for him beside Titian and Velasquez, even beside Goya. He was in no sense a great painter, but he is a national figure comparable to Dr Johnson or Trollope, of whom we may well be proud. He was an excellent craftsman, trained in the discipline of the silversmith's shop. He painted better every year of his life. He was frivolously versatile, always hankering, like poor Benjamin Haydon, for the heroic and the sublime. Haydon is honoured today only for *Waiting for the Times*. Hogarth's Bristol altar-piece is disregarded, his *Marriage à la Mode* has given continuous pleasure for 200 years and has inspired generations of worthy disciples.

The school which Hogarth founded may be defined as the detailed representation of contemporary groups, posed to tell a story and inculcate a moral precept. The figures are not merely caught and preserved in certain attitudes; previous and subsequent events are implicit in the scene portrayed. Hogarth's moral lessons are commonplace, commonsensical: that extravagance leads to destitution, debauchery to madness, crime to the gallows, loveless marriage to infidelity and so on. It remained for the more delicate sentiment of the Victorians to refine on these maxims. Holman Hunt's *Awakened Conscience* deals with a deeper experience than a dose of venereal disease. Augustus Egg's *Past and Present* gives a more poignant revelation of deserted childhood than the Countess's crippled orphan. There is more pathos in Orchardson's bridegroom than in the Earl. Frith's *Derby Day* is better composed and better painted than *The March to Finchley*. But Hogarth was the rude originator of these refined works and shares our gratitude.

Review of *Hogarth's Progress*, by Peter Quennell. *Time and Tide*, 9 July 1955.

He was pure Cockney, intolerant of everything foreign. English painting, so far as it has excelled at all, has done so in inverse relation to the influence of Italy and France. I do not know of any foreign painter except Svoboda who rivalled the English School in their own *métier*. Comparable Parisians of the nineteenth century tended towards the lubricious or the allegorical. There is one corner of the artistic field that will remain for ever England.

In writing Hogarth's life, Mr Quennell has had a task which few will envy. Hard-working craftsmen give little scope for the biographer. All that can be told of Hogarth's affairs is contained in Austen Dobson's admirable article in the *Dictionary of National Biography*. His full-length study, which until now has held the field, is largely padding. So, indeed, inevitably, is Mr Quennell's. The difference is that whereas Dobson's padding makes rather dull reading, Mr Quennell's is entirely enjoyable. He knows eighteenth-century London, particularly its underworld, very well indeed. Any account of Hogarth's day-to-day existence must be largely conjectural. Mr Quennell has taken the occasion to give a rich, detailed conspectus of the streets and taverns, theatres and political controversies, in which Hogarth worked and from which he drew his illustrations. Often there are pages on end with no direct reference to the hero of the story, but they are vivid, elegant pages and they help us to an understanding of his art.

. THE DEATH OF PAINTING .

'From today painting is dead,' cried Paul Delaroche in 1839, when first shown a daguerreotype. He spoke too soon. For two generations there was life – vigour, sometimes – in the stricken body. Even today in odd corners painters may still be found plying their ancient craft for the pleasure of a few impoverished private patrons. But for the professional critics, the public committees, the directors of galleries, the art is indeed dead, picked white; not a smell survives. It is noteworthy that a Frenchman first saw the significance of this French invention. France was the scene of the death agony. Delaroche's prognosis was sound enough. But it was based on a false diagnosis.

Nearly twenty years later an Englishman wrote: 'Photography is an enormous stride forward in the region of art. The old world was well nigh exhausted with its wearisome mothers and children called Madonnas . . . its wearisome nudities called Nymphs and Venuses . . . Then a new world slowly widens to our sight, a very heaven compared to the old earth . . . There will be photograph Raphaels, photograph Titians. . . .'

That was the prospect Delaroche feared. Here were a box, a lens, a bath of salts and with them the common man could effortlessly accomplish all that the

The Saturday Book: No. 16, ed. John Hadfield (London, 1956). Quotations from artists in this essay are taken from Robert Goldwater and Marco Treves, *Artists on Art: From the XIV to the XX Century* (New York, 1945).

great geniuses of the past had attempted. For until the present century the whole history of European painting was determined by man's striving to reproduce and arrange visual appearances. The critics of the last fifty years have been busy in imputing quite different motives to the Masters and in identifying quite different achievements. There is no evidence of these preoccupations in the rather sparse documents. Most of the letters and recorded precepts of the Masters deal with prices, models and technical devices. When they speak of their aims they are unanimous. Leonardo da Vinci wrote: 'That painting is most praiseworthy which is most like the thing represented' and: 'When you wish to see whether your picture corresponds with that of the object presented by nature, take a mirror and set it so that it reflects the actual thing, and then compare the reflection with your picture.' Nicholas Hilliard wrote: 'Now knowe that all painting imitateth nature or the life in everything.' Piero della Francesca: 'Painting is nothing but a representation of surfaces and solids foreshortened or enlarged.' Poussin: 'Painting is nothing but an imitation of human actions . . . one may also imitate not only the actions of beasts but anything natural.' In the court of Louis XV it was disputed whether two perfect painters, observing the same scene, would not produce identical pictures, painters by inference differing only in their faults. There were certainly at different periods some differences of opinion about the rights of selection of the artist, about the modifications he might make in his model in the interest of ideal beauty, what details he might eliminate in the interest of grandeur. Painters represented things they had never seen, such as cherubim on the wing. Some, such as Bosch, portrayed pure fantasy but all the objects were imagined as concrete, visible and tangible and painted as such. It was never questioned that the painter's prime task was to represent. Actual illusion was never achieved except in amusing toys – dog-eared papers apparently pinned to the wall so that the fingers itch to remove them – but there is no reason to doubt that had a full-scale *trompe l'oeil* ever been effected, it would have been applauded without reserve.

Today high honours and high prices are given to the practitioners of 'non-representative art'. Patronage is in the hands of people who no longer seek joy in possession; the directors of public galleries conceive it as their duty to instruct by exemplifying 'movements', however repugnant they may find the task. In the early days of the Post-Impressionists there were ingenious journalists who tried to demonstrate that the new painters were logically developing the discoveries of the Masters; that true aesthetic emotion had always existed in some unexplored subconscious area and was only at that moment (*circa* 1911) becoming articulate; that all original artists had begun by shocking the Philistine. As the scrupulously accurate drawing of Holman Hunt and the early Millais looked 'deformed' to Dickens, so a few years were needed before the common man could see Léger with new eyes. That particular bit of humbug has not worn well. In the last fifty years we have seen the drawings of savages, infants and idiots enjoying fashionable favour. The revolutionaries have grown old and died. No new eyes have grown in new heads. The division between the painting and sculpture of this century and its predecessors has become more pronounced, as more observers in other spheres recognize the evils of the time. There have been no sensational recantations of the kind prevalent among political writers, but the critics on the whole now admit that while Giotto and Tintoretto and Rembrandt and Degas were all in their enormously different ways practising the same art, the activities – call them what you will – of Léger belong to an entirely different order. Can this revolution be attributed to photography?

That invention certainly failed in the claims originally made for it. It has been a humble assistant to the Arts. There are mosaics and frescoes so placed that they can be seen imperfectly and then only with great fatigue. Photography has disclosed new beauties in these. The camera can reveal certain things that are invisible to the naked eye, such as the hitherto unrecognizable stains on the Holy Shroud at Turin. As in the classic hypothesis of the apes typing eternally until they write the sonnets of Shakespeare, the millions of plates exposed have inevitably, but quite fortuitously, now and then produced an attractive composition. But in its direct relations with painting, photography has never been a rival. The allegorical groups and costume-pieces produced in the fifties and sixties – such as Rejlander's celebrated *The Two Ways of Life* and Mrs Cameron's illustrations to *The Idylls of the King* – are what Delaroche feared, and they proved to be wholly ludicrous. The mortal injury done to painters was something quite other; it was both technical and moral.

In technique it was the instantaneous snapshot, not the studio exposure, which proved revolutionary. Movements which before had eluded the eye were arrested and analysed. The simplest example is that of the galloping horse. Draughtsmen had achieved their own 'truth' about the disposal of its legs. The camera revealed a new truth that was not only far less graceful but also far less in accordance with human experience. Similarly with the human figure. In posing a model a painter was at great pains to place her. His sense of composition, her sense of comfort, the feasibility of maintaining and resuming the pose, were important. It was a frequent complaint of young artists that their elders were content with the repetition of art-school clichés. They struggled to build up from sketches entirely novel attitudes. Then came the camera shutter to make permanent the most ungainly postures. The 'slice of life' became the principle of many compositions at the end of the nineteenth century. At the same time 'gum prints' were invented by the photographers, a process by which the surface of painting was imitated. For a decade or more painting and photography were very close. There are 'gum prints' by the Parisians Demachy and Bucquet made at the turn of the century which at first glance may be mistaken for photographs of Impressionist canvases. How far the founders of Impressionism worked from snapshots is conjectural. Their followers were quite open in the matter. Sickert used to translate photographs into paint in just the same way as Victorian ladies translated paint into needlework – and in both cases with very pretty results.

Many early photographers, among them the herald of the 'photograph Titians' quoted above, were unsuccessful painters. There was a fair livelihood to be made out of the new device, especially by a man with the air of an artist; nothing comparable, certainly, to the splendid earnings of the popular painters, but the photographer did not have to work for it, as they did. Perhaps no painters in history worked so hard as the eminent Victorians. They knew little of the easy student days of *Trilby* or of the versatile apprenticeship of the Renaissance. Painting had become a profession, respectable, rewarded, specialized. They trained as hard as for the law or for medicine, and they kept in training through the long years of rich commissions and hereditary honours. The physical exertion of covering their great canvases was immense. They used 'assistants', but very furtively. Not for them the teeming studios of Rembrandt or the factory of Alan Ramsay. The English patron who was paying two or three thousand pounds for a picture demanded that it should be all the artist's own work.

Photography provided the ideological justification for sloth. The camera was capable of verisimilitude; it was not capable of art; therefore art, the only concern of the artist, was not verisimilitude. Verisimilitude was what took the time and trouble. Art was a unique property of the spirit, possessed only by the artist. You could be awfully artistic between luncheon and tea. So the argument ran.

In 1877 Ruskin denounced Whistler's pretentious *Nocturne in Black and Gold* with the felicitous expression: 'a coxcomb flinging a pot of paint in the public's face.' The prospect of enlarging this opinion in court was 'nuts and nectar' to him. 'The whole thing,' he wrote to Burne-Jones, 'will enable me to assert some principles of art economy which I've tried to get into the public's head, by writing, but may get sent over all the world vividly in a newspaper report or two.' Alas, that great projected trial came to nothing. Ruskin was too ill to appear. Whistler was given contemptuous damages without costs; Ruskin's costs were paid by public subscription. But it was not the hoped-for triumph of high principle. The pert American scored some verbal points and gentle Burne-Jones reluctantly gave evidence that Whistler's work lacked 'finish'. This clearly was not the point at issue with the early and life-long adulator of Turner. What a tremendous occasion had Ruskin at the height of his authority and eloquence stood up to warn the world of the danger he acutely foresaw! Something as salutary as Sir Winston Churchill's utterance at Fulton, USA, and perhaps more efficacious. By a curious aberration of popular history the trial was for more than a generation represented as a triumph of Whistler against the Philistines. Today, it is reported, there is an honoured American painter who literally does 'fling' pots of paint at his canvas. What would Whistler have to say about that? Ruskin, we may be sure, would be serenely confident in his early judgment.

The German demagogues of the thirties attempted an exposure of 'decadent' art, so ill-informed and ill-natured and allied to so much evil that honourable protests were unheard or unspoken. The art dealers were able to appeal to a new loyalty; if one hinted that Klee was the acme of futility one proclaimed oneself a Nazi. That phase is ended. Today we need a new Ruskin to assert 'some principles of art economy'. First, that the painter must represent visual objects. Anatomy and perspective must be laboriously learned and conscientiously practised. That is the elementary grammar of his communication. Secondly, that by composition, the choice and arrangement of his visual objects, he must charm, amuse, instruct, edify, awe his fellow men, according as his idiosyncrasy directs. Verisimilitude is not enough, but it is the prerequisite. That is the lesson of the photographer's and of the abstractionist's failure.

. DR WODEHOUSE AND MR WAIN .

An investigation has lately been made in the book-trade to determine which literary critics have most influence on sales. I remember the time when the *Evening Standard* was undisputed leader. A good review there by Arnold Bennett was believed to sell an edition in twenty-four hours. The claim was exaggerated, as I learned to my disappointment when he kindly noticed my first novel. The ensuing demand was, I think, something between two and three hundred, but I wonder whether any critic today has so large and immediate an influence. At the same period his colleague on the *Daily Express* was D. H. Lawrence, then at the height of his powers. Things have changed. The Beaverbrook press is no longer listed as having any influence at all.[1] The *Observer* heads the poll, with the *Sunday Times* as runner-up.

The *Sunday Times* has a larger circulation than the *Observer* and is read, I should have thought, by people with just as much money to spare for book-buying. It may be that the *Sunday Times* critics are occupied with less interesting books – natural history, the biographies of Anglican clergymen, reprints and military history seem to get more attention there than new works of imagination – but the chief credit must go to personalities. Sir Harold Nicolson's urbane essays could appear in either paper indifferently. It must be the young lions of the *Observer* whose voices are heard in the shops and libraries. It so happens that the issue of the *Observer* which records their triumph includes a note by one of them, Mr John Wain, which illuminates their aims and methods.

He had previously reviewed *French Leave*, the latest work of a master I have

Spectator, 24 February 1956.
1 Nancy Spain, the *Daily Express*'s book reviewer and leading literary critic of the Beaverbrook press, replied to this assertion with 'Does a Good Word from Me Sell a Book?' *Daily Express*, 17 March 1956, p.6. She claimed that a notice from her had caused Alec Waugh's *Island in the Sun* to sell 60,000 copies, which dwarfed 'the total first edition sales' of all Evelyn's titles. Her figures were wildly wrong. Waugh sued for libel, and on 20 February 1957 was awarded £2,000 damages.

all my life revered, Mr P. G. Wodehouse, CMG, D.Lit., and concluded with the judgment: 'sooner or later the record will have to be taken off.'

Mr Wain, I believe, is a very young man; Dr Wodehouse I know to be old. To remind an old man that his time is nearly up seemed to me caddish, and I wrote to say so. Mr Wain replied: 'It is not *criticism*, of course, to defend a poor book by pointing out that the author is an elderly man, or to maintain that anyone who has written a *lot* of books must be a great author, but then Mr Waugh is not a critic.' Now in my uncritical way I thought *French Leave* a delightful book but that was not the point I was trying to make. I simply objected to Mr Wain's manners. That he does not deign to notice. Integrity is all. Considerations of common decency must not stand between the young critic and his high purpose. I had come up against that redoubtable person, the 'dedicated man'. It is rather alarming to one trained in a laxer school.

Years and years ago, before it attained its present magisterium, I was one of the regular reviewers on the *Observer*. We used to scramble round Miss Garvin's office trying to make off with the expensive art books. We were far from being dedicated, but we had certain old-fashioned ideas of fair play. One of them was that you did not abuse a book unless you had read it. If a writer got a notice which said 'Mr So-and-so's numerous admirers will find much to enjoy in his latest volume . . .' he could be sure that the reviewer had taken it straight round to the second-hand dealer without opening it. On the other hand if one had wasted a day reading the book, it was fair game. One could revenge oneself for the irksome experience by destroying it piecemeal. These conventions seem not to be observed today.

Mr Wain condemns *French Leave* as a 'poor book'. I wonder how carefully he read it. As I pointed out to him, he entirely failed to notice the existence of one of the subsidiary characters, complaining of 'the absence of any mention of England' when in fact there was the clever caricature of an English civil servant. He had another complaint. 'Mr Wodehouse has slipped up . . . in making him' (the hero) 'an author scrawling away in a garret. That convention has gone out. Starving authors aren't romantic figures any more; they just stand in line with all the other floperoos.' Now the character to which Mr Wain refers was far from starving. He was an industrious freelance, who could not indeed immediately afford to marry, but was able to lend his father substantial sums of money and had already completed a novel which in the course of the narrative became a best-seller. He was moreover a Frenchman living in Paris, where garrets abound. 'Floperoo' is an unfamiliar expression to me.[1] I take it to mean 'failure'. Dr Wodehouse's hero was on the eve of enormous success, but even had he not been, I cannot for the life of me see the force of Mr Wain's complaint. Unsuccessful authors must scrawl away somewhere – attic, basement, mezzanine. What does 'stand in line' mean? Literally queue for the dole?

---

1 'Floperoo' was a P. G. Wodehouse term for a spectacular failure on the stage. Its opposite was a 'socko'. See P. G. Wodehouse and Guy Bolton, *Bring on the Girls* (London, 1954).

And does 'all the other floperoos' refer only to other unsuccessful writers or to failures in every walk of life? No wonder young writers starve if they give up scrawling and just hang about street corners with other unemployed youths.

Perhaps I am doing Mr Wain an injustice but I rather suspect that what he resents is that Mr Wodehouse's hero, although he has not yet reached the heights of reviewing for the *Observer*, has a large and diverse circle of friends. When I was a young floperoo I knew quite a number of successeroos (if that is the correct term) and got on quite well with them. 'That convention,' Mr Wain assures us, 'has gone out.' He believes, I take it, in a strictly stratified society in which Doctors, like Mr Wodehouse, should not consort with Failed BAs like me. That, I think, explains his severe sentence: 'Mr Waugh is not a critic.' If he had said I was not a good critic, I would have understood. But not a critic at all, of any kind?

In a civilized society everyone is a critic. Mr Wain and his young friends have tried to make our flesh creep with revelations of the new barbarism which lurks in academic by-ways. They greatly scared one veteran novelist who accepted the grim picture too literally.[1] But there is really no great cause for alarm. Even in the happiest days of the past it was only a small part of the population who fostered the arts and graces. That world still exists and is the proper milieu of the writer. In that world the most acute and influential criticism is uttered in private conversation by people with no identifiable qualifications. Is Mr Wain totally unaware of the existence of these critics? Does he regard them as imposters because they have not taken classes in English Literature? Does he really believe that one must hold a diploma from some kind of college before one can voice an opinion?

Before he and his friends attempt to introduce rigid trades-unionism in the arts, they might reconsider their own interests. Mr Wain is not only a reviewer on the *Observer*; he is an aspiring novelist and poet. At the moment we have the diverting spectacle of a ship-yard which stands idle because wood-borers and metal-borers cannot decide which of them shall bore holes in composite plates of metal and wood. Literary restrictive practices can only prolong Mr Wain's exile in the territory he seems to find so disagreeable.

---

1 Somerset Maugham had recently abused the new generation of lower-middle-class, university-educated writers in highly offensive terms.

. A REMARKABLE HISTORICAL NOVEL .

> All, all of a piece throughout,
> Thy chase had a beast in view;
> Thy wars brought nothing about;
> Thy lovers were all untrue.

These lines, little quoted fifty years ago, have lately become hackneyed as describing our recent history. They come poignantly to mind in relation to imperial Germany. We cannot complete them:

> 'Tis well an old age is out
> And time to begin a new,

because we know that, in that particular area, everything which came after 1914 was a degradation from its degraded antecedent. The Kaiser's Germany – very much the Kaiser's with his personal omnipresence in private, social and political life, his sharp, press-lord's observation of the high and the humble alike; Berlin, capital of Philistia, gross modern growth among pine and sand, with its savage, perverted military and its gluttonous Jewish bourgeoisie; the south, still with its principalities, its sentimentally Catholic, sentimentally feudal nobility, with their French chatter and their amateurish experiments with the natural sciences – all this is a world far more remote than the Athens of Pericles or the Rome of the Borgias. About this world, written with an air of authority which compels acceptance, a novel has just appeared by a new writer of remarkable accomplishment.

So that this shall not appear as a notice of unrelieved, and therefore perhaps rather dubious, praise, let me state at once where it seems to me to fall short of extreme excellence. There is a certain clumsiness in the telling of the story that reveals the unpractised hand. The time-sequence is unnecessarily disturbed. There was no need, for example, to tell us of Edu's bankruptcy in the first pages; it would have kept. Moreover there is a narrator, a grandchild, who pops her nose into the crack of the door and occasionally, very seldom, addresses us in the first person giving us information she could not possibly have possessed. There is a descent, rather past the middle, where we have too much talk between Sarah and Caroline, as though the author had taken a deep, unaccustomed draught of Henry James and become momentarily intoxicated. There is, to my mind, a slight improbability in the mechanics of the final (pp. 348– 50) catastrophe. There is some theological uncertainty. The remarks (p. 188 and p. 354) given to conventional papists: 'Is it not insisting on error, this making images of what is itself illusion?' and 'It is presumption even to talk of being saved,' properly belong respectively to a Hollywood Buddhist and a despairing Jansenist. But when these few blots have been noted there remains a

Review of *A Legacy*, by Sybille Bedford. *Spectator*, 13 April 1956.

book of entirely delicious quality. The plot is intricate and admirably controlled. The theme is not superficially original; two families vastly dissimilar, the
one Jewish, inartistic millionaires, the other slightly decadent Catholic aristocrats, become joined in marriage. That sort of situation has been employed
often enough before. But here everything is new, cool, witty, elegant, varying
in range from the horrors of Prussian military education to the farce of
monkeys in the Kaiserhof Hotel. The scenes of the baptism of the Jewish
heiress are uproariously funny and totally free of offence to either religion.
There is no hint of (odious, cant word) nostalgia in the book. The lovable,
civilized 'hero' is ruthlessly stripped and exposed. Only Gottlieb, the butler,
maintains his ascendancy uncompromised. The rest are 'all, all of a piece
throughout'; frauds and failures and each event in the elaborate structure has a
direct causal connection with the revelation of them.

We know nothing of the author's age, nationality or religion. But we gratefully salute a new artist.

. A STORY WITH A MORAL .

For forty-five years, the full reading-life of most of us, there has been an
unbroken series of novels by Sir Compton Mackenzie. He has written much
else, but it is primarily as a novelist of great versatility, ranging from high
romance, through satire to farce, that we honour him. This year he has given us
something substantial and new and ambitious; a morality. Everything he writes
sets us an example of elegance and sound workmanship. In *Thin Ice* he points a
moral and an apt one. He has taken as his theme one which, despite the
strenuous discussion it always arouses, has contributed little to English literature: that of the homosexual male.

There are many highly competent English books by homosexuals, but until
very lately their authors cautiously falsified their emotions and experiences by
transposing them into terms of the relations between men and women. Their
influence has been malign, for many young people have got their first ideas of
love from these novels and plays, believing they were reading realistic studies of
the normal processes of sex, when in fact something quite different was being
portrayed.

There is a radical difference between heterosexual and homosexual relationships. It is not, as is often suggested, that one man likes fat women, another
thin, a third prefers young men – a mere question of what constitutes an
attractive 'type'. 'Normality' is certainly an almost meaningless expression.
The absolute norm is an abstraction from which all men vary in greater or less
degree. Moral theologians postulate a Natural Law and from it deduce a code
of the licit and illicit that corresponds very slightly with the common observation of human behaviour. Much that seems 'normal' is forbidden, much that

Review of *Thin Ice*, by Compton Mackenzie. *Sunday Times*, 10 June 1956.

seems repugnant or absurd is allowed. The vagaries of human lust are fully catalogued. They have been publicized and we have become less xenophobic in condemning sexual eccentricity. Indeed, there is a popular tendency to demand 'fair shares' in toleration. 'I didn't choose to be born a sadist. Why shouldn't I have my bit of fun same as anyone else?' We recognize the fallacy in the plea of the child-killer. We tend to accept it in less horrific cases. It is, unless I greatly misread him, Sir Compton's intention to utter a temperate and sage call to order.

'Compassion' is merely the Latin for 'sympathy', but the words have grown far apart. Sir Compton has no sympathy for his hero. He has compassion. He entrusts the narrative to an entirely conventional observer who retains undiminished his youthful affection for the hero even when he fully recognizes the depths under the thin ice on which he cuts his elegant figures.

From Balliol in 1896 until the 'blitz' in 1941 we follow the career of Henry Fortescue, clever, ambitious, well born, well off, one of many 'future prime ministers' who disappoint expectations. Women find him attractive. He is known as a 'woman-hater', which in late Victorian times bore no stigma of unnatural vice. He knows that to disclose his real character would be to ruin his career, so, apart from a single escapade in Morocco, he maintains rigid self-control. His career fails for other reasons. He professes a patriotism, an imperialism, a concentration on foreign affairs and particularly on the affairs of the Levant, for which the politics of this century give little opportunity. It is when he realizes that there is no seat for him in the Cabinet that he becomes first indulgent and then reckless in his lawless pleasures. It is this aspect of lawlessness, with the concomitant of blackmail, which characterizes the life of the homosexual.

Other recent novels, notably *Hemlock and After* and *The Heart in Exile* have given more alarming revelations of this teeming underworld of male prostitution. I suspect that Sir Compton has been to these sources, or to those like them, for his brief glimpses. It is clearly a region as strange and repulsive to him as to his narrator. One scene, the arrest of the politician in Chapter XV, was common gossip during the latter stage of the war. It is delightful to see this highly diverting anecdote, which was unlikely to find its way into the protagonist's reminiscences, so admirably preserved for posterity.

There have been many novels about politicians whose careers were ruined by moral weakness. The theme of *Thin Ice* is more subtle and more significant; that of a man whose moral character is ruined by political failure. For Sir Compton unobtrusively illustrates the neglected truth that every moral and immoral act is an act of will. It is in many ways a great inconvenience (though there are manifest compensations) to have 'unnatural' sexual appetites. In the correspondence which filled the papers lately on this subject, it seemed to be assumed by many writers that temptation and sin were one and the same thing. Sir Compton gently and wisely expounds the deterioration of a human character. When the war comes Fortescue is so set in his vice that although there is now full, distinguished scope for his talents, the narrator can only conclude that his death in an air-raid was a happy deliverance.

The imaginative writing of the old has certain rare and attractive qualities. One is the entry of death. It is not a violent intruder. It is the stranger, half known already, who waits for all. The characters of *Thin Ice* die away one by one with little fuss, though some, the narrator's wife among them, leave permanently bereaved hearts. Her death and that of the hero's brother are accidental, but they *complete* their lives. Fortescue goes out with a bang, unregretted. It is as though the lion, in one of the cautionary tales of childhood, had made his sudden, exemplary pounce. There is another fragrantly old-fashioned feature in the story. Some of the characters improve with age, they grow wiser and kinder and more refined. One does not often see this process recorded in current fiction, though it is not totally unknown in life.

. A POET OF THE COUNTER-REFORMATION .

The century following Cranmer's consecration is unique in our history as being the only period in which any considerable numbers of English had the will and the opportunity to die for their religious beliefs. These beliefs were various, many mere fancies and aberrations. One tenet was common to nearly all: that it was the duty of the civil authority to punish doctrinal error. None of the martyrs, I think, can properly be claimed as suffering for 'freedom of worship'. Neither the brutality of their treatment nor the courage with which they endured it is a measure of the truth of their opinions. During the few years of Robert Southwell's ministry when Roman Catholics were being arrested and executed with intensity, there were other sufferers. Francis Kett (mistakenly dubbed Robert by Father Devlin in the text, and John in the index), the Anglican clergyman whom Burghley caused to be burned at Norwich, proclaimed that Christ and his apostles were at that moment alive in Judea. He died blithely but has left no spiritual progeny to honour him. Nor has William Hacket, the eccentric preacher who had himself crowned as 'King Jesus' in Cheapside. Indeed, I suppose that today it would be impossible to find a bishop and rather difficult to find any communicant member of the Church of England who holds the views for which Latimer was burned.[1] His famous, if

---

Review of *Life of Robert Southwell*, by Christopher Devlin. *Spectator*, 22 June 1956.

[1] The quatercentenary of the Oxford Martyrs occurred on 16 October 1955, and (the then) Professor Hugh Trevor-Roper wrote an article, which was sharply critical of Roman Catholicism, for the occasion: 'The Oxford Martyrs', *Spectator*, 14 October 1955, p.484. Waugh's assertions seem intended as a provocative reply to that article. An acrimonious controversy (not involving Professor Trevor-Roper) followed in the *Spectator* from 29 June to 10 August 1956. This controversy merged into two others on somewhat related matters, and the last (with Professor Trevor-Roper) ended only on 6 October 1956.

spurious, last words have not been fulfilled. But Roman Catholics hold the faith for which their martyrs suffered then, for which in other lands they have suffered and are still suffering, generation after generation. It must not, then, be held against them as tediously rancorous that they rejoice to keep them in remembrance.

The Jesuits in particular are conspicuously industrious in preserving and completing the records of the heroes of their Society. Father Christopher Devlin has made a welcome addition to the series with his *Life of Robert Southwell*, the Elizabethan priest, poet and martyr who has not previously been the subject of a full biography. From his own researches and those of his scholarly predecessors he has assembled all the facts that are known, and supplied an up-to-date and interesting commentary. The records are far from complete. Some conjecture and much ingenious inference were needed to make the story clear. From the detailed and closely argued narrative there emerges a personality of great nobility, intelligence and spirituality.

Southwell was a man, heart and soul, of the Counter-Reformation. In the time of Henry VIII the resistance to the Reformation had been a conservative rear-guard. Campion's generation had seen such rapid changes of royal policy that they were sceptical of any permanent settlement. Each had depended on his own conscience and his own foresight in deciding what sacrifices were required of him. Southwell was twenty years younger than Campion. It was plain in his generation that the Church of Elizabeth and Cecil, though bearing the marks of improvisation, had become a permanent feature of their regime, with which compromise was impossible. Southwell and his fellows were missionaries under an implacably hostile government and they suffered no doubts of the kind which were so variously solved by the generation who took their degrees under Mary Tudor. They were a new generation. 'The greatest number of papists is of very young men,' Burghley wrote to Elizabeth in 1584, with the bitterness of the ageing revolutionary. Parents who themselves had no appetite for sacrifice sent their sons abroad to be educated in the old faith. Southwell was one of these. At the age of 15 he went to the English College at Douay. He came of a rather raffish but influential family. His father was illegitimate but his kinship was acknowledged by many of the leading members of the governing clique. There had been a fortune but it was frittered away in the courts of law. In any age Southwell would have become a priest or monk. His education brought him under the Jesuits and he immediately conceived the ambition to follow the martyrs of the Society into England. His desire for martyrdom was explicit. The aim of his spiritual training was to make himself worthy of this vocation.

The course of Jesuit training is rigorous and uniform, contrived to annihilate self-will while stimulating natural aptitudes, to canalize the whole personality into the service of God by obedience to superiors. It might be expected that the result would be a type. In fact, then and now, the most diverse personalities emerge from the process. John Gerard and William Weston, whose lives have lately been admirably edited by Father Philip Caraman, were contemporaries of Southwell, similarly trained. All three are sharply distinct personalities. There was an undoubted tinge of melancholy in Southwell which never produced lassitude in his active life, but found expression in his poetry. This poetry, privately circulated during his lifetime and later collected and published, enjoyed great contemporary esteem and has found many later admirers. Like his prose, it is in the fashion of his age, not the fashion, perhaps, most sympathetic to modern readers. He was twelve years older than Donne and about the same age as Shakespeare, but he was already in prison when Shakespeare was first talked about. Father Devlin plausibly argues that the greater poet was familiar with his work. The Jesuit noviceship and the life of a priest in hiding are not the best schools for lyric poetry. Southwell's aim was to turn the themes and manners of contemporary love-poetry to edifying ends.

His life as a student, priest and missionary follows the course of his fellows. Father Devlin leads us to the final, inevitable climax through a great accumulation of detail – the rows among the refugees, the spies and adventurers, the priest-holes, the devoted hosts and the traitors, all are now familiar. The determining public events were the Babington plot and the Armada. After 1588 it was plain that there would be no official re-establishment of the old religion. The priest became essentially the sacrificial victim and it was a role to which Southwell ardently aspired. His tortures were particularly savage and this book throws light on the very ugly personal confidence that subsisted between Topcliffe and the Queen. It is no longer possible to represent Elizabeth as innocently blind to what her servants were doing.

Father Devlin's *Life* will be the standard work. I am not sure that I follow his arithmetic on page 60 or the significance of the Plenary Indulgence mentioned on page 70. It is a pity, I think, that he does not always make it clear whether he is translating from the Latin or quoting original English. But the book is a treasury of valuable information. It is not intended to be popular. No doubt a lively epitome will one day be made for general reading.

. MAX BEERBOHM .
A LESSON IN MANNERS

Because of his early precocity and his open old-fashioned scorn of the new royal circle, of the new, popular writers of the Edwardian era, of Arnold Bennett and of H. G. Wells, because of his antiquated elegance in dress, Max Beerbohm came to be regarded as a man of the 1890s. In fact his full flowering was in the 1920s. He wrote little then, but it is the decade of his best collections of essays, of his most brilliant drawings, exhibited at the Leicester Galleries, of the publication of *A Survey* (1921), *Rossetti and his Circle* (1922), *Things New and Old* (1923), *Observations* (1926).

Atlantic, September 1956. First printed *Sunday Times*, 27 May 1956.

He lived abroad, and from being a ubiquitous man-about-town he had become a secluded and exclusive celebrity. On his rare visits to London everyone strove to meet him. I was not one of the young men to whom invitation cards came in great profusion – I was the author of one light novel and a heavy biography – but on one of these later visits I managed to find myself in his company.

To say that I was invited to dine with him by my solicitor gives a wrong impression. I had no solicitor in those happy days. There were no japanned deed cases painted with my name in E. S. P. Haynes's office. He had acted for me, it is true, in a single disagreeable piece of legal business, but he gave me far more in oysters and hock during its transaction than he charged me in fees. He was the most remarkable of solicitors, a man who actually enjoyed the company of literary men of all ages and reputations. A second Watts-Dunton? the reader will ask. Not a second Watts-Dunton. Haynes did not seek to restrain the pleasures of his clients; however extravagant, he applauded and promoted them.

I kept no diary then. I think it must have been in the spring of 1929 that I received the invitation to dine *en famille* in St John's Wood to meet Max Beerbohm. I came with joy, for Max Beerbohm was an idol of my adolescence to whom every year had deepened my devotion. It was my first visit to Mrs Haynes. Hitherto my meetings with Haynes had been in a subterranean bar in Chancery Lane. Now I saw him at home, in a home that might have come straight from the pages of du Maurier's *Punch*; Mr Vandyke Brown ARA at home.

As soon as I entered the drawing-room I realized why I had been asked; I was by far the youngest man present and I was there to provide a lively partner for the youngest Miss Haynes. Everyone else was illustrious, each an idol of mine. It was my first sight of Hilaire Belloc and of Maurice Baring. Either of these on any other night would have been a prodigious treat, but my eyes and ears were for Max. He was very polite and quiet. I stood far off with the youngest Miss Haynes, who had been dandled on the knees of these resplendent beings and regarded them as jolly old buffers. Preposterous to record, she seemed genuinely more interested in me and my friends than in them.

In the dining-room the separation persisted. Max sat far away, and between us hung the barrier of elderly intimacy and allusion. How well everyone talked and how loudly! All save Max. How they laughed and chaffed! What robust vocabularies, what rare knowledge, what exuberant fancies vollied and thundered between me and the object of my devotion! How splendidly lacking they were in any sort of side! What capital good fellows they were! And how Max enjoyed them, and they him! Every now and then with perfect timing, but quite inaudibly to us at the end of the table, the gentle exquisite inserted his contribution. How joyously Belloc and Baring acclaimed him! Admirable wine circulated. I spoke freely to Miss Haynes about Robert Byron and Harold Acton. Then the ladies left us, and the chairs were about to be drawn up when there irrupted two or three youngish men who (with their womenfolk, now in the drawing-room) had been 'asked in later'. Chairs drew apart again. More glasses were brought. The decanter went from hand to hand. It was a memorable evening, but through it all thrilled the faint Panpipe of disappointment. When at length I left I had nothing to remember of Max Beerbohm; a 'Good evening' and a 'Good night'. I returned to the club where I lived, slightly drunk but slightly crestfallen.

It was there that I was vouchsafed a second chance. I found that club a convenient place to sleep, but already my then fast, smart preferences were alienating me from it. It was the genial resort of respectable men of letters, where the spirit of Edmund Gosse still reigned in the morning-room and the younger members seemed mostly to be employed by the BBC. The truth must be told, I felt rather superior to the place. And there in the hall next day at one o'clock, watch in hand, a host evidently expecting a guest, stood Max Beerbohm. He did not wear the tall hat and tubular coat of the Nicholson portrait; he was military rather than aesthetic in his dandyism. But he was smart as paint.

I sidled forward wondering whether to accost him or not. He observed my movement, smiled and held out his hand. I remarked that the previous evening had been very pleasant. He agreed and added that he greatly looked forward to seeing the portrait on which he understood I was at work. He had heard Tonks speak of it with unusual warmth. In that awful moment his friend arrived. I slipped away broken. No luncheon for me that day; rather the Hamam Baths, which in that happy epoch existed for just this purpose – to soothe the wounded heart.

Under that exotic cupola I sprawled and sweated; I plunged into the raftered hall where the bust of 'Sligger's' father gazed down on mobled mankind. I dozed through the afternoon and at sundown had hot buttered toast and whisky and soda. Then, a better man, I returned to the scene of my disaster to dress for the evening.

I was greeted by the porter with a letter addressed – could it be? – in the fine little handwriting which fills the spaces of the famous drawings. How I wish I had kept it! Part of the anarchy which I then professed was a disdain for personal records. I remember the gist but not the inimitable diction. It was an apology. Max Beerbohm was growing old, he said, and his memory played tricks with him. Once in his own youth he had been mistaken by an elder for someone else and the smart troubled him still. He reminded me that he knew my father well and had seconded him in days before I was born for this very club. He said he had read my novel with pleasure. He was on his way back to Italy. Only that prevented him from seeking a further meeting with me.

It was an enchanting document. More exciting still was the thought that, seeing my distress, he had taken the trouble to identify me and make amends.

Good manners were not much respected in the late twenties; not at any rate in the particular rowdy little set which I mainly frequented. They were regarded as the low tricks of the ingratiating underdog, of the climber. The test of a young man's worth was the insolence which he could carry off without mishap. Social outrages were the substance of our anecdotes. And here from a remote and much better world came the voice of courtesy. The lesson of the master.

. SOMETHING FRESH .

This is a complicated, subtle and, to me at least, an intensely interesting first novel. I do not think that it is totally successful. Miss Spark has attempted something very difficult. There are elements of *gaucherie* which a duller, more experienced novelist would have avoided. But at a time when 'experimental' writing has quite justly fallen into disrepute, her book is highly exhilarating.

She has attempted, consciously or unconsciously, to impose one on the other and to combine two distinct themes, each with its own leading character. The first theme is the mechanics of story-telling, the second a case-history of insanity. The result is not easy to describe. First there is a story. A lively, likeable, old-age pensioner of gypsy descent lives alone in a Sussex cottage. She will accept no help from her daughter who is married to a prosperous, pious merchant. Her grandson, a man of indecent curiosity improbably employed as a sport-commentator on the wireless, is curious to know how she 'manages'. He discovers that she is the head of a gang of jewel-smugglers who use preposterously elaborate means of secrecy. Here, baldly stated, is the germ of a conventional mystery story. The plot thickens to inspissation. For no plausible reason the chief agents of the gang are the husband and son of a protégée of the daughter, once employed as the detective-grandson's nursery governess. The London agent is a bookseller, a Belgian baron with black blood and an interest in black magic, who has been the lover of the bigamous wife of the first agent. This wife is also the business partner of the homosexual brother of the pious, prosperous son-in-law. Moreover, the first nursery-governess wife turns up as matron of the hostel to which the former mistress of the detective-grandson is sent when she is received into the Church from which he has apostatized. It is all rather absurd and, I presume, is meant to be absurd. The point is that the mechanics of story-telling operate in the same way for absurd as for plausible stories. The interest is in the relationship between author and character. Every novelist, good or bad, must know the odd stages of intimacy and independence in which he deals with his 'creations'. Sometimes he is drawing directly on his own experience, recording what he has observed of men and women about him; usually his experiences have become so digested in the imagination that no identifiable portrait results. Sometimes he is in control, forcing his characters

Review of *The Comforters*, by Muriel Spark. *Spectator*, 22 February 1957.

into situations convenient for his theme. Sometimes the characters assume responsibility and he finds himself following them anxious and bewildered many paces behind. During composition extraneous elements intrude and are sometimes accepted, sometimes extruded. Miss Spark reveals the whole process. The importance to the various members of the family of the grandmother's nefarious activities gives reality to the artificial construction. Her theme enables her to assemble a brilliant series of passages describing the manners and customs of modern English Roman Catholics.

Now comes the feature which makes *The Comforters* such difficult and such rewarding reading. The narrator is the neurotic ex-mistress of the detective-grandson. Between them there subsists love and loyalty which will eventually result in marriage. Meanwhile the narrator, herself an important character in the story, goes off her head. The area of her mind which is composing the novel becomes separated from the area which is participating in it, so that, hallucinated, she believes that she is observant of, observed by, and in some degree under the control of, an unknown second person. In fact she is in the relation to herself of a fictitious character to a story-teller. It so happens that *The Comforters* came to me just as I had finished a story on a similar theme[1] and I was struck by how much more ambitious was Miss Spark's essay and how much better she had accomplished it.

When I say that she is not totally successful, I mean that, though every page is of vivid interest, there is, or so it seems to me, some confusion between the real and the actual. There is, for instance, at the end, a death which gets into the papers and is the subject of legal inquiry, which can only be the fantasy of the narrator's disordered mind. It is never quite clear in which world, that of the novel or that of actuality, each event occurs. The only book I can think of which has any affinity with this is *Cards of Identity*. That was in many ways more elegantly written, but it had a basic futility which *The Comforters* escapes. Throughout all the narrator's aberrations she has a fixed point of reference in her religious faith. Real sacrilege (or the idea of it) shocks her in quite a different way from her imagined terrors, and the obligation of following the rudimentary discipline of her faith is more compelling than the desire to evade the control of the imaginary director.

I fear I have given a most inadequate account of this very difficult book. In spite of its basic obscurity the surface is alight with happy passages. The scallywags who, mostly, comprise the cast are deliciously portrayed. It is a thoroughly *enjoyable* work. I can't think, by the way, why it is called *The Comforters*.

---

1 *The Ordeal of Gilbert Pinfold* (1957).

. RANDOLPH'S FINEST HOUR .

No one who knows Mr Randolph Churchill and wishes to express distaste for him should ever be at a loss for words which would be both opprobrious and apt. When, in May 1955, the *People* described him as 'chief among' those who 'have not seen fit to fight openly for seats but prefer to be paid hacks, paid to write biased accounts of the campaign' (the general election), they attacked a man who had made himself obnoxious to them, in one of the rather few places in which he was entirely impregnable. It was a preposterous comment which in the slow processes of the law at last brought them into the courts in October 1956. Any man, and particularly a poor man, who has the courage to risk his money and expose himself to cross-examination in order to defend his reputation against the misrepresentations of the rich and powerful press is sure of a sympathetic hearing. Mr Churchill was awarded £5,000 and it was a very popular win indeed. Now he has published a full account of the affair.

It all, in Mr Churchill's chronology, dates back to September 1953, when he was asked to propose the health of the editor of the *Daily Mirror* at a public luncheon. Mr Churchill, rather than refuse, took the opportunity to arraign the guest of honour and a number of absent newspaper proprietors on the charge of pornography. I wish I had been there. It sounded a first-class joke. But apparently it was the first skirmish in a holy war which Mr Churchill felt himself inspired to lead and he was much annoyed to find that *The Times* newspaper did not take him seriously. Off he went to Manchester next month and amplified his charges before the Publicity Association. Still no report in *The Times*. He issued his two speeches as a pamphlet. W. H. Smith and Sons refused to sell it. Back he went to Fleet Street in November and preached to the Forum. There was, he believed, a conspiracy to silence him. That is always the complaint of the crank, but in this matter Mr Churchill had an important and popular cause. I think he makes a plausible case.

Mr Ainsworth, the editor of the *People*, was one of the men whom Mr Churchill named as a leading pornographer. Nineteen months later Mr Ainsworth libelled him in the singularly infelicitous terms quoted above. Fifteen months later he, or someone else, paid £5,000 for his clumsiness.

Throughout the two days' trial the rival barristers exchanged the customary polite references to one another's brilliant advocacy, but to the lay reader it seems that the deciding factors were Mr Ainsworth's diffidence in appearing personally – a fastidiousness in sharp contrast to his literary activities – and Mr Churchill's exuberant and dominating eloquence. Indeed, he set an example of style and diction to both counsel. Mr Fearnley-Whittingstall, in opening, spoke of 'nailing a lie to the mast' and began his final speech with the cryptic exclamation, 'Yo ho ho and a bottle of rum tactics.' Mr Gilbert Paull, in his final speech for the defence, said: 'It was not the attacks on Mr Ainsworth that

Review of *What I Said about the Press*, by Randolph Churchill. *Spectator*, 22 March 1957.

got his (Mr Ainsworth's) goat,' while Mr Churchill, in the sustained oration which, with occasional prompting from the cross-examining counsel, comprised his performance in the box, never strayed from the thin second growth of the Augustan grove save to penetrate at moments into the solid wood which his father frequents. There is even at times a touch of the fire and precision of Hilaire Belloc. Sometimes poor Mr Paull edged in a word and got soundly snubbed. '*Q*.: Is it criminal to call you a hack? *A*.: I am not suggesting it is criminal – this is a civil action, Mr Paull.' Even the judge received scant attention at times. '*Q*.: I am suggesting to you that the language shows a complete lack of – *A*.: You would rather I wrote what people like – Mr Justice Jones: Let counsel finish the question. *The Witness*: You were complaining about the language I used, etc.' [My italics.]

Unable to call any witness for the defence, Mr Paull resorted to the futile expedient of searching Mr Churchill's other writings in order to show him as equally intemperate as Mr Ainsworth. Mr Churchill firmly kept him to the issue that he complained, not of the violence of Mr Ainsworth's language, but of the falsehood of the allegations. Poor Mr Paull made a sad show of pretending to take with great seriousness expressions that were patently ironical or facetious. In the Punch-and-Judy dialogue Mr Churchill scored every time. It was his own personal triumph. But, reading it, one is left at the end with a certain disgust.

Mr Churchill got his damages. Counsel and solicitors got their fees. The jury dispersed, no doubt, with satisfaction at seeing justice done and a rich, unlovely commercial undertaking lose some of its huge profits. But who, one wonders, really pays? Mr Churchill's is one among a crop of recent libel actions,[1] some trivial, some, like the Duke of Norfolk's, very grave, in which heavy damages have been awarded. But do the libellers ever suffer at all? Libel can be a graver delinquency than pornography. Nearly twenty years ago a bright, young magazine, *Night and Day*, was ruined and extinguished by a libel action brought by a rich corporation.

Does anyone in the modern world of the great newspapers experience the slightest setback in his profession, does any journalist, editor or owner smoke a single cigarette the fewer as the penalty for his nasty and illegal practices? The time, I think, is ripe for the restoration of the pillory.

. UNSOLVED MYSTERY .

It has long been known to the almost limitless circle of his acquaintances that Mr Douglas Woodruff was preparing a treatise on the Tichborne case. Others

---

1 Waugh had won a libel action against Nancy Spain and the Beaverbrook press on 20 February 1957.

Review of *The Tichborne Claimant: A Victorian Mystery*, by Douglas Woodruff. *Spectator*, 21 June 1957.

have started later and finished before him. In 1899¹ when the great project was a mere germ in his precocious young mind, Mr J. B. Atlay produced a legal study, mainly of the first, civil action. In 1936 when Mr Woodruff's researches were well advanced, Lord Maugham published a further book, again concentrating mainly on the civil action and examining its records in the assumption that justice was done but done at far too great cost of time and money. Mr Woodruff worked on in the intervals of his other multifarious activities quite undiscouraged, slowly amassing more and more quaint details which had escaped the notice of his brisk, professional rivals. Some observers doubted whether the great work would ever be completed. Now it is before us and it is a splendid monument to his perseverance and skill. Some slight internal evidence of haste may be found in the present edition; the five corrigenda which disfigure the table of contents are a small part of the misprints; there are occasional repetitions and infelicities of diction which patient revision will correct. It is to be hoped that they are receiving attention, for this book is certain to be the final, classic account of the case.

And what a case it was, fascinating in every aspect!

The Tichbornes are genealogically one of the most illustrious families in the country. Horace Round admitted them to his tiny circle of genuine, ancient pedigrees. In the middle of the last century they were rich, having added to their original estates in Hampshire valuable London property of their distant connections the Doughties. There was, however, a paucity of male heirs. Three brothers in turn succeeded to the baronetcy. The third had two sons, Roger and Alfred. Roger was believed to have been lost at sea; Alfred, having succeeded, died in 1866, leaving a posthumous son during whose infancy the estates were being held in trust, when there appeared from Wagga Wagga in Australia a man claiming to be the lost uncle Roger. He arrived in England on Christmas Day 1866. It was not until 10 May 1871 that his case opened. It occupied the courts for 103 sittings until 6 March 1872 and cost the Tichborne family £92,000. The defence plausibly identified the claimant with a Wapping butcher named Orton. The claimant was then committed for perjury and after another enormously protracted trial he was sentenced to seven years on two counts, the terms to run consecutively. He was released on ticket-of-leave in 1884 and lived until 1898 still asserting his claim.

Mr Woodruff lucidly arranges the complex of conflicting evidence, but even under his witty guidance there are stiff passages. To the juries, particularly that of the civil case which had been carefully selected from among the educated and responsible, the burden of listening day after day was intolerable, and it is plain that they cut it short out of sheer boredom and exasperation at the first moment when a piece of conclusive evidence seemed to be before them.

On the claimant's first appearance he was recognized and accepted by his

---

1 Woodruff was born in 1897, and Atlay's book was published in 1917. Presumably the date should read 1917.

mother, the family doctor, the solicitor, many old servants, neighbours and tenants, by officers and men who had served with Roger in the Carabineers. Apart from his mother, the family instantly rejected him even before they had examined his claim. It was not only the fortune that was at stake, it was family honour. The claimant was vulgarly unprepossessing, disreputable, probably criminal, and he was married to a totally illiterate woman who had already borne an illegitimate daughter to another man. Moreover, he was irreligious and his occasional ludicrous attempts to employ the language of the family's faith – he subscribed a letter to his mother, 'May Blessed Maria have mercy on your soul' – showed that he was completely out of touch with it. This injection of Popery into the affair was the source of much of the claimant's popularity. It was the *idée fixe* of Dr Kenealy, who got himself debarred by the violence of his defence in the criminal trial. It was a strong influence on the two or three Members of Parliament who consistently supported him. The claimant was for a long time the hero of the newly enfranchised lower class whose discontent had not yet been canalized into orthodox socialism. They had a deep, inarticulate resentment against a system of law which seemed to be organized expressly to preserve the propertied classes. A later generation of working men would not be particularly concerned to restore a lost aristocrat to his possessions. But class-consciousness in mid-Victorian times was more capricious. Hard words were spoken at the trial about butchers; much scorn was poured on the claimant for his plebeian traits. To the common people it seemed that a man like themselves was being persecuted simply because he was like themselves. And in the background there continually flitted the sinister, black figures of the Jesuits. So great was the popular excitement that Dr Kenealy got into Parliament well over the heads of the two orthodox candidates as the champion of the claimant. Hence, partly, the extremely severe sentence at the criminal trial. Cockburn[1] had prejudged the case and imprudently expressed his opinions before he came to judge it and he was resolved that the case should end in his court.

The propertied classes had every reason to feel alarm. None of them would be safe if they were at the mercy of adventurers who might claim their possessions and leave them vindicated no doubt but crippled by costs. Normally such impostors were kept from the courts by the expense, but the claimant had devised the expedient of selling bonds at a discount, promising to pay 100 per cent or more interest on money lent him in the event of his success. If that became a practice, no one was secure. Worse still, the claimant made the assertion, wantonly false, it seemed, and abominable even if true, that he had seduced his first cousin, now a respectably married woman. This particularly outraged decent opinion and explains much of the strong language used from the bench. Thus for more than a decade the case became one of national importance, with some affinities to the Dreyfus case but with two vital differ-

---

1 Lord Cockburn, Waugh's great-great-grandfather.

ences: the Dreyfusards had all the money they needed and Dreyfus was certainly innocent. The claimant was penniless and probably guilty.

Mr Woodruff has taken as subtitle: *A Victorian Mystery*, and his great contribution to the literature of the subject is to demonstrate that it is still a mystery, not the cut-and-dried exposure of an impudent fraud as is generally supposed. Coleridge, who led for the family in the civil case, described the claimant as 'the cleverest man' he had ever met in the courts. This opinion is baffling, for during the 35,000 questions of his cross-examination he seems to reveal himself as a booby. Though of medium height, he weighed nearly twenty-eight stone, drank heavily and was afflicted by a tape-worm; these physical disabilities may account for the daze in which he seems to have been enveloped. Cockburn remarked that it would be paradoxical to evince his ignorance of Roger Tichborne's youth as evidence of his honesty. It is nevertheless inexplicable that if he were the scheming criminal he was represented as being he should have neglected to inform himself on matters that were easily accessible. He went to Preston, for example, and did not trouble to visit Stonyhurst where he claimed to have been at school. His answers when questioned about his schooldays were preposterous. On the other hand, he did seem to remember a number of odd and unimportant details which could not possibly have been known to a Wapping butcher who had never met Roger Tichborne. The identification of the claimant with Orton leaves as many discrepancies and improbabilities as with Roger Tichborne.

Cockburn's summing up was pure advocacy. He was determined that the punishment should be exemplary and that the case should never be reopened. Nor was it, despite a steady trickle of evidence which seemed to tell in the claimant's favour. There was a lunatic in Australia, shut up under the name of Cresswell, who might have been Orton. Men wrote in to say that there *had* been survivors from the shipwreck in which Roger Tichborne was supposed to have perished. Other evidence suggested that the master had stolen the ship and sailed into Australia under a false name. There was a close connection between the claimant and bush-ranging. Were Orton, the claimant and Castro two men or three men or one man? Did Tichborne shoot Orton, or Orton Tichborne? In the Australia of the sixties men were known by nicknames and borrowed and discarded surnames indifferently. There was a great deal of shooting and stealing. The claimant clearly had a shady past. He may innocently have supposed that no questions would be asked about it and finally have had to face the alternative of a conviction for perjury or for some much graver crime in Australia.

The dissipated, despondent Roger Tichborne who is revealed in his letters had moods of self-disgust when he wished to disappear. If he survived the voyage in the *Bella* it is quite in keeping with his character that he should have been content to remain dead until his continued financial failure and the prospect of fatherhood made him think once more of home.

It is not to be expected that anything further will transpire. Mr Woodruff has provided a magnificent encyclopaedia of the whole incident which will kindle the imagination and curiosity of generations of readers.

. OP. XV .

It is more than thirty years since Miss Compton-Burnett published her first novel and revealed to the world her brilliant and peculiar talent. If my memory serves the revelation was gradual. No prominent critic trumpeted his 'discovery' of her. There was no dizzy succession of reprints. Her renown spread in intimate, fastidious circles as each reader sought to communicate and share his delight. I who lived (and live) rather far from fastidious circles was not drawn into the almost secret society of her admirers until the publication of *Brothers and Sisters* in 1929. Since then I have remained steadfastly devoted, but because of the impact of first love *Brothers and Sisters* has for me a unique eminence and I tend to regard it as quintessential of her art. Not that there has been any great change in her matter or manner. She has established her own enclosed garden in which in due season her flowers unfold, each perfectly true to type and almost identical. I have never got on with Professor Tolkien's 'Hobbits'. Those who do, I presume, enjoy something of the same experience as the readers of Miss Compton-Burnett, the entry into a timeless Wonderland directed by its own interior logic, not distorting, because not reflecting, the material world.

Miss Compton-Burnett's readers have now, I think, greatly multiplied. I wonder whom they comprise. Her fellow-writers certainly, for her technical skill is masterly. In the thirties a number of English novelists, reacting perhaps against the vogue for Proust, sought to tell their stories as much as possible in dialogue. Mr Henry Green is one of the most notable of these but he quite often allows himself the luxury of rich and poetic descriptive passages. Miss Compton-Burnett austerely restricts herself to the minimum of bare stage directions. She is the least sensuous of writers. There is no flavour of food or wine, no scene-painting of landscape or architecture, no costume, no visual image even of the characters; ages are stated; height, bulk, strength or infirmity gently suggested; sometimes a moustache or a beard is mentioned, but there is never anything approaching a portrait. In her latest novel, *A Father and His Fate*, one character only is given a line or two of physical description and that because she is a newcomer and therefore remarkable in the close family circle.

The family is the theme of all Miss Compton-Burnett's creation, men and women who have grown up together knowing one another, and no one else, so intimately that huge assumptions are accepted unexpressed and the continuous conversation is allusive. 'No one can speak in this house without meaning

Review of *A Father and His Fate*, by Ivy Compton-Burnett. *Spectator*, 16 August 1957.

too much,' says one of the characters in her latest book. The reader must guess what statements are frank, what are ironical. Most are ironical. These families live in an unspecified era before the invention of motor-cars and telephones. Sometimes they are bourgeois, more often gentry. All live in the country in substantial houses, with plenty of servants and governesses and 'companions'. Domination is the theme; the subservience of those born to be paid to those born to pay – 'You could not have had a better mistress.' 'No, sir, as I am called to a position that entails one.' – the subservience of women to men, of poor relations to their benefactors; the subservience of all to one imposing matriarch or patriarch. Nothing that happens outside the household has any real exis-tence. Miss Compton-Burnett's usual plot is an intrusion from the outer world which threatens the stability of the family.

The plot of *A Father and His Fate* runs true. The father, in the big house, has three daughters; his brother's widow in the dower-house has three sons, the eldest of whom, Malcolm, is his heir. Enter a disruptive orphan. Malcolm becomes engaged to her. The Father and Mother leave for a journey abroad. Anything may happen outside the defences of home. In fact a curious ship-wreck occurs from which the Father returns without the Mother. Father takes Malcolm's orphan. Mother returns, not drowned, but living on an allowance of banknotes anonymously sent her from a neighbouring village. The orphan is sent back to marry Malcolm. She does so, but reveals that Father has been paying Mother to keep away. She has a baby, Father's not Malcolm's, disap-pears; Malcolm marries Father's daughter. Baldly stated the plot is rather absurd – as indeed are the plots of most works of art. Related by Miss Compton-Burnett in conversation (almost all the action takes place offstage) it is irresistibly beguiling. It is often said by both admirers and detractors that her dialogue is unprecedented and inimitable. There is, however, one popular English book, first published in 1913, which has a remarkable affinity. The plot is a numerous family in a large country house with an odd butler, a ridiculous tutor, a disinherited half-brother and a lost will. This is how they speak:

'I cannot think it dutiful of you, Dorothea, to call either your parents or myself *passing old* or *tough*. I don't see what comfort you could expect us to find in such epithets. . . .'

'I am only thinking of what the servants would say.'

'You will not hear what their servants say, Emily.'

'But I shall know they are saying it all the same. . . .'

'Emily,' said Mr Chubb in agitated tones to his sister-in-law, 'are you aware that your back hair is all caked in mud?'

'No, Thomas, I was not; and I think it very unkind of you to tell me. Now I shan't be able to enjoy my lunch for thinking of it.'

'It is not noticeable from the sides or from the front so no one at table will be able to perceive it.'

'But it is not that I care about. The servants will all be standing behind me.

You must take the first opportunity to mention our accident, Thomas.'

Try those extracts on one of Miss Compton-Burnett's admirers. Then tell her that they are from Mrs Henry de la Pasture's *The Unlucky Family*.

. ANYTHING WRONG WITH PRIESTLEY? .

In the *New Statesman* of 31 August Mr J. B. Priestley published an article entitled 'What was wrong with Pinfold?' 'Pinfold', I should explain, is the name I gave to the leading character of my last book, a confessedly autobiographical novel which had already been reviewed (very civilly) in the literary columns of that curiously two-faced magazine. The contrast is notorious between the Jekyll of culture, wit and ingenious competitions and the Hyde of querulous atheism and economics which prefaces it. Mr Priestley's article appeared in Hyde's section. He is not concerned to help me with my writing, as he is so well qualified to do, but to admonish me about the state of my soul, a subject on which I cannot allow him complete mastership. With 'Let Pinfold take warning' he proclaims in prophetic tones, and with the added authority of some tags from Jung, that I shall soon go permanently off my rocker. The symptoms are that I try to combine two incompatible roles, those of the artist and the Catholic country gentleman.

Which of those dangers to the artistic life, I wonder, does he regard as the more deadly. Not living in the country, surely? Unless I am misinformed Mr Priestley was at my age a landed proprietor on a scale by which my own modest holding is a peasant's patch.

Catholicism? It is true that my Church imposes certain restrictions which Mr Priestley might find irksome, but he must have observed that a very large number of his fellow writers profess a creed and attempt to follow a moral law which are either Roman Catholic or, from a Jungian point of view, are almost identical. Mr T. S. Eliot, Dame Edith Sitwell, Mr Betjeman, Mr Graham Greene, Miss Rose Macaulay – the list is illustrious and long. Are they all heading for the bin?

No, what gets Mr Priestley's goat (supposing he allows such a deleterious animal in his lush pastures) is my attempt to behave like a gentleman. Mr Priestley has often hinted at a distaste for the upper classes but, having early adopted the *persona* of a generous-hearted, genial fellow, he has only once, I think, attempted to portray them. On that occasion, of which more later, he showed a rather remote acquaintance, like Dickens in creating Sir Mulberry Hawke. It is the strain of minding his manners that is driving poor Pinfold cuckoo. 'He must,' writes Mr Priestley, 'be at all times the man of ideas, the

Spectator, 13 September 1957. On 14 September a *Times* leader deplored this row.

intellectual, the artist, even if he is asked to resign from Bellamy's Club' (a fictitious institution that occurs in some of my books). Mr Priestley's clubs must be much stricter than mine. Where I belong I never heard of the committee inquiring into the members' 'ideas'. It is true that we are forbidden to cheat at cards or strike the servants, but for the life of me I can't see anything particularly artistic in either of those activities.

Naturally I hunger for Mr Priestley's good opinion and would like to keep my sanity for a few more years. I am an old dog to learn new tricks but I dare say I could be taught an accent at a school of elocution. I should not find it beyond me to behave like a cad on occasions – there are several shining examples in the literary world. My hair grows strongly still; I could wear it long. I could hire a Teddyboy suit and lark about the dance halls with a bicycle chain. But would this satisfy Mr Priestley? Would he not be quick to detect and denounce this new *persona*? 'There was Waugh,' he would say, 'a man of humane education and accustomed to polite society. Tried to pass as Redbrick. No wonder he's in the padded cell.'

I do not flatter myself that Mr Priestley's solicitude springs solely from love of me. What, I think, really troubles him is that by my manner of life I am letting down the side, all eleven of them whoever they are whom Mr Priestley captains. 'If authors and artists in this country,' he writes, 'are not only officially regarded without favour but even singled out for unjust treatment – as I for one believe – then the Pinfolds are partly to blame. They not only do not support their profession; they go over to the enemy.'

I say, Priestley old man, are you sure you are feeling all right? Any Voices? I mean to say! No narcotics or brandy in your case, I know, but when a chap starts talking about 'the enemy' and believing, for one, that he is singled out for unjust treatment, isn't it time he consulted his Jungian about his *anima*? Who is persecuting poor Mr Priestley? Mr Macmillan does not ask him to breakfast as Gladstone might have done. His income, like everyone else's, is confiscated and 'redistributed' in the Welfare State. Tennyson's life was made hideous by importunate admirers; Mr Priestley can walk down Piccadilly with a poppy or a lily, but he will be unmolested by the mob who pursue television performers. Is this what Mr Priestley means by unjust treatment? Pinfold, he says, is vainly waiting for a message from Bonnie Prince Charlie. Is it possible that Mr Priestley is awaiting a summons to Windsor from Queen Victoria?

Mr Priestley is an older, richer, more popular man than I, but I cannot forbear saying: 'Let him take warning.' He has had some sharp disappointments in the last twelve years; perhaps he would call them 'traumas'. The voices he hears, like Pinfold's, may be those of a wildly distorted conscience. There was, indeed, a *trahison des clercs* some twenty years back which has left the literary world much discredited. It was then that the astute foresaw the social revolution and knew who would emerge top dog. They went to great lengths to suck up to the lower classes or, as they called it, to 'identify themselves with the workers.' Few excelled Mr Priestley in his zeal for social justice. It is instructive to reread his powerful novel *Blackout in Gretley*, which was written at a very dark time in the war when national unity was of vital importance. Its simple theme is that the English upper classes were in conspiracy to keep the workers in subjection even at the cost of national defeat. The villain, Tarlington, is everything deplorable, a man of good family and of smart appearance, a Conservative, the director of an engineering works, a courageous officer in 1914 – and, of course, a German spy. *Blackout in Gretley* is like *The Hill* in reverse; all morals derive from social origin. The police are a fine body of men but the chief constables are Fascist beasts. Two attractive women in the same fast set are equally suspect; but one turns out to have been a disorderly waitress before her respectable marriage; she has a heart of gold. The other is the niece of Vice-Admiral Sir Johnson Fund-Tapley and, of course, a traitor. Only two workers show moral delinquency; of these one turns out to be a German officer in disguise; the other, and more wicked, is – a Roman Catholic. Even the bad food at the hotel is ascribed to the fact that it is managed by a retired officer. 'This country has the choice during the next two years,' a virtuous character says, 'of coming fully to life and beginning all over again or of rapidly decaying and dying on the same old feet. It can only accomplish the first by taking a firm grip on about 50,000 important, influential gentlemanly persons and telling them firmly to shut up and do nothing if they don't want to be put to doing some most unpleasant work.'

Came the dawn. Mr Priestley was disappointed. No concentration camp was made for the upper classes. Nor have the triumphant workers shown themselves generous or discerning patrons of the arts. Gratitude, perhaps, is not one of their salient virtues. When they feel the need for a little aesthetic pleasure they do not queue at the experimental theatre; they pile into charabancs and tramp round the nearest collection of heirlooms and family portraits; quite enough to inflame the naked artist with an itch of persecution mania.

. SAHIBS AND SOLDIERS .

The First Hundred Thousand was not strictly a novel but it was unmistakably the work of a novelist. 'The characters are entirely fictitious,' said the author's note, 'but the incidents described all actually happened.' Was it, I wonder, the first book of its kind; one which, instead of a single hero, portrayed a group and, instead of a plot, described the behaviour of this heterogeneous group in a common predicament; an invention which the film-makers were to adopt fifteen years later when they struck a mean between story and newsreel in the planned and rehearsed 'documentary'?

'Retrospective view' of *The First Hundred Thousand*, by Ian Hay ('Best-Sellers of the Century – 15'). *Observer*, 6 April 1958.

One writes of the book in the past tense for it is now out of print and few people under the age of 50 can have read it. In 1915 and 1916 it heartened a considerable part of the nation, schoolboys and aunts predominantly, but front-line soldiers too. Its successors, *Carrying On* (1917) and *The Last Million* (1918) appeared in a world where propaganda was already recognized as a function of the state; they lacked the innocence and spontaneity of these early sketches taken in the off-hours of active soldiering. *The First Hundred Thousand* was a highly professional version of the thousands of inadequate, inarticulate letters which were being written home from training-camp and trench. It told people everything they wanted to know, in a tone they wanted to hear, about the routine and accidents of what was then an entirely unfamiliar manner of life.

Ian Hay (Beith) was already a popular novelist when he joined 'Kitchener's Army'. *Pip* and *A Knight on Wheels* were triumphs of healthy, prosaic, middle-class, humorous romance with an affinity to the works of Mr P. G. Wodehouse in his early years before the afflatus of fantasy carried him into Literature. One is apt to think nowadays of Kitchener's Army as being composed of very young men. Ian Hay was 36 when he was commissioned in the Argyll and Sutherland Highlanders, too old to see the war out as a regimental soldier, but in a very happy place for observation during the first year, midway between the senior officers who had seen service in South Africa and the recruits fresh from civilian life. He had, moreover, some military experience as commanding officer of a public school OTC. He had therefore particular advantages in recording the humours and sorrows of his battalion from its first shambling round the barrack square without arms or uniforms until its decimation at Loos.

The first year of the First World War is laid out as in the pages of *Punch*. As in *Punch*, serious cartoons are interspersed among the jokes. There is the prevalent genial contempt for politicians, particularly for pacifists and radicals and trade unionists, which grows indignant but never savage as the dangers and endurances of active service thicken. Discipline is irksome to those who in civilian life have 'had at their beck and call a Radical MP who, in return for their votes and suffrage, had informed them that they were the backbone of the nation and must on no account permit themselves to be trampled upon by the effete and tyrannical upper classes.'

One of the officers has been the prospective Conservative candidate for a safe Liberal seat:

> My opponent [he says], whose strong suit for the last twenty years has been to cry down the horrors of militarism and the madness of national service and the unwieldy size of the British Empire, is now compelled to spend his evenings taking the chair at mass meetings for the encouragement of recruiting. On these occasions I always send him a telegram he has to read out on the platform. . . . *All success to the meeting and best thanks to you personally for carrying on in my absence.*

Former miners are digging trenches under fire:

At home several thousand patriotic Welshmen . . . were going on strike for a further increase of pay. . . . It was one of the strangest contrasts that the world has ever seen. But the explanation thereof, as proffered by Private Mucklewame, was quite simple and eminently sound. 'All the decent lads are oot here.'

As in *Punch* of the time, there is fervent loyalty to the Crown. Private M'Slattery, an insubordinate soldier, is permanently reformed by a Royal inspection. An officer in the front line says:

I can't say I have ever noticed Staff Officers crowding into the trenches at four o'clock in the morning. If I ever do meet one performing such a feat I shall say: 'There goes a sahib – and a soldier! and I shall take off my hat to him.' 'Well, get ready now,' said Bobby. 'Look.' Two figures in the uniform of the Staff are picking their way amid the tumbled sand-bags. One was burly and middle-aged. His companion was slight, fair-haired and looked incredibly young. The younger officer – he was a lieutenant – noticed Captain Blaikie and saluted him gravely. Captain Blaikie did not take his hat off as he had promised. Instead he stood suddenly to attention and saluted, keeping his hand uplifted until the slim, childish figure had disappeared round the corner of the traverse. It was the Prince of Wales.

Pure Bernard Partridge, no doubt, but with the difference that the foregoing observations were not chosen at the table in Bouverie Street but on active service. It was Ian Hay's peculiar strength and weakness to see and feel in all sincerity precisely what the patriotic part of the country wished to see and feel.

The frontispiece of *The First Hundred Thousand* makes no concession to the art of Bruce Bairnsfather whose 'Old Bill' was already one nationally accepted, unromantic version of the fighting man. It shows a kilted regiment swinging along in column of fours. Highlanders are always rather dear to many English hearts. Ian Hay made full appeal to this sentiment. A chieftain dies gallantly. Private soldiers when they forget orders say: 'I canna mind. I had it all fine just noo, but it's awa' oot o' ma heid.' All the fun (and it is, in various forms, a persistent element in English humour) that can be wrung from otherwise commonplace sayings being put into dialect is here used to adorn the jokes of army life.

These jokes differ little from one war to another, or from one regiment to another. It is highly laughable at the time when the sergeant-major scores a 'possible' on the wrong target; when the Pay Corps credits a subaltern with 1s. 4d. field allowance on the grounds that, when he shared his room in barracks, one half of him must have slept out; when another subaltern salutes a military policeman in mistake for a general; when a facetious company commander posts a parody of orders in the ante-room when the colonel is out to dinner; when the field telephone fails (in training); when the French liaison officer inquires about English politics. These things delighted Kitchener's Army as they delighted the conscripts of the Second World War. Do they bear transcription? In Ian Hay's case I think that up to a point they do. They have the confident gusto and topicality of the very best, second-class raconteur.

As the story approaches its climax it becomes more exciting. The schoolmasterly tendency to issue terminal reports – 'We are now as fit for active service as seven months' relentless schooling can render us. We shall have to begin all over again, we know, when we find ourselves up against the real thing, but at least we have been thoroughly grounded in the rudiments. . . . We have ceased to regard obedience as a degradation . . . etc' – is suppressed and an appreciable air of suspense is created before the battle. The battle itself is authentic. Why then is the book out of print? Why does one not advise the young to read it or seek to present it as a forgotten period piece?

The fault lies in its soldierly qualities. Everything in it is conducive to good order and military discipline. The funny books of the Second War were mostly written about the slums of the Army. The heroes of Mr Alan Hackney and Mr Maclaren-Ross have no regimental spirit; they regard their officers as lunatics and crooks: they have no wish to 'do their bit' or 'carry on'. They contribute nothing to their country's victory. But they are deliciously funny, especially to those who were more fortunate in their military adventures.

Ian Hay's heroes are the stuff that won the war, but Ian Hay's mind was too commonplace to discern more than their soldierly qualities. Mild eccentricities they have, both officers and men, but the theme of the book is that these eccentricities can be tamed and directed to the common good. The colonel says of them: 'They're a rough crowd and a tough crowd: but they're a stout crowd. By gad! we'll make them a credit to the Old Regiment yet.'

Ian Hay with all sincerity was occupied with being a credit. It happens that in the last month I have been reading (in the course of writing a biography) a large collection of letters written in 1914 and 1915 by twenty-odd unusually intelligent ex-undergraduates in Kitchener's Army to an Oxford don. Only one, it is true, was a Highlander, but all were in regiments with long-established pride – the Foot Guards, the Rifle Brigade, the 60th, the county infantry. Most of the writers died gallantly, but I find in their letters something very much more familiar than I found in *The First Hundred Thousand*. They are more acrimonious, more despondent, more concerned with leave and old friends, more critical of fellow subalterns and chaplains, more conscious of the proximity of death than any of the 'Bruce and Wallace Highlanders'. Ian Hay represented the least interesting heroes and victims of the First World War.

. HANDS OFF SMITH .

The Dictionary of National Biography with all its few defects is an essential part of the writer's professional equipment. It is also a series of beguiling bedside books. Logan Pearsall Smith (whose memoir is not one of the best features of the latest volume – surely some sharper definition could have been found for

Review of *Dictionary of National Biography 1941–1950*, ed. L. G. Wickham Legg and E. T. Williams. *Spectator*, 19 June 1959.

Trivia than 'short pieces'?) used in periods of depression to retire with it and read through volume by volume for weeks on end. Only the most harassed hack is content to put the book back when he has read the article he sought. To continue reading is to find the most delicious incongruities; to go, for example, from Francis Thompson to Sir Henry Thompson, the apostle of cremation, famous for his 'octaves' – dinners of eight courses, consumed by eight eminent men, beginning at eight o'clock. But, of course, the great work exists primarily as a library of reference. Like the *Oxford English Dictionary*, it was the conception of a Scotchman in the eighties. Elderly men speak of the OED as 'Murray's'. I have never heard the DNB called 'Smith's' but it is vexatious to find the founder's name now dropped for the first time from the title page. George Smith was no scholar. He was a rich man whose fortune derived from many sources besides publishing. He was born five years after Queen Victoria and died four months before her. At the age of 58 he decided to erect a monument to posterity. Other European states had subsidized biographical dictionaries of their worthies. Nothing of the kind had been attempted in the United Kingdom since 1793, when the *Biographica Britannica* came to an end at the letter F. Smith was typical of his time and people in regarding this undertaking as the proper sphere of private munificence. He found two admirable editors in Leslie Stephen and Sidney Lee and gave them their head. People have attributed to his national sentiment the extraordinary prevalence of Scotch divines among the names chosen for immortality. I think a more likely explanation is that a great many notables of the eighties were grandsons of the manse, and that they saw to it that their ancestors were commemorated. Smith gave a great part of his fortune to the enterprise and his widow continued the work after his death. Her volume, the second supplement covering the deaths of the first decade of the new century (all eminent Victorians), was the last in the great tradition. Sidney Lee still edited it. It comprises over 2,000 pages. The volume published in 1927, covering the years 1912–21, was a wretched shadow. The editors pertly dismissed their predecessor's work as a 'bold and attractive experiment'. The work was now in the hands of dons and *pietas* was not fashionable at the high tables of the twenties. But decency began to reassert itself. From 623 pages in 1927, the work grew to 962 in 1937 and to 968 in 1949. Now for five guineas we are offered 1,031. It is very good value. Instead of a heartening welcome *The Times* newspaper has set up a cry for 'revision'.

Have we so soon forgotten the fate which befell the *Encyclopaedia Britannica* after its eleventh edition? This is not the age of reformation but of defence, when every man of goodwill should devote all his powers to preserving the few good things remaining to us from our grandfathers. If by 'revision' *The Times* meant elaboration and extension, one could only applaud its intention and marvel at its naïve ignorance of the conditions of publishing. There are names, such as Gerard Hopkins, whose fame grew too slowly for admission. Much new material has been revealed about many of the subjects of every age, but particularly of the Victorian. If some new George Smith were to appear with a million or so pounds he would indeed deserve to have his name kept on the title page fifty years after his revision. But this is not what *The Times* meant. Cut it down, spice it up, stick in some snaps from the *Picture Post* 'library', bind it in plastic, hawk it from door to door – that is what 'revision' would mean today. Chuck it, Haley.

But indignation at this shabby suggestion must not lead to the other extreme of encouraging the new young editor, Mr E. T. Williams, to think he has yet recovered full Victorian standards. He and his former colleague have chosen the names well, both of writers and subjects, but many of the articles lack the completeness and precision of their predecessors. It is for facts, not for opinions, that we go to the DNB. The more accomplished the writers in general literature, the less they seem able to master the dry, impersonal style required for this work. Mr Leslie Hartley's biography of Margot Asquith, Mr Christopher Sykes's of Robert Byron and Mr Betjeman's of Berners, for example, lack the classic touch. Mr Reynolds on Baden-Powell and Mr Wylie on Gandhi, on the other hand, provide models Lee and Stephen would have approved. I do not know what has been the editorial practice of Mr Legg and Mr Williams, but I suspect that they decided how much space should be given to each subject and then allowed the contributor to fill it as he thought best. This was not Lee's method. 'I never knew before,' he wrote in 1884, 'how many words might be used to express a given fact. I read piles of manuscript, cutting right and left, and reducing some copy to a third of its length.' Mr Williams seems to be content to let his contributors give a general personal impression. He has not been embarrassed by a surfeit of fact.

Can it be that Mr Weaver's innovation in 1937 of allowing contributors to append their names has had a subtly deleterious effect? There was no secret of authorship before, but the use of initials, which could be identified by the curious, set a proper proportion between subject and writer. Signed articles insinuated a hint of journalism.

It would be easy to go through this volume pointing out omissions; for example, to complain that no account of Mrs (Eugenie) Strong is complete that does not mention her early beauty and her late fanatical devotion to Mussolini. But that is not the purpose of this article. May I instead offer some unsolicited advice to the editor for future use? Let him impose a strict minimum of the facts required. There should be an exact catalogue of the subject's achievements; in the case of a writer his bibliography; of an artist the present position of all his major works (the list of rooms decorated by Rex Whistler is notably inadequate). Of his private life there should be the *addresses* where he was born, lived and died and the position of his grave; his ancestry and progeny; his religious beliefs, if any; his social circle (Robert Byron's and Rex Whistler's friends were of great importance to them and to their work. No indication is given of the kind of people they lived among); education, illnesses and income. It is important to know which of the worthies had private means, how much they earned, how much they left. Height and weight (at different ages). Only when all the basic information has been provided should the writer (if at all) be allowed to express his opinions. There is no reason why some more concise form, even perhaps in the manner of *Who's Who,* might not be used. Why, for instance, write: 'He was placed in the second class of classical Honour Moderations and in the subsequent year was in the first class of *Literae Humaniores*,' when '2nd Mods, 1st Greats' meets the case? In this way space could be found for the inclusion of more names. Sidney Lee was well aware that the chief value of the DNB lay in its records of the relatively obscure. Long articles on prime ministers do not take the place of their biographies. It is when one's curiosity is aroused by the statue of a forgotten local worthy or when one seeks, say, to identify the schoolmasters and tutors who influenced a life of greater interest, that one turns most gratefully to the DNB. There are some crashing bores in the present volume, but few of the dim who found their little place in earlier volumes. Does it seem intolerably neo-Fascist to suggest that, in cases where names do not give a clear indication, colour and race should be mentioned? To take an imaginary example: if we are told that someone married a Miss da Silva of Colombo, it would be interesting to know if the lady was Portuguese or Sinhalese. Mr Arthur Marshall makes a valuable innovation in the latest volume by telling us how to pronounce 'Brazil, Angela'; to rhyme with 'dazzle'. There are many surnames, e.g. Blakiston and Jowett, whose various holders have preferred to pronounce them differently. A phonetic rendering of all doubtful names would be a valuable addition.

The question of candour cannot be so confidently resolved, but I am inclined to think that here Mr Williams might allow himself some slight freedom from Victorian restraint. There is no one alive now, I suppose, who would be hurt by a clearer picture of Lord D'Abernon's management of the Ottoman Bank. Lord Wavell's account of Wingate, appearing after Mr Sykes's biography, reads very mealy-mouthed. Does the description of James Agate as 'a hedonist in the best sense' cover all his pleasures? A public man's morals are not his private concern because they affect the achievement for which he is celebrated. Much can be done by innuendo. How is one to distinguish in reading of a man whose last fifteen years were spent in seclusion whether he spent that time prayerfully 'making his soul' or in an alcoholic stupor? An article in the DNB is written for posterity, not, like an obituary, for contemporaries, but it is read by contemporaries. How can Mr Williams reconcile his two duties of decency and candour? I can see no solution unless it be that of the house-agent. If he does not mention the view from the west bedrooms you may be sure there is a sewage farm immediately below them. Perhaps there should be a form: 'The above was sober, honest, chaste, maritally faithful, sexually normal, courageous, sweet-smelling,' and so on through the list of unmentionable failings, which should be attached to the foot of each article. The omission of any particular would be recognized as significant by regular readers.

All this is but to suggest the dignity and delicacy of Mr Williams's position.

He is on his own now (I understand) at a turning point of the history of the DNB. He has a splendid crop of characters in the present decade. May I beg him to restore the spirit (and the name) of George Smith to his next volume?

. THE HAND OF THE MASTER .

Once, when I was 14 and he was 45, I was taken to visit Edward Johnston at Ditchling. I had lately won an 'Art' prize at school with an illuminated collect the letters of which were carefully drawn with a fine steel nib. Edward Johnston took me into his work-room, beautifully described in this biography, took a turkey quill and cut it into a chisel-pointed pen. Then, to show how it was used, he wrote a few words for me in what is now called his 'foundational' hand. I treasure that piece of writing. But still more I treasure the memory of the experience of seeing those swift, precise, vermilion strokes coming to life. It was a moment of revelation analagous to that recorded by Eric Gill: 'the first time I saw him writing, and saw the writing that came as he wrote, I had that thrill and tremble of the heart which otherwise I can only remember having had when first I touched her [his wife's] body or saw her hair down for the first time, or when I first heard the plain-chant of the Church or when I first entered the Church of San Clemente in Rome or first saw the North Transept of Chartres.' It was the awe and exhilaration of the presence of genius.

Edward Johnston's name is known only to thousands of the tens of thousands who revere his great pupil, Gill. His influence is ubiquitous and unacknowledged except by experts. Every schoolboy who learns the 'italic script', every townsman who reads the announcements of the underground railway, everyone who studies the maps attached to modern travel books is seeing in the light of Johnston. So complete has been his triumph in the last fifty years that our taste now calls for something 'gamier' in typography. It has been the irony of Johnston's achievement – just as the Socialist Party which began as a protest against industrialism now finds itself in the thick of it – that his cult of simplicity, which in his own work accentuated the brilliant idiosyncrasy of his craftsmanship, has led to the stark tedium of mechanical repetition. He was conscious of this dismal development in his lifetime. 'My block letters for the UD (underground), originally intended to be printed from wood types, have been printed by means of a rapidly moving rubber "blanket" which finally rounded off all the square corners.' He was spared the realization of the world of 'plastics' in which the tradition of craftsmanship seems finally to be foundering.

Johnston was not only a maker; he was a thinker, sometimes to the neglect of his work. He never followed his associates into the Catholic Church. He was so

Review of *Edward Johnston*, by Priscilla Johnston. *Spectator*, 24 July 1959.

good and holy and odd that he never felt the need of it. His youngest daughter has produced a portrait that seems to me very near perfection, keeping a happy balance between his domestic and professional affairs, hiding none of his exasperating peculiarities, but revealing a singularly pure and lovable artist.

. ASPIRATIONS OF A MUGWUMP .

I hope to see the Conservative Party return with a substantial majority. I have bitter memories of the Attlee–Cripps regime when the kingdom seemed to be under enemy occupation. I recognize that individually some of the Liberal candidates are more worthy than many of the Conservatives, but any advantage to them can only produce deplorable instability. I have met, seen or heard very few leading politicians; of those I know the Conservatives seem altogether more competent than their opponents.

I have never voted in a parliamentary election. I shall not vote this year. I shall never vote unless a moral or religious issue is involved (e.g., the suppression of Catholic schools). Great Britain is not a democracy. All authority emanates from the Crown. Judges, Anglican bishops, soldiers, sailors, ambassadors, the Poet Laureate, the postman and especially ministers exist by the royal will. In the last 300 years, particularly in the last hundred, the Crown has adopted what seems to me a very hazardous process of choosing advisers: popular election. Many great evils have resulted but the expectation of a change of method in my lifetime is pure fantasy.

Crowned heads proverbially lie uneasy. By usurping sovereignty the peoples of many civilized nations have incurred a restless and frustrated sense of responsibility which interferes with their proper work of earning their living and educating their children. If I voted for the Conservative Party and they were elected, I should feel that I was morally inculpated in their follies – such as their choice of Regius professors[1]; if they failed, I should have made submission to socialist oppression by admitting the validity of popular election. I do not aspire to advise my sovereign in her choice of servants.

Spectator, 2 October 1959. Contribution to a symposium of election comments.

1 Professor Hugh Trevor-Roper (now Lord Dacre) had been appointed Regius Professor of Modern History at Oxford by Harold Macmillan in 1957. Waugh wrote to his daughter Margaret on 2 October 1959, 'I enclose my election address. I think it is funny to hold up Trevor-Roper as Macmillan's great folly instead of Suez or Cyprus. . . .' On 7 March 1961 Waugh wrote to *The Times*, 'We do not hold the title of "Regius Professor of History" in great awe . . . these professorships were instituted for the propagation of the political views of the government of the time . . .'

. I SEE NOTHING BUT
BOREDOM . . . EVERYWHERE .

It is presumptuous to interpret what Mr Vincent Cronin has cleverly called 'the deaf and dumb language of Providence'. All I can do is predict what will be the character of the next decade, if present tendencies continue uninterrupted.

I must confess that I face the immediate future with gloomy apprehensions. I am not the least nervous about the much-advertised threats of the nuclear scientists: first, because I can see nothing objectionable in the total destruction of the earth, provided it is done, as seems most likely, inadvertently. If it is done in malice someone will have behaved culpably. But every well-instructed child knows that the world is going to end one day. The only certain information we have on the subject is that the catastrophe will be fiery and unexpected: the only certain instructions, that we must live every day as though it were to be our last. Secondly, because I believe scientists and publicists enjoy a sense of importance when they make our flesh creep. I well remember the nonsense that was talked in 1938 by the experts on chemical and bacteriological warfare; the wholesale massacres that were threatened from aerial bombardment. And thirdly, because I do not think the next world war will break out in the period we are discussing.

No, what I fear is not alarm but boredom. I am thinking primarily of this kingdom. In other parts of the world there will no doubt be appalling events. The foundation of empires is often an occasion of woe; their dissolution, invariably; and I believe that the peoples of Asia and Africa who have lately enjoyed British rule are in for great distress. But I believe that in this country we have settled down to a period of stagnation which will last just about ten years. I have no fears of political upheaval or of the oppression foreseen by George Orwell for 1984. We endured a full socialist regime, with all its features – one-party government, control of industry, imprisonment without trial, forced labour in the mines, and so on – from 1940 to 1945. The Socialist Government very slightly alleviated it; the Conservatives rather more. The Labour Party will continue its useful function of posing annoying questions to Ministers but I do not think the electorate will ever again vote them into authority.

At the moment it is popular to talk of universal affluence and increased comfort. It is worth noticing that this enrichment is enjoyed by only a part of the nation; the largest, but, I think, the least interesting. Almost everyone I know is much worse off. I, for example, was earning about £3,000 a year in the middle thirties. I see from the official figures lately given by the Financial Secretary to the Treasury that in order to enjoy the standard of living I had in 1938 I must now earn £20,750. I find it hard work to earn half that amount and my income has, on paper, greatly increased. Those whose incomes have

Daily Mail, 28 December 1959. Part of a series of predictions about the 1960s.

remained the same are, notoriously, very much more impoverished. Numerically, as voters, this almost submerged class are of small importance; they will dwindle in the coming decade.

I do not think that the newly enriched will continue to get much richer, but they have been trained to accept universal privation. All that upsets them is to see someone else better off. Financially we are moving towards a classless society. The morbid attention that is at the moment being paid to the minor nuances of social distinction – an attention evident not only in popular newspapers but in grave weeklies – is a sign of the weakness, not of the strength, of the social order. The British, until now, have been the most elaborately stratified people in Europe. It may be a good or a bad thing to be classless; it is certainly un-British.

The most dismal tendency I see is that with our class-system we are fast losing all national character. It was thought absurd by many and detestable by some, but it was unique and it depended for its strength and humour and achievements on variety: variety between one town and another, one county and another; one man different from another in the same village in knowledge, habits, opinions. There were different vocabularies and intonations of speech; different styles of dress. Now all those things that gave the salt to English life and were the raw material of our Arts are being dissolved. When I was last in the Tate Gallery there was exposed a series of casts from a work by Matisse, showing the disappearance of a human figure. The first showed the clumsy but recognizable back of a woman; the last a mere absurdity; and between them the earnest student could study the stages of dissolution in the master's mind. Something like this is happening to the English.

They are already hard to find in London. No one lives there who is not paid to do so. You will find strange faces and strange tongues in the streets; tourists in the hotels; and there are no private houses. Do I exaggerate? Perhaps there are still a score where more than a dozen can sit down to dinner. I do not pretend to be a popular man-about-town. My knowledge comes second-hand, but I believe that London society has ceased to exist; all hospitality is now commercial or official.

The essence of society was not, as is often represented, that it provided a setting for political and financial intrigue. It was the world where people amused themselves, and at the same time exercised a gentle discipline, imposing a standard of manners on its members and those who emulated them, distinguishing between fame and notoriety in its protégés, keeping the bumptious in their places, insisting on good workmanship from its tradesmen. It was an institution as essentially English as the monarchy. London society has disintegrated. Those who should comprise it are scattered; most have retreated to their country houses. The rest are dispersed from central Africa to the West Indies. Those who should enliven it are stultifying and vulgarizing themselves before the television. This has happened and I see no possibility of restoration.

All this makes unwelcome reading for the editor of a newspaper whose business is to make every day new and exciting. How will he fill his columns in the next decade? I see nothing ahead but drab uniformity. The motor-car has already destroyed its own usefulness. Suppose, as seems most unlikely, it once more is rendered mobile by making the whole country into a speedway and a car-park, there will be no inducement to go anywhere because all buildings will look the same, all shops sell the same produce, all people say the same things in the same voices. Foreign travel will be scarcely more attractive for the elderly and experienced. One went abroad to observe other ways of living, to eat unfamiliar foods and see strange buildings. In a few years' time the world will be divided into zones of insecurity which one can penetrate only at the risk of murder and tourist routes along which one will fly to chain hotels, hygienic, costly and second-rate.

The Arts? Here one cannot, thank heaven, speak confidently. We have in a lifetime seen painting and sculpture come to a dead stop all over the world, but the human spirit may rise in reaction. But suppose we in England do produce a genius in the next ten years, will he stay with us? The rewards will be negligible. There will be no cultured world to entertain and encourage him. I think he will leave us as so many others have done in recent years. It is a sorry civilization that exiles instead of honouring its artists. He will decamp not, primarily, for flattery and fleshpots, but simply because the sort of community we all see coming will afford no stimulus to his work. If he remains, it will be as an outlaw.

The underworld will always be with us. At its present rate of growth it should surpass American proportions in 1965 and Sicilian in 1980. The editors can take comfort here. Strikes and crimes of violence will still be news all through the leaden decade. One day, I suppose, we shall be asked to read as the most exciting event of the century about the adventures of some American or Russian who has sat on the moon in a sealed capsule. Heavens, how boring.

But in about 1970 I expect to read of the outbreak of the next world war. Most of my countrymen will welcome it as an escape from the slavery of boredom. Poor beasts, they will have forgotten. But they will soon learn. The epoch will end in another bout of socialism more severe than the Churchill–Attlee terror of the early forties.

. THESE ROMAN SCANDALS .

For more than 2,000 years Rome has been 'The City', the unique capital of the western world. Like the heart of a man, it has always been torn from within by faction and threatened from without by the barbarian.

At the present time the great barbarian threat is from the cinema and, closely associated with it, from the new type of tourists who come neither as art lovers nor religious pilgrims but as pleasure seekers. For these a nasty quarter has sprung up in and about the Via Veneto. An ill-considered law has lately closed the brothels, which were discreet, inexpensive and disciplined, and their place has been taken by gaudy nightclubs. They constitute a minute part of the city which receives disproportionate attention.

Romans of all classes are still immeasurably more moral and dignified than the people of London or Paris or New York. Italy still has no divorce. Shortly after the war there was a strong movement to introduce it. Now opinion has greatly changed. But there is a small set to which a negligible number of the nobility belong, consisting mostly of cosmopolitans and the cinema world, which gets a great deal of public attention.

Just as English matrons like to spend their Sundays reading about crimes of violence to which they are not the least addicted or even tempted, so there is an eager public for gossip about the goings-on of the 'Via Veneto set'. More than a dozen weekly papers flourish on this appetite. The chief of them, *Lo Specchio*, publishes an index of the names mentioned in each issue. All this causes dismay not only to the authorities of the Church, and the topic has lately become concentrated in Fellini's film *La Dolce Vita*.

At the moment this film is the staple of all conversations. The story is disconnected and consists of a series of episodes in the life of a gossip-writer. The Romans, and the people of other cities where it has been shown, are very angry about it. It has been neither censored nor censured by the Church, though many pious people are very much shocked. Controversy is mainly on two counts – the treatment of the Roman aristocracy, who take themselves seriously and are, in fact, mostly serious people, and of the Church.

Mr Fellini has no close personal associations with either subject. What he understands perfectly and portrays brilliantly are the worlds of the cinema and of journalism. The Italian cinema industry was founded by Mussolini, but did not find its powers until after his murder. Cinecitta, the cluster of studios on the outskirts of Rome, is very modest compared with Culver City. They give irregular employment to about 2,000 people. I watched Mr Rossellini directing a film with calm authority with the help of one cameraman and two electricians in a set which had to be approached almost on all fours in a corner under the scaffolding of another stage. It was all most unlike the huge spaces and multitudinous assistants of an American studio.

The best and only purely light-hearted incident in *La Dolce Vita* is the arrival of an American film star in Rome, and the highest achievement of the film is the band of press photographers who, like a ballet chorus, caper and creep through all the scenes, comic or tragic. There Mr Fellini is totally at home. Another group satirized is intellectual Bohemia in a scene which, my intellectual Bohemian friends assure me, is quite absurd.

For the scene of high society the Odescalchi Palace, where I am sure no orgies have taken place for some centuries, was hired for an orgy. This caused a scandal, which was increased by the employment as actors of a genuine butler and one or two genuine aristocrats. It is a commonplace for Italian directors to employ peasants and slum-dwellers to act their own lives. It is new for people of higher position. Some of them agreed to play in *La Dolce Vita* for the fun of it, not realizing quite what sort of film would result. The committee of the Italian nobility – a body of rather vague authority constituted largely to prevent people, after the official abolition of titles in 1945, from using titles which they had not inherited – published a solemn rebuke to the aristocrats who took part.

But the main issue is the religious one, and I can only say that as a conventional Catholic I saw nothing objectionable. The film opens with a helicopter carrying a statue of Christ to a new church. It flies over the city, passing Romans of every kind, cheering schoolchildren, sun-bathing women, and so on. Some wonder who Christ was. The next religious episode was the exploitation by press and television of a supposed miraculous appearance of Our Lady to some children. Such events do occur not infrequently in many parts of the world. The clergy are represented as sceptical, attempting to subdue the popular hysteria, and finally remaining to bury a man who has been brought dying to the scene in the hope of a miraculous cure and abandoned when rain disperses the crowd. There was nothing irreverent there. The satire was directed entirely against the press and the photographers.

Finally, there was a scene at dawn in the Odescalchi Palace when the revellers returning from the orgy in the garden are suddenly confronted by the priest, followed by the old grandmother, on their way to Mass. The two members of the family break away from their guests and soberly follow the little procession into the chapel. That seemed to me a very moving moment. It was a reminder that Rome is for most Christians the capital of Christendom and that behind all the hubbub the essential population are industrious and pious: you cannot escape the motor-cycles in Rome, but you can very easily escape the Via Veneto and find the silent houses where scholars and seminarists are at work. The city has absorbed and civilized succeeding waves of barbarian invasion. It will conquer again in its own good time.

. NOW, WHY CAN'T BRITAIN HAVE A CASINO AT THE END OF EVERY PIER? .

The visit to Homburg was a great mistake. I went there as a sentimental pilgrim to see the first creation of François Blanc, the Frenchman who founded Monte Carlo.

I was misled by antiquated guide-books to expect a place of faded mid-Victorian charm. In 1840 when Blanc and his brother first took the place in hand it was one of the poorest of the tiny independent principalities of Germany. In 1872, when he was expelled by the Prussians, it was the most fashionable gambling resort in the world and the profits of the casino had seeped into every cottage in the state. It was here that Russians came with sacks

Daily Mail, 29 March 1960.

of bullion and some of them, such as Dostoievsky, with nothing but obsessive hope. It is an historic spot and I had never been there.

The journey afforded a chance to explore an unfamiliar entry into Italy, up the Rhine via Harwich and the Hook of Holland, through Frankfurt to Milan – the route of many conquering armies. Seats were booked in the Reingold Express. I have long advocated the superior comfort and convenience of railways over aeroplanes. But the primary law of travel is: first catch your train. The Reingold Express does not wait for its English passengers. Our ship was late. This cannot be a very rare occurrence for British Railways have a leaflet ready printed to suggest alternative trains. On a day of bitter cold we found ourselves changing trains at Rotterdam, Utrecht, Duisburg and Cologne; no restaurant-cars; never time enough at any station for a meal. At length, six hours after we had expected to arrive, we came to Homburg in the dark, in a snowstorm; no porter or taxis.

Next morning when we walked out to see the town we found that the Air Force had nonchalantly demolished the old casino in 1945. Gambling has started again after seventy years' suppression in a plain, new building which smelled of onions and cabbage. The stakes were negligible. The clientele local. No trace remained of the flamboyant François Blanc.

Monte Carlo remains his monument. He planned it and named it and after the Prussians closed the gaming-houses of the Rhineland, he made it world famous. He realized the secret of advertising that is now commonplace – the identification of a name with a product. From 1877 when the last Swiss casino closed until 1930 when governments suddenly became avid for foreign currencies, Monte Carlo was the only place in the civilized world which enjoyed public, legal gambling. And it has kept up appearances – the appearances of the 1880s.

Once one's attention is fixed on the green cloth there is not much to choose between Monte Carlo and the hideous establishment at Enghien. But it was one of Blanc's principles that his customers should not only be fleeced; they should be delighted. He created a resort where people would stay for pleasure – not merely swoop in and out in a moment of greed. Gambling stimulates expenditure. Those who win are easily lured to the jewellers. Those who lose, who have seen large sums whisked away by the croupiers' rakes, are glad to find some tangible return for their money. The fashionable shopkeepers of Paris and London opened branches in Monte Carlo. Blanc provided hotels, singers, ballet and pigeon-shooting. (This last was regarded askance at first for fear the accessibility of firearms might promote suicide.) And this policy has been followed by his successors.

The casino know they will always win in the end. Their aim is to keep their customers in the place. The story is told of a great American magnate who visited the casino at the beginning of the century. He was yachting and had one evening to spend there. He had never seen roulette before; after watching a few turns his sharp brain grasped all the factors. He sent a message to the director saying he was willing to play if for the evening the limit was removed from the maximum stake. The director asked only one question: 'Is he sitting or standing?' 'Sitting.' He agreed. The millionaire played for several hours and lost heavily.

What the casino dislikes is the rich man who makes a single huge haphazard throw and decamps with his winnings. What it likes best is the man who thinks he has a 'system'. Method is another matter. Most gamblers have a method which gratifies their sense of order. There is a system by which you stake 143 units on each turn in the strong hope of winning one. It is printed in a pamphlet on sale near the casino. I am no mathematician, but I think I see a catch in it.

Happy gamblers do not worry about arithmetic. They believe in the moods of fortune; in their individual luck being in or out, in the inexplicable disposition of certain numbers to turn up more often than others at certain periods. Games of chance are not subject to calculation but to intuition. I have no talent for them. I play a little and lose a little. I go often to Monte Carlo for simple love of the place.

For one thing, it has one of the best hotels in the world. The Italians specialize in omniscient and omnicompetent concierges. The Greeks have an admirable order of 'little ones', who may be small boys or elderly men, who are always at hand to go on errands. But at Monte Carlo if one comes from Italy or Greece one rejoices at one's return to the *haute cuisine*. It is not native to the coast, where fish stews, excellent in their way, are the reigning dish. It was part of François Blanc's civilizing mission to introduce classic French cooking to the frugal Italianate Monegasques and to supplement the drab little wines of the district with importations from his homeland, from Burgundy and from Champagne. And the tradition survives. There are now first-class restaurants in and around Monte Carlo, but nothing to tempt the serious eater from the kitchen Blanc founded.

It is in the winter that Monte Carlo is most itself. Then it is purely European, without an American within hearing. The Italians are the most numerous and the highest gamblers. There are more cold days than the authorities will readily admit, but lifts and an underground passage join the hotel to the casino. No one need expose himself to the bad weather and usually in January and February it is sunny and windless.

Every cinemagoer must now be as familiar with the topography of the terraces, the little harbour, the castle and the casino as with his own home town. The Condamine, the front of the yacht-basin, has, alas, been wrecked in the past few years but the casino itself, its gardens and theatre are just as Blanc left them. From the shrine of St Devote to the embowered railway station it is all pure prettiness without a hint of Art anywhere. There are times, particularly after a tour of Italy, when one is surfeited with Art. Masterpieces exalt and refine and inspire, but their constant proximity can become oppressive. There is not, so far as I know, anything remotely resembling a work of art in the whole principality. For a short time this starvation diet is highly exhilarating. All in all Monte Carlo is the prime achievement of pre-1914 sweetness of life.

Why, one asks, can we not reproduce it in England? We are an orderly people who would readily respond to the discipline of a casino. Rich and poor gamble constantly. The curious aberration of thinking gambling immoral has lasted more than a hundred years. No moral theologian supports it. There was a time, indeed, when it seemed imprudent; a time when diligence and thrift could be the foundation of a fortune. Now the state makes the accumulation of wealth impossible except by luck or cunning. The state manipulates its coinage and its funds in a way which impoverishes its subjects as no casino would dare to treat its customers. Taxation and death-duties have loaded the wheel with zeros. Gambling is no longer even imprudent. Anti-gambling laws began with King Louis Philippe in 1832. They spread throughout the world. Now few civilized countries maintain them. English seaside resorts are the most dismal in the world. Why can we not have a casino at the end of every pier?

. SINKING, SHADOWED AND SAD – THE LAST GLORY OF EUROPE .

Venice is the most beautiful city in the world. It is not very old as the great cities of Asia count time. It is about the same age as London. Moralists of the last century used to draw comparisons between the two places – mercantile, maritime and imperial – and warn Londoners that they might decline like the Venetians if they gave way to luxury and ostentation.

London has not declined. Goodness knows there is little luxury and no ostentation there today. We avert our eyes from it in shame. And Venice remains the object lesson in a very different sense from that predicted by our great-grandfathers. If every museum in the New World were emptied, if every famous building in the Old World were destroyed and only Venice saved, there would be enough there to fill a full lifetime with delight. Venice, with all its complexity and variety, is in itself the greatest surviving work of art in the world.

The Venetians came to their hundred islands from the mainland as a refuge from the invaders from the north. And a place of refuge it has remained. Everyone knows that there are no wheeled vehicles in Venice, but only those who have experienced it can appreciate what that means. There are now motor launches. The gondoliers have almost priced themselves out of existence. There are now scarcely a dozen private gondolas.

Not many of the palaces are in the hands of the families who built them. Some, like the Rezzonico, are museums; some, like the Labia, have been restored and occupied by foreigners; most are divided into apartments. The two chief hotels have built themselves unobtrusively ugly new wings. You will find grumblers to tell you that Venice is not what it was. Don't believe them.

Daily Mail, 30 March 1960.

On this, the latest of several visits, I came for the first time in January when it is 'out of season' for foreigners and the Venetians themselves feel most at their ease. It was chilly and damp and misty and I saw the city in a new aspect; one of poetic melancholy and mystery. It is not essentially a summer city. Most of its festivals occur in winter. In the great days of the republic the nobles used to retire from their huge frescoed halls and spend the cold weather cosily in mezzanine flats. In July and August they moved to villas along the Brenta Canal and in the hills. No one who could afford to go away spent the summer in Venice. That is an American craze which began in my lifetime. Spring is an exquisite season, but, alas, too popular. I would sooner get rather wet in the streets and find many of the pictures indoors rather obscure (only two buildings have introduced modern lighting) than live in a crowd.

Never believe anyone who tells you he 'knows' Venice. You can 'do' it in less than a month, studying and enjoying all that the guide-books recommend. And that is at the same time both an education and an inebriation. But the Venetians themselves are the last to claim that they 'know' their city. It is divided into six areas, whose boundaries are inextricably confused, and even today, I am told, there are Venetians who have never been outside their own *sestiere*. Each church, each well-head, is the centre of a distinct community.

How can one give an impression of the Venetians? Perhaps they are what Romans were between 1815 and 1870. But there is something of the East in the modesty of the women and the gravity of the men. This, which 200 years ago was the city of gambling and carnival, is now, outside Spain, the acme of decorum. No public love-making, no brawling, no showy clothes; withdrawn yet still traditionally cosmopolitan.

I went to tea in one of the few palaces still fully occupied by the original family – one which has not only magistrates of the republic but a canonized saint in its pedigree. Half a dozen of us were there in the high frescoed hall. Because I was English all spoke in my language, easily, colloquially, allusively, almost without accent. They compared T. S. Eliot and Anouilh in their treatment of Thomas à Becket; they spoke of the breeds of English cattle. No one there had spent more than a week or two in England. It was an ease with the world such as one once found and no longer finds in Paris; and this is a city with no diplomatic corps, a provincial city comparable, I suppose, in financial and political importance to Swansea.

Later I went into another milieu to call on a local journalist; a man, I suppose, not very well off. We met at a statue and he led me through tunnels and alleys – in Venice there is no rich or poor quarter – until we emerged at his house, drab enough from the outside; an English municipal council would no doubt condemn it to demolition; under an arch, into a yard, and we were in a fifteenth-century arcade, up a staircase and we were in a delicate little room of eighteenth-century rococo plaster work such as antiquarian societies in England will create a fruitless hullabaloo about when they are doomed to destruction. In Venice they exist everywhere, out-of-sight, uncounted.

The Venetians are the most conservative people in Europe, and by a strange paradox they are at the moment deprived of self-government for fear they should turn Communist. They have no *podestà* (mayor) but are ruled by a Prefect sent from Rome. All their civil servants and most of their police come from Naples and Sicily. They got bored with politics at the end of the eighteenth century. Since then they have been ruled by French, Austrians, Piedmontese. They are far too wise and experienced to fuss. But they guard their own city fiercely.

Two years ago there was a plot to erect a 'modern' house, designed by the American, Wright, on the Grand Canal. The Neapolitan officials had given their consent. Then the Venetians and their foreign friends became aware of the danger and the thing was stopped. There is only one ugly building in Venice today – the campanile of St Mark's. It has stood there in defiance of proportion and elegance for 500 years. In 1902 it collapsed. A heaven-sent opportunity, one would say, to clear the thing away. Not at all; the Venetians patiently built an exact replica.

The present Pope was Patriarch of Venice before his election. The Venetians are proud and pleased; pleased especially because it was rumoured that he had designs to demolish Sansovino's screen in St Mark's. 'He had to go of course,' they say, 'but he was a good man, so we sent him to Rome.'

And yet they dare not have an election in Venice for fear that they should turn up a Communist. The reason is ironical and significant. Mussolini and his finance minister went to great pains to restore the prosperity of Venezia. At Mestre and Marghera on the mainland they created new industrial suburbs which were to be the glory of the Fascist regime. They, of course, have turned solid Communist. But the Venetians still have their refuge from them in their own islands, and the horses of Lysippus look down from the porch of St Mark's not at all surprised or alarmed by what they see.

But the city is sinking. Every year, by a few inches, it subsides into its lagoon. Not in my time nor, I pray, in my children's, but one day it will silently disappear. With it will go the last glory of Europe. I hope there will still be someone alive to remember the now hackneyed lines of Wordsworth: 'And when she took unto herself a mate, she must espouse the everlasting sea.'

. MARRIAGE A LA MODE - 1936 .

There is a phrase current among blurb-writers, originating I suppose in some dark corner of Cambridge (Mass.) or Cambridge (Eng.), which identifies certain books as inviting study 'on more than one level'. I am not sure what they think they mean by this beyond the obvious statement that some readers are

Review of *Casanova's Chinese Restaurant*, by Anthony Powell. *Spectator*, 24 June 1960.

more intelligent and better informed than others and will therefore better appreciate the writer's meaning. If they mean that the books they admire are replete with esoteric allusions, symbols and allegories, the natural conclusion is that (Holy Scripture apart) they are inferior exercises in the art of communication. Some novelists no doubt do play with such conceits. Mr Anthony Powell is a happy example of a writer who works on a single level.

He is slightly my junior in years. I have few reasons to desire longevity. One of them is the hope that I (and he) may be spared to see the completion of the fine sequence which he calls *The Music of Time* and to sit (or lie) back to read it continuously, for the annual instalments he provides, eagerly expected and keenly enjoyed, do put something of a strain on an already faltering memory. The main characters, the brilliantly contrived dramatic episodes, the aloof and tolerant tone, the precise expression – all these remain with us during the long periods of waiting, but the minor characters, Max Pilgrim, for instance, or Chips Lovell, tend, in my mind at least, to diminish and almost to disappear. Moreover Mr Powell is not content to manipulate a single already numerous and diverse cast; more and more characters appear in each book, all intricately but tenuously connected with their predecessors. To borrow again from the blurb-writers' vocabulary, I do not think these characters exist fully 'in the round'. They can be observed from one position only. We cannot walk round them as statues. They present, rather, a continuous frieze in high relief, deep cut and detailed.

The present book, more than any of its four predecessors, owes its value to its position in the series. It could not, I think, be greatly enjoyed by a reader ignorant of what has gone before. I enjoyed it rather less than them for a variety of reasons. The new characters are musicians and are (to me) much nastier and therefore less interesting than the painters, writers and men of the world with whom Mr Powell has dealt until now. There is a common scold whom I found so repellent that she stood out from the general easy-going acceptance of the bizarre which Mr Powell has hitherto successfully inculcated. These may be complaints of the squeamish but all Mr Powell's devotees will, I am sure, feel disappointment in being denied their annual treat of Widmerpool. We wait and wait for him to appear, confident that he will precipitate one of his great catastrophes. At last we see him; he says a few words; he retires. And those few words leave us for the first time with a faint doubt of his reality. Could they really have been spoken by a man in his twenties?

> 'For a man to have shared one's education is, in my eyes, no special recommendation to my good graces. I suppose I could have formed some early impression of his character and efficiency. I regret to say that few, if any, of my school contemporaries struck me sufficiently favourably for me to go out of my way to employ their services.'

An elderly understudy seems to have usurped the peculiar overcoat. It is Mr Bultitude addressing Dr Grimstone. Moreover, Widmerpool is represented as aspiring to be part of the shadow court of Fort Belvedere. This adds a further improbability. There were some queer fish in what the Archbishop of Canterbury denounced as an 'exotic circle' but, surely, no one remotely like Widmerpool.

The abdication of King Edward VIII is appropriately given greater emphasis than the Spanish Civil War; appropriately, because the theme of this book is marriage. In its four predecessors the theme was success and failure in the various competitions of life, polarized in the success of the grotesque Widmerpool and the failure of the charming Stringham. Now Mr Powell's characters are less concerned with money and reputation. They are married and fretting under the restraints and disillusions of their state. What one is not told, and needs to know in order to understand them, is what they mean by marriage. None of them avows any religious belief or traditional, ethical code; they have no dynastic ambitions of family alliances or heritable properties; no expectation of life-long companionship. All believe that marriage is terminable at will; most of them marry more than once. How do they distinguish the relationship from other forms of concubinage? That they do make a distinction is apparent from the gravity with which they discuss it, but Mr Powell gives no hint of its origin and character. Is it purely superstitious and atavistic? The narrator writes:

> To think at all objectively about one's own marriage is impossible, while a balanced view of other people's marriage is almost equally hard to achieve with so much information available, so little to be believed. Objectivity is not, of course, everything in writing; but even casting objectivity aside, the difficulties of presenting marriage are inordinate. Its forms are at once so varied, yet so constant, providing a kaleidoscope, the colours of which are always changing, always the same. The moods of a love affair, the contradictions of friendship, the jealousy of business partners, the fellow feeling of opposed commanders in total war, these are all in their way to be charted. Marriage, partaking of such – and a thousand more – dual antagonisms and participations, finally defies definition.

Mr Powell owes us something more solid than this evasion of the novelist's duty if he expects us to sympathize with the anxieties of his creations.

Casanova's Chinese Restaurant is a cheap resort which some of the characters occasionally frequent. Nothing of importance to the story happens there. The incongruity of the name, which came about through the combination of two dissimilar establishments, tickles the narrator's fancy, but it is not easy to see why Mr Powell chose it as the title of the book.

Having made these few ungrateful comments I must deny any suggestion that the book is a failure. Mr Powell knows very well what he is doing. All long works of literature have their periods of apparent stagnation. His purpose will become clear in subsequent volumes. Taken by itself it seems to me to lack structure, but no doubt it has an essential part in the grand design. Nor does it lack its own high drama. We have to wait for it. It is all in the third section, page 129 to page 190; the occasion is the performance of a symphony composed by one of the new characters and the party given to celebrate it by Mrs Foxe, Charles Stringham's mother, at which many of the old characters are gathered.

It is invaded by Charles Stringham, who is now recognized as an alcoholic and held in gentle restraint by 'Tuffy', Mrs Foxe's former secretary. The scene of Stringham's drunken but controlled mockery of the nagging Bohemian wife, of his momentary domination of the group and of his final act of non-resistance to Tuffy's authority, is as finely conceived and finished as anything Mr Powell has written anywhere.

Nor should this book be regarded merely as an interim report of progress for in it the author has slyly inserted a sentence which I think will prove to be the key of the whole work. On the second page the narrator observes: 'In the end most things in life – perhaps all things – turn out to be appropriate.' It is this realization that separates the five novels Mr Powell wrote before the war from those he has written after it. The first were brilliant studies of the grotesque; in the later books the characters behave as anarchically but they are seen as cohesive. They have not merely the adventitious connection of crossing the path of a single observer; they all hang together apart from him. There is homogeneity and rule in apparent chaos; and this is in the natural order of experience. No eschatological sanctions are invoked. In this essential respect Mr Powell's position may well be defined by contrasting it with that of his contemporary, Mr Graham Greene. Mr Greene's characters never know anyone. Their intense, lonely lives admit of professional acquaintances, lovers and sometimes a single child but they are never seen as having ramifications of friendship, cousinhood and purely social familiarity. Their actions are performed under the solitary eye of God. Mr Powell sees human society as the essential vehicle of the individual. Everyone knows everyone else, perhaps at the remove of one. Everyone's path crosses and recrosses everyone else's. There are no barriers of age or class or calling that can divide the universal, rather cold intimacy which the human condition imposes.

. THE ONLY PRE-RAPHAELITE .

Mrs Cuthbert – Diana Holman-Hunt – is much younger than I but genealogically we are of the same generation, having a great-great-grandfather in common. By the circumstances of her upbringing she might belong to an earlier generation, for her childhood was spent almost alone with her two grandmothers. With one she made her home, at the other's she made occasional visits. The first was conventional, frivolous, self-indulgent and, it appears, rather cold-hearted. The other (*née* Waugh), the widow of the painter, was emotional, pious, stout-hearted, well-read and reckless of personal appearance. I knew her, but not well. I had tea with her in her sparsely inhabited, richly furnished house in Melbury Road and listened eagerly to her reminiscences of the Pre-Raphaelites, delighting in her strong intellect and sharp

Review of *My Grandmothers and I*, by Diana Holman-Hunt. *Spectator*, 14 October 1960.

expressions, but I was totally ignorant, as I suppose were most of her guests, of the extraordinary features of the ménage which her granddaughter here delightfully reveals. It is 'Grand', Mrs Holman Hunt, who dominates the book. Mrs Freeman, the maternal grandmother, might be any well-to-do woman of the period. Mrs Holman Hunt would have been extravagantly original in any age.

The book, *My Grandmothers and I*, has already been noticed in the *Spectator*, where it provided the theme for an essay on domestic servants. If it is now treated as an excuse to write about Holman Hunt, homage must first be paid to the great skill of the author. In her preface she describes her work as 'true in essence, but not in detail' and there are a number of obscurities and discrepancies that will puzzle a reader who treats it as a source of biography. Dates and ages are usually left vague. Impressive characters such as 'Big Aunt' loom into the story as they must have done in the child's life without introduction or full identification. It is the secret of the book's charm that the author has not sought to elaborate her memories with research. Adult curiosity remains unsatisfied. How much money, one would like to be told, did 'Grand' leave? Her extreme parsimony was clearly due to choice rather than to necessity. But were the gold coins in the drawer real sovereigns? Was the father, who makes a brief and endearing appearance, running through the modest but far from negligible family fortune? When and where did 'Grand' adopt ritualistic practices so alien to her presbyterian origins? Simeon Solomon died before Diana Holman-Hunt was born. His name had been expunged from the memoirs of the period. Can 'Grand' really have hoped to encounter him and relieve his destitution during the period of the First World War? Can she really have been ignorant of the causes of his downfall? How old was the Duke of Gloucester and how old the author when she invited him to go fishing in Kensington Gardens? But these problems cease to tease when the book is accepted for what it is – a triumphant re-creation of a child's memories.

Mrs Holman Hunt had long been widowed when the granddaughter became aware of her and, no doubt, had developed her peculiarities in loneliness. Not that she was a recluse. Her social life was vigorous and varied but in her later years it seems to have been confined to the hours of daylight. Once the burglar traps had been set the little household retired hungry to their comfortless rooms and the old woman was left with her memories. What reverence the English painters and writers of the nineteenth century excited and perpetuated among their womenfolk! 'Grand' copiously and regularly weeping over the slab in St Paul's Cathedral which covered her husband's ashes; 'Grand' tenaciously defending, and training a third generation to defend, his just claims to have been the originator of Pre-Raphaelitism; 'Grand' literally labelling the tea cups out of which eminent Victorians had drunk; can we hope to see such *pietas* among the relicts of our modern painters? Nor was she, singular in so much else, unique in this. The great men of the mid-Victorian era imposed themselves on their immediate posterity when no apparatus existed to record their spoken words. They imposed not only their achievements but their reticence. Whatever their weaknesses and doubts they did, almost all of them, regard themselves as the custodians of morality. We know very little of their private lives, particularly of their pleasures. Some traces have been left of their early manhood – of smoking-parties, boating-parties, an easy cameraderie in lending and borrowing money, but from the moment they marry we are given only a record of professional triumphs and official honours. Rossetti was a man of flagrantly Bohemian habits but his brother William succeeded in obliterating almost every trace. Of Holman Hunt we know less than of any of them. We have his own fascinating autobiography (the second, two-volume, fully illustrated edition of which, incidentally, was paid for by 'Grand') but apart from that almost nothing. His works, he believed, ensured his immortality. Perhaps it is prurient to ask for more. Perhaps in this prurient age more attention would be paid to his works if we knew more of his life than he was prepared to disclose.

'Grand' was in a somewhat ambiguous position. She was the sister of his first wife at the time when such marriages were illegal in England. Ten years elapsed between the two marriages during much of which time Hunt was abroad and alone. One is reminded of Augustus Egg who ended his days in Algiers with a wife whom, the official biographer states, he was, to his regret, unable to present to his friends. Did Hunt have any escapades in his young manhood in Palestine? We know nothing of his courtship. Had he taken the younger sister's fancy at his first wedding? Her descriptions of his full, scented beard are distinctly amorous – as indeed they should be. But one wonders what went on in the years of his widowhood and how he finally settled for 'Grand'. Not, apparently, as I had always supposed, partly to provide a second mother for Cyril. He, according to 'Big Aunt', was soon sent packing by 'Grand'.

There can be no one alive today who can claim Hunt's friendship. There were few at the time of his death, and there are not many anecdotes of him in the reminiscences of the period. He does not seem to have been a likeable man. My father, who got on with most people, stayed with him as a young man when Hunt was at the height of his fame and found him impenetrably aloof. Mrs Plunket Greene, who knew him in her childhood, reported him as cruel and pompous. The charge of cruelty was based on the story that he had starved an animal to death in his garden to paint the *Scapegoat* – a less hilarious incident than Diana Holman-Hunt's description of his boiling a horse. Max Beerbohm represents him as plebeian in appearance and patronizing in manner. After the age of 30 he seems to have made or kept no close friends. But 'Grand' certainly doted on him, and his son Hilary unexpectedly remembers him as an indulgent father who was constantly getting him out of scrapes. His portrait of himself suggests the saint and the sage.

His character will, presumably, remain enigmatic. His works remain and they are, I suppose, the least appreciated of any comparable painter's. When I was last in Birmingham his superb *Shadow of Death* lay in the cellars of the city Art Gallery. He was, beyond question, the original Pre-Raphaelite and the only one to pursue throughout his whole life the principles of his adolescence. Pre-Raphaelitism in popular use has come to connote picturesque mediaeval-ism of the kind exemplified in the watercolours of the 1860s which Rossetti painted under Ruskin's direction. Pre-Raphaelitism to Hunt meant the intense study of natural appearances devoted to the inculcation of a lofty theme. He was obsessed with the structure of objects (hence his attempts to reduce the horse to a skeleton) and with the exact tincture of shadows. While his contemporaries in France, whom he regarded with loathing and contempt, sought to record a glimpse, he sought to record months of intense scrutiny. Their works are eagerly sought by the modern *nouveaux riches*; Hunt's are probably of less value than when they were painted. It must be admitted that they are ugly, compared with the Italian and Flemish masters he professed to emulate. He was in his work, as apparently in his life, notably lacking in the wish to please. He rejoiced in defying contemporary standards of prettiness (except in a very few deplorable cases). Why does not the present age rejoice with him? A kind of cataract seems to seal the eyes of this half-century, which has accepted with relish monstrosities of every sort, to the invention, accomplishment, untiring vitality and dedicated purpose of these great and often hidden masterpieces.

. DON'T TELL ALFRED .

It is nine years since Miss Nancy Mitford published a novel. In the meantime she has devoted herself to history, producing two studies whose charm and lightness of touch almost concealed the extent and accuracy of knowledge which illuminated them. Her last novel, *The Blessing*, though eminently read-able and sparkling with feminine fun, was, we may now admit, a slight disappointment, reminiscent of her earlier work rather than of the two post-war books with which her true literary career began. (How agreeable for a writer not to be chidden with the loss of early promise.) We can without offence now admit the relative failure of *The Blessing* because in *Don't Tell Alfred* she has written her most mature and satisfactory story, expunging the slight taint of the fashion-magazine which was discernible to the captious in *The Pursuit of Love* and *Love in a Cold Climate*.

The best advice that can be given to a young writer of comedy is: 'Never kill your characters'. This for two reasons: first, the frankly commercial: library readers like to resume where they left off and meet old and loved acquaintances. Mr P. G. Wodehouse's characters are not only immune from death but from advancing age. Secondly, artistically; very few novelists indeed, and those not notably the best, are able to 'create' more than a limited cast. In social life it

Review of *Don't Tell Alfred*, by Nancy Mitford. *London Magazine*, December 1960.

is usually the bores and parasites who 'know everyone', it is the rarer spirits who confine their friendship to a *bande*. In general this is true of novelists. The huge 'canvas', the crowded cast, have less to offer than the constant, intense observation of a single limited milieu. Miss Mitford killed Fabrice Sauveterre and had to resurrect him under the name of Charles-Edouard de Valhubert; she killed Linda, and now we find her again, eyes swimming with tears for suffering animals, as Northey in *Don't Tell Alfred*. We have almost all the old friends *in propria persona* – Uncle Matthew, Davey Warbeck, even the ineffable Dexters, older but very much alive, entering the circus-ring at the crack of Miss Mitford's whip and performing their routine with glittering precision. Lady Montdore is dead, as also Aunt Emily; neither much to be mourned. The Bolter remains off-stage but exercises her potent influence. Monsters, clowns and acrobats are all back under the Big Top with a few new modern attractions.

The series of turns which follow one another with brilliant management comprises the outrageous vicissitudes of diplomatic life in Paris. We are asked to accept, and readily do so, an initial absurdity. Alfred Wincham, it may or may not be remembered, was the almost invisible don whom Fanny, the narrator of the first two books, happily married. He held the chair of Pastoral Theology and made rare, aloof entrances in his little house which constituted a *pied-à-terre* in Oxford for the Radlett children and Lady Montdore. We were once told he was elected Warden of his college but Miss Mitford gaily disregards this and in her present book he is still Professor and still in St Aldates. He was a socialist and it is now revealed to the reader that he is one of the faceless men who really govern England. On the strength of having worked with Ernest Bevin during the war – presumably in sending forced labour to the mines and factories – and having furtively but regularly lunched at Downing Street with Mr Attlee, he is appointed by a Conservative Prime Minister as British Ambassador in Paris. We have Miss Mitford's word for this transition and do not demur. At first it seems that the theme of the book is to be the conflict between dowdy Fanny and the outgoing ambassadress, the beautiful Lady Leone, who has made the historic mansion a pleasure dome for her intimates.[1] Fanny will win because she holds the cards. The realistic Parisians will transfer their affections quickly enough from the brilliant exile to the holder of power. International affairs will be recognized as more important than bizarre picnics. That is, indeed, the theme of the first sixty hilarious pages which constitute a delightful short story. In this case it is Uncle Davey who comes to the rescue and when we realize that that episode is over, we tend to expect that he is to become the Jeeves who unfailingly provides the solution to the series of predicaments; but in fact he fades into valetudinarianism and is not particularly important in the later stages of the book. The story takes a different turn when it concerns the behaviour of Fanny's four ghastly sons. Although ostensibly a theologian, Alfred appears to have brought up his family in total ignorance of the truths of religion. It is not very surprising to anyone except Fanny that they turn out to be cranks, cads and crooks. Alfred in an uncomfortable moment of truth expresses genuine dismay. It seems, at several points, that the theme of the book is to be the contrast between Northey – the social-secretary cousin, the reincarnation of Linda ('Oh you are lucky to be so kind'), the irresistible Radlett – with her cousins in whom the wish to please is totally absent. But a vague belief that boys will be boys and that any generation is in revolt against its elders and betters eventually soothes the mother's anxieties. There is an excellently rendered farcical conclusion which should not be revealed to the reader. Two other subplots run through the narration – the entirely delicious relations between Northey and a French politician, and the journalist who maliciously misreports everything for an English press-lord. This character lacks authenticity merely by his physical appearance. There is no good reason why he should not look just as Miss Mitford describes him. Somehow he does not carry conviction. Has she, perhaps, out of respect for the law, disguised someone of quite other physical characteristics?[2]

The great, heartening, feature of *Don't Tell Alfred* is that it is incomplete. So many problems are left unresolved, so many characters have been left in the air, that one may confidently look for a sequel.

Has the book, then, any unifying quality? Yes, it is a socialist tract, the most explicit that Miss Mitford has yet offered us. She has never dissembled her subversive opinions but until now she has preferred to work in the class-war as what used, in her youth, to be called 'a fifth columnist'. Now she has come into the open. She is no longer concerned to exacerbate class-feeling by troubling the middle classes in matters of diction. Here she is writing of the centre of European polity. Once she displayed a schizophrenic social scene. There was on one side the Borelies and Kroesigs, coarse capitalists pretending to aristocracy, and on the other a fairyland of French dukes, every one of whom was an insatiable lover, an expert on women's clothes and on eighteenth-century bronzes; between them a dying world of eccentric, emotional, animal-loving English. Now after a long sojourn in Paris she is even willing to admit that there may be moments of tedium in the highest French society. That, for Miss Mitford, is a Canossa and she is doing public penance.

The 'Pull to the East' is something so powerful that a mesmerist must be employed to counteract it. The young of the West look forward to no future; jazz and ill-earned money are their sole occupations. Dexter returns (can we doubt it?) as a spy for Russia. The 'European Army' is an absurdity. The Americans, whom ill-wishers have hitherto contented themselves with describing as bores and barbarians, are now represented as a doomed race; bewildered, drugged, dieted, psychoanalysed, suicidal.

'Have you been committing again?' was the question, referring to adultery, with which Miss Jessica Mitford tells us she used to greet her brother. Miss Nancy Mitford is the last of the 'committed' novelists.

1, 2 When Lady Diana Cooper left the British Embassy in Paris, she set up house at Chantilly in seeming rivalry to the incoming ambassadress. Lady Diana was greatly worried by the reports of the Paris correspondent of the *Evening Standard*, Sam White.

. AN IRISHMAN IN THE MAKING .

I have been asked by the new head of the family to record some memories of my contemporary, the late Earl of Longford. I accede gladly for he and his siblings are bound to me by long friendship, but I do so with some difficulty because they are themselves so articulate and fertile. Nothing I know of their heredity or environment explains the singular literary florescence of the Pakenham family. Almost every member has published a book; many of them are auto-biographical and Edward Longford's childhood has been very fully chronicled, directly and indirectly.

His later years were lived entirely in Ireland in the company and in the service of his fellow countrymen. These services, not only to literature and the drama but to sport – he was for a time joint Master of Hounds though not himself an actual follower: to politics – he was in the Senate: to the revival of local craftsmanship – he maintained a tweed manufactory: to the social life of Dublin, where he spent more time than in his seat in Westmeath – all these activities have already been gratefully acknowledged. It only remains for me to fill the gap of the time I knew him best in the early 1920s and 1930s.

At Oxford he was remarkable for his independence. He belonged to no set and was entirely free of the temptation which afflicted most undergraduates to cut a figure of one kind or another. He belonged, I think, to no clubs; certainly not to the Bullingdon where his younger brother was a popular member; nor to the bacchanalian Hypocrites; nor, despite his early and enduring devotion to the theatre, to the OUDS. He rarely went down to London and never appeared in the ballroom. His only intemperance was political. It was the time when Irish Home Rule was still a bitter question and he supported the unpopular cause with reckless audacity which, on the night of the Wilson murder, led him to Mercury.

Undergraduate convention at that time reinforced the proctorial rules to make an almost impassable barrier between the men's and the women's colleges. Edward became unofficially engaged to a charming and clever 'under-graduette' (as they were then dubbed), Miss Christine Trew, whom he married when he came of age. Together they formed a lifelong partnership of shared enthusiasms. Mrs Trew had a house in Oxford. Friends of Edward's had to be acceptable to both mother and daughter. When Edward and Christine married and settled at Pakenham, Mrs Trew accompanied them. The solid, castellated house was redecorated in the oriental style, and was the scene until 1939 of large summer house parties, deeply memorable to all the participants, whose character is not easily conveyed without an inappropriate hint of the ludicrous.

Edward and Christine were not the primary movers in these festivities. They opened their house and extended its traditional hospitality to the friends of the younger Pakenhams. Oxford was in general the common bond between the

Observer, 12 February 1961.

guests. Dons then young and in uproarious spirits, writers then little known to the public, originated escapades and impostures to *épater* the neighbours. Many courtships were conducted there. I had the impression that, when the last of us left, Edward and Christine watched us go with something of the relief with which fond parents wave their obstreperous children back to school.

Not that Edward ever held aloof from the junketing. He had a particular relish for singing to his own organ accompaniment, Anglican hymns alternating with anti-English ballads. I have seen at Pakenham what I have seen nowhere else, an entirely sober host literally rolling about the carpet with merriment. Edward soon became uncommonly stout, a condition which caused him no self-consciousness, which, I think, he never took any steps to relieve. His butler and attendant footmen would gravely bestride the spherical form in its velvet smoking suit as they carried their trays. Edward had the gracious habit of tipping his guests on their departure by making bets which he knew he would lose, so that he bore the expense of our visits.[1]

The Dublin literary world has been described by Mr Cyril Connolly as 'warm and friendly as an alligator pool'. Over this dangerous enclosure Edward and Christine floated serenely indifferent to the snapping jaws below. It is not difficult to become a public figure in Dublin. It is rare to be regarded with real esteem and affection. That, with Christine's constant support, was Edward's achievement.

. BRITISH WORTHIES .

I must not pretend to have read every word of this book, but I have devoted a happy morning to it – a longer time than most reviewers of fiction give to their material – and I can state with confidence that it will sustain the high reputation of its 112 predecessors. If a trend is discernible, it is one towards sobriety. Thirty years ago there were contributors who sought to amuse; few today. Sir Osbert Sitwell still adds admonition to autobiography and now 'advocates compulsory Freedom everywhere, the suppression of Public Opinion in the interest of Free Speech and the rationing of brains without which there can be no true democracy', but most of those elected for inclusion are content to set out their claims to celebrity without adornment. Fewer, it seems to me, apart from the Anglican clergy, admit to hobbies. It is remarkable, though scarcely credible, that a few men still claim 'motoring' as a 'recreation'.

Who's Who is an essential document for ADCs and attachés whose duty it is to scan official visitors' books. It is also an excellent work for casual perusal, titillating curiosity on many points. Why is Sir Ranulph Twisleton-

---

1 According to 'The Talk of the Town', *Daily Express*, 11 January 1930, p. 5, Waugh won £2 from Lord Longford by climbing the pinnacle of a tower. The amount paid to guests corresponded to the height reached, and Waugh had intrepidly scaled the second highest point.

Review of *Who's Who 1961*. *Spectator*, 24 March 1961.

Wykeham-Fiennes listed under F and Adm. the Hon. Sir R. A. R. Plunkett-Ernle-Erle-Drax under P? How are the entrants chosen, particularly the foreigners? The book begins with a Finn and ends with a German. It is far from being exclusively British. What do the lesser breeds do to qualify? Sampling at random there seems to be an element of caprice in the selection.

It is said that there is keen competition to be admitted. Sometimes there may be an advantage in being there. Foreign hotel managers keep it handy; but against that must be set the appalling vulnerability to beggars and research students. It is significant that a great number of entrants give accommodation addresses of agents and banks.

It is interesting to observe how very few of the entrants, even those who owe their chief fame to it, admit to broadcasting. Mr Betjeman does not, nor Lord Boothby, though both own up to their publications. Lord Kinross candidly admits his weakness. Mr Ian Fleming, with commendable modesty, does not even name his books. 'Various novels of suspense', he is content to call them. Everyone who has respectable war service is explicit about it. Reticence is shown about wives. Some contributors name all, some only the most recent, some none at all. *Who's Who* is not as directly revealing as Burke, but there are discoveries to be made even here. Who would have guessed that Mr Godfrey Winn, in the days when he was, as he himself describes it, 'star columnist' of the *Daily Mirror* and when all his domestic affairs seemed open to us, had all the time an older brother who is now a judge of the High Court, Queen's Bench? What English novelist has the orders of the White Lion (Czechoslovakia) and the Oaken Crown of Luxemburg? What is Marshal Zhukov's address? These are a few of the points of interest in this admirable volume.

. CHESTERTON .

The publishers claim for *Chesterton: Man and Mask* that it is a book of which Chesterton would have approved. There is certainly nothing in it – except perhaps the disparagement of Belloc – likely to cause positive offence, but it has two features which might have displeased its subject. First, its genesis. It is the thesis for a doctorate. The writing of theses has become a very prominent part in the American educational process, not only by aspiring doctors but, it seems, at high schools. Research is no longer confined to recondite subjects and foreign texts; popular modern work is investigated with equal zeal and greater ease. The fashion bears hard on contemporary writers, particularly if they are Catholics, for there are not a great number of modern Catholic writers in English and it is natural for Catholic teachers to direct their pupils towards them. Even the dimmest are beset by importunate adolescents: 'I have chosen you for English. Please tell me what first influenced you to write.' Chesterton did not live to suffer from the craze but he is a writer of the modern world to this

Review of *Chesterton: Man and Mask*, by Garry Wills. *National Review*, 22 April 1961.

extent, that it is a grave reproach to suppose that his work needs elucidation. A writer who cannot make his meaning clear to his own generation and their immediate successors is a bad writer. Chesterton, of all men of our times, wrote especially for the common man, repeating in clear language his simple, valuable messages.

A second cause which Chesterton might have for complaint is Mr Wills's literary style. It is not uniformly bad. Indeed, again and again he shows himself capable of constructing a grammatical, even an elegant, sentence. But not always – and the jargon of the lecture room keeps slipping in – 'existential', 'dialectic', 'normative', 'experiential', 'complementarity' – in a way which would have set the teeth on edge in the head of the old journalist.

Chesterton was notoriously inaccurate; Mr Wills thinks wilfully so. He not only applauds but emulates this trait. It would be tedious to pick out all his errors. Let two suffice. He says that the author of the 'Heroic Poem in Praise of Wine' wrote 'nothing but the shortest poems'. In his brief account of the Marconi scandal he introduces three mysterious characters named 'Isaac and Samuel Rufus and Henry Isaacs' whom the astute reader may tentatively identify as Rufus and Godfrey Isaacs and Herbert Samuel.

These criticisms made, one can turn to Mr Wills's virtues. He is a young man without the dandyism proper to his years, but he is also free of adolescent prurience. The title *Man and Mask* raised apprehensions of an attempt at exposure. It has become commonly accepted nowadays that any man's idiosyncrasies of appearance or manner are a disguise deliberately adopted to conceal some fear or vice. *Persona* is one of the cant terms of modern criticism, and modern critics regard it as their function to strip their subject of its protective mask. They should take notice of Max Beerbohm's *Happy Hypocrite*. The mask, the style, *is* the man.

Mr Wills to his great credit shows no inclination to expose Chesterton. There are questions which do titillate curiosity: what, if any, were his homosexual adventures at the Slade? To what extent, if at all, was he ever in danger of becoming a serious drunkard? The obesity which he bore like a *panache* must have been morbid. The physical health of an artist, like his financial means, is something which a critic may reasonably consider an influence on his work. How much was Chesterton, how much Belloc, really driven by financial need to the over-production which oppressed them both? How much was it the product of a nervous restlessness and sloth? For profusion can be slothful. It requires more effort to do a small thing really well than do many things carelessly. Mr Wills, with commendable restraint, denies himself the investigation of these problems. He concerns himself very little with the events and circumstances of Chesterton's life. He has contented himself with a study of his written work and has been assiduous in pursuing it in all its huge ephemeral bulk.

There used (and I daresay there still is) to be a company of ladies at the Hollywood film studios whose task it was to tell stories to the directors and producers who lacked the aptitude of reading. They used to peruse all the literature of their time, contemporary and classic, and spin a comprehensive yarn to the assembled company. Now and then they would strike a spark from those flinty imaginations and a voice would proclaim: 'That's for me. Go buy it.'

Mr Wills has performed a similar service for Chesterton. He has read everything and he presents us with a conscientious, if clumsy, précis. He begins his book by suggesting some questions that require solution. He then plods through his work taking it, book by book, poem by poem, essay by essay, and telling us what it is about. At the end he honestly admits failure. 'This book,' he admits, 'opened with a series of questions which, when I wrote the first pages, I hoped in some measure to answer. Now I know that is impossible.'

As a small boy I possessed a book called *The Conjuror at Home* which opened with the valuable advice: 'Never tell your audience in advance what you propose to do. It may not come off.' Mr Wills might have heeded this advice. If he had said in his opening chapter: 'I propose to read everything Chesterton ever wrote and prove that I have done so', we should have applauded his stamina. If his examiners merely require evidence of hard reading, he deserved his doctorate *cum laude*, for Chesterton's output was vast, as is also (it comes as a surprise to this reviewer to learn) the volume of critical studies written about him. It is hard to conceive that Mr Wills's exegesis will greatly illumine the general reader.

For him, as for this reviewer, Chesterton is primarily the author of *The Everlasting Man*. In that book all his random thoughts are concentrated and refined; all his aberrations made straight. It is a great, popular book, one of the few really great popular books of the century; the triumphant assertion that a book can be both great and popular. And it needs no elucidation. It is brilliantly clear. It met a temporary need and survives as a permanent monument. Besides this, Chesterton wrote a number of memorable and delightful verses, notably *Lepanto*. He was a lovable and much loved man abounding in charity and humility. Humility is not a virtue propitious to the artist. It is often pride, emulation, avarice, malice – all the odious qualities – which drive a man to complete, elaborate, refine, destroy, renew, his work until he has made something that gratifies his pride and envy and greed. And in doing so he enriches the world more than the generous and good, though he may lose his own soul in the process. That is the paradox of artistic achievement.

It was a happy chance that Chesterton lived before the era of television. His gifts, his amiability, his very simple eccentricities would have tempted him to become one of the great performers on that damning machine. He lived on the edge of the chasm. Men still had to express themselves in writing until Chesterton was too well habituated to literature to learn new tricks. Living today his words would be lost, his prestige prodigious and his renown brief.

. AN ACT OF HOMAGE AND REPARATION TO P. G. WODEHOUSE .

Last year, when Mr P.G. Wodehouse attained the age of 79, the Americans, with their natural, exuberant generosity, celebrated his eightieth birthday with a declaration of homage signed by most of the best-known writers of the English tongue. Now, with the real occasion almost on us, we, his former compatriots, may prepare our own proud, national salute, but first there is some unfinished business between us, an old and lamentable quarrel to be finally and completely made up and forgotten.

This is an apt occasion, an anniversary.[1] Twenty years ago on 15 July 1941 listeners to the BBC Home Service Postscript were shocked to hear a virulent denunciation of this honoured artist as a collaborator with the enemy.

From his captivity in Germany he had made five recordings describing his experiences as a civilian prisoner of war. A negligible number of people in this country heard any of these talks. All we knew was what the journalist who acted as spokesman of the Minister of Information told us. He described Mr Wodehouse as a gambler and an 'old play-boy' who had remained in France after the débâcle for 'fun'; who had then been 'stealthily groomed by Dr Goebbels for stardom and the limelight of quislings', had 'pawned his honour for the price of a soft bed'; who had 'fallen on his knees and worshipped Hitler'.

Little indication was given of what Mr Wodehouse had actually said. The only words quoted as his had not in fact occurred in the broadcasts at all but were the invention of an American newspaper reporter. Mr Wodehouse was denounced as a traitor and a contrast was held up to our admiration: a man described as displaying 'true splendour of heart'. It is a poignant experience to recall the echo of those years of delusion. Who was this paragon? – Dmitrov, the Bulgarian Communist.

Let it be said at once that no one connected with the BBC had any responsibility for this utterance. All the Governors formally protested against it; one of them, I believe, who was a friend of the Prime Minister of the time, went to him personally to ask him to override his Minister's judgment. They were rebuffed, and the incident provides a glaring example of the danger of allowing politicians to control public communications, a power they had usurped during the war and have now, as we all know, relinquished.

The Postscript did not have the effect designed for it. Some innocent hearers believed what they were told and were incensed. Some high-spirited young airmen set out for Le Touquet to demolish Mr Wodehouse's villa but, as

Sunday Times, 16 July 1961. Text of broadcast over Home Service of BBC, 15 July 1961.

1 Waugh suggested eight years earlier in a letter to the *Daily Mail* (24 November 1953) that the BBC should invite '. . . the originator of their war-time attack to make an apology' to Wodehouse.

562 . CONTRA MUNDUM

sometimes happened, they pranged the wrong target.[1] I was elsewhere and otherwise engaged at the time. The impression I got later from my friends who had heard the broadcast outburst of 15 July was a sense of vicarious guilt that we had descended to the methods of our enemy in our official propaganda.

Both Broadcasting House and *The Times* newspaper received weighty protests, headed by the Poet Laureate in his capacity as President of the Society of Authors. Anyone who knew anything of Mr Wodehouse knew that he never gambled and that so far from being a 'play-boy' he was one of the most diligent of living writers. We knew that at the time of the fall of France civilians had been exhorted to stay where they were and not get in the way of the retreating armies. There was honour rather than shame in a civilian who let himself be taken prisoner. Later it transpired that the 'soft bed' to which his advanced age at length entitled Mr Wodehouse was paid for, not by Dr Goebbels, but by his own earnings – the continental royalties on the translations of his earlier books.

Even before the truth was made public most of his fellow countrymen were content to believe that the charge of kneeling to worship Hitler was preposterous. Many of Mr Wodehouse's most ardent supporters were serving in the Armed Forces and therefore precluded from public expression of their indignation. A great volume of protests came from the universities and from fellow writers. But they were not entirely unanimous, and it is significant of that shabby time that most of those few who supported the attack did so on grounds not of patriotism but of class. The speaker had emphasized the fact that the names represented by Mr Wodehouse's initials are rather imposing. It was well known that Mr Wodehouse, like Shakespeare, drew most of his characters from the upper class and their servants. One correspondent in a newspaper led the hunt beyond the author to these characters, whom he described as 'moneyed and bored, the breeding ground of fascism'. 'The embryo of the fascist mentality,' he said, 'was recorded in his whole set of characters.' The conception of Mr Mulliner and Lord Emsworth as potential Eichmanns would be too grotesque to deserve mention were it not a symptom of that diseased period.

In England, as in other countries, during the last war there were men and women who sought to direct the struggle for national survival into proletarian revolution and to identify the enemy with their own upper classes. Few people, I suppose, now remember that there was at that time an authentic Nazi propagandist who broadcast in English. His harsh accents were very different from those usually associated with the nobility. But the people in charge of our morale insisted on dubbing him 'Lord Haw-Haw'.[2] The attack on Mr Wode-

---

1 When revising *Wodehouse at Work* Mr Richard Usborne attempted to verify this story but came to the conclusion that it was untrue. See 'Shooting Down a Wodehouse Story', *Evening Standard*, 12 November 1975.

2 The name 'Lord Haw-Haw' was first given to Norman Baillie-Stewart, who spoke with an exaggerated upper-class accent; it was transferred to William Joyce when he replaced Baillie-Stewart as chief Nazi propagandist.

house conformed to this conspiracy to identify aristocracy with treason. It should, however, to their abiding honour be recorded that in 1944, when the monstrous suggestion was made that Mr Wodehouse should be prosecuted, two socialists, George Orwell and Mr Muggeridge, were among the first and most effective of his defenders.

It was not until 1954, when in its October and November issues the magazine *Encounter* published the text of the notorious broadcast, that the full truth became clear. As his friends had always confidently believed, there was in them no political implication of any kind, no mention of Hitler or of the Nazi system. The nearest he came to comforting the enemy was to suggest that they were human beings, neither admirable nor lovable, but human. He recounts with obvious candour and with his own unique humour his experiences from the moment of the arrival of the conquering army at Le Touquet to his eventual internment in a prison, where, by being elected president of the library, he was able to resume his life's work as a writer of fiction. He had no preferential treatment except what his fellow captives voted him. Throughout his transit across Europe he bore with admirable good humour privations which would have been severe for a man half his age, and suffered from the incompetence and officiousness of those in whose charge he was travelling. At a time when the whole world was disposed to regard the German Army as an irresistible machine, he described its rear echelons as manned by the muddled and ineffectual. He tells how, after days of futile parades at which the prisoners were counted and re-counted, one of his fellows remarked that after the war he proposed to buy a German soldier, keep him in the garden and count him six times a day.

Mr Wodehouse's broadcasts were not calculated to engender respect for the Germans, nor hate. That was his offence in the eyes of the official propagandists of the period. He revealed that civilian prisoners had slightly endearing nicknames for their gaolers – 'Pluto, Rosebud, Ginger and Donald Duck'; that like most prisoners of war they were able to organize some modest recreations for themselves. Our rulers at the time, like our enemies, were dedicated to fomenting hate. They would have had us believe that the whole German nation comprised a different order of creation from ourselves. Mr Wodehouse's simple diversion from their party line was what was represented as 'kneeling in worship' of Hitler.

Dmitrov followed his calling to his nasty end. Mr Wodehouse lives in prosperity, honour and fertility, alas, not among us, his fellow countrymen. Why bring up again after twenty years this ugly moment of official aberration?

'It is now time to regard the incident as closed.' George Orwell wrote that in 1944, but there is a hideous vitality in calumny. Justice *seems* to have been done. Innocence *seems* to have been established. But always there is some mean or ignorant mind ready to reassert the lie. I have seen it again and again in the course of the last ten years insinuated into reviews and gossip paragraphs. It is therefore with great pleasure that I take this opportunity to express the disgust that the BBC has always felt for the injustice of which they were guiltless and their complete repudiation of the charges so ignobly made through their medium. If Mr Wodehouse is by any chance listening in his distant western island of refuge, I would say: you have always given great evidence of magnanimity. You tell me you have met and conceived a liking for the man who twenty years ago did you so grave an injury. Will you please extend your forgiveness to everyone who ever spoke or thought ill of you?

That being said, we can turn to the happier theme of greeting him on his approaching eightieth birthday. A man of my age, twenty-two years younger than Mr Wodehouse, has grown up in the light of his genius. By the time that I went to school his stories were established classics and in the nursery I was familiar with my elder brother's impersonations of Psmith. I have possessed a complete set of his works, now sadly depleted by theft. I still await with unappeasable appetite the publication of each addition to the *oeuvre*. And this is no recondite hobby, it is shared by thousands.

The first thing to remark about Mr Wodehouse's art is its universality, unique in this century. Except for political claptrap few forms of writing are as ephemeral as comedy. Three full generations have delighted in Mr Wodehouse. As a young man he lightened the cares of office of Mr Asquith. I see my children convulsed with laughter over the same books. He satisfies the most sophisticated taste and the simplest. Belloc, to the consternation of Hugh Walpole, forthrightly declared him to be the best prose writer of the age; Ronald Knox, most fastidious of scholars and stylists, rejoiced in him. At the same time his translations are enormously popular among the Norwegians, a people who have not as yet fully evolved their own literary language and are, they admit, quite unconscious of the nuances of dialogue. They read him for his plots. The Americans are notoriously capricious in their laughter and change their style of joke as often as their style of interior decoration. But they still read Mr Wodehouse.

What is the secret of his immortality? One essential, of course, is his technical excellence achieved by sheer hard work. He is the antithesis, for example, of Ronald Firbank, whose haphazard, hit-or-miss innuendoes sparkle and flutter in and out of critical attention. Mr Wodehouse is an heroically diligent planner and reviser. He has confided very little of his personal affairs to the public, but in 1953, he authorized the publication of his letters to an old school friend, Mr W. Townend, who arranged them into a fascinating book entitled *Performing Flea*. They cover, intermittently, thirty years of his working life and in them he reveals his literary method. We find a man occupied, one may say obsessed, by construction.

Most of us who rejoice in his work do so primarily for the exquisite felicity of the language. That, it seems, is a minor consideration to the author. Either it comes to him unsought, an inexplicable gift like Nijinsky's famous levitations, or it is a matter on which he is so confident in his own judgment that he does not trouble to mention any hesitations he may experience. From his letters he seems to write, as the Norwegians read, for the plot.

He has done much work in collaboration for the theatre and his mind is set upon the story as a series of effective scenes. He thinks of his characters as being on stage or off. Every exit and entrance is deliberately contrived. In 1924 he wrote: 'I class all my characters as if they were living, salaried actors . . . The one thing actors – important actors, I mean – won't stand is being brought on to play a scene which is of no value to them in order to feed some less important character and I believe this isn't vanity . . . They kick because they know the balance isn't right.'

In 1937 we find him writing:

It looks as if the *Saturday Evening Post* are taking it for granted that they are going to buy the story but they felt that the early part needed cutting. 'Too many stage waits' was what Brandt said. And when I looked at it, I saw they were right. Here is the layout as I had it. (1) Bertie goes to see his Aunt Dahlia. (2) She tells him to go and buy flowers for Aunt Agatha who is ill. (3) Bertie goes back to his flat and she rings him up and says she forgot to say that she has another job for him – which will necessitate a visit to an antique shop. (4) Bertie goes to flower shop and gets into trouble. (5) Bertie goes back to his flat and sobs on Jeeves's shoulder. (6) Bertie goes to antique shop and gets into more trouble. Now, can you imagine that I had written that part quite a dozen times, and only now spotted that it ought to go like this: (1) Bertie goes to Aunt Dahlia. She tells him to go to antique shop. (2) Bertie goes to antique shop and plays the scene which originally took place in flower shop, then plays the antique shop scene. It cuts out fifteen pages without losing anything of value. And what I'm driving at is that isn't it ghastly to think that after earning one's living as a writer for thirty-seven years one can make a blunder like that. Why on earth I kept taking Bertie back to the flat, where nothing whatever happened, I can't think. This, the revision, necessitated five days of intense work.

That extract, typical of many of these letters, shows not only the master's industry but his humility. Writers on the whole are a vain and irascible people who do not take kindly to criticism, still less to direction. For professional literary critics Mr Wodehouse has no great respect and that for the very good reason that, as I know from long personal experience, his books are almost impossible to review. It is easy enough to compose a general dissertation about his idiosyncratic art, but as year by year each book appears there is singularly little to be said about it except to acknowledge the event gratefully and joyously.

Mr Wodehouse's prestige has been founded on his readers rather than on his critics, but he is essentially a professional man who seeks to satisfy his clients and he takes as his clients those who sign the cheques, the editors and publishers. This is an American rather than a European attitude. We in Europe look on editors and publishers as necessary and often very agreeable middle-men between ourselves and our readers. We think of ourselves as the guardians of our own reputations. American editors regard themselves as employers, and many sharp misunderstandings arise when European writers publish their work in the New World. Mr Wodehouse has never expressed any annoyance, rather gratitude, at what in Europe would seem irksome presumption. Indeed, he attributes the superiority of American magazines to this editorial interference:

> Practically every English magazine [he wrote] would buy any sort of bilge provided it was by somebody with a big name as a novelist. The reason the *Saturday Evening Post* was always so darned good was that Lorimer never fell into this trap . . . the Boss was an autocrat all right but, my God, what an editor to work for! He kept you up on your toes. I had twenty-one serials in the *Post*, but I never felt safe till I got the cable saying each had got over with Lorimer.

Of the dedicated craftsman there is abundant evidence in his letters; of the artist very little. Of his method of writing, as distinct from composing, his only hint is in 1946, when, apropos of the loss of momentum which he experienced in later life, he wrote: 'I find I have a tendency to write a funny line and then add another, elaborating it when there is no necessity for the second bit. I keep coming on such bits in the thing I'm doing now, I go through the story every day and hack them out', but the magic which produces the funny line remains incommunicable.

There is, as the extracts I have quoted show, a notable difference between his style in writing letters and writing for publication, and I should say that his exquisite diction, as natural as birdsong, is a case of genuine poetic inspiration. I don't believe Mr Wodehouse knows where it comes from or how; wherever he is, in luxury or in prison, he is able to sequester himself and, as it were, take dictation from his daemon.

One can date exactly the first moment when he was touched by the sacred flame. It occurs half-way through *Mike*, written in 1910. Collectors prize as bibliographical rarities such early works as *William Tell Told Again* and *Swoop*, but it is impossible to discern in them any promise of what was to come. Then in Chapter XXXI of *Mike*, which was then being serialized in the *Captain* and had run an easy course of agreeable, conventional schoolboy fiction, Psmith appears and the light is kindled which has burned with growing brilliance for half a century. Psmith himself is not the greatest of his creations, but he is the first, and Mr Downing's quest for the boot in Chapters XLIX, L and LI is one of the great scenes of comic literature. Was Mr Wodehouse himself aware, I wonder, that he had crossed the mysterious frontier?

I am not in his confidence, but I suspect some of his notable lack of side comes not only from beauty of character but from a genuine failure to recognize his own immeasurable superiority to other writers who 'got over with Lorimer' and sold their wares to the *Saturday Evening Post*. I do not believe that in his own work he distinguishes between a contrived character like Ukridge and an inspired one like Bertie Wooster. It is, perhaps, in the nature of inspiration that the recipient is unaware of its operation. I believe that Mr Wodehouse is still a little puzzled at the awe in which he is held by connoisseurs of English prose. He was genuinely abashed when he received his honorary doctorate at Oxford – so much so that he gives evidence of believing that the ceremony took place in Cambridge. When Mr Sean O'Casey described him as 'English literature's performing flea' he said: 'I believe he meant to be complimentary, for all the performing fleas I have met have impressed me with their sterling artistry and that indefinable something which makes the good trouper', and he used the appellation as the title of the book from which I have been quoting. It is not, primarily, the 'good trouper' that we revere; not even 'the sterling artist'; it is the 'indefinable something' which makes the poet; which, in Housman's famous image, raises the hairs on our cheeks as we shave.

There was a cocky young reviewer a year or two ago who publicly debased himself by stating that Mr Wodehouse was out of date. In that young man's sense, he has never been in date. He inhabits a world as timeless as that of *A Midsummer Night's Dream* and *Alice in Wonderland*; a world inhabited by strange transmogrifications.

I said just now that he wrote mainly of the upper classes and their servants. That needs modification. Of his three distinctive cycles that of Blandings is aristocratic; that of Mr Mulliner middle class, and that of Wooster an intricate combination of moneyed leisure and desperate impecuniosity. None have any identity with the real life of any period. Mr Wodehouse's characters are not, as has been fatuously suggested, survivals of the Edwardian age. They are creations of pure fancy – and I use pure in both its senses. Mr Wodehouse must know as well as anyone else what are the amorous adventures of young, rich bachelors in London. His 'young men in spats' pursue an ideal of courtly love. The word 'spats' recalls us to realms of fantasy. They have not been part of the normal costume of a young man about town these forty years. They are still worn at the Drones Club, and the Drones, with its swimming bath and its smoking concerts, its 'Old Beans' and 'Old Crumpets' touching one another for fivers, has no correspondence at all with any London club of any period. Mr Wodehouse was an early member of Buck's Club. He knew exactly how young men talked: the language of the Drones was never heard on human lips. It is all Mr Wodehouse's invention, or rather inspiration.

They fall in love impetuously and ardently, these figures of Mr Wodehouse's imagination. Their sole failure of chivalry is the occasional mercenary pursuit of an heiress. Seduction and adultery are unknown among them. But they are capable of most other moral lapses. They fall into rages. They get drunk. They smuggle. They rob. They commit arson. They kidnap. They blackmail. They even resort to violence – quite a number of innocent and guilty alike, even the police, get knocked on the head. Professional criminals abound, but they are not the brutes of recent fiction, still less of real life. There are horrific aunts in plenty, but they are not the aunts of 'Saki' Munro. All, whatever the delinquencies attributed to them, exist in a world of pristine paradisal innocence.

For Mr Wodehouse there has been no Fall of Man; no 'aboriginal calamity'. His characters have never tasted the forbidden fruit. They are still in Eden. The gardens of Blandings Castle are that original garden from which we are all exiled. The chef Anatole prepares the ambrosia for the immortals of high

Olympus. Mr Wodehouse's idyllic world can never stale. He will continue to release future generations from captivity that may be more irksome than our own. He has made a world for us to live in and delight in.

When that solemn day comes in three months' time, Mr Wodehouse, when you keep your eightieth birthday, please remember that all your old compatriots will be thinking of you with unique and unqualified gratitude.

. FOOTLIGHTS AND CHANDELIERS .

A parlour-game question: what middle-aged Englishman displays the following attributes: 'Our foremost arbiter of taste' (New Statesman), 'One of the unassailables of our time' (Daily Mail), 'The Horace Walpole of our time' (New York Evening Sun)? Give it up? Then how about this: 'The Byron of the camera' (Life)? Of course. The answer is Mr Cecil Beaton, who has published a selection from his diaries, interspersed with reminiscence, covering the years 1922–39.

It is a fairly attractive production, interspersed with the author's line-drawings and a number of plates which seem to be arrayed without relevance to the text. It tells the story of the early years of a man unashamedly on the make. Mr Beaton reveals himself as a young man consumed by worldly ambition, not for power nor for creation; he simply wanted to get himself known and accepted. As a child he was stage-struck; as an adolescent society-struck. There was no great difference between the footlights and the chandeliers. Both revealed worlds of make-believe where everyone looked his best and talked cleverly. Mr Beaton recounts as many painful and humiliating mishaps as Mr Pooter, of whose diary these pages sometimes remind us, but he climbed steadily to the head of his profession as a portrait photographer until, as a fit climax to this book, he received the command of the Queen Mother, then the Queen, to make the charming series of studies of her at Buckingham Palace – a sitting which his beguiling personality prolonged from twenty minutes to three hours.

In later life he has earned renown as a theatrical designer. He did little in that line before the war. He got the Americans to buy his drawings. But his rise to popularity and prosperity was essentially as a photographer. He had the knack, so grossly lacking in his juniors, of making his subjects look attractive and elegant. His camera carried him into the presence of the famous and the beautiful and, once there, he often established himself in warm friendship. There was between the wars a society, cosmopolitan, sympathetic to the arts, well-mannered, amusing, above all ornamental even in rather bizarre ways, which for want of a better description the newspapers called 'High Bohemia'.

Review of *The Wandering Years*, by Cecil Beaton. *Spectator*, 21 July 1961.

There Mr Beaton shone. The record of these 'wandering years' ought to be enchanting. Perhaps it will enchant others; alas, not me. There was a gift lacking at his christening. Sir Arthur Bryant writes: 'Cecil Beaton is not only an artist – he can write.' The publisher gives no date for this opinion. Mr Beaton is tireless in self-education. He may lately have learned a new art. I can only say that, judging from this book, most of which is twenty years old, he can't write for toffee. Neither in verbal expression nor in literary construction does he show any but the feeblest talent.

The work is heterogeneous. There are passages from the diaries in which he recorded (not, surely, for publication?) his early, naïve aspirations and despairs. There is a theme, lately popularized by Mr John Betjeman, of the conflict of an aesthetic son with a philistine father, and of the subsequent remorse. Here and, still more, in the descriptions of family tragedy, I find him highly embarrassing, not because such themes are necessarily improper, but because they require a delicacy and restraint, which Mr Beaton lacked, to dignify them. Mr Beaton is aware, and sadly comments on the fact more than once, that despite his ever-widening success and popularity there were certain cold people who regarded him as slightly absurd. He went so far as to take lessons from Mrs Patrick Campbell in order to acquire a deeper tone of voice. Mr Noël Coward gave him unsolicited advice about discretion in dress and deportment. Apropos of this propensity of his to attract ridicule, I may, perhaps, be excused for correcting his memory on a small point. It is, I confess with shame, true that a crony and I behaved cruelly to him at our Hampstead private school. He was an extremely pretty little boy. The spectacle of his long eyelashes wet with tears was one to provoke the sadism of youth. His offence was that he was reputed to enjoy his music lessons. The bullying of little Beaton was not, as he suggests, an isolated incident, but repeated many times. Our chief sport was to stick pins into him. And it did not stop, as he suggests, because 'if it is possible to put up an authoritative front or assume an aggressive attitude in turn, then the bully himself will be the first to collapse,' but because my companion in this abomination and I were caught out and soundly beaten for it by a master. This lapse of memory makes me wonder whether his account of his ducking at Wilton is entirely accurate. I was not there, but I remember the eyewitness accounts which circulated in London a day or two later. They were more farcical than the account given here.

Mr Beaton belongs to the last generation to whom it was still possible to travel freely in a world not yet much despoiled by politicians and tourists. He took full advantage of his opportunities and saw many spectacles of beauty. It is in his attempts at descriptive passages that his lack of literary skill is most apparent. When he uses words that are at all recondite – 'pristine', 'allegiance', 'novitiate', 'funicular', for example – it is too often apparent that he does not know their meanings. Many of his sentences are stilted. 'Few people have yet stirred themselves; business has not been embarked upon.' Why not: 'Few have yet stirred; business has not begun'? 'The Château itself, begun in the sixteenth century, has seen many subsequent additions in the intervening years.' Either 'subsequent' or 'in the intervening years' is redundant. It is a pity that Mr Beaton, instead of taking lessons in elocution (most people, anyway, enjoyed his voice), did not engage a literary tutor.

He is at his best when he is writing in a cheeky, slangy way about people. Here I find him highly amusing when he is describing people I don't know – the brawl in Hollywood, for example, or the working habits of Bébé Bérard – but I met a great many of his characters and knew many of them well, and I find his portraits flat; not dull, but two-dimensional. They would be, to me, unrecognizable but for their names (and he is rather odd sometimes about even these, referring to married women and widows as if they were divorcées – 'Mrs Beatrice Guinness', 'Mrs Venetia Montagu'). I don't think it is simply a case of having a different vision. I don't think that in his early days he was really interested in people except when they were on the stage. He noticed their clothes and their peculiarities and noted scraps of dialogue, but he seemed unaware of their having an existence apart from him, of having a past or ties of kinship, except so far as they were referred to in newspapers, or a future. He lived in the present moment and the present company without historical sense. He had no curiosity, he tells us, about his own grandparents. He shrank from maturity and remarks with great satisfaction of a friend, aged 33, that he is 'mentally several years younger' than when they last met. Ancient buildings existed for him purely as a picturesque setting, not as monuments to a continuing past. It is perhaps significant that one of the artists to excite his highest rapture was the manipulator of a Greek shadow-show. Nor, despite much lack of reticence, does Mr Beaton display full candour. He seems sometimes to eavesdrop on himself and report what he has learned. I do not hear the authentic note of self-revelation even in his most shy-making confidences. For these reasons I do not think he qualifies for the title, bestowed on him by the *Sunday Times*, of 'memorialist'. I don't think people of the future will turn to him to elucidate the condition of his age.

. MEGNIFICENT MR KAPLAN .

In the mid-1930s Europeans became aware of the new and exhilarating humour and technical precision of the *New Yorker*. One of the most brilliant and original of the writers of that decade was young Mr Leo Rosten, who was reading for his PhD at Washington. He had previously taught in a night school for adults on the West Side of Chicago. Drawing on his experiences there and writing in the name of 'Leonard Q. Ross' he created Hyman Kaplan, a unique and enduring figure of pure fun. He has since published a second series, equally beguiling, under his own name. Pan Books give no reason for preserving the pseudonym. *The Education of Hyman Kaplan* is not particularly apt for

Review of *The Education of Hyman Kaplan*, by Leonard Q. Ross, Pan Books. *Observer*, 6 October 1961. Waugh reviewed the first edition of the book for *Night and Day*, 11 November 1957.

paper covers. It is not a work to be read and thrown away, but to be kept at the bedside and constantly resorted to. When it first appeared, in 1937, I wrote: 'Immensely funny and all the better for being taken in large doses . . . a lovely book.' My zest has not become dull in the intervening years.

It is not at all easy to define the qualities which make it so memorable. It comprises a series of brief incidents in an English class for immigrants. Mr Rosten transposed the scene from Chicago to New York because, he says, 'stories about immigrants in a night school just have an irresistible tropism for that marvellous carnival of city.' The students come from many nations and trades. Their sole common feature is that English is a foreign language to them and they are desperately keen to master it. Stated baldly, the jokes consist of puns and of 'howlers'; the comic foreigner, lost in the complexities of English idiom, was a standard *Punch* figure for more than a century.

Hyman Kaplan and his companions in class are that, but translated into poetry and a wild disorder of logic comparable to 'Alice'. They are seen through the eyes of their instructor, Mr Parkhill, who is as eager to teach as they are to learn, whom they revere, for whose favour they fiercely compete, who almost loves them but leaves them night after night baffled and defeated. His is the lowest class. Those who satisfy him ascend to Miss Higby. Mr Parkhill is dealing with those who are barely literate in any tongue and have picked up such English as they know with imperfect ears from imperfect speakers.

In what Mr Rosten calls 'the antic freedom of phonetics' the words 'I ate the bread' can become 'I hate the brat'. 'Dialect,' as he says, 'is not transcription. Nothing is more depressing than a passage of broken English exactly transcribed. The "accurate ear" for which a writer is praised, is as inventive as it is accurate.' Mr Parkhill's method of teaching, fraught with the dangers of rivalry and animosity, is to invite his pupils to correct one another's mistakes. It is in these skirmishes that Mr Kaplan is always in the wrong and always victorious.

'Well,' began Miss Mitnick yet a third time, desperately, ' "animated" is wrong. "Your *animated* brother, Hymie"? *That's* wrong.'

She looked at Mr Parkhill with a plea that was poignant. She dared not look at Mr Kaplan, whose smile had advanced to a new dimension.

'Yes,' said Mr Parkhill. ' "Animated" is quite out of place in the final greeting.'

Mr Kaplan sighed. 'I looked op de void "enimated" *spacial*. It's minnink "full of life", no? . . . Vell, I falt *planty* full of life ven I was wridink de ladder.'

Miss Mitnick dropped her eyes, the rout complete.

'Mr Kaplan!' Mr Parkhill was left to fight the good fight alone. 'You may say "She had an animated expression" or "The music has an animated refrain." But one doesn't say "animated" about one's *self*.'

The appeal to propriety proved successful. Mr Kaplan confessed that perhaps he had overreached himself with 'Your animated brother'.

'Suppose we try another word,' suggested Mr Parkhill. 'How about "fond"? "Your *fond* brother – er – Hyman"?' (He couldn't quite essay 'Hymie'.)

Mr Kaplan half closed his eyes, gazed into space and meditated on this moot point. ' "Fond", "fond",' he whispered to himself. He was like a man who had retreated into a secret world, searching for his Muse. ' "Your fond brodder,

Hymie."' He shook his head. 'Podden me,' he said apologetically. 'It don't have de *fillink*.'

'What about "dear"?' offered Mr Parkhill quickly. '"Your *dear* brother", and so on?'

Once more Mr Kaplan went through the process of testing, judgement and consultation with his evasive Muse. '"Dear", "dear". "Your dear brodder, Hymie." Also no.' He sighed. '"Dear", it's too *common*.'

'What about –'

'Aha!' cried Mr Kaplan suddenly, as the Muse kissed him. His smile was as the sun. 'I got him! Fine! Poifick! Soch a void!'

The class, to whom Mr Kaplan had communicated some of his own excitement, waited breathlessly. Mr Parkhill himself, it might be said, was possessed of a queer eagerness.

'Yes, Mr Kaplan. What word would you suggest?'

'"Megnificent!"' cried Mr Kaplan.

Admiration and silence fell upon the class like a benediction.

The last words are the conclusion of Mr Kaplan's examination paper: 'ps. I don't care if I don't pass. I *love* the class.' The reader can gratefully echo them. Mr Kaplan has been a potent force for European–American understanding for twenty-five years. In Europe we are apt to identify the United States with the tourists who visit us. It is salutary to remember that a great part of the population have fled from us and have no ambition to return.

. SLOTH .

The word 'Sloth' is seldom on modern lips. When used, it is a mildly facetious variant of 'indolence', and indolence, surely, so far from being a deadly sin, is one of the most amiable of weaknesses. Most of the world's troubles seem to come from people who are too busy. If only politicians and scientists were lazier, how much happier we should all be. The lazy man is preserved from the commission of almost all the nastier crimes, and many of the motives which make us sacrifice to toil the innocent enjoyment of leisure, are among the most ignoble – pride, avarice, emulation, vainglory and the appetite for power over others. How then has Sloth found a place with its six odious companions as one of the Mortal Sins?

Theologians are the least rhetorical of writers. Their vocabulary is elaborate and precise, and when they condemn an act as a mortal sin they are not merely expressing disapproval in a striking phrase. They mean something specific and appalling; an outrage against the divine order committed with full knowledge and consent which, if unrepented before death, consigns the doer to eternal loss of salvation. Prelates and preachers may be found who use the words irresponsibly. One sometimes sees proclamations in which the faithful are

The Seven Deadly Sins, ed. Raymond Mortimer. (London, 1962.) First printed *Sunday Times*, 7 January 1962.

exhorted to vote in an election or refrain from an entertainment 'under pain of mortal sin'. Moral theologians give little support to such utterances. Indeed many speculate that, the sanctions being so awful and the conditions so stringent, very few mortal sins have ever been committed. We only know that Hell is there for those who deliberately choose it. Shall we go there for lying too long in the bath or postponing our letters of congratulation or condolence? Obviously not. What then is this Sloth which can merit the extremity of divine punishment?

St Thomas's answer is both comforting and surprising: *tristitia de bono spirituali*, sadness in the face of spiritual good. Man is made for joy in the love of God, a love which he expresses in service. If he deliberately turns away from that joy, he is denying the purpose of his existence. The malice of Sloth lies not merely in the neglect of duty (though that can be a symptom of it) but in the refusal of joy. It is allied to despair.

There is a well-known pathological condition of religious melancholy in which the sufferer believes himself to be eternally damned through no particular fault of his own but by the ineluctable whim of the Almighty. In recent years, with the waning of Calvinist eloquence, this aberration seems to have tended to shed its religious trappings, but there are recognizable traces of it in some of the utterances of the 'beatniks'. Despair of this kind is not Sloth. Sloth is the condition in which a man is fully aware of the proper means of his salvation and refuses to take them because the whole apparatus of salvation fills him with tedium and disgust.

It is, one might suppose, a rare condition most often found among those who have dedicated themselves to a specifically religious vocation for which they find themselves unworthy, and not the prime temptation of men living in the world. Sixty years ago it would have been pedantic to treat of it in a secular journal, but, curiously enough, in this generation the man of Sloth, in all his full theological implications, has become one of the stock figures of stage and novel. The protagonists of these popular spiritual dramas, French, English, American, sometimes priests, are spoken of as having 'lost their Faith' as though Faith were an extraneous possession, like an umbrella, which can be inadvertently left behind in a railway-carriage; but in fact their predicament is quite different from that of their unhappy great-grandfathers who, confronted with plausible arguments that the universe took longer than six days in the making, decided that the whole foundation of their religion was spurious. These new apostates do not wrestle with historical and philosophic doubts; they simply lapse into 'sadness in the face of spiritual good'.

The plainest representation of this depth of Sloth, and the one likely to be freshest in the reader's memory, is Querry, the central character of Mr Graham Greene's recent novel, *A Burnt-Out Case*. He is an eminent architect who, like the less well-known writer, Morin, created by the same richly gifted writer, is sickened by the applause of admirers who persist in attributing his achievements to a love of God he has ceased to exercise. Love of his fellow men also dies in him. Eaten by apathy, self-pity and the sense of futility he tries to escape to the most remote refuge in central Africa where there happens to be a leper settlement. Here he dies a ludicrous death. The only change in him has been a twinge of affection for a servant and, at the instigation of an atheist doctor, an interest in the erection of some new sheds.

The author's intention, as in most of his later books, is obscure. Does he mean us to recognize in these feeble stirrings of humanity an act of the will which a theologian would recognize as contrition? We must not impute damnation to a human soul. With fictitious characters we are free to speculate. I should say that on the facts given us by Mr Greene, Querry was guilty and in Hell. He is one of a rather large company of modern fictitious characters. The fact that they have so captivated the artists and the public of the day suggests that the problem is not so recondite as might have been supposed. It must not be thought I am accusing Mr Greene of Sloth. Artists often express vicarious experiences (most erotic writing is the work of the impotent). It would be impossible for a man who was really guilty of Sloth to write about it, for he would be incapable of the intense work required to produce a novel like *A Burnt-Out Case*.

So much for the Sloth of the theologian, technically dubbed *accidia* (or *acedia*). There is no true classical term for this state, not because it was unknown to the ancients, but because it was too commonplace to require identification. The last centuries of European paganism before the revelation of Christian joy were sunk deep in *accidia*. Now that paganism is returning we see the symptoms again. Can we accuse our listless and torpid contemporaries of Sloth in the sense defined above? I think not, because the great majority have been deprived by the state of religious instruction. The phrase 'spiritual good' is totally foreign to them, and they lack the full knowledge of its nature which is an essential element in the commission of mortal sin.

There are, however, very near parallels, especially in those whose calling has a superficial resemblance to monastic life, the armed services. These men accept higher standards of obedience than civilians and are expected on occasions to make greater sacrifices. 'Browned-off' and 'bloody-minded' troops present a type of Sloth. I have seen soldiers in defeat who could not be accused of laziness. They were making strenuous exertions to get away from the enemy. Nor were they impelled by fear. They had simply become bored by the mismanagement of the battle and indifferent to its outcome. There were ill-found camps and stations in the war where men refused to take the actions which would have alleviated their own condition, but instead luxuriated in apathy and resentment. There was a sense of abandonment there which, though it was not recognized as such, was theological in essence; instead it found expression in complaints, just or unjust, against the higher command and the politicians.

It was suggested above that we were not putting ourselves in danger of Hell by indolence but, just as he is a poor soldier whose sole aim is to escape detention, so he is a poor Christian whose sole aim is to escape Hell. Besides *accidia* there is *pigritia*, plain slackness, which is a deflection from, if not an outrage against, the divine order. This increasingly is a national characteristic, so closely allied to our national virtues of magnanimity and good temper as to be at times barely distinguishable from them. It is strange, in an age when the conscience is directed so constantly to social aims, that this vice so largely escapes censure, for if, as has been said, the personal motives of industry may be base, the consequences of idleness on society are conspicuously deleterious.

It is a fault about which we are particularly liable to self-deception. Almost all the men and women in England proclaim themselves to be busy. They have 'no time' to read or cook or take notice of the ceaseless process of spoliation of their island or even to dress decorously, while in their offices and workshops they do less and less, in quality and quantity, for ever larger wages with which to pay larger taxes for services that diminish in quantity and quality. We have voted for a Welfare State but are everywhere frustrated because we are too lazy to man the services; too few school teachers, too few hospital nurses, too few prison warders. That way lies national disaster; but the subject of this essay is moral, not political. There is something unattractive about those who gaze out of their windows for long periods studying the idleness of the navvies 'at work' outside. Let me speak of my own trade.

Since I first set up as a writer nearly thirty-five years ago I have witnessed a lamentable decline of power in all the processes of literature. The period between the delivery of a manuscript to the publishers and its appearance for sale as a book is now about three times what it was in my youth, as also is the period between ordering a book from a shop in the provinces and receiving it. The standards of printing have deteriorated. Compositors, equipped with mechanical devices unknown to their illustrious predecessors, are ruthless in setting up gibberish and preserving it against proof corrections.

But it ill becomes authors to complain of the mechanics. We are ourselves in a situation peculiarly apt for self-deception, for there is no one except ourselves who can accuse us of idleness. The actual process of writing is laborious and irksome. We sit at our desks for, say, two hours and emerge with a thousand deathless words. But if we sit at our windows smoking, observing the birds, who is to say that we are not deep in aesthetic rumination? If we lounge in a foreign café, who is to say we are not 'collecting material'? Not the Commissioners of Income Tax.

You must know us by our works. How many of us display the 'hard gem-like flame' with which, for example, Max Beerbohm in his day illuminated even the columns of the *Daily Mail*? How many resolve that nothing shall leave the workshop which is not as perfectly finished as our talents allow? How many have simply given up the effort to plan and complete and adorn a work of art? Endowed with the most splendid language in the world, most of the young writers seem intent to debase and impoverish it.

Their elders do not set them a high example. If one considers the list of those who, twenty years ago, would have been expected to be now at the height of their powers, one finds a pitiably small band of survivors and those mainly men and women of the previous decade. The rest concern themselves with appearing on television, collaborating in film-scripts and attending congresses where they call attention to the lack of prestige they are accorded. Of the hard, long work of actually writing books, most have despaired. How many reviewers, even in the respectable papers, read the book sent them with close enough attention to retail their plots or arguments without mistakes of pure laziness?

It may be noted that in the Arts profusion, as much as sterility, may be evidence of laziness. Those huge novels from North America are not the product of diligence; hard labour would refine and clarify them. Some writers, it is said, leave this to their publishers, presenting them with trunk-loads of typescript from which a précis is made in the office. This is not a common trouble in this country. Here we suffer rather from the imposture of writers who produce their rough notes and sketches as finished work and pretend to a unity in what are mere scraps of articles and lectures.

These are some of the evidence of Sloth in a single trade in a country where the vice is widely prevalent. They may seem of minor importance in the history of national decline but they are symptomatic of the whole disease, and literature was formerly the one art in which we could claim equality with (if not superiority to) the rest of the civilized world. Sloth is not such an innocent weakness as at first glance it appeared.

It is easy to find explanations of modern laziness. All the 'glittering prizes' of success have lately become tarnished. The company in the room at the top has lost the art of pleasing. But Sloth is not primarily the temptation of the young. Medical science has oppressed us with a new huge burden of longevity. It is in that last undesired decade, when passion is cold, appetites feeble, curiosity dulled and experience has begotten cynicism, that *accidia* lies in wait as the final temptation to destruction. That is the time which is given a man to 'make his soul'. For few of us the hero's and martyr's privilege of a few clear days ending on the scaffold; instead an attenuated, bemused drifting into eternity. Death has not lost its terror in the new clinical arctic twilight. In this state we shall have to face the last deadly assault of the devil. It is then, perhaps, that we shall be able to resist only by the spiritual strength we have husbanded in youth.

. LUTHER .
JOHN OSBORNE'S NEW PLAY

Mr John Osborne has no one but himself to blame for the sobriquet of 'angry young man' which is attached to him in the popular press. It was, no doubt, because he saw the young Luther as a similar malcontent of ill-controlled violence of expression that he was attracted to his story. But there were other features of the theme which made it appropriate. For one thing Mr Osborne's strong talent is for uninterrupted monologue. His characters are too uncivil to indulge in anything that can be called conversation. They shout one another down. And there is very little opportunity for monologue in contemporary, realistic drama. The best – indeed the only really good feature of *Look Back in Anger* was the opening harangue by the cad–hero to his patient wife. That could not be repeated in a second play. But the pulpit provides an admirable stage property for just the sort of composition in which Mr Osborne excels and in *Luther* he takes full advantage of it.

There was, perhaps, another attraction – the hope of shocking. In Britain this fell flat because the number of Britons specifically calling themselves 'Lutheran' is negligible. The Protestant sects are mostly Calvinist by origin and their members do not, in any case, frequent the theatre. The Anglican Church, strongly Lutheran at its foundation, has in the last century tended to deny its pristine loyalties. Very few Britons have been brought up to revere Luther as a man of religion. Moreover two generations have grown up with a strong antipathy to everything German and do not easily accept as a hero a man who has the reputation of being one of the founders of German nationalism. But this condition does not pertain to the same degree in the United States of America, where it seems probable that many will be shocked to Mr Osborne's satisfaction by the portrayal of a pious leader as a foul-mouthed and, eventually, traitorous agitator.

One does not resort to the theatre (or to the novel) to learn history. It may be accepted that the dramatist (and novelist) is entitled to lay the emphasis where he will, to select among his sources the incidents most suitable to his purpose and, where more than one version exists, to prefer the more picturesque. He may also invent where his invention does not contradict established fact. Mr Osborne has not always followed these precepts. There was little need for invention. Luther's true history is so dramatic and so fully recorded that deviation is otiose. It is significant that where Mr Osborne most grossly falsifies his facts, he most weakens his effect. For example he has written a first-class scene for Tetzel (which in London was brilliantly played) showing him selling indulgences. But by the time Luther met Cardinal Cajetan at Augsburg, Tetzel was, in fact, dying in disgrace at Leipzig. Mr Osborne introduces him in a subordinate and ineffectual role into the Augsburg conversations, spoiling

Review of *Luther*, by John Osborne. *The Critic* (USA), February–March 1962.

his part and depriving himself of the opportunity to present, as was sorely needed, a cynical Italian Renaissance churchman. This part he has to give to Pope Leo and he chooses to diminish that great if not very edifying pontiff by giving him the tastes and manners of a sporting stock-broker.

Again, Staupitz, Luther's friend in the monastery and sometime sympathizer, died in 1524 fully reconciled to the Church. Mr Osborne produces him in 1530 as a lachrymose and still undecided dotard.

The chief point at issue between Luther and the Church was the doctrine of Grace and Justification by Faith. There are few dramatic possibilities in this dispute which would, indeed, be quite unintelligible to the majority of a modern audience. It is legitimate for Mr Osborne to choose the more risible point of spurious relics, but he does so in a way that suggests Luther was original in his denunciations, which had been common for generations.

The great dramatic moment of Luther's life, of course, was his burning of the Papal Bull. After that the decision of the Diet of Worms was (artistically) an anticlimax. On that occasion he came under the secular ban of the Empire and its importance is that the political independence movement of the German princes enabled him to escape unpunished. Mr Osborne gives us two scenes of defiance, the latter much less forceful than the first.

There is a further question of aesthetic propriety. There is always an easy laugh to be had by making a clergyman swear. Mr Osborne puts a considerable number of obscenities into Luther's mouth, most (if not all) taken from his recorded words. But were these expressions obscene at the time? If sixteenth-century Germans habitually employed them without offence, merely as a form of emphasis, they should be translated into the equivalent English. If Luther was exceptionally foul-mouthed it is proper to suggest this. Personally, I am too ignorant to judge. Certainly in London the impression received was that many of the audience were titillated by the spectacle of a clergyman talking in a way inconceivable in a modern clergyman. And that is bad art.

Mr Osborne's first act gives us a convincing picture of a young monk attempting to find salvation by rule. Prayer is the essence and purpose of monastic life. Either from egotism or impatience Luther was frustrated in prayer and attempted to fill this bottomless deficiency by scrupulous observances. And despaired. In the second act we see him inflated with confidence in his own interpretation of scripture as the sole means of salvation; thus led unavoidably into collision with the Church, both in its divine, incorruptible nature and its earthly, corruptible nature. In the last act Mr Osborne is at a loss for a dramatic conclusion and falls back on a scene of domestic seclusion which is much at variance with the facts. The further Luther escaped from orthodoxy and discipline the more presumptuous he became. Mr Osborne shows him as having grown sceptical of the value of his revolution at a date when he had before him a decade in which he became 'the Pope of Wittenburg', claiming and exercising in his small dissident region all the authority Leo had enjoyed; more, indeed, for he issued a dispensation for bigamy to a particularly discreditable supporter.

Mr Osborne, following his proletarian sympathies, makes much of Luther's encouragement of the savage repression of the peasants by their overlords. It was an outrage typical of the age and place but it was to some extent provoked. It was quite consistent with Luther's previous career that he should inflame and exculpate the acts of revenge. If the dramatist wished to show the corruption of his hero's character he could have drawn on his exhortations to persecute Jews and Anabaptists because there he was denying the principles of private judgment in religious opinion for which he was originally so strong. Instead we are given the more commonplace spectacle of revolutionary turned conservative of which, of course, there are numerous historical examples. Luther was never a revolutionary in this way. He was an opportunist politically who saved his skin by supporting the anarchic princes against the homogeneous empire of Christendom.

In his dislike of his leading character the dramatist even denies him the convivial, even generous, rumbustious qualities he undoubtedly possessed and makes him a whining, snarling hypochondriac.

But Mr Osborne's main weakness is what always enfeebles men without religion when they attempt religious subjects. Mr Osborne simply does not know whether prayer has an object. He sees monastic life as harmless and congenial to certain temperaments, as futile and irksome to others. He does not know if there is a God. A Catholic would agree that the Church needed reformation and point to the Council of Trent as the means God appointed for the process. A Lutheran, presumably, would say that God was displeased by the devotional habits and doctrinal refinements of his worshippers and inspired a group of Germans to start again on a new and better plan. Mr Osborne does not know whether God is involved in his story. Were the young Luther's prayers barren because he was following an unsatisfactory liturgy or because all prayer is barren except as auto-suggestion? That is the central problem which Mr Osborne shirks.

But when all these defects have been noted it must still be asserted that *Luther* is a composition altogether more valuable than all the nonsense of the *nouvelle vague*. It is a piece of stage craft in a sound tradition with many highly exciting and amusing episodes.

. THE PRIVATE MAN .

The following pages comprise a deeply felt and plainly worded Call to Order by an American who represents no political party or organization. He is, as his title defines him, a 'private man'; one accustomed to authority and responsibi-

Commentary in *The Private Man*, by T. A. McInerny. New York, 1962.

lity and imbued with the traditions of his native New England. He is disquieted at the influences which he sees as predominant in many quarters of his own country and of her European allies and his aim, like the younger Cato's, is to recall his contemporaries to the fading virtues of their ancestors. He is making a personal act of protest, and, to that extent, I must dissociate myself from him in the way that editors disclaim responsibility for the opinions of their correspondents. I lack first-hand knowledge of the social, economic and political conditions of America; I sometimes dissent from the conclusions he makes from his observations in England; the History, from which he draws his illustrations, is not precisely the History I was taught, either in conspectus or in detail; but I gladly accept the invitation to write this preface because the problems which the author raises are those which vex conservatives all over the world.

More than sixty years ago, in what seemed the height of the capitalist era, King Edward VII startled a Mansion House banquet by quoting: 'We are all socialists nowadays'. Now, when socialism under one guise or another is spreading everywhere, it is not altogether extravagant to say: 'We are all conservatives'. Progess, as it has been understood since the eighteenth century, has proved a disappointment. For every gain there has been a compensating, or even preponderating, loss. Former 'progressives' suspect that they have gained all that is attainable and are in danger of losing it, while others believe that for a century the 'spirit of the age' has been moving in a wrong direction. Christendom, the West, the Free World – call it what you will – is on the defensive; its division from the opposed communist world is absolute. There is now no place for the honest dupes of 1930s and '40s. We know what communism is and either accept or reject it in its totality. This is a wholesome clarification. We know that the qualities we value are not natural gifts but human achievements which must be preserved with effort and sacrifice. This was recognized in the 1950s. But now, in the present decade, many are conscious of a new danger. In war, it is notorious, opponents soon forget the cause of their quarrel, continue the fight for the sake of fighting and in the process assume a resemblance to what they abhorred. We are all conservatives but what exactly are we striving to conserve? Looking over our shoulders from the ramparts do we see the unconquered citadel already in decay? This, if I read Mr McInerny rightly, is his central theme, the exploration of which takes him to the roots of human society.

Civilization is, under God, the free association of free men. Man is born in a family and by nature should be fed and taught in a family until he is of an age to take on the responsibilities of parenthood. A man's true freedom is in direct proportion to his power to control the production of the necessaries of family life. The State is an association of families who by reason of kinship or contiguity find it convenient to share corporate duties. The usurpation by the State of the free man's prerogatives is a universally observable process whether the ostensible form of association is autocracy, as in Hitler's Germany and the 'emergent' peoples of former colonies, oligarchy as in Russia, or a popularly elected President and Congress as in the USA and, from time to time, in France.

Since the early years of the Industrial Revolution there have been individual prophets who have been dimly aware of this trend towards servility. Ruskin and William Morris believed it could be averted by socialism; Belloc and Chesterton, by distributism. In both cases there was nostalgia for an idealized Middle Ages. They saw as the great social evil the regimentation of the poor by avaricious employers who were controlled and often capriciously ruined by the manipulations of international financiers. No one doubts that there were evils crying for correction, but the great private fortunes accumulated at the cost of human hardship were not all squandered in private indulgence but found their way into benevolent endowments and fructified all over the world in new enterprises. Moreover the physical hardships of the Victorian miner or factory-hand were not more severe than those of the peasant. The evil was primarily moral: the loss of independence and self-respect in the new industrial conurbations. The new Gradgrind is the State and, unlike Gradgrind, the State does not make a fortune.

Mr McInerny does not speak of the abstract 'State'. He prefers to speak of the 'Public Man'. In England we see our enemy not in the flamboyant politician but in the anonymous and invisible bureaucrat, but conditions are similar. In both our countries it is the policy of governments to diminish the stature of the private man. They threaten to treat all men as the capitalists of the last century treated their newly urbanized dependants.

Theoretically there is a vast difference between the United States and the United Kingdom. My country is not a democracy. It is a monarchy, aided by two houses of parliament, one of which, of lesser importance, is predominantly hereditary and therefore richly representative of the 'private man' in all his idiosyncrasies. The United States are the first child of the revolution which destroyed France; there all authority comes from below. In my country the Crown is the consecrated fount of honour, the head of an established Church, the source of legal, naval, military and diplomatic appointments, the redresser of grievances and the punisher of crime. A loyal subject may cast his vote for a candidate to the House of Commons under the pretence that he is tendering the monarch humble advice in the choice of counsellors. Power is delegated from above, not from below – in theory. But in practice we suffer most of the ills of oppression by the majority that Mr McInerny deplores in his own country. The majority, the public man, the common man, the State, the spirit of the age – the many headed, many named monster knows that the strongest force opposed to him is property. Our great-grandparents used to speak of a modest inherited fortune as 'an independence'. Property enabled a man to perform unremunerative public services, to practise the arts, to defy his rulers. The State destroys private property in three ways; first, by literally robbing the widow and orphan by confiscating bequests; secondly, and more insidiously, by so taxing earned incomes that saving is impossible – in most trades and professions in most countries a man is allowed to enjoy a considerable part of his earnings if he squanders it on travel and entertaining; thrift alone is penalized; thirdly, the State has the power to debase the coinage, a process euphemistically called 'inflation' which in simple terms means paying the majority more than they earn.

It has often been pointed out that Liberty and Equality are irreconcilable conceptions. The three historic catch-words of the revolution which still stand inscribed on the public buildings of France suffered in esteem in the aftermath of the Second War. To the soldiers of the victorious armies 'Liberation' meant theft – 'I've just liberated a case of brandy'; 'Fraternity' meant fornication – 'Going fratting tonight?'; while Equality meant for the civilian the ration-book and uniform want. Men are not naturally equal and can only seem so when enslaved. In antiquity even the slaves were able to exercise their varying superiorities.

By introducing a uniform system of education and by seeking to make it universal and compulsory, the State is attempting to minimize natural superiorities. The precocious child is regarded as a problem and his development is, when possible, stunted. The child from a quiet and studious home is seen to have an advantage over his fellows whose parents are rowdy and illiterate; work out of school hours is therefore discouraged. Even examinations, thought by the progressives of the last century to be a defence against privilege, are now denounced in the consultations of schoolteachers as introducing an unhealthy spirit of competition into education. In most modern States the governments aspire to destroy the independent schools, which notoriously foster individuality and responsibility.

It would be paranoiac to suppose that there is an organized conspiracy. The 'spirit of the age' is observed in action, but no doubt many public men and bureaucrats are consciously aware that their tasks would be easier if mankind lost its diversity and became wholly docile in accepting what is represented to it as its own good; and when, as constantly happens, a decision has to be made between the opposed claims of liberty and equality, their choice instinctively favours equality. But in this the rulers betray themselves.

When a servile state has been achieved and man has 'nothing to lose but his chains', there is a fatal weakness from without and from within. Men will only fight for what they love. The more uprooted they are from their essential loyalties, the more the control of their own lives and families and the pride in their possessions are taken from them – so much the more readily will they fall victim to attack from nations which have not been so enervated.

Moreover the more pusillanimous they grow in defending their private lives, the more capricious will they become in their choice of rulers. When the State – the public man – claims credit for all benefits, it must accept responsibility for all misfortunes. A people who have forfeited their privacy will easily succumb to rogues and charlatans who promise a change of condition. They will know they have been cheated and turn on any surviving minorities that are pointed out to them as the origins of their malaise. Revolution and persecution will follow their odious course.

The State (ideally, we believe) is the free association of free men. Man develops his highest natural faculties in society. Men are distinguished by the variety and degree of their natural faculties. Therefore the proper structure of a healthy State is pyramidical. The organic life of society should be a continuous process of evolving an aristocracy. In a healthy society there should be no impassable barriers of hereditary caste keeping down the individual; recruitment into the aristocracy should be fostered; nor should there be rigid privilege which preserves in authority men who prove themselves unfit for it; but, by and large, the most valuable possession of any nation is an accepted system of classes, each of which has its proper function and dignity. At the head – I am not sure that McInerny would agree with me in this particular – is the fount of honour and justice; below that men and women who hold office from above and are the custodians of tradition, morality and grace; when occasion arises ready for sacrifice but protected from the infection of corruption and ambition by hereditary possession; the nourishers of the arts, the censors of manners. Below that the classes of industry and scholarship, trained from the nursery in habits of probity. Below that manual labourers proud of their skills and bound to those above them by common allegiance to the monarch. In general a man is best fitted to the tasks he has seen his father perform.

Neither Mr McInerny nor I can hope to see such a State in its completeness – it has never existed in history nor ever will; but both our nations are yearly drifting further from this ideal. It is not enough to say: 'this is the spirit of the age' and to deplore it, for the spirit of the age is the spirits of those who compose it and the stronger the expressions of dissent from prevailing fashion, the higher the possibility of diverting it from its ruinous course.

. HERE THEY ARE, THE ENGLISH LOTUS-EATERS . . .

We are the wrong ages, my daughter and I – 19 and 58 – for the kind of adventurous travel which I once enjoyed, but for the past two months we had certainly been travellers rather than tourists.

We bore on our bodies the bites of many insects and the bruises from being thrown about in very small ships in very rough waters. We had walked and climbed on rough trails. We had had an Indian hunter with us to shoot our dinner. The men who helped us on our way had been district commissioners not tourist agencies. We had not endured the hardships of explorers, but we had been far from the smooth routes prepared for foreign visitors.

All this came to an end in Trinidad when, after a violent crossing from

Daily Mail, 20 March 1962.

Guiana in a half-empty cargo ship, we found ourselves in Port-of-Spain confronted with the large and luxurious French liner in which we had booked our return passage.

It was a startling transition; not from one world to another but from the real world into make-believe – the world of the 'pleasure-cruise'; a very agreeable world indeed. It is only in this century – I think since the First World War – that shipping lines have put themselves out to attract passengers who have no destination but merely wish to sleep and eat free of cares, and every now and then open their eyes on unfamiliar territory.

We slipped on board to find a community already firmly established. The nationalities, mostly French and English with a few Germans, were sharply divided and stratified among themselves. The game of identifying celebrities from the passenger-list had been played out in the early cold days of the trip. Now each little set had established its bridge table, its corner of the bar, and its daily habits.

The food was delicious; the service solicitous. My daughter and I felt like intruders from outer space. We had the evidence of some small alligators caught on Christmas Day on the Brazilian frontier to remind us that we had really quite lately roughed it, but we settled down happily to the lotus-eating.

There was an early film – Buster Keaton or Harold Lloyd? – which showed an invalid millionaire landing from his yacht during a revolution in a Central American republic. As he passed up the main street in his bathchair he gravely saluted the men who were falling shot around him, supposing them to be bowing. It was rather in this fashion that we went ashore at our various ports of call. Everywhere an efficient tourist organization which transcended world affairs took us in charge, beguiled us and returned us to our ship sharp on time as ignorant of the country we had visited as though we had been under an hypnotic trance.

At Caracas the windows were still unglazed after a riot two days earlier. We jammed the streets of the old town while we visited the tomb of Bolivar – the great anarch who created all the insoluble problems of South America – then were whisked away to a huge, modern, totally characterless hotel where we lunched and bathed as though we had been at Miami. 'Who does Venezuela belong to?' a lady tourist asked me.

Haiti is ruled by gangsters. Its country districts pullulate with witches and secret societies. At the time of our visit, as is usual, batches of officers were on trial for plotting to assassinate the President. Abysmal poverty exists in close proximity to showy but precarious wealth. We were packed into closed cars and driven through the residential suburbs of Port au Prince, up the hills to a shop selling carved wood and water-colour paintings where a drum-and-rattle band greeted us; back into the cars to another shop selling identical works of art, enlivened by a similar band; back into cars to yet a third hillside shop of the same kind; then back to the ship. We had done Haiti.

So the tour went on, from island to island, and very pleasant it was too.

There is no reason to feel superior. The tourists are paying heavily and getting good value for their money. They do not wish to learn anything about the troublesome modern world. They suffer there for nearly eleven months of the year. At home they are short of servants and generally perplexed by post-war conditions. During these cruises they can recapture what they think they remember of the placid thirties.

For the tourists are mostly elderly. Travel brochures represent, in vivid colours, swimming pools where the young and beautiful recline and sport. There was nothing like that in our ship nor, I daresay, is there anywhere. The pleasure-cruise is essentially an old folks' outing, and old folks may not look pretty in bathing-dresses, but they have learned in a happier age how to enjoy themselves. Hence the excellence of the kitchen.

There were few romantic scandals on board. We were mostly too old for that. We had our drunks and we had the mild English social competition. 'No, we didn't go on the excursion,' people would say. 'We just dropped in to luncheon with friends' and later shyly revealed that they had been to a Government House or an embassy.

We had the mild English ironies of observing what frightful objects our fellow passengers had bought on shore.

No doubt the French, too, had their animosities. They kept shaking hands all the time as though being reconciled after long estrangements. But we were a thoroughly happy ship until the Great Shadow fell. I do not think that the French were at all affected by this blight. I am quite sure the Germans were not. But during the last three days of the voyage while skies were darkening and winter clothes were being pressed, almost every English face was overcast with anxiety. It was not the rough water of the Bay of Biscay, nor the natural regret that six weeks' jaunt was over. It was not the impending discomforts and duties of home life. It was not the parting from new-made friends or the anticipation of family reunion. It was something which strikes far deeper into the English conscience – the Problem of Tipping.

It is not a thing that has ever worried me. I like to be capricious in the matter, following no rule except my own inclination. I do not actually say, 'This is for yourself, my good man. Do not spend it on strong drink,' but I feel rather as though I were presenting prizes at a school sports; rewards for skill and for effort based on close observation of form. I daresay I often give less than is expected, quite often more. I regard it as a purely personal whim.

Not so the vast majority of my country people, whose senses of justice, propriety and pride are hopelessly confused. Patriotism and social status are deeply involved too; the wish to conform, the uncertainty of the valid rules. Few of them except the very rich are actively parsimonious, but they are haunted by the belief that it is vulgar to be lavish. They have seen those who are manifestly less impressive than themselves enjoying favoured treatment. They do not wish to compete with such outsiders. Still less do they wish to prejudice their country's prestige by giving less than the Germans. This was particularly poignant in a French ship.

It is notorious that the French happily accept lower tips from Frenchmen than from foreigners. It is also notorious that the French have no delicacy about expressing disappointment in this matter. Where an Englishman will raise his eyebrows, the Frenchman will break into voluble reproach. The half-knowledge of the French tongue with which most English are equipped renders them specially vulnerable in a dispute. Men are, on the whole, more apprehensive than women, and it was an elderly man who broached the subject as we sailed from Lisbon.

'I suppose it's time we began to think of this business of tipping. Have you decided what you're going to do?' On the last night, in the English Channel, a harassed lady asked me: 'Have you done the Sordid yet?'

Between these extremes were a series of furtive consultations. One woman compiled a list as though for Christmas shopping. Her anxiety was that she might forget someone: 'Once in the night I rang for some Vichy water. A steward came whom I've never seen before or since. How can I track him down?' 'Rest assured,' I said, 'that anyone with claims on you will present himself in good time.' Then there were the alarmists. 'I've just heard So-and-so say that he means to give his cabin steward 10 per cent of his passage money. Surely that can't be right? My cabin cost £600.' And those anxious to be just. 'We have two table stewards. Each does as much work as the other but one is the senior. Shouldn't they have the same amount?'

And there was the problem of the *maître d'hôtel* who in the last days had been ostentatiously eager to please, spooning out double helpings of caviare and lighting flares of *crêpes Suzette* all over the dining saloon. Surely he could not be given less than his under-strappers. And what of the head steward, an aloof man, who sometimes vouchsafed a patronizing nod. 'Is he too grand to tip?' 'Nobody except the captain is that.'

So it went on until at last English feet touched English soil and English hands touched English silver. There the island race felt at ease. Would they, I wonder, have been happier during those last days of *angst* if they had lived under an ordinance forbidding tipping? I doubt it. Passengers by aeroplane do not look notably contented. I think this national neurosis tends to distract them from the annoyances of homecoming.

For those who suffer acutely I can offer one piece of advice. There is an edifying sentence written by I know not whom, Stevenson, perhaps: 'I shall not pass this way again . . .' and is to be [*sic*] found illuminated and framed and branded in poker-work by many simple hearths. Its sentiment is that in our brief passage through life we must endeavour to leave behind us smiling faces. I would counsel tippers to remember those words: 'I shall not pass this way again.' Perhaps you will. Then you will meet welcome or hostility in precise proportion to what you have disbursed. But if you are quite sure you will never see these people again, it does not matter how black their looks or how opprobrious their comments at your departing back.

I was exhilarated to see it announced that Pan Books has commissioned a treatise on etiquette. The firm issues very large editions very cheaply, and clearly knows its business. There must, therefore, be once more a wide popular curiosity on matters of decorum.

I say 'once more' for England in her century of supremacy was a great market for such works. Then, all over the country, prosperous new families were emerging who wished to learn the social habits of those who had been rich longer. It was assumed, without full justification, that a certain code of behaviour was uniformly observed in polite society; that this code could be learned by study and everyone would then be at ease with everyone else.

These Victorian manuals make excellent reading and give some impression of the pleasures and pains of the well-to-do. They also, the best of them, inculcate high principles of morals and manners; higher principles, I suspect, than were always observed. The books were ridiculed; people would deny having even seen them; but they sold like hot cakes.[1]

This 1962-style manual I find bleakly depressing. The photograph of the authoress does not invite confidence. She is young and pretty, not at all, in appearance, the dragon who should frighten us into better behaviour. In normal civilizations it is the old who are the custodians of the tribal customs. It is their duty to transmit them. The young can enjoy flouting them until they themselves age, when they will find they revert to the conventions they were first taught. Moreover, manners are especially the need of the plain. The pretty can get away with anything. The publishers should have chosen an ugly, elderly, ill-tempered woman to write their book; or better, a man, for women are naturally Bohemian, while men honour convention.

Victorian books were addressed to the rich who wished to mix with the aristocracy. Our modern authoress, Miss Maclean, provides tips for the poor; such as: 'Where parents can't afford the uniform at a grammar school the local education authority in most districts is empowered to make a grant.' She advises hostesses at a reception: 'Buy your drinks at the local off-licence.' The idea of dealing regularly with a wine merchant is strange to her chosen public. Of the celebration of coming-of-age she remarks: 'Where, as so often today, 21-year-olds have more money to spare than their parents, they throw the party themselves – anything from a sophisticated cocktail party' (what can that be?) 'to a dancing to records beer-and-cheese affair.'

Review of the *Pan Book of Etiquette*, by Sarah Maclean. *Daily Mail*, 12 April 1962.

1 When writing 'Manners and Morals' Waugh consulted Victorian manuals such as: 'The Man in the Club Window.' *The Habits of Good Society: A Handbook of Etiquette for Ladies and Gentlemen: With Thoughts, Hints, and Anecdotes Concerning Social Observances; Nice Points of Taste and Good Manners; and the Art of Making Oneself Agreeable: The Whole Interspersed with Humorous Illustrations of Social Predicaments; Remarks on the History and Changes of Fashion; and the Differences of English and Continental Etiquette*. (London: James Hogg and Sons, n.d.)

Those with plebeian accents are advised to 'cultivate the BBC type. Less exaggerated than the so-called "Oxford accent".' Those without taste in furniture and decoration are urged to 'study the home magazines'. She notes some of the fruits of Miss Nancy Mitford's light-hearted but deleterious excursion into social discipline, and prints a brief list of expressions which are 'U' and 'non-U', but she herself is cheerfully and shamelessly independent of such niceties. Her readers are the contemporary representatives of the characters of the immortal *Diary of a Nobody*. Social historians will note the dismal declension of the lower-middle class from the days of Pooter to those of Jimmy Porter. Mr Pooter lived in an agony of social uncertainty, but his standards of comfort and decency were immeasurably higher.

The publishers claim that this book 'covers every social activity'. There are many quarters where etiquette is still firm – diplomacy, the services, the learned professions, the older universities, field sports, the sea, clubs, gambling, for example, all have their own man-made codes of politeness. Miss Maclean is silent about them, and quite reasonably. She is writing primarily for urban office- and shop-girls in whose lives a wedding is the one formality and whose social embarrassments occur at rare visits to expensive restaurants.

In matters of the kitchen she is not an unfailing guide. It is kind of her to tell us that *'tripe'* in French means 'tripe': not so kind that *osso buco* (marrow-bone) is 'veal stewed with dry white wine'. She instructs us how to eat a bizarre dish which she calls 'caviare served with an omelette'. Can this be some modern degradation of the classic *caviare aux blinis*?

She makes a gruesome analysis of what, I dare say, are prevalent customs. Engaged couples, she tells us, 'go off for weekends alone together'. 'The modern world is not so censorious as it was in the 1920s' (a notoriously lax decade). 'The modern bridegroom usually expects the bride to pay her whack towards the honeymoon.' 'Christenings usually take place within the first three months for the purely practical reason that an older child may prove a difficult armful.' Of Miss Maclean's numerous advisers none, obviously, was acquainted with the paedo-baptist controversies.

No doubt all that she says – and she acknowledges the kindness of 'very many people' who helped her 'garner the facts' – corresponds to some deplorable habit observed somewhere, but, surely, the very fact of any girl buying this book is evidence of her wish to do a little better, not in display but in propriety?

If they wish to abandon all social conventions, their way is clear: they need merely follow the 'beatniks'. But they would not be consulting Miss Maclean if this was their ambition. The press is full of the doings of very rich Levantines on their yachts. These cannot be emulated except in the feverish imagination, but there still exist in England a few unobtrusive households which precariously preserve the traditions of a happier and healthier age. It is to these that a book on etiquette should lead.

As soon as the advertising agents adopt a phrase it becomes universally odious. The words 'Gracious Living' cannot be spoken without apology. They were never, as far as I know, in civilized use. It is sad that the vulgarity of the term should have extended to the thing indicated. The need now is for a call to order.

For generations the English have been the least ceremonious of nations. That was because we enjoyed complete self-confidence in our order. We preserved, behind our easy-going and eccentric ways, a basic decorum. It is time we awoke to the danger of finding ourselves a people of slatterns and louts.

Morality and etiquette have little connection, but it is worth noticing that vices were sometimes avoided for fear of social disgrace. What was 'not done' was, in fact, not done, and Society exercised sanctions against gross offenders. There is no such thing today as ostracism. There was much hypocrisy in the ruin of Parnell, Wilde and Dilke, but this was not, as was pretended in the 1920s, a middle-class Victorian triumph. Byron and Beckford were driven abroad in an aristocratic age. Earlier Wilkes lost his seat in Parliament for writing indecent verse. Society was the guardian of certain elementary decencies and discretions.

Nowadays in London on the rare occasion when a hostess proclaims she will not have a man in her house again, she merely means she has had a private tiff with him or, more likely, grown bored; never that he had bilked of his card debts or been convicted of crime in the courts. The modern clergy are shy of threatening hell fire. Their admonitions to higher morality are no longer reinforced by the appeal to convention.

But the call to order I plead for is something quite superficial. A matter of style of living. In the decade before the war European fashions were set largely by homosexuals. They are naturally nonconformist and their influence was to remove almost all the formalities which still survived, but they had their own kind of elegance and standards of politeness. 'The sons of Belial had a glorious time' and most people were grateful to them for making everything so gay and ornamental. Then came the 1940s, first the war, after it the Cripps–Attlee terror. Domestic servants dwindled and the tradition of their training quite ceased in many parts of the country. As a result a generation has now grown up who have never experienced – yes, let me use the accursed words – 'Gracious Living'.

There are now no longer shortages of food and clothes; new mechanical devices do the work of many servants. But England shows least sign of any war-damaged country of recovering its decencies of living. English women were proverbially dowdy, but they were well-scrubbed. Englishmen were the best dressed in the world. Foreigners came hundreds of miles to buy their clothes with the simple ambition of looking like English milords. English tailoring is still good. But one of the sharpest impressions one gets when returning from abroad is of the slovenliness of men, young and old, who can well afford to be properly turned out.

It is not a matter of expense. Clothes cost much more, but there is no reason why they should require a larger proportion of a man's income. A respectably dressed man in the street carries, I suppose about £150 of clothes, and everything except his tie and his socks should last him fifteen years, if he takes care of it. Few men now have valets. Relatively few did after 1914. Young, penurious men took care of their clothes and even on occasions polished their own shoes. Look at the feet of young men today. I have lately observed one in a London club, well-born, well-married and not poor, whose sole was flapping loose from his shoe.

There were two men a hundred years apart – Beau Nash and Beau Brummell – who have become historic for their influence on fashion. Both were of modest origins and small fortune. Nash took over the management of Bath and made it a centre of civility. Brummell in the larger world personified the transition from splendour to elegance. Splendour, under its gold lace, was often dirty. Brummell brushed his teeth and changed his linen three times a day. London needs both a Nash and a Brummell.

. MANNERS AND MORALS – 2[1] .

One simple reform which is needed is the return of the habit of dressing in the evening. The homosexuals of the thirties eschewed conventional starched shirts, but they took pains to dress up fancifully and they looked jolly pretty. Nowadays, as often as not, young men arrive at dinner in the clothes they have worn all day, and quite often arrive half-drunk because they have been sweating in a cocktail party up to the last minute. If they had been home, bathed and got themselves into a dinner-jacket or evening dress they would be altogether more agreeable companions. Hostesses, theatre-managers and restaurateurs should insist on this. It might cause momentary resentment, but young men would soon learn that evening dress is perfectly comfortable and that wearing it puts them in a festive mood.

It is unforgivable to arrive drunk. It is a reflection on your host. If he gives you bad wine or too little – and he will certainly be encouraged to both these economies if his guests arrive full of gin – refuse further invitations. It is also unforgivable to get drunk when most other people are sober. That is what night-clubs are for. It is for the host to decide whether he wants to make a heavy drinking evening.

Young men in London expect to be fed most evenings. If it is explained to

Daily Mail, 13 April 1962.

1 The *Daily Mail* advertised the second part of 'Manners and Morals' with this teaser: 'Tomorrow – "Women smoking in the streets should be placed under close arrest."' However, nothing about women smoking was printed. Waugh wrote to Peters, 23 April 1962: 'The *Daily Mail* gravely mutilated the second of the articles on modern manners. I know that it is no good complaining.'

them that those with weak heads must not drink all that is offered and that their popularity depends on their deportment, they will mend their ways. Still more it should be impressed on the greedy that they must not call for what is not offered. I have heard youths at a London ball, which was flowing with good champagne, demand to be supplied with spirits.

In the mutual contempt of host and guest, which has become a deplorable feature of English life, it is the host who holds power. The guest, however welcome, is there on his sufferance.

There were never more bathrooms in England than there are today and never so many dirty necks and finger-nails in both sexes. Heaven knows what horrors lie hidden below the clothes. A few girls who work as mannequins are professionally clean; countless others should be sent to bed supperless. In this the Americans are immeasurably the superiors of the English. There was a time when we used to laugh at the supposedly dirty habits of continental Europeans. The laugh (if it is funny) is now on us.

The Londoners have made their town so unpleasant that all who have families or friends in the country migrate every Friday evening. Forty years ago there were many people who spent Sunday in London and made a very agreeable day of it. Now there is a vast exodus.

They carry little luggage, these weekenders, and treat the country as, to the disgust of the inhabitants, we used to treat the South of France. A countryman, even if he does not go to church on Sundays, as he usually does, wears a dark suit to suggest that he has been. These urban invaders sprawl about in pyjamas in the summer, in corduroy and sweaters in the winter. Early on a summer morning I have seen a banker at Mass in a country village wearing sandals and an open shirt as though he were at St Tropez.

Hostesses should realize that they have authority. It is not their business simply to feed the horde but to tame it.

There are other simple rules which the new Nash and Brummell should enforce. Invitations should be promptly answered and, when accepted, kept. I was appalled last year to observe that for a large coming-of-age party the invitations were accompanied by a stamped and addressed postcard printed with a form of acceptance or refusal. Hostesses apparently despair of getting answers from their young friends.

The telephone, that pernicious device, is responsible for much. People leave all arrangements vague in the knowledge that they can always ring up at the last moment and change them. The telephone should never be used except among intimate friends and, I suppose, in commerce. I do not know how much real value it is in offices. It seemed to me to cause a great deal of misunderstanding and waste of time in the army.

Apropos of the telephone, it should be noted that the caller is in the position of the suppliant. He cannot expect to burst in unannounced whenever it suits his convenience. He must expect to be kept waiting. In the days when I myself had a telephone I found that certain bumptious businessmen had the habit of employing secretaries to make their calls for them. I would be led to the pantry, where the instrument was housed, to hear: 'Mr Waugh? Just a moment, please. Mr Brute wants you and he is speaking on the other line.' The only reply to such treatment is to ring off immediately.

The great difference between our manners and those of the Americans (on the whole a better-mannered people than ourselves) is that theirs are designed to promote cordiality, ours to protect privacy. Most Americans like to meet as many people as possible. Most Englishmen are content with a restricted acquaintance. Friends should take care before effecting an introduction to discover that both parties wish to meet.

Some races have the disconcerting but practical habit of announcing their own names loudly on being introduced. We do not do that here. It is all the more important for the introducer to impress the names of the introduced. It is not uncommon for the very young to know one another only by their Christian names. The surname is what identifies. A general prohibition on the use of Christian names outside the family, if it could be enforced, would be healthy and also revive the excellent old habit of conferring nick-names. No one must suppose that he has been introduced to anyone else because he is familiar with the face.

Historically ceremony and etiquette are the revolution against barbarism of peoples developing their civilization. They can also be the protection of those in decline; strong defences behind which the delicate and valuable are preserved. The Chinese and the Byzantine empires are examples of civilizations preserved century after century by good manners. These islands are at the present time in danger of lapsing into their state of 1,400 years ago, when the Romans had deserted them and chivalry was yet to come.

My generation has not set a good example of defence. Let the young man the walls.

. ELDORADO REVISITED .

One of the many sharp differences between my generation of English writers and our successors' was that we got about the world. Robert Byron, Mr Graham Greene, my brother Alec, Mr Christopher Sykes, Mr Peter Fleming, Lord Kinross – to name a few of my own acquaintance – spent much of their youth in enterprising and arduous journeys. To find in the atlas a place about which one knew absolutely nothing, to go there for that very reason, was our preparation for what seemed likely to be a sedentary middle age.

For some – Mr Greene in particular – the habit has proved ineradicable. I now regret having neglected so much of the then civilized world, now given over to tourists or terrorists. I regret the time and money wasted in clambering over

National Review, 9 October 1962. First printed *Sunday Times*, 12 August 1962.

the glaciers of Spitzbergen when I might have visited the temples and palaces of Indochina, but it was a more exhilarating occupation than attending literary congresses at whose sessions, it seems, modern young writers see the world. One of the places I visited during that unencumbered decade was the hinterland of British Guiana – Raleigh's Eldorado. Thirty years afterwards I went back.[1]

In 1932 you might scan the English newspapers in vain for mention of that remote dependency. Now the Guianese are persuaded that they are of vital significance in world affairs. They would be disconcerted to learn how little the average educated Englishman knows about them. Their problems are acute and form, in their way, a microcosm of universal unrest. Moreover their problems are insoluble.

The first remark to greet the returning stranger was usually: 'You must find a great many changes.' The answer, during the first weeks, was: 'Compared with my own country, the changes are negligible.' Not for three generations has British Guiana been a colony in the generally accepted sense. There are British and Canadian expatriates who work there, and intend to retire elsewhere. Guianese of pure white stock, with roots in the country, are almost exclusively Portuguese. They form (with the Chinese) a small, educated and, in a few cases, moderately prosperous bourgeoisie. No agitator can denounce a class of 'settlers'; nor can he claim that national lands have been usurped. The original inhabitants are some 25,000 tribal Indians (now dubbed Amerindians) out of a population of half a million. Nor can the agitator claim that the land is held by armed force. One company of British infantry represents the entire might of empire.

To speak of Guianese 'nationality' is an orator's trick persuasive at councils of the United Nations, but meaningless on the spot. The main population is part Negro and part Indian; the latter are the latest comers, mostly from Bihar. The races seldom mixed in the past and are now fiercely antagonistic to one another.

Nor has the territory any geographical unity. Five great but barely navigable rivers divide it from north to south; except on the coast there is no communication from east to west. Four distinct areas comprise the narrow alluvial strip between the estuaries, forest, swamp and the open highlands of the Brazilian border. The territory is the size of England, but its half-million inhabitants are densely crowded into the coastal strip. The efficiency and devotion of the colonial sanitary service has, by eliminating many formerly endemic diseases, greatly aggravated the problem. There is now poverty and unemployment but, even so, the condition of the poorest is better than that of the poor of most states in Central and South America. A century-and-a-half of British rule has preserved them from the calamities which befell the 'liberated' colonies of Spain and Portugal. The Guianese politicians are now demanding sovereignty.

1 Waugh first visited British Guiana in December 1932. *Ninety-Two Days* and *When the Going was Good* record his adventures.

A visit to their sovereign neighbours and to Haiti would be more instructive to them than their jaunts to New York.

'You must find a great many changes'; not in the white, wooden houses and pleasant avenues of Georgetown and New Amsterdam, not in the forests and rivers. The cattle trail to the highland savannahs, up which I once rode for many weary days, is now impassable. An air service carries the meat of the Rupununi to the coast and brings up tinned milk, rum and such luxuries as the ranchers can afford. Bread has appeared there. Also jeeps. These greatly impede communications. Thirty years ago every ranch had its corral of ponies which were freely lent to the traveller from stage to stage. It was heavy, hot riding but, starting before dawn, as the sun set one reached one's destination. Now the jeep is often out of repair and the cost of petrol onerous, and there are few ponies. Only the Amerindian bullock carts still follow the old, slow ways.

A new town, self-contained, well planned, with many amenities for the senior staff and high wages and salubrious conditions for all, has sprung up in the bush where there was only a ramshackle mining camp thirty years ago. It is called Mackenzie and is the creation of a Canadian firm which extracts bauxite. Highly efficient automation and the superior quality of the raw material enable it to keep pace with its colleagues in other countries. An engine costing nearly a million dollars moves a thousand tons of surface-sand an hour and is manned by a crew of ten. The plant works ceaselessly day and night. The balance of prosperity is delicate. There are many other sources of bauxite in other parts of the world. Revolution on the Cuban model could result in complete closure at Mackenzie.

The other big industry is sugar. Here the Guianese are at a great disadvantage to their competitors. A benevolent company, with wide and deep ramifications in the commercial life of the colony, controls what were once private estates and still bear the picturesque names of their former proprietors. Booker's have set up their own welfare state in the last twenty years, but they cannot modify the hard facts that the price of sugar is as artificial as that of diamonds, that the plantations lie below sea level so that their expenses in drainage, irrigation and conservation are far higher than those of more favoured territories, and that they depend on subsidy mainly controlled by the United States. The labour on the sugar estates is almost entirely (East) Indian, and at Mackenzie, Negro.

What changes did I find remarkable in British Guiana? Not the new bauxite town, not the jeeps on the savannah, not the air-conditioning in Georgetown. The great change was something more typical of the modern age than any of these things. It was the growth of hate.

Thirty years ago the Guianese had been down-at-heel, lackadaisical, easy-going. Now there is something new and ugly; something that is popularly called 'political consciousness'. There is no consciousness of 'colour' in Guiana. Indeed, I attended a performance of an Australian comedy in which the cast of amateurs was bizarrely mixed, all speaking in accents which differed from pure BBC English to broad Creole, and a black girl playing the mother of a white daughter, so that throughout the play I assumed her to be a nanny and was puzzled to find a proletarian Australian served like a patrician Virginian.

But racial antipathy is rampant and new – the direct result of the attempt to introduce representative government on the basis of universal suffrage. 'You coolie man go home in the ship that brought you'; 'You black man, wait, we make you slave like you belong', is a typical street altercation. Guiana must be the only place where you find a Negro advocating apartheid.

The sage of Buxton, Mr Sidney King, is no crank but a sad, imaginative Negro, a former Minister of Education. He wishes to see the two communities constitutionally separated, each with its own government. For the Negroes have lately become aware of the fact that they have been outbred by the Indians and are in a numerical inferiority which will grow more marked in the next generation. Given independence, they believe, they will find themselves in an Indian colony. This realization overshadows the hopes of independence to which the Negro party is committed in its programme; individually and privately most of them admit that they would prefer Crown Colony status. At present the Negroes greatly predominate in the police and in the local defence volunteers. If the Indians are to give full effect to their victory at the polls, they must raise their own militia or invite a communist garrison from Cuba or elsewhere to replace the British detachment.

In religion the Negroes, Amerindians, most of the Chinese and, of course, the Portuguese are Christian, while the Indians are Hindus with a minority of Mohammedans. In social habit the Negroes are improvident, intemperate, adventurous, gregarious. They either live in the towns or seek their fortunes (usually disastrously) in the spare diamond and gold fields up the rivers. The Negroes emigrate. The Indians stay at home with deep attachment to the soil; they are frugal and polyphiloprogenitive.

Neither race has in general any ideology. It so happens that the Prime Minister, Dr Jagan, who has captivated his fellow Indians, is a Marxist with many close bonds with the Communist Party. He has lately expelled the anti-Communist member of his Cabinet, Mr Rai. His supporters know nothing of these foibles, but believe he can in some unspecified way enrich them. Such wisdom and responsibility as exist in Guianese politics belong to the Portuguese Party, who can never hope to attain power under a system of popular suffrage.

Such are the intractable problems which win Guiana an occasional paragraph in the foreign news. No collection of people could be less 'ripe for democracy' or even for one-party dictatorship. It is with a sense of relief that the visitor escapes from the claustrophobic, steamy, haunted atmosphere of the coast into the hinterland.

There, thirty years – 300 years for that matter – have made little change. The forests still teem with animals, reptiles and insects. The Amerindians still travel in their dugout canoes and fish with the bow and arrow. They have guns and never miss a shot. They are clothed and Christianized, but they still live the secluded lives which Raleigh first disturbed.

Unlike the compact, stockaded villages of Africa, the Amerindian settlements are a haphazard litter of huts, each almost out of sight of its neighbour. Rum has reached them, and their drinking parties are now often briefer and fiercer than their former slow, dull, traditional bouts of intoxication with their fermentations of cassava. They fear that the black men will eat their children. Few of them have seen an East Indian. 'We have two loyalties, to the Queen and to the missions. We want to be left alone,' a chief told me. In the beautiful swamp country of the Moruka they have ancestral memories of 'liberation', for there among their multitude of islands, they took refuge from Venezuela when they lost the protection of the Spanish crown. They talk of returning, if they lose the Queen's protection. And on the savannah they talk of crossing to Brazil rather than fall under the rule of the coast people.

In the Rupununi almost every position of authority is held by the descendants of one man, a Scotsman named Melville, and his two Amerindian consorts (one of whom is still alive). They are not rich. Their rule is not comparable to that of the old ranchers of the Argentine or Mexico. They are simply the accepted leaders of the scattered community. Their ramifications of cousinship defy the genealogist.

To end this sketch on a happier note, the transformation of Boa Vista should be mentioned. Thirty years ago this settlement on the Rio Branco, four days' stiff ride into Brazil, was the desperate dead end where the outlaws of the country came to die. There was no symbol even of law. There was no means of livelihood. Every man carried a revolver – the only man in regular employment was a gunsmith whose speciality was to file the mechanism of these weapons so as to give them 'hair-triggers'; every man had malaria, and most had syphilis. They lay all day in their hammocks, hating one another and shaking with fever. Now, by a whim of the federal government, it has become a state capital. It has 15,000 inhabitants. Each of the rapidly succeeding governors (four last year) has left his mark in grand, unfinished and abandoned buildings. There is a regiment of soldiers, a busy mission school and hospital, a large hotel which has no food or (when I was there) water, and almost no visitors.

Government officials have quartered themselves there. All who are employed are government officials. Their small salaries reach them irregularly from remote Brasilia. There is nothing to buy. They seem to subsist entirely on water-ices and cigarettes. They have a bishop and two churches and electric light for an hour or two most evenings.

But unlike their odious predecessors they are all smiling and welcoming. The girls are pretty and smart. Murder is comparatively rare. As long as the money arrives from the central government they are a happy people. It is too easy, with Guiana in mind, to condemn all state interference. In Boa Vista, preposterously perhaps but effectively, the state has been beneficent. It is just conceivable that something of the kind could happen in Eldorado.

. COLLECTORS' PIECES .

Enthusiasm for Victorian taste is not, as I sometimes see suggested, a modern fad. When, forty years ago, my friends at the university organized an exhibition of Victorian *objets d'art*, they were repeating on a grand scale what they had already attempted more modestly at school, and were imitating what had earlier been done in London. Arnold Bennett had a Victorian dining-room earlier still. M. Cocteau came very late to the movement. Mr John Betjeman threw his strong talents for popular communication into an esoteric but well-established movement of which Robert Byron was a prime mover and Mr Harold Acton, his brother William and Mr Mark Ogilvie-Grant were active supporters.

There was an element of jocularity in those early days, the wish to scandalize parents who had themselves thrown out the wax-flowers and woolwork screens which we now ardently collected. But the taste was habit-forming and grew with feeding. Smart decorators began to put high prices on the charming pieces of *papier mâché* which could still be picked up for a few shillings in provincial junk shops. But it was chiefly as objects of ornament that Victoriana were valued. Mr Betjeman was largely responsible for the enjoyment of Victorian architecture which immigrants to this country have transformed into a serious, critical science. It is only, I think, in the last year or two that *Country Life* has admitted buildings later than 1840 to its studies of great houses. The little revolution is now complete in aesthetic circles and with its established respectability may lose some of its enthusiasts. But there has been, so far as I am aware, a scarcity of books on Victorian furniture.

Here are two appearing in the same season and covering the same ground. The hesitant buyer may ask: which? The answer is: both. The more costly has 282 illustrations, the other 135. Miss Aslin provides four colour plates, Mr Whineray one. Both books would be better without any. In present conditions first-rate colour reproduction is prohibitively expensive, the second-rate is disagreeable; in particular the travesty of the Talbert cabinet in the Victoria and Albert Museum introduced by Miss Aslin. The black and white reproductions are almost all excellent in both books and, happily, there is little duplication. Certain pieces, such as the Chevy Chase sideboard, inevitably appear in both but in general the selections are complementary. Mr Whineray has the exclusive enjoyment of Lady Rosse's interior of 18 Stafford Terrace. Miss Aslin alone has Lord Wraxall's superb collection. Mr Whineray has succeeded to the accumulated learning of R. W. Symonds, to whom he pays suitable tribute. Miss Aslin has done all her own research. Mr Whineray shows more knowledge – or at any rate more interest – in the technicalities of craftsmanship. Neither writer, it seems to me, is quite certain what sort of reader is addressed; whether the collector and dealer or the uninitiated who still has to

Review of *Victorian Furniture*, by R. W. Symonds and B. B. Whineray and *19th Century English Furniture*, by Elizabeth Aslin. *Spectator*, 19 October 1962.

be persuaded to look with new eyes on things hitherto disregarded. Neither, it seems to me, is absolutely confident in taste, either in reprobation, apology or praise.

There are discrepancies, which only the expert can resolve. The Castell Coch washhand stand is attributed by one to Burges, to Chapple by the other. Mr Whineray illustrates a wood-carving machine of 1845 and asserts that such apparatus was used on a large scale throughout the second half of the century. Miss Aslin dates its prevalence a generation later. Mr Whineray has one misleading sentence. He writes: 'By 1880 Max Beerbohm in an essay could write of the aesthetes "hurling their mahogany into the streets."' What he meant to say was that in 1894 Beerbohm wrote of the aesthetes of 1880 doing so. He himself was eight years old in 1880. I hope that Miss Aslin is mistaken in her belief that William Morris never designed furniture himself. There is a small carved and painted armchair attributed to Morris which stands in the foreground of Sylvia Gosse's etching of her father (reproduced opposite p. 276 of Evan Charteris's *Life and Letters of Edmund Gosse*). I was brought up to believe that this was designed by Morris for Rossetti, was indeed fitted to him like a pair of trousers in his middle-aged obesity, with the hard little triangular cushion especially devised to support the small of his back. I should be sorry to find my leg had been pulled.

Neither author, I am sure, would make any claim to having produced a definitive treatise. Sources are abundant and research is in its infancy. What, I wonder, has happened to the circular cut-glass table which in 1939 was on sale in Clifton for £500; a stupendous work, destroyed, perhaps, by enemy action? The Tinted Venus was resurrected. There must be very many notable works waiting to be found. One longs for a catalogue and analysis of the more important works which were ingeniously constructed from fragments of Tudor carving, not as fakes but as original creations from old material, much more worthy of interest than the modern 'sculptors'' assemblages of bits of machinery. (The few pew-ends of Mr Betjeman's poem preserved and made up into a chair.) But one may congratulate both authors on having produced very agreeable interim picture books and on having written valuable commentaries on their illustrations.

The task was anything but light. In the profusion of nineteenth-century trade catalogues there is a baffling confusion of nomenclature. The simple round table which is a staple of all Victorian rooms goes under a variety of titles. Seeing it, in one of these books, described as a 'loo-table', a child said to me: 'What very large lavatories they must have had.'

Any attempt to distinguish 'styles' is frustrated by the fact that identical popular models were produced year after year for half a century. No one in the late Victorian period would be told at an emporium that 'classic' was 'out', 'Tudor' or 'Gothic' was 'in'. A bewildered young couple setting up house would, in the Tottenham Court Road, find themselves in a wilderness of furniture in every conceivable 'style' and every degree of elaboration; the materials of the world, the decorative fancies of the world, all funnelled into the capital of the world; transmogrified and often enough exported again to the tropics where had grown the original dark timbers, so that still in mosques and oriental palaces one may find, reverently preserved among the treasures of centuries, gimcrack grandfather clocks and 'balloon-backed' chairs from the mass production of the East End of London. Most, of course, remained at home to fill the new middle-class houses that were covering the environs of the cities. It is of small interest except to the social historian and it may mislead him. We must not suppose the Victorians as a community of Podsnaps sunk in the contemporary. Most families of the middle class possessed inherited furniture of an earlier age and, not wishing to cut any sort of dash, valued it with piety. In the upper class the splendid collections of the eighteenth and of earlier centuries which survive today in the great houses are evidence that they did not follow the mode. Rather they introduced new aids to comfort among the more austere legacies of their forebears. An examination of the few photographs of late Victorian interiors of country seats usually reveals, almost hidden among a jungle of contemporary upholstery, potted palms and exotic importations, the original fine pieces designed for the rooms by Kent and Adam and Hepplewhite. I suppose that if a century hence a stage-designer wishes to portray the dwelling of a well-to-do Englishman of 1962 he will search the pages of the magazines devoted to women's interests and study those interiors I often see portrayed where the living quarters comprise a single glass enclosure on various levels fitted with metal furniture and decorated with 'mobiles'. Perhaps such places exist outside the imagination of 'art editors'. I can only affirm I have never set my nose in one. I therefore rather doubt whether the furnished rooms illustrated in Victorian catalogues often came into existence. What did happen was that from time to time families bought additions which they thought would go with what they already had.

The great exception was 'Art Furniture'. Soon after the Queen's accession there came the great divide before which almost everything made was a thing of beauty and after which almost everything was increasingly ugly. In that crisis there emerged a series of aesthetic movements ranging in scope from 'the Firm' of the Pre-Raphaelites to the devastating planned inhumanity of the Glasgow school; customers of high pretension would engage artists to design rooms and whole houses for them. At the same time there persisted almost until 1939 highly skilled and very costly craftsmen who could produce on order monuments to their 'patrons'' idiosyncrasies. It is for these works that the private collector must race to anticipate the dead hand of the museums, luckily not yet very grasping. The ordinary run of Victorian furniture, to which rather too much attention is paid in both these books, is of no more interest than the 'planned obsolescence' of modern motor-car design.

. WITHOUT STOPPING TO THINK . . . .

The contemporary English literary world may be conveniently divided into: those who can write but cannot think, those who can think but cannot write, and those who can neither think nor write but employ themselves at international congresses lecturing on the predicament of the writer in modern society.

Nancy Mitford, by her choice of title, puts herself in the first class. Modesty constrained her to alter the original verse which runs:

> He flabbergasts the human race
> By gliding on the water's face
> With ease, celerity and grace.
> But if he ever stopped to think
> Of how he did it, he would sink.

These lines are more applicable to the writer than her adaptation of them, in which she makes the first and third lines read: 'She aggravates the human race . . .' and 'Assigning each to each its place.'

That she does not think is, in a sense, apparent. Most mature adults have adopted habits of thought which may loosely be dubbed a 'philosophy'; their opinions, however erroneous or extravagant, are consistent, and one can generally predict how they will decide in the questions of their time. Not so Miss Mitford. She is purely idiosyncratic, a survival of the time before feminism when it was thought feminine to be capricious. She is a socialist with a horror of egalitarianism, an expatriate with deep roots in the English countryside, a cosmopolitan with disdain for all people except a tiny section of the French.

She grew up in the years before girls of good families went to the universities. She is far better read in the subjects that interest her than most graduates. Her syntax is shaky. But her essential quality is that she can write. Whether telling a romantic story or displaying the fruits of her laborious inquiries into the history of seventeenth- and eighteenth-century France, she is readable. Some dons may disparage this gift. It is the first requirement of all literature.

In *The Water Beetle* she has collected fourteen essays most of which have been published in various, dissimilar periodicals. The contribution which will be new to most readers (it has been circulated privately) is the diary of a pilgrimage she made in 1954 to the corpse of Stalin, whom she describes as the 'dear old soul' who 'saved her bacon'. It is typical of her whimsical ways that she describes the queue, full of Chinese, at the tomb and remarks that Russians stand in it for six hours, and six pages later writes: 'The only queue I saw while in Russia was at Zagorsk – a crowd waiting for holy water.'

But this accumulation of short pieces brings only delight. Perhaps she has been at work polishing them. They seem not only as fresh as when they first

Review of *The Water Beetle*, by Nancy Mitford. *Sunday Telegraph*, 21 October 1962.

appeared, but sharper, too. The skill of the water beetle is speed of movement. Here she glances from a reminiscence of her own childhood to that of Augustus Hare; from Scott's last expedition to the Antarctic to her own euphoria in a French château; from a discussion of modern clothes to an appraisal of Saint-Simon. And she does it all with ease, celerity and grace. There is no putting on of a grave face and the caution: 'Now, to be serious.' All is told in the same gay, artless, artful manner as though in one of those *salons* whose demise she tearlessly regrets.

She is serenely capable of such innocent *gaffes* as describing Oates's disappearance into the blizzard as 'suicide'. Her love of Louis XV is as sweet and impersonal as a schoolgirl's for a film actor. Like all the English abroad she sincerely believes that she is not a 'tourist', even in Russia where that condition is obligatory. She is entirely oblivious of all moral and spiritual judgments. Her conventions are of her own devising; she attributes them to a world of her own imagination. She constantly flabbergasts the present reviewer. When most of our writers have sunk, she will still be gliding on the water's face. We all owe her a welcome and deep gratitude.

. THE MIDDLE PASSAGE .

Mr Naipaul is an 'East' Indian Trinidadian with an exquisite mastery of the English language which should put to shame his British contemporaries. He has shown in his stories – particularly in *The Suffrage of Elvira* – that he is free of delusion about independence and representative government for his native land. Humour and compassion are the qualities inevitably and most justly predicated of him.

In *The Middle Passage* he has attempted the direct narrative of a journey in the Caribbean such as many writers of other races and religions have attempted. His peculiar position as returning expatriate may be compared to that of Irish and Italian Americans who revisit the homes of their ancestors. There is conflict between the intimacy and sympathy of his origins and the satiric detachment of the foreign observer. It is not surprising that he is at his best when describing other places than Trinidad. There he is depressed by the second-rate and second-hand which haunt him. He was also, presumably, among his own kin with their susceptibilities always in mind. He therefore lapses into generalities as though he were addressing an international literary congress on the 'predicament' of the West Indian writer. He has much of interest and significance to say, but those who relish his novels will be happiest when he reaches the mainland. Here he fell under the spell of Dr Jagan, but without becoming oppressively partisan, and was not content to remain on the coast but travelled upcountry as far as the Venezuelan border and beyond the

Review of *The Middle Passage*, by V. S. Naipaul. *Month*, November 1962.

Takutu into Brazil. In these areas an Englishman enjoys some advantages over the 'East' Indian, which he lacks on the coast, and finds himself on easier terms with the Portuguese, black 'pork-knockers', missionaries and Indians (now called Amerindians). These last confound all strangers of any race, but the Englishman has the bond of religion with them and their confidence born of generations of, on the whole, congenial intercourse. But Mr Naipaul travels with the artist's eye and ear and his observations are sharply discerning. He ends his journey on the North Shore of Jamaica – that horrendous suburb of Miami which has rapidly sprung up and will, it is to be hoped, as rapidly dissolve. Mr Naipaul is everywhere conscious that the history of the Caribbean is replete with atrocities. He offers little hope (as can no honest traveller in those lands) that a new era of love and plenty is about to open.

. THE SAME AGAIN, PLEASE .

It is unlikely that the world's politicians are following the concluding sessions of the Vatican Council with the anxious scrutiny given to its opening stages in 1869. Then the balance of power in Europe was precariously dependent on the status of the Papal States in Italy; France and Austria directly, Prussia indirectly, and the Piedmontese kingdom particularly, were involved in their future. Even Protestant England was intent. Gladstone had his own, personal, theological preoccupations and was in unofficial correspondence with Lord Acton, but Lord Clarendon, the Foreign Minister, and most of the Cabinet studied the dispatches of their agent, Odo Russell (lately selected and edited with the title of *The Roman Question*), and pressed him for the fullest details. Manning was privately dispensed of his vow of secrecy in order that he might keep Russell informed. Queen Victoria ruled as many Catholics as Anglicans, a section of whom in Ireland were proving increasingly troublesome.

The Council, as is well known, adjourned in dramatic circumstances which seemed to presage disaster. Subsequent history confirmed its decisions. The Paris Commune obliterated Gallicanism. Bismarck's *Kulturkampf* alienated all respectable support of the dissident Teutons. All that Odo Russell had consistently predicted came about in spite of the wishes of the European statesmen.

The consultations, resumed after their long recess and dignified by the title of the Second Vatican Council, are not expected to have the same direct influence outside the Church. The popular newspapers have caught at phrases in the Pope's utterances to suggest that there is a prospect of the reunion of Christendom. Most Christians, relying on the direct prophecies of Our Lord, expect this to occur in some moment of historical time. Few believe that moment to be imminent. The Catholic aspiration is that the more manifest the true character of the Church can be made, the more dissenters will be drawn to make their submission. There is no possibility of the Church modifying her defined doctrines to attract those to whom they are repugnant. The Orthodox Churches of the East, with whom the doctrinal differences are small and technical, are more hostile to Rome than are the Protestants. To them the sack and occupation of Constantinople for the first half of the thirteenth century – an event which does not bulk large in the historical conspectus of the West – is as lively and bitter a memory as is Hitler's persecution to the Jews. Miracles are possible; it is presumptuous to expect them; only a miracle can reconcile the East with Rome.

With the Reformed Churches, among whom the Church of England holds a unique position, in that most of its members believe themselves to be a part of the Catholic Church of the West, social relations are warmer but intellectual differences are exacerbated. A century ago Catholics were still regarded as potential traitors, as ignorant, superstitious and dishonest, but there was common ground in the acceptance of the authority of Scripture and the moral law. Nowadays, I see it stated, representative Anglican clergymen withhold their assent to such rudimentary Christian tenets as the virgin birth and resurrection of Our Lord; in the recent prosecution of *Lady Chatterley's Lover* two eminent Anglican divines gave evidence for the defence, one of them, a bishop, in the most imprudent terms. Another Anglican dignitary has given his approval to the regime which is trying to extirpate Christianity in China. Others have given their opinion that a man who believes himself threatened by a painful death may commit suicide. Aberrations such as these, rather than differences in the interpretation of the Augustinian theory of Grace, are grave stumbling blocks to understanding.

It is possible that the Council will announce a definition of the *communicatio in sacris* with members of other religious societies which is forbidden to Catholics. Rigour is the practice of some dioceses, laxity of others. There is no universal rule, for example, about the celebration of mixed marriages. On the other hand, some French priests, in an excess of 'togetherness', are said to administer Communion to non-Catholics, an imprudence, if not a sacrilege, which can only be reprobated. The personal cordiality shown by the Pope to Protestants may well be the prelude to official encouragement to co-operate in social and humanitarian activities, which would remove the bitterness from a condemnation of association in the sacraments.

The question of Anglican Orders is unlikely to be raised, but it is worth noting that the conditions have changed since their validity was condemned. Then the matter was judged on the historical evidence of the Reformation settlement. But since then there have been goings-on with *episcopi vagantes*, Jansenist Dutch and heterodox eastern bishops, with the result that an incalculable proportion of Anglican clergymen may in fact be priests. They may themselves produce individual apostolic, genealogical trees, but the results will be of little interest to the more numerous Protestant bodies to whom the Pope's paternal benevolence is equally directed.

A Catholic believes that whatever is enacted at the Council will ultimately affect the entire human race, but its immediate purposes are domestic – the setting in order of the household rudely disturbed in 1870. There are many questions of great importance to the constitution of the Church which do not directly affect the ordinary Catholic layman – the demarcation of dioceses, the jurisdiction of bishops, the setting to contemporary uses of the powers of the ancient religious orders, the changes necessary in seminaries to render them more attractive and more effective, the adaption of missionary countries to their new national status, and so forth. These can safely be left to the experience and statesmanship of the Fathers of the Council. But in the preliminary welcome which the project has enjoyed during the past three years there has been an insistent note that the 'Voice of the Laity' shall be more clearly heard and that voice, so far as it has been audible in northern Europe and the United States, has been largely that of the minority who demand radical reform. It seems to me possible that many of the assembled Fathers, whatever their own predilections, have an uneasy feeling that there is a powerful body of the laity urging them to decisions which are, in fact, far from the hopes of the larger but less vocal body of the faithful.

I speak for no one but myself, but I believe I am fairly typical of English Catholics. The fact that I was brought up in another society does not embarrass me. I have been a Catholic for thirty-two of what are technically known as my 'years of reason'; longer, I think, than many of the 'progressives'; moreover, I think that a large proportion of European Catholics, despite their baptisms and first communions, are in fact 'converts' in the sense that there came to them at some stage of adolescence or maturity the moment of private decision between acceptance and rejection of the Church's claims.

I believe that I am typical of that middle rank of the Church, far from her leaders, much farther from her saints; distinct, too, from the doubting, defiant, despairing souls who perform so conspicuously in contemporary fiction and drama. We take little part, except where our personal sympathies are aroused, in the public life of the Church, in her countless pious and benevolent institutions. We hold the creeds, we attempt to observe the moral law, we go to Mass on days of obligation and glance rather often at the vernacular translations of the Latin, we contribute to the support of the clergy. We seldom have any direct contact with the hierarchy. We go to some inconvenience to educate our children in our faith. We hope to die fortified by the last rites. In every age we have formed the main body of 'the faithful' and we believe that it was for us, as much as for the saints and for the notorious sinners, that the Church was founded. Is it our voice that the Conciliar Fathers are concerned to hear?

There are three questions of their authority which sometimes come to our attention.

One is the Index of Prohibited Books. I have been told that its promulgation depends on the discretion of the diocesan bishop. I do not know if it has been promulgated in my diocese. It is not at all easy to obtain a copy. When found, it is very dull, consisting largely of pamphlets and theses on forgotten controversies. It does not include most of the anthropological, Marxist and psychological theses which, uncritically read, might endanger faith and morals. Nor, as is popularly believed, does it include absurdities like *Alice in Wonderland*. There are a few works, such as Addison's Essays, which one expects to find in any reputable home and several which are compulsory reading at the universities, but in general it is not a troublesome document. Sartre's presence on the list provides a convenient excuse for not reading him. But there is an obvious anomaly in preserving a legal act which is generally disregarded. I think most laymen would be glad if the Fathers of the Council would consider whether the Index has any relevance in the modern world; whether it would not be better to give a general warning of dangerous reading and to allow confessors to decide in individual cases, while retaining particular censorship only over technical books of theology which might be mistaken for orthodox teaching.

A second point is the procedure of ecclesiastical courts. Most laymen spend a lifetime without being involved with them, just as they live without acquaintance with criminal proceedings. Cases of nullity of marriage are, however, becoming more common and much vexation and often grave suffering is caused by the long delays which result from the congestion of the courts and from their laborious methods. The layman does not question the authority of the law or the justice of the decisions; it is simply that when he finds himself in doubt, he thinks that he should know in a reasonable time his precise legal status.

Thirdly, it would be satisfactory to know the limits of the personal authority held by the bishop over the laity. No vows of obedience have been made. Not in England, but in many parts of the world it is common to see a proclamation enjoining the faithful 'on pain of mortal sin' to vote in a parliamentary election or abstain from certain entertainments. Have our bishops in fact the right to bandy threats of eternal damnation in this way?

As the months pass and the Council becomes engrossed in its essential work, it is likely that the secular press will give less attention to it than it has done to its spectacular assembly. The questions for discussion are a matter of speculation to all outside the inner circle but there is a persistent rumour that changes may be made in the liturgy. I lately heard the sermon of an enthusiastic, newly ordained priest who spoke, perhaps with conscious allusion to Mr Macmillan's unhappy phrase about Africa, of a 'great wind' that was to blow through us, sweeping away the irrelevant accretions of centuries and revealing the Mass in its pristine, apostolic simplicity; and as I considered his congregation, closely packed parishioners of a small country town, of whom I regard myself as a typical member, I thought how little his aspirations corresponded with ours.

Certainly none of us had ambitions to usurp his pulpit. There is talk in northern Europe and the United States of lay theologians. Certainly a number of studious men have read deeply in theology and are free with their opinions, but I know of none whose judgment I would prefer to that of the simplest parish priest. Sharp minds may explore the subtlest verbal problems, but in the long routine of the seminary and the life spent with the Offices of the Church the truth is most likely to emerge. It is worth observing that in the two periods when laymen took the most active part in theological controversy, those of Pascal and Acton, the laymen were in the wrong.

Still less did we aspire to usurp his place at the altar. 'The Priesthood of the Laity' is a cant phrase of the decade and abhorrent to those of us who have met it. We claim no equality with our priests, whose personal failings and inferiorities (where they exist) serve only to emphasize the mystery of their unique calling. Anything in costume or manner or social habit that tends to disguise that mystery is something leading us away from the sources of devotion. The failure of the French 'worker priests' is fresh in our memories. A man who grudges a special and higher position to another is very far from being a Christian.

As the service proceeded in its familiar way I wondered how many of us wanted to see any change. The church is rather dark. The priest stood rather far away. His voice was not clear and the language he spoke was not that of everyday use. This was the Mass for whose restoration the Elizabethan martyrs had gone to the scaffold. St Augustine, St Thomas à Becket, St Thomas More, Challoner and Newman would have been perfectly at their ease among us; were, in fact, present there with us. Perhaps few of us consciously considered this, but their presence and that of all the saints silently supported us. Their presence would not have been more palpable had we been making the responses aloud in the modern fashion.

It is not, I think, by a mere etymological confusion that the majority of English-speaking people believe that 'venerable' means 'old'. There is a deeply-lying connection in the human heart between worship and age. But the new fashion is for something bright and loud and practical. It has been set by a strange alliance between archaeologists absorbed in their speculations on the rites of the second century, and modernists who wish to give the Church the character of our own deplorable epoch. In combination they call themselves 'liturgists'.

The late Father Couturier, the French Dominican, was very active in enlisting the service of atheists in designing aids to devotion, but tourists are more common than worshippers in the churches he inspired. At Vence there is a famous little chapel designed in his extreme age by Matisse. It is always full of sightseers and the simple nursing sisters whom it serves are proud of the acquisition. But the Stations of the Cross, scrawled over a single wall, are so arranged that it is scarcely possible to make the traditional devotions before them. The sister in charge tries to keep the trippers from chattering but there is no one to disturb; on the occasions I have been there I have never seen anyone in prayer, as one always finds in dingy churches decorated with plaster and tinsel.

The new Catholic cathedral in Liverpool is circular in plan; the congregation are to be disposed in tiers, as though in a surgical operating theatre. If they raise their eyes they will be staring at one another. Backs are often distracting; faces will be more so. The intention is to bring everyone as near as possible to the altar. I wonder if the architect has studied the way in which people take their places at a normal parochial Mass. In all the churches with which I am familiar, it is the front pews which are filled last.

During the last few years we have experienced the triumph of the 'liturgists' in the new arrangement of the services for the end of Holy Week and for Easter. For centuries these had been enriched by devotions which were dear to the laity – the anticipation of the morning office of Tenebrae, the vigil at the Altar of Repose, the Mass of the Presanctified. It was not how the Christians of the second century observed the season. It was the organic growth of the needs of the people. Not all Catholics were able to avail themselves of the services but hundreds did, going to live in or near the monastic houses and making an annual retreat which began with Tenebrae on Wednesday afternoon and ended about midday on Saturday with the anticipated Easter Mass. During those three days time was conveniently apportioned between the rites of the Church and the discourses of the priest taking the retreat, with little temptation to distraction. Now nothing happens before Thursday evening. All Friday morning is empty. There is an hour or so in church on Friday afternoon. All Saturday is quite blank until late at night. The Easter Mass is sung at midnight to a weary congregation who are constrained to 'renew their baptismal vows' in the vernacular and later repair to bed. The significance of Easter as a feast of dawn is quite lost, as is the unique character of Christmas as the Holy Night. I have noticed in the monastery I frequent a marked falling-off in the number of retreatants since the innovations or, as the liturgists would prefer to call them, the restorations. It may well be that these services are nearer to the practice of primitive Christianity, but the Church rejoices in the development of dogma; why does it not also admit the development of liturgy?

There is a party among the hierarchy who wish to make superficial but startling changes in the Mass in order to make it more widely intelligible. The nature of the Mass is so profoundly mysterious that the most acute and holy men are continually discovering further nuances of significance. It is not a peculiarity of the Roman Church that much which happens at the altar is in varying degrees obscure to most of the worshippers. It is in fact the mark of all the historic, apostolic Churches. In some the liturgy is in a dead language such as Ge'ez or Syriac; in others in Byzantine Greek or Slavonic which differs greatly from the current speech of the people.

The question of the use of the vernacular has been debated until there is nothing new left to be said. In dioceses such as some in Asia and Africa, where half a dozen or more different tongues are spoken, translation is almost impossible. Even in England and the United States where much the same language is spoken by all, the difficulties are huge. There are colloquialisms which, though intelligible enough, are barbarous and absurd. The vernacular used may either be precise and prosaic, in which case it has the stilted manner of a civil servant's correspondence, or poetic and euphonious, in which case it will tend towards the archaic and less intelligible. The Authorized Version of the Bible of James I was not written in the current tongue but in that of a century earlier. Mgr Knox, a master of language, attempted in his translation of the Vulgate to devise a 'timeless English', but his achievement has not been universally welcomed. I think it highly doubtful whether the average church-goer either needs or desires to have complete intellectual, verbal comprehension of all that is said. He has come to worship, often dumbly and effectively. In most of the historic Churches the act of consecration takes place behind curtains or doors. The idea of crowding round the priest and watching all he does is quite alien there. It cannot be pure coincidence that so many independent bodies should all have evolved in just the same way. Awe is the natural predisposition to prayer. When young theologians talk, as they do, of Holy Communion as 'a social meal' they find little response in the hearts or minds of their less sophisticated brothers.

No doubt there are certain clerical minds to whom the behaviour of the laity at Mass seems shockingly unregimented. We are assembled in obedience to the law of the Church. The priest performs his function in exact conformity to rule. But we – what are we up to? Some of us are following the missal, turning the pages adroitly to introits and extra collects, silently speaking all that the liturgists would like us to utter aloud and in unison. Some are saying the rosary. Some are wrestling with refractory children. Some are rapt in prayer. Some are thinking of all manner of irrelevant things until intermittently called to attention by the bell. There is no apparent 'togetherness'. Only in heaven are we recognizable as the united body we are. It is easy to see why some clergy would like us to show more consciousness of one another, more evidence of taking part in a social 'group activity'. Ideally they are right but that is to presuppose a very much deeper spiritual life in private than most of us have achieved.

If, like monks and nuns, we arose from long hours of meditation and solitary prayer for an occasional excursion into social solidarity in the public recitation of the office, we should, unquestionably, be leading the full Christian life to which we are dedicated. But that is not the case. Most of us, I think, are rather perfunctory and curt in our morning and evening prayers. The time we spend in church – little enough – is what we set aside for renewing in our various ways our neglected contacts with God. It is not how it should be, but it is, I think, how it has always been for the majority of us and the Church in wisdom and charity has always taken care of the second-rate. If the Mass is changed in form so as to emphasize its social character, many souls will find themselves put at a further distance from their true aim. The danger is that the Conciliar Fathers, because of their own deeper piety and because they have been led to think that there is a strong wish for change on the part of the laity, may advise changes that will prove frustrating to the less pious and the less vocal.

It may seem absurd to speak of 'dangers' in the Council when all Catholics believe that whatever is decided in the Vatican will be the will of God. It is the sacramental character of the Church that supernatural ends are attained by human means. The interrelation of the spiritual and material is the essence of the Incarnation. To compare small things with great, an artist's 'inspiration' is not a process of passive acceptance of dictation. At work he makes false starts and is constrained to begin again, he feels impelled in one direction, happily follows it until he is conscious that he is diverging from his proper course; new discoveries come to him while he is toiling at some other problem, so that eventually by trial and error a work of art is consummated. So with the inspired decisions of the Church. They are not revealed by a sudden clear voice from heaven. Human arguments are the means by which the truth eventually emerges. It is not really impertinent to insinuate one more human argument into the lofty deliberations.

. DRINKING .

In my childhood wine was a rare treat; an adult privilege to which I was admitted on special occasions. At my school there was no tabu against drinking (as there was against tobacco). Housemasters occasionally made a mild grog or cup for senior boys. I remember being embarrassed when one Ascension Day (a whole holiday) my companion got very drunk on liqueurs at a neighbouring hotel. It was at the university that I took to drink, discovering in a crude way the contrasting pleasures of intoxication and discrimination. Of the two, for many years, I preferred the former.

I think that my generation at Oxford, 1921–24, was the last to preserve more or less intact the social habits of the nineteenth century. The ex-service men of the First War had gone down. Undergraduate motor-cars were very few. Women were not seen except in Eights Week. Oxford was still essentially a market-town surrounded by fields. It was rare for a man to go down for a night during term. The generation after ours cherished closer links with London. Girls drove up; men drove down. Cocktail shakers rattled, gramophones discoursed jazz. The Cowley works enveloped the city. But in my day our lives were bounded by the university. For a brief Indian summer we led lives very much like our fathers'.

In the matter of drink, beer was the staple. I speak of undergraduates of average means. There were a few rich men who drank great quantities of champagne and whisky; a few poor men who were reputed to drink cocoa. The average man, of whom I was one, spent £100 a term and went down £300 in debt. Luncheon was served in our rooms with jugs of beer. Beer was always

The Compleat Imbiber – 6: An Entertainment, ed. Cyril Ray. (London, 1963.)

drunk in Hall. At my college there was the custom of 'sconcing' when a breach of decorum, such as mentioning a woman's name or quoting from a foreign tongue, was fined by the provision of beer for the table. At one time I used to drink a tankard of beer for breakfast, but I was alone in that. It was drawn and served without demur. The Dean of my college drank very heavily and was often to be seen feeling his way round the quad in his transit from Common Room to his rooms. There were occasions such as bump-suppers and 'smokers' when whole colleges were given up to bacchanalia. In my first year there was a 'freshers' blind' when we all got drunk on wines and spirits and most of us were sick. Some white colonials got obstreperous and the custom was given up. All drinks were procurable at the buttery but the bursar scrutinized our weekly battels and was liable to remonstrate with a man whose consumption seemed excessive. My friends and I had accounts with wine merchants in the town, relying on the buttery for beer and excellent mild claret, which was the normal beverage at club meetings held in undergraduate rooms. No one whom I knew ever had a bottle of gin in his rooms. I remember only one man being sent down from my college for drunkenness and that not his own; late at night he hospitably passed tumblers of whisky out of his ground-floor window to a friend in the lane, who was picked up insensible by the police. I always thought it a harsh sentence. The poor fellow had come 3,000 miles from the United States to imbibe European culture.

There were six or seven clubs with their own premises; some, like the Grid, highly respectable, others, Hogarthian drinking dens. The most notable of the dens was named the Hypocrites, in picturesque Tudor rooms over a bicycle shop in St Aldates (now of course demolished). There the most popular drink was red Burgundy drunk from earthenware tankards. A standing house rule was: 'Gentlemen may prance but not dance.' The oddest of these clubs with premises was the New Reform at the corner of the Cornmarket on Ship Street. This was subsidized by Lloyd George in the belief that it would be a nursery for earnest young Liberals. It became a happy centre of anarchy and debauch. Habits of extravagance grew and in my last year we drank a good deal of champagne in mid-morning at the New Reform and scoffed from the windows at the gowned figures hurrying from lecture to lecture. There was a vogue for whisky and crumpets at tea-time in the Union. I think it is no exaggeration to say that, in my last year, I and most of my friends were drunk three or four times a week, quite gravely drunk, sometimes requiring to be undressed and put to bed, but more often clowning exuberantly and, it seemed to us, very funnily. We were never pugnacious or seriously destructive.[1] It took very little to inebriate at that age and high spirits made us behave more flamboyantly than our state of intoxication really warranted. Not many of us have become drunkards.

1 See Anthony Powell, *Infants of the Spring* (London, 1976), p. 154: 'Evelyn Waugh . . . was excluded [from the Hypocrites Club] at this period for having smashed up a good deal of the Club's furniture with the heavy stick he always carried.'

We were not discriminating. In a novel I once gave a description of two undergraduates sampling a cellar of claret. I never had that experience at that age. Indeed I do not think that at 20 I could distinguish with any certainty between claret and burgundy. Port was another matter. The tradition of port drinking lingered. Many of the colleges had ample bins of fine vintages of which undergraduates were allowed a strictly limited share. Port we drank with reverence and learned to appreciate. The 1904s were then at their prime, or, at any rate, in excellent condition. We were not ashamed (nor am I now) to relish sweet wine. Yquem had, of course, a unique reputation. Starting to drink it in a mood of ostentation, I was led to the other white Bordeaux. Tokay was then procurable and much relished. Bristol Milk and a dark sherry named Brown Bang were also favourites. We tried anything we could lay hands on, but table-wines were the least of our interests. We drank them conventionally at luncheon and dinner parties but waited eagerly for the heavier and headier concomitants of dessert.

Nowadays, I am told, men privately drink milk and, when they entertain, do so to entice girls. It is tedious for the young to be constantly reminded what much finer fellows their fathers were and what a much more enjoyable time we had. But there you are; we were and we did.

. WILLIAM ROTHENSTEIN .

Sir William Rothenstein has been dead for nearly eighteen years. The publication of this book is an act of piety; a happy assertion of the principle that everyone of eminence is entitled to an official biography. It is also a reminder to a younger generation of the many remarkable qualities of a man who is now seen largely through Max Beerbohm's eyes. Rothenstein wrote his own copious memoirs whose success greatly sweetened his old age when his reputation as a painter was in temporary eclipse, but he left behind a mass of valuable papers to be sorted and selected by a later hand. The biographer first chosen died before his task was completed; before it was scarcely begun. Mr Speaight has made an entirely new work fulfilling with industry and tact all that could be expected of him. He has the great gift, allied perhaps to that of the actor, of throwing himself into the part. Who could be more different than St Thomas of Canterbury, Hilaire Belloc and Rothenstein? With each of these Mr Speaight has shown a sympathy which approaches identity. He is able, for example, to rebuke his subject for ignorance of 'the fundamental work on design being done in Finland' in the early 1920s. Who, I wonder, apart from Mr Speaight, was aware of these developments? When he takes up a subject he does so with a proper air of mastery.

Review of *William Rothenstein*, by Robert Speaight. *Month*, January 1963.

He was, he confesses, in some doubt about how to dub his subject. He decided, no doubt on the best advice, to call him 'William'; a mistake I think. Surnames were much used particularly by painters in Sir William's era. I doubt his ever being addressed as 'William', but Mr Speaight is rather free with Christian names. It is not always immediately apparent whether 'John' refers to Augustus John or to Sir John Rothenstein. This, and the peculiar metaphor of 'unstitching a cenacle' are the trivial complaints a captious reader can make. There is, however, a graver quarrel with the publishers. This is a costly book. The sloth and clumsiness of binders is notorious. Many American publishers despair of inserting plates at the appropriate places and sew in an illustrated supplement. This deplorable fashion is preferable to Messrs Eyre and Spottiswoode's indiscriminate insertion of illustrations far from the relevant text. For three guineas they should offer something better.

Max Beerbohm has left an indelible impression of Rothenstein as the exotic invader of the nineties, coming not from Bradford but the studios of Paris, captivating all the notables of his time. Mr Speaight has undertaken the task of exhibiting him more completely as the dedicated painter, teacher and champion of countless causes. I met him only once. He came to my house just before the Second War, when he was in retirement. He at once made for a painting I had lately acquired for something under £10 by a totally unknown Victorian artist, a robust Philistine who had nothing in common with Rothenstein's own aspirations or his associates. My contemporaries describe it as 'amusing'. Rothenstein at once began to praise it, not with the strained politeness of a guest confronted with something odd but judiciously, as if he were appraising the work of one of his own pupils. Indeed he expressed regret that few of his pupils could paint so well; extraordinary evidence of receptiveness still lively in old age and ill-health.

Rothenstein knew everyone of importance in his age, many of them intimately. In their choice of company artists of all kinds are especially vulnerable. Their ease (and consequently their work) depends on it. There are those who surround themselves with their inferiors and protect themselves from criticism in a circle of sycophants and those who are happiest with their peers. Rothenstein was eminently of the second class and he paid for his preference by constant friction with talents as strong as his own and with conflicting tastes. He was ever generous in praise of others, ever affectionate, but he would not be bullied into opinions he did not sincerely share. In the great disintegration of aesthetic standards that began in the second decade of the century and was completed in the fourth, when the fashionable critics competed in absurdity, Rothenstein remained firm and as a result fell out of favour both with pundits and patrons. His unpopularity was relative. Public honour came to him. His works were collected and dispersed all over the world. He was in constant demand at banquets and on the wireless. But contemporaries no abler than he were acclaimed where he was not. His influence, so potent in speech, did not find expression in the canvases of his pupils. His natural melancholy and irritability as Mr Speaight well shows, were accentuated by this neglect. It is safe to prophesy that recognition is not far off. When the trash which modern taste has obliged his son to introduce into the Tate has been relegated to the cellars, Rothenstein's work will come into the light. This process of restoration will be greatly expedited by Mr Speaight's admirable book.

. SPLENDID VOLUMES .

Ruari McLean's book is addressed austerely and exclusively to the collector. There are no biographical anecdotes, few individual judgments. It is a textbook superseding Courtenay Lewis's handsome but unsatisfactory *Picture Printing in England*.

Collectors will receive *Victorian Book Design and Colour Printing* with mixed emotions. First there is the ignoble grudge that anything should occur to enlist wider interest in their recondite pleasures. In the past thirty years they have watched prices rise from shillings to guineas. The good collector is not gratified by the enhanced value of his possessions; he wishes to complete his collection, and, hitherto, the ornamental books of the nineteenth century have been some of the few objects of beauty within the means of the poor. We do not want a craze to start. Secondly, there is chagrin at the gap here revealed in our present collections and the revelation of the existence of unsuspected superior copies of what we have – for example Shaw's *Illuminated Ornaments* adorned with gold leaf.

But the dominant emotion is one of gratitude to the author for his valuable, indeed absolutely necessary, labours on our behalf in cataloguing the treasures still to be sought. We may think he overrates Noel Humphreys at the expense of Owen Jones. We may regret that he is less than precise in explaining the process which produced what are inadequately known as the *papier mâché* bindings. We may point to the quality of his own colour plates as glaring examples of the regression from the standards of a hundred years ago. But all these are the quibbles of envy. Mr McLean has produced the book we needed in an admirable form.

Most men of my age grew up believing that the art of printing was rediscovered by William Morris at the end of the nineteenth century and the art of lettering a decade later by Edward Johnston. Then with almost guilty pleasure we found for ourselves some of the gems of mid-Victorian book design. We were disposed to keep the secret to ourselves. Chromolithography is a sensual taste or distaste. Some recoil from the opaque pigments. Once you have been caught by their charm you do not give a fig for aquatint. The weight of those splendid volumes predisposes them to destruction. 'Loose in Covers' is the

Review of *Victorian Book Design and Colour Printing*, by Ruari McLean. *Sunday Telegraph*, 10 March 1963.

booksellers' common note on those which were backed by perishable preparations of rubber. Only a few had sewn linen guards. Awful destruction took place during the 'salvage drive' of the last war. Almost too late a committee devoted itself to rescuing doomed volumes for sale. These formed the nucleus of many of the private collections today.

Mr McLean's highly competent compilation will set us, as they say, 'targets'. It comes not so much to strengthen our approval of our own judgment as to spur us to hunt wider for these lovely things while they are still procurable.

. AN APPRECIATION OF POPE JOHN .

In a dark and chilly epoch the short reign of Pope John XXIII was memorable for light and warmth, qualities generated by his own personality.

Among historic institutions the papacy is unique in its variety of human character. In other religions and cultures there have been dynasties of priest-kings, but these have been remote figures seldom seen or heard by their devotees, moving in the measure of elaborate ritual, leaving little record of individual peculiarities. The popes, in contrast, have lived in the thick of affairs and in most cases have left a deep impress on their contemporaries. In its twenty centuries the throne has been held by many saints and a few rascals; ascetics and epicures, scholars, statesmen, warriors, weaklings and heroes. There have been periods when observers have confidently predicted the extinction of the system; they have always been confounded by its emergence from the shadows with renewed strength.

John, from the first days of his election, was conspicuous for his spontaneous affability. The newspapers of the world were quick to recognize this lovable trait and to emphasize it almost to the exclusion of other more important qualities. John was represented as a jolly old fellow who was more at ease with his gardener than with ambassadors, a simple, warm-hearted yokel with little patience for the niceties of theologians and lawyers. This was a totally distorted picture.

He was always written of as 'a peasant'. In fact, he came of a class which has no counterpart in most parts of the world. His family, the Roncalli, is one of the basic families of the district around Bergamo in northern Italy. Many small holdings of land have been uninterruptedly in their possession for centuries. In the course of time some branches rose to the nobility; others – the product of large families and limited property – sank to being artisans and labourers, but the kinship was recognized and honoured. Pope John's father was landless at the time of his birth, but soon owned his own house – a substantial stone

Saturday Evening Post, 27 July 1963.

building – and the surrounding land. His family was not rich but it was never in need. Its strongest characteristic was identification with the ancestral soil.

Pope John's birthplace, Sotto il Monte, is about five miles from Bergamo. Until his election to the papacy John returned there every year, renewing his family life. Angelo Roncalli, the future pope, was born on 25 November 1881, the third of thirteen children. At the age of 11 his parish priest obtained a place for him in the seminary at Bergamo. The curriculum at the seminary was wide and general – Latin, Greek, mathematics, history, geography, literature, physics and chemistry. Roncalli excelled, with the result that he was picked to go to Rome for his theological studies. He went there in 1900, a holy year, so that his first sight of Rome was at a time when it was full of pilgrims from all over the world – the concrete evidence of the universality of the Church.

In June 1915 he was called to the colours and served in the medical corps in Bergamo near the front line. He had under his care the garrison troops, the wounded and dying in the hospital and the civilian refugees. While he was Patriarch of Venice he recalled those years, writing to acknowledge the greetings of a congress of chaplains, 'I thank God that I did my military service. . . . How much I learned about the human heart during this time, how much experience I gained, how much grace I received to be able to dedicate myself to my duties.'

Such were the future pope's early years, spent entirely in Italy and mostly in the district of his birth, but more varied in experience than those of many churchmen. His middle life was filled with a succession of appointments of increasing importance admirably executed. In all he showed the character formed at Bergamo – charity, prudence, humility and – a rare virtue in his age – hope.

At the age of 40 he was called to Rome to the Congregation for the Propagation of the Faith, which supervises the work of Catholic missions. Pius XI on his succession raised him to the rank of Protonotary Apostolic. His main task in this office was to further the papal policy of recruiting native clergy in the mission countries. In 1925, at the age of 43, he was appointed apostolic visitor to Bulgaria with the rank of archbishop. This was the beginning of nineteen years' work in what may be called the Byzantine world, now freed from the Turks who left behind them, besides many Mohammedans, a complex of Christian communities sharply antagonistic to one another. Archbishop Roncalli was thus able to study at first hand the disastrous fragmentation of Christendom. In 1935 he was transferred to Constantinople as delegate to Turkey and Greece. When the Germans conquered Greece, Roncalli exerted himself to mitigate the distress of the occupation.

He would have been content to end his days in the Levant, and the summons in December 1944 to be nuncio in Paris was far from welcome. For some time he supposed it to be a clerical error, but to Paris he went, finding himself dean of the diplomatic corps in a city agitated by all the problems of renewing its vitality and haunted by the spirit of revenge. Most of the French Church hierarchy had collaborated in various degrees with Marshal Pétain. There were demands from the Communists for wholesale dismissals. Roncalli urged patient judicial examination of the evidence; tempers cooled, truth prevailed, and in the end he accepted the resignation of only three of the thirty-three who had been denounced.

In January 1953 he was made a cardinal and shortly after was appointed Patriarch of Venice. This in all expectation should have been the final stage of his career. He considered it so. An English visitor at his table raised his glass and said, '*Auguri Eminenza* [Good luck],' to which he answered, chuckling, '*Perchè dire "Auguri" a me? Io sono già Arcivescovo, già Cardinale – non c'è piu niente di aspettare. Ho già tutto* [There's nothing more to look for. I have everything].'

When in October 1958 he went to the conclave to elect a successor to Pius XII he was nearly 77. None of those who speculated on the next pope ever mentioned Cardinal Roncalli. It was not until the twelfth ballot that Roncalli, to general surprise, appeared with the requisite majority. He was the oldest man to be elected in 200 years. His name was scarcely known to most of the faithful. It was widely assumed that he was a *Papa di passaggio* – a stopgap while the curia unravelled the threads of authority which had become knotted in the preceding decade of autocracy. From the first days of his reign he dispelled all such misconceptions. He proved the most active physically of any of his recent predecessors and the most youthful in mind.[1]

He had a deep reverence for the office of the papacy. It is said that when, in his dreams, he found himself in a predicament, he used to say, 'I wonder what the pope would do about this,' only to awaken to the grave conclusion, 'But *I* am the pope.'

His choice of name was strikingly original. Previous Johns had not cut very fine figures in history. One of them, in fact, never existed at all. John VIII has the macabre distinction of being the first pope to be murdered (as distinct from martyred), a fate in which he was followed by both John X and John XII. John XIX is reputed to have offered to sell the primacy of Christendom to the Patriarch of Constantinople.

It is said that Roncalli chose the name John simply because it was his father's, and that explanation is consonant with his temperament, but it is not entirely fanciful to see a deeper meaning in his choice. There had been no Pope John for more than 600 years, and the new reign was intended to cast back to the age of Giotto and Fra Angelico. Marxism, nationalism, rationalism, the Enlightenment, the Reformation and the Renaissance – all these accretions of problems were to be peeled off. For too long too many churchmen had been, of necessity, too grimly defensive, too strictly conventional. Pope John, ever since he left home, had lived in a tumultuous world. His deep reading of history showed him that there was nothing uniquely menacing in his age; in one place

1 Waugh disliked Pius XII's liturgical and other changes and, when John XXIII was elected, wrote: 'I have a crush on the new Pope . . . he looks good for twenty-five years placid inactivity.' See *Letters*, 2 November 1958.

or another the Church has always been persecuted, has always been threatened by traitors from within ; it is her natural condition. 'We sometimes have to listen,' he said at the Ecumenical Council, 'to the voices of people who, though burning with zeal . . . say that in our era, in comparison with past eras, everything is getting worse . . . as though at the times of former councils everything was a full triumph for the Christian idea and life and for proper religious liberty. We disagree with these prophets of doom. . . . In the present order of things divine Providence is leading us to a new order of human relations which, by men's own efforts and even beyond their expectations, are directed toward the fulfilment of God's superior and inscrutable designs.'

In many countries the chief prophets of doom are found among the young. The words of the opening psalm of the Mass, *'ad Deum qui laetificat juventutem meam'* ('to God who giveth joy to my youth'), have an ironic ring in a generation of beatniks and rancorous students. A very old man was needed to recall the world to the joy of youth.

As Bishop of Rome, he went about his diocese as none of his predecessors had done for a hundred years. On one of his first days in the Vatican he was walking in the garden when some labourers approached him to kiss his ring. In accordance with Pius XII's standing order, they were told by the guards to keep back. 'Why are you doing that?' Pope John asked.

'For security, your Holiness.'

'But I would not have hurt them.'

He visited prisons, hospitals, colleges, churches as freely as he had done in Venice. He visited the death-bed of the (Protestant) British minister. He went for unexpected visits as far as Assisi and Loreto. Wherever he went he fell into easy, genial conversation. The press of the world followed his movements with respectful delight.

He also opened the Vatican wide to those who might have been suspect as opponents. In Venice he had said, 'I must never refuse to admit anyone. For all I know he may be coming to confess his sins.' As pope, some limits had to be made on the number of audiences. The almost daily passage which his predecessors had made through the state chambers between ranks of devotees, each eager to kiss their rings, was a physical strain which he relieved by receiving large numbers while seated. To them he gave his blessing and a brief, often jocular, address. He privately received leading Protestants and talked with them frankly and cordially. There was nothing unique in this. Most of the popes have had visits of courtesy from men of all religions.

What was unusual was the number who now sought admittance. It was taken as a symptom of a wide, contemporary aspiration toward the reunion of Christendom. He disconcerted some of his court by receiving Khrushchev's son-in-law and daughter, thus emphasizing that his goodwill extended to the entire human race.

His memorable public work was the calling of the Second Vatican Council. This was entirely his own initiative. No one had petitioned for it. No one had expected it. It is as yet too early to judge the achievements of this great assembly. In the past, general councils have usually been held against someone or some tendency; to condemn error and define revealed truth. Pope John saw his council as essentially a joyous gathering of friends who had much to discuss of mutual concern. No dogma was in dispute; the questions were those of discipline and liturgy. It was not, as was reported, specifically a council of reunion. Churches independent of Rome had no place among the fathers. They were represented by observers, kept well informed of the otherwise secret proceedings but given no voice in the discussions. The pope believed that the more the true character of the Church was made evident, the more historic prejudices and misconceptions must disappear. It was a surprise to the non-Catholic observers, who had grown up to think of the Roman Church as authoritarian, to find how free the criticism and argument was among the fathers.

Before the recess Pope John hinted that he might not be present when the council reassembled in the autumn. Early in 1963 it was noticed that he was paler, thinner and more easily fatigued, but he continued with his duties. At Eastertide he issued the encyclical *Pacem in Terris*, which epitomized his aims.

This document is unique in that it is addressed to all mankind, not, as usual, only to the faithful. The pope, in effect, was calling for the ending of the Cold War. Under Pius XII the Church had inspired resistance to the Communist world with the result that many naïve Catholics had assumed that any government that opposed Communists had a holy cause.

In particular Pius had given his encouragement to the many priests and bishops under Communist rule who were suffering various degrees of restraint. All the Catholic world of the West looked with admiration at these solitary heroes, but in their own countries a generation was growing up that knew little of them. The pope's care was for the spiritual welfare of all his flock. He had to decide whether this was best promoted by the symbolic but powerless witnesses to the faith. He came to believe that concordats with hostile governments do more good than intransigent opposition. He made it known that he wished to recall these resolute men. It was a hard decision, the fruits of which cannot yet be seen.

But *Pacem in Terris* is not a document of appeasement. It is a restatement in general terms of the traditional Christian principle of the primacy of the individual and his family over the state, which is the antithesis of Communism.

There are some who quoted in the pope's last months, 'Woe unto you, when all men shall speak well of you.' No pope for centuries enjoyed such acclaim among non-Catholics. But John will be remembered as the man of hope. His successors will determine how many of his hopes were chimerical and how many a result of his perception.

. THE DUCHESS OF JERMYN STREET .

Many attempts were made during her long life to portray the character of Rosa Lewis. She captivated the imagination and curiosity of Londoners – transient or permanent – of many kinds. It was most desirable that a definitive study should be made before she passed into legend. Here it is, written by one who knew her well, enjoyed her confidence, understood her idiosyncrasies and had also the skill and patience to investigate the authentic sources.

This is the portrait of an era as well as of one of its protagonists.

My own connection with Rosa was tenuous. I first met her at about the same time as Mrs Fielding. I had not then started on the profession she abhorred. I was introduced into the Cavendish by Mr Alastair Graham, who is mentioned in this book, and welcomed as one of the moneyless young men whose wine was charged to the bills of older and richer customers. Five years later I was expelled with the words: 'Take your arse out of my chair, Lulu Waters-Waugh.' (Rosa was at the time engaged in a row with a contemporary of mine named Lulu Waters-Welch. She liked, as Mrs Fielding points out, to confuse names.) Our brief acquaintance was largely vicarious. I stayed at the Cavendish once and spent several jolly evenings there, but I was never an habitué; I was seldom in London and the character I drew from her in my second novel was mostly derived at second-hand from the anecdotes and imitations of my friends. Thus, when it was suggested that I should write her life, I knew I was incapable. Mrs Fielding, as will be seen in the following pages, was the obvious person to take it on.

She has succeeded as no one else could. It was a task of the utmost difficulty. We are nearing the centenary of Rosa's birth. Legends, which she did little to dissipate, proliferated about her early years and the fascination of this book lies almost as much in the falsehoods that are exposed as in the truths which research has established. There was the further difficulty that Rosa excelled in the two *métiers* in which triumph is most transient and most incommunicable. She was a great cook in the classic tradition and she was a great cockney clown. There are few people now alive who tasted her quail pudding. Those now in middle age knew her as a richly comic entertainer whose jokes, lacking her timing and tone of voice, tend to vanish when set down in print.

Mrs Fielding, it seems to me, has been brilliantly successful both in evoking the Edwardian era before her own birth, when Rosa was working strenuously to achieve her unique position, and in reporting the later years which she knew so intimately, when Rosa had abandoned the kitchen and was the sharp, garrulous hostess to a diverse, but never dull, company. Mrs Fielding gives us the picture of two ages, one created in the imagination, one keenly observed; more than this she gives the first full, true portrait of a warm-hearted, comic and totally original woman.

Preface to *The Duchess of Jermyn Street: The Life and Good Times of Rosa Lewis of the Cavendish Hotel*, by Daphne Fielding. (London, 1964.)

. THE MAN OF PROPERTY .

John Galsworthy died in 1933 with more official decorations and greater universal respect than have ever been accorded to any English novelist. His surviving contemporaries cherished his friendship. In modesty, generosity, devotion to his art, scrupulous regard for his honour in public and in private affairs, munificence and stoic self-restraint he was a faultless representative of his nation and was recognized as such from Budapest to Stockholm and in many parts of the United States of America. He was eagerly read by foreigners as providing textbooks by which English habits could be learned and English character judged, but he was not read in England by the younger generation of writers. Ironically he had come to be identified with the very class and character whose deficiencies he had set himself to expose. His books have always found readers but not, in the last forty years, among those interested in the art of the novel. Perhaps a younger generation will atone for the neglect of his immediate successors.

The Man of Property is the foundation of his *oeuvre*. It was begun in 1902 when he was in the seventh year of his nine years' passionate but furtive liaison with the wife of a cousin. The circumstance is vital to the book. Those who knew him best described this affair, which eventually became a serenely happy marriage, as the experience which made him an artist. He was a man of conventional upbringing and conventional tastes, educated in classics and the law, an athlete and a sportsman, and surrounded by a numerous, long-lived, prosperous and conventional family. His illicit love, occurring in the heart of this circle, alienated him from them – not from his father, who was kept in ignorance of it, nor from his sisters, who were sympathetic, but from the cousins and their allies, whom he came to regard as constituting a solid, powerful, impermeable barrier against the free happiness of the human spirit. 'The Forsytes' were not, for him, a single family. They were a class whose values were all material and quantitative, who were actuated solely by the obsession of property. Adultery is in the plot of *The Man of Property* but its theme is the representation of a class. In other books and in his plays he successfully portrayed other classes, but 'the Forsytes' and all they stood for were his special creation.

Gilbert Murray wrote to him in 1922, when the Forsyte books appeared in a single volume:

> It is a wonderful achievement of yours to have created this Saga. The rum thing to me is that, after reading it all and admiring it and loving it, I don't feel that I know in the least what a Forsyte is like, and am not conscious of having seen one. I believe you have a queer poetical method which simulates realism in order to attain beauty.

This is a profound criticism. *The Man of Property* opens in the year 1886, when Galsworthy was 19 years old. Most of the characters are old or middle-aged.

Introduction to *The Man of Property*, by John Galsworthy. New York: The Heritage Press, 1964.

They are seen through the eyes of youth and they are described sixteen years later when they have become the embodiment of the frustration of his love. To the social historian they pose the question: did they ever exist? Their obsession with urban commercial matters is not an English characteristic. None of them goes into the navy, the army, politics, the Church, the colonial service, which were in Victorian times the normal means by which families of rising wealth entered the gentry. Until 1918 it was the normal aspiration of every Englishman to become a gentleman. (Galsworthy himself was eminently one.) Commercial origins were obscured. Those of the commercial families who could afford it tended to buy or build themselves houses on agricultural properties far from the source of their incomes and to assume the privileges and obligations of the squirearchy. Soames Forsyte's move from London is the activating event of the story. He is dubbed by his relations 'the man of property'; they ridicule him for setting up as a gentleman. But in fact he is merely building an expensive villa in the purlieus of London on a modest plot of ground which he does not even own freehold. It does not ring true. Or rather, in Gilbert Murray's words, it is a queer poetical method simulating realism.

The English commercial class has been variously treated by the great novelists. Dickens's Podsnaps and Veneerings are prototypes of the Forsytes. But there is one great difference between them: their stability. In Victorian novels the disagreeable plutocrat almost invariably goes bankrupt. In the Edwardian age in which Galsworthy began his great work, wealth seemed indestructible. In the post-war era in which he finished it, it was revealed once more as precarious. One lifetime spanned the whole of British plutocracy. But *The Man of Property* was written in the heyday of security; it is tragedy in the Greek fashion where Nemesis is inescapable, and Nemesis is property itself. This explains the conclusion against which Galsworthy's sage adviser, Edward Garnett, vainly protested.

When Galsworthy wrote the book he intended a single complete tragedy. He notes August 1918 as the time when he decided to make it the opening of a series. He had destroyed the manuscript in 1913, thinking it to be something of no greater importance than his other multifarious writings. The extension of the work has won it millions of readers but it has impaired the classical finality of the original conception. He was in later life to identify many features of the narrative with his own family life. These revelations tend to impair the reader's appreciation of the imaginative vigour of his creation.

The plot is finely constructed. We are presented with a family, shown them in full detail in all their ramifications. There has been one domestic scandal – young Jolyon's – sedulously ignored. There is one rather shaky member – Dartie. Otherwise they are all prosperous and self-satisfied. There is a beautiful stranger, Mrs Soames,[1] who is appreciated as an ornament. It is recognized that she is not entirely happy in her marriage; the depth of her detestation of her husband is not known, nor are its causes ever made evident. Into this circle

1 i.e. Mrs Soames Forsyte. Presumably 'Irene Soames' below should read 'Irene Forsyte'.

comes 'the Buccaneer', artistic, improvident, passionate – all that the Forsytes are not. He becomes the lover of Irene Soames. He is an invention, someone to take the place which in real life Galsworthy occupied.

The drama of Galsworthy's own love affair was heightened by the fact that he was himself a Forsyte, no buccaneer, one of the circle he was disrupting. Galsworthy conscientiously attaches to Bosinney all the attributes, even unconventional dress, which a Forsyte would expect in an artist. He is arrogant towards the Philistine. He is also, alas, quite humourless. In the action at law which is the crisis of the story, the reader may well sympathize with Soames. Bosinney may have had talents – it is hard to visualize the villa with its glazed court, columns and purple leather curtains – but costing is an essential part of an architect's equipment. To mislead a client in the matter (while seducing his wife) argues grave professional impropriety. Galsworthy's celebrated fairness of mind is seen in the judge's summing up. Bosinney is not designed to attract unqualified admiration. Does he carry conviction?

Edward Garnett, in a series of penetrating letters quoted in H. V. Marrott's compilation, urged Galsworthy against the final episode. To a man of Galsworthy's upbringing and nature the catastrophe – professional discredit, bankruptcy and above all the shock of the forcible possession of a mistress by her husband – might well produce despair. A man such as Bosinney has been represented would take it all much more lightly. He and Irene would have crossed the Channel with her jewels and muddled along somehow. But two factors prevented this plausible solution. First, the artist's 'queer poetical method simulating realism'. Galsworthy had set out to write a tragedy, not a comedy of manners. The victims had to be duly sacrificed. And they were to be sacrificed to the ineluctable god of Galsworthy's creation – Forsytism. The lovers had defied powers too strong for them. The intruder must be destroyed, the captive returned to her odious prison. That was the law of life as Galsworthy saw it in the harrowing uncertainties of his nine years' ordeal.

. THE LIGHT THAT DID NOT WHOLLY FAIL .

Kipling was born in 1865. It seems probable that the two books under review are the first of many which will commemorate the centenary and, one may hope, will do greater justice to his singular talents than did his obituaries.

He died at an unfortunate time. For twenty years he had been continuously ill; he had suffered bitter bereavements and he had seen the course of history deflected from the direction of all his early aspirations. His writing was not merely neglected but scornfully attacked by the literary critics of the time.

Review of *Kipling's Mind and Art*, ed. Andrew Rutherford and *Aspects of Kipling's Art*, by C. A. Bodelsen. *Sunday Times*, 22 March 1964.

When he died King George V was also on his death-bed and the greater public event overshadowed his obsequies. In the coming year there is ample opportunity for amends.

Neither of these books is likely to do much to reawaken proper respect. Professor Bodelsen is respectful enough. He is a Dane and therefore untainted by the social and political prejudices which jaundiced an earlier generation of English and American critics, but his scholarly thesis has the limited object of elucidating the obscurities of some of Kipling's late and least-known work. This he fulfils patiently and plausibly and his book will no doubt be of great value to the writers of theses. In particular he examines in detail the story of 'Mrs Bathurst' which never puzzled the present reviewer for the good reason that he never read it. The Professor has little to say about the characteristic works for which in his time Kipling was revered and reviled.

Mr Rutherford is a lecturer at Edinburgh. He has compiled a number of essays dating from 1936 to 1963 and has himself contributed an essay on Kipling's regard for army officers which contains the dubious suggestion that the boisterous camaraderie of the barracks and of service reunions was homosexual in origin. Of the other components of the book two are already well known, Mr Edmund Wilson's and George Orwell's. Mr Wilson is handicapped by his nationality in fully understanding the English character. He is ignorant of our class system and of our education. It is entirely absurd to speak of Kipling's 'snobbishness' – he who sang the praises of the lower and lower-middle class, the non-commissioned officers, the 'railway folk', the engineers of the tug and the tramp-steamer and who pungently scorned the life of leisure and privilege; who refused all public honours and lived, except when his work as a war correspondent demanded it, in simple seclusion.

Mr Wilson, naturally enough when writing for his fellow countrymen but rather tediously for Englishmen, spends much of his space in examining Kipling's experiences in the United States. George Orwell wrote in 1942 at the height of his revulsion from what he regarded as the feeble hypocrisy of English socialist journalism. If he were alive today he would no doubt derive much ironic amusement from the changed position in popular esteem of the Boers in this half-century from that of the gallant little people fighting for their homesteads and way of life to that of the villains of apartheid. Almost all the contributors to Mr Rutherford's book find it necessary to describe Kipling as odious, sometimes finding psychological excuses for him on the popular assumption that all delinquency is a misfortune of upbringing.

Few, if any, survive who knew Kipling well before the First World War. He does not seem to have been a very lovable man except to a very small, vanished circle. It is a mistake, I think, to quote Arnold Bennett's second- or third-hand anecdote of his insinuating himself into the confidence of the officers of a liner and then making them the subject of an official complaint. That does not ring true. But it may be admitted that he seemed touchy and truculent. Many writers are. Kipling was certainly not odious in the way that Rimbaud or

Rousseau were. Max Beerbohm's pictures of him as a ranting vulgarian should be qualified by recognition of his love of France and of French literature.

Much is made of the unhappy five years of his childhood at Southsea. He was indeed abominably treated but he regularly visited the entirely happy household of the Burne-Joneses and he was triumphantly rescued from his 'aunt' as soon as his mother realized the state of affairs. He himself refers to the ordeal but as something he has survived, strengthened for the hardships of life. At school he was one of a dominant and defiant set. His seven subsequent years in India were more damaging to him as an artist.

Contrary to much American opinion, popular journalism is not a good training for literature. It was some years before Kipling rid himself of the bad habits he learned on the Lahore *Gazette*.

Mr Wilson describes him as 'a newspaper man who had access to everything', thus revealing complete incomprehension of the position of a reporter in the sharply stratified society of British India. It was in those years of drudgery and snubs that his bitterness, as well as his vulgarities of style, were rooted.

'The Light that Failed' gives a clear exposition of his views on popularity, prestige and technical mastery. Kipling, I think, made no distinction between art and craftsmanship; it is the job well done that he admires. The hero of 'The Light that Failed' seems to have been a bad painter but he is rebuked only when, to please the dealers, he cleans and smartens up a soldier in the line. Kipling was conscious of a 'demon' or *daimon* who entered him from outside and directed his work. Most story-tellers are aware of this influence. They do not know where they are tending; worse, they fear the ending of this guidance from some undiscovered place in their minds. In Kipling's case the disputes of his critics about 'verse' and 'poetry', 'bad good poetry' and 'good bad poetry', have little significance. He was very industrious and very prolific. It is idle to expect to be equally pleased by all he wrote. There is undoubtedly in many of his stories a disagreeable relish for cruelty (though negligible compared with many much-praised modern writers).

Orwell makes the point that his reproductions of proletarian speech are 'stylized' and false and attributes this to a patronizing superiority. Certainly the line 'When 'Omer struck 'is blooming lyre' is ridiculous. The speaker would be ignorant both of Homer and lyres, but in general the stylization of the demotic is something most writers have been compelled to. Soldiers swore continuously and monotonously. It would have been impossible in his age to print a transcription of their real speech. It seems to me doubtful that English writers have ever succeeded in reproducing the speech of the poor. The language of Jane Austen's characters differs little from that of their counterparts today, but Sam Weller, Kipling's soldiers and the figures of modern popular drama speak distinct and different tongues.

Mr Noël Annan provides a valuable examination of Kipling's conception of 'the Law' and Society. 'He was hardly interested,' he writes, 'whether the customs or morality or religion were right or wrong. For him all that mattered was that they existed.' This judgment goes to the heart of Kipling's character. He was a conservative in the sense that he believed civilization to be something laboriously achieved which was only precariously defended. He wanted to see the defences fully manned and he hated the liberals because he thought them gullible and feeble, believing in the easy perfectibility of man and ready to abandon the work of centuries for sentimental qualms.

Kipling had no religion. Christianity had been shown him in a repulsive form and he rejected it for life. The God of the Old Testament, Allah, Mithras, the Architect of the Universe, even Christ, blunder vaguely into his narrative as convenient myths. He seems to have known little of Hinduism. Most of his 'natives' are Mohammedan. The Christian Incarnation and the Redemption did not exist for him as positive facts. He seems sometimes to have believed, sometimes not, in some form of personal immortality. A great many artists have suffered this deprivation and survived, aesthetically. Not Kipling. He wanted divine sanction for his 'Law', he wanted to participate in symbolic ceremonies, he clung to the conception of a sacred text. He had affinities with Belloc – superficially in his love of France and Sussex, technically in his rollicking metres, deeper in his scorn of politicians and his regard for private and national honour. But he lacked Belloc's Faith and that was a primary need in him that he disastrously failed to satisfy.

. ALFRED DUGGAN .

The death of Alfred Duggan in April of this year brought an abrupt end to a literary career which was in many respects unique.

In recent years we have become so familiar with the spectacle of personal frustration and disaster in the artistic life that we have come almost to regard it as normal. Scott Fitzgerald and Dylan Thomas are typical of many less famous and less gifted writers who began with early brilliance and popular recognition only to find in early middle age that their powers were exhausted and that nothing remained for them except self-pity and drunkenness. Alfred Duggan, on the contrary, spent his youth and early manhood as a rake. Of all my contemporaries he seemed one of the least likely to succeed. Lest I should seem to be betraying the memory of the dead, let me say that a few months ago I wrote to him to ask whether, in some memoirs I was writing, I might describe his early escapades, and was given ungrudging permission to go ahead. Had we been told forty years ago, when we first became friends, that I should now be pronouncing a panegyric on him, we should both have been totally incredulous. He was 47 when he published his first novel, *Knight with Armour*, and in the fourteen succeeding years he produced the *opus* of a full lifetime. He emerged from his years of dissipation with his mind acute, his remarkable memory unimpaired and a prose style already perfectly fitted for his use.

Most writers begin clumsily with experiments they live to regret. Alfred came into action fully equipped and, it seemed, fully exercised in arms. He wrote fifteen historical novels, one of which, *Count Bohemond*, will appear posthumously, three biographies and seven historical studies for young readers. His repute grew steadily in the most diverse quarters. Reviewers became increasingly respectful. It seems to me that a talent so independent of fashion is certain to attract more and more admirers in the future and to establish him safely in a high place among the writers of his period.

In his lifetime he scrupulously avoided publicity and eschewed all the literary gatherings which provide less industrious craftsmen with the opportunity of self-advertisement. Some biographical information is therefore not out of place now.

His father was a rich Argentine of Irish descent who died during Alfred's childhood. His mother was the beautiful daughter of an American diplomatist. She brought him, his younger brother and his sister to England for their education and in 1917 married Lord Curzon, almost the last of the grandee English statesmen, then a member of the Inner War Cabinet, and, it seemed, a future Prime Minister. Alfred thus grew up in the heart of high political society, living in his stepfather's four great houses and himself enjoying a large fortune left him by his father. As I have suggested above, he made no attempt to use these advantages – then very considerable – to advance himself to positions of influence and power. Neither at Eton nor at Balliol did he show application for work. He lived rather flamboyantly for pleasure, alternating between the hunting field and the night-club. Lord Curzon was more perspicacious than his tutors and friends and discerned the great talents which seemed to be running to seed. Alfred also travelled widely, particularly in the Levant where he early began to study the remains of the Crusaders, visiting many castles which were then quite unknown except to a handful of adventurous experts. His fortune dwindled and finally disappeared. Alfred accepted his changed circumstances with dignity and without repining. Instead of his former extravagant pleasures he read – not with any ambition to professional scholarship, but from interest in his subject – mediaeval military history. To the observer it seemed he was merely listlessly passing his time during his long sessions in the library at Hackwood, but all he read became sharply recorded in his memory, so that when at last his pent-up creative powers found expression he could draw on a great store of detailed knowledge.

At the age of 20 he professed Marxism and atheism, but after a few years he returned to the Church of his childhood and for the last thirty-five years of his life was a devout, if, at first, a wayward, conservative Catholic.

With his abandonment of Marxism Alfred became a fervent patriot of the kingdom of his adoption. In 1939, though older than the normal age of recruitment, he enlisted as a private soldier and contrived to get himself posted to Norway in a company of volunteers for hazardous service. He endured the great hardships of the retreat in 1940, an experience which impaired his hitherto strong physical constitution and, no doubt, hastened his death. Invalided out of the army, he chose to serve his country at the bench of an aeroplane factory. In 1953 he married and for the eleven remaining years led a life of complete domestic happiness and unremitting industry in the seclusion of Herefordshire. He entirely overcame his inherited weakness, partly by the aid of a physician, partly by his power of will, partly by his new-found love as a husband, but essentially, I believe, from supernatural grace. It is, as I said before, the antithesis of the popular pattern, but it should be remarked that even in the time of his dissipation there was always a *gravitas* in him, a dignity and courtesy which transcended his weakness.

Such in brief was his life, known to only a few friends. His work stands as his memorial. He spoke of it with a detached modesty which sometimes gave the impression of cynicism. When asked why he habitually treated of obscure persons and periods instead of with subjects more likely to excite popular interest, he would answer, with less than candour, that the scantiness of sources in the Dark Ages relieved him of the labours of research. In fact, he was a dedicated artist who was at ease in remote times.

This century has been prolific in historical novels, many garish, some scholarly. I know of none which give the same sense of intimacy as Alfred's – as though he were describing personal experiences and observations. There is never anything in his work that is romantic, picturesque or sensational. It is accurate and infused throughout with a dry irony that is peculiarly his own. His religious faith is implicit in all he wrote. He was never an apologist or pro-pagandist, but he recognized the Church as being the only proper milieu for mankind. He also recognized mankind as being constitutionally unworthy of the divine promises and he maintained a genial tolerance of the defects of human nature. I think that one of the formative influences in his life was his stepfather's purchase and restoration of Bodiam Castle in Sussex. He followed that process with intense interest and from that went on to his long study of other mediaeval fortifications and to the details of arms and tactics. His first book begins at Bodiam with a knight riding East under the cross. His last ends with the triumph of Christian arms in Jerusalem. He intended to write a further book about Tancred. The Crusades were always in his mind, though he strayed into pre-Christian history very successfully. *Leopards and Lilies*, the story of the Angevins, written in 1954, was the latest historical period with which he dealt. The Renaissance and the Reformation and the Counter-Reformation were all strange to him. Romans and Normans, the worlds of empire and chivalry, were the natural founts of his imagination. Modern history he regarded with calm despair.

It would be tedious to give a list and précis of all Alfred's books. They are there to be studied by all whose taste is not debauched by modern excesses; lucid, plausible stories, humorous, wry and exact. A particular palate is required for their savour. To those who seek bawdy and sentimental tales, they will not appeal. Every reader will find his own favourite among them. For me, *Conscience of the King*, published in 1951, is outstandingly characteristic of the author. It deals with the age of King Arthur, far removed from the romances of Malory and Tennyson, the very dark age in Britain after the Romans left when the heathen barbarians were everywhere flooding in; an age which, I think, Alfred identified with our own. The hero is Cerdic, a very base man, the founder of the royal house of Wessex, through whom, by Matilda, our present royal family are descended. Cerdic was a Roman, an apostate Christian, who came to terms with the invading savages. Their manners revolt him, but he survives. At the end he is left reflecting that he has done the best possible for himself. He has no inkling of the days when his posterity will rule half the world. He wishes Romans were still here, but he has survived them. 'I would like to talk to a well-educated and intelligent man before I die,' he considers, 'but I know that is quite impossible.' And then comes the Duggan glint of irony. 'There is one thing that worries me, especially when I lie awake at night. Suppose all that nonsense [Christianity] that my brother Paul used to preach is really true after all?'

That seems to me the quintessence of Alfred, first in his imaginative entry into an entirely strange world, in his recognition of that world as being the progenitor of our own and in his view of both Cerdic's world and ours in the only light that makes them intelligible – the light of eternity.

. CHANGES IN THE CHURCH .
QUESTIONS FOR THE 'PROGRESSIVES'

Sir, – Like all editors you justly claim that you are not responsible for the opinions of your correspondents and claim credit for establishing an open 'forum'. On the other hand you write of 'exploding renewal' and 'manifest dynamism of the Holy Spirit', thus seeming to sympathize with the northern innovators who wish to change the outward aspect of the Church. I think you injure your cause when week by week you publish (to me) fatuous and outrageous proposals by irresponsible people.

Father John Sheerin is neither fatuous nor outrageous but I find him a little smug. If I read him correctly he is pleading for magnanimity towards defeated opponents. The old (and young) buffers should not be reprobated. They have been imperfectly 'instructed'. The 'progressive' should ask the 'conservative with consummate courtesy' to re-examine his position.

I cannot claim consummate courtesy but may I, with round politeness, suggest that the progressives should re-examine their own? Were *they* perfectly instructed? Did they find the discipline of their seminaries rather irksome? Did

Catholic Herald, 7 August 1964.

they think they were wasting time on the Latin which they found uncongenial? Do they want to marry and beget other little progressives? Do they, like the present Pope, think Italian literature a more enjoyable pursuit than apologetics?

The distinction between Catholicism and *Romanità* has already been stressed in the American journal *Commonweal*. Of course it is possible to have the Faith without *Romanità* and to have *Romanità* without the Faith, but as a matter of recorded history the two have kept very close. 'Peter has spoken' remains the guarantee of orthodoxy.

It is surely (?) a journalistic trick to write of 'the Johannine era'. Pope John was a pious and attractive man. Many of the innovations, which many of us find so obnoxious, were introduced by Pius XII. Pope John's life at Bergamo, Rome, in the Levant, at Paris and Venice was lived with very meagre association with Protestants until, in his extreme old age, he found himself visited by polite clergymen of various sects whom he greeted, as he did the Russian atheists, with 'consummate courtesy'.

I do not believe he had any conception of the true character of modern Protestantism. I quote from an article in *Time* magazine of 10 July:

> The one persuasive way of referring to Jesus today is as a 'remarkably free man'. After the Resurrection the disciples suddenly possessed some of the unique and 'contagious' freedom that Jesus had. In telling the story of Jesus of Nazareth, therefore, they told it as the story of the free man who had set them free . . . He who says 'Jesus is love' says that Jesus' freedom has been contagious . . . Van Buren concludes that Christianity will have to strip itself of its supernatural elements . . . just as alchemy had to abandon its mystical overtones to become the useful science of Chemistry.

These words are not those of a Californian crank but of a clergyman of the 'Episcopal Church' of America, who derive what Orders they have from the Archbishop of Canterbury. I am sure that such questions were not raised on the much-publicized meeting of the Archbishop and Pope John.

Father Sheerin suggests that Catholic conservatism is the product of the defensive policy necessary in the last century against the nationalistic-masonic-secularism of the time. I would ask him to consider that the function of the Church in every age has been conservative – to transmit undiminished and uncontaminated the creed inherited from its predecessors. Not 'is this fashionable notion one that we should accept?' but 'is this dogma (a subject on which we agree) the Faith as we received it?' has been the question (as far as I know) at all General Councils. I have seen no evidence that Pope Paul had anything else in mind when he summoned the present Council.

Conservatism is not a new influence in the Church. It is not the heresies of the sixteenth and seventeenth centuries, the agnosticism of the eighteenth century, the atheism of the nineteenth and twentieth centuries, that have been the foes of the Faith turning her from serene supremacy to sharp controversy. Throughout her entire life the Church has been at active war with enemies from without and traitors from within. The war against Communism in our own age is acute but it is mild compared with those fought and often won by our predecessors.

Finally, a word about liturgy. It is natural to the Germans to make a row. The torchlit, vociferous assemblies of the Hitler Youth expressed a national passion. It is well that this should be canalized into the life of the Church. But it is essentially un-English. We seek no 'Sieg Heils'. We pray in silence. 'Participation' in the Mass does not mean hearing our own voices. It means God hearing our voices. Only He knows who is 'participating' at Mass. I believe, to compare small things with great, that I 'participate' in a work of art when I study it and love it silently. No need to shout. Anyone who has taken part in a play knows that he can rant on the stage with his mind elsewhere. If the Germans want to be noisy, let them. But why should they disturb our devotions?

'Diversity' is deemed by the progressives as one of their aims against the stifling *Romanità*. May they allow it to English Catholics.

I am now old but I was young when I was received into the Church. I was not at all attracted by the splendour of her great ceremonies – which the Protestants could well counterfeit. Of the extraneous attractions of the Church which most drew me was the spectacle of the priest and his server at low Mass, stumping up to the altar without a glance to discover how many or how few he had in his congregation; a craftsman and his apprentice; a man with a job which he alone was qualified to do. That is the Mass I have grown to know and love. By all means let the rowdy have their 'dialogues', but let us who value silence not be completely forgotten.

Your obedient servant,
Evelyn Waugh

. THE MAX BEHIND THE MASK .

Because of its successful dramatization and frequent reissue in different forms, *The Happy Hypocrite* is, I suppose, the most widely known of Beerbohm's works, though it is neither his most brilliant nor most characteristic. That fairy story, it will be remembered, is the exact counterpart to *The Picture of Dorian Gray*. Wilde imagined a young man portrayed in early beauty. His life is increasingly vicious, but only the painting reveals the horrible deterioration of his character. Until death the hero retains the spurious glow of innocence. Lord George Hell in *The Happy Hypocrite* is an aging rake who prosecutes an idyllic love affair with a young girl under the disguise of a youthful mask. When it is finally torn from his face the ravages of age and debauchery are found to

Review of *Max*, by Lord David Cecil and *Letters to Reggie Turner by Max Beerbohm*, ed. Rupert Hart-Davis. *Atlas*, January 1965.

have totally disappeared. He has become what his innocent love has made him.

In his eagerly awaited biography, *Max*, Lord David Cecil makes a point of Beerbohm's early assumption of a mask, demure, elegant, passionless, which he wore all his life so that it became an essential part of his character. Lord David does little to unmask him. Indeed there is no reason to suppose that the mask hid anything. It was a part of his exquisite wardrobe. There were no dark secrets any more than there were deformities under his beautifully cut frock coats.

The writing of the biography was a difficult task. Beerbohm's life was happy and uneventful. For the most part Lord David has been content to tell it in tactfully chosen, familiar extracts from his subject's own writing. The connecting passages present a problem. Beerbohm's own literary grace was so complete that the juxtaposition of another hand must inevitably make a crude contrast. Any attempt to emulate the master's own style would have been disastrous. But Lord David has an easy, Whiggish negligence of grammar which gives the happy illusion that he is reading aloud in the drawing-room and occasionally pausing to comment colloquially on the entertainment. A disagreeable reviewer might hold up to reprobation numerous sentences of Lord David's which offend against even colloquial syntax; but to do so would be to miss the point of his achievement just as much as to complain of the narrow scope of Beerbohm's own genius.

For Beerbohm was a genius of the purest kind. Some English writers, he said, were weight-lifters; others jugglers with golden balls. There were, he believed, rather too many weight-lifters – and today he would have to add contortionists, freaks and buffoons to the literary circus.

I am told that the young, and especially the young who have fallen under the dire influence of the Cambridge School of English Literature, dismiss Beerbohm with contempt. How much high pleasure they miss! It is reasonable to impute an element of envy. The word 'satire' has now been usurped by guttersnipes. Our popular caricaturists are content with types. Few of them, one must suppose, have any personal acquaintance, as Beerbohm had, with their subjects. Every phrase and line of his is a rebuke to them. After his very early days, when he gambolled with an ornate and consciously absurd vocabulary, he wrote supremely well. His essay on Venice, originally an article in the *Daily Mail*, is a model not only of imaginative observation but of variety of structure. It is, I believe, the best travel sketch ever written. In narration he was less happy except in 'Maltby and Braxton'. I confess to qualms about 'The Dreadful Dragon of Hay Hill' and 'William and Mary'. As Lord David points out, Beerbohm had his own, exquisite, sharply circumscribed universe within which he was 'incomparable' and from which he very rarely strayed. But Lord David writes primarily as a biographer rather than as a critic, and he has assembled all the available facts in a way to leave us grateful.

Beerbohm's was an odd environment as the youngest of a large, diverse family. His father, a German-Balt by origin, without, as has been supposed,

Jewish blood, married his deceased wife's sister, so that the elder members were closer than half-brothers and half-sisters. They ranged in character from the famous, flamboyant, improvident actor-manager Sir Herbert Beerbohm Tree to the sister who became an Anglican nun (in an order which allowed a considerable freedom). There was a ne'er-do-well, a dandified brother who drifted round the casinos of Europe losing money; another brother who disappeared in Australia and was said to have married a Negress; a methodical housekeeping sister; the mother who lived to great old age and could not be restrained from perpetual hospitality. There were others, less notable, and at the tail came Max, a type of the child of late love, selfish, self-sufficing, affectionate, cool, surprisingly tough, saturated in the wish and ability to please.

Until his marriage at the age of 38 he lived at home, cosseted by all. They started in easy circumstances but grew poorer. Max was at times near penury. Had he been well-off his case would have been a normal one – a more versatile Logan Pearsall Smith, a more gifted Gerald Berners – but he was, I think, unique in guarding his tiny, brilliant genius against all corruption at the price of frugality which at times approached privation. He relished luxury when it was offered him by Philip Sassoon, Northcliffe or Lady Desborough, but he never aspired to riches. Indeed, it is constantly surprising to learn how little he was paid. At his first exhibition of caricatures after the First World War we find him exhilarated at making £1,000 for the fruit of eight years' work. Most of his most brilliant drawings fetched less than £50 each. 'I have a public of 1,500,' he said at the height of his fame.

Lord David provides more information than has hitherto been available about Beerbohm's love affairs, but they still remain (and are likely to do so forever) in deep obscurity. Is it prurient to wish we knew more? At Oxford and in his first years in London his male friends, with the exception of Rothenstein, were almost all homosexual. He did not share their pleasures, but he was fully aware of them and used the slang of the clique, referring to 'renters' (male prostitutes) and 'mulierasts' (heterosexuals). He was captivated by Wilde but had begun to see through him long before his fall. His objection was not moral, merely aesthetic; Wilde was growing gross and arrogant. His only fear was that closer friends, such as Ross and Reggie Turner, might get into trouble with the police.

There came his 'crush' on Cissy Loftus; then his strange, prolonged 'engagement' to an unsuccessful American actress, Grace Conover. Then his brief 'engagement' at Dieppe to the passionate Constance Collier. Did they go to bed? Did they experiment and fail? Finally there was his long, devoted marriage to the elusive, fastidious Florence Kahn. A *marriage blanc*? Lord David does not tell us, because he does not know. Nor can anyone ever know. Beerbohm remarked of Ruskin that it was surprising he should marry without knowing he was impotent. But the question is of little importance in an artist of Beerbohm's quality.

Lord David has not been well served by his publishers, Constable. The illustrations are undated; the index is contemptible. Mr Hart-Davis's edition of Beerbohm's letters to Reggie Turner is a model of editorship. It is his misfortune that the collection should appear simultaneously with the biography. Lord David has been through it first and skimmed some of its riches, but he has chosen to eschew all references and most dates, so that it is a great pleasure to turn to the scrupulous text of Mr Hart-Davis.

Reggie Turner had a peculiar position in relation to Beerbohm. Slightly older, better off, accounted by all the better talker, he failed completely as a writer and lived in a cosmopolitan half-world while Beerbohm was basking in fashionable favour. He never repined. His devotion to Beerbohm remained untainted by envy and graced by constant small acts of munificence. Beerbohm wrote to him with complete intimacy and Turner preserved that side of the correspondence. It is to be regretted that his letters to Beerbohm are lost. As it stands, the present volume is a valuable text, an essential complement to Lord David's biography. Every library should have both. Taken together they provide as clear a picture of Beerbohm as we are likely to get.

. THE SPIRIT OF EDITH SITWELL .

This last posthumous book of Edith Sitwell's is described as her 'autobiography'. The word does not seem entirely apt but it is difficult to provide an alternative. The book was written while she was ill and in pain during the last months of her life. It comprises anecdotes, essays in criticism and extensive quotations from her own work and that of others. 'I do not refer,' she writes in the Preface, 'to any of my dearly loved living friends. I trust I have hurt nobody.' This is a laudable, final disposition but her friends may regret the self-imposed reticence which leaves so many of her characters pseudonymous or anonymous, for she was throughout life a controversialist in the class of Whistler. No game was too great or too small for her unnerving marksmanship and her delicate compassion was qualified by a zest for combat.

Her brother Osbert has left a rich and elaborately planned memorial to the brilliant family of which she was the eldest, giving their father, Sir George, an immortality in which the fantasies of Edith had a great part. The reviewer has had the delight of some thirty-five years' friendship with them and he still finds it impossible to discern the precise moments of their becoming air-borne, when prosaic memory yields to poetic fancy.

Taken Care Of is not, to outward appearance, a planned book. It seems rather that, knowing her end was near, Edith Sitwell composed a synopsis to explain to later readers the origin and development of her poetic life. It can be roughly

Review of *Taken Care Of*, by Edith Sitwell. *Sunday Times*, 4 April 1965.

divided into her dedication to her muse, her compassion for suffering humanity, her scorn of humbugs, her delight in the comic contradictions of life.

In youth she suffered excessively from discouragement. Neither parent appreciated her genius. Her father resented her sex, her mother her unconventional beauty. Had she been a son and heir, had she been a pretty débutante . . . But she was not. And when she achieved independence it seemed that everyone was conspiring to interrupt and frustrate her work. Because she had herself been discouraged in youth, she was extravagant in her generosity towards (often) undeserving aspirants. For many years she regarded herself as duty-bound to defend any artist who came under attack, especially one of her siblings.

Her compassion was strong in her long before she became formally Christian. The two wars caused her greater grief than they did to more active participants. She was taken by a stunt photographer to the slums of Los Angeles and the experience seared her. Towards the end of her life her compassion remained as keen, but she began to accept the possibility of the spiritual value of accepted suffering.

She had much to endure from humbugs – the more as she became more famous. Her brothers enjoyed a wide social life. To her the world of the rich and fashionable was a trap to distract her from the unremitting labour of her poetry, and she recoiled with loathing.

It seems that at the end of her life, now full of honours, she still had bitter memories of the harsh and foolish things that were said of her early work, and she was at pains to elucidate what had been obscure in her first technical experiments. She had a relish for display which the audiences of the USA fully appreciated. She dressed unconventionally and dramatically, asserting her striking, idiosyncratic looks against the 'ugly duckling' which her parents saw in her.

The dignity of fame and the charity of religion tempered her ferocity as an antagonist. It is to be hoped that some PhD thesis-writer will choose her earlier controversial work as a subject. In the book under review there is rather little of it: a description of Wyndham Lewis, some sharply drawn quotations from the Cambridge literary school, and a fierce denunciation of *Lady Chatterley's Lover* which makes the reader wish that the prosecution in that much muddled case had called literary witnesses, who abounded, to the worthlessness of that work instead of leaving the jury with the impression that an endless succession of dons and parsons supported the defence without a dissentient opinion – these are the few occasions when Edith Sitwell in this book gives us a sample of her formidable power to expose the absurd.

She was an early patron of Mr Cecil Beaton, who contributes many photographs to the book.

. FIZZ, BUBBLY, POP .

Some years ago I had the happy experience of joining a miscellaneous company of English politicians, peers, novelists and journalists on a tour of Champagne. We had been invited to Rheims by the vintners for the blessing of a stained-glass window they had presented to the cathedral. The ceremony was stripped of most of its dignity by the irreverence of the French press photographers but the days of hospitality were memorable. We perambulated the huge archaic cellars of Pommery and the formal gardens of Moët; the elaborate processes of the *vendange* and vintage were demonstrated.

We were entertained in the houses and offices of many local magnates whose names had hitherto been abstractions on the labels of their wines. They are an outstandingly handsome set, the champagne barons and baronesses, mostly the descendants of the nobility of other provinces who, a hundred years ago, migrated to this bleak region and married the heiresses of the original simple farmers of the land and then, not content, as most fortune hunters would be, to live at ease, took charge of their wives' dowries, learned the business and enormously increased its value.

Everywhere we were regaled with bottles, some of dignified age, some in turbulent youth. We had a thundering good time. It must therefore seem ungrateful to say that it was several weeks before I again drank champagne. An illusion of adolescence had been dissipated. Until that lavish beano, I had held that champagne was the ideal beverage for any hour of the day and night and for every physical condition. Now I am obliged to admit that the French know better and that it is a wine for (frequent) occasional use.

Champagne is in a sense the most modern of wines. It claims a monastic origin but, in fact, it was little known outside its own district until the Russian invasion at the fall of Napoleon. The history of the Widow Clicquot, which has been charmingly written by Princesse Jean de Caraman-Chimay[1], wife of one of the present senior partners of the firm, is typical of the great champagne houses.

Mme Clicquot, née Ponsardin, was a bourgeoise of Rheims. Born twelve years before the revolution, widowed before Austerlitz, she inherited a property in which viticulture was a growing concern. Her father was a Jacobin; she the ancestress of three dukes. Throughout her long widowhood she devoted herself to perfecting the processes of manufacture and to selling her wine abroad. Her rivals were also prospering.

Early in the nineteenth century champagne became the symbol of prosperity and gaiety and so it has remained in the darker and duller succeeding century.

Vogue (New York), 1 September 1965.

1 Properly Princesse Jacqueline. Waugh supplied a preface for, and partially rewrote the English translation of, her book, *The Life and Times of Madame Veuve Clicquot-Ponsardin* (Curwen Press, London, 1961).

It is a manufactured wine owing less to nature and more to human skill than any wine in France. It is inimitable. Gruesome attempts have been made to produce an equivalent. It is almost indestructible and will stand changes of temperature and physical agitations that would ruin a Bordeaux or a Burgundy; still more a port. Champagnes of the same brand and year are identical in Épernay, Hollywood and Tokyo. In the early years of the export trade horrible things appeared in the bottles – *yeux de crapaud* and *couleuvres* – and the correspondence of the rival agents is full of anxiety about the condition of delayed cargoes. Patient scientific investigation has cured all that.

Today one can be completely confident of finding every bottle clean to the last drop. I do not remember ever finding a bad cork. In extreme age the wine loses its fizz, and sometimes darkens in colour and takes on a flavour of Madeira. There are those who relish it in this condition. During the war it was discovered that one of the London railway hotels still had a bin of flat, brown, sixty-year-old champagne, still priced as it had been in its youth. There in the mornings through the ravages of the bombs a little group of coeval gourmets used to meet and sip in great content.

By its nature champagne can be produced only on a large scale. The hereditary skills of the various workers have to be fertilized by great capital investment. In the course of the last 150 years, Rheims, once the sacring place of the kings of France, has become the centre of one of its most important export industries. A handful of families owns and manages the entire business. Each has its own trade secrets and each produces a wine of its own character. When you find a genuine champagne bearing a label that is not well-known, you can (I think) be sure that it is the product of one of the great houses which it is reluctant to sell under its own name; sometimes, but not always, an inferior wine, sometimes merely a surplus part of the regular production.

Many London wine merchants have wine bottled for them in Rheims or Épernay which they sell under names of their own at lower prices than the famous brands. These they recommend for use at balls and weddings, but they are worth the experiments of serious drinkers who may sometimes be surprised by finding a vintage of high quality under an unfamiliar title.

The champagne vintners like those of the Douro can blend their wines to satisfy the tastes of their customers. In the years before 1917 the Russians were the most important, and they liked it sweet. Sugar was added before fermentation. In many parts of Europe a wine only slightly less sweet than the Russian is still preferred, but in this century the words 'sweet champagne' have acquired a pejorative sense suggestive of the bordello, while 'dry' fatuously suggests sparkling wit. English and Americans are guilty of the modern flight from sweetness which is driving into neglect the finest Sauternes, hock and even port.

I have seen a ghastly (I hope false) report that the incomparable Château d'Yquem is now making a dry wine for New Yorkers who are proud of the name but can not enjoy its riches. Pink champagne also has a *louche* reputation –

ballet shoes and *cabinets particuliers*. Sometimes I believe it is ordinary white wine with some tasteless colouring matter added. Veuve Clicquot Rosé on the other hand is a rare, splendid and quite distinct wine.

Most of the wines of Champagne are made from a mixture of black and white grapes. There are, however, the delicious *Blancs de Blancs*, the best of which are very slightly sweet and *crémant* instead of *mousseux*. These have the great advantage that they can be tossed down in bumpers without the impediment which the fizz causes in the normal gullet. There are also, of course, the still white wines of the district, *champagne nature*, delicate and refreshing, which I have very rarely met outside France.

But for most of the world champagne means 'Fizz', 'Bubbly' or 'Pop', the international symbol of high living. I began this essay by stating that it should be a matter of frequent occasional use, sometimes as the last of many wines at a formal banquet, but best 'discussed' – to use an antiquated term – in privacy. For two intimates, lovers or comrades, to spend a quiet evening with a magnum, drinking no apéritif before, nothing but a glass of cognac after – that is the ideal. At midnight with a light supper, then too it is excellent.

There are those – I am no longer of them – who find a pint sustaining in midmorning, drunk in solitude after one's letters are answered before facing the social trials of the day. The worst time is that dictated by convention, in a crowd, in the early afternoon, at a wedding reception.

Since the austere forties people in England have realized that champagne is relatively inexpensive. It has the great advantage to the host that the hard-drinking young do not much like it. They look for whisky. If they find it, they are irremovable and after an hour or two become boisterous or even truculent. When only champagne is offered them, honour has been satisfied and they soon slink off disappointed.

Champagne parties, I am told, are now taking the place of cocktail parties. No skilled barman is needed. The wine, when spilled, does little damage. Neat devices are on the market with which half-empty bottles can be sealed for future use. But, however convenient and inexpensive these assemblies, they have a disadvantage that should be noted; they smell. Many things that are very good in the mouth, such as Camembert cheese, can be offensive to the nose. Champagne is one of them and, like cheese, should be taken on a full stomach. To enter a house at seven, when it is full of people who have eaten nothing for some hours, who have drunk champagne and are obliged by the noise and press to shout into one another's faces, makes one long for the wholesome, gross reek of rum grog.

But this is not the note on which to end an act of homage to one of the great man-made goods that has not only survived into our day but actually thrived and become refined. Lament the modern age as we will. Declare with justice that we can no longer build or paint; that we have made all but the most remote corners of our countryside uninhabitable and destroyed the charms of travel. But in one thing we have it better than our great-great-grandfathers – the copious bounty of the harvest on those chilly battlefields of Champagne and of the invention and industry in the dank chalk caves where miles of bottles lie maturing for our delight.

. PORTRAIT OF A HEAD .

All schoolmasters, for good or ill, attain a certain immortality; the memories of their idiosyncrasies remain sharper than those of subsequent acquaintances. J. F. Roxburgh had all the gifts and charms to captivate the adolescent. He may well be remembered as the last of the great headmasters who created a school and imposed on it his own ethos. Something like 3,000 men must have grown up under him; not less than 1,000 must have had their tastes and habits formed by him. It seems probable that in the modern development of English education we shall not see his peer.

In writing his biography the present Provost of King's has done more than perform an act of *pietas*. He presents an admirable portrait of an admirable man. I do not see how the book could be bettered nor can I conceive of any pupil of his at Stowe or at Lancing who would willingly neglect to read and possess it.

Roxburgh was not an innovator or an experimenter. Certain features of his own boyhood at Charterhouse seemed to him undesirable and reformable, in particular the exaggerated deference paid to those proficient at cricket and football, but in general education he sought to transmit the culture he had himself received, while spreading happiness among all who came under him. Greek, Latin, French and English Literature (and diction) up to the end of the nineteenth century – these, he believed, made a full man. He was singularly well equipped to impart them both by his *panache* and his deep genuine affection for all his pupils. He became a Conservative in politics. He was faithful to the social order in which he had been reared. Every hour in his form room was exhilarating. He was not a profound scholar and he did not, as do many schoolmasters, concentrate his attention on a few boys who promised university distinctions.

He was my sixth-form master at Lancing. After that our ways led apart and I knew him only as a brilliant propagandist in the newspapers. It comes as a startling revelation that at the time when he seemed at the height of prosperity, with members of the royal family gracing all his functions and himself living in spacious style worthy of the Dukes of Buckingham, he suffered constant embarrassment about the finance and the control of the school which was only one of a consortium with which he had little sympathy.

At Lancing, as a layman, he had no part in the religious education with

Review of *Roxburgh of Stowe*, by Noël Annan. *Observer*, 17 October 1965.

which we always supposed him to be at variance. Indeed, consciously or unconsciously, he did much to shake conventional faith. The Provost describes him in the pulpit and even suggests that there was a time when he considered taking holy orders. At Lancing he passed for an agnostic.

He was abnormally industrious and wore himself out prematurely by his attention to duty. He was a weary and perhaps disillusioned man at the end. The two great wars of his lifetime struck hard at both personal friendships and philosophic principles. He left no body of writing. He was not, I think, personally ambitious except to carry out in style the tasks entrusted to him. Style was the man, but infused everywhere with compassion and affection.

The Provost of King's has put all who knew him in a deep debt for his masterly treatment of an elusive subject. I trust the book will run to many editions. When it does Gitt's on p. 47 should be changed to Gibb's. Also the position of his standing desk should be moved from his private study to his housemaster's room in Sanderson's.

. CHRONOLOGICAL LIST OF OCCASIONAL WRITINGS NOT PRINTED IN THIS VOLUME .

L.= letter to the editor
R.= review

L. *Lancing College Magazine*, November 1921, p. 83.

L. *Lancing College Magazine*, March 1922, p. 31.

'The Union' (reports of debates). Cherwell, 31 January, p. 28; 7 February, p. 46; 14 February, p. 60–1; 21 February, p. 76; 7 March, p. 111; 15 March 1922, p. 127. Unsigned.

'The Union' (reports of debates). *Oxford Fortnightly Review*, 21 October, pp. 13–14; 4 November, pp. 25–6; 18 November, pp. 41–2; 2 December 1922, p. 56. Last two unsigned.

'Rugger Night'. *Isis*, 7 February 1923, p. 8. L.

'The National Game'. *Cherwell*, 26 September 1923, pp. 174, 176.

Sub-editor of *Isis* for spring term, 23 January–12 March 1924.

'The Union' (reports of debates). *Isis*, 6 February, p. 13; 20 February, p. 19; 27 February, p. 10; 12 March, p. 15; 7 May, p. 12; 22 May, p. 34; 28 May, p. 21; 4 June 1924, p. 16.

R. of film of Ibanez novel. *Isis*, 30 January 1924, p. 6.

R. of films *Robin Hood* and *The Little Milliner*. *Isis*, 6 February 1924, p. 16.

R. of film *Pagliacci*. *Isis*, 14 February 1924, p. 17.

R. of film *If Winter Comes*. *Isis*, 20 February 1924, p. 28.

R. of film *Woman to Woman*. *Isis*, 27 February 1924, p. 6.

R. of film *The Four Horsemen*. *Isis*, 5 March 1924, p. 24.

Reviews for *Bookman* (London), unidentifiable. See *Diaries*, 27 August, 7 September and 8 September 1927.

R. of *English Letter Writers*, ed. R. Brimley Johnson. *Bookman*, March 1928, p. 328.

'D. G. Rossetti'. *Times Literary Supplement*, 17 May 1928, p. 379. L.

R. of Robert Paltock, *The Life and Adventures of Peter Wilkins*. *Observer*, 9 December 1928, p. 8.

'Old-Fashioned Drinks'. *Daily Express*, 21 December 1928, p. 5.

'Careers for Our Sons: Revelations Concerning the Street of Ink'. *Passing Show*, 19 January 1929, p. 22.

'Careers for Our Sons: Shop-keeping'. *Passing Show*, 9 February 1929, p. 16.

R. of W. R. Fuerst and S. J. Hume, *Twentieth Century Stage Decoration*; D. Morand, *Monumental and Commercial Architecture of Great Britain*; E. B. Hovell, *Indian Sculpture and Painting*; P. Koechlin and G. Migeon, *Oriental Art*; M. Salamon, *Fine Print of the Year, 1928*; G. Smith and F. Bengar, *The Oldest London Bookshop, 1728–1928*. *Observer*, 17 February 1929, p. 9.

'Matter-of-Fact Mothers of the New Age'. *Evening Standard*, 8 April 1929, p. 7.

R. of Henry Green, *Living*; Allan Hillgarth, *Change for Heaven;* Inez Holden, *Sweet Charlatan*. *Vogue* (London), 4 September 1929, p. 43.

'Let the Marriage Ceremony Mean Something'. *Daily Mail*, 8 October 1929, p. 12.

R. of Arthur Symons, *From Toulouse-Lautrec to Rodin*; Ana M. Berry, *Art for Children*; Ana M. Berry, *Animals in Art*; W. G. Raffe, *Poster Design*; Sir John Soane, *Lectures on Architecture*; Francis Carruthers Gould, *Nature Caricatures*. *Observer*, 12 January 1930, p. 6.

'A Searchlight on a Classic. No.2; *Tess*, as a "Modern" sees it'. *Evening Standard*, 17 January 1930, p. 7.

'Recommendation to those who wish to preserve Oxford', in souvenir programme of a matinee held 28 February 1930 for the Oxford Preservation Trust, p. 15.

R. of Terence Greenidge, *Degenerate Oxford?* in *Fortnightly Review*, March 1930, pp. 423–4.

'I Prefer London's Night Life'. *Daily Mail*, 5 April 1930, p. 10.

'Advice to the Rich'. *Daily Express*, 10 April 1930, p. 12.

R. of Norman Douglas, *How About Europe?* in *Week-end Review* (London), 31 May 1930, pp. 426, 428.

REVIEWS IN THE *GRAPHIC*, 31 MAY – 25 OCTOBER 1930, ALL UNDER TITLE 'THE BOOKS YOU READ'

R. of Charles Graves, *–And the Greeks*; Doris Arthur Jones, *The Life and Letters of Henry Arthur Jones*; Roy Campbell, *Adamastor*; Alan Sims, *Anna Perenna*; Norman Douglas, *How About Europe?* 7 June 1930, p. 543.

R. of Daphne Salt, *Strange Combat*; Daphne Muir, *The Last Crusade*. 14 June 1930, p. 588.

R. of V. Sackville-West, *The Edwardians*; Sir Lionel Cust, *King Edward VII and His Court*. 21 June 1930, p. 661.

R. of M. G. Eberhart, *While the Patient Slept*; Virgil Markham, *Shock!*; Ivy Low, *His Master's Voice*; Tyline Perry, *The Owner Lies Dead*; Alice Campbell, *Spiderweb*; Valentine Williams, *The Knife Behind the Curtain*; postscript replying to Charles Graves's letter of 22 June about Waugh's review of his book. 28 June 1930, p. 715.

R. of A. P. Herbert, *The Water Gipsies*; G. D. H. and M. Cole, *Burglars in Bucks*; Colette, *Mitsou*; Alec Waugh, '. . . *Sir*,' *She Said*; B. Causton and G. G. Young, *Keeping It Dark*; Maurice Baring, *Robert Peckham*. 5 July 1930, p. 33.

R. of Ethel Mannin, *Confessions and Impressions*; J. Keith Winter, *Other Man's Saucer*; W. R. Burnett, *Iron Man*; Charles Williams, *War in Heaven*; Clemence Dane and Helen Simpson, *Printer's Devil*. 12 July 1930, p. 75.

R. of Dorothy Sayers and R. Eustace, *The Documents in the Case*; A. Fielding, *The Craig Poisoning Mystery*; Leonard Falkner, *Murder Off Broadway*; Jesse Collings, *Please Meet Alphonse*; Francis Yeats-Brown, *Bengal Lancer*; Owen Tweedy, *By Way of the Sahara*; Harold Dearden, *The Mind of the Murderer*. 19 July 1930, p. 122.

R. of John Buchan, *Castle Gay*; Gilbert Frankau, *Martin Make-Believe*; Naomi Royde-Smith, *The Island*; Thomas Wolfe, *Look Homeward, Angel*; W. B. Maxwell, *To What Green Altar?*; John Erskine, *An Experiment in Sincerity*. 26 July 1930, p. 173.

R. of A. Conan Doyle, *The Edge of the Unknown*; J. S. Viereck, *Glimpses of the Great*; H. J. Massingham, *The Friend of Shelley*; Stephen Graham, *The Death of Yesterday*; Oliver Madox Hueffer, *Some of the English*. 2 August 1930, p. 206.

R. of A. E. W. Mason, *The Dean's Elbow*; E. V. Lucas, *Down the Sky*; Anon., *Waac Demobilised*; Philip Gibbs, *The Wings of Adventure*; Cecil Roberts, *Havana Bound*; Hermione Flatau, *Drama in Mount Street*; T. S. Stribling, *Backwater*. 9 August 1930, p. 247.

R. of Theodore Dreiser, *Color of a Great City*; Sisley Huddleston, *What's Right with America*; Umberto Nobile, *With the 'Italia' to the North Pole*; M. A. Murray, *Egyptian Sculpture*. 23 August 1930, p. 317.

R. of Vicki Baum, *Grand Hotel*; Rose Macaulay, *Staying with Relations*; Elmer Rice, *A Voyage to Purilia*; Paul Bloomfield, *Quite Contrairy; Famous Novels of Today* (an omnibus volume); *Ethel M. Dell Pullman*. 27 September 1930, p. 509.

R. of Evelyn Waugh, *Labels*; Dominique Dunois, *The Natural Mother*; Robert

Gathorne-Hardy, *Laceburg Manor*; Johannes Haller, *Philip Eulenberg: The Kaiser's Friend*; Richard F. Russell, *Foreword to Life*. 4 October 1930, p. 25.

R. of Somerset Maugham, *Cakes and Ale*; John Dos Passos, *The Forty-Second Parallel*; Margaret Kennedy, *The Fool of the Family*. 11 October 1930, p. 74.

R. of Arnold Bennett, *Imperial Palace*; Louis Marlow, *The Lion Took Fright*; Dorothy Sayers, *Strong Poison*; Gregory Baxter, *Death Strikes at Six Bells*. 18 October 1930, p. 121.

R. of Osbert Sitwell, *Dumb Animal*; Charlotte Haldane, *Brother to Bert*. 25 October 1930, p. 174.

R. of Catherine Carswell, *The Life of Robert Burns*; Dorothy Walworth, *They Thought They Could Buy It*; E. L. Woodward, *The Twelve Winded Sky*. 8 November 1930, p. 277.

'Famous Authors on Marriage Morals'. *John Bull*, 5 July 1930, pp. 20–1.
'Address Snobbery'. *Daily Mail*, 12 July 1930, p. 8.
'A Gambling Holiday'. *Daily Mail*, 19 July 1930, p. 10.
'The Old Familiar Faces'. *Daily Mail*, 2 August 1930, p. 8.
'Parties One Likes'. *Daily Mail*, 15 August 1930, p. 8.
'Schoolboys Who Do Not Grow Up'. *Daily Mail*, 30 August 1930, p. 8.

DESPATCHES TO *THE TIMES* FROM ABYSSINIA BY-LINED 'FROM OUR SPECIAL CORRESPONDENT'

'The Abyssinian Coronation: Duke of Gloucester at Jibuti'. 27 October 1930, p. 12.
'The Abyssinian Coronation: Duke of Gloucester's Arrival'. 29 October 1930, p. 13.
'British Air Mission in Addis Ababa'. 30 October 1930, p. 13.
'Duke of Gloucester in Abyssinia: Presents to the Emperor'. 31 October 1930, p. 14.
'The Statue to Menelik'. 3 November 1930, p. 12.
'Coronation Banquet in Abyssinia: 30,000 Guests'. 5 November 1930, p. 13.
'Emperor's Procession in Addis Ababa'. 6 November 1930, p. 13.
'The Abyssinian Festivities: Emperor's Picnic Party'. 7 November 1930, p. 13.
'Review at Addis Ababa: Capering Military Bards'. 8 November 1930, p. 11.
'The Abyssinian Celebrations'. 10 November 1930, p. 11.
'End of Abyssinian Celebrations'. 13 November 1930, p. 13.

DESPATCHES TO THE *DAILY EXPRESS* FROM ABYSSINIA BY-LINED '"DAILY EXPRESS" SPECIAL CORRESPONDENT'

'British Airmen in Abyssinia'. 30 October 1930. Manchester edn.
'Dancing Priests at Emperor of Abyssinia's Coronation'. 4 November 1930, p. 3.
'Raw Beef Feast: Grandfather Clock on Tomb of an Emperor'. 5 November 1930, p. 3.
'Ethiopian Emperor at Church: Chiefs in Lion Skins as Escort'. 6 November 1930, p. 19.

'A Journey to Abyssinia'. *Graphic*, 130 (22 November 1930), p. 350.
'A Journey to Abyssinia – Alarums and Excursions'. *Graphic*, 130 (13 December 1930), p. 504.
'British Policy in Aden: A Conference of Tribal Chiefs'. *The Times*, 17 March 1931, p. 13.
'It's High Time Someone Called the Bluff About the Flood of Central European Romances' (r. of Franz Werfel, *The Hidden Child*; G. B. Stern, *The Shortest Night*;

James Kenward, *John and David*; E. Phillips Oppenheim, *Simple Peter Cradd*). *Evening Standard*, 23 July 1931, p. 18.

R. of Thomas Moult, *Saturday Night*; J. M. Frank, *The World Against Mary*; Ladbroke Black, *Some Queer People*; John Doe, *Eye Witness*. *Evening Standard*, 20 August 1931, p. 14.

'Vile Bodies' (re dramatization of novel). *Evening Standard*, 25 August 1931, p. 9. L.

R. of H. H. Houben, *The Call of the North*, Jan Welzl, *Thirty Years in the Golden North*. *Spectator*, 18 June 1932, p. 869.

R. of Peter Quennell, *A Superficial Journey*; Wyndham Lewis, *Filibusters in Barbary*; Alan Pryce-Jones, *People in the South*; Jan and Cora Gorden, *Three Lands on Three Wheels*. *Spectator*, 6 August 1932, p. 186.

R. of A. S. Wadia, *The Call of the Southern Cross*; Kasimir Edschmid, *South America*; George Bröchner, *A Wayfarer in Denmark*; Leonard Matters, *Through the Kara Sea*; Waldo Frank, *Dawn in Russia*. *Spectator*, 1 October 1932, pp. 412, 414.

R. of Violet Hunt, *The Wife of Rossetti*. *Spectator*, 8 October 1932, p. 449.

R. of Penryn Goldman, *To Hell and Gone*; Julian Duguid, *Tiger-Man*; Amelie Posse-Brazdova, *Sardinian Side-show*; Lowell Thomas, *Kabluk of the Eskimo*; Robert Gibbings, *Iorana!*; Walter Bayes, *A Painter's Baggage*. *Spectator*, 18 November 1932, pp. 703, 705.

'My Escape from Mayfair'. *Daily Mail*, 29 March 1933, p. 10.

'The Shadow Frontier Line'. *Daily Mail*, 12 May 1933, p. 10.

'Debunking the Bush'. *Oxford and Cambridge Magazine*, December 1933, pp. 406–7.

'Rough Life'. *Virginia Quarterly Review*, January 1934, pp. 70–7.

'Farewell, 1933'. *Harper's Bazaar* (London), January 1934, pp. 52, 94.

R. of Albert Gervais, *A Surgeon's China*; Rawdon Hoare, *Rhodesian Mosaic*. *Spectator*, 12 October 1934, p. 538.

R. of Geoffrey Moss, *A Box of Dates for Children*. *Spectator*, 23 November 1934, p. 24.

'Some After-Thoughts on Wedding Week: Did We Overdo it?' *Sunday Referee*, 2 December 1934, p. 12.

R. of L. M. Nesbitt, *Desolate Marches*. *Spectator*, 19 July 1935, p. 106.

DESPATCHES TO THE *DAILY MAIL* FROM ABYSSINIA

'Drilling the Emperor's Volunteers'. 27 August 1935, p. 10.

'Rains Ending in Abyssinia'. 29 August 1935, p. 12.

'Evelyn Waugh on Abyssinian Troop Movements'. 3 September, 1935, pp. 11–12.

'Abyssinians Move to the "Front"'. 6 September 1935, p. 7.

'British Guard at Addis Ababa, Secrecy Drama'. 7 September 1935, p. 11.

'Italian Consuls Withdrawn'. 9 September 1935, p. 18.

'More Abyssinian Troops Moving, Civilians Reported Leaving Two Towns'. 10 September 1935, p. 12.

'Germans Send Home Women'. 11 September 1935, p. 12.

'Emperor's Raw Beef Banquet'. 13 September 1935, p. 13.

'Abyssinia Call to 750,000'. 14 September 1935, p. 5.

'Emperor Sells Honours'. 16 September 1935, p. 9.

'Abyssinian Troops Rebuked, Reluctant to Go to the "Front"'. 17 September 1935, p. 7.

'Belgian Recruits in Abyssinia'. 18 September 1935, p. 12.

'Consuls Held Up, Safe Conduct Refused by Abyssinians'. 19 September 1935, pp. 11–12.

'Abyssinian View, Emperor Advised to Accept Terms'. 20 September 1935, p. 14.

'Emperor and Rome Envoy Meet at "End-of-Rain" Ceremony'. 23 September 1935, p. 9.

'Abyssinian Mobilization Order'. 24 September 1935, p. 14.
'Abyssinians Luxury Gaol'. 25 September 1935, p. 19.
'Abyssinia Chiefs, Why They Accept the Emperor's Rule'. 26 September 1935, p. 14.
'Abyssinia Pomp, Emperor's Review at Today's Feast'. 27 September 1935, p. 14.
'Abyssinia Waits, Mobilization Decree at Any Moment'. 1 October 1935, pp. 13–14.
'Emperor's Protest, Italian Troops in Salt Desert'. 3 October 1935, pp. 13–14.
'Throbbing Drums Call Abyssinians to War'. 4 October 1935, p. 13.
'Addis Ababa Curfew, Italian Legation Isolated'. 5 October 1935, pp. 11–12.
'Emperor's Guards Yell for Blood'. *Sunday Dispatch*, 6 October 1935, p. 17.
'Emperor's Guard Ordered to Leave for Ogaden'. 7 October 1935, p. 14.
'Adowa's Value, Abyssinia Says Not a Strategic Point'. 8 October 1935, p. 14.
'Women's Wish to Fight'. 10 October 1935, p. 15.
'Count Vinci's "Holiday", Italy Breaks off Relations'. 11 October 1935, p. 15.
'Count Vinci Leaving Today'. 12 October 1935, p. 7.
'Count Vinci Kept Under Guard'. 14 October 1935, p. 9.
'Unruly Troops Denied Rifles'. 15 October 1935, p. 9.
'"Holy War" on Italians'. 16 October 1935, p. 7.
'Abyssinia and Settlement Talks, Cession of Provinces "Impossible" '. 17 October
    1935, p. 13.
'War Cry to Emperor, "Kept Back Too Long"'. 18 October, 1935, p. 11.
'Count Vinci Stays On'. *Sunday Dispatch*, 20 October 1935, p. 15.
'Orators in Relays'. 21 October 1935, p. 9.
'Exiled Minister's Return'. 22 October 1935, p. 9.
'Egyptian Prince in Addis Ababa, To Take Red Cross Corps to Front'. 23 October
    1935, p. 9.
'Abyssinia Offensive Expected Today'. 28 October 1935, p. 13.
'General Nasibu's March'. 29 October 1935, pp. 13–14.
'Breaches Made in Walls of Harar'. 31 October 1935, p. 14.
'Abyssinians Fight Each Other, 70 Dead in Night Mistake'. 1 November 1935, p. 14.
'Gloomy "Joy Day" in Addis Ababa'. 4 November 1935, p. 4.
'Briton's Radio Post, Chief of Abyssinian Station'. 5 November 1935, p. 18.
'Salary Cuts in Addis Ababa'. 7 November 1935, p. 15.
'Prince of 19 to Act for Emperor'. 8 November 1935.
'Fear of Air Attack on Emperor'. *Overseas Daily Mail*, 9 November 1935, p. 5.
'Emperor Calls a War Council'. 13 November 1935, p. 12.
'Emperor's Week of Prayer'. 14 November 1935, p. 15.
'Abyssinian Ruler's Pledge, "I will shed my blood for my People"'. 19 November 1935,
    p. 9.
'Anarchy in Abyssinian Army Centre'. 19 November 1935, p. 14.
'Abyssinian Ban on Wireless'. 24 November 1935.
'Abyssinians' Big Sicklist'. 25 November 1935, p. 7.
'"Impregnable" Road to Addis Ababa'. 26 November 1935, p. 9.
'Emperor on Way to Front'. 30 November 1935, p. 12.
'Emperor in Dessye, Women Repair Roads for His Arrival'. 3 December 1935, p. 14.

'Home Life is So Dull . . .' *Sunday Express*, 1 December 1935.
R. of Peter Fleming, *News from Tartary*. *Spectator*, 7 August 1936, p. 244.
R. of Ladislas Farago (ed.), *Abyssinian Stop Press*. *Spectator*, 2 October 1936, p. 554.
'Marie Bashkirtseff' (r. of Dormer Creston, *Fountains of Youth*). *Morning Post*, 9
    October 1936, p. 18.
R. of P. G. Wodehouse, *Laughing Gas*. *Tablet*, 17 October 1936, pp. 532–3.
R. of Paul H. Emden, *Regency Pageant*; R. H. Mottram, *Portrait of an Unknown
    Victorian*; Roy Strachey (ed.), *Our Freedom*. *Morning Post*, 6 November 1936, p. 16.

R. of Elaine Sanceau, *Indies Adventure*. *Morning Post*, 24 November 1936, p. 16.
R. of Mortimer Durand, *Crazy Campaign*. *Tablet*, 5 December 1936, p. 784.
R. of Aldous Huxley, *The Olive Tree*. *Morning Post*, 15 December 1936, p. 18.
'Books for Christmas'. *Spectator*, 18 December 1936, p. 1077.
'Christmas at Bethlehem'. *Tablet*, 19 December 1936, p. 861.
'Christmas at Bethlehem'. *Tablet*, 2 January 1937, p. 26. L.
'Christmas at Bethlehem'. *Tablet*, 9 January 1937, p. 62. L.
'Italian Reprisals in Addis Ababa'. *The Times*, 12 March 1937, p. 17.
'In preparation . . . Hostesses and housebreakers get ready for the Coronation'. *Nash's Pall Mall Magazine*, April 1937, pp. 8, 10–11.
'A Letter of Advice to a Lady Threatened with Invasion from the Antipodes'. *Harper's Bazaar* (London), May 1937, pp. 64–5, 158.
'Gilded Youth: Evelyn Waugh talks about class in the Commons'. *Nash's Pall Mall Magazine*, May 1937, pp. 8, 10–11.
'Cad Architecture'. *Nash's Pall Mall Magazine*, June 1937, pp. 8, 10–11.
'Barabbas, Publisher'. *Nash's Pall Mall Magazine*, July 1937, pp. 8, 10–11.

REVIEWS IN *NIGHT AND DAY*, 1 JULY–23 DECEMBER 1937

R. of Margaret Barton, *Tunbridge Wells*; E. C. Large, *Sugar in the Air*; G. E. Trevelyan, *Two Thousand Million Man-Power*. 1 July 1937, pp. 32–3.
R. of Murray Constantine, *Swastika Night*; A. L. Rowse, *Sir Richard Grenville of the Revenge*; William Tejling, *The Pope in Politics*; Julius Lips, *The Savage Hits Back*. 8 July 1937, pp. 24–5.
R. of Owen Rutter, *Triumphant Pilgrimage*; M. Sandoz, *Old Jules*; Herbert Clyde Lewis, *Gentleman Overboard*. 15 July 1937, pp. 25–6.
R. of Peter Chamberlain, *Sing Holiday*; Paul Cohen-Portheim, *The Spirit of Paris*; John Drinkwater, *Robinson of England*. 22 July 1937, pp. 24–5.
R. of E. T. Bell, *Men of Mathematics*. 5 August 1937, pp. 23–4.
R. of W. H. Auden and Louis Macneice, *Letters from Iceland*; Philip Thornton, *Dead Puppets Dance*. 12 August 1937, pp. 25–6.
R. of Horace McCoy, *No Pockets in a Shroud*; Michael Arlen, *The Crooked Coronet*. 26 August 1937, pp. 26–7.
R. of Ella K. Maillart, *Forbidden Journey*; Dr Johnston Abraham, *99 Wimpole Street*. 2 September 1937, pp. 26–7.
R. of Arthur Calder-Marshall, *The Changing Scene*; Dave Marlow, *Coming, Sir!* 9 September 1937, pp. 25–6.
R. of J. A. Spender, *Men and Things*. 23 September 1937, pp. 24–5.
R. of Max Miller, *Mexico Around Me*; G. E. P. Collins, *Makassar Sailing*; A. J. Marshall, *The Black Musketeers*. 30 September 1937, pp. 26, 28.
R. of Pamela Hansford-Johnson, *World's End*; Kenneth Allott and Stephen Tait, *The Rhubarb Tree*; Frederic Prokosch, *The Seven Who Fled*. 7 October 1937, p. 29.
R. of *May the Twelfth: Mass Observation Day-Surveys*. 14 October 1937, pp. 28, 30.
R. of Ernest Hemingway, *To Have and Have Not*; Terence Greenidge, *Tin Pot Country*. 21 October 1937, pp. 28–9.
R. of Julian Pine, *Rotten Borough*; Eric Linklater, *The Sailor's Holiday*; William Lamb, *The World Ends*; G. M. Young, *Daylight and Champagne*; H. E. Bates and Agnes Miller Parker, *Down the River*. 28 October 1937, pp. 24–5.
R. of T. O. Beachcroft, *The Man Who Started Clean*; Patrick Balfour, *Lords of the Equator*; Siegfried Sassoon, *The Complete Memoirs of George Sherston*; Neil Stewart, *The Fight for the Charta*. 4 November 1937, pp. 24–5.
R. of Ethel Firebrace, *Autobiography; Press Gang*; Leonard Q. Ross, *The Education of*

Hyman Kaplan; Freya Stark, *Baghdad Sketches*. 11 November 1937, p. 23.

R. of V. Sackville-West, *Pepita*; Sir Ronald Storrs, KCMG, *Orientations*; Stephen Tennant, *Leaves from a Missionary's Notebook*. 18 November 1937, pp. 28, 30.

R. of John Betjeman, *Continual Dew*; Charles Prior, *So I Wrote It*. 25 November 1937, pp. 24–5.

R. of Lord Clonmore, *Pope Pius XI and World Peace*; James Laver, *Taste and Fashion*; Earl of Ilchester, *Chronicles of Holland House, 1820–1900*. 2 December 1937, pp. 24–5.

R. of A. F. Tshiffely, *Don Roberto*; Hesketh Pearson and Hugh Kingsmill, *Skye High*. 16 December 1937, pp. 25–6.

R. of J. R. Clynes, *Memoirs*; C. P. Rodoconachi, *No Innocent Abroad*. 23 December 1937, pp. 24–5.

'Variety'. *Nash's Pall Mall Magazine*, September 1937, pp. 8–9.
'Equitation'. *Harper's Bazaar* (London), October 1937, pp. 58–9, 106, 108.
'Teresa Higginson'. *Tablet*, 11 December 1937, p. 803. L.
'Foreword' to Stuart and Vera Boyle, *The Rise and Fall of Mr Prophitt*. (London: Chapman and Hall, 1938.)
'The Oxford Arctic Expedition' (r. of Alexander R. Glen and Noel A. C. Croft, *Under the Pole Star*). *Tablet*, 15 January 1938, pp. 80–1.
'Wedding Presents'. *Harper's Bazaar*, April 1938, pp. 70, 112, 116.

REVIEWS IN THE *SPECTATOR*, 15 JANUARY 1938– 24 MARCH 1939

R. of Christopher Isherwood, *Lions and Shadows*. 160 (25 March 1938), p. 538.

R. of Archibald Lyall, *Black and White Make Brown*. 8 April 1938, p. 640.

R. of Cicely Hamilton, *Modern England*; Beverley Nichols, *News of England*. 22 April 1938, pp. 714, 716.

R. of Sacheverell Sitwell, *Roumanian Journey*. 20 May 1938, p. 924.

R. of Frank Tilsey, *First Things First*. 160, (20 May 1938), p. 930.

R. of Lord Elton, *Among Others*; Lord Dunsany, *Patches of Sunlight*; David Edstrom, *The Testament of Caliban*; Walter Starkie, *The Waveless Plain*; John Van Druten, *The Way to the Present*. 17 June 1938, pp. 1112, 1114.

R. of Lettice Cooper, *National Provincial*; Robert Nicolson, *Love is a Sickness*; Herbert Kahan, *Apollo Flies*; James Hanley, *Hollow Sea*. 24 June 1938, p. 1162.

R. of *The Country Citizen* by 'The Countryman' (Robertson Scott). 8 July 1938, p. 54–5.

R. of Herbert Tichy, *Tibetan Adventure*; John Hanbury-Tracy, *Black River of Tibet*; Dana Lamb and June Cleveland, *Enchanted Vagabonds*; Theodora Benson, *In the East My Pleasure Lies*; James Ramsey Ullman, *The Other Side of the Mountain*. 29 July 1938, p. 207.

R. of Hilaire Belloc, *Return to the Baltic*. 2 December 1938, pp. 964, 966.

'To See the Queen'. *Vogue* (London), 25 May 1938, pp. 51–2.
'From London to Budapest, British and Irish Pilgrims Welcomed in European Countries'. *Catholic Herald* (London), 27 May 1938, p. 1.
'Is Oxford Worth the Money?' *Sunday Dispatch*, 10 July 1938, p. 12.
R. of *The Ladies of Alderley*, Nancy Mitford (ed.). *Tablet*, 23 July 1938, p. 110–12.
'Muddling Through'. *Harper's Bazaar* (London), December 1938, pp. 79, 94.
'BBC Bulletins'. *The Times*, 20 February 1939, p. 8. L.
'Journey to a War'. *Spectator*, 21 April 1939, pp. 674–5. L.
'Mr Evelyn Waugh and the *Daily Mail*'. *Tablet*, 19 August 1939, p. 250. L.
R. of C. S. Jarvis, *The Back Garden of Allah*; Gerald Reitlinger, *South of the Clouds*;

William J. Makin, *Caribbean Nights*; Mora Gardner, *Menacing Sun*. Spectator, 25 August 1939, p. 300.

R. of J. B. Priestley, *Rain Upon Godshill*; Howard Spring, *Heaven Lies About Us*; James Bridie, *One Way of Living. Spectator*, 1 September 1939, p. 331.

'1st RM Battalion'. *The Globe and Laurel*, May 1940, p. 227.

'1st RM Battalion'. *The Globe and Laurel*, June 1940, p. 279.

R. of Charles B. Cochran, *Cock-a-doodle-do. Spectator*, 19 December 1941, p. 582.

'Why Not War Writers?' *Horizon*, December 1941, pp. 437–8. L.

'Snobbery and Titles'. *Spectator*, 8 May 1942, p. 443. L.

R. of Eric Baume, *I've Lived Another Year*; Hector Bolitho, *War in the Strand. Observer*, 23 August 1942, p. 3.

R. of Enid Starkie, *A Lady's Child. Tablet*, 19 August 1942, p. 250.

L. re Alfred Wallis. *Horizon*, March 1943, p. 214.

'Hilary A. St George Saunders'. *Book-of-the-Month Club News*, May 1943, pp. 5–6.

'Religion in State Schools'. *New Statesman*, 2 October 1943, p. 217. L.

'Religion in State Schools'. *New Statesman*, 16 October 1943, p. 251. L.

'Church and State in Liberated Croatia'. Public Record Office, 17 May 1945, Section 4, Balkan States, Confidential (16805), R 5927/1059/92.

'Picasso and Matisse'. *The Times*, 20 December 1945, p. 5. L.

R. of Osbert Sitwell, *The Scarlet Tree. Tablet*, 10 August 1946, p. 74.

'The Jesuit Who Was Thursday: An Examination of Mrs Trollope's "Father Eustace"'. *Tablet*, 21 December 1946, pp. 338–9.

'Foreign Travel for Young Writers'. *The Times*, 17 April 1947, p. 5. L.

'The Last Days of Hitler'. *Tablet*, 28 June 1947, p. 335. L.

'The Pieties of Evelyn Waugh'. *Bell*, July 1947, p. 77. L.

'A Visit to America'. *The Times*, 6 November 1947, p. 6. L.

L. to Cyril Connolly explaining themes of *The Loved One*, in 'Introduction'. *Horizon*, February 1948, pp. 76–7.

'Evelyn Waugh Upholds Knox Version'. *Universe*, 27 February 1948, p. 6. L.

'Mr Waugh on the Catholic Novelist'. *Duckett's Register*, March 1948, p. 3. L.

'Christian Prayer'. *The Times*, 21 May 1948, p. 5. L.

'Christian Prayer'. *The Times*, 25 May 1948, p. 5. L.

R. of *The Eighteen-Nineties: A Period Anthology Chosen by Martin Secker. Month*, January 1949, pp. 59–60.

'Monsignor Knox's Old Testament: A Literary Opinion'. *Month*, July 1949, pp. 41–3.

'Elected Silence'. *New Statesman and Nation*, 20 August 1949, p. 197. L. Three further letters under same title: 3 September 1949, pp. 245–6; 10 September 1949, p. 274; 17 September 1949, p. 302.

Foreword to Thomas Merton, *Waters of Silence*. (London: Hollis and Carter, 1950.)

'Mulled Claret'. In *As We Like It: Cookery Recipes by Famous People*, ed. Kenneth Downey. (London: Arthur Barker, 1950.)

'A Card from Evelyn Waugh' (explanation of refusal to contribute to *Cherwell*). *Cherwell*, 24 April 1950, p. 17.

R. of Robert Gathorne-Hardy, *Recollections of Logan Pearsall Smith. English Review*, January 1950, pp. 61–2.

R. of Malcolm Muggeridge, *Affairs of the Heart. Tablet*, 195 (4 February 1950), pp. 91–2.

'Electric Sanctuary Lamps'. *Tablet*, 196 (9 September 1950), p. 215. L.

'Matisse Builds a Church'. *Tablet*, 196 (2 December 1950), p. 486.

R. of Osbert Lancaster, *Façades and Faces. Tablet*, 196 (9 December 1950), p. 509.

'The South Bank at Night'. *The Times*, 24 May 1951, p. 5. L.

'The Claque'. *Sunday Times*, 12 August 1951, p. 8. L.

'Saint Helena'. *Tablet*, 198 (3 November 1951), p. 324. L.

'Saint Helena'. *Tablet*, 198 (17 November 1951), p. 364. L.

'The Importance of Mr Maugham'. *Sunday Times*, 13 January 1952, p. 8. L.

'Tax on Dollar Earnings'. *The Times*, 6 February 1952, p. 5. L.

'Taxation of Authors'. *The Times*, 24 May 1952, p. 7. L.

R. of Rex Whistler, *The Königsmark Drawings*. *Time and Tide*, 33 (6 December 1952), pp. 1456–7.

'Mr Waugh Replies'. *Sunday Express*, 14 December 1952, p. 3. L. about Tito's visit.

'Marshal Tito's Visit'. *Spectator*, 189 (19 December 1952), p. 846. L.

'Farewell to a Saint'. *Picture Post*, 58, No. 4 (24 January 1953), pp. 16–18.

'Tito and Stepinac'. *New Statesman and Nation*, NS 45 (31 January 1953), p. 122. L.

'Marshal Tito's Visit'. *Sunday Times*, 1 February 1953, p. 6. L.

'Religion in Yugoslavia'. *Sunday Times*, 15 February 1953, p. 6. L.

'Tito and Stepinac'. *New Statesman and Nation*, NS 45 (28 February 1953), p. 233. L.

'President Tito's Visit'. *The Times*, 24 March 1953, p. 9. L.

R. of Patrick Leigh Fermor, *A Time to Keep Silence*. *Time and Tide*, 34 (20 June 1953), p. 824.

'Modern Missions'. *Sunday Times*, 26 July 1953, p. 6.

'P. G. Wodehouse'. *Daily Mail*, 24 November 1953, p. 4. L.

'Sir Thomas More'. *New Statesman and Nation*, NS 46 (12 December 1953), p. 762. L.

'Sir Thomas More'. *New Statesman and Nation*, NS 47 (2 January 1954), p. 16. L.

'Sir Thomas More'. *New Statesman and Nation*, NS 47 (16 January 1954), p. 70. L.

'Conditions in Goa'. *The Times*, 24 March 1954, p. 9. L.

R. of Helen Angeli, *The Pre-Raphaelite Twilight*. *Spectator*, 192 (23 April 1954), pp. 498, 501.

R. of Lord Stanley of Alderly, *Sea Peace*. *Time and Tide*, 28 April 1954, p. 1145.

'Hilaire Belloc'. *New Statesman*, NS 48 (3 July 1954), p. 16. L.

'Painter and Patron: Responsibilities to One Another'. *The Times*, 17 July 1954, p. 7. L.

'Self-Denial'. *Truth* (London), 15 October 1954, p. 1279. L. replying to 'Profile: Evelyn Waugh Among the Ruins', 8 October 1954, pp. 1242–3.

'In the Movement' (re literary movements of 1930s and 1950s). *Spectator*, 8 October 1954, p. 434. L.

'A Star for Silence'. *The Times*, 28 April 1955, p. 13. L.

'Drunk in Charge'. *Observer*, 15 May 1955, p. 12. L.

'After "Family Portrait": Selections from the Next Popular Controversy'. *Punch*, 25 May 1955, p. 632.

'Graham Greene'. *Catholic Herald*, 3 June 1955, p. 2. L.

'Stonor'. *Tablet*, 206 (16 July 1955), p. 66. L.

'Statues in London'. *The Times*, 20 July 1955, p. 9. L.

'Men of Waugh'. *Spectator*, 22 July 1955, p. 121. L. in reply to Lord Noel-Buxton.

R. of Norton B. Crowell, *Alfred Austin, Victorian*. *Sunday Times*, 4 September 1955, p. 5.

'Victim of a Hoax?' *Catholic Herald*, 16 September 1955, p. 2. Signed, 'Mrs Teresa Pinfold'. L. in humorous defence of *Cracks in the Cloister*.

R. of Caresse Crosby, *The Passionate Years*. *Sunday Times*, 23 October 1955, p. 5.

R. of Alfred Duggan, *God and My Right*. *Spectator*, 195 (18 November 1955), p. 667–8.

R. of Graham Greene, *The Quiet American*. *Sunday Times*, 4 December 1955, p. 4.

Preface to Robert Hugh Benson, *Richard Raynal, Solitary*. (Chicago: Henry Regnery, 1956.)

Preface to Lord Sudley, *William: or More Loved than Loving*. Second edn. (London: Chapman and Hall, 1956.)

'P. G. Wodehouse'. *Observer*, 12 February 1956, p. 12. L.

'A Final View'. *Four Quarters* (LaSalle College), 5, No. 3 (March 1956), pp. 18–19. L. commenting on creative writing.

R. of J. F. Powers, *Presence of Grace*. *Commonweal*, 63 (30 March 1956), pp. 667–8.

R. of *The Autograph Edition of the Works of P. G. Wodehouse. Sunday Times*, 3 June 1956, p. 4.

'Matisse Reliefs'. *The Times*, 20 June 1956, p. 11. L.

'A Poet of the Counter-Reformation'. *Spectator*, 197 (13 July 1956), p. 63. L.

'A Poet of the Counter-Reformation'. *Spectator*, 197 (27 July 1956), p. 143. L.

'Deification and Clarification', *Spectator*, 197 (3 August 1956), p. 178. L.

'Deification and Clarification'. *Spectator*, 197 (10 August 1956), p. 206. L.

'Deification and Clarification'. *Spectator*, 197 (24 August 1956), p. 261. L.

'Popish Plotters'. *New Statesman and Nation*, NS 52 (1 September 1956), p. 243. L.

'Papist Plots'. *New Statesman and Nation*, NS 52 (15 September 1956), p. 312. L.

'Popish Plots'. *New Statesman and Nation*, NS 52 (29 September 1956), p. 377. L.

'Mighty Old Artificer'. *Spectator*, 197 (2 November 1956), p. 608. L.

R. of Devendra P. Varma, *The Gothic Flame. Spectator*, 198 (10 May 1957), p. 622.

'A Tribute to Ronald Knox'. *Sunday Times*, 1 September 1957, p. 7.

'Monsignor Ronald Knox'. *Tablet*, 210 (7 September 1957), p. 194. L.

'Mgr R. A. Knox'. *Sunday Times*, 8 September 1957, p. 4. L.

Preface to Ronald Knox, *A Spiritual Aeneid*. (London: Burns and Oates, 1958.)

Preface to Earl of Wicklow, *Fireside Fusilier*. (London: Hollis and Carter, 1958.)

'Mgr R. A. Knox'. *Tablet*, 211 (7 June 1958), p. 536. L.

'Mgr Knox on St Teresa'. *Catholic Herald*, 11 July 1958, p. 2. L.

'A True Father in God'. *Sunday Times*, 12 October 1958, p. 10.

R. of R. A. Knox, *Literary Distractions. Spectator*, 201 (17 October 1958), p. 523.

'On Wine'. *The Pan Book of Wine*. London, 1959, pp. 9–13.

Preface to Eric Newby, *A Short Walk in the Hindu Kush* (New York: Doubleday, 1959), pp. 11–12.

R. of Vincent Brome, *Frank Harris. Spectator*, 202 (20 February 1959), p. 268.

'Ronald Knox: The Quintessence of Oxford'. *Tablet*, 213 (2 May 1959), p. 419.

'Vindicating À Kempis'. *Catholic Herald*, 8 May 1959, p. 2. L.

'An Unposted Letter'. *The Times*, 17 June 1959. L. re Mgr Knox and atomic bomb.

'Social Distinctions'. *The Times*, 19 September, 1959, p. 7. L.

R. of Leo Rosten, *The Return of Hyman Kaplan. Spectator*, 203 (16 October 1959), p. 525.

'Mr "C"'. *New Statesman and Nation*, NS 58 (24 October 1959), p. 546. L.

'X Marks the Spot'. *Spectator*, 203 (30 October 1959), p. 598. L. in reply to critics of 'Aspirations of a Mugwump'.

'The Life of Ronald Knox'. *Tablet*, 213 (7 November 1959), p. 970. L.

R. of Truman Capote and Richard Avedon, *Observations*; Yousef Karsh, *Portraits of Greatness. Spectator*, 203 (20 November 1959), pp. 728–9.

R. of *The Life of Christina of Markyate. Spectator*, 203 (4 December 1959), pp. 840–1.

Preface to Hilaire Belloc, *Advice*. (London: Harvill Press, 1960.)

'In the growing cult of sun-worship I pity the helpless Briton', *Daily Mail*, 28 March 1960, p. 8.

'Thank Heavens for DDT'. *Daily Mail*, 31 March 1960, p. 13.

R. of Peter Anson, *Fashions in Church Furnishings, 1840–1940. Spectator*, 204 (22 April 1960), pp. 580–1.

'A Bishop's Rebuke'. *The Times*, 5 July 1960, p. 13 L. re attendance of Catholics at civic ceremonies in Anglican churches.

R. of Peter Quennell, *The Sign of the Fish. Spectator*, 205 (8 July 1960), p. 70.

R. of Anthony Carson, *A Rose by Any Other Name. London Magazine*, 7 (September 1960), pp. 76–7.

'Opponents – They Meet as Friends'. *Sunday Dispatch*, 6 November 1960.

'Lady Chatterley'. *Spectator*, 205 (18 November 1960), p. 771. L.

R. of Ronald Knox, *The Occasional Sermons*, ed. Philip Caraman. *Spectator*, 205 (25 November 1960), pp. 858–9.

'Evelyn Waugh Replies'. *Encounter*, 15 (December 1960), p. 83. L. in reply to Frank Kermode, 'Mr Waugh's Cities'.

'The Death Penalty'. *Spectator*, 204 (9 December 1960), p. 936. L.

'The Death Penalty'. *Spectator*, 204 (16 December 1960), p. 955. L.

'Who Deplores It?' (re use of foot-notes rather than end-notes). *Sunday Times*, 12 February 1961, p. 34. L.

Preface to Jacqueline de Chimay, *The Life and Times of Madame Veuve Clicquot-Ponsardin*. (London: Curwen Press, 1961.)

R. of Ronald Chapman, *Father Faber*. *Sunday Times*, 29 January 1961, p. 27.

R. of Frank Arnau, *Three Thousand Years of Deception in Art and Antiques*. *Spectator*, 206 (3 March 1961), p. 300.

'Nihil Obstat'. *The Times*, 7 March 1961, p. 13. L.

R. of Daphne Fielding, *The Adonis Garden*. *Spectator*, 206 (23 June 1961), p. 928.

R. of Muriel Spark, *Voices at Play*; Daniel Pezeril, *Blessed and Poor*. *Spectator*, 207 (7 July 1961), pp. 28–9.

'Publishers'. *Observer*, 9 July 1961, p. 18. L.

'P. G. Wodehouse'. *Sunday Times*, 30 July 1961, p. 18. L.

R. of Simona Pakenham, *Pigtails and Pernod*. *Sunday Times*, 10 September 1961, p. 25.

'Old Men at the Zoo'. *Spectator*, 207 (13 October 1961), p. 501. L.

'Indexes' (in novels). *The Times*, 16 October 1961, p. 13. L.

R. of Loelia, Duchess of Westminster, *Grace and Favour*. *Spectator*, 207 (20 October 1961), p. 551.

R. of Graham Greene, *In Search of a Character*. *Spectator*, 207 (27 October 1961), pp. 594–5.

R. of Muriel Spark, *The Prime of Miss Jean Brodie*. *Cosmopolitan*, 152 (February 1962), p. 38.

'My Father'. *Sunday Telegraph*, 2 December 1962, pp. 4–5.

Preface to Anthony Carson, *Travels, Near and Far Out*. (New York: Pantheon, 1963.)

'The Dialogue Mass'. *Tablet*, 217 (16 March 1963), p. 292. L.

'The Council: Phase One'. *Tablet*, 217 (7 September 1963), p. 969. L.

'The Council: Phase One'. *Tablet*, 217 (21 September 1963), p. 1017. L.

'What is Expendable?' *Tablet*, 217 (28 September 1963), p. 1044. L.

R. of Jessica Mitford, *The American Way of Death*. *Sunday Times*, 29 September 1963, p. 36.

Preface to Alfred Duggan, *Count Bohemond*. (London: Faber and Faber, 1964.)

'Understanding the Conservatives' (in the Catholic Church). *Commonweal*, 80 (7 August 1964), pp. 547–8. L.

'Using English in the Latin Mass'. *The Times*, 8 August 1964, p. 7. L.

'Reactions to Evelyn Waugh'. *Catholic Herald*, 28 August 1964, p. 4. L.

R. of Gale Pederick, *Life with Rossetti*. *Sunday Telegraph*, 8 November 1964, p. 20.

'A Suggestion for Mr Waugh'. *Commonweal*, 81 (4 December 1964), pp. 352–3. L.

'Clive and Cook' (re social status of empire builders). *Sunday Telegraph*, 10 January 1965, p. 13. L.

'Evelyn Waugh's Impressions of Spain'. *Venture*, 2 (February 1965), pp. 58–63.

R. of Pope John XXIII, *Journal of a Soul*; Kurt Klinger, *A Pope Laughs*; Henri Fesquet (ed.), *Wit and Wisdom of Good Pope John*. *Sunday Telegraph*, 7 March 1965, p. 21.

'An Aid to Participation?' *Tablet*, 219 (24 April 1965), p. 473. L.

'Fides Quaerens Intellectum'. *Tablet*, 219 (31 July 1965), p. 864. L.

'Edwardian Life'. *Spectator*, 6 August 1965, p. 176. L.

'Some Modest Proposals from Illinois' (concerning proposed changes to liturgy). *Tablet*, 18 September 1965, p. 1040.

'A Post-Waugh Insight' (reply to criticism of his conservatism). *Commonweal*, 7 January 1966, p. 391.

INDEX

1. Page numbers prefixed by letters refer to: review – R; introduction – I; preface – P; forward – F; or commentary – C.

2. 'n' after a page number refers to a footnote on that page.

3. Entries referring to the Introductions to each section are in parentheses.

4. Under 'Waugh, Evelyn' the reader is referred back only to the Introductions, except for the titles of his books. Where these are indexed elsewhere, (EW) has been placed after the title.

DATE DUE